# A Way Through the Woods

## The Scovilles of East Haddam, Cornwall, and Norfolk, Connecticut

Compiled and Written by Janice (Billian) Falvey

Middletown, Connecticut

A Way Through the Woods: The Scovilles of East Haddam, Cornwall, and Norfolk, Connecticut

© 2022 Janice (Billian) Falvey, Middletown, Connecticut
All rights reserved.

Front cover image *New England Homestead* by Samuel Lancaster Gerry (1813–1891). This work is in the public domain in its country of origin and other countries and areas where the copyright term is the author's life plus 100 years or fewer.

Map of Litchfield opposite the *Table of Contents* is in the public domain as it was created by a US Census Bureau employee in the course of his duties.

ISBN: 978-0-578-37202-0

Book design by Sarah E. Holroyd (https://sleepingcatbooks.com)

*Dedication*

*In loving memory of my mom and dad*

*And the following people and organizations who assisted me along the way . . .*

The Cornwall Historical Society, especially the late Michael Gannett.

The Godfrey Memorial Library, Middletown, Connecticut. Especially the late Doris Post and Barbara Tierney.

The Norfolk Historical Society, especially Richard Byrne, who was gracious enough to bring my husband and I to the "Dean Lot" (also known as *Intervail Lot Number 43).* This is a deeply wooded area where Reuben Dean had his property, and where his brother-in-law and my ancestor, Ithamar Scoville, lived.

The countless genealogical friends I made along the way over the many years of research, who not only helped me with my research but also shared their own documents and photos. To them I am deeply indebted.

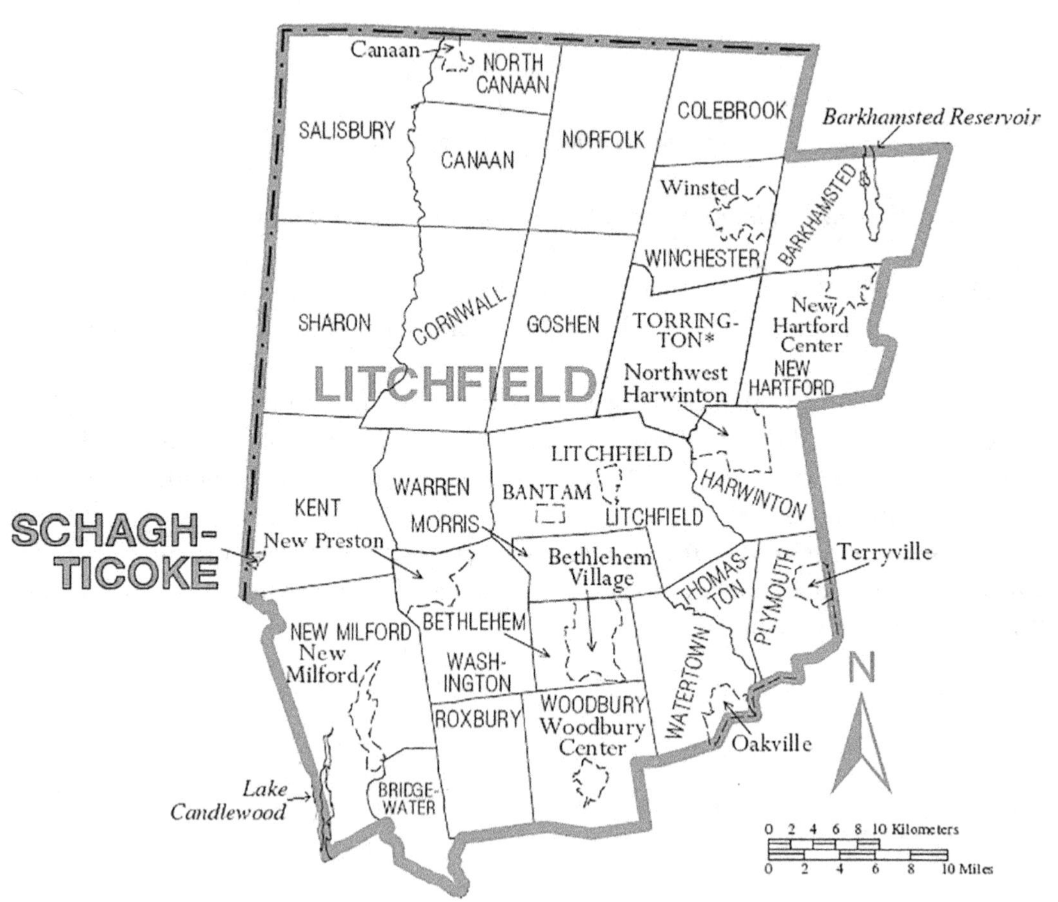
Canaan
NORTH CANAAN
SALISBURY
CANAAN
NORFOLK
COLEBROOK
Barkhamsted Reservoir
Winsted
BARKHAMSTED
WINCHESTER
SHARON
CORNWALL
GOSHEN
TORRING-TON*
New Hartford Center
NEW HARTFORD
LITCHFIELD
Northwest Harwinton
LITCHFIELD
HARWINTON
KENT
WARREN
BANTAM
LITCHFIELD
MORRIS
SCHAGH-TICOKE
New Preston
Bethlehem Village
Terryville
THOMAS-TON
PLYMOUTH
NEW MILFORD
New Milford
BETHLEHEM
WASH-INGTON
WATERTOWN
N
ROXBURY
WOODBURY
Woodbury Center
Oakville
Lake Candlewood
BRIDGE-WATER
0 2 4 6 8 10 Kilometers
0 2 4 6 8 10 Miles

# Table of Contents


**Preface** ix

**The Origin of the Name Scoville** 1

**The Immigrant Ancestor—Arthur Scoville[1]** 3

**First Generation** 9

1. ***Stephen[1] Scoville*** (Arthur) 9

**Second Generation** 16

2. ***Stephen[2] Scoville*** (Stephen,[1] Arthur) 16

**Third Generation** 24

3. ***Timothy Scoville[3]*** (Stephen,[2] Stephen,[1] Arthur) 24

**Fourth Generation** 36

4. Timothy Scoville[4] (Timothy,[3] Stephen,[2] Stephen,[1] Arthur) 36
5. ***Ithamar Scoville[4]*** (Timothy,[3] Stephen,[2] Stephen,[1] Arthur) 46
6. Ira Scoville[4] (Timothy,[3] Stephen,[2] Stephen,[1] Arthur) 55
7. Triphene/Triphena Scoville[4] (Timothy,[3] Stephen,[2] Stephen,[1] Arthur) 90
8. Roxalana Andrews (Thankful Crocker) 93

**Fifth Generation** 107

9. Philo Scovill[5] (Timothy,[4] Timothy,[3] Stephen,[2] Stephen,[1] Arthur) 107
10. Amasa Scoville[5] (Ithamar,[4] Timothy,[3] Stephen[2], Stephen[1], Arthur) 116
11. Lodema[5,] Scoville (Ithamar,[4] Timothy,[3] Stephen,[2] Stephen,[1] Arthur) 126
12. Almira Scoville[5] (Ithamar,[4] Timothy,[3] Stephen,[2] Stephen,[1] Arthur) 134
13. ***Franklin Scoville,***[5] (Ithamar,[4] Timothy,[3] Stephen,[2] Stephen,[1] Arthur) 144

**Sixth Generation** 154

14. i. Charles Foote Scoville[6] (Amasa,[5] Ithamar,[4] Timothy,[3] Stephen,[2] Stephen,[1] Arthur) 154
15. ii. Mary Lord Scoville[6] (Amasa,[5] Ithamar,[4] Timothy,[3] Stephen,[2] Stephen,[1] Arthur) 167
16. i. Silas Kelsey[6] (Almira,[5] Ithamar,[4] Timothy,[3] Stephen,[2] Stephen,[1] Arthur) 176
17. ii. Clarissa Kelsey[6] (Almira,[5] Ithamar,[4] Timothy,[3] Stephen,[2] Stephen,[1] Arthur) 181
18. iii. Melissa Kelsey[6] (Almira,[5] Ithamar,[4] Timothy,[3] Stephen,[2] Stephen,[1] Arthur) 189
19. iv. Philo Kelsey[6] (Almira,[5] Ithamar,[4] Timothy,[3] Stephen,[2] Stephen,[1] Arthur) 212
20. i. Irene Scoville[6] (Franklin,[5] Ithamar,[4] Timothy,[3] Stephen,[2] Stephen,[1] Arthur) 214
21. ii. ***Charles Martin Scoville[6]*** (Franklin,[5] Ithamar,[4] Timothy,[3] Stephen,[2] Stephen,[1] Arthur) 219
22. Julia Rebecca Scoville[6] (Franklin,[5] Ithamar,[4] Timothy,[3] Stephen,[2] Stephen,[1] Arthur), 232
23. iv. William Harrison Scoville[6] (Franklin,[5] Ithamar,[4] Timothy,[3] Stephen,[2] Stephen,[1] Arthur) 240
25. vi. Lucius Edwin Scoville[6] (Franklin,[5] Ithamar,[4] Timothy,[3] Stephen,[2] Stephen,[1] Arthur) 254

**Seventh Generation** 264

26. i. Franklin "Frank" Scoville[7] (Charles Foote,[6] Amasa,[5] Ithamar,[4] Timothy,[3] Stephen,[2] Stephen,[1] Arthur) 264

27. ii. Mary Jane Scoville[7] (Charles Foote,[6] Amasa,[5] Ithamar,[4] Timothy,[3] Stephen,[2] Stephen,[1] Arthur) 270

28. i. Susan Jane Benson[7] (Clarissa Kelsey,[6] Almira Scoville Kelsey,[5] Ithamar,[4] Timothy,[3] Stephen,[2] Stephen,[1] Arthur) 272

29. ii. Henry N. Benson[7] (aka Horace Benson, Niles Horace Benson) (Clarissa Kelsey,[6] Almira Scoville,[5] Ithamar,[4] Timothy,[3] Stephen,[2] Stephen,[1] Arthur) 279

30. ii. Frank Flint [7](Melissa Kelsey,[6] Almira Scoville Kelsey,[5] Ithamar,[4] Timothy,[3] Stephen,[2] Stephen,[1] Arthur) 282

31. Charles Franklin Kelsey[7] (Philo Kelsey,[6] Almira Scoville,[5] Ithamar,[4] Timothy,[3] Stephen,[2] Stephen,[1] Arthur) 288

32. Philo Lewis Kelsey[7] (a.k.a. Lew or Lewis) (Philo Kelsey,[6] Almira Scoville,[5] Ithamar,[4] Timothy,[3] Stephen,[2] Stephen,[1] Arthur) 291

33. Albert A. Scoville[7] (Charles Martin,[6] Franklin,[5] Ithamar,[4] Timothy,[3] Stephen,[2] Stephen,[1] Arthur) 295

34. ***Agnes R. Scoville***[7] (Charles Martin,[6] Franklin,[5] Ithamar,[4] Timothy,[3] Stephen,[2] Stephen,[1] Arthur) 297

35. George Henry Raidart[7] (Julia Rebecca,[6] Franklin,[5] Ithamar,[4] Timothy,[3] Stephen,[2] Stephen,[1] Arthur) 304

36. Frank Ellsworth Scovill[7,] (William Harrison,[6] Franklin,[5] Ithamar,[4] Timothy,[3] Stephen,[2] Stephen,[1] Arthur) 307

37. Minnie Irene Scoville[7] (William Harrison,[6] Franklin,[5] Ithamar,[4] Timothy,[3] Stephen,[2] Stephen,[1] Arthur) 316

38. Cora Irene Scoville[7] (Albert Franklin,[6] Franklin,[5] Ithamar,[4] Timothy,[3] Stephen,[2] Stephen,[1] Arthur) 335

39. Charles Merritt Scoville[7] (Albert Franklin,[6] Franklin,[5] Ithamar,[4] Timothy,[3] Stephen,[2] Stephen,[1] Arthur) 345

40. Florence Mabel Scoville[7] (Albert Franklin,[6] Franklin,[5] Ithamar,[4] Timothy,[3] Stephen,[2] Stephen,[1] Arthur) 355

**Eighth Generation** 358

41. i. Charles Mittean Scoville[8] (Franklin,[7] Charles M.,[6] Amasa,[5] Ithamar,[4] Timothy,[3] Stephen,[2] Stephen,[1] Arthur) 358

42. ii. George Albert Scoville[8] (Franklin,[7] Charles M.,[6] Amasa,[5] Ithamar,[4] Timothy,[3] Stephen,[2] Stephen,[1] Arthur) 361

43. iii. Harry Franklin Scoville[8] (Franklin,[7] Charles M.,[6] Amasa,[5] Ithamar,[4] Timothy,[3] Stephen,[2] Stephen,[1] Arthur) 363

44. iv. Gilbert Lafayette Scoville[8] (Franklin,[7] Charles M.,[6] Amasa,[5] Ithamar,[4] Timothy,[3] Stephen,[2] Stephen,[1] Arthur) 365

45. v. Mabel M. Scoville[8] (Franklin,[7] Charles M.,[6] Amasa,[5] Ithamar,[4] Timothy,[3] Stephen,[2] Stephen,[1] Arthur) 366

46. vi. Ethel May Scoville[8] (Franklin,[7] Charles M.,[6] Amasa,[5] Ithamar,[4] Timothy,[3] Stephen,[2] Stephen,[1] Arthur) 367

47. Agnes[2] Mary Billian[8] (Agnes,[7] Charles Martin,[6] Franklin,[5] Ithamar,[4] Timothy,[3] Stephen,[2] Stephen,[1] Arthur) 370
48. Fred Joe Billian[8], (Agnes,[7] Charles Martin,[6] Franklin,[5] Ithamar,[4] Timothy,[3] Stephen,[2] Stephen,[1] Arthur) 374
49. **Ernest Clarence Billian**[8] (Agnes,[7] Charles Martin,[6] Franklin,[5] Ithamar,[4] Timothy,[3] Stephen,[2] Stephen,[1] Arthur) 378
50. Wilbur Henry Raidart[8] (George Raidart,[7] Julia Scoville,[6] Franklin,[5] Ithamar,[4] Timothy,[3] Stephen,[2] Stephen,[1] Arthur) 383
**The Case of Philo C. Scoville 387**
**The Account Book of Ira Scovill 400**
**Index 420**

# Preface

The focus of this work is based on years of research regarding my Scoville ancestors and some of their descendants. As a child, I loved listening to the stories about the "old days." It wasn't until 1979 that I began my research into this family. In the beginning, there was some confusion as to whether my great-grandmother's surname was "Schofield" or "Scoville." To clear up this confusion, I ordered my great-grandmother's death certificate, which not only provided me with the correct surname—Scoville—but also the name of her father, and I was off and running.

Since I started this journey in 1979, I have gathered many primary and secondary sources along with speculations, probabilities, and theories. In 1981, I ordered the book by Jennie M. (Scoville) Wheeler Holley, *Arthur Scovel and His Descendants in America 1660–1900,* (pub. 1941, by Tuttle Publishing Company, Inc.). Her work was my main source of information prior to the inception of the Internet and genealogical websites such as Ancestry®. My research also included writing to many historical societies and libraries, hiring a professional genealogist, visiting cemeteries, as well as going to the Connecticut State Library in Hartford and the Godfrey Memorial Library in Middletown (a place where I was a "frequent flyer").

While I have also researched the various lines on both my paternal and maternal lines, I always came back to my Scoville ancestors. Anyone who has done genealogical research is aware that there are always those brick-walls and gaps that you just can't seem to fill. There is so much erroneous information out there on the Internet and I have tried my best to cite my sources within this book. If any information herein hasn't been proven by a primary source, or at least a secondary source, I notate it as such.

In addition, it must be noted that there are two distinct Scoville families that arrived in New England circa 1660—John Scovil and Arthur Scoville. They are the conjectured sons of Richard and Mary Scoville of County Dorset, England. Arthur is presumably the older brother of John, and since they did immigrate approximately at the same time, it is likely that there is a close connection between these two men. This will be explained futher in the section titled *The Immigrant Ancestor—Arthur Scoville.*

There are two books that have been published regarding these two Scoville immigrants. The book on Arthur has already been mentioned. The book on the John Scovill line was written by Homer W. Brainard, *A Survey of the Scovils or Scovills in England and America,* (published 1915).

If you (the reader) have done any research on the Scoville line, you may have found that there is much erroneous information on these two families, often combining the two *distinct* families into one family tree.

I have been asked, "Why write a genealogical book when everything can be found online." My answer to that question is, "Yes, you can find dates and places online, but much of what I have in this work is *not* online." Our ancestors are much more than a vital record.

For the sake of consistency, I will use the spelling *Scoville* unless the actual document has it spelled in an alternative way. Additionally, this is not a complete work on the descendants of *Arthur Scovel,* but only a select group of ancestors that I have come to "know" through my own research.

# The Origin of the Name Scoville

In the northwest part of France, near Caen, is a small village (or commune, as they refer to it in France) by the name of Escoville. This is the seat of the name "Scoville." This is proven out by the fact that the earliest known person of that name was referred to as "de Scoville." This would refer to a territorial name meaning "of" Scoville (Escoville).

No records have been located of a man named de Scoville in the Domesday Book in 1086[1] when William the Conqueror ordered that a survey be taken. The primary purpose of this survey was to determine what taxes would be owed to King Edward the Confessor. If someone with the name of de Scoville had come over from Normandy during the conquest in 1066, he must have been someone without a title or any significance. It is also possible that the person with this name may have migrated to England some years later and would have not have been named in the Domesday Book.

It wasn't until the year 1194 that de Scoville appears in the records. One Ralph de Scoville was a knight who owned a number of farms worked by tenants in Wiltshire, Somerset, and Hants. Sir Ralph de Scoville's manor was located in Turveston—now known as Turweston, which is located in the County of Buckinghamshire. There are two other records for Ralph de Scoville appearing in 1215 and 1227, but the contents of these records are not known to this writer (see Homer W. Brainard's extensive work on the Scoville family in his work, *A Survey of the Scovils or Scovills in England and America,* which can be found online through various websites for a more detailed account of Ralph de Scoville).

There was another set of Scovilles who had settled in County Dorset, seated on the southern coast of England in the parish of Corfe Castle. This is where it is believed that the immigrant ancestors (Arthur and John) came from. By the time of the births of Arthur and John Scoville the "de" was no longer in use (from the available records reviewed). It appears that the use of the "de" before the name Scoville disappeared sometime in the 1200s.

The Scoville books that were published in 1915 and 1941, respectively, suggest that the parents of Arthur and John Scoville were Richard and Mary (Cook) Scoville.

Richard Scoville is said to have lived at "Whole Place" in the parish of Shapwick, Somerset, England (Somerset is located on the western coast). Charles A. Hoppin, who wrote an article entitled *The Scovilles of Wessex* (which was published in Chapter I of the Homer W. Brainard book), was certain that Richard and Mary Scoville were the parents of Arthur and John. The problem I have with this pronouncement is the fact that neither Arthur nor John Scoville named any of their children "Richard" or "Mary." The old naming patterns were typically followed as thus:

1st son—Father's father
2nd son—Mother's father
3rd son—Father
4th son—Father's eldest brother

1 https://en.wikipedia.org/wiki/Domesday_Book

1st daughter—Mother's mother
2nd daughter—Father's mother
3rd daughter—Mother
4th daughter—Mother's eldest sister

While not everyone followed this prescription for naming their children, it was used more often than not, at least until the nineteenth century. Ever since the publications of the aforementioned books, many people have used Richard and Mary Scoville as the parents of Arthur and John on their family trees. While it is possible, there isn't any proof one way or the other.

It must also be noted that there isn't a direct linear line from Arthur and John Scoville to Ralph de Scoville or any other Scoville person that lived in England since the earliest times. The gaps in the early genealogy of the Scovilles are wide and varied. Perhaps one day the mystery of this family will be revealed.

# The Immigrant Ancestor—Arthur Scoville[1]

We can see from the previous chapter on the origin of the name of Scoville that much work went into finding out where our Scoville ancestors came from and who the parents of Arthur were. In this section, the discussion is on whether Arthur Scovil and John Scovil were brothers. The foregoing information comes from Charles R. Eastman,[2] who compiled several works on the Scoville family.

Arthur Scovel is said to have been born probably in County Dorset, England, between 1635–1640; he died in Middletown, Connecticut, on February 7, 1706/07. It's thought that he may have married in England to Joanna______, whose parentage and date of death are unknown, although there are indications that her death took place in Middletown in the fall of 1678. It has been conjectured that Arthur married a second time, but no record of the name and date of that second marriage has been found.

We do not know exactly when Arthur Scoville came to New England, but it was perhaps circa 1660. He came too late for the great Puritan migration and hence did not immigrate for religious reasons. It is possible that, in some way, he was connected to the Commonwealth in England and, seeing that the collapse of the Commonwealth was imminent, decided to emigrate before the monarchy was restored; it is also possible that he moved for economic reasons. Since no records have been found clarifying the reason for his immigration, this is all a matter of conjecture.

Arthur first settled in Boston, where his first five children were born between 1662–70. Their sixth child, John, was probably born in Connecticut Colony in 1671/2. No other children were born to Arthur and Joanna besides these six as is clearly evidenced by Middletown land records, and of these six, two daughters named Elizabeth died in infancy.

Arthur had removed with his family from Boston to Middletown in the fall of 1670, and would seem to have lived there with his family continuously for the next eight or nine years. But a remarkable document dated September 24, 1678, indicates that, for reasons unknown, he described himself as "of Lyme," and attempted to entail upon his four children all of his real property in Middletown, without granting them power to make alteration thereof. The effect of the document was virtually a will, and very different from an ordinary conveyance. For some reason, Arthur apparently did not care to sell his holdings in Middletown lands, but nevertheless transferred the title to them by deed of entail. His intention in doing so cannot be discovered from the deed itself, although the language indicates that he had sufficient reasons.

> Out of consideration of that natural affection and love which I have in bear onto my well-beloved children, Arthur, James, John, and Elizabeth Scoville, and also for

2 Eastman, Charles Rochester (1868–1918), *Scoville Family Records A Preliminary Brochure*; (1910), 15–20. This compilation is now in the public domain.

> divers good causes and considerations now thereunto especially moving, I do give, grant and confirm unto them all my rights, interest and propriety in my land and housing in Middletown, & all of these parcells [sic] and I bought of William Biggs and John Warner....... to have and to hold from the day of my death forever, they to have it by equal proportions as many as shall be living.[3]

It must be noted that none of his children were of age in 1678—Arthur, the oldest, being but fourteen years of age.

What is significant is the fact that, although a certain personal property is given or bequeathed to his eldest son, Arthur,[1] in a quasi-will just cited, no mention is made of his wife, Joanna, and the natural inference is that she was at that time already deceased. If we assume that that was the case, Arthur's removal to Lyme in 1678, with four young children on his hands in his home broken up, becomes readily intelligible. Lyme was then a flourishing community, more populous than Middletown, and numbered among its inhabitants several families from Boston in vicinity, some which may have been previous acquaintances of Arthur.

Assuming that this was the case, it would not be surprising for him to have remarried and made a new home for himself. There is strong presumptive evidence to show that this is what happened. Some arguments in favor of this conclusion are stated as what is known to date with the available records.

Whatever may have been the immediate purpose of the semi-will or deed of entail[4] as mentioned above, it was revoked by Arthur a decade later, as shown in Middletown land records on the date of October 8, 1688, and was declared by him over his signature to be utterly void and of non-effect. Whether or not he was legally empowered to cancel this instrument, there can be no doubt that such was his intention, nor can we doubt that he had sufficient motives prompting its revocation. There is no proof that he returned to Middletown to live at this time, or at any time subsequently unless shortly before his death, which occurred on February 7, 1706/07, and he may have been there merely on a visit.

Regardless, immediately after Arthur's decease a disagreement among his heirs arose in regard to the Middletown property, which dispute was only settled by an appeal to the governor and council for the appointment of arbitrators. Thus, Middletown land records[5] contain the following:

> ...for as much as James Scovel and John Scovil, William Borden and Nathaniel Hudson for themselves and their heirs have made choice of us whose names are underwritten to arbitrate the differences relating to their father Arthur Scovel's deceased lands in Middletown...[6]

---

3 This deed is recorded in the First Book of Records at Middletown.

4 In English common law, fee tail or entail is a form of trust established by deed or settlement that restricts the sale or inheritance of an estate in real property and prevents the property from being sold.

5 Middletown Land Records, Vol: 2; 170.

6 The document is dated March 2, 1705/06, thereafter, follows award and very minute division.

The William Borden and the Nathaniel Hudson named in the foregoing petition were husbands respectively of Elizabeth Scoville, daughter of Arthur and Joanna, and of Rachel, widow of Arthur's eldest son Arthur. The estate of Arthur was not administered through either the Hartford or New London probate court, but it is self-evident from the petition cited above that no other persons besides the four who are named had any share in the Middletown lands. This must be regarded as proof positive that Arthur and Joanna Scoville had no other children living in 1678 besides those mentioned in the deed of entail recorded in the fall of that year, and if any were born afterward they did not participate in the division of Middletown's real property. This detailed discussion is a matter of importance to determine the origin of one Stephen Scovil of Lyme, who has caused the early genealogists on this line many speculations as to his parentage.

The wife of Stephen Scovil[1] was Sarah, daughter of Thomas and Hannah (Brockway) Champion, who was born at Lyme, March 8, 1687/8, from which it is fair to assume that her husband was born several years earlier, say between 1680 and 1684. In that case he would have been 21 to 25 years old, and his wife Sarah not yet 18 at the time of their marriage in November 1705. The greater part of their lives was passed at Lyme, probably on the settlement then known as North Society, near the present village of North Lyme, but about the year 1724, the family removed to Hadlyme parish of East Haddam, some four miles distant from North Lyme, and remained there.

To determine Stephen's[1] origin, it is necessary to frame some kind of hypotheses, and a choice is presented of these alternatives. Either we may regard the obscure "William Scovil" of Dr. Fields[7] mention as a real personage, and punitive father of Stephen, or else we must suppose that Arthur Scoville of Boston, Middletown, and Lyme to have been his father, probably by a second marriage after the death of his wife Joanna—keeping in mind, however, that there is no public record of a second marriage, nor of the death of his first or conjectural second wife.

In the one case we are obliged to acknowledge that there is absolutely no proof of the existence of a William Scoville at any time so early as that reported by Dr. Fields, either in Haddam or at East Haddam, nor yet at Lyme, where the records have been carefully researched by Mr. Brainard[8] and others. There has not been found any progenitor of the same generation as Arthur and John anywhere in the Connecticut colony who owned real property, or died leaving an estate to be administered, so far as can be discovered from contemporary sources. Under the circumstances, the alleged early settler (William Scovil) of Haddam, who is reported to have removed from Hartford "not far from the year 1668" fades into a more or less nebulous personage—in fact a non-entity.

With John[1]and "William Scovil" eliminated, there remains only Arthur, who described himself of "Lyme" in 1678 and likely lived the rest of his life out there to be considered as the possible parent of Stephen.[2]

No one can suppose the latter to have been an immigrant colonist, and absolutely no other heads of families bearing the Scovil patronymic are known to have been in this country

7 Charles Eastman does not expand on who Dr. Fields was.

8 Brainard, Homer W., *A Survey of the Scovils or Scovills in England and America*, (1915).

toward the close of the century besides Arthur and John. Stephen[1] was of a later generation than theirs, and if he did not belong to one or the other of their households, it is impossible to account for his origin. John's family is excluded, by virtue of documentary evidence, therefore Stephen[1] can be assigned only to the family of Arthur. The reasons for regarding him, provisionally at least, as son by a second marriage, are these:

1. The fact that he must have been born at a later date than that of September 1678, at which time Joanna probably was dead, since neither real or personal property was bestowed on her by the deed of entail on file at Middletown, or any provisions made for her maintenance.
2. Had Stephen been the son of Arthur and Joanna, he would undoubtably have shared in the distribution of his father's estate and joined in with the other heirs in the petition for appointment of arbitrators in the dispute that arose among the heirs following Arthur's decease.

The fact that there was a disagreement among the heirs is significant. It implies that the question was raised that a problematical deed of entail is to be construed as having customary affect, or whether it was no longer operative after having been revoked by Arthur, or after he had attempted to revoke it. It may be held to imply, also, that Stephen's[1] rights were involved considering that he was an heir, but that the dispute was terminated so far as his individual claims were concerned, probably by private agreement with the other heirs before the matter was submitted to arbitration. Or, since his name does not appear along with the other petitioners, we may suppose that on coming of age, or at the time of his marriage in Lyme a few months prior to Arthur's decease, he had already received his portion of the patrimony. Having explained these difficulties, there remains but one valid objection to this hypothesis, which is the fact that no record exists of Arthur's second marriage, nor of the death of his conjectured second wife, which must have occurred prior to his own decease. These omissions can only be attributed to the likelihood of careless record keeping, destruction of the records by fire or vermin, or some other reason why these records do not exist. The recordkeeping of Lyme was no different than in many other New England towns in those early days—they were carelessly kept or otherwise defective.

It may be objected by some that the foregoing arguments are not conclusive and that there isn't sufficient evidence justifying the claim of a relationship between Arthur and Steven[1] Scovil as father and son. The following suppositions will (hopefully) show that they were indeed related.

First: It was the common custom of the day for Christian names to be perpetuated in the male line from one generation to the next. When there were several sons, the first born was fairly certain to be named after his father or paternal grandfather, and the next eldest after some other near relative, often a maternal uncle or grandparent. That the father of the two immigrant colonists was named *John* may be considered probable from the fact that this is the only Christian name which reappears in common among the children of both Arthur and John Scovil. As with the family of Stephen,[1] we find that his eldest son was Stephen,[2] and his second son was named Arthur.[2] One would be hard pressed to see this as merely a coincidence.

Second: A deed bearing the date of December 22, 1715, from Peter Pratt to Stephen Scovil, was acknowledged in the presence of two witnesses: William Borden and Joanna Scoville. This would seem to be a significant fact or an extremely singular coincidence that both persons were near kinsfolk of Arthur Scovil. William Borden was the son-in-law and husband of Elizabeth,[1] Stephen's[1] supposed half-sister. Joanna, a minor witness, was the daughter of John[1] Scovil, who married Mary Lucas and the supposed niece of Stephen. Among the entire population of Lyme, why should these connections of Arthur Scovil witness a deed in favor of Stephen[1] Scovil unless they were at the same time relatives?

Third: A son of the same Stephen[1] Scoville, Thomas[2] by name, married in 1749 Jerusha, daughter of James[1] Scovil of Wallingford, and great-granddaughter of Arthur. At about the same time another of Stephen's[1] sons, Nathan,[2] removed from Hadlyme parish to Wallingford, and purchased land near Notch Mountain adjoining that of the aforementioned James[1] Scovil. Hadlyme to Wallingford are some distance apart,[9] and communication was not easy in those days. Yet the two Scovil families must have been intimately acquainted to permit the above events taking place, and this acquaintance was probably due to the fact of a previously existing relationship between the parties.

Fourth: In the year 1735 Stephen[1] and the same James[1] Scoville of Meriden-Wallingford are associated in the purchase of a tract of land in Harwinton. Neither of them located there but appear merely to have invested together in a business enterprise. James[1] eventually sold his holdings, and Stephen[1] gave his in turn to his son Ezekiel,[2] who settled in that region. The point to be emphasized here is that these heads of families, living some distance apart, had business dealings severally or together even in more remote regions of the state and can scarcely be supposed to have joined in these negotiations with each other except as a result of their mutual relationship.

Finally: To sum up the conclusions that have been reached as to Stephen's[1] parentage, all available information appears to indicate that Stephen[1] Scovil of Lyme and Hadlyme was the son of Arthur, the immigrant ancestor; the son likely the product of a second marriage after the death of Arthur's first wife, Joanna, and the date of his birth may be assigned within the interval of 1680–1684, and that there is no proof of the existence of a William Scovil at Haddam or elsewhere in the colony of the same generation as Arthur and John, the two settlers, nor is there proof of the existence of any other Scovil progenitor excepting these two who is capable of being regarded as a parent of Steven. John Scovil of Waterbury and Haddam could not have been Steven's father, and by process of exclusion Arthur *must* have been.

***Children of Arthur and Joanna Scovil***

i. Elizabeth, b. Dec 1, 1662; d.y.

ii. Arthur, b. Jun 24, 1663/64; d. Jun 24, 1694, m. Rachel________; she m. second Nathaniel Hudson.

iii. Elizabeth, b. Sep 18,1665; d.y.

9 In our current road and highway system, the distance between these two points is 42.2 miles. It may have been much further during the 1700s due to the condition of the roadways and the fact that many "roads" were just pathways.

iv. Elizabeth, b. Mar 18, 1667; m. William Borden of Lyme, Connecticut.

v. James, b. Jun 13, 1670; m. Hannah________.

vi. John, b. abt. 1672 in Middletown; m. Mary Lucas.

***Child of Arthur Scovil and Conjectured Second Wife***

1. vii. **Stephen**,[1] b. 1680/84 in Lyme; m. Sarah Champion..

# First Generation

## *1. Stephen[1] Scoville (Arthur)*

Born about 1680 to 1684, probably in Lyme; died in East Haddam, Hadlyme parish, between May 20 and 30, 1752; married 4 November 1705, Sarah Champion, born in Lyme 8 March 1687/88; she was living in 1745, death date is unknown. She was the daughter of Henry Champion and Hannah Brockway of Lyme.

As mentioned in the previous chapter, we know that Stephen bought thirty acres of land in 1724, which was bounded by what was known as the "Commons."[10] Years later the "Commons" became the parish of Hadlyme. The Society of Hadlyme was formed from the East Haddam Society and Lyme Third Society in October 1742. A copy of the original record is below:

> At a General Assembly holden at New Haven on 14th Day of Oct. Ano: don-1742 Upon the memorial of Isaac Willey, Stephen Scovil, John Comstock and other members of the First Society in East Haddam in Lyme preferred to this Assembly in May Last.... This Assembly do Enact, Decree, and Order that ye said Isaac Willey, Stephen Scovil, John Comstock and the Rest of the Inhabitants of the Parish hereafter Described be and they are here by Imbodyed and made one District Ecclesiastical Society by the name of Hadlyme...[11]

Hadlyme is on the easten shore of the Connecticut River and is in the northwest corner of the Town of Lyme and was settled much earlier, circa 1685, at a place referred to as Creek Row, where the settlers established their homesteads. The men who first settled there were John Bates, a man with the last name "Cone," Daniel Brainard, a man with the surname of "Gates," Nicholas Ackley, Samuel Spencer, and others. By the year 1700, there were thirty families living in East Haddam. It is not known with certainty that Stephen Scoville was born in East Haddam but it's possible that this family removed from Lyme to this area in early stages of the settlement.

From the Grantor/Grantee records of East Haddam[12] you will note that Stephen[1] was involved with buying and selling property, as was his son Stephen,[2] and other members of his family.

| Grantor | Grantee | Date of Transaction | Book/Page |
|---|---|---|---|
| Scoville, Stephen | Scoville, Hezekiah | January 28, 1741, | 5/4 |
| Scoville, Stephen | Williams, Philip | April 8, 1751, | 4/98 |

10 East Haddam Land Records, Vol: 1. 556. Connecticut State Library, Hartford, Connecticut.

11 *History of Middlesex County, Connecticut With Biographical Sketches of Its Prominent Men,* (1884, New York, J.B. Beers & Co. 36 Vesey Street. No one author is ascribed to this work.

12 East Haddam Grantor/Grantee List 1704–1910, [mf#312; mf#0004110] General Index—East Haddam, Connecticut State Library, Hartford, Connecticut.

| Grantee | Grantor | Date of Transaction | Book/Page |
|---|---|---|---|
| Scoville, Stephen | Town of E.H. | May 15, 1750, | 4/35 |
| Scoville, Stephen | Abner Bangs | April 8, 1751, | 4/202 |
| Scoville, Stephen | Town of E.H. | June 20, 1751, | 5/8 |

Most of these transactions took place a year prior to Stephen's death. There is no description of said properties as it is an index only; however, I have added the book and page numbers should anyone want to review these land records for themselves.

One can ascertain that this branch of the Scovilles were just regular folk working long hours in all kinds of weather at various trades:[13] keeping food on the table and raising their families. A small glimpse into the life of Stephen comes from his association with his father-in-law, Thomas Champion.

According to Hempstead's diary,[14] Stephen Scoville was "engaged in the manufacture of planks and staves."

Thomas Champion was engaged in the ownership and management of a sawmill situated in the Eight Mile River in the town of Lyme.[15] It is likely that Stephen was associated with his father-in-law in this venture. The Eight Mile River is a considerable stream, which is formed by two branches, one in the town of East Haddam and the other in the town of Salem. This waterway flows into the Eight Mile River Cove, sometimes referred to as Hamburg Cove, near the village of Hamburg. In times past, during the shad season,[16] the early settlers could catch shad by the thousands. Through this cove, or perhaps at Ely's Wharf, a mile below on the Connecticut River, the export of shad could be handled. It appears that Stephen also owned land along Beaver Brook, which may be an indication that he was also involved in the fur trade; this area is near the present village of North Lyme.

Stephen Scoville became a member of the Hadlyme Church in 1745/6; his wife, Sarah, was admitted to full communion in the First Church of East Haddam on December 19, 1731. The family would have had to travel some six miles to the north to worship there. About the year 1742, a church was gathered in Hadlyme,[17]and Sarah became a member of this church.

---

13 A good source of the daily life in the 1700s, see *Diary of Joshua Hempstead*, readily available for purchase on Amazon.

14 *Diary of Joshua Hempstead of New London, Connecticut, Covering a Period of Forty-Seven Years, From September 1711 to November 1758*; (year)1715, May 19. 46; "Joshua [ ] & Stephen Scophills [sic] at Lyme to buy plank.

15 Trowbrige, Francis Bacon, *The Champion Genealogy: A History of the Descendants of Henry Champion, of Saybrook and Lyme, Connecticut, Together with Some Account of Other Families of the Name. (1891).* Lyme Records, Vol: III, 141.

16 Spencer's Haddam Shad Shack is a Landmark and Historical Place. The old building is still there. There is also a Shad Shack Museum in Haddam-Killingworth. Shad is the State Fish of Connecticut and has been harvested since 1662.

17 "The [Ecclesiastical] Society of Hadlyme was incorporated in Oct. 1742 and was thus called because it was partly from Lyme. The church was organized with ten male members, on the 26th of June 1745, and on the 18th of the succeeding September, the Rev. Grindall Rawson, who had been

Several of the Scoville children, who were now adults, were baptized by its pastor and became members about 1746. The book *The Church Records of Hadlyme, Complete List of Members 1745–1913* (page 54) shows Stephen and Sarah Scoville as members. Hadlyme is where the family remained until the death of Stephen in 1752. At the time of Stephen's death, this couple had been married forty-seven years and they raised ten children together in relative comfort for this time period. Additionally, all their children lived into adulthood in a time when the mortality rate for children was high due to illnesses, epidemics, and/or from accidents.

Stephen Scoville wrote his will, which was approved on July 7, 1752. We do not have the exact date of death, only that it was between May 20 and 30, 1752. He would have been between 72 and 76 years old at the time of his death. Because of his age and the fact that mortality was near, he wrote out his will.[18]

The Will of Stephen Schoval[sic][19]

> In the name of God amen. I Stephen Schoval of East Haddam in the county of Hartford and colony of Connecticut; calling in mind my mortality and that it is appointed for all man wants to die, and being a perfect in memory, for which I desire to bless God, I do now make this my Last will and Testament, and firstly I do give my soul into the hands of God that gave it in my Body to be Buried with decent Christian Burial and Respecting what a Estate God hath blessed me with al[sic] here: I do after all my lawful Debts are paid by my executor here after mentioned, I give and bestow in manner and form as follows This Twentieth day of May Annoque Domini 1752.
>
> Imprimis. Unto my Beloved wife Sarah Schoval I do give an bequeath to use in my House and Lands and Tenements During her Remaining my widow, and that Provided my son Thomas Schoval Behave well toward her, that he shall have the Improvement thereof and live with her, allowing her Therefore an Honorable maintenance out of the same; and provided he or his Heirs and etc. (?) shall abide to perform the same as above, he to have it after her Disease, whom with my wife I do ordain executors of this my last will and Testament and here [it is] to be understood that she keep sundry movables as she shall judge needful for her to keeping House so long as she lives.
>
> To my beloved son Stephen Schoval besides what I have already given him I do give him Ten shillings old Tenner to be paid by my Executors [within] suitable time after my Decease. To my beloved son Arthur Schoval, I do give besides what I have already given him Ten shillings of old Tenner are paid as above. With respect to my beloved sons and daughters, viz. Ezekiel Schoval, Hezekiah Schoval, Daniel Schoval, Sarah Brockway, and Mary Beckwith; I do give my movables to be equally divided,

---

minister several years at South-Hadley, Mass., was installed their pastor." Taken from the online website "Historic Buildings of Connecticut" by David Dudley Field. The information on the website comes from his book: *A Statistical Account of the County of Middlesex, in Connecticut* (1819).

18 Stephen's will can be found at the Connecticut State Library, [case#2678 & 5126]. Now also available via Ancestry.

19 The will is copied verbatim as it appears in the original.

considering what each of them had as portion when they Divide, and that their Brother Nathan Schoval[20] is to come in with them in the Division Equal as above as may be mentioned hereafter [ ] this is to be noted that mothers to keep such as she shall need to keep house with all till her Deceased, and yn Divided. Unto beloved son Thomas Schoval I do give in bequeath my Tenements and land after my wife's Disease as above sd, or to come in the possession thereof before provided his mother should marry again. . . .

To my Beloved son Nathan Schoval, I do give to come in with his other Brothers and Sisters mentioned together as equal part of my movable estate within the same Terms and in the same manner as before mentioned of them.

Signed, Sealed, Published and Pronounced this to be my Last will and Testmt, canceling all former wills and Testaments. In Testimony whereof I do set my hand and seal the Day and Date before mentioned. . .

Signed
Stephen Scovill

Ephraim Fuller
her
Sarah X Smith
Mark
Mary Fuller
Grindal Rawson.

The will was probably written by Rev. Grindal Rawson, pastor of the Hadlyme church, who was also one of the witnesses. The witnesses personally appeared before Joseph Spencer, Justice of the Peace, and provided the will, which was approved, allowed, and ordered to be recorded July 7, 1752.

The total estate was valued at £168–8p-6d, and the inventory appears to have been undertaken by Samuel Crosby, Christopher Holmes, and Nathaniel Beckwith.

The inventory list is entered as I imagine the person or persons taking the inventory would have by walking through each room and noting each item:

| | | |
|---|---|---|
| Castor Hat | Blue Straight body coat | another pair of brown leather breeches [sic] |
| 2 great coats | two vests | pair of boots and spurs |
| 2 pair of shoes | 2 pair buckles | Blue and black stockings |
| Another pr stockings | 1 Holland shirt | another shirt |
| Flannel check shirt | check woolen | 2 pair linen drawers |
| 1 Holland cap | one Holland handkerchief | two caps |
| 1 pair mittens | Silk handkerchief | 6 ½ yards tow cloth |
| 5 yards ditto | | |

20 Nathan was the last-born child of Stephen Scoville and Sarah Champion. He (Nathan) had removed to Wallingford-Meriden (CT) before 1757.

This clothing inventory shows a man with work clothing as well as those for church and visiting.

The inventory taker had moved from the kitchen area to a bedroom or bedrooms. There are implements for shoe making as well as for knitting clothing. There is a "Great Chair" likely reserved for the head of the household, or a guest or person of importance. There are no drinking mugs noted but a "wine glass" is listed. It would appear the Scoville home had three beds with assorted sheets and coverlets.

| | | |
|---|---|---|
| A Great Chair | 2 small chairs | 2 ditto |
| 1 brass kettle | 1 pewter quart | 2 pint basons [sic] |
| 1 pewter platter | 5 pewter spoons | old pewter |
| 1 wine glass | 5 vials | 3 bottles |
| 1 earthen platter | 4 wooden dishes | 6 wooden plates |
| 1 iron skillet | 2 knives and forks | 1 box of iron and heaters |
| 1 piggin[21] | 1 pair of small steel yds. | 1 churn |
| 5 prs knitting needles | 1 butter tub | iron candle stick |
| 1 hetchel[22] | 1 iron pot and hooks | frying pan |
| grid iron | tongs and slice | meat fork and lamp |
| 2 trammels[23] | 2 sheets and tablecloth | 1 sheet |
| 1 napkin | 1 line[sic] sheet (linen?) | 1 flannel blanket |
| 2 sheets | 1 coverlet | bed bolster and pillow |
| 2 bedsteads and cord | another bed | bed tick and bolster |
| 6 coverlets, one rag loom | | |

Additionally, there are eight books listed:

| | | |
|---|---|---|
| 1 Testament | 1 Psalm book | 1 Account book |
| 1 Psalter | 3 small bound books | 1 catechism |

As in many colonial households of some means, listed are books that would reflect the colonial period, i.e., Testament, Psalms, and then an account book. But what of the "three small bound books"?

We know that Stephen could read and write (as he signed the will), but could all the family members read and write? Or just the males? Without existing journals, diaries, or letters from the females in the family, this is a question that remains without an answer.

The next group of items recorded are the provisions within the household along with raw materials:

21 A "piggin" is a small wooden pail with one stave extended upward as a handle.

22 A flax hetchel or hatchel is a tool to comb the flax fibers over a bed of nails.

23 A hook to take vessels out of the fire.

| | | |
|---|---|---|
| 11 pounds tobacco | 1 cedar tub | 3 pounds flax |
| 2 old casks | 3 ½ pounds of coverlet yarn | 4 ¾ pounds of woolen yarn |
| 3 pounds wool | 2 axes and a froo[24][sic] | meal sleve[25] |
| 2 ½ bushels of wheat | 2 bushels Indian corn | 2 ½ bushels of override(?)meal |

In this section there are pounds of wool, yet there is no mention of a spinning wheel or loom for weaving. In the inventory of Sarah Champion Scoville's grandfather, Henry Champion, a spinning wheel was listed. Perhaps the wool and yarn were spun at the Champion home in Lyme. Because this family was of some means, they may have had hired girls to do this type of work. In her book *Our Own Snug Fireside, Images of The New England Home, 1760–1860,* Jane C. Nylander states, "Routine chores assigned to hired girls included most of the heavy indoor work."[26] This would include spinning.

Conversely, there is mention of eleven pounds of tobacco, yet no mention of a pipe in the inventory. Since Stephen was engaged in the sawmill and the fur trade, there is no reason to doubt that he also planted tobacco to be sold in the marketplace.

We now come to the farming implements and tools:

| | | |
|---|---|---|
| Tap borer[27] | 1 small gimlet and hammer | pr old chisels |
| 1 great auger | 1 chain and clews (?) | 1 cap ring |
| cart boxes and hoops | harness | 2 guns |
| 1 dye tub | 1 set plow irons | another chain |
| 1 sickle | | |

The family's livestock consisted of a horse, 1 dark red cow and calf, another cow, and two swine.

Lastly, the will notes the house and the land:

| | |
|---|---|
| Dwelling house | £25 |
| Barn | £9 |
| 3 acres of land | £51 |
| 17 acres of land | £42–10p |
| 15 ½ acres of land | £28 |
| 1 ¾ acres of land | £4–10p |

We know that Sarah was alive at the time of her husband's death as she is mentioned in his will. Perhaps she went to live with her son Thomas, who was in charge of "behaving well toward her," or she remained in the home where she had lived for some forty-seven years of her marriage and raised all their children.

24 An unknown item.

25 Could possibly be a sieve.

26 p. 50–51

27 A tool used for boring tapping holes in casks.

Upon Stephen's death, Sarah would have been at least sixty-five years of age. Thomas Scoville (*Stephen,*[1] *Arthur*) moved to Lempster, New Hampshire, around 1775, which is when he sold his property in Hadlyme.

We do not know if his aged mother would have made the trip to New Hampshire, but it is doubtful she would have been left on her own as Thomas would stand to lose his inheritance if he did not follow his father's instructions "to treat her well and care for her." It is also possible that Sarah had died by the time Thomas left to pursue a life first in New Hampshire and then Orwell, Vermont. I have not found a will for Sarah, nor any other records that would have provided any clues to the approximation of her death.

The federal census did not begin until 1790 (although there was a special census in Vermont for 1788), however, no image is available on Ancestry for the 1788 Vermont census; at any rate, Sarah would have been over a hundred years old to have been listed in this census.

### *Children of Stephen Scoville and Sarah Champion*

Born in East Haddam, Connecticut:

2.

- i. Stephen[2], b. 20 Aug 1706; m. Rebecca Millard
- ii. Sarah, b. 11 Sep 1708; m. 27 1739, John Brockway of Lyme (William, Wolston), b. 10 May 1697, his second wife. She died at Lyme 12 Jun 1770.
- iii. Arthur, b. about 1710; m. Phoebe Willey.
- iv. Ezekiel, b. 12 Jun about 1712; m. Mindwell Barber.
- v. Hezekiah, b. about 1714; m Mary Gates.
- vi. Hannah, b. about 1716; bap. as an adult at Hadlyme, Jan 1745. Probably died before her father as she is not mentioned in his will.
- vii. Daniel, b. about 1718; married Miriam Chamberlain; second Lucy Beckwith. No issue from either marriage.
- viii. Mary, b. about 1720; m. Joseph Beckwith.
- ix. Thomas, b. 16 June 1722; m Jerusha Scoville.
- x. Nathan, b. about 1727; bap. As an adult, Jan 1745/6; m. Mary

# Second Generation

## 2. *Stephen[2] Scoville* (*Stephen,[1] Arthur*)

Born in Lyme or East Haddam 20 August 1706; died in East Haddam shortly after 13 April 1778; married Rebecca Millard on 16 January 1729, at East Haddam. She was the daughter of Thomas Millard and Rebecca________[28] also of East Haddam.

The Millard family has been documented, although not to any great lengths. From an article published in *The American Genealogist* in 1946 by Wyman, Matthew Millard was the son of Humphrey Millard and Elizabeth Smith, born September 30, 1680. The records of Reading, Massachusetts, have the elder Millard living there as early as 1676, where his name is given as "Humphrey Miller." Humphrey had been a soldier in King Phillip's War[29] and it is said he was involved in the Great Swamp fight in December 1775.

When the war ended, he married Elizabeth Smith, the daughter of Matthew Smith of Woburn, Massachusetts, on September 12, 1677, at Cambridge, Massachusetts.[30] This couple had four children between 1678 and 1684—two sons and two daughters, with only the sons, Thomas and Matthew Millard, surviving into adulthood.

Thomas Millard had removed from Massachusetts to Connecticut after selling his farm in Charlestown, Massachusetts, in 1724/25, and settled in Millington parish, which lies in East Haddam, Connecticut. Thomas is said to have been a weaver by trade in Massachusetts and likely plied his trade in Millington as well.

Thomas made out his will on July 26, 1728, and had just turned fifty years old on the 23rd of June. Perhaps he was in poor health when he made out his will as Thomas died on October 17, 1728, in East Haddam and in the probate records he is listed as "Thomas Miller" of "Haddam East Society."[31] His estate was inventoried by John Spencer, John Church, and Jabez Chapman. The land inventory was worth £762–10–00. The will reads in part:

---

28 Many articles and genealogical websites have recorded Thomas' wife's surname as "Dutton," however, in an article from *The American Genealogist* (aka TAG) on the Millard family disputes this. Vol. 22,23,24 of TAG (1946–47) 205–206. Article written and researched by Edward Church Smith and Philip Mack Smith. *Outline for a Genealogy of the Family of Humphrey Millard of Reading, Massachusetts.* However, the will of Thomas Millard references the land that he is giving to his son, Matthew Millard: "I give him the other half of the aforesaid lott that lyes between me and brother Dutton . . ." The term "brother" could refer to a brother-in-law or a fellow member of a church. Since the Millards are not the scope of this research, I have not delved into this any further.

29 Bodge, George Madison, A.B., *Soldiers In King Philip's War: Being a Critical Account of That War with A Concise History of the Indian Wars of New England From 1620–1677*; (1896 and 1906). One of the men listed on the roster is Humphrey Millard.

30 *Massachusetts Compiled Marriages 1633–1850;* Ancestry.

31 Hartford Probate Records, Vol. XII, [146-7-8]. Connecticut State Library, Hartford, Connecticut.

> I, Thomas Miller of Hadam [sic] . . . give his wife Rebecca Miller on third of land, moveable estate, son Thomas Miller land "between the lands of Brother Dutton and the Lott [sic] which I now dwell, etc., . . . son Matthew Miller, son John Miller and daughter Rebecca Miller money, authorized Ensign John Church and Jebez Chapman to divide land; wife Rebecca and son Thomas executors; witness John X Spencer, Isaac Eylley, Jr., Samuel Dutton.

The will was proved on November 3, 1728. The court appointed Rebecca to be the guardian of her children Matthew, age 19, and John, age 15, on April 1, 1729; and then on December 13, 1728, she was made guardian of her daughter Hannah.[32]

Daughters Rebecca, Elizabeth, and Hannah received money from their father's estate but that does not mean that they had control of it as we see with daughter Rebecca (wife-to-be of Stephen Scoville).

Rebecca was twenty-two years old at the time of her father's death. He left her £65, however, her brothers oversaw paying her this amount per the instructions of the will. Her sisters, Elizabeth and Hannah, presumably were left similar amounts, which would likely go towards their dowries.

Not much is known of Stephen's daily life. Like many men of his time, he performed multiple occupations. He likely farmed some of his land and may have also worked in the sawmill as did his father before him. He bought and sold land and may have leased some of his land for additional income. He was a carpenter, tended to livestock, planted, and cared for the crops, went to church. He may have been in the militia, as men were required to do. Stephen and his sons would have spent much of their time outdoors in all kinds of weather. Conversely, the women of the family would be involved with the household duties, caring for the sick, tending to a kitchen garden, making clothing, etc. The early colonial families may have seemed to do nothing but work, however, they did enjoy games, quilting parties, and storytelling, depending upon the time of year.[33]

The actual date of Stephen's death is not known, however, it is believed to be sometime after he made out as will on April 13, 1778. Stephen would have been seventy-two years of age at this time.

> . . . to each children [sic] one shilling. To son Samuel Scovel ten shillings together with what I have already given him. To my son Timothy ten pounds of my personal estate together what I have already given him. To the heirs of my deceased son, Henry, Henry, and Mary four pounds out of my personal estate; to my son Stephen Scovel all my lands and buildings thereon standing, reserving his mother's use of same;

---

32 *Guardianship: A Misunderstood Probate Term,* posted by the Ancestry Team on January 14, 2016. The article can be found in Collections, Research. It states in part, "It isn't uncommon to find children with guardians even with the mother still living . . . a woman didn't have the legal standing herself to represent even her own children."

33 Nylander, Jane C, *By Our Own Snug Fireside: Images of The New England Home, 1760–1860,* (1993).

> also, my iron crowbar and draft chain. To my children Samuel, Timothy, Stephen, Rebecca, Elizabeth and my grandchildren Henry and Mary seven shillings lawful money, to be equally divided between them. Son Timothy and daughters Rebecca and Elizabeth to be residuary legatees. Son Stephen to be executor.

His will was dated April 13, 1778, and proved at Colchester, March 7, 1780.

### *Children of Stephen Scoville and Rebecca Millard*

Born in East Haddam:

i. Stephen, b. 19 Sep. 1729; d. 29 Sep. 1751, in Cornwall, Litchfield, Connecticut.

In 1738, the land in Cornwall had gone up for sale, and by 1742 there were forty-five names on the tax list. While Stephen is not mentioned on this list, he had an interest in settling there. His Millard relatives had already removed to Cornwall and Stephen had made the long trip to settle there. However, his plans were cut short as he died at the age of twenty-two years. It is unknown whether he died from an illness or from an accident. I have not found any reference to the cause of his death. In *The History of Cornwall* by E.C. Starr, Starr does mention *a* Stephen Scoville as dying in 1739 from a "bite from a mad cat," however, this is too early for the Stephen we are discussing here. Whether from illness or accident, Stephen did leave a will to provide for his younger siblings in the way of land in Cornwall.[34] The following is the inventory for his estate.[35] All spelling is exactly as it is in the original records.

> 1 beaver hat, 1 shirt, 1 shirt, 1 pr of leather bretches, a straight bodyed coat and vest, 1 pair stockens, 2 pr brass buckles, 1 pair camblet bretches, 1 pair mittens, a limming hook, one chest, seventy acres of rough land

There is no mention of a bed, eating implements, or any creature comforts. He had the barest of necessities and "seventy-acres of rough land." Since his uncles Thomas and Matthew Millard had already settled in Cornwall, he likely boarded with them until he could build a place of his own.

The distribution of his estate occurred on February 23, 1757. The co-administrators of the estate were his brother Samuel and father, Stephen Scoville.

The seventy acres of rough land is described in the distribution of the estate.

> . . . in said Cornwall being [ ] a part on the Second part the 26th lot of the 4th Division which lot was laid out to the Reverend Mr. Solomon Palmer.[36] The said acres bounds as follows: Beginning at the East corner of the 25th lot. From that runs North 39–30, West 16 chains 65 links to a chestnut Stadle which is the North East corner of said

34 His death may have been caused by illness seeing that he made out a will at such a young age.

35 Litchfield Probate District, town of Cornwall, 1752, [No. 5126]. Connecticut State Library, Hartford, Connecticut.

36 Recorded in the Cornwall Proprietor First Book of Records, [folio 112].

lot; Thence West 9 degrees West 10 chains 95 links to a heap of stones on the south bound bounds begun at [ ] containing 12 acres and [ ] besides allowances for the highway.

The distribution to his brothers and sisters:
To Rebecca Scoville—nine acres of the estate
To Timothy Scoville—nine acres of the estate
To Henry Scoville—eight acres and a half
To Elizabeth Scoville—eleven acres
To Irena Scoville—eight acres
To Stephen Scoville—seven acres
To Samuel Scoville—twelve acres

ii. Samuel Scoville b. 29 Sep. 1731; d. 14 Jan. 1808, Cornwall. He married his first wife, Ruth Squires, about 1755.[37] He married his second wife, Mary Rowland, in Cornwall.

***Children of Samuel Scoville and Ruth Squires***

All born in Cornwall:

a. Jacob, b. 6 Nov 1756; m. Ruhamah (Jennings) Emmons.
b. Samuel, b. 8 Nov 1758; Mary Emmons; #2 Sarah_______. Removed to Vermont.

***Children of Samuel Scoville and Mary Rowland***

c. Joseph, perhaps b. 1765; d. aft. 1788.
d. Daniel, b. Oct 1768; m. Lois Rockwell.
e. Jonah, birth, death, and marriage unknown; is said to have removed to northeast Ohio.
f. Ezra, b. Oct 1768 (twin?); d. Jan. 1813;[38] m. Tryphena Terrell.
g. Stephen, birth date is unknown; he died in 1783.
h. Anna, b. abt. 1770; d. 26 Oct 1847, Coventry Ville, New York. She married Christopher Still Moses Stork. He was the son of Moses Stork and Eunice Mason and was born in Branford, Connecticut. As an adult, Christopher was a tanner, shoemaker, and farmer. Christopher and Anna's eldest children were born in Connecticut, but they soon removed to Coventryville, New York, where all their other children were born and raised. Christopher was one of the men who organized the First Congregational Church in Coventryville in 1805. According to *The History*

37 Ruth Squires was the daughter of Rev. Jonathan Squires of Plainfield, Connecticut.

38 You will note that many of the Scovilles that were living in Cornwall died between January–February 1813 due to the "spotted fever" epidemic. In the spring of 1812 until 1813 an entire section of New England was "scoured by a fearful epidemic," called "spotted fever" and later "malignant fever." It is now believed that this disease was cerebro-spinal meningitis, which was thought *not* to be contagious at the time.

*of the Town of Coventryville*, by Oliver P. Judd, Christopher's mother, Eunice, and two of his brothers also removed to Coventryville, while their father, Moses, was off at sea. Moses did not join them; he had been a man of the sea for too long to want to settle out in the wilderness. Moses Stork went back to the sea and never returned.

*Their Children*

*a. i.* Jonathan, b. abt. 1774; m. Salome Hoskins.

*b. ii.* Lois, birth, marriage, death dates are unknown; m. Dilly Howe and lived on Sharon Mountain (Connecticut).

*c. iii.* Sarah, bap. 18 Oct 1772.

***Children of Stephen Scoville and Rebecca Millard continued . . .***

iii. Rebecca, b. 25 Nov 1773; m. Medad Thornton.

iv. Sarah, b. 7 Mar 1736; d. 15 Aug 1736.

3. v. **Timothy**,[3] b. 20 Sep 1737; m. Thankful Crocker.

vi. Henry, b. 16 Mar 1740; d. in Bolton, Connecticut, after 15 Feb 1763; m. Martha Taylor; she the daughter of David and Martha (Ferry) Taylor; b. 29 Sep 1738 in Bolton; bap. 17 Dec 1738; d. at Bolton after 1775.[39] She married second, John Hale, 29 Sep 1768.

Henry served in the French and Indian War 1758/59 and possibly later. He served in the Second Regiment, Third Company under Capt. Nathan Whiting and Lt/Major Joseph Spencer. His name was found in the roster in the book *Connecticut Soldiers, French and Indian Wars, 1755–1762*, pages 35 and 129.

We know that Henry was still living as of Feb. 15, 1763, as he quit-claimed one-seventh interest in his deceased brother's land (Vol. II, p. 367, Cornwall Deeds). Henry lists himself as of "Bolton," and as having received to his "full satisfaction of Timothy Scovel of East Haddam, four pounds fifteen shillings lawful money. . . . to forever release Quit Claim unto said Timothy Scovel and his heirs assigns forever." This is the land that the eldest brother, Stephen, had left to him. Henry Scovel personally appeared and signed the document. The witnesses were Benjamin Trumble and Alex Phelps.

Henry was only twenty-three when the deed was signed and little else is known of his short life. Two children were born to this couple: Mary, born? and Henry, baptized at Bolton July 5, 1761; m. Sarah______.

vii. Sarah, b. 15 May 1742; d. Aug 27, 1749.

viii. Elizabeth, b. 28 Jan 1744.

ix. Hannah, bap. Jan 1745/46 at East Haddam First Church.

x. Irene, b. 20 Jul 1748.

xi. Stephen Scoville born Jan 4–15, 1752, East Haddam; died 27 Jan 1813, in Cornwall;[40]

39 *Connecticut Church Record Abstracts 1630–1920,* Ancestry.

40 Millard, Ebenezer Sherwood, *Diary and Account Book;* [call#974.62 c8mi, main vault 13]—"Mr. Stephen Scovel departed this life on Tuesday the 27th of January 1813 in the 62nd year of his life after a severe illness of about 10 days." Connecticut State Library, Hartford, Connecticut.

he married his cousin, Mary Scoville (*Arthur,[2] Stephen,[1] Arthur*) on or before 1778, likely in East Haddam. A birth date and death date for Mary have not been discovered; she had a brother, Abner, who was born in 1738, but there are no birthdates for sisters Phoebe and Sarah (who married Asahel Rogers). We can speculate that Mary was born sometime in the 1740s or the early 1750s.

This couple was in Cornwall by October 24, 1785, as a land record was recorded there (Cornwall Land Record 4/285), and Stephen's will was recorded October 9, 1813. This couple had several children who were deaf. Not much else is known about of this family.

***Children of Stephen Scoville and Mary Scoville***

i. Levi U. Scoville, b. abt. 1780, East Haddam; d. 25 Jul 1855, Cornwall; m. (1) Olive Merrill; she b. abt. 1779; d. 6 Feb 1830, Cornwall. He m. (2) Sally______; b. circa 1789 in New York; d. 21 Oct 1875, Cornwall. From Theodore S. Gold's book *Historical Records of the Town of Cornwall, Litchfield, Connecticut,* published 1904, page 259 comes the following: "From Stephen [Scoville] descendant of Levi, who was deaf and dumb[41]; and Sylvester, his son, who still occupies the old homestead."

Levi was a good farmer, and a man of remarkable intelligence for a deaf and dumb, before he had any modern advantages of education. He had no difficulty in communicating with his neighbors by natural signs so apt that all could understand. He was a regular attendant at church, and it was said, he knew what the minister had to say."

***Children of Levi Scoville and Olive Merrill***

All children likely born in Cornwall:

*a. i.* Ransley, nothing more is known.

*b. ii.* Harriet Eliza, b. 1805? d. 13 May 1885, Cornwall; probably the Harriet Eliza listed on the special 1880 census for Cornwall of "Defective, Dependent and Delinquent Classes." Listed as "deaf since birth." She was living with her brother Sylvester during this time.

*c. iii.* Artemus, b. 1810; d.? m. Amanda Ford on 30 Oct 1836.

*d. iv.* Mary Elizabeth, birth, and death dates unknown; m. Luther B. Harrison[42] in Cornwall on 30 Dec 1828; Luther B. Harrison, b. abt. 1805. They removed to Palmyra, Michigan.

*e. v.* Stephen, b. abt. 1813; death? m. Sabrina Wraight, b. abt. 1819.

*f. vi.* Sylvester Merrill, b. abt. 1816; d. 27 Oct 1897; m. Harriet Winans on 27 May 1824; m. #2 Mary Lane.[43]

*g. vii.* Olive Merrill, b. 7 Sep 1823; nothing more is known.

---

41 I have copied this entry verbatim from Gold's book. Please remember that it was not a "politically correct" society at that time, and the term "deaf and dumb" was commonly used.

42 Luther B. Harrison was the son of Luther Harrison and Rachel Johnson of Cornwall, Connecticut.

43 Marriages and death dates for Artemus, Mary Elizabeth, and Sylvester come from the *Barbour Vital Records* and the *Connecticut Vital Records Index of Deaths 1897–1968* found online at the Connecticut State Library, Hartford, Connecticut.

***Children of Stephen Scoville and Mary Scoville continued . . .***

ii. Irene, d. 2 Feb 1813 (likely from the "spotted fever" epidemic).

iii. Rebeckah, her birth and death dates are unknown.

iv. Mary, birth date unknown; d. 30 Dec 1803; m. David Wickwire.

### *The Beginning: Western Land for Sale*

On the second Thursday in October 1737, the Connecticut General Assembly enacted, "The act for the Ordering and Directing the Sale and Settlement of all Townships in Western Land."[44] This act would give specific rights of seven townships that would be sold at public auction during a specific period.[45] The town of Cornwall contained 384[46] acres and was one of the townships that would be on the auction block. The auction occurred in 1738 at the Fairfield Courthouse. According to Elijah Allen, each proprietor that purchased land in "said town" had to build a house "at least eighteen-foot square" and fence "six acres of land."[47] The new landowner had to remain on the land for "three years commencing after two years aforesaid."[48] So began the settlement of Cornwall Connecticut.

When the Connecticut general assembly decided to put Cornwall land up for sale, they designated that there would be fifty-three rights divided on the east side of the Housatonic River. The first meeting of the proprietors was held in Hartford, Connecticut, on September 6, 1738. Five men were chosen to lay out fifty acres for each proprietor as well as to decide where the roads would be and how wide. The five early proprietors were: Benajah Douglas, Joseph Waler, Joseph Kilbourn, Joseph Allen, and Samuel Roberts.

One of the more important aspects of a new community was the ministry. Before any land was put up for public auction, the ministry was to have the first three rights: one for the minister, one for the support of the school in the town, and the ministry had one right. The rest was sold at public auction. However, many of the original thirty-eight settlers had sold their rights, perhaps as an investment or sold them because they were not able to keep them.

I suspect that most of the early settlers had purchased this land sight unseen. Were they dispirited by what they saw? For this was a land of rolling hills, rocky soil, severe thunderstorms, and long, harsh winters. Many of the people who had come from the settlements along the Connecticut River were used to the fertile soil that had been abundant, but was now over-farmed and was becoming too crowded. The settlers that decided to remain in Cornwall and reached their plot saw nothing but trees. If the newcomer was fortunate, he found a lane that

44 Starr, Edward C., *The History of Cornwall, Connecticut*, 35.

45 Gannett, Michael R., *The Distribution of the Common Land of Cornwall, Connecticut, 1738–1887*, (Cornwall Historical Society, 1990), 18–20. Mr. Gannett provides a more detailed description on how Cornwall's land was distributed.

46 Starr, Edward, C., *The History of Cornwall*. This figure comes directly from Mr. Starr's book. The actual acreage of Cornwall is 29,504 acres (based on current records). The 384 acres is likely the amount of acreage that was auctioned off in the early stages.

47 *Ibid*

48 *Ibid*

his ox-drawn wagon could be driven down. The new landowner had to cut down the numerous trees and burn brush, build his house, and plow a garden. Once done, there would be acres of stumps doting the landscape. From the very first dig the settler likely hit rock. Some of these "rocks" were actually large boulders hidden beneath the ground. Here is what Elijah Allen had to say about the topography of Cornwall: "To a stranger it is somewhat Romantick [sic] as being interspersed with Hills and Dales."[49] The Reverend Dr. Styles, upon seeing the town, was asked his opinion of it and the Reverend commented, "Nature exhausted all her store to throw up rocks but did no more."[50]

The rocky land could be a curse, but once they were dug up, many of these stones were utilized by the settler in marking his boundaries, as well as to keep his animals in. To this day, the rocks that were dug up by the early settlers can still be seen throughout this area and other towns of Litchfield County.

The land that was once cleared by the sweat of men and oxen is now forested again. The walls of stone now hidden by acres of trees still wrap around the Cornwall countryside in a snake-like fashion as a testament to the perseverance of our ancestors.

By the year 1742, they were now forty-five names on the tax list that generated £1,433. One of these men—Matthew Millard—had originally bought of "Jonathan Patterson and Stephen Bissell" and was one of the largest landowners in Cornwall. At the first town meeting, Matthew Millard had the distinction of finding a minister for the newly formed town. In early New England, the minister was an honored member of the community as well as a role model who acted as the head of his own household and his congregation.

Matthew Millard had gained respect within the early community of Cornwall.[51] He was a man of some means and is on the list of Cornwall citizens as having owned livestock valued at £35 in 1742.[52] Matthew was sixty-two years old when he left an established community to strike out in a land that was remote with only 45 people living there.[53] We can only speculate on his reasonings for removing to such an area so late in life. In the seven years that he was a resident of Cornwall, he established himself to be the largest landowner in the town; he had been given the water rights to Cream Hill Lake and built himself a home on the west side of Town Street across from Judge Burnham. Matthew Millard died in Cornwall on September 14, 1749, at the age of sixty-nine years and is buried in the Allen Cemetery, a mile north of Cornwall Village.[54] Matthew's nephew, Stephen Scoville, followed his uncle to Cornwall and purchased land but didn't live long enough to settle there. Stephen in turn left property in Cornwall to his siblings, hence the beginning of the Scoville family in Cornwall.

---

49 Allen, Elijah, *Cornwall in 1801,* (Cornwall Historical Society). 1985.

50 *Ibid*

51 A person would have to have some standing in the community to be asked to pick someone as important as the minister.

52 To give some perspective, the value of the livestock in today's market would be $7,697.

53 By 1790, Cornwall's population had grown to 1,470 inhabitants. There were probably others that were not counted, i.e., Indigenous People and the African Americans who may have resided in this town at that time.

54 The information on the death and burial place comes from Starr's *History of Cornwall,* 416.

# Third Generation

### 3. *Timothy Scoville*[3] *(Stephen,*[2] *Stephen,*[1] *Arthur)*

Born 20 August 1737, East Haddam, Connecticut; died 30 January 1813, Cornwall, Connecticut.[55] His first marriage was to Thankful Crocker on 3 September 1760, in East Haddam; she born 27 January 1732/33, Colchester, New London, Connecticut, and died in Cornwall March 1781.[56] She was the daughter of James Crocker and Alice Swift.

Timothy Scoville was the last of the brothers to arrive in Cornwall. As previously recounted, his first brother, Stephen, left him nine acres when Timothy was twenty years old in 1757 and was then unmarried. The grantor/grantee lists from 1704–1901 show many Scovilles either as landowners or witnesses to deeds, particularly in the years between 1740–1750. When checking the land records for East Haddam, there isn't any evidence to indicate Timothy ever owned land in East Haddam prior to his removal to Cornwall.[57]

Timothy grew up on or near the land his grandfather had settled in Hadlyme parish. This is the land that was given to Timothy's father (Stephen[2]) to settle and raise his family. Timothy was the fifth child of eleven and the third son of Steven and Rebecca. Most likely, Timothy's father was a farmer, although like the men of his time, he had more than one skill. It is also probable that Stephen Scoville worked alongside his father and brothers on their land. Each generation was the same: the boys learned the skills of their fathers, uncles, and male neighbors; conversely, the daughters would help their mother in the kitchen and the garden and help with the younger children. Sometimes children would be bonded out to other families to work in their households. This was a common practice for boys and girls of that era. It is unknown whether any of the Scoville children were living in other households for a period of time as we lack the necessary documentation to provide such information to us.

The federal census didn't begin in Connecticut until 1790, and until 1840, only the head of the household was named. On the census reports for the aforementioned years, we can only see by the "tic" marks to designate how many males and females were in the household at any given time. These marks do not indicate what relationship these people had to the head of the household. This makes it difficult to prove a relationship and it can only be speculated how the household members were related. A "family" could consist of the parents, their children,

---

55 Two sources of the death date of Timothy are Ebenezer Sherwood Millard's *Diary and Account book, 13,* "Mr. Timothy Scovel and Mrs. Wickwire both died on Saturday, the 30th of Jan. 1813," and the newspaper *Connecticut Mirror,* Monday, March 8, 1813 issue and lists those that died of the "prevailing epidemic," in Cornwall: Mr. Stephen Scovill, aged 62; Mr. Timothy Scoville, aged 77; in Goshen, Mrs. Triphena Carrier, daughter of Timothy Scovill.

56 The death information is from Starr's *History of Cornwall.* No official vital record has been discovered regarding her death.

57 In Colonial America a male under the age of twenty-one could not buy or sell land without restriction until he reached his majority.

grandchildren, grandparents, aunts and uncles, as well as orphan children, outside help, such as hired girls or boys and farmhands—all in one household. One can imagine the complexity of such a household with many diverse personalities; however, the responsibility of the people in the household and authority always fell to the head of the family.

How and where did Timothy Scoville meet Thankful Crocker? This is one area of research where it is virtually impossible to find information. We know that Thankful's birth was registered in Colchester; however, her family may have lived in the Westchester section of Colchester. Without getting into the complete genealogy of the Crocker family, Thankful was the daughter of James Crocker[58] (*Jonathan,[1] John*) and Alice Swift (*Jireh,[1] William*). This couple had removed from Barnstable, Massachusetts, to Colchester about 1724.

The first land record for James Crocker is found in 1728 from "Samuel Fuller to James Crocker."[59] On the same day as the first transaction between Samuel Fuller and himself was another transaction, from "Andrew Carrier to James Crocker."[60]

The first transaction in 1728 was for a home lot house and 299 acres of land. By November 1, 1736, the Crocker household now swelled to seven children including Thankful, who was about eighteen months old at this time.

James Crocker then sold the land he had bought in 1728 from Samuel Fuller to Nathan Williams (did this family move to a larger home to accommodate the growing family?). Seven years prior to Thankful's marriage to Timothy, Thankful's father, James Crocker "of Colchester" made a gift to his son James of "30 acres of the West side of my farm I now live on."[61] This land bordered south on the Colchester–East Haddam line. This brings us back to how Timothy and Thankful met. It is conceivable that while Thankful may have lived some distance from the Millington parish area of East Haddam, it was still close enough to the border of East Haddam turnpike for a young Timothy to go courting.

As I have mentioned before, I've never found any land transactions for Timothy and once this couple was married, they likely lived with either the Scoville or Crocker families. This was not an uncommon practice as many couples waited weeks or even months before leaving the "parental home and going housekeeping."[62] In addition, when Thankful married Timothy she brought into the marriage a daughter from a previous relationship by the name of *Roxalana Andrews*.[63] Thankful was also six months pregnant with her second child at the time her marriage to Timothy—their first child having been conceived sometime in March 1760.

I've cross-checked all the Crocker entries for Colchester, Connecticut, in the Barbour Vital Records and could not find a man with the last name of *Andrews* who married a Thankful

58 From the Crocker family comes our Mayflower ancestors: Elizabeth Tilley, John Howland, and Richard Warren.

59 Colchester Land Records (herein CLR), Vol: 22:820; 1 home lot house, 299 acres. Connecticut State Library, Hartford, Connecticut.

60 CLR, Vol: 22:619.

61 CLR Vol: 62:388.

62 Nylander, Jane C., *Our Own Snug Fireside: Images of The New England Home, 1760–1860,* (1993), 60.

63 *Barbour Vital Records* for Colchester: "Andrews, Roxalana, 24 July 1758, d. Thankful Crocker."

Crocker. Also note that in the Barbour Vital Records for the birth of Thankful's daughter Roxalana, Thankful is listed as "Crocker" *not* Andrews. She may have had to name the father of her child, which was a common practice so that the father of the said child would provide for him/her and that the mother and child would not have to go to the town for financial help. There were other women named Thankful Crocker in the Crocker genealogy, but none had married a man with the last name of Andrews or had a daughter named Roxalana. Proof that this Roxalana was the daughter of Thankful Crocker and was raised as a Scoville will be discussed further in this study (see the chapter on the *Fourth Generation* for more on Roxlana).

Timothy's brother, Samuel, had gone to Cornwall as early as 1754, most likely spending time there to clear the land and to "settle for three years commencing after two years aforesaid." By 1761, Samuel Scoville had married Ruth Squires in Cornwall and had permanently settled there. There were nine acres of land waiting for Timothy—land he had inherited from his older brother Stephen. The young couple (Timothy and Thankful) probably discussed among themselves with their respective parents about their decision to pack up whatever goods they had to begin their journey to the Western Lands of Litchfield County, leaving family and friends in East Haddam and Colchester.

This couple was in Cornwall by September 13, 1762, as their third child, Timothy,[4] was born there on that date.[64]

I have not been able to ascertain the exact route that the early settlers to Cornwall took; they may have taken a route from East Haddam and would have had to cross the Connecticut River. Perhaps they took the ferry from Haddam or Chester (Connecticut) to make the initial crossing. From there they may have followed a road through Middletown and westward and, at some point in their journey, they would have followed a trail west before they arrived at their destination.[65]

An assembly was held in Hartford in May 1760 that the highways from Simsbury through the towns of New Hartford, Barkhamsted, Winchester, Colebrook, and Norfolk "should be cleared and made feasible for traveling . . . by the 20th of November 1761."[66] The so-called highways did not resemble our modern highways. They were typically one-lane roadways of dirt and grass. Some of these lanes still exist in the small towns in Litchfield County.

Once they arrived in Cornwall, it was imperative that a house be built to accommodate this family. It's possible that they were staying with one of their Scoville or Millard relatives in Cornwall until that could be accomplished. Many of the early settlers to Cornwall built log cabins, but as time went by the homes were typically known as a "cape," a one- or one-

64 The place of Timothy's birth is confirmed by Cornwall Vital Town Records, Vol. 1. Family History Library (herein FHL) [film#151243]; "Timothy Scovel, son of Timothy Scovel and Thankful his wife born Sept. 13th A.D. 1762."

65 On our modern roadways, it is 66.4 miles from East Haddam to Cornwall and takes approximately 1 hour and 28 minutes to get there.

66 Trumbull, James Hammond, and Hoadly, Charles Jeremy, *The Public Records of the Colony of Connecticut 1636–1776, With the Journal of The Council War, 1675 to 1678, Connecticut General Assembly, County of Safety,* Anonymous et. al; 3 Vols., 82 (1850) This work is in the public domain.

and-a half- story house with three or four rooms around a central chimney; the size of the homestead was usually 10 x 14 or 15 x 16 square feet. If the family was financially able, many of the houses were added on to as the family grew.

As noted in the previous chapter, Timothy was one of eleven children; granted, some of the older siblings may have been out of the household and on their own by the time Timothy was born, but there were still many people living in one household. To put this in some perspective, Timothy's mother, Rebecca, like most women of her time, had children in two-year intervals. This means that for twenty-three years of her life, Rebecca was either pregnant or nursing a child. So having a home that could contain these large families was important.

Timothy Scoville, along with his brothers, lived in North Cornwall on or near Towne Road, in the area not too far from Yelping Hill. *The History of Cornwall, Connecticut*[67] states: "Timothy settled just above the Mills place, lived and died where they settled and is buried in South Cornwall Cemetery." Even today, the area is sparsely populated. One can only imagine the solitary living in the 1760s. As a young man, Timothy may have obtained some rudimentary schooling as he could sign his name; however, learning life skills would have taken precedence as he would one day have to make a living for himself and his family. Spring would bring the tilling of the rocky soil to plant, collecting sap from sugar maples, tending the animals, clearing the land, and many other duties. The freshly cut trees would be brought to a sawmill for wood to build or to sell. The rocks would be used for animal enclosures and for stone walls. In Joshua Hempstead's book regarding his daily life up to 1758, you see the cycle of daily tasks: getting the apple trees ready in March; digging and drawing up stones (this seemed to be a year-round job); plowing, planting, harvesting, repairing—the list goes on and on. Although our lives are much easier than they were in the 1700s, we also have the same cycles year after year, but the tasks are eased by modern technology.

The first land record found for Timothy in Cornwall is in 1765[68] with Levi Crocker "of Kent for consideration of twenty-five pounds lawful money received in my full satisfaction of Timothy Scofel of Cornwall... fifteen acres of land which I purchased of Ezra Tyler and Mary, his wife excepting five acres which I have sold to my brother Jonathan of said Cornwall." Levi and Jonathan are certainly the brothers of Thankful Crocker, who followed many other families to Cornwall.

There were two land transactions in 1770 in Cornwall where Timothy was the grantor: February 12[69] and May 19, 1770.[70] The first transaction was selling "two certain pieces of land to Heman Swift."

The land was "bounded as follows (viz) South on Heman Swift [ ] land, East on Palmer's land, and part on Elisha Swift of Kent belonging to Stephen Scovel deceased it being the Home Lot that I now live on containing fifteen acres together with my dwelling house thereon

67 Starr, E.C., 259.

68 Cornwall Land Records, recorded October 30, 1765. [Vol: 2/366]. Connecticut State Library, Hartford, Connecticut.

69 *Ibid,* Vol.3/153.

70 *Ibid,* Vol. 5/170.

standing with all the loose boards in and about said House[71], the other said pieces is two seventh parts of a sixty-seven acre lot of land that lately belonged to Stephen Scovel deceased which he had late of Cornwall one of which in parts was set off to me in distribution of his and Stephen's estate and other part to my brother Henry Scovel, deceased which I purchased of him the said Henry."

This deed was signed by Timothy Scovel.

The second parcel was sold to John Howe "of Cornwall," a "certain tract of land lying in said Cornwall," which he had bought of Samuel Wilcox. This parcel was the 38th lot of the 5th division and is described in the usual manner that occurred during this time: "beginning at a heap of stones which is the southeast corner of the 38th lot," etc. The rest of the document mentions links and chains and more heaps of stones—this is how the land was surveyed during this time.[72]

For some reason Timothy signed with his mark (X) instead of his signature. The witnesses were Thomas Russell and Francis Brown.

*[My note: land records may be an overlooked source by a family researcher; however, they are important in the fact that they may hold a key to a family relationship. Reading land records may not be the most exciting part of your research, yet I have found proof of several ancestors and collateral lines using this tool.]*

On the 20th day of September 1777, Cornwall Land Records volume 3/410 shows another transaction with Samuel Wilcox as the grantor and Timothy Scovel as the grantee. This was for sixty acres of land in Cornwall and Timothy paid "one-hundred pounds lawful money" for this property. The land that Samuel Wilcox had purchased from Thomas Humphries was a tract farm and a highway ran through the same property. This deed was signed by Samuel Wilcox and witnessed by Ebenezer Simmons and Samuel Scovel.

Three more land records exist where Timothy either bought or sold land between the years 1786 and 1808. On April 28, 1786, (Cornwall Land Record, Vol.5/84) Stephen Scovel (this is the Stephen born 1752) "of Timothy, sold three acres for three pounds."[73]

This land bordered Daniel Harrison's land, as well as Timothy's and Stephen's. The deed was signed by Stephen Scovel and witnessed by Nathaniel Bristol and Elijah Allen.

A deed was recorded on February 21, 1792, of one John Reed "of Cornwall" to Timothy Scovel "of Cornwall" regarding the 25th lot in the 7th division of land in Cornwall. "This land was bounded West on Samuel Scovel's land, North partly on Ephraim Jackson's land, and partly on Daniel Harrison's land, East and South on Timothy Scovel's land containing thirty-five acres . . . with appurtenances thereof unto him the said Timothy Scovel . . . John Reed do for myself, heirs, executors and admin Covenant with the said Timothy Scovel, heirs,

---

71 Regarding the mention of "loose boards"—does this mean the house was not completed?

72 Rogers, James Allen, *Early Lands of the Rogers Family in the Foxton Area (Millington Society) of East Haddam, Connecticut,* (2006). This work is a good source on early surveying methods as well as deciphering the Rogers family in East Haddam.

73 At the time of this record, currency was still referred to as the British pound sterling. It wasn't until April 2, 1792, that the United States Congress created the United States dollar as the country's standard unit of money.

etc., that at and until the ensealing these presents I am well seized of the premises as a good indefeasible estate in fee simple; and have good right to bargain and sell the same in manner and farm as is above written: and the same if free from all encumbrances whatsoever . . .

"Signed by John Reed and witnessed by Samuel Deming and Edward Rogers."[74]

Clearly the deed is different from other transactions that have been recorded for Timothy Scoville. This transaction is a covenant, which is a formal agreement (or promise) to do or not do a particular act that is stipulated between the two parties. In other words, after John Reed had purchased the property, the transaction could not be made void, defeated, or canceled by any past event, or error or omission either by Timothy, his heirs, or any of his executors.

The last deed was recorded in Cornwall, on April 4, 1808,[75] whereby "Timothy Schovel of Cornwall . . . for the consideration of one-thousand dollars received to my full satisfaction of my son Ira Schovel of Cornwall . . . a certain tract of land in said Cornwall lying in two pieces—the first piece is the Homestead on which I now live . . . bounded Westerly on Highway in part and on Joseph Scovel's land, part southerly on Jacob Scovel's land, East on Stephen Scovel's land in part and on Joel and Luther Harrison's land in part and northerly on said Joel and Luther Harrison's land. The second piece bounds easterly on Highway southwardly on Joseph Scovel's land westwardly on said Joseph Schovel on Abraham and Oliver Hotchkiss' land and north on said Joel and Luther Harrison's land containing about 100 acres of land, being the same more or less, with the buildings thereon."

[Note: The names within this deed, Joseph and Jacob Scoville, are the nephews of Timothy, the sons of his brother Samuel. The Stephen Scoville mentioned in this deed is the Stephen born 1752 and died 1813. The Harrisons were neighbors of the Scovilles for some time.

Timothy signed with his mark: Timothy X Schovel. The deed was witnessed by Stephen Scovel and Luther Harrison. The deed was received and recorded on March 22, 1809/1819(?) (the date is hard to read, but since Timothy died in 1813, the year of this transaction is likely 1809.]

At an annual town meeting on December 11, 1775, Timothy (with several other men) was elected to be a surveyor of highways for the following year. On December 4, 1780, he again was elected to be a surveyor of the highways along with his brother Samuel for the following year. The surveyors of highways were persons chosen to supervise the adult male inhabitants of their respective districts, in constructing and maintaining roads.[76] No other records for Timothy have been found in the town meeting minutes as having been elected to any other position for the town of Cornwall.

Timothy was taxed from 1763–1804. There are incomplete Grand Lists records from 1805–1807, and it is unknown whether Timothy[1] was listed as being taxed for those years; however, by 1808 (where the Grand List is complete) he is not listed right through to 1813, when he died.

74 Cornwall Land Records, Vol.6/116.

75 *Ibid,* Vol.9/296.

76 Definition from *Cornwall Documents Town Meeting Minutes 1740–1875,* transcribed with notes by Michael R. Gannett, originally published in 1994 by the Cornwall Historical Society and reprinted in 2003.

Timothy had sold off his property to his son, Ira, in 1808 and we see Ira Scoville on the Grand Lists beginning in 1804–1815. After selling his property in 1808 to his son, Timothy probably lived with Ira until his death.

This is only my speculation as I have no proof of this, however, if he had lived somewhere else, I imagine he would've been assessed a tax.

By the year 1775 the family had grown to seven children—the last one was baptized in 1774. The first two children (Ruth and Rush) born in East Haddam had died in infancy. According to E.C. Starr's account in his book *History of Cornwall,* he states that Thankful Scoville died March 1781. In *my* research, I have not found any other source indicating her date of death. Among some of the descendants of Timothy, we have pondered whether Timothy had married two or three times. If Thankful died in 1781, who are the two females listed on the 1790 census? This census poses a problem because it does not give the approximate ages for females; only the males have an approximate age attached to them. The process of elimination among the children also poses difficulty for the simple fact we do not know anything about the daughters Ruhamah or Asube. One of the females on the 1790 census *could* be Triphene; again, this is merely speculation.

Timothy's household in 1790 Cornwall:

*Free White Persons—Males 16 and over—2*
*Free White Persons—Females—2 (no approximate ages given)*

When we review the 1800 census for Cornwall, we see the following:
Timothy's household:
*Free White Persons—Males—45 and over—1—Timothy*
*Free White Persons—Females—45 & over—1—first or second wife?*

We can ascertain that the male age forty-five and over is Timothy. He would have been sixty-three years old at the time of the census. And what of the female? Is this Timothy's wife? But is this Thankful, or a wife from a second marriage? As previously mentioned, Thankful is said to have died in March 1781. To muddy the waters a little more, there is a death record for March 1801, which states: "The wife and grandchild of Timothy Scovel."[77] Note that this death of the wife of Timothy in 1801 also is said to have occurred in March, just as it is recorded that Thankful died in March 1781. Was there a transcription error by Starr giving Thankful's death as 1781 instead of 1801? Or is it just a coincidence that both women died in March? It would be surprising for a man to wait twenty years to remarry in Timothy's day, especially if he still had young children at home.[78]

On September 13, 1801, Timothy Scoville remarried to a woman named Sarah Rogers[79] in the parish of Millington, East Haddam, Connecticut. This marriage took place six months either *after* the death of Thankful (say March 1801) or the unknown second wife whom

77 From my personal collection of records from the CSL on microfilm. Cornwall records.

78 If Thankful died in 1781, she would have been forty-nine years old at the time of her death.

79 *Connecticut, Church Record Abstracts, 1630–1920,* [images, Ancestry].

Timothy married after Thankful died in 1781.

The identity of Sarah Rogers (who married Timothy Scoville) is complicated by the fact that there are many women named Sarah Rogers located in and around East Haddam, Connecticut, during this timeframe. An additional question needs to be asked: why did Timothy return to his hometown to remarry? Were there no available women in Cornwall? This would have been quite a journey for a man of sixty-four years of age to make—a round trip of over one hundred miles.

The Rogers family was well known in the East Haddam area, specifically the area then known as Foxtown (Millington Society). The book by James Allen Rogers, *Early Lands of the Rogers Family in the Foxtown Area (Millington Society) of East Haddam Connecticut,* suggests a possibility of the identity of the Sarah Rogers who wed Timothy Scoville. There was a woman by the name of Sarah Rogers who was born October 23, 1766, who *may* have been the daughter of John Rogers and Sarah Borden. Sarah would have been twenty-nine years younger than Timothy, but this would not have been an uncommon occurrence during this period in history. In addition, there were no other women named Sarah Rogers from this area who would be of marriageable age.

Listed below are women named Sarah Rogers who could be the second or third wife of Timothy Scoville.

*Candidate #1*

The records found online (which are held by the Church of the Latter-Day Saints) state that the Sarah Rogers who was born on 23 October 1766, in East Haddam, Connecticut, was the daughter of John Rogers and Sarah Borden. John Rogers and Sarah Borden were married on 1 June 1758 (this marriage was recorded in the Millington Church Records). The following children of this couple were baptized at the Millington Church East Haddam on 13 October 1765: Dorothy, Gordon, and Roswell. However, a baptism for Sarah Rodgers has not been located after her birth in 1766. It is possible that this record is lost to time, the minister failed to record it, or she died as an infant or small child. No other information has been found on this Sarah Rogers.

*Candidate #2*

A Sarah Scoville (*Arthur,*[2] *Stephen,*[1] *Arthur*), birthdate unknown, married Asahel (Asael [sic] Rogers[80]of East Haddam, on March 12 (or 15), 1769. On page fifty-nine in the *Addenda* section of the Rogers book, by Mr. Allen, Asael [sic] Rogers is listed as being of "Other East Haddam Rogers Families," but this particular line has not been developed.

Asahel Rogers is named in the deed[81] of Daniel Scoville (Stephen,[1] Arthur), which reads as follows:

80 This information comes from two sources: *Arthur Scoville and His Descendants 1660–1900* and the *East Haddam Second Society Millington Church Records.* These records are in my personal possession; the latter provided by a professional genealogical researcher at the Connecticut State Library, Hartford, Connecticut.

81 East Haddam Records, [Vol. XI, 25]. *Ibid.*

> To all people to whom these Presents shall Come Greeting. Know ye that we Ezekiel Scovel of Waterbury and Nathan Scovel of Wallingford, both of New Haven County and Stephen Scovel, Marcus Cole, Phoebe Cole his wife, Stephen Scovel the 2nd, Mary Scovel his wife, Joseph Beckwith and Mary his wife, as Asahel Rogers and Sarah Rogers his wife of the County of Hartford of the State of Connecticut, and Abner Scovel, Thomas Scoville of the State of New Hampshire for consideration of Sixty Pounds Lawful money by us in hand received to our full satisfaction of Thomas Scovel the second of Lampster (Lempster) in the county of Cheshire in the State of New Hampshire, do Quitclaim, release and make over all our right and title and interest in all land and buildings being in lying in the township of East Haddam that came to us by heirship out of the estate of Daniel Scovel late of said East Haddam, deceased, in Hartford County and said Connection, etc.

This document is signed by Ezekiel Scovel, Nathan Scovel, Stephen Scovel 2[nd], Joseph Beckwith, Mary X Scoville (her mark), Mary Beckwith. The deed is dated March 10, 1778.

Who was Daniel Scovell [sic] in the aforementioned land deed? Daniel was the son of Stephen[1] (*Arthur*) and had been born circa 1718 and died in East Haddam in 1761. He married twice (Miriam Chamberlain and Lucy Beckwith). Daniel did not leave any issue by either marriage. The *Scovel* book by Holley states with regard to this deed: "Seventeen years after his death his heirs, who were his brothers and sisters, conveyed all his estate in East Haddam to Thomas Scovell, 2[nd] (*Thomas,*[2] *Stephen,*[1] *Arthur*)[82] of Lempster, N.H."

On page twenty-four of *Arthur Scovel and His Descendants 1660–1900*, by Holley, it states that Phoebe Cole and Sarah Rogers—who were the daughters of Arthur Scovel (*Stephen*[1], *Arthur*)—had gone to Nova Scotia "eleven years before,"[83] which would be approximately 1767. In addition, the Holley book states that Sarah Scovel married Asahel Rogers in East Haddam in 1769. The timeframe that Holley mentions whereby Asahel Rogers and his wife, Sarah, left for Nova Scotia is in error. If Sarah Rogers was in Nova Scotia circa 1767, she must have come back to Connecticut as she married Asahel Rogers in East Haddam in 1769. While I did not find a reference of Asahel Rogers in Nova Scotia, there is a reference of Sarah's brother Abner Scoville. He is listed on the *Deed Records 1764–1950*[84] in Black River, Kings County, Nova Scotia—Section 1, Stone 60. This is an index only; the actual record was not available.

Using the same website (as I did for Abner), there is no record of an Asahel/Asa Rogers in this part of Nova Scotia. It is possible that the Scoville/Rogers families did go to Nova Scotia as a family group, but Asahel died there, and Sarah Scoville Rogers returned to her home in East Haddam and then remarried to her cousin Timothy in 1801(?).

The Arthur Scovel[2] (*Stephen,*[1] *Arthur*) family is not well developed. Sarah Scoville Rogers' eldest brother, Arthur, is said to have been born circa 1735 (Abner, circa 1738; Phoebe, circa 1740; Sarah, circa 1742, and Mary, circa 1744).

---

82 The Thomas listed as "2[nd]" is Thomas son of Thomas Scoville.

83 This reference is eleven years prior to the 1778 deed.

84 Kings County (Nova Scotia) Historical Society. The name is written as "Schofiell/Schofill."

There are a number of unsourced data regarding the birth and death dates of Asahel and Sarah Rogers on Ancestry.

One record has a Sarah Rogers born 10 April 1741 and died 23 October 1823 in East Haddam; another has Asahel Rogers born about 1740 and died 6 April 1778, Valley Forge, Chester, Pennsylvania. While these are possibilities, without a source to follow it's impossible to prove or deny.

*Candidate #3*

Lastly, the deed given to Ira Scoville in 1808 by his father Timothy states in part that Ira agreed to support his father's widow, Sarah Scoville, in "sickness and health during her natural life." The deed also records that she was provided "one good riding horse and two cows." The witnesses to this deed are Clarissa Burnham and Rhoda Burnham. Who are these women and why did they witness the deed?

Living in Cornwall at the same time as Timothy was one Noah Rogers, who left a will in 1810[85] in Cornwall, Connecticut, which mentions his wife, Rhoda Rogers, son Noah Rogers, Jr., grandson Noah Rogers (son of Noah Rogers, Jr.), daughters Abigail, Clarissa J., Amanda, Sarah, and Rhoda. No married surnames are given for his five daughters. The land was bequeathed to his grandson, Noah Rogers, Jr. Is the Sarah Rogers, the daughter of Noah Rogers, the same Sarah Rogers who married Timothy Scoville?

Further research showed that this Sarah Rogers, daughter of Noah Rogers, could not be the wife of Timothy Scoville.

Records show that this Sarah Rogers (born in 1768 and died August 12, 1845)[86] in Cornwall, had married Oliver Burnham on October 17, 1787, also in Cornwall.[87] He died on April 30, 1846, in said town.

Oliver Burnham was a selectman and a judge in Cornwall at various times in his life. Clarissa and Rhoda, who witnessed the deed, probably did so because they were the daughters of Oliver Burnham and Sarah (Rogers) Burnham. They likely performed the task of being witnesses when their father needed one for legal documents.

We are left with two possible candidates for the wife of Timothy Scoville (eliminating Sarah, daughter of Noah Rogers). Research into this conundrum over the years has not provided any additional evidence. Researching the Rogers line has been very difficult because of the commonality of the name. Even the name "Asahel"—while it may be a very uncommon name in our time—was not that uncommon in Asahel's time, and cross-checking any available data for him has also proved unfruitful.

Currently, it appears that Sarah Rogers, the conjectured daughter of John and Sarah (Borden) Rogers, is still the best candidate for one of Timothy's wives. Sarah Rogers was from the same town as Timothy, and the Scoville and Rogers families would have been well

85 Connecticut State Library, [microfilm#1022356, box #703 PD] Cornwall, Litchfield 1810 [#4962].

86 *The Charles R. Hale Collection of Connecticut Cemetery Inscriptions.* [images, Ancestry].

87 The birth, marriage, and death dates for Oliver Burnham come from the *Barbour Collection.* Ancestry.

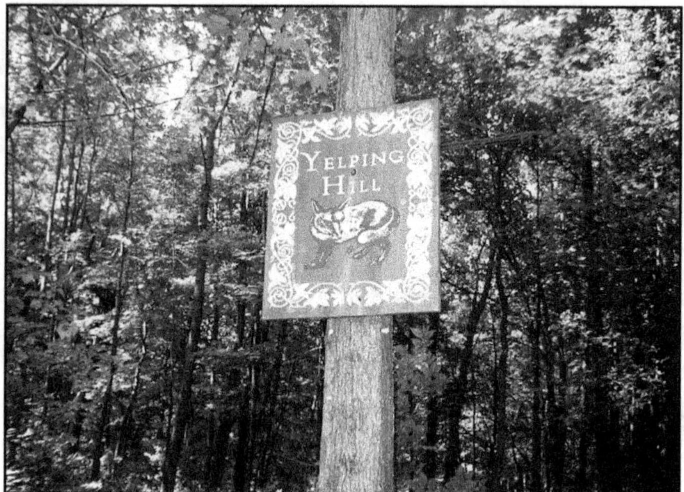


A sign designating that you are now in the Yelping Hill area of Cornwall, Connecticut. Photo taken by the author in 2001.

acquainted because of the proximity of where they resided.

It was certainly not uncommon for a man to marry multiple times, especially if there were still young children in the household, as was the situation in this case. A man would seek out another helpmate to care for the home and children while he, the head of the household, needed to provide for his family. If Thankful did indeed die in 1781 the oldest child at this time was their son Timothy, who was age nineteen. At the age of nineteen, Timothy[2], served six months as a substitute for his father in the Revolutionary War. The elder Timothy would have been forty-two at that time and perhaps he felt it would be a great hardship to leave his family to serve; or he or his wife Thankful were not well at the time. In any event, with Timothy[2] out of the household, that left the next eldest son, Ithamar, age fifteen, to help around the homestead.

Little is known of Timothy and his wife Sarah after 1808. On 30 January 1813, at the age of 76, Timothy succumbed to the "spotted fever"[88] disease and was buried in the South Cornwall Cemetery.

***Children of Timothy Scoville and Thankful Crocker***

i. Ruth, b. 8 Dec 1760, East Haddam; d. 16 Feb 1764, Cornwall.
ii. Rush, bap. 1761, Colchester, Connecticut;[89] d. East Haddam.
4. iii. Timothy,[4] b. 31 Oct 1762, East Haddam; d. 13 Sep 1845, Hector, Tompkins Co., N.Y.; m. Chloe Kelsey.

Children born/bap. in Cornwall:
5. iv. **Ithamar,**[4] b. 7 Aug 1764; d. 30 Oct 1831, Norfolk, Connecticut; m. unknown.

88 *Spotted Fever Epidemic in New England in 1812: Serious in Rockingham,* published on the web and the information was based on *The Connecticut River Valley in Southern Vermont and New Hampshire,* historical sketches, Rutland, VT, Tuttle Co., Marble City Press, (1929).
89 CLR. Connecticut State Library, Hartford, Connecticut

6. v. Ira,[4] b. 25 Sept 1766; d. aft. 1 Jun 1840; Loraine Co., Ohio; m. Ruth Knapp.
vi. Ruhamah, b. 25 Sep 1766[90] (twin?); nothing more is known.
vii. Asube/Arube, bap. 25 Oct 1766[91]; nothing more is known.
7. viii. Triphene,[4] bap. May? 1772;[92] d. 2 Mar 1813, Goshen, Connecticut; m. Elisha Carrier.
ix. Philo, bap. 9 Oct 1774;[93] nothing more is known.

***Child of Thankful Crocker***

8. *i. Roxalana/Roxylana Andrews,[4] b. 24 Jul 1758, Colchester, Connecticut; d. 14 Jul 1839, Norfolk, Connecticut; m. 24 Feb. 1780, in Norfolk to Reuben Dean; he b. 22 Feb. 1752, Philipse Patent, New York; d. 14 Jul 1836, Goshen, Connecticut.*

I have not found any records of additional children born to Timothy's speculative second wife or to Sarah Rogers Scoville.

---

90 FHL [film #1516243], Cornwall Vital Town Records, Vol. 1; her name is written as "Rume," a diminutive of Ruhamah, and the record clearly states "born on." Her birth was not recorded until May 11, 1767. *Ibid.*

91 Baptismal Records for Cornwall, 1755–1892, First Congregational Church Records, 5 & 6. Clearly states "Daughter to Timothy Scophel." *Ibid.*

92 *Ibid*, 3 & 4.

93 *Ibid*, 5 & 6.

# Fourth Generation

### *4. Timothy Scoville[4] (Timothy,[3] Stephen,[2] Stephen,[1] Arthur)*

Born 13 September 1762, Cornwall,[94] Litchfield, Connecticut; died 25 December 1845, Hector, Tompkins Co. NY; married 1 January 1789[95] Salisbury, Connecticut, Chloe Kelsey, daughter of William Kelsey and Hester Chapman. She born 13 April 1762, Westbrook, Middlesex Co.,[96] Connecticut; she died 29 October 1849. Both are buried in the Presbyterian Church cemetery, Peach Orchard (Hector), now part of Schuyler Co. NY.

The first mention of Timothy (other than the vital records) is in the Revolutionary War records. When a soldier signed up for a certain enlistment period, they were promised to receive compensation as a "bounty" at the end of their time in service. The bounty was either paid in money or land. They also received a monthly salary: privates earned about six dollars, sergeants eight dollars, and a captain twenty dollars.

In June 1779, under Captain Belts and Colonel Sherman's regiment, Timothy saw battle at Verplanks Point on the Hudson River and at Morristown and Staten Island, New York, and was discharged in December or January as his six months were up.

Timothy continued his service as he again enlisted in June 1780 for a three-month stint under Captain Perner and Colonel Samuel Canfield at Horse Neck, Connecticut, and was a guard "on the lines" in White Plains, New York.

In March 1781 (the same month and year that his mother, Thankful, is said to have died), he once again enlisted as a substitute for his father for three months. In 1782, he signed up for a twelve-month stint under Captain Nathan Stoddard and Colonel Canfield[97] against the "cowboys."[98] He was stationed at Morrisana and other places in New York.

During his twelve-month term, Timothy was also stationed at Fort Waterbury (aka Fort Stamford), Stamford, Connecticut. According to the website *Fort Stamford Park*, "The British were in control of Long Island and New York, and it only took an hour to sail across the Long Island Sound; raids on the people in Stamford and the surrounding areas were a constant threat."[99] The people of said town constantly requested protection from Governor Trumbull, and after a serious raid on Darien by the British, the governor and the Safety Council decided to erect a permanent fortification. Under the direction of General Waterbury, "the troops

---

94 Cornwall Vital Town Records, Vol.1, [LDS film #1516243]. Connecticut State Library.

95 From Chloe Scoville's deposition seeking Timothy's pension.

96 Claypool, Edward A., *A Genealogy of the Descendants of William Kelsey Who Settled at Cambridge, Mass. In 1632, at Hartford, Conn., in 1636, and at Killingworth, Conn., in 1663. (1928–1947)*. 298.

97 Revolutionary Pension Records, [#W19006]. National Archives and Records Administration.

98 The term "cowboy" is a reference to the Tories.

99 See www.fortstamfordpark.org for the full article.

began construction of the fort on October 4, 1781."[100] The fort was in operation until 1783 when the Treaty of Peace was signed.

Timothy was also stationed in White Plains (New York) for a time. There is a story of Timothy Scoville that, while scouting (being the head of his party), he discovered six "cowboys" in a door-yard and called his party to "come on!" The "cowboys" threw down their muskets and ran off. Timothy gathered up all the arms himself and carried them to his comrades.[101]

The pension records for Timothy are very difficult to read. According to the deposition, Timothy was given a discharge from Captain Betts of the Continental Army.

By the time of the deposition, Timothy no longer had his discharge papers; regardless, he was granted a pension after the Court of Common Pleas had taken many depositions from those who had served with him, as well as friends and family members. Once this had been accomplished, the Court of Common Pleas was satisfied that he had been a soldier in the Revolutionary War.

The following declaration was taken on October 1832:

> Declaration of Timothy Scoville
>
> State of New York, Tompkins County
>
> On the third day of October and the year of our Lord one-thousand eighteen hundred and thirty-two, personally appeared in [ ][102] court before this Judge of this Court of Common Pleas of the county of Tompkins [ ] Timothy Scovill a resident of the Town of Hector and said County of Tompkins and State of New York aforesaid aged seventy years and [ ] who being first duly sworn and [ ]. To [ ], doth in his oath [ ] the following declaration in order to attain(?) the [ ] of this act of Congress [ ] June (?) 7, 1832.
>
> That in the month of May or June in the year 1779 he was living with his father Timothy Scoville in the town of Cornwall in the county of Litchfield in the state of Connecticut and that his said father Timothy Scoville was drafted as a [ ] and to [ ] for six months and that his [ ] [ ] and as a substitute for his said father [ ] into the service of [ ] [ ] [ ]in [ ] [ ] draft under Captain Betts and Col. [ ] and in General Huntington's Brigade and [ ] and he was living when called into service in the Town of Cornwall in the County of Litchfield and the State of Connecticut.
>
> That [during? ] the Revolutionary War he was living in the Town of Salisbury in the State of Connecticut until in or about the year one-thousand eighteen hundred and four (?)when he removed to the town of Green in the County Chenango State of New York at which [time?] he enlisted four years at the end of which time he removed to the town of Hector in the then County of Seneca now County of Tompkins and State of New York when [he?] has? [ ].

100 *Ibid*

101 This information came from an article found in a book; regrettably, I failed to cite the source.

102 The open brackets designate that a portion of the document is illegible.

That he was first called into service as a substitute for his father in the year 1779. That in the year 1780 he in listed as a volunteer as a private that in the spring of the year 1781 he went into the service as a substitute for [ ] Thomas Gould(?).

That in the year 1779 his [ ] and Captain bets company in Colonel Hinman's regiment and General Huntington's Brigade—[the rest of this portion is completely illegible].

That he was born in the year 1762 in the town of East Haddam in the state of Connecticut in the month of September of that year. That he has a record of his age and his family Bible.

The rest of the document gives information on where he was during his time in the service, however, it is too difficult to decipher the handwriting. The document is signed by Timothy Scovill.

Deposition From Ira Scovill

State of New York, County of Tompkins

Ira Scovill of the Town of Hector in said County of Tompkins, being duly sworn deposes says he is sixty-six years of age is a brother of Timothy Scovill recollects of his brother being in the United States service during the Revolutionary War and believes that he was absent in the service the length of time set forth in his declaration and Department in further says that the Alexander M. Comstock, David Tyler[103], Timothy Scoville in this department all live in the same neighborhood. Sworn in subscribed the 28th day of August 1832.

Signed
Ira Scovill

[ ] Halsey, Judge of the Court of Common Pleas for Tompkins County

And the said Court do hereby declare their opinion after the investigation of the matter and after putting the interrogatories prescribed by the War Department, that the above named applicant was a Revolutionary Soldier and served as he states, and the court further certifies that it appears to them that Alexander M. Comstock who has signed the proceeding certificate and Departition is a clergyman resident in the Town of Hector, and that David Tyler and Ira Scovill, who has also signed Departitions are residents in said Town of Hector and are credible persons and their statement is entitled to credit.

J. Samuel [ ] Clerk of the Court Common Pleas

The following people gave their depositions on behalf of Timothy Scoville:

David Tyler—son-in-law & neighbor.
Alexander M. Comstock—Clergyman & neighbor.
Samuel Scoville—brother.

103 David Tyler is a son-in-law of Timothy Scoville.

Ira Scoville—brother.
Levi Miles—Lived in Cornwall. Levi and Timothy had enlisted together.

Some of the more interesting reading came from the depositions from Chloe Scoville when she applied for Timothy's pension after his death in 1845.

Chloe Scoville—alluded to their marriage date of January 1, 1789, in Salisbury.
Augustus Ely—son-in-law
Reuben Smith—he states that he was present at their marriage and had been acquainted with both parties before their marriage.
Richard Smith—he was a playmate of Timothy and Chloe's children and knew them all his life.

There were several other depositions given by those who served with Timothy. Because Timothy had misplaced/lost his discharge papers, the War Department really wanted to make sure he was who he said he was and served his country during the war. Eventually, he was awarded a pension for his service. When Timothy died, Chloe had to apply for the pension to continue receiving funds.

As noted, there were many depositions taken for Chloe to continue receiving Timothy's pension. This is based on the records of *U.S. Revolutionary War Pensioners, 1801–1815, 1818–1872.*[104] Chloe began receiving a pension in March 1846 and the amount of $28.32 would be received twice a year (March and September) and ended at her death in 1849.

With the war over, Timothy returned home to Cornwall (he was now in his twenties and likely wanted to start a family of his own) and on January 1, 1789[105] he married Chloe Kelsey, who was at that time of Salisbury, Connecticut. She had been born in Westbrook, Connecticut, which is situated on Long Island Sound.

Chloe's parents were William Kelsey and Hester Chapman.[106] William Kelsey had been born in Killingworth, Connecticut, and then his family moved to Westbrook, where he married Hester Chapman, and it is where all of their children were born. As the Kelsey book points out, the family removed to Salisbury sometime after May 1768.[107] Salisbury is situated in the northwest corner of the state and the area is made up of extensive hills in deep valleys mostly of granite and limestone. The area is well known for its rich production of iron ore. Little else is known about the Kelsey family.

104 *Ledgers of Payments, to U.S. Pensioners Under Acts 1818–1858—From Records of the Office of the Third Auditor of the Treasury. Records Group Title: Records of the Accounting Offices of the Department of the Treasury; Record Group: 217; Series Number: T718; Roll Number: 17.* National Archives, Washington, D.C.

105 The day and month have not been found in any of the records consulted for this marriage.

106 Claypool, Edward A., *A Genealogy of William Kelsey Who Settled at Cambridge, Massachusetts in 1632* (1928–1947) 115.

107 *Ibid*

The early years Timothy's marriage is sketchy at best. I have not been able to locate Timothy on the 1790 census as he may have been living with his parents, Timothy and Thankful. The elder Timothy is listed as living in "Cornwall," with four people in the household. Excluding Timothy and Thankful, there is *one free white male aged 16 and over* and a *free white female*—no age given. Since the 1790 census does not list the names of household members (only the head of household) the other male and female *could be* two of Timothy's younger siblings. Conversely, there is only one William Kelsey that I could find on the census, but this William is living in Litchfield, Litchfield County, Connecticut, with seven people in the household. Two of these *could* be Timothy and Chloe; however, I have not found any mention of the Kelsey family living anywhere other than Westbrook and Salisbury. Since the Kelseys are not the focus of my research, I have not delved into the records of this family, and based on what I have seen and read, the earlier researchers into this line did not fare any better with discovering any additional data on this family after their removal to Salisbury.

In the book by James H. Smith *History of Chenango and Madison Counties, New York,* we find Timothy Scoville as having arrived in Smithville Flats circa 1799 as a millwright, and there he built the "first sawmill in the town." According to the above-mentioned book, the "sawmill did not stand for many years but went to decay." By 1800, Timothy and his family were back in Cornwall as he is listed on the 1800 census[108] there:

Free White Males <10—1 (Philo)
Free White Males 26–45—1 (Timothy)
Free White Females <10—3 (Olive, Mary, Hester)
Free White Females 10–16—1 (?)
Free White Females 26–45—1 (Chloe)
Free White Females 45 and over—1 (likely Hester Chapman Kelsey)

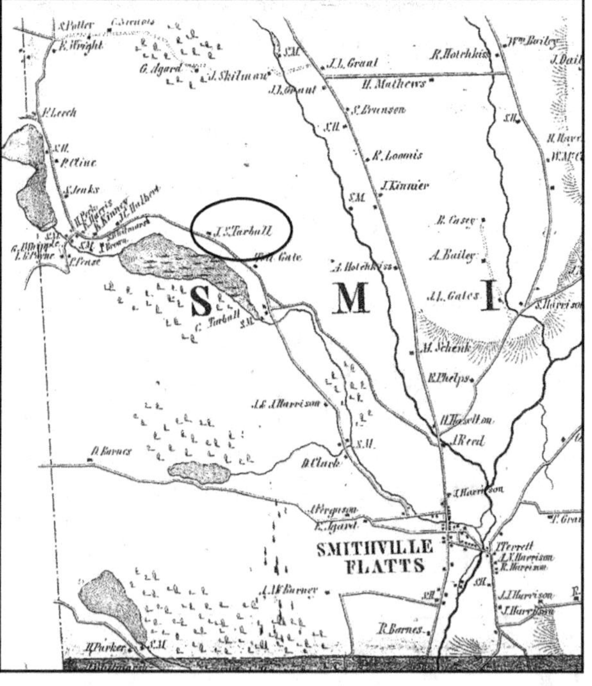


Timothy shows up on the Cornwall Grand List for 1801 as having been taxed ninety-four dollars. After 1801 he is no longer in Cornwall.

(See the name "J.S. Tarball" on the map. This is approximately where Timothy Scoville's sawmill was located.)[109]

108 Gannett, Michael R., *Cornwall Grand Lists, 1742–1820 and Cornwall Censuses 1790–1800–1810–1820, Compiled by Michael R. Gannett.* 1800 U.S. Federal census for Cornwall, Litchfield Co., CT, 105 (Cornwall Historical Society) 2003.

109 Fagan, L., *Map of Chenango County, New York,* (L. Leal, Norwich, NY 1855). Found online

There is a gap between the years 1802–1805 whereby I have not discovered where Timothy and his family were. The Scovell book by Holley mentions that he resided in Burlington, Vermont, but I have not found any records there. Mrs. Holley corresponded with many people to gather information for her book and some of that information may be erroneous. I have not spent too much time looking into a connection with Timothy in Vermont as I believe that this may be a wild goose chase.

What drew Timothy to remove to Hector, New York? This is a question I cannot answer succinctly; perhaps it was that he had heard of a new settlement there where the land was good for farming (unlike Cornwall).

The early settlers were constantly on the mov, just as his forebearers had been, removing from East Haddam to Cornwall; Timothy continued the trek "west" for better opportunities.

From the *History of Tioga, Chemung, Tompkins and Schuyler Counties, New York*[110] comes the following:

> HECTOR, NY
> Is the southwest corner township of the Military Tract and forms the northeast corner town of the county. From the lake, on its entire western outline, rise rocky bluffs, nearly perpendicularly, to the height of from 50 to 100 feet, except the points of land that jut into it at the mouths of the various streams which empty into the lake. From this elevation the land rises in a gradual slope to from 500 to 700 feet above Seneca Lake, and from 1200 to 1400 feet above tide. The surface is a rolling upland, much broken by deep valleys and high ridges. The soil consists mostly of clay, or sandy and gravelly loam. The inhabitants are mostly engaged in agricultural pursuits. On the western slope, bordering on the lake, the soil is particularly adapted to the culture of fruit, and much attention is given to the raising of peaches, plums, and grapes, which are raised in large quantities, and of fine quality.

What *is* known of Timothy is that he was in Schuyler County in 1805, as a reference to him states that "Timothy Scoville came from Chenango County [in] 1805 and settled where J.B. Kinan now lives. He afterwards moved to Hector Hill and bought twenty-six acres."[111] The record reads as follows:

> ... Timothy purchased land in the town of Hector for the consideration of a dollar from the trustees of the Gospel and School. The description of the land is given as "lot" 44, town of Hector, part of a subdivision #2 and said great Lot 44, beginning with 13 chains and 48 links to stake and thence east 19 chains 48 links to place beginning containing 26 acres. The witnesses to this record were Lewis Owen and James L.S. Goudin.

---

through *Mills Along the Genegantslet Creek in Chenango County, New York*, posted by John H. Bock (2015). http://www.sawbiz.com. Accessed 2021.

110 Everts and Ensign; 616.

111 Everts and Ensign, *History of Tioga, Chemung, Tompkins and Schuyler Counties (1879)* 622; found on Schuyler Co. NY Genealogical Resources (sites.rootsweb.com).

As we've seen in prior land records for some of the Scovilles in Connecticut, the surveying records for plots of land are described as measured in "links" and "chains." The July 2018 edition of the *Backbone Ridge History Group*[112] newsletter explains the Gunter Chain:

> Edmund Gunter, an English mathematician, and astronomer described a surveyor's chain with 100 links—measuring 66 ft (22 yards or 4 poles) all together. This design, one sq. chain equals 484 sq. yards; ten sq. chains equal one acre and eighty chains equal a mile. Gunter's design proved to be popular in England.

The Gunter Chain method was used to survey military lots in Tompkins County, New York, in the eighteenth century.

From an article in *The Backbone* entitled "The Potomac Road, The Backbone of The Backbone," by Marsha E. Smith,[113] "she traced the Potomac Road through the records from Reynoldsville to the county line." From the present-day road map, with an old plat map from the mid 1800s, she found that while many of the roads had been "smoothed out in places," they remained the same for the most part.

She went on to say that an old Town Meeting Minute book gave a glimpse into the "happenings" in the town of Hector (i.e., "school records, records of chattel mortgages, and road survey records and petitions"). When the earliest settlers arrived in the area, they likely followed the old "Native American" trails as well as "General Sullivan's trail." Her review of the Town Meeting minutes for Timothy Scoville include the following:

> Starting in Reynoldsville, Potomac Road begins in the north east corner of Lot 54, it transverses in the south west corner of Lot 45, transects a small corner of Lot 44, travels north a bit adjacent to the lot line through Lot 34, where midway through the lot it turns east and then follows the boundary lines between Lots 34 and 35, continuing the path north between Lots 24 and 25, Lots 14 and 15, and finally between Lots 5 and 6 where it ends at the Seneca County border.
>
> No. 65. Survey of public Highway beginning at the highway between Lots No. 45 and 54 20 chains west of Southwest corner of 45 thence [north and west] to a road running from Timothy Scovilles to Joel Reynolds. Recorded Jan'y 10th 1817.
>
> No. 129. Courses and distances for an alteration in the road leading from Ira Reynolds passed Timothy Scovills, to wit, Beginning in the highway two rods east of the N.E. corner of said Scovills [ ] thence S. 34ø E. 20.00, thence S. 40ø E. [ ] its intersection with the old trout [ ] [ ] where it leaves said Scovill's [ ] March 25th, 1825. Recorded 28th March 1825.

And lastly:

112 Backbone Ridge History Group. This is a very informative newsletter on Hector, NY, and its people. www.backboneridgehistorygroup.com. Accessed March 11, 2020.

113 The Backbone History Group newsletter, 2015 Spring Edition. 5.

136. This may certify that we were called on to examine the Road lately altered beginning at Joshua Smiths and running North westerly through Timothy Scovels where it intersects the old road on the oath of twelve freeholders that said alteration is useless and unnecessary and we therefore hereby certify that we consider the record of the above alteration as null and void and of no effect April 25th, 1825. Recorded June 30th, 1825.

A map of Lot 44 is shown in the section of Ira Scoville.

Once this family settled in Hector, they became involved with the organization of the Presbyterian Church. On September 15, 1809, the Presbyterian Church was constituted by the Revs. Charles Mosher and William Clark, and five days later the church was organized in Hector, New York, with Timothy and Chloe becoming early members. At a meeting of the male members of the church "on the 23rd day of February 1810, Timothy Scoville and Thomas Morten were elected trustees of said church."[114]

Timothy was clearly committed to the Presbyterian Church,[115] as was his wife. An article in *Presbyterianism in New England,* by Dr. Henry M. Dexter felicitously describes "the New England" way as a "Congregationalized Presbyterianism, or a Presbyterianized Congregationalism which had its roots in the one system, and its branches in the other."

Presbyterians in the United States[116] came largely from Scottish immigrants, Scotch-Irish immigrants, and from New England Yankee communities that had been originally Congregational but changed because of an agreed-upon "Plan of the Union of 1801" for frontier areas.

The Kelsey family may have been one of those Scotch-Irish families already alluded to and Timothy and his family became a part of that church culture.[117]

The first Presbyterian church had been erected in 1718 in Peach Orchard, which is in the northwest part of Hector; it contained three churches, forty dwellings, and about one hundred and fifty people. The local Indigenous Peoples had orchards in the vicinity and there was a large peach orchard when the town was first settled, hence the name.

Chloe Scoville was also a committed member of the church as she was one of the "constituent members of the Presbyterian Church in Peach Orchard [New York]"[118] and remained a member for the rest of her life.

---

114 Finch, Jesse Howell, 1889–1968 (main author), Fisher, Carl W. (added author) and Swick, Harriet Jackson (added author), *Some Cemeteries Between the Lakes Country (portions of Seneca, Schuyler, and Tompkins Counties, N.Y.*; Vol. 2, 337.

115 Loetscher, Frederick L., *Presbyterianism in Colonial New England, Part* 1; Journal of the Presbyterian Historical Society (1901–1930) Vol. 11, No. 2 (June 1921) 85–86.

116 Presbyterianism in Colonial New England, Part 1.

117 This is pure speculation on my part and I do not have any documented proof that this family was Scotch-Irish.

118 Pierce, Henry B., *History of Schuyler County.* (Everts and Ensign, Philadelphia), 1879.

It is said that the church was raised with the "use of ardent spirit." The church raising was enough to stimulate the people, so proud they were of their house of worship.

While Timothy was living in Hector, he had family members in Cornwall who died in 1813: his father, his sister, a nephew, and his uncle. Did he travel back to Cornwall or was the sad news brought to him by mail? Both would have been troublesome as travel was rough, and the mail was unpredictable. There were postal roads, however, Hector was still very much a wilderness. It is possible that a post rider dropped off a letter to an inn or a tavern to inform Timothy. Likely, it was too late for him to do anything since the "spotted fever" epidemic killed quickly and the burials took place as soon as possible—usually the next day. It must have troubled Timothy deeply to lose so many family members in such a short span of time.

≈

Timothy's family is found living in Hector on the 1820, 1825, 1830, and 1835 censuses; however, I have not been able to locate him on the 1810 or 1840 census records, using many variants of the spelling of the last name.

The 1820 census gives the following family dynamic:

Free White Males—45 & upwards—1 (Timothy)
Free White Females—10–16—1(?)
Free White Females—16–26—1(?)
Free White Female—45 & upwards—1 (Chloe)

In 1825 Timothy was living on the same piece of land as is shown on the special New York census.[119] This was the twenty-six acres (Lot 44) of land that he purchased for a dollar. This land was now improved upon.

1 male (inc. head)—1qualified to vote
3 females (inc. head)—2 females unmarried between 16–45
26 acres of improved land
12 cattle; 1 horse; 17 sheep; 6 hogs
12 yds fulled cloth, 18 yds flannel _______cloth
50 yds linen of cotton ______yr.

The three women spent a good part of the year weaving cloth. Flax was likely grown on the twenty-six acres to make the linen cloth and the seventeen sheep were shorn and the wool was also spun.

The following year, in September 1826, Laura Scovelle [sic], Augustus Ely, and Timothy Scoville were examined and approved to be admitted to the church.[120]

Augustus Ely was the son-in-law of Timothy Scoville, having married Timothy's daughter Olive. Laura Scoville was likely the daughter of Timothy's brother Ira, who also lived in Hector.

---

119 1825 State Census—Hector, Tompkins County, NY; [images, Ancestry].

120 *First Presbyterian Church Records, Hector, New York, 1809–1924.* (author unknown)

The last census where I can locate this family is in 1835 for Hector:

Timothy Schofield
4 males (inc. head—2 subjects to military, 3 qualified to vote)
1 female (inc. head—under 45)
40 acres of improved land
14 cattle; 3 horses; 20 sheep; 4 hogs
18 yds fulled cloth; 6 yds flannel; 12 yds cotton—in yr.

Again, we only have the name of the head of household—Timothy. Who are the four males? Based on all information available, Timothy and Chloe had only one son, Philo, who had been out of the household for a long time and was living in Ohio. The four males could have been relatives and/or hired hands to help with the property. The other curious item is the "female" listed as being "under 45." At the time of this census Chloe would have been seventy-three years old. It is possible the census taker put the tic mark in the wrong box, or the transcriber of said census made an error in recording the data. Nevertheless, we can see that Timothyhad increased his acreage as well as the number of livestock he owned. However, the amount of cloth produced *decreased*. The daughters Olive and Hester had married and had families of their own, and daughter Mary (Polly) had died in 1826; this left the spinning and weaving to Chloe to handle.

Timothy died on December 25, 1845, and is buried in Lot #18 in the Hector Presbyterian Church Cemetery. His obituary was published in the *Ithaca Chronicle* on December 31st and states the following:

> At his residence in Hector, on the 25th inst., Mr. Timothy Scoville in the 84th year of his age. Mr. Scoville has been a member of the Presbyterian Church in Hector for many years. He fought faithfully the battle of his country during the Revolution, and he fought more faithfully the good fight of faith. His life was praying [a] consistent useful life; and his death was a peaceful and praying death. As a husband and father, he was kind and affectionate, yet notwithstanding all the ties which bound him to earth, the infinite wise Being, who we trust loved him better than any earthly friend, called him down to his early tabernacle, and enter into the rest which remained to the people of God.

As a well-respected member of the community and as a man of great faith, Timothy Scoville, a farmer, received the highest praise in his obituary.

Five years later, on the twenty-ninth day of October 1849, Timothy's wife Chloe died at the age of "87 yrs. 6 m. & 16 d's" as it is inscribed on her headstone.

### *The Children of Timothy Scoville and Chloe Kelsey*

9. i. Philo,[5] b. 30 Nov 1790, or 1791[121] in either Salisbury or Cornwall; d. 5 Jun 1875, Cleveland, Ohio; m. Jemima Bixby 16 Feb 1819, Ellsworth, Mahoning, Ohio.

121 I have not been able to find an actual birth/baptismal record for Philo and have seen his year of birth as 1790 or 1791. His headstone states he was born in 1791. His biography indicates he was born in Salisbury, Connecticut, which is probable since his mother's parents lived in said town and the young couple may have lived with them for a time.

ii. Olive S., b. 31 Jan 1793 likely in Cornwall; d. 6 Mar 1880, Watkins, Schuyler, N.Y.; m. Augustus Ely 7 Nov 1812, Tompkins Co., N.Y.

iii. Mary (Polly), b. 27 Mar 1795, likely Cornwall; d. unm. 16 Jan 1826, Hector, N.Y. buried in Presbyterian Church Cemetery near her parents.

iv. Hester Kelsey, b. 30 Nov 1800, likely Cornwall;[122]d. 26 Mar 1834, Hector, N.Y.; m. (1) Nathan Gardner Case on 25 Dec. 1817 (probably in Hector); m. (2) David Rich 30 Oct. 1826, in Hector; he b. 18 Jan 1798; d. 21 Apr 1849. He m. (2) Mary W______.

## 5. ***Ithamar Scoville***[4] *(Timothy,[3] Stephen,[2] Stephen,[1] Arthur)*

Born 7 August 1764;[123] died 10 October 1831[124] in Norfolk, Connecticut; married unknown name; probably died after 1830 in Norfolk.

Ithamar is my brick-wall ancestor with whom I have spent countless hours and years scouring the records online, in person, hiring genealogists, etc. To this day, his life is somewhat of a mystery. As I write this (2022), the name of his wife has not been discovered—not even a first name. This search began in earnest in 1980 and at this point, I believe she will remain a mystery. Some years ago, I thought it would be helpful to develop a timeline for Ithamar to have a visual record of what information I have and where the gaps were—it has been a useful tool.

Unlike previous biographical information on my ancestors prior to Ithamar, I intend to develop Ithamar's information as a timeline as I did so many years ago. Perhaps anyone who may read this in the future will see something that I have missed.

### *TIMELINE AND NOTES FOR ITHAMAR SCOVILLE*

1764—7 August—Cornwall—Ithamar is born.

1780—24 February—Ithamar's half-sister Roxalana marries Reuben Dean in Norfolk.[125] Ithamar was sixteen at this time. Also note that Reuben became an integral part of Ithamar's life as the years went by.

1781—March—Ithamar's mother, Thankful, dies [see Timothy[1] and Thankful, Third Generation regarding this death].

1781–1782—Ithamar's brother, Timothy, enlists for a three-month stint in Rev. War

---

122 Father Timothy is on the 1800 census for Cornwall, Connecticut.

123 Cornwall, Connecticut Town Vital Records, Vol. 1, FHL [ film#1516243] "Ithamar, Son of Timothy Scovel & Thankful, his wife born August 7th, 1764, Recorded October 30th, 1765. Mr. John Pierce Town Clerk."

124 *Communicants, Baptisms, Marriage, Deaths 1816–1873*, located in a back room of the Norfolk Library, Norfolk, Connecticut. After about 25 years of searching for Ithamar's death date, it was suggested to me by a Norfolk historian to write to the library because he knew that they kept some documents in a "back room." Finally, Ithamar's death date was located. The death date comes from *Norfolk Church Records, Vol. III, "Only those who have no Grave- Stone."*

125 A deposition by Reuben's brother (regarding Reuben's Rev. War service) confirms that Roxalana was considered a "Scoville," and she always went by the name Scoville.

[Timothy's service records].

1783—15 January—Ithamar's maternal grandmother, Alice Swift, dies in Westchester, Connecticut. [Mayflower Births and Deaths, Ancestry].

1785—7 November—Ithamar's maternal grandfather, James Crocker, dies in Westchester, Connecticut [*Ibid*]. His will, which is online, is not helpful as to mentioning any family members.

1788–1789—Ithamar marries in either Cornwall or Norfolk [conjecture].

1790—Ithamar (and his brother Ira) are not found as heads of households on the 1790 Federal Census; not in father's household (according to the ages listed for the people in Timothy's home); not found as heads in any U.S. households for this year in any state where the census was taken.

1790—A male child born to Ithamar and ? [based on the 1800 census].

1791—30 November—Amasa Scoville born—probable son of Ithamar and ? Will expound on this further.

1794—Cornwall—Ithamar and brother Ira are listed on the Grand Tax lists—likely heads of their own households by this time [*Cornwall Grand List 1742–1820 and Cornwall Censuses 1790–1820,* compiled by Michael R. Gannett, Cornwall Historical Society, 2003].

1794—Lodema/Lodemia Scoville born—a probable daughter of Ithamar and ?

1796—5 October—Ira Scoville purchases "of Elihu Canfield" 50 acres in Norfolk called "Intervail Lot 43." This parcel of land is an important piece of the puzzle regarding this family. Land passed back and forth between Ithamar, Amasa, Lodema, Roxalana, and Ira Scoville, which shows some sort of family relationship [Norfolk Land Records].

1796—Almira Scoville born—probable daughter of Ithamar and ?

1797—5 January—deed received (Intervail Lot 43) [Norfolk Land Records].

1800—Federal Census, Norfolk—Ithamar Scoville, 26–45; "wife" 26–45; 1 "son" under 10; 1 "daughter" under 10. While the family numbers do not match up with the births of four children that I have noted above, two of the children may not have been counted or were in someone else's household at the time of the enumeration.

1801—March, Cornwall—the wife and grandchild of Ithamar's father Timothy die. It is unknown who the parents of this grandchild are.

1801—13 September—Ithamar's father remarries in East Haddam to Sarah Rogers. Parentage not confirmed.

1802/03—Norfolk—A son is born to Ithamar and his unnamed wife [based on the census records]. Name of child unknown.

1803—Norfolk—Ira Scoville sold the **west** end of the Intervail Lot 43 to Reuben Dean. This piece of land was bounded east on Ithamar Scoville, north on Jabez Bacon, west on Joshua Beach, and south on Jesse Benton.[126]

1804—Cornwall—Ira Scoville is back on the tax rolls—month and day is unknown.

1804—Norfolk—Ithamar sells the **east** half of the Intervail Lot 43 to Daniel Pettibone [a neighbor on the 1800 census]. Did Ithamar return to Cornwall? If he did, he is not mentioned on any of the tax records. He does show up, however, on the 1810 census in Cornwall. He sold this property for $217.00.

126 Norfolk Land Records, Vol. 7, 246. Connecticut State Library, Hartford, Connecticut.

1804—2 June, Norfolk—deed received.

1806—31 August, Norfolk—"Amasa Scoville and Ledem[ia]" Scoville are baptized and are listed as "adopted" children of Reuben Dean and _______.[127] My theory is that Amasa and Lodema/Lodemia Scoville were baptized as older children and not as infants. I also believe that these were the children of Ithamar and his wife. No other Scoville families have an Amasa or Lodemia as their children.

1800–1810—A son born to Ithamar and wife [based on census records].

1809—29 August, Norfolk—Franklin Scoville born to Ithamar and wife. This is the only proven/documented child of this couple.[128]

1810—Cornwall, Federal Census—Ithamar is back in the town of his birth. The census reads as follows:

Head of Family: Ithamar Scoville

Free White Males <10—4 (born say 1800–1810) (three unnamed "sons" and Franklin)

Free White Males 26–45—1 (Ithamar)

Free White Females 10–16—1 (born say 1794–1800) (perhaps "daughter" Almira Scoville)

Free White Females 26–45—1 ("wife")

1811—8 April, Norfolk—Nathaniel Dickinson for "consideration of three-hundred dollars received in full satisfaction of Joshua Beach . . . the land and premises . . . lying in Norfolk . . . bounded on the land of Amasa and Lodema Schovil . . . being the same land formerly owned by Ithamar Schovil containing thirty acres be the 'same more or less.'"[129]

1811—21 November, Cornwall—Ithamar purchases three acres of land from Charles F. Jackson for fifteen dollars. This parcel was on the line between Cornwall and Canaan, otherwise on Joel and Luther Harrison's land.[130]

1811—28 December, Cornwall—deed received.

1812—Approx. date—Amasa Scoville marries Lucy C. Foote—perhaps in Torrington or Wolcottville, Connecticut, as this is where Lucy was from.

1813—27 January, Cornwall—Ithamar's uncle Stephen Scoville dies of the epidemic.

1813—30 January, Cornwall—Ithamar's father, Timothy, dies of the epidemic.

1813—1 February, Cornwall—A son of Ithamar dies age 10—likely the son who was born 1802/03 and the one mentioned in E.C. Starr's *History of Cornwall*—Starr does not name this son. He also likely died from the epidemic (page 524).

---

127 *Baptisms, Marriages, Burial and List of Members Taken From Church Records of the Rev. Ammi Ruhamah Robbins, First Minister of Norfolk, Connecticut 1761–1813*. This book was regarding the *Commemoration of the One Hundred and Fiftieth Anniversary of the Organization of the Church, December 24, 1760,* and was printed for Carl and Ellen Battelle Stoeckel (1910). 67.

128 Death certificate for Franklin confirms that Ithamar was his father; ironically, there is no request for the mother's name on this certificate of death.

129 Norfolk Land Records, Vol. 9, 308.

130 Cornwall Land Records, Vol. 9, 217.

1813—2 March, Goshen—Ithamar's sister, Triphene, dies age 38 of the epidemic.[131]

1813—29 May, Goshen—Lodema Scoville "of Norfolk" marries Elisha Carrier "of Goshen." Elisha was the widower of Triphene Scoville, who was the proposed aunt to Lodema and Ithamar's sister.

1814—10 January, Cornwall—the Town of Cornwall prosecutes a claim against Norfolk "for the support of Ithamar Scovel and his family." The meeting minutes:

> At a Special Town Meeting legally warned and held at the North Meeting House in the Town of Cornwall on the 10th day of January, A.D. 1814, John Calhoun Esq. was chosen Moderator. Voted that an Agent be appointed to prosecute a claim of the Town of Cornwall against the Town of Norfolk for support afforded to Ithamar Scovil and his family, inhabitants of said Norfolk, before he was removed to the Town of Norfolk by a warrant from the Civil Authority. Voted that Oliver Burnham Esquire to be the Agent of the town for the purpose mentioned in the foregoing vote. And lastly voted that this meeting be dissolved. Attest: William Kellogg, Town Clerk.[132]

According to the notes by Mr. Gannett, (who transcribed the meeting minutes) of the Cornwall Historical Society, each town was responsible for the welfare of its own paupers, but there were many intertown disputes over which were the proper hometowns for the migrant paupers; the State reimbursed towns for keeping paupers who were not Connecticut inhabitants.

Warnings out of town was a method used in the New England communities to pressure or coerce "outsiders" to settle elsewhere. The Board of Selectmen of a town issued such warnings, which were served by the constable upon any newcomer who might become a town charge. When persons were warned out of a town, they were not necessarily forcibly removed. The first warnings out were recorded on June 6, 1654, in the village of Rehoboth, Massachusetts. The practice was common throughout the early Colonial Period but died out in the early 19th century.[133]

Ithamar had been born and raised in Cornwall and lived in that town when he was not living in Norfolk. There is nothing in the Meeting Minutes that gives us a glimpse into what happened to this family for them to be considered "paupers." Did the War of 1812 impact the Connecticut economy? Was Ithamar not an astute farmer? Could he not work the land due to illness or physical disabilities? Of course, there are other less favorable attributes of our ancestor's personalities that could have been the problem, but without knowing for certain, I will not speculate here.

---

131 Connecticut Town Death Records, pre-1870 (Barbour Collection); Connecticut Courant, Tuesday, March 2, 1813; Vol. XLIX.

132 Gannett, Michael R., *Cornwall Documents Town Meeting Minutes 1740–1875, Transcribed with Notes.* Cornwall Historical Society, reprinted 2003.

133 Wikipedia article. Cited were the works of *Warning Out in New England,* Josiah Henry Benton (W.B. Clarke Company, 1911); George Tilton, *History of Rehoboth,* (Boston, 1918); Leo Titus, Jr. *Titus, A North American Family History* (Baltimore, 2004).

1814—2 April, Cornwall—Ithamar sells his land that he had purchased in 1811 for fifteen dollars to John Bradley "of Norfolk."[134] Ithamar probably sold this land to raise money to support his family. Ithamar signed the document with an X.

1814—Norfolk—"[The] U.S. Treasury assessed $45 to Ammas [sic] Scovel and Lodema Scovel—nine acres, no house-tax was for out buildings only."[135] Note that Lodema is referred to as "Scovel" not Carrier, even though she had been married for some four years.

1815—28 April—An infant of Elisha Carrier and Lodema Scoville died.[136]

1815—20 May—Elisha Carrier and Lodemia Carrier "of Goshen" sell back to Amasa Scoville the two pieces of land that Amasa had quit-claimed to them in 1806 (witnesses Birdsey Oviatt & JP Moses Lyman).

1815—24 July, Cornwall—Ithamar and family were once again "legally warned out," and suit or suits "may be necessary against the Town of Norfolk."[137]

1816—Known as the "year without a summer;" heavy frosts, snow, and all-around cold weather right through the summer. Crops failed and people went hungry. Many removed to other states.

1817—11 March—Amasa Scoville "of Torrington" sold to Roxalana Dean, wife of Reuben Dean, nine acres of land in Norfolk, bounded south on Jesse Benton, east on Caleb and Joel Beach, west on Joshua Beach and is the "land and all land Ira Scoville deed to myself and Lodema Scoville." Lodema had already conveyed her nine acres to Amasa.[138]

1820—Norfolk, Federal Census—the census was begun on the first Monday in August (August 7th).

Ithamar's household consisted of all males. Note that Ithamar's neighbor is his brother-in-law, Reuben Dean.

> Free White Males between 16–18—1 (born say between 1802–1814). Could this be Philo C. Scoville? (See the chapter on The Case of Philo C. Scoville)
> Free White Males < 10—3 (one being Franklin)
> Free White Males 45 & up (including head)—1—(Ithamar)
> (No tic mark for any females in the family)

1826—15 March, Norfolk—A James Scoville dies, age 22, born say 1804, buried in an unmarked grave.[139] Could this be a son of Ithamar? The name James doesn't fit the naming patterns of this family and I have not been able to discover who this James is.

1830—Norfolk, Federal Census—A "Thomas" or "Thamar" Scoville and "wife" age 60–70 years are enumerated. These ages certainly coincide with the age of Ithamar in 1830 (68 years). Note that there isn't a Thomas Scoville living in Norfolk at this time and Thomas is not a name used by my Scoville family line.

---

134 Cornwall Land Records, Vol. 9, 365. Connecticut State Library, Hartford, Connecticut.

135 Connecticut Historical Society records.

136 Goshen First Congregational Church Records, Vol. 2, 46; sex and name of child is unknown.

137 *Cornwall Documents Town Meeting Minutes 1740–1875.*

138 Norfolk Land Records, Vol. 1, 10:231, MF#1213 #1168–69.

139 Norfolk Church Records, Vol. III, "Only those who have no Grave Stone."

A review of the early census records reveals that Ithamar's name is variously written as Thamar, Jhama, Thamos. I am confident that the man named in the 1830 census in Norfolk is my fourth great-grandfather, Ithamar. Also of note is that Reuben Dean is living next door to Ithamar in 1830 as well.

The "wife" who is enumerated on the 1830 census is not on the 1820 census. If this is the same woman, she could have been counted in someone else's household in 1820 (while visiting) or was not counted at all for whatever reason.

1831—10 October, Norfolk—Ithamar Scoville dies age 67 yrs. 2 mo. 3 d.

Ithamar is buried in an unmarked grave, as previously stated. There is no record of Ithamar being buried in any of the cemeteries in Norfolk (or Cornwall, for that matter). In May 2002, Richard Byrne of the Norfolk Historical Society was very gracious in receiving permission by the current owners to show us the area where my ancestor once lived. Richard was our "tour guide" as he had grown up in the area and hiked in these woods a good part of his life, and during these hikes, he made many discoveries over the years. This area is heavily wooded and at the time of our hike the forest was just coming alive with greenery.

Richard had some interesting things to show us—remnants of the past. The area was known as "Dean's Farm" (when Reuben Dean was living there). At the time of our visit, we were shown the well that still exists on the property today and, across from it, a cabin where the barn once stood. The cabin had been used by the Boy Scouts for many years. There are stairs in the cabin that are said to have come from Reuben's barn; however, to my untrained eye, they looked like the type of narrow stairway that would have been in a home in the early part of the nineteenth century.

Apple trees still exist on the property and there are Barberry bushes growing where the settlement once was. These bushes are not native to Connecticut and may have been planted there at some point or self-seeded, as they are now considered an invasive plant species. Richard also showed us a "road" (that is merely a pathway now) where maple trees were planted on either side and this "road" goes over a small bridge. While we were there, I imagined my ancestor going back and forth on this road and over the bridge. We were deep into the forest now; no cars could be heard or any other motorized vehicle. Even the birds were quiet as they often are in a forested area—the one thing that we did hear (or thought we heard) was a sound of a bear. It was off in the distance and, thankfully, we didn't see it!

We were shown many of the remnants of pits where colliers made charcoal—perhaps this is a job that Ithamar was involved in. There were also parts of cellars, stone walls, and remains of outbuildings that dotted the landscape.

While all the things we had seen so far had been interesting, the one area that captured me the most was what Richard was to show us next.

A small area on this property had unmarked graves: two "headstones" and two footstones. We were told that these graves had been dug up many years past and it is said that the male was at least six feet tall and that there were a woman and two children also buried there (where the footstones are located). Richard had no knowledge as to who was buried here but I knew it couldn't be Reuben or his wife because they are buried in a cemetery in Norfolk. While I have no proof that these graves are of Ithamar and his family, it would seem reasonable to presume it could be since:

1. We know he was buried in an unmarked grave; and
2. That he and his family were poor.

It wasn't uncommon to find people buried on their property and, while it is uncertain whether he still owned any land, he *was* living next door to his brother-in-law Reuben, who seemed to have a close relationship with him, and Reuben may have had them buried on his own property.

Overlooking part of Intervail Lot 43 is a man-made pond that occurred long after Ithamar lived there. Below is the photo of Dean's well.

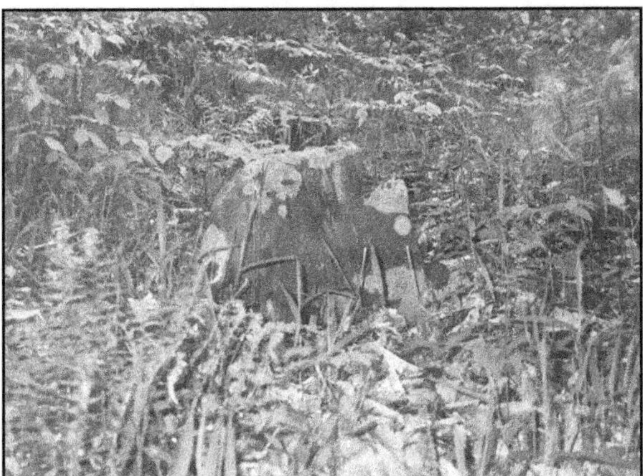

One of the headstones on the Dean property.

Photo of one of the footstones.

This photo shows all the graves together. Because of the undergrowth it is hard to see them all clearly. The second footstone is where the white "dot" is. Oddly, the cloudy spots only showed up on the area where we took photos of the graves; the rest of the photos came out fine. I don't know if it is a developing flaw or not.

A copy of the Proprietor's Map of Norfolk, Connecticut, showing where the Dean property was located (the lower left-hand corner).

Lastly (and as I previously mentioned), I cannot find a record for the woman who married Ithamar Scoville. A professional genealogical researcher suggested that I check the ten neighbors of my ancestor, as these neighbors may hold a clue as to the identity of the woman who became Ithamar's wife.

While there are exceptions to every rule, in most cases, a man would look within his own town or village for a prospective spouse.

When Ithamar was living in his father's household in Cornwall, their neighbors were the Harrisons, Beaches, Stevens, and Pettibones as well as others who lived within the "neighborhood." So far, I have not been able to connect any of the daughters of these families as having married anyone with the surname of Scoville.

It is also a mystery where Ithamar was in 1790. He would have been married by that time (based on when his first child was born). Early in my research, I was taken off the trail as a couple of books (the Scovel book by Holley and History of Cornwall) both stated that Ira and Ithamar "went west." I suppose it all depends on what "west" means. Ithamar's brother, Ira, *did* remove to New York, and I guess you can say that New York is "west." However, Ithamar moved no further than Norfolk, Connecticut.[140]

140 Again, much of the information in the Arthur Scovel book by Holley was given to her by descendants whom she had corresponded with. One instance is where it states that Ithamar had gone with his brothers west, but if so, he returned to Connecticut and settled at Falls Village, Connecticut, in the town of Canaan at a place called "Ithamar's garden." If Ithamar ever lived in Falls Village, I have not been able to find a record of such. From all available sources he lived in Cornwall and Norfolk.

As we've seen, land records can hold clues to family relationships, as in the case of Intervail Lot 43. In other land records I have not been able to find anything that gives any relationship with Ithamar. While I do not want to go into a lengthy list of what I've checked, I will just say that I have looked at countless probate records, estate packets, court records, vital records, etc. Most of the major discoveries (like Ithamar's death) cannot be found online (i.e., Ancestry) or even in the Connecticut State Library, which holds a plethora of records.

I speculate that Ithamar's unnamed wife was born between 1764–1773 and died sometime after 1830. These possible birth years of their children are based on the available census records.

**_Children of Ithamar Scoville and Unnamed Wife_**

i. A male, b. between 1790–1800, probably Norfolk. Name unknown.

10. ii. Amasa,[5] b. Nov 1791, Norfolk; d. 7 Oct 1842 Wolcottville, Connecticut; m. Lucy C. Foote in Torrington; she b. Nov 1795 in Torrington to Col. Samuel Foote and Lucy Lord; d. 5 Oct 1863, Chicago, Illinois.

11. iii. Lodema,[5] b. circa 1794, probably Norfolk; d. 1873 Brimfield, Portage, Ohio; m. 29 May 1813, Goshen, Elisha Carrier; he b. abt. 1768; d. Aug 1844, Brimfield, Portage, Ohio.

12. iv. Almira,[5] b. circa 1796 probably Norfolk; d. 31 Jan 1868, Maine, Broome, New York; m. abt. 1820 in Austerlitz, Columbia, New York, to Horace Kelsey, Baptist Minister, he b. 21 Apr 1798, New Marlborough, Berkshire, Massachusetts; d. 22 Oct 22, 1890, Barton, Tioga, New York.

v. A male, b. circa 1803/04, probably Norfolk; likely the son who died 21 Feb. 1813, age nine/ten in Cornwall.

13. vi. **Franklin,**[5] b. 29 Aug. 1809, Norfolk; d. 11 Jul 1901, Pine Meadow, Connecticut; m. 6 Oct 1830, Norfolk, Amarilla Hotchkiss; she b. 17 Jan 1810, Norfolk; daughter of Oliver Hotchkiss and Rebecca Sturdevant; d. 6 Jun 1882, Pine Meadow, Connecticut.

## *6. Ira Scoville[4] (Timothy,[3] Stephen,[2] Stephen,[1] Arthur)*

Born 25 September 1766,[141] Cornwall; died sometime after 1840[142] in either Ohio or Michigan; he married about 1794 in either Cornwall or Norfolk, Connecticut, to Ruth Knapp; she born 28 July 1774, Connecticut, possibly to Timothy Knapp and Ruth Cowles;[143] died 28 February 1871, Berlin Township, Erie, Ohio.

Like his siblings, Ira was probably born in Cornwall. There is no information on his early

141 For some reason, Ira is not listed with his "twin" sister Ruhamah on the record of births in Cornwall. He is clearly a son of Timothy Scoville and Thankful Crocker as recorded in a land record. Baptismal Records for Cornwall, 1755-1892, First Congregational Church Records pgs. 5 & 6.

142 Ira Scoville appears on the 1840 census for Ohio, but he has not been found on the 1850 census. He likely died between these two censuses.

143 The parents of Ruth Knapp have not been proven, however, they name their fourth child "Ansel/Ancil *Cowles* Scoville." The genealogy of the Knapp family by Alfred Averill Knapp, *Nicholas Knapp Genealogy*, (1953) gives the parents of Ruth as Timothy Knapp and Ruth Cowles.

life and, like his brother Ithamar, he doesn't appear on the 1790 census in any state where the census was taken. Ira may have married Ruth as early as 1794, however, their first child was not born until 1801; it's likely that the marriage occurred closer to the time of the first child's birth.

As documented in Ithamar Scoville's timeline, his brother Ira Scoville purchased fifty acres of land called the "Intervail Lot 43" in 1796. Ira probably had removed to Norfolk and lived on part of the land he had purchased, but he also had land in Cornwall as he is listed on the Cornwall Grand Lists for years 1794, 1804, 1808, 1809, 1810,[144] 1813, 1814, and 1815 (keeping in mind that some of the lists are missing or incomplete). According to the town meeting minutes for Cornwall, Ira was also selected as a surveyor of the roadways for "the year ensuing" November 8, 1813.

The information for Ira is the typical census record and land records, however, one of the more fascinating and interesting pieces of information is that Ira kept an account book that has survived approximately 219 years and is in the hands of some of his direct descendants. Ira's account book gives a glimpse into his daily life and is something that we don't often get to experience when researching our early ancestors. His account book will be given in its entirety at the end of this book.

In 1806, Ira—"of Cornwall"—sells some land in Norfolk to Amasa and Lodema Scoville. This is the same land that shows up in the timeline for Ithamar Scoville. The land was sold for "one-hundred and twenty-four dollars" and bordered Joshua Beach's land and is known as Intervail Lot 43. The description of the land is recorded as from a "heap of stones" in the east line of the highway and so forth. Also mentioned are measurements chains and links to a "birch tree." Ira set his "seal" on the sixteenth day of June 1806. Witnesses were Betsy Pettibone and Oliver Burnham, Justice of Peace and Joseph Clark, Town Clerk recorded that the deed was received on June 17, 1806.

On the same day, Ira Scovil sold to Reuben Dean for "two-hundred dollars one piece of land lying in said Norfolk containing twenty-two acres and is to be taken off the west end of a certain lot of land Number 43 of said Norfolk being the same lot I purchased of the said Ira Scovil the deed being recorded in the records of Norfolk 8th Book Page 272 . . ."[145] Reuben Dean set his "seal" and the deed was signed and witnessed by the same people and on the same day as the deed for Amasa and Lodema.

In 1808, Ira's father, Timothy "Cornwall," for "one-thousand dollars" received:

> . . . of my son Ira Schovil of Cornwall, aforesaid, Do give grant, bargain and confirm unto said Ira Scoville his Heirs and Assigns forever one certain piece of land of said Cornwall lying in pieces, the first piece is the Homestead on which I now live and bounds as follows: Westward on highway in part and on Joseph Scovel's land in part Southerly on Jacob Scovel's land, Easterly on Stephen Schovel's land, in part and on Joel and Luther Harrison's land, in part Northerly on said Joel and Luther Harrison's land; the second piece bounds Easterly on Highway, Southerly on Joseph Scovel's

144 Ira is listed on the 1810 census for Cornwall.

145 Norfolk Land Records, Vol. 8, 479.

> land, Westwardly on Joseph Schovel, on Abraham and Oliver Hotchkiss[146] land and North on Joel and Luther Harrisons land, containing about one-hundred acres of land, be the same more or less with the Buildings thereon.[147]

The witnesses to this record were Stephen Scovel and Luther Harrison. Timothy Scovel signed with his mark. Once again, the Justice of Peace is Oliver Burnham and the instrument was received and recorded on March 22, 1813, with William (?) Kellogg as the Registrar.

It is not known whether Timothy and his wife continued to live on the property that he had sold to his son. Unfortunately, reading the 1810 census for Cornwall is not helpful because the names are recorded in alphabetical order: Scovel—Stephen, Levi, Ithamar, Joseph, Timothy, Ira, Jacob, and Jonathan, in which case we do not know who lived next door to one another.

In Timothy's household there were two people enumerated: a Free White Male—45 & over; and a Free White Female 45 & over.[148] This would have to be Timothy and Sarah (Rogers) Scoville.

On the 24th day of April 1809, Ira Scovel "of Cornwall" for "one-hundred fifty-five dollars" received in "full satisfaction of Joshua Beach of Norfolk . . . to his Heirs and Assigns forever, one certain piece of land lying in said Norfolk."[149] This is the land that he sold to Amasa "Scovil" and Lodema "Schovel" in 1806.

On August 1, 1810, the census takers began their treks across Connecticut to record the citizens of the cities, towns, and villages. Cornwall was still a wilderness.

Starting in 1800, the enumeration was carried out under the direction of the Secretary of State and, until 1840, the marshals reported the results to him.[150] These were conducted door to door and, in a place like Cornwall, it must have been difficult as the homes and farms could be at a great distance from one another. The census taker may find no one at home and had to decide whether to come back another day. Sometimes they would even try to get the information from young children or make a guess! And even if a head of household gave the information, it does not necessarily mean the information was accurate.[151]

The 1810 census for Ira Scoville is as follow:

Free White Males < 10—1 (Ancel Cowles Scoville or Ira Bradford Scoville?)
Free White Males—26-45—1 (Likely Ira Scoville)
Free White Females < 10—2 (three daughters should be recorded here)

---

146 Oliver Hotchkiss' daughter Amarilla Hotchkiss, married Franklin Scoville, grandson of Timothy Scoville.

147 Cornwall Land Records, 1802–1809, Vols. 8–9, Vol. 9, 296. Connecticut State Library [Reel #598, FHL #000396]. I added some grammatical marks for clarity. These grammatical marks do not appear in the actual record. I have used the spelling "Scoville" as it appears in the deed.

148 Compiled by Michael R. Gannett, Cornwall Historical Society. *Cornwall Grand Lists 1742–1820, Cornwall Censuses. 1790, 1800, 1810, 1820,* Cornwall, Connecticut Federal Census, 1810.

149 Cornwall Land Records, Vol.9, 70. Connecticut State Library, Hartford, Connecticut.

150 *Twenty Censuses Population and Housing Questions 1790–1980.* U.S. Department of Commerce, Bureau of the Census.

151 Szucs, Dennis Loretto and Wright, Matthew, *The Source: A Guidebook to American Genealogy,* third edition published 2006. The article on the census can be found online: wiki.rootsweb.com.

Free White Females—10–16—2 (unknown who the two females are)
Free White Females—26–45—1 (Likely Ruth Knapp Scoville)

Despite what appears to be an inaccuracy of the 1810 census, the only child who cannot be accounted for as reaching adulthood is Ancel Cowles. More on this later.

On the 12th day of March 1813, an indenture of lease[152, 153] was drawn up between Ira Scovil and Sarah Scovel. The document reads as follows:

> This indenture of lease made this 12th day of March in the year of our Lord 1813, by and between Ira Scovil of Cornwall in Litchfield County and State of Connecticut of the one part and Sarah Scovel said Cornwall, widow of Timothy Scoville late of Cornwall deceased, of the other part, witnesseth that they said Ira Scovil for and in consideration of five-hundred dollars already received in behalf and on account of the said Sarah Scovel in part of the consideration a deed given to me by my Hon. father Timothy Scovel late of said Cornwall deceased, and all of all other conditions and things to be observed, done and performed on the part of said Sarah Scovel, hath demised, grantee and to confirm farm(?) letter unto her the said Sarah Scovel, the whole of the lands and buildings and other appurtenances thereon standing which lie in Cornwall that was deeded to me by my said father Timothy Scovil and is founded and described by said deed dated the fourth day of April 1808 reference thereto being lands containing about one-hundred acres of land.
>
> To have and to hold the above demised, grantee and farm letter promises to her the said Sarah Scovel during the term of her natural life to use, occupy and improve to her own use she committing no unnecessary waste on said premises, and it is agreed by the said Sarah Scovel of the second part that the said Ira Scovel of the first part shall use and improve the whole of said leased premises so long and on condition that he shall at all times keep, provide for and feed on said farm and for the use of said Sarah Scovel one good riding horse and two cows during the pleasure of said Sarah and in all things will and honorably support said Sarah in sickness and in health and at his own proper charge and expense provide for and support her the said Sarah according to her age and condition in life, and on condition the said Ira Scovel shall so well support said Sarah during her said natural life and at her decease pay all funeral charges, then the said Ira Scovil to have the said riding horse and cows. And it is further agreed and understood that if at any time during the life of said Sarah, the said Ira Scovil or his heirs should fail or neglect to fulfill all and singular the conditions before mentioned, then the said Sarah to have full right and possession of said leased premises and said horse and cows to her own use and improvement during her said Life and said Ira and his heirs debarred any use therein during the life of said Sarah.

152 "Any deed, contract, or sealed agreement between two or more parties." *Collins English Dictionary 5th Edition*, (first published 2000, Harper Collins Publishers 1979, 1986, 1991, 1994, 1998).

153 Cornwall Land Records, Vol. 9, 476.

In witness whereto we here unto set our hands and seals at Cornwall the 12th day of March in the year of our Lord 1813.

Signed, Sealed and Delivered the presence of Clarissa Burnham, Rheda [Rhoda] Burnham
Ira Scovil
Sarah X Scovel

Ira and Sarah personally appeared before the Justice of the Peace, Oliver Burnham, and the document was received, entered, and recorded on March 22, 1813, by William Kellogg, Registrar.

This indenture of lease is very explicit on how Ira's stepmother was to be treated or all would be forfeited.

Ira and his family remained in Cornwall for approximately two years more after this indenture was signed and sealed. Sometime after 1815 he removed to Hector, Tompkins County, New York. His brother Timothy had been living there for some time, and perhaps that is why he removed there. Ira's father had entrusted him to handle the affairs of his estate and that of his stepmother. While Timothy was the eldest (living) son and typically would have been the one to be called on to be the executor of his estate; he was too far away to perform such duties. The next in line would have been Ithamar, but it doesn't appear he was qualified to handle such important duties, so that left Ira.

I do not believe that Ira would have left Sarah Scoville on her own in Cornwall per the instructions of the indenture. It is also unknown whether Sarah remarried and a record of such an event has never been discovered. If she had, it is likely she would have remained on her property in Cornwall. My theory is that she went with her stepson to Hector, New York, and to expand on this, a Sarah Scoville is mentioned in the *First Presbyterian Church* records (Hector, New York) as having died 11 January 1826. My theory is that this *is* the wife of Timothy Scoville, and stepmother of Ira.

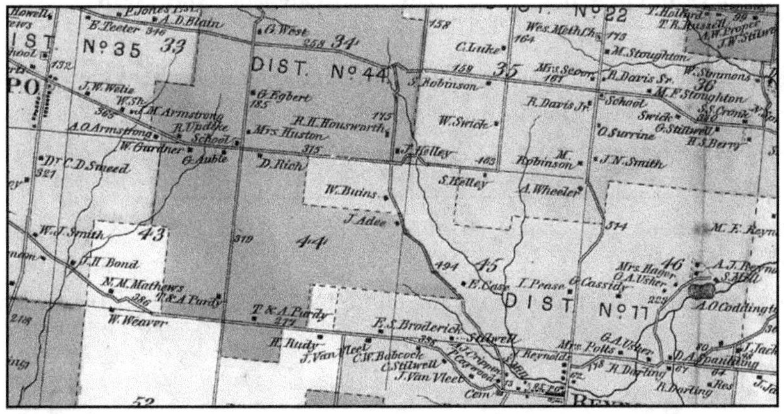


The map[154] above shows Great Lot 44 in Hector. This is where Timothy settled and is

154 Town of Hector 1874 map. Military Lots 43, 44, 45, 46—This is from the Backbone Ridge website (maps) backboneridgehistorygroup/maps. Unfortunately, I could not reproduce a map showing Lots 44 & 34. You can go on the Backbone website to see the area. Map printed with

where the property that contained the twenty-six acres is located. Unfortunately, I have not been able to find a map showing all the people who lived in this section. This area is now part of the Finger Lakes National Forest.

Besides the fact that Ira's brother was living in Hector, was there another reason to leave Connecticut? In Sidney Perley's book *Historic Storms of New England,*[155] in the chapter entitled "The Cold Summer of 1816," he describes it as the "coldest summer known to have been experienced in New England."[156] It was also called "poverty year"[157] (and more recently, "the year without a summer"). This name was given because of the destruction of crops, and many of the farmers were "brought to want."[158] Throughout the summer months there were various areas of frost and snow and there was a severe drought in the northwest section of New England. The fruit trees would begin to bloom but then they would freeze; birds would die because of this unusual weather. The areas that were affected the worst were Maine, Vermont, and New Hampshire. According to Mr. Perley's book, the weather had not been as extreme in Rhode Island and Connecticut, but even there, the "season was somewhat backward, but the crops were not so materially affected as they were farther north."[159] Regardless, living off the land in Cornwall was difficult and when the opportunity presented itself, Ira headed "west" to the fertile soil in Hector. This would not be the last time that Ira would move to another state.

Record keeping in New York was very poor during the early years and, other than the 1820 census and a record of a deed in 1836, I have not found any other data for Ira or his family. There is no information I could find as to whether they belonged to a church or if Ira was involved with the goings on in the town as his brother Timothy was.

The 1820 census for Hector, New York:[160]

Free White Males < 10—3 (probably Milo and Myron)
Free White Males—10-15—1 (probably Ira Bradford)
Free White Males—45 & over—1 (Ira)
Free White Females—10—15—1 (perhaps Laura)
Free White Females—16-25—1 (perhaps Amanda)
Free White Females—45 & over—2 (likely Ruth and Sarah)

I contend that the second female aged forty-five and over in Ira Scoville's household is his stepmother, Sarah. I contend that the Sarah Scoville who died January 1826 in Hector is most likely to be the Sarah Rogers who had married Timothy Scoville.

---

permission from Backbone Ridge History Group.

155 First published in 1891 by Salem Press Publishing and Printing Company, Salem, Massachusetts; it was reprinted under copyright 2001 by Memoirs Unlimited, Inc., Commonwealth Editions. 171

156 *Ibid*

157 *Ibid*

158 *Ibid*

159 *Ibid, 178*

160 National Archives and Records Administration, [Roll M33 76, Image 25.] Census began on August 7, 1820.

The state census for Hector, New York, in 1825 shows that there were five males in the household and two females; however, since I have not viewed this record myself, I am relying on an email from a fellow researcher back in 2001 and the early state censuses are not available anywhere online.

By the time of the 1830 census, there is only one woman enumerated in the sixty to sixty-nine age bracket, and that would be Ruth Scoville.

1830 census for Hector, New York:[161]

Free White Males—10–14—1 (probably Myron)
Free White Males—15–19—1 (probably Milo)
Free White Males—60–69—1 (Ira)
Free White Females—60–69—1 (likely Ruth)

On April 12, 1836, Ira Scoville and his wife, Ruth Scoville of Hector, Tompkins County, New York, sold to George Egbert (also of Hector, New York) for $800 fifty acres of land being part of Lot #34 in Hector.[162] Ira Scovill signed the deed and Ruth Scovill signed with her mark. Curiously, the judge, Caleb Smith, examined Ruth separately from her husband, Ira, to make sure that she had "executed the said conveyance freely and without any fear or compulsion of her husband." Ruth acknowledged that she signed the conveyance "freely and of her own will." I have never seen this terminology before when reading other deeds where the judge of record interviews the wife separately to make sure she is "on board" with selling the property.

The selling of this land was the precursor for the Scovilles to move once again—this time further west to Rochester, Lorain County, Ohio. Ira Scoville wa, at this time, seventy years old. What drove him to want to traverse hundreds of miles to start over again? A current map shows Hector, New York, and Rochester, Ohio, approximately 351 miles apart. Rochester, Ohio, sits on Lake Erie and was so named after the town of Rochester, New York.

This part of Ohio was called at the time the Connecticut Western Reserve. In the early settlement of the colonies, no one knew how far the land extended. As a result of this, some colonies, including Connecticut, received "vague charters of conveyance," which implied that a particular colony had a right to the land far to the west.

Because of the many disputes between the states regarding boundary rights, the newly formed federal government had to step in to settle the disagreements that arose. On September 13, 1786, Connecticut "relinquished its claims except for a 120-mile-long strip of land along Lake Erie, called the Western Reserve.[163] Ira Scoville and his family may have gone about 200 miles to the west to Lake Erie and traveled to Rochester via the waterway instead of the overland route.

According to *History of Lorain County, Ohio: With Illustrations & Biographical Sketches of Some of Its Prominent Men and Pioneers*,[164] Rochester township was settled about the year

161 1830 Federal Census [images, Ancestry].

162 From Deed Book JJ, 459–460 Tompkins County Courthouse—County Clerk's Office. Sent to me by Gary Scovill, a descendant of Ira Scoville.

163 See full article by Barbara Austen: *New Connecticut on Lake Erie: Connecticut's Western Reserve*, connecticuthistory.org, a program by Connecticut Humanities.

164 Williams Brothers, 1879, 286.

1827 by a man named Dodge, and by the 1840 census, Rochester had a population of about 200 citizens.

The last census that Ira was enumerated on was the 1840 census for Rochester and he would have been about seventy-four years of age (although the census records have him in a different bracket).

1840 census for Rochester, Ohio:[165]

Free White Males < 5—3
Free White Males—20–29—2
Free White Males—60–69—1 (Ira Scoville)
Free White Females < 5—2
Free White Females—20–29—2
Free White Females—50–59—1 (Ruth Scoville)
Persons employed in agriculture—3

Ira's son, Ira Bradford, lived next door to his parents and I suspect some of the people counted in Ira's household may be grandchildren, or others who may have been in this household on the day the census taker came. Ira Bradford's family was also enumerated on the same day, so it is possible some of these people may have been counted twice.

A record for Ira Scoville's death has not been discovered. He is not found after 1840 and it is not certain where he died, although it is likely to have occurred in Ohio. Ruth Scoville lived to the age of ninety-seven, and after Ira's death, she can be found in the censuses living with various relatives. In 1870, Ruth is living with her daughter Amanda and her husband, David Knapp, in Berlin Township, Erie County, Ohio. She died the following year on February 28, 1871.

I haven't determined the parentage of Ruth Knapp by a primary source record. I originally deduced that perhaps Timothy Knapp and Ruth Cowles may be her parents because of the middle name of Ira and Ruth's first-born son—Ansel *Cowles*; however, I have found conflicting information regarding this couple. One source (via Ancestry) states that Timothy Knapp and Ruth Cowles married in 1792. If this is the case, they couldn't be the parents of Ruth, who was born in 1774. An alternative source (and likely more accurate) comes from a descendant of Daniel Tyler[166] (husband of Amanda Scoville, daughter of Ira and Ruth Scoville). The descendant of Daniel Tyler concluded that Ruth's parents were, indeed, Timothy Knapp and Ruth Cowles. Timothy Knapp was born about 1750 in Connecticut and married Ruth Cowles about 1773 in Litchfield (Connecticut). Ruth Cowles Knapp was born March 25, 1750 in Canaan (Connecticut) and was the daughter of Joseph Cowles (1715–1806) and Ruth Woodruff (1719–1748).

In checking other possibilities for Ruth's parents on the Family Search site, someone had Elnathan Knapp and Lydia Barber as Ruth's parents, but again, this couple did not marry until 1788. I suspect that Ruth may be related (through her father) to the Knapps from Danbury, Connecticut, where some settled in and around Norfolk, Litchfield, Connecticut,

165 1840 Federal Census [Images, Ancestry].

166 Daniel Bickford of Richmond, Virginia, provided the information on the parents of Ruth Knapp.

in the mid-1700s. As did *my line* through a Sturdevant/Knapp marriage (*Hannah,[4] Caleb,[3] Samuel,[2] Caleb,[1] Nicholas Knapp the immigrant ancestor*).

While I personally believe that Timothy Knapp and Ruth Cowles are the parents of Ruth Knapp Scoville, more research is required to confirm or disprove her parentage through primary source records.

### *Children of Ira Scoville and Ruth Knapp*

i. Clarissa[5] (*Ira,[4] Timothy,[3] Stephen,[2] Stephen,[1] Arthur*), bap. 27 Aug 1801[167] Norfolk; d. perhaps New York or Ohio; m. perhaps Philo Clemmons, b. perhaps circa 1793 Connecticut??

There is some mystery regarding two of the daughters of Ira and Ruth Scoville. Clarissa is one of them (Dimmis is the other). Some online family trees have her name as "Clarissa Jane," however, when she was baptized, she is simply recorded as Clarissa. Whether the second name "Jane" came into existence at a later time, or is another person completely, is one of many questions for this daughter.

Clarissa was baptized with her sister, Dimmis, on 27 August 1801. They may have been twins (just as her father Ira Scoville was likely a twin to his sister Ruhamah). The fact that they were baptized in 1801 ***does not*** mean that they were born in 1801. As in the parlance of today: Norfolk was (and still is) out in the boonies. Having a minister on hand to baptize your child was few and far between. Dimmis and Clarissa could already have been five, six, or seven years old by the time that they were baptized.

Some years ago, a woman contacted me believing that Clarissa may be her ancestor, and that she may have married a man named Philo Clemons. She knew I was a long-time Scoville researcher and looked to me to see if I had any information. I did not. Of course, this piqued my interest and I started poking around to see if I could find anything that may assist her.

The first thing I recalled was that there was a man named Philo Clemons listed in Ira Scoville's account book.[168] This entry may not mean anything on its own, however, as this entry is approximately 1803, when Ira was living between Cornwall and Norfolk, Connecticut, which would mean that Philo Clemons was also living in the same proximity.[169]

To go a step further, a Philo Clemons is also listed on the 1820 census for Hector, New York, at the same time that Ira Scoville was living there. In fact, Philo Clemons, Ira, and Timothy Scoville, as well as Ira's son-in-law (David Tyler) were neighbors. So, what does this mean? Could it be that Philo Clemons is a possible husband for Clarissa Scoville? As mentioned before, when people removed to another state, they generally did so in family groups, and if Philo Clemons and Ira Scoville and his family were all in Connecticut and New York at the same time, it would present a good case for a possible marriage between these two people.

---

167 *Baptisms, Marriages, Burials and List of Members Taken From the Church Records of The Reverend Ammi Ruhamah Robbins, First Minister of Norfolk, Connecticut, 1761–1813*. Printed for Carl and Ellen Battelle Stoeckel, 1910; 62

168 Ira Scoville's account book is included in this work.

169 There is no mention of any Clemons families in Gannet's books on Cornwall, and there is no mention in Starr's *History of Cornwall* or Crissey's *History of Norfolk*.

Let's review the 1820 census for Hector, New York, for Philo and the woman who is proposed to be is wife. The household consisted of two males under 10 (born between 1810–1820), one male between 26–44 (born between 1776–1794), one female under 10 (born between 1810–1820), and one female between 16–25 (born between 1795–1804). These ages would certainly "fit" Philo and Clarissa.

One of the males listed as "under ten" on the census *may* have been Philo T. Clemens,[170] who was born circa 1816 in New Preston, Litchfield County, Connecticut, and the other male *may* have been Lyman Clemons, born 12 April 1822 in New York.[171] Philo *may* have been in Connecticut in 1816 and he certainly was in Hector, New York, in 1820, so it is not a far stretch to think that a second male on this census could have been born in 1822 in New York.

The census records for 1830 and 1840 were also checked, with the name Clemons being spelled in various ways. It has been a tedious task to determine the correct family. A man named Philo Clemons was found in Coventry, Chenango, New York, and one in Prattsburg, Steuben County, New York. The other men named Philo just didn't seem to fit the profile as they were enumerated in the southern states, and it is highly unlikely the family resided there.

The 1830 census for Coventry, New York, lists the following:

1 male—50–59 (born 1771–1780)
2 females—10–14 (born 1816–1820)
3 females—15–19 (born 1811–1815)
1 female—20–29 (born 1801–1820)
1 female—50–59 (born 1771–1780)

Based on the ages of the inhabitants in the 1830 census the profiles do not appear to be the same as the Philo Clemons of Hector, New York, in 1820. It has been discovered that the Philo Clemons family on the 1830 and 1840 census in Coventry, Chenango, New York, was born in 1771 and died in 1849 in Coventry. His wife was Sarah Clemons.[172] We can now eliminate this family from our inquiries.

So where is the Philo Clemons who is the person of interest here?

On the 1830 census for Prattsburg, Steuben, New York, is also a man named "Philo Clemons." What is interesting about this particular fellow is his next-door neighbor—Ira Bradford Scoville, the son of Ira Scoville, and the brother of Clarissa Scoville.

The adults in this group were born between 1791–1800—this would seem to fit the profiles of the Clemons family in 1820 in Hector, New York. There are also five males and three females of various ages within this family unit.

When we look at the 1840 census for Philo Clemons in Prattsburg, New York, the family unit is smaller, and Ira Bradford is no longer his neighbor. The family unit has three young females in the household. The adults are listed as aged between "50–59," so born between

---

170 Philo T. Clemons was the administrator of the estate of Lewis Clemons of "Thomaston, Litchfield, Connecticut," who was born 1796 and died 1873. Lewis Clemons may be the father of Philo T. Clemons. *Connecticut, U.S., Wills and Probate Records, 1609–1999.* Ancestry.

171 Birthdate given by a poster on Ancestry—no proof of birth, baptizing, and the like.

172 Find A Grave, Chapel Cemetery, Coventry, New York.

1781–1790. These dates of birth are off slightly compared to the 1820 and 1830 census reports. There are two more census reports available for a Philo Clemons in Prattsburg—the 1850 federal and the 1855 state censuses.

With the 1850 census we finally get to see all those named in the household. Philo Clemens [sic] b. 1792, Connecticut; Mary E. Clemens, b. 1792, Connecticut. There is a woman named Maria Parker, aged 33, with young children also named Parker in this household. Perhaps Maria is their daughter? The family before Philo is the Riley Clemens family. He is aged 29 and living with his "wife and children." Is this a son of Philo Clemons?

Is Mary E. Clemens the first or second wife of Philo?

The New York State Census for 1855[173] shows a "Philo Clemons," age 59, born in Connecticut and living with the Ezra C. Bramble family as a boarder in Prattsburg, Steuben County. He stated that he "resided in city or town 40 yrs." and is listed as a "border." The 1855 census does not ask whether the individual is married or widowed. The fact that the age of Philo is close enough to a birth year of 1793 (if, indeed, this date is accurate in and of itself) and the fact he gives his birthplace as "Connecticut" make this Philo a possibility of being the one who *may* have married Clarissa Scoville.

The obvious question is, is this Philo Clemons in Prattsburg in 1830, 1840, 1850, and 1855 the same Philo Clemons who lived in Hector, New York, as a neighbor of Ira Scoville?

A Philo Clemens was also found in a death record on Ancestry: Philo Clemons, born 1793, Milford, CT; died August 3, 1868, Burr Oak, St. Joseph, Michigan;[174] widowed. His age was given as 75 yrs., 6 months, 1 day. This would mean he was born 2 February 1793. He died from "paralysis" and was a "farmer."

While this data is promising, I have to refer back to the account book kept by Ira Scoville, where he mentions Philo Clemons in 1803. The Philo Clemons whom Ira mentioned cannot be the same person of the same name who was born in 1793, as that Philo would have been just ten years old.

Lastly, another individual on Ancestry has a Philo Clemons as the son of Isaac Clemons and Susan Rogers. This person states that Clarissa Jane "Scofield" was the daughter of Ira and Ruth Knapp Scoville. This couple has a son, Lyman Clemons, born 12 April 1822 in New York and died 4 January 1894 in Rheims, Steuben, New York; married 10 November 1844 (per Bible record) Druzilla Frost (1821–1890). There were no sources provided other than the Bible record, which may or may not be a primary source.

A much more diligent search is needed to narrow down all the men named Philo Clemons, and if a Philo Clemons did, in fact, marry Clarissa Scoville, daughter of Ira and Ruth Scoville.

This narrative has been exclusively about a man who may have been the husband of Clarissa Scoville, yet we know nothing more about Clarissa (other than her baptismal record). She may not have even lived to adulthood! As far as I have been able to ascertain, Ira Scoville did not leave a will. If he had, we would have been able to approximate or know for certain where and when he died. Ruth Knapp Scoville lived a very long life, but she did not leave a will either.

173 All census records regarding Philo Clemons and Philo T. Clemons come from Ancestry.

174 It must be noted that Riley Clemons is also buried in Burr Oak, St. Joseph, Michigan, as is Philo—Find A Grave.

If one or the other had left a will, it may have provided clues regarding Clarissa. Land records may be the only way forward to prove or disprove once and for all the existence of these two people as a couple.[175]

ii. Dimmis,[5176] *(Ira,[4] Timothy,[3] Stephen,[2] Stephen,[1] Arthur)* bap. 27 Aug 1801[177] in Norfolk; died after 1860, perhaps in Waterloo, Black Hawk, Iowa, or Buffalo, New York;[178] m. 28 Oct 1813, in Cornwall[179] to Fredrick Maine[180]; he b. abt. 1793, perhaps in Kent,[181] Litchfield, Connecticut; d. after 1855, probably in New York.

Prior to "discovering" the marriage record for Dimmis Scoville, I could not find any information on her. The marriage record is significant in the fact that this is only the second time a person of this name is mentioned in the records some twelve years after her baptism—no other Dinnise/Dimmis Scoville or any alternate spelling has been discovered in Cornwall, Norfolk, or anywhere else in Litchfield County, Connecticut. My contention is that the daughter of Ira and Ruth Scoville—named *Dimmis*—is the same person who married Fredrick Maine and this one record may dispel the erroneous information that exists for Fredrick Maine on the Internet.

In our ancestor's time, it was common for a marriage to take place in the hometown of the bride. Dimmis's father, Ira Scoville, lived alternately between Cornwall and Norfolk, Connecticut, and during the time of the marriage, Ira was certainly living in Cornwall, as shown in the 1810 census, and he is listed on the tax lists for said town.

Frederick Maine is also listed on the grand list[182] in 1814 and was being taxed $3.92, and then in 1815 he was taxed $70.32. The amount he was taxed in 1815 suggests he had made improvements to his property. Ira is also on the tax list for Cornwall during this time (as previously mentioned). By 1816 Ira Scoville and Frederick Maine are no longer mentioned on the tax rolls for Cornwall or anywhere else in Connecticut. We know that, as in the previous

---

175 Just a note: while I did not provide footnotes for the various census and death records, they are easy enough to find via Ancestry.

176 In the records that are available, the name "Dimmis" can be found written as Demis, Dennis, Damaras, etc.

177 *Baptisms, Marriages, Burials and List of Members Taken From the Church Records of The Reverend Ammi Ruhamah Robbins, First Minister of Norfolk, Connecticut, 1761–1813.* Printed for Carl and Ellen Battelle Stoeckel, 1910; 62.

Please note that the fact that these two daughters were baptized on the same day does not confirm that they were twins. Clarissa and Dimmis could have been toddlers, or even older, when they were baptized. Children that had not been baptized could all be rounded up for baptism the next time the preacher came to town—especially in such a rural area as Norfolk.

178 Obituary notice for Dimmis's daughter, Saran Ann (Main) Miller in the *Waterloo Evening Courier*, November 1910.

179 The marriage record was discovered among the "miscellaneous" records held at the Cornwall Historical Society.

180 This name is alternately spelled *Maine or Main.*

181 Frederick/Fredrick Main may have been the son of Jonathan Main and Sarah Hall of Kent.

182 "Cornwall Grand Lists 1742 - 1820" Gannett, Michael R.

narrative on Ira, the family left for Hector, New York, around 1816. When someone removed to another part of the country, they typically did so in family groups. It would seem probable that Fredrick Maine and his family also left (Connecticut) at the same time. But where was Fredrick prior to this time and what do we know about him? The online sources and the Maine genealogy claim that he was the son of Jonathan Main and Sarah Hall. This couple married on August 30, 1773, in Kent, Litchfield County, Connecticut.[183] The only child attributed to this couple is a daughter named Lydia, who was born December 18, 1773, in Kent.

Jonathan Main had removed from Stonington, New London, Connecticut, to Kent. A John Main is listed on the 1790 census there (page 59), as well as a Jonathan Main. Two other Main families were enumerated in Kent: Caleb Main and Hannah Main.

I mention this because all the information I have seen online (whether through Ancestry, Family Search, or individual family trees) gives Fredrick's place of birth as "Hartford," Connecticut. I have never found an *actual* record of Fredrick Maine showing that he was born there through vital records, Church records, etc. and I cannot find any Main/Maine families living in Hartford on the 1790 census.

All Main families listed on the 1790 census in Connecticut:

Ezekial—Bristol, Hartford Co., CT
Thomas—Ashford, Windham Co., CT
Caleb—Kent, Litchfield Co., CT
Hannah— " "
Jonathan— " "
John— " "
Russell—Woodbridge, New Haven Co., CT
Ezekial—Harwinton, Litchfield Co., CT
Elias—Willington, Tolland Co., CT

There were twenty families with the spelling Main**e** enumerated in New London, New London County, Stonington is part of New London County. This is likely the seat of the Main/Maine families in Connecticut.

Many of the online, unsourced records continue to state that Fredrick Main(e) was born September 18, 1793, in Hartford, Hartford County, Connecticut. Frederick is said to be the son of Jonathan Main(e) and Sarah Hall (or Morgan?). This family is in Kent, Litchfield, Connecticut, in 1790. The family had been living in this town since 1773. Perpetuating the myth of Hartford as the birthplace of Frederick is just not logical.

In the book by Algeron Aiken Aspinwall, *The Descendants of Eziekiel Main of Stonington, Connecticut* (published 1954), he states the following:

> Jonathan Maine (son of John) and Sarah (Morgan) Maine was born February 12, 1743, Stonington. Served in the Revolutionary War. Land was deeded to him by his father in Kent in 1778. He lived there until 1809, when he removed to Port Byron, Cayuga County, New York. He married in Kent, August 30, 1773, as the

183 Kent (Connecticut) Vital Records, Vol. 2–40.

> church records show to Sarah Hall. He may have had another marriage as one of his grandsons thinks his grandmother's name was not Sarah. The only child shown on the records for Kent, is a daughter Lydia, but the US census of 1790 shows that he was living at Kent and his family consisted of four males under 16, and five females, probably his wife and four daughters. His descendent gives the names of his children as below, (omitting Lydia) there must have been a son and daughter not given on this list—Frederick's birth is given by a descendent as having been at Hartford, Connecticut, so perhaps he lived there for a time before moving to Port Byron. Their children: Lydia, b. Dec. 12, 1773; Rufus, abt. 1775; Daniel; Samuel, 1778 or 1779; Huldah; Polly; Frederick, b. Sept. 8, 1793; Betsy, m. John Lewis.

Frederick's mother, Sarah, would have been about forty-eight years old at his birth, and one last child was born when she was approximately fifty. If it weren't for the fact that Jonathan Main removed to Port Byron, New York, I wouldn't have given credence to Frederick being born to this couple as most women during this time were no longer birthing children at forty-eight and fifty years old!

Jonathan Main shows up on the 1800 census in the Town of Kent[184] and the family consisted of one male under 10 (Frederick?); one male 10–16; one male 45+ (Jonathan); one female under 10 (Betsey?); two females 10–16 (Polly and Huldah?); one female 16–26 (Lydia?); and one female 45+ (Sarah).

By 1810, the Jonathan Main family is in Locke, Cayuga County, New York.[185] It is possible that Frederick went with his family to Locke, as he was seventeen years old at the time of their removal. If he did, he came back to Cornwall to marry Dimmis in 1813. He would have been twenty-years old and soon would be old enough to own land, which is why he is on the Grand Tax Lists previously mentioned.

I do not know where Fredrick and Dimmis were between 1815–1819; they may have remained in Cornwall, however, by 1820 they were listed as living in Mentz, Cayuga County, New York, with a family of five: one male in the age bracket of 26–40 (Frederick); one female 16–25 (Dimmis), and two males under 10. This couple's neighbors were Rufus Maine and Jonathan Maine (brother and father?).

In addition to the 1820 census, Frederick is also mentioned in Ira Scoville's account book. Ira and his family were living some forty-three miles south in Hector.

I contacted the Town Historian for Mentz, New York, to see if Frederick owned land there and she could not find any records or deeds. The only records that are available are the census records (1820, 1830, 1840, 1850, and 1855). This family remained in Mentz, at least per the census records. They could have conceivably resided in another town such as Port Byron, but they are never listed on the census for that town or any other town. Whether Frederick and

---

184 1800 Federal Census, Kent, Litchfield Co., Connecticut, FHL: 205619 [m32;Roll:2; Sheet: 702; Image: 55].

185 1810 Federal Census, Locke, Cayuga Co., New York, FHL: 0181385 [Roll: 31; Sheet; 1120; Image: 00028]. The Town of Locke was formed in 1802 from the Town of Genoa (formerly called "Milton") and is seated at the southern end of Oswego Lake.

Dimmis lived in Hector prior to the 1820 census (which began on August 7, 1820) is also an unknown. Ira Scoville recorded his transaction with Frederick in May 1820.

The 1840 census shows a family of ten—six males and four females—one of each being Frederick and Dimmis. There were two involved with agriculture, one employed in manufacture or trade, and one in navigation of canals, lakes, and rivers.

By 1850, we have the names of all those living in the household:

> Frederick Main, age 57 [born say 1793], carpenter, real estate value: $500, b. Connecticut.
> Laura? Main, age 16 (female), b. New York.
> Chauncy Main, age 20, (son?), b. New York.
> Laura Main, age 10, (daughter?), b. New York.

It is impossible to read the second entry. I tried comparing the handwriting from this enumerator to his other entries, but he has too many swirls and loops to determine what the first letter of this name is. It could be an "L" and "S" or an "A," but since there were only two daughters born to this couple—Sarah Ann and Laura (and Sarah Ann would have been approximately thirty years old at the time of the 1850 census)—the second person in the household must be Laura Main, who would have been sixteen at the time of the 1850 census; the younger Laura Main may have been a granddaughter of Frederick.

Where is Dimmis in this record? She was not counted with her own family. I checked the census records for 1850 for all her children except Perry I. Main and Frederick A. Main, as I could not locate them on the 1850 census. Dimmis could not be located. She could have been visiting or just was not counted. However, she was still living as she does show up on the New York State census for 1855 in Mentz:

> Frederick Maine, 61, b. CT, carpenter, married, resided in said county 40 years
> Demas Maine, 61, wife, b. CT, married, resided in said county 40 years
> Laura Maine, 20, child, b. Cayuga, [marriage section left blank] resided in said county 20 years
> Ellen Welch, 3, grand child? [first word is faded], b. Cayuga, resided in said county 3 years

After 1855, Frederick is no longer listed on any census records. He presumably died between the 1855 census and the 1860 census. New York did not start mandating death certificates until 1880 and it took a while for all municipalities to become compliant (as an example, Port Byron vital records do not start until 1884/85). Checking the available records that are online (Mentz Church Cemetery), there is no record of anyone with the last name of Main/Maine. It is possible that he was buried in another cemetery, but a record of such has not been discovered.

All records that I have seen have the date of death for Frederick Maine as 1853, in Hartford, Connecticut. At the time that I was researching this family all known sources were checked; that is, Connecticut State Library through their Barbour collection did not yield a death record for Frederick in Hartford or anywhere else in Connecticut. The same can be said for the cemetery records that are also available at the library and online. We know that he was still living in 1855 as recorded in the census, and I would question why a man who had lived in Mentz, New York, for some forty years would suddenly appear in Hartford and die there. I could not find any Main relatives living in or around Hartford. The death date and place for Frederick appear to be erroneous and without any basis of fact. This misinformation has been perpetuated for years and needs to be corrected.

Some years ago, I did attempt to correct this information with a direct descendent of Frederick. However, this person was adamant as to the veracity of the online account of the family and a Bible record that she claims was kept by a descendent of Jerome Maine (the eldest son of Frederick and Dimmis) and is recorded in the "Higginbotham Family Bible." This is all well and good, *if* the recorded information took place at the time of the birth or death of each individual.

How many generations removed were these Bible entries made? Were they made at the time of the occurrence or a generation or two later based on great-grandpa's memory? Many scholarly historians have changed their opinions on whether Bible entries can be considered as primary source evidence. Their reasoning is based on several factors: 1. For the information to be considered primary, you must know who recorded the information; 2. What is the publication or copyright date of the Bible? 3. What type of pen and ink were used to record the information? Is the writing instrument consistent with the period when it was written?[186] 4. Does the handwriting appear to be all done around the same time and by the same person?

~

On the 1860 census for the Twelfth Ward in Buffalo City we see Dimmis living with her daughter and son-in-law: Henry W. Miller and Sarah Ann (Main) Miller. Dimmis is listed as age sixty-five and is working as a "domestic." Her birthplace is given as "Connecticut." In addition to Dimmis Main, her son (and Sarah's brother) Chauncy is also residing in this household.

The New York State census for 1865 does not show Dimmis in the Miller household or any other household of her children and I could not find her on the 1870 or 1880 census. I can only speculate that Dimmis died sometime after 1860.

The death of Dimmis's daughter, Sarah Ann Miller, is recorded in the *Iowa Deaths and Burials 1850–1990.*[187] The death record confirms that Sarah Ann Miller's father is Frederick Main and her mother is "Dennis Scofield."

The obituary for Sarah Ann Main Miller on the next page was found in *The Daily Times* (Davenport, Iowa). She was buried on November 11, 1910.[188]

After reviewing the preponderance of evidence for Frederick Main and Dimmis (Scoville) Main, I conclude that Frederick *was* born in Connecticut, most likely in Kent as that is where

---

186 You can review these entries for yourself on Ancestry. Just go to the Public Records section and enter "Frederick Main" and you will be able to find a copy of the Bible entries and make your own decision.

187 *Iowa, U.S., Death and Burials, 1850–1990.* FHL: 1561085; Reference: 4771.

188 Page: 2.

WATERLOO, Ia., Nov. 12.—Ninety years and one month old yet with mind keen and active to the last, Mrs Sarah Ann Miller passed away at the home of her daughter, Mrs John Hubbard, 219 Lafayette stret, with whom she had made her home for the past twelve years.

his parents removed to prior to his birth (there is no proof of his birth or death in Hartford, Connecticut), and that he likely died in Mentz sometime after the 1855 census and is buried there or in Port Byron, date of death and cemetery are unknown.

I also conclude that Dimmis Scoville was, in fact, the daughter of Ira Scoville and Ruth Knapp, (based on her baptismal record) born in Norfolk, Litchfield County, Connecticut (**not** Port Byron, New York as alluded to by the descendants of Fredrick Main); that she married Frederick Main in Cornwall in 1813 and lived there until 1815/16 and may have removed to Hector, New York, for a short spell, but afterwards lived in Mentz, New York, with her family. I further conclude that, after Frederick's death, Dimmis lived with her daughter and son-in-law in Buffalo, New York, and may have lived in Waterloo, Black Hawk, Iowa, where she died sometime after 1860.[189]

Please note that I have not confirmed all marriage and death dates of the individuals listed:

### *The Children of Frederick Main and Dimmis Scoville*

*a.i.* Jerome B., b. 10 May 1814,[190] probably in Cornwall; d. 2 Feb 1893;[191] m. Abigail Harnden; date unknown; she died 11 Aug 1869, perhaps Port Byron, NY. This couple lived primarily in Mentz, Port Bryon, and in 1860 in the Village of Jordon, Onondaga, New York. Jerome is listed on the 1870 Erie, Pennsylvania, City Directory as living as a boarder at the Pet. House. He is described as a "cooper."

*b. ii.* Infant son, unnamed. Died 5 Apr 1816, probably Cornwall, age 12 days;[192] (This child would have been born about March 24, 1816.)

*c. iii.* Perry J., said to have been born 18 Nov 1816—(is this feasible?). The unnamed child (#2 above) was born 24 Mar 1816. Perry Main would have to have been conceived shortly thereafter and would have been born at the eighth month of pregnancy. The other alternative is that this date of birth is wrong, or perhaps Perry Main was a twin also born on March 24th and survived? He married (1) Anna B. Shaw; (2) Matilda Dennison. He is listed on the 1880 census for

189 According to the descendant of Dimmis (whom they refer to as "Damarius") she died in 1884 in Union City, Erie, Pennsylvania. I have checked the cemetery records for Union City and she is not listed.

190 Online records indicate that he was born on May 10, 1813; however, that would have been five months before his parents married—I don't see that as a reasonable assumption. Seven months after their marriage makes more sense.

191 Headstone inscription via Ancestry.com.

192 Hale Collection of Cemetery Inscriptions, Connecticut, Ancestry.com.

Titusville, Crawford, PA, with wife Matilda. Next door is his brother Norman. In 1870 he is listed in the Erie Co., Pennsylvania, City Directory as living on High Street and his occupation is a "cooper."

*d. iv.* Sarah Ann, b. 6 Oct 1820,[193] perhaps in Mentz or Port Byron, NY; d. 9 Nov 1910, Waterloo, Blackhawk, Iowa; m. Henry W. Miller, 3 July 1842,[194] Mentz or Port Byron; he is said to have been born in Albany, NY, about 1821; d. 1900 Waterloo, IA.

*e.v.* Daniel M., b. 26 Jul 1822, perhaps Mentz or Port Byron, NY; d. 7 Feb 1916, Cook County, IL.; m. Azuba_______; b. about 1824, NY.; d. unknown; in 1860 they were living in Arcadia, Wayne, NY. He is listed as a "master cooper."[195] Some of Daniel's brothers were also employed as coopers at one time or another per occupations listed on the census reports and/or death certificates.

*f. vi.* Frederick A., b. 19 May 1823—(I don't know if this individual belongs here).

*g. vii.* Norman, b. 16 Mar 1826, Mentz or Port Byron, New York; d. 9 Sep 1912, Ripley, Chautauqua, New York; m. Ruth Miller. He is listed as a "boatman" on the 1855 census.

*h. viii.* John D., b. 2 Mar 1829, probably Mentz or Port Byron, NY; d. unknown; m. Lydia Rensier; listed on the 1855 census for Mentz, NY, and on the 1880 for Union City, Erie, PA. He is listed as a "laborer" and working in a grocery store.

*i. ix.* Chauncy V., b. 21 Jul 1830, probably Mentz or Port Byron, NY; d. 5 Apr 1914, Union City, Erie, PA,[196] and is buried in Evergreen Cemetery in Union City. He is said to have been married three times: (1) Jane ______; (2) Carrie E. Cornell (1852–1886); (3) Martha Clark Ackerson, m. 23 Jun 1887. I was able to locate him on the 1850, 1865, 1870, 1880, and 1900 censuses, and on the 1910 census he is listed as a "widower" and is living in the household of Victor Blaskeley and is a "boarder." Chauncy's occupation was alternately given as "laborer" or "cooper."

*j. x.* Laura M.; b. abt. 1834;[197] d. unknown; m. unknown. Possible child is Ellen Welch, b. abt. 1852 in Cayuga, New York (per 1855 census). A cursory search via Ancestry and Family Search did not provide anything further on Laura. A more thorough search will need to be done by someone interested in this line.

iii. Amanda,[5] (*Ira,[4] Timothy[3], Stephen,[2] Stephen,[1] Arthur*) b. 15 Jan 1802, in Norfolk, CT;[198]

---

193 Her obituary notice in the *Waterloo Evening Chronicle* gives her date of birth as October 9th, same year.

194 Sarah's death and marriage dates come from the obit notice.

195 A cooper is a maker or repairer of casks and barrels.

196 Pennsylvania Death Certificate, via Pennsylvania Historical and Museum Collection and Ancestry.com.

197 Online Public Trees on Ancestry indicates that Laura's birthdate is December 16, 1834. There is no source allocated to this date.

198 The date of birth for Amanda comes from her obituary, which was published in the *Sandusky*

bap. 12 Jul 1802[199] in Norfolk; d. 8 Feb 1892, Ogonz, Ohio.[200] She m. (1) on 10 Oct 1820, Hector, NY,[201] to Lewis Tyler,[202] b. 23 Apr 1795, NY; d. 3 Jan 1845, Prattsburg, Steuben, NY. His death was caused by a tree falling on him. He is buried in the Old Cemetery, Prattsburg, NY; she m. circa 1847 (2) David Knapp, b. 8 Aug. 1802; d. 1872, Berlin, Erie, Ohio. Amanda Scoville and Lewis Tyler had ten children, all likely born in New York.

***The Children of Lewis Tyler and Amanda Scoville***

*a. i.* Ira Lewis, b. 12 Jul 1821.
*b. ii.* Daniel Henry, b. 4 May 1823.
*c. iii.* Harriet Loisa, b. 28 May 1825.
*d. iv.* George Washington, b. 3 Jul 1827.
*e. v.* Merry Melinda, b. 5 Sep. 1830.
*f. vi.* Sylvia Corkin, b. 6 Apr 1833.
*g. vii.* Charles Dwight, b. 22 Nov. 1836.
*h. viii.* Martin Quick, b. 28 Oct. 1837.
*i. ix.* A. D., b. 1 Feb. 1842.
*j. x.* Sarah Jane, b. 7 Jan. 1844.

As we've learned, Amanda's family removed from Norfolk, Connecticut, to Hector, New York, and this is where she met and married her first husband, Lewis Tyler. Sometime after their marriage the couple removed from Hector, New York, to Steuben County, living in the towns of Wheeler and Prattsburg. This couple is found on the 1830 census for Wheeler, and they are living in Prattsburgh in 1840.[203]

The 1840 census for Prattsburg for Lewis Taylor [sic] as follows:

Free White Males < 5—2—(born about 1835–1840) (Charles D. b. 1836, Martin Q. b. 1837)
Free White Males 10–14—1 (born about 1826–1830) (George W. 1827)
Free White Males 15–19—2 (born about 1821–1825) (Ira Lewis b. 1821, Daniel H. b. 1823)
Free White Males 40–49—1 (born about 1791–1800) (Lewis Tyler b. in 1795)
Free White Females 5–9—2 (born about 1831–1835) (Merry M. b. 1830? Sylvia C. b.1836?)

---

*Register,* February 23, 1892, 2; Hayes Presidential Library—Fremont, Ohio.

199 Baptism date is from the records of the *Church of Christ, Norfolk,* Connecticut, compiled by the Rev. Ammi Ruhamah Robbins, 1761–1813, 41.

200 *Rutherford B. Hayes Presidential Center Obituary Index,* 1810s—2016. Ancestry.

201 Source not documented.

202 Lewis Tyler is said to be the son of Daniel Tyler (b. 1768; d. March 8, 1826). The Tylers and the Scovilles were neighbors in Hector, Tompkins County, New York. This information was confirmed through the estate papers of Daniel[2] Tyler.

203 Note that Lewis's last name is written as "Taylor," however, I believe this is the Tyler family based on the number of people in the household and ages thereof.

Free White Females 15–19—1(born about between 1821–1825) (Harriet L. b.1825)
Free White Females 30–39—1 (born about 1801–1810) (Amanda Scoville b. 1802)

Two of their children (A.D. and Sarah Jane) are not listed as they were born after the 1840 census.

In 1835 we find the David Knapp family, who are living in a neighboring town of Addison, Steuben County, New York:[204]

Head of Household—1 (David?)
Number of Males—1 (Charles W.?)
Number of Females—4 (Jerusha, Sophia, Sarah, and ??)
Married Females less than 45—1(Flavia?)
Unmarried females 16–45—0

David's first marriage to Flavia[205] likely occurred sometime around 1820/21 as their first daughter, Jerusha, was born about 1821/1822. This daughter married David Abrams in 1844 and they were living in Trumbull County, Ohio, on the 1880 census. She is listed as being born in New York. She is also listed on the 1910 census in Ravenna, Portage County, Ohio, age 86 and living with her daughter and son-in-law.

The second child is Sophia, who was likely born November 3, 1826, in New York; she married Spencer John Mattoon July 16, 1846; she died April 7, 1891[206] in Waupun, Dodge County, Wisconsin.

Spencer Mattoon was the son of Levi Mattoon. I found this couple on the 1850, 1860, and 1880 censuses living in Chester, Dodge County.

The last two children born to David and Flavia are Charles W. Knapp and Sarah Knapp Kasson; the search for these two children proved to be unfruitful.

---

204 This information was sent to me by a fellow researcher, and I do not have the source to cite here.

205 Hubbell, Homer Bishop, *Dodge County Wisconsin Past and Present,* (S. J. Clarke Publishing Company, 1913); 328–329. This book profiles some of the early settlers to Dodge County. One of these settlers is Spencer J. Mattoon, and states the following: " Spencer J. Mattoon came to Wisconsin in the fall of 1844 from Portage, Ohio, and settled in the town of Chester on a farm he owned for many years, which at the time consisted of two hundred and ten acres. In 1846 he married Sophia Knapp, a native of the State of New York. She was the daughter of David and Flavia Knapp . . ."

206 The vital information comes from a family chart via Ancestry. This information is not backed up by any sources.

The 1840 census[207] for Prattsburg, New York, also lists a Sophia Knapp as "head of the household." Her household consists of the following:

Head of Household—50–59 (born between 1781–1790) Sophia Knapp
One male—40–49 (born between 1791–1800)
One male—10–14 (born between 1826–1830)
One male—15–19 (born between 1821–1825)

Could this be David Knapp's mother living in her own household? The other persons in the household could be children, grandchildren, a brother?

Lewis Tyler is said to have died on January 3, 1843(?), in Prattsburg[208] by a tree that fell on him. I do not have any other details about this, as the documentation I had for this cannot be found; but suffice to say, Amanda became a widow with children to support and the last child (Sarah Jane) having been born in 1844. Sometime after Lewis Tyler's death, Amanda Scoville Tyler remarried David Knapp. He is presumed to be the same David Knapp who lived in Addison and Prattsburg, New York.

There is a David Knapp who was born August 8, 1802. While two census reports have him having been born in New York, I believe that he may have been born in Norfolk, Connecticut; however, the only records I have found of a David Knapp in Norfolk are from three marriage records that are recorded in *Baptisms, Marriages, Burials, and a List of Members Taken From the Church Records of Reverend Ammi Ruhamah Robbins Who Was the First Minister of Norfolk 1761–1813*:[209]

David Knapp and Abigail Case—married June 15, 1794
David Knapp and Sophia Dodge?—married December 28, 1797
David Knapp and [ ] Knapp—married July 1799

A family tree located on Ancestry suggests that David Knapp was the son of David Knapp (1715–1838) and Sophia Dodge (1779–1849). I find this improbable as David Knapp (the elder) would have been eighty-seven at the time of (the younger) David Knapp's birth and would have been 123 years old at death! The death date may be correct, but the birth information is clearly erroneous. There is also another family tree that states "Lucinda Mann" as the wife of (the younger) David Knapp. My sense is that much of the information from individual family trees for David Knapp have been cobbled together by using other people's trees and trying to make the information "work." None of these trees have any sources attached to them.

As of this writing I have been unsuccessful in locating David Knapp, Amanda Tyler, or Amanda Knapp on the 1850 census.

It is not until 1860 that I have been able to locate them living in Fairfield Township, Huron County, Ohio.[210] Only three persons are listed in the household: David, age 58; Amanda,

207 1840 census, *Prattsburgh, Steuben, New York;* Roll: 341; Page: 254; FHL: 0017207. Ancestry.

208 On Family Search, a record indicates that "Louis Tyler" died in 1843 as opposed to 1845 (the date that I have). However, this record provides no source and is written on an index card and cannot be used as primary evidence of his death.

209 79 & 80.

210 1860 census, *Fairfield Township, Huron County, Ohio;* Roll: M653_991; Page: 341; FHL: 803991.

age 58; and Sarah, age 14. This Sarah could not be David's daughter from his first marriage, however, if this is the Sarah born to Lewis Tyler and Amanda Scoville in 1844, she would have been sixteen years old in 1850. The disparity in ages on the census is a common occurrence, depending upon who is giving the information and the person's memory at the time of enumeration.

David and Amanda had removed from New York and gone west about 1858 (see obituary notice for Amanda). David Knapp had purchased land in Fairfield Township, Huron County, in the spring of 1858 and later they had removed to Berlin Heights, Erie County, Ohio.

By 1870 this couple was living in Berlin Township, Erie County, Ohio:

David Knapp, age 67, b. New York
Amanda Knapp, age 68, b. Connecticut
Ruth Scoville, age 90, b. Connecticut

This census shows an aging couple caring for Amanda's mother, Ruth. The following year, Ruth Knapp Scoville died on February 28, at the age of ninety-six years and seven months in Berlin Township, Erie County, Ohio, and according to the *Find A Grave* website, she is buried in McMillen Cemetery in Huron, Erie Co., Ohio.

Amanda's husband died on February 23, 1872. David Knapp is listed as "69 years, 6 months, and 15 days old;" this would confirm that his birthdate was August 8, 1802.

The cause of his death was due to "bone in artery." I can only surmise that he may have broken a bone, which may have severed an artery and he subsequently bled to death?

David Knapp's estate was probated January 26, 1872[211]and his "inferred death date" is given as "1872." His will names Amanda Knapp (wife), Charles W. Knapp (son), Sarah Kasson (daughter), Jerusha Abrams (daughter), Sophia Mattoon (daughter), and Jonathan S. Howard (executor).[212] I believe these children are from David Knapp's first marriage as daughter Sophia Knapp Mattoon was born circa 1826[213] and couldn't be the child of Amanda and David.

After the death of her husband, Amanda moved in with her daughter Sylvia Howard and her son-in-law, Jonathan.[214] The 1880 census for Berlin Township includes Amanda, age "78," listed as "mother-in-law" and born in "Connecticut." She lives with this family until her death, at age ninety, on February 8, 1892, in Ogontz, Ohio.

The obituary reads as it was originally written:

> Ogontz—Mrs. Amanda Knapp, aged mother of Mrs. J. Howard died Monday morning February 8. The funeral services were held at the house the following Wednesday at 10 a.m. Internment in the cemetery at Berlin Heights. Amanda Knapp

211 *Ohio, U.S., Wills and Probate Records, 1780–1998;* Case: 519; Will Record, Vol:1–2, 1853–1878. Ancestry.

212 Jonathan S. Howard was the son-in-law of Amanda Scoville Tyler Knapp. Amanda's daughter, Sylvia C. Tyler, married in 1889.

213 Amanda Scoville Tyler was busy having children with Lewis Tyler during this timeframe.

214 His name is alternately given as either "Jonathan" or "John S." Howard on the census records.

was born in Connecticut January 15, 1802. When she was 15 years old, she came with her parents to Thompkins County New York. In 1820 she was united in marriage to Lewis Tyler. 10 children blessed this union, six at home survive her, two sons and four daughters. After 25 years of companionship death claimed her husband. She remained a widow until 1847 when she was married to David Knapp, with whom she lived until 1872, when death again left her alone. The deceased has been a resident of this state since 1858 and was highly respected by all who had an an acquaintance with her. The children wish to return heartfelt thanks to all who kindly gave their services during their bereavement.

Both Amanda and David Knapp are buried in Riverside Cemetery, Berlin Township, Ohio.

David Knapp *may* be the son of David Knapp and Sophia Knapp. Two clues may suggest this: 1. Sophia Knapp was living in Prattsburg, Steuben, New York, in 1840, and 2. David Knapp and his wife name a daughter "Sophia"—perhaps after his own mother?

These clues, while weak, may be a jumping-off point for further study.

iv. Ancel Cowles Scoville,[5] (*Ira,*[4] *Timothy,*[3] *Stephen,*[2] *Stephen,*[1] *Arthur*) bap. 5 Oct 1805, Norfolk, Connecticut.[215] Through much diligent research over the years, nothing more can be found on this individual outside of his baptismal date. Other descendants of Ira Scoville have played a part in this research with the same results. He may have died young, and that is why no further records are available.

v. Ira Bradford Scovill[5216] (*Ira,*[4] *Timothy,*[3] *Stephen,*[2] *Stephen,*[1] *Arthur*) b. 16 Apr 1807, Norfolk, Connecticut, d. 18 Nov 1863, Pioneer, Williams, Ohio; m. abt. 1829 to Harriett Dennison, b. 10 Dec 1806, New York; d. 6 Apr 1879, Pioneer, Williams, Ohio.[217]

The first record I have of Ira Bradford living on his own comes from the 1840 census for Rochester, Loraine County, Ohio. There is an Ira Scovel listed on the 1830 census for Lima, Livingston County, New York; while the age for the male would "fit" Ira B., the two other persons in the household do not.

Ira Bradford Scovill

215 His name is written as "Anfel-Cowles Scovil, son of Ira and Ruth Scovil," *from Baptisms, Marriages, Burials and List of Members Taken From the Church Records of the Reverend Ammi Ruhamah Robbins, First Minister of Norfolk, Connecticut, 1761–1813.*

216 Ira Scovill and his descendants spelled their surname without the "e."

217 Photo courtesy of the late Alyce Smith.

Ira Bradford is living next door to his father, Ira, in Rochester, Ohio, in 1840:

Free White Persons—male—<5—1 (likely Cyrus Sawyer, b. 1839)
Free White Persons—male—5–10—1 (likely William H., b. 1835)
Free White Persons—male—30–40—1 (Ira Bradford, b. 1807)
Free White Persons—female—5–10—1 (likely Hester E., b. 1832)
Free White Persons—female—30–40—1 (likely Harriett, b. 1806)

By 1850, Ira Bradford Scovill and his family were living some seventy-three miles south in Homer Township, Medina County, Ohio. The census for that year (1850)[218] lists Ira B. as a "farmer" and the value of his real estate is $819.00. Along with his wife, Harriet, there are five children in the household: Hester, William, Albert S., John M., and Wesley D.

Ira Bradford lived in Homer with his family for ten years, but was on the move again as, by 1860,[219] the family shows up in Bridgewater, Williams County, Ohio. Ira Bradford made his living as a farmer and on the census report his real estate is valued at $600, while his personal estate is valued at $200. The family once again is made up of wife, Harriet, William, Cyrus S., Hester (written as "Wester"), John M., and Wesley.

Three years after moving to Bridgewater, Ira B. died on November 18, 1863. All available records that I have seen state that Ira Bradford died in Pioneer, Williams County, Ohio. Pioneer is approximately six miles and somewhat northeast from Bridgewater. If Pioneer was indeed his death place, it can only be speculated why he was there. A burial place has not been found for Ira Bradford and it is possible he was buried in an unmarked grave.

The map of Bridgewater (1864) on the following page shows the property of Ira B. Scovill; Section 13, heirs of Ira Bradford Scovill.

Ira Bradford's wife, Harriet,[220] lived until April 6, 1879. She was living with her son William H. Scovill in Bridgewater in 1870.[221] Like his father, William H. was listed as a "farmer" and was likely working the farm that his father had worked prior to his death. Living next door was her son Cyrus and his family.

Harriet is buried in Pease Cemetery in Pioneer along with her son Wesley.

### *The Children of Ira Bradford Scovill and Harriet Dennison*

*a.i.* Albert, b. 28Apr 1830, Hector, Tompkins, New York; bap. 20 Feb 1831, Prattsburgh, Steuben Co., New York; d. 13 Aug 1833.

*b. ii.* Hester E., b. 25 Nov 1832, Hector, Tompkins, New York; d. 23 Dec 1899, Wayland, Allegheny, Michigan; m. Ezekiel Benjamin Smith, 11 Jan 1863, Hillsdale, Hillsdale Co., Michigan.

*c. iii.* William H., b. 1835, Hector, Tompkins, New York; d. Jul 1899, Birchtree, Shannon, Missouri; m. Rosanna Light, 31 Dec 1871, Bridgewater, Williams,

218 1850 census, *Homer Township, Medina, Ohio;* Roll: 709; Page: 166b. Ancestry.

219 1860 census, *Bridgewater, Williams Co., Ohio,* Roll: M653_1052; Page: 95; FHL: 805052. Ancestry.

220 A photo of Harriet Denison Scovill can be found on Ancestry, the original shared by the username: scorak.

221 1870 census *Bridgewater, Williams Co., Ohio;* Roll: M593_1282; Page: 30A. Ancestry.

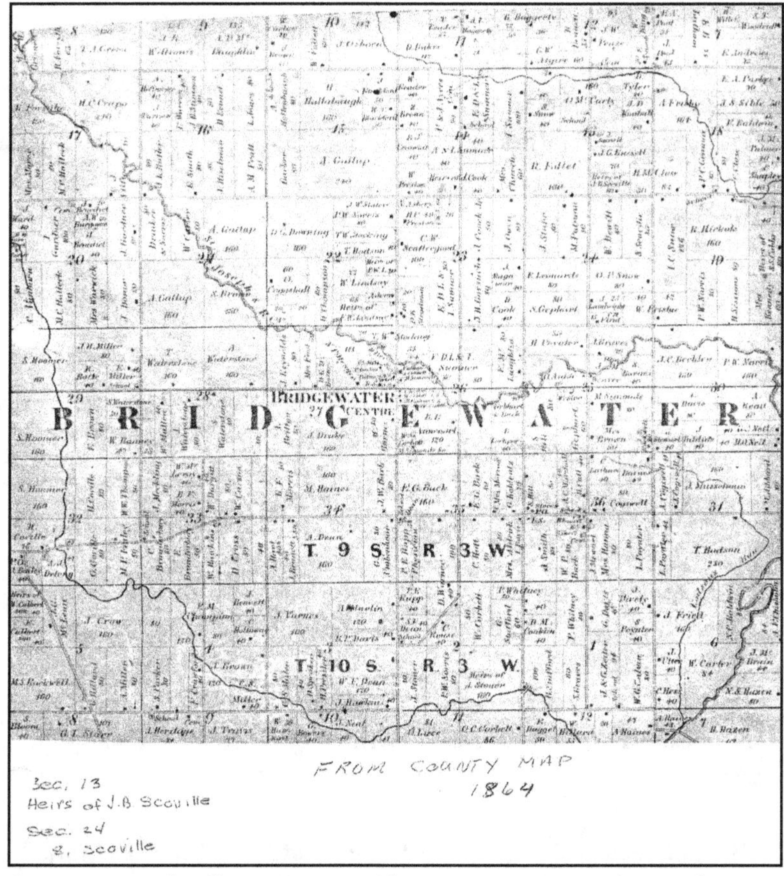


Conveyances of Williams County, Ohio. Section 13; Town 9; South Range 3 West; Bridgewater, Township.

Ohio. William H. was living in Putnam, Ohio, in 1880 (as per the census) and he is listed as "teaching school." He is said to have been a "pastor," but I could not find a record of him on the census listed as such. He may have been a lay preacher. More research would need to be done to find a reference of this.

*d. iv.* Cyrus Sawyer, b. 12 Mar 1839, Rochester, Lorain, Ohio; d. 13 Apr 1893, Bridgewater, Williams, Ohio; m. (1) Mary Victoria Clark, 1 Sep 1861, Ashland, Ohio;[222] m. (2) Mary Joanna Vanderhoof, 2 Nov 1867,[223] Homer, Medina, Ohio. She was born 1845, Ohio. The obituary notice for Cyrus from the 21 April 1893 edition of the *Pioneer Tri-State Alliance* newspaper. The obituary was written by his brother, Rev. William H. Scovill.

My dear brother, Cyrus Sawyer Scoville was born in Rochester, Lorain County, Ohio, March 12, 1836. In the fall of 1845, when he was six years old, his parents removed to Penfield, Lorain County, where his father worked in a sawmill until 1848, when he moved to Ashland County, where he resided (except for 2 years in

222 *Ohio County Marriage Records, 1774–1993*; Film# 002074386; Ancestry.

223 *Ibid, Film#000423820*

Homer, Medina, Co.,) until the spring of 1858 when he came to Williams County where he has lived ever since.

He learned the carpenters trade in Lorain County, and for many years spent the most of his time working at the business. He experienced religion over 30 years ago and joined the M. E. Church and was a faithful earnest worker in the church as long as he was able to go to the house of God. He was severely afflicted with tumors on his body and limbs several years, which caused the amputation of his right arm, in the cutting out of his limb a very large one. A gathering came in his head and pressed his eye, so it had to be taken out. About the middle of March began to grow worse and lost his speech so he could not speak more than a few words at a time. He lingered until April 13th half past 11 P.M. when he passed away to the land of eternal rest. Our loss is his eternal gain.

*It will not be long until I pass over the river and meet the dear brother on the Golden paved Streets of the New Jerusalem nevermore to part.*[224]

Through this obituary notice we have a few more clues to the life of Cyrus' father, Ira Bradford, and where and when he lived and worked. While obituary notices are not considered a primary source, since the brother of Cyrus gave this information, it may be more accurate as he was an eyewitness to these events, as he was the older brother. The birth year for Cyrus is suspect; not only does his headstone gives his birth year as 1839, but other online genealogical sources do as well.

***The Children of Cyrus Sawyer Scovill and Mary Victoria Clark***

*aa. i.* Ellsworth Mitchell, b. May 1863; m. Artie Guise.

*bb. ii.* Ulysses Sidney, b. 18 Nov. 1868, Ohio; d. 20 Aug 1963; m. Lillian Guise; she born Feb. 1873, Ohio.

***The Child of Cyrus Sawyer Scovill and Mary Joanna Vanderhoof***

*cc. iii.* Everett Bradford, b. 5 Dec.1875; m. Sarah Belle Scoville, 16 Dec. 1897.

***The Children of Ira Bradford Scovill and Harriett Dennison continued . . .***

*e.v.* John Mitchell, b. 19 Jul 1841, Rochester, Lorain, Ohio; d. 12 June 1927, Oakville, Delaware, Indiana; m. 14 Sep 1865, Lydia Rebecca Bear, Pioneer, Williams, Ohio. She b. 5 Jul 1843, Pioneer; d. 26 May 1923[225], Oakville, Delaware, Indiana. From the federal census records between 1870–1920, John and his family were on the move:

224 A copy of the obituary was sent to me by the late Alyce Smith many years ago. It was published in the *Pioneer Tri-State Alliance* newspaper.

225 I have also seen reference that Lydia died in 1926 as opposed to 1923 and the death place listed as Kankakee, Illinois. This reference comes from Ancestry.com under *Illinois Deaths and Stillbirth index 1916–1947.* This reference lists her husband as John M. Scoville, and her maiden name is given as "Bear."

1870—Union, Branch, MI—farm laborer
1880—Madison, Williams, Ohio—produce dealer
1900—Montpelier, Williams, Ohio—railroad laborer
1910—Superior, Williams, Ohio—coach cleaner (railroad)
1920—Prairie, Henry, Ohio—no occupation listed—owns home free and clear

John Mitchell is buried in Woodlawn Cemetery, Springport, Henry, Indiana, as is his wife, Lydia. Their children:

a*a*. *i*. Charles Loren, b. 1 Nov. 1866.

b*b*. *ii*. George Sawyer, b. 25 Aug 1868, Pioneer, Bridgewater Township, Williams Co., Ohio; d. 3 Mar 1959, Kalamazoo, Michigan; m. Ruby Sema Marshall, Oct. 1905, Nebraska; b. 11 Jul 1885, Williamsburg Township, Phelps, Nebraska; d. 29 Jan 1962, Chicago, Ill. This couple divorced around 1920.

*f*. *xi*. Wesley Wells, b. 1844, Rochester, Lorain, Ohio; d. 25 Dec 1863, Pioneer, Williams, Ohio. [Note that the date of death is only a month after his father's and occurred in the same town.] Since Wesley was only nineteen when he died, he did not leave a trail of records.

***Children of Ira Scoville and Ruth Knapp continued . . .***

vi. Laura Scoville[5] (*Ira,[4] Timothy,[3] Stephen,[2] Stephen,[1] Arthur*) b. 2 Feb 1809/10, Norfolk, Connecticut; d. 7 Sep 1866, White House Station, Lucas, Ohio; m. George Smith, circa 1835; he b. 15 Jan 1802; d. 6 Mar 1873.[226]

You will not find an official date of birth for Laura Scoville as there is no record of her ever existing in any of the records as the daughter of Ira and Ruth Scoville. It wasn't until 2001 that a fellow Scoville researcher by the name of Dan Bickford brought this to our attention. He referenced an entry in the E. C. Starr book *A History of Cornwall, Connecticut* (1926, page 505), which reads: "Ira Scoville's child baptized July 22, 1810." No gender is given. He then pointed to the 1820 census for Hector, Tompkins County, New York:

Free White Males < 10—3 (probably Milo and Myron)
Free White Males 10–15—1 (probably Ira Bradford)
Free White Males—45 & over—1 (Ira)
Free White Females—10–15—1 (Laura)
Free White Females—16–25—1 (Amanda)
Free White Females—45 & over—2 (likely Ruth and Sarah)

The next clue was the 1825 census for Ira Scoville in Hector, which gives five males in the household (Ira, Ansel C., Ira B., Milo, and Myron) and two females (Ruth and Laura—Amanda was married and out of the household by this time).

George Smith shows up on the 1840 census for Rochester, Lorain, Ohio, and there were eight people in the household.

---

226 Birthdates for Laura and George were based on their age, month, and day of death using the birthdate calculator: https://longislandgenealogy.com/birth.html

Free White Males—<5—1
Free White Males—5–9—1
Free White Males—10–14—1
Free White Males—30–39—1 (George)
Free White females—<5—1
Free White females—5–9—1
Free White females—10–14—1
Free White females—20–29—1 (Laura)

The family is again living in Rochester in 1850. George is stated to have been born in New Jersey and his occupation is given as a "farmer." His family consisted of his wife, Laura, and the following children: Burr Smith (1836), Mary Smith (1836), Chauncey Smith (1840), George Smith (1840), Ann Smith (1842), and Eli Smith (1846).

From the 1850 census, it appears that George and Laura were married about 1835. If so, she would have been fifteen years of age in the 1825 New York census and age ten in the 1820 census; this would indicate that she would have been the child baptized in 1810 listed in *A History of Cornwall.*

So far, all we have is speculation that Laura Scoville Smith was the daughter of Ira Scoville and Ruth Knapp. It's not until the 1860 census that her identity connection is revealed and confirmed. Even though this census does not ask the relationship between all the parties, I cannot see a valid reason why an eighty-three-year-old woman (Ruth Knapp Scoville) would be living with this family unless she was related in some way. I contend that Laura Scoville was the daughter of Ira and Ruth Scoville based on the information we have to date.

In 1866, Laura died, and George sold his property in Lorain County in 1867.[227]

Whether Ruth continued to live with her son-in-law is not known. We know that she *was* living with her daughter Amanda in 1870; however, in 1870 George Smith was living in Brighton, Lorain County, Ohio, with the Hugh Mosher family and he was age sixty-five. Again, there is no indication what relationship he had to this family. Interestingly, it does give his real estate value of $3,000, so he must have still owned land somewhere in Ohio.

George and Laura are buried in Ripp Cemetery, Waterville Township, Lucas County, Ohio. Laura's headstone reads that she died aged 56 yrs., 7 mo. September 7, 1866; George's stone gives his age at death as 71 yrs. 1 m. 22 days on March 6, 1873. Because of the commonality of the surname, I have not delved further into this family or their children.

### *Children of George Smith and Laura Scoville*

1. Burr Smith, b. abt. 1836. Listed on the 1880 census in Canaan, Madison, Ohio, with wife Almina/Alvina/Almira, and Edward Lewis. She b. Nov 1841. Their children:
   *a. i.* Chauncey, b. Sep. 1860; m. Emily J.; b. Nov. 1860.
   *b. ii.* George
   *c. iii.* Mary
2. Mary Smith, b. abt. 1838

227 This information was provided to me, but I cannot cite its source.

3. Chauncey Smith, b. abt. 1840
4. George Smith b. abt. 1842
5. Ann Smith, b. abt. 1844
6. Eli Smith, b. abt. 1846. Listed on the 1870 census in Waterville Township, Lucas County, Ohio.

vii. Milo Scovill[5] (*Ira,*[4] *Timothy,*[3] *Stephen,*[2] *Stephen,*[1] *Arthur*) b. 9 Apr 1815, Cornwall, Litchfield, Connecticut; d. 6 Mar 1896, Farmersville, Livingston, Missouri; m. (1) 19 Oct 1834, Sandusky, Erie, Ohio, Cynthia Crawford; b. 20 Mar 1816, New York; d. 26 Dec 1850/51,[228] Amboy, Michigan; m. (2) 4 Sep 1852; Mary Routson, b. 13 Mar 1831, Fayette County, Pennsylvania, d. 5 Feb 1892, Livingston, Missouri.[229]

Milo Scoville and his second wife, Mary Routson.

The first record of Milo Scovill living on his own is on the 1850 census[230] in Amboy, Hillsdale County, Michigan (I could not find an 1840 census that lists him as the head of the household). At this time, his first wife, Cynthia Crawford, is listed. As with almost all the descendants of Ira[1] Scoville, they were on the constant move from one town to another or one state to another. There were always new opportunities opening and this group of Scovills were not afraid to make that leap of faith to begin anew.

Outside of the census records, Milo Scovill is also mentioned in *History of Amboy,* in the online genealogical website genealogytrails.com. He is mentioned as being one of the early settlers of Hillsdale County prior to 1850.[231]

A record of the First Methodist Episcopal Church indicates that in February 1851, Rev. Newland Sampson organized a Protestant Methodist Society of about fifteen members.

228 Other online references on Ancestry indicate she died in 1851.

229 Dern, John Philip and Wadner, Marjorie, *Rauenzahner to Routson, A Family on the Move,* (Picton Press, May 1, 1997), 57. The identity of Milo's second wife was not known for some time until her maiden name was discovered by a descendant via the book on the Routson family. Mary is a descendant of Johan Ludwig Rauenzahner (1711–1778).

230 To avoid redundancy, all census records noted here come from Ancestry.

231 This photo used with permission by a descendant of Milo and was sent to me many, many years ago.

Among them were Milo Scovill and Cynthia Scovill. Another reference indicates that in 1856 a Methodist Episcopal class was formed in which Milo and Cynthia took part. This must be an error since Cynthia died in 1850 or 1851.

The *History of Hillsdale County, Michigan with Illustrations and Biographical Sketches of Some of Its Prominent Men and Pioneers*[232] mentions Milo Scovill as a "landowner in 1851, Section 10, Town 9, Range 2, 40 acres." He was elected a "juror" and a Justice of the Peace in 1868 and 1871, and a Commissioner of Highways in 1853, 1854, 1860, 1867, and 1870.

We find Milo still living in Amboy in 1860 with his second wife, Mary, and family. Milo is still occupied as a farmer with a real estate value of $600, and a personal estate of $329.

The Agricultural 1860 census shows that Milo owned "25 acres" of improved land and "15" acres of unimproved land, as well as "4 milch cows; 4 oxen; 5 sheep; 6 swine," the value of which was $259. There were 12 bushels of wheat, 8 bushels of Rye, 130 bushels of Indian corn, 26 bushels of oats, and 18 pounds of wool. The value of his farming implements was "$38."

On September 11, 1861, Milo enlisted in Company F of the 11th Michigan Infantry[233]—he was forty-six years old at this time. He was promoted to a "full corporal" on May 1, 1862, and was mustered out due to disability on August 27, 1862, in Nashville, Tennessee. A copy of his discharge papers states that he was a corporal under Captain S. B. Smith.

His discharge papers confirm that he was born in Litchfield County, Connecticut, and was age forty-seven years. He was 5′ 8 1/2″ tall and had blue eyes and gray hair. It also mentions that he was "unfit" for duty for "40" days.

The surgeon (W.N. Elliott) wrote the following as to the reason why he was discharged:

> I certify that I have carefully examined the said Milo Scovill of Captain S. B. Smith's Company and find him incapable of performing the duties of a soldier because of chronic diarrhea and general disability, his age being such that the recuperation powers are not sufficient to endure camp life.

Without going into detail on camp life during the Civil War, suffice it to say that it was hard even for the young members to endure. They were out in all kinds of weather, had an insufficient diet, and the water would often not be fit to drink. For a man of Milo's age, it would've been so much more difficult. There are no records to tell us how he felt about being discharged, but he did return home to Amboy to his family and resumed his life as a farmer.

In 1870 the family was still living in Amboy, but sometime before the 1880 census they moved to Cream Ridge Township, Livingston, Missouri. Milo was now sixty-five years of age. What drew him to move again is unknown (on our modern-day highway system the trek between Amboy, Michigan, and Livingston County, Missouri, is 581 miles). This couple lived out the remainder of their lives in Cream Ridge Township. On February 5, 1892, Mary Routson Scovill died, and she is buried in Ward Cemetery located in Farmersville, Livingston County. Four years later, Milo died on March 6, 1896, and is buried in Ward Cemetery.

---

232 Everts and Abbott, (Philadelphia, published 1879) 297–299.

233 *U.S. Civil War Records and Profiles, 1861–1865*; Film#M545, Roll 37. Ancestry.

***The Children of Milo Scovill and Cynthia Crawford***[234]

*a.i.* George William Scovill,[6] b. 12 Jul, 1835.

*b. ii.* Ransom C. Scovill,[6] b. 22 Apr 1837, Rochester, Lorain, Ohio; d. 2 Feb 1926, Frontier, Hillsdale, Michigan; m. (1) 20 Nov 1859, Hillsdale Co., Ohio, Adelaide Fuller; b. 28 Apr 1840, Rensselaer Co., New York; d.o. Isaiah Fuller and Electa Boardman; d. 24 Mar 1895, m. (2 ) 16 Jan 1896, Mary J. Vanderhoef Scoville—widow of Cyrus Sawyer Scovill.

Ransom served with the 18th Michigan Volunteers, Co. F during the Civil War. His length of service was two years, ten months, and sixteen days. He was mustered out on June 10, 1865. Ransom is buried in Sebring Cemetery, Hillsdale County, Michigan.

***The Children of Ransom Scovill and Adelaide Fuller***

*aa. i.* Alfred Scovill,[7] b. 1861; d. 1927; m. Minnie Sipes 22 Feb 1894, Frontier, Michigan.

*bb. ii.* Dora Scovill,[7] b. 1866; d. 20 Apr 1886, Cambria Township, Hillsdale Co., Michigan; m. Chauncy Watkins. Buried Wyllys Sebring Cemetery. Dora died giving birth to her first child, Orlyn C. Watkins. Her headstone reads:

*"Alas! How changed that lovely flower*
*Which bloomed and cheered my heart*
*For fleeting comforts of an hour*
*How soon we are called apart*
*Just in the morn of life*
*But we'll cherish here thy memory*
*My own, my angel wife."*[235]

*cc. iii.* Mary E. Scovill,[7] b. 3 May 1869. Mary never married and was ill for most of her adult life.

*dd. iv.* Danvers B. Scovill,[7] b. 1 Jul 1869; d. 1948; m. Rena Decker, 4 Nov 1897, Branch, California.[236]

*ee. v.* Sara Belle Scovill,[7] b. 18 Jan 1872; m. 16 Dec 1897 Frontier, Hillsdale, Michigan; m. Everett B. Scovill; d. 21 Nov 1925, Hillsdale, Hillsdale, Michigan.

*ff. vi.* Herbert C. Scovill,[7] b. 16 Oct 1873; m. 15 Oct 1884, Inez Hinkle, Woodbridge Township, Michigan.

*gg. vii.* Letica Electa Scovill,[7] b. 25 Jan 1883; d. 1967; m. George Wolfe.

***The Children of Milo Scoville and Cynthia Crawford continued . . .***

*c. iii.* Almyra/Almira Sabrina Scovill,[6] b. 22 Nov 1838.

---

234 The birthdates for all the children come from the Bible records of Mary R. Scovill. The Bible was purchased October 14, 187__. The entries are all in the same handwriting (the handwriting for the last two entries is different). The Bible (I believe) is in the hands of a descendant, Dale Burney. Not primary evidence, but likely the correct birthdates.

235 Copied from the headstone and submitted by Gary Scovill.

236 *Michigan County Marriage Records, 1822–1940.* FamilySearch through Ancestry.

Left–right standing: Viola, Sarah, Herbert, Danvers, Mary
Seated: Lettie (Electra), Ransome (Scoville), Adelaide, Alfred

Left–right rear: Mabel, Mary, Electa S. Wolf, George Wolf, Rena Decker Scovill, Danvers, Viola S. Touse, Frank Touse, Luzene, Sarah, Lillian (Guiss) Scovill, Ila, Herbert, Ulyss, Inez (Hinkle) Scovill
Seated: Minn (Sipes) Scovill, Harry Scovill, Fred, Ross, Clayton, Joanna S. Scovill, Ransom, Ancil, Everett, Fred or Lehah Scovill
Both photos courtesy of the late Gary Scovill (1934–2020) of Hillsdale, Michigan.

*d. iv.* Ancil Milo Scovill,[6] b. 16 Jul 1840, Rochester, Lorain, Ohio; d. 2 Apr 1910, Columbia City, Indiana; buried Vestaburg, Montcalm, Michigan; m. (1) Nancy M. Eddinger about 1876; born 12 Apr 1855; d. 21 Nov 1901, Montcalm, Michigan; m. (2) 10 Jul 1908, in Whitley, Indiana, Lucy Saurman/Sourman; d. 27 Mar 1910, age 72, in Columbia City, Indiana.

Ancil Milo Scovill also entered service during the Civil War on August 21, 1861, with the 1st Regiment, Michigan Calvary, Co. E as a private.[237] At this time he was twenty-one years old, 5′ 10 1/2″ tall, with blue eyes, light hair, and a light complexion.

His occupation was as a farmer, and his birthplace was Hillsdale, Michigan.[238] According to the military records, Ancil Milo was on the muster roll in November and December of 1863, but was then discharged on December 23, 1863, by "virtue of re-enlistment as Vet Volunteer provisions [ ] No. 191 W. C. Services 1863, Washington, D.C."

On December 24, 1863, he is on the rolls in Stevenbury, Virginia. It appears he re-enlisted for a "period of three years." He was paid a bounty of $402, and by 1865 he is listed as a "teamster" with the Brig train "since Nov. 10, 1864."

In June 1865 he was on extra duty Brig Quartermaster "since June 1, 1865." On July 1, 1865, Fort Leavenworth, Kansas, it states "deserted," however, the charge of desertion against Ancil Milo was dropped and removed on July 6, 1865, "under the provisions of the Act of Congress," approved July 5, 1884. The discharge certificate was furnished by the Adjutant General's office December 27, 1884. The dishonorable discharge "heretofore issued to this man is canceled."[239]

Ancil Milo is listed on the 1880 census with his first wife, Nancy, daughter Lula, and son Sawyer in Madison Township, Williams Co., Ohio.

***The Children of Milo Scoville and Mary Routson***

*e.v.* Newlin Sampson Scovill,[6] b. 8 Sep 1853, Michigan; d. 28 Apr 1922, Kansas City, Jackson, Missouri; m. (1) Mary L. Entricon, 1873; (2) Florence Octavia Lyon, 4 Mar 1891, Livingston, Missouri.

*f. vi.* Almanzor Scovill,[6] b. 11 Jun 1855, Hillsdale, Michigan; d. 16 May 1923, Ponca City, Lincoln, Oklahoma; m. Mary Alis Johnson 2 Dec 1882, in Missouri.

*g. vii.* Myron Leroy Scovill,[6] b. 15 Jul 1857, Livingston Co., Missouri; d. 29 Dec 1936, Ponca City, Lincoln, Oklahoma; m. 1883, Rosa Isabella Helf (1859–1910).

*h. viii.* Edith Arminda Scovill,[6] b. 20 Dec 1858, Amboy, Michigan; d. 6 Oct 1934, Seattle, Washington; m. 1883, Otis Duff[e]y, (1861–).

*i. ix.* Ulisus [sic]Grant Scovill,[6] b. 28 Jul 1863, Hillsdale Co., Michigan; d. 26 Aug. 1863, Hillsdale, Michigan.

*j. x.* Edward Everett Scovill,[6] b. 2 Dec 1864, Hillsdale, Michigan; d. 13 Apr 1869, Hillsdale, Michigan.

*k. xi.* Lucy Jane Scovill,[6] b. 19 Nov 1867, Michigan; d. 28 Jan 1916, Logan Co.,

---

237 From *U.S. Civil War Soldiers, 1861–1865*. The 1st Calvary Regiment was formed Sept. 13, 1861, with a muster date of March 10, 1866. Ancestry

238 Ancil Milo was born in Rochester, Lorain Co., Ohio, *not* Hillsdale, Michigan, as it has been purported.

239 A descendant of Ancil Milo stated that Ancil would often show up at his father's house alone. He would stay a while and then leave, but it is not known where he went when he left.

Oklahoma; m. 1886, Livingston, Missouri, George Helf (1862–1928).

*l. xii.* Edmund Cameron Scovill,[6] b. 26 Sep 1867, Hillsdale, Michigan; d. 14 June 1940, Omaha, Sarpy, Nebraska; m. 1896 Winifred ______ (1867–1951).

*m. xiii.* Eulalia Amanda Scovill,[6] b. 24 Sep 1872, Missouri; d. 5 Oct 1890, Cream Ridge Township, Livingston, Missouri.

*n. xiv.* Burton Baldwin Scovill,[6] b. 14 Nov 1873; d. 22 Oct 1874.

≈

viii. Myron Scovill,[5] *(Ira,[4] Timothy,[3] Stephen,[2] Stephen,[1] Arthur)* b. 10 Jan 1818, Hector, Tompkins, New York; d. 13 Mar 1876, Rochester, Lorain, Ohio; m. Martha Wheeler, 9 Nov 1837, Rochester, Loraine, Ohio;[240] b. 25 Feb 1820, Brighton, Lorain, Ohio; d. 25 Oct 1901, Rochester, Lorain, Ohio; she m. (2) 14 Jul 1878, Lorain County, Ohio, Nathan Noble.[241]

Not much is known about Myron except what has been found from the basic information, i.e., birth, marriage, death, and census records.

This family is on the 1850 census as living in Brighton with two children: Edward and Lewis. Myron is listed as a "farmer" with the value of his real estate being $800.

Ten years later, they are still in Brighton. The family has grown to three children: Edward, Lewis, and Mary. Myron is still listed as a "farmer" with his real estate having increased to $1,500 and a personal estate of $373.

Myron was referred to as "Rev. Myron Scovill," but it is not until 1870 when his occupation is listed as a "Minister of Gospel." (It is thought that he and his family may have belonged to the Rochester Center Congregational Church while living in Rochester.)

As of 1870, the family was now living in Jeromesville, Ashland, Ohio. The only child in the household is Mary, age fourteen. Myron is no longer listed with any real or personal estate values; however, in 1874 Myron is listed as owning land in French Creek, Brighton, Ohio.[242] Two years later, Myron died at the age of fifty-eight.

On July 14, 1878, Martha Scovill remarried to Nathan Noble. According to the 1850 census for Nathan, he was listed as a "clothier" and living in Litchfield, Medina, Ohio, with his parents, born about 1811 in New York. I have been able to locate him on the census until 1880, when he was now married to Martha Scovill and living in Litchfield, Ohio.

By 1900 Martha was living with her son, Lewis, back in Brighton and is listed as a "widow," Nathan having died in 1897.[243] Because of Martha's and Nathan's ages at the time of their marriage, there were no children born to this couple.

---

240 *Ohio County Marriage Records, 1774–1993;* Original data: *Marriage Records. Ohio Marriages.* Various Ohio County Courthouses. Ancestry.com. "Martha Wheeler, female, marriage date, 9 Nov. 1837, Lorain, Ohio; Spouse: Miran [Myron] Scavit [Scovill].

241 *Ibid.* Film: 000378294.

242 *U.S. Indexed County Land Ownership Maps, 1860–1918, Ohio, Lorain.* Ancestry.

243 *Rutherford B. Hayes Presidential Center Ohio Index, 1830s–2011.* Ancestry.

***The Children of Myron Scovill and Martha Wheeler***

1. Edward J. Scovill,[6] b. 1844, probably Brighton, Lorain, Ohio; d. 11 Dec 1891, Brighton; m. Ella Sankey, 3 May 1871;[244] she born 1851. Edward J. Scovill served in Co. F, Ohio 12th Calvary Regiment. This couple lived in Avon, Lorain Co., Ohio, in 1880.
2. Amanda Scovill,[6] b. 8 Oct 1840; d. Dec 25, 1844.[245]
3. Lewis Scovill,[6] b. 13 Oct 1846, Brighton, Lorain, Ohio; d. 30 March 1930, New London, Huron, Ohio, and is buried in the Rochester Station Cemetery. The census records for Lewis show that in 1880 he was living with his brother Edward in Avon, Lorain, Ohio. In 1900 he was living alone in Brighton and was a "farmer." By 1910 he was still living in Brighton on Center Road South, and he owned his farm free and clear. He was the only one in the household. I have not been successful in locating Lewis on the 1920 census. The 1930 census was begun on April 1st of that year and, since Lewis died two days prior to that census, he is not listed. Lewis remained a bachelor.
4. Almina M. Scovill,[6] b. 5 Jan 1851, Ohio; d. 2 Jun 1852, Ohio. Buried in Rochester Station Cemetery.
5. Mary Almira Scovill,[6] b. 7 Dec 1856, Rochester, Lorain, Ohio; d. 24 Sep 1939, New London, Huron, Ohio; m. 27 Nov 1873, Summit County, Ohio,[246] Charles Gudson Farmer; b. 14 Jul 1846, Hopkinton, Saint Lawrence, New York,[247] to Charles Terrien Farmer and Rosalie Beourne. Prior to his marriage, Charles served with Co. F, 13th NY Calvary during the Civil War. After this couple's marriage they were residing in Swan Creek, Fulton, Ohio (according to the 1880 census). By 1900 they had removed to Clarksfield, Huron, Ohio. Their destination was New London, Huron, Ohio, where they are listed on the 1920 and 1930 census.

On Oct. 12, 1923, Charles died. Mary may have gone to live with one of her children after his death. Mary died sixteen years later on September 24, 1939, in New London, Ohio. Like the majority of Scovills from this line, they are buried in Rochester Station Cemetery. This couple had the following children:

*a. i.* Bertha L. Farmer Cummings[7]—1875–1955
*b. ii.* Fred Farmer[7]—1877–1877
*c. iii.* Arthur Myron Farmer[7]—1879–1950
*d. iv.* Pearl M. Farmer—1882 [7]–1882
*e. v.* Hazel Blanche Farmer Breckenridge[7]—1884–1961
*f. vi.* Mabel Farmer[7]—1886–1886
*g. vii.* Charles Claude Farmer[7]—1888–1969
*h. viii.* Ivy Leona Farmer—1889[7]–1891

---

244 *Ohio County Marriage Records, 1774–1993;* Original data: *Marriage Records. Ohio Marriages.* Various Ohio County Courthouses. Ancestry.

245 The birth and death dates for Lewis, Amanda, Almina M., and Mary Scovill come from *Cemetery Inscriptions of Lorain County, Ohio,* (1980), 419–424, which were transcribed by volunteer Kathy Groner. Rochester Station Cemetery.

246 *Summit County, Ohio, Marriage Records, 1840–1980.* Ancestry.

247 Information comes from a descendant of Charles Farmer (Robert Farmer 1928–2010).

*i. ix.* Lewis McKinley Farmer[7]—1892–1951
*j. x.* Ruth Farmer [7]—1894–1984
*k. xi.* Harry Ernest Farmer [7]—1898–1985

### 7. *TRIPHENE/TRIPHENA SCOVILLE*[4] *(TIMOTHY,*[3] *STEPHEN,*[2] *STEPHEN,*[1] *ARTHUR)*

Bap. May? 1772;[248] the actual date of baptism is illegible. The *History of Cornwall*, by E. C. Starr, also states that she was baptized 1772, so perhaps she was born a few months earlier, or even at the end of 1771. She died 2 Mar 1813, in Goshen, Connecticut; m. Elisha Carrier in about 1798,[249] likely in Cornwall, Litchfield, Connecticut. Elisha Carrier was born circa 1768, probably in Connecticut. I have been unsuccessful in locating his date of birth or his parentage. There were several Carrier families in Colchester, New London, Connecticut, but I have not been able to match him up with any family to date. One possibility is an Elisha Carrier, b. 13 Jan 1767, Colchester, who was the son of Thomas Carrier and Rebecca Sears.[250]

Elisha (born 1767) married Mary Fuller on January 22, 1795, in Millington Society, East Haddam. This marriage would be cutting it close if this is the same man who married Triphena Scoville. Checking the usual sources online proved unfruitful. A further examination of records at town repositories would need to be done.

A man named Elisha Carrier first appears in Cornwall records in 1798,[251] where he is listed on the tax rolls. He was the only male in the household and was between the age of 21–70.

Elisha was taxed the sum of $67.00. Elisha is on each consecutive tax record in Cornwall except the year 1802. By 1808 he is no longer on the tax rolls in Cornwall as the family had moved to Goshen, Litchfield, Connecticut.

While still in Cornwall they were counted on the 1800 census:

Free White Persons males 26–45—1 (Elisha)
Free White Person males <10—1 (born between 1790–1800)
Free White Persons females <10—1 (born between 1790–1800)
Free White Persons females 26–45—1 (presumably Triphene)

In 1805, Elisha Carrier sold land in Cornwall to Joseph Scovil, also of Cornwall:[252] "one certain piece of land in Cornwall containing about three acres, be the same more or less, bounded as follows viz. South and Western Highway, North on Canaan Line and East on

248 See footnote 78.

249 This is pure speculation. I have not been able to find a marriage record for this couple. It may have occurred a few years earlier, as per the 1800 census there are two children "under 10," so a marriage could have happened any time between 1790–1799.

250 *Carrier Genealogy*, compiled by Barbara Brown of The Colchester Historical Society, typewritten sheets, date unknown; 12.

251 Gannett, Michael R., *Cornwall Grand Lists 1742–1820 and Cornwall Census Records, 1790–1820;* 96 (Cornwall Historical Society, 2003).

252 *Cornwall, Connecticut Land Records 1802–1809*, Vols. 8–9, Vol. 8, 236; Connecticut State Library Reel #598; FHL #0003961.

land belonging to Luther and Rachel Harrison." The deed was signed on November 27, 1805, in the presence of Oliver Burnham and Rhoda Burnham. Oliver Burnham—as we've seen in previous land records—was the Justice of the Peace in Cornwall.

There is another land record between Elisha Carrier and two other persons in 1806. This concerned land in Canaan. Elisha had received $200.00 from Salmon Hunt and David Taylor for "certain tracts or parcels of land containing fifty acres of land, be the same more or less, two of said pieces lying in Canaan, the other in Cornwall, the first piece lying in Canaan purchased of Isaac Dean as by his deed recorded in Canaan Town Records, Book 6, Page 84 [?]. The second lying in said Canaan purchased from Sarah Watson for Bounds reference to be had to her Deed on said Records. The third piece lying in Cornwall for the Bounds reference to be had to my Deed of Isaac Hugg [?] recorded on said Cornwall Records Book 7, page 239 with the buildings standing on said land."[253]

There must have been some problem with this land transaction as David Taylor, Rafel Hunt 2nd, Salmon Hunt, and Amos Hunt, "all of Canaan," brought a judgement against Elisha to the sheriff of Litchfield County. The case was heard in the Court of Common Pleas "holden" at Litchfield on "4th of Tuesday of March 1806." The gentlemen recovered some of their losses in the sum of "96 dollars and 94 cents."

The cause for the judgement against Elisha is not known, but it was not the last time that Elisha was involved in a court matter, as will be noted later.

The 1810 census still shows this family living in Goshen:

Free White Persons males 10–16—1 (the same "son" listed on the 1800 census <10)
Free White Persons males 26–45—1 (Elisha)
Free White Persons female <10—1
Free White Persons female 10–16—1 (the same "daughter" listed on the 1800 census <10)
Free White Persons female 26–45—1 (presumably Triphene)

I have never discovered any names for this couple's children, although I may have found a good candidate for a son of this couple, and will expand on this further.

Like most men of the time (and the rural area in which he resided), Elisha pursued his livelihood as a farmer, as this is his occupation in later census reports.

Sometime in late January, Triphena was stricken with "spotted fever," and she succumbed to this illness on February 3, 1813,[254] as did her father and uncle and many others. Triphene was thirty-eight years old at her death. Her burial place is likely unmarked in Goshen, Connecticut.

It is now believed that the "spotted fever" epidemic was Cerebrospinal-Meningitis.[255]

253 *Ibid*, 239.

254 *Connecticut Courant (1791–1832)*, 31; "At Goshen Mrs. Triphena Carrier, wife of Elisha Carrier, and daughter of Timothy Scoville, all of the prevailing epidemic." Also note that some people died the very same day of this disease. Pro Quest Historical Newspapers online via Connecticut State Library.

255 See vermontgenealogy.com for complete article. While Connecticut had many cases of

During the time that this epidemic took place (1812–1813), this disease was not thought to be contagious.

As an aside, a recipe for the so-called cure for the spotted fever was as follows:

> To one quart of lime add one gallon of water. To one quart of tar, add two quarts of water. Let these stand in separate vessels until they froth, skim the froth, pour them together. To this mixture add eight ounces of saltpeter, four ounces of opium—take a glass when going to bed and repeat the same in four or five hours.[256]

During their marriage this couple did have at least two children—a boy and a girl. One candidate as a possible son is Rufus Carrier. By chance I found this information while searching for Elisha Carrier on the 1830 Connecticut census.

Elisha was living in Warren, Litchfield, Connecticut, during this time, and next door to him was one Rufus Carrier. Per the headstone inscription[257] for Rufus, he was born in 1808. The accuracy of this birth year has not been confirmed, but suffice it to say, it is possible that Rufus is the "son" enumerated on the 1810 census as a male "of 10 and under 16." Anyone who has worked with census records knows that the accuracy of birth years given to the census taker is often unreliable.

Rufus Carrier "of Kent"[258] married Betsy Weeks (1801–1898) "of Goshen" on September 24, 1828, officiated by Rev. Silas Ambler.[259] As mentioned in the previous passage, the 1830 census shows both Elisha and Rufus living as neighbors. Ironically, they both removed to Brimfield, Portage County, Ohio, at approximately the same time. Based on what has already been said, I conclude that Rufus and Elisha were close relatives, if not father and son.

Rufus Carrier had a short life, as he died in Brimfield in 1838 at approximately thirty years of age. In their short marriage, Rufus and Betsy had the following children:

*a. i.* George W. Carrier,[260] b. Dec 1829, Connecticut; d. 30 Dec 1914, Brimfield, Portage, Ohio; m. (1) Elizabeth______; m. (2) 10 Sep 1867, probably in Brimfield, Helen M. Jones. George W. served in the 7th Ohio Infantry during the Civil War. George and Helen had six children: Lillie, Lorain, Mary, Myra, Newton E., and Nina B.

---

"spotted fever" it was much worse in Vermont.

256 This "remedy" was found in the papers of Capt. Charles Church, a wealthy leading citizen of Westminster. I do not know if Capt. Church formulated this "potion" himself or not, but if you can survive taking this concoction, you can survive anything!

257 Rufus Carrier is buried in West Lawn Cemetery, Brimfield, Portage Co., Ohio.

258 Kent, Litchfield County, Connecticut.

259 *Barbour Collection*

260 After the death of his father, Rufus, George was sixteen and appointed a guardian, Reuben Hart, on 7 February 1846. *Guardian Case file on microfiche [abstract].* Much of the information on the Carrier family comes from CGRS Certified Genealogical Record Specialist, Donna J. Redhead Gruber. Portage County Probate Court Records, Portage County Historical Society and Portage County Recorder. Report provided July 10, 2004.

*b. ii.* Darrius Carrier, b. 1831, Connecticut; d. 1863, Knoxville, Tennessee. He was a private in the Civil War and was not married at the time of his enlistment. He is buried in West Lawn Cemetery, Brimfield, Ohio.

*c. iii.* Alice L. Carrier, b. 1834, Connecticut; d.1888, Brimfield, Ohio; m. John H. Glass "of Prussia,"[261] he b. circa 1820. Alice is buried with the rest of her family in West Lawn Cemetery, Brimfield.

*d. iv.* Mary Carrier, b. 1837, Connecticut; d. 1875, Brimfield, and is buried in Brimfield in West Lawn Cemetery. The headstone inscription does not list a married name for her.

Betsy Carrier never remarried after Rufus's death and was living with her daughter Alice and her husband in 1880.

≈

After the death of Elisha's wife, Triphene, Elisha remarried his wife's niece, Lodema Scoville. The continuation of the life of Elisha Carrier and Lodema Scoville will be carried on through Lodema, ancestor number eleven (11) of this record.

### *8. Roxalana Andrews (Thankful Crocker)*

Born 24 Jul 1758, Colchester, New London, Connecticut; died 14 Jul 1839, Norfolk, Litchfield, Connecticut; married 24 Feb 1780, in Norfolk, Litchfield, Connecticut, to Reuben Dean; he born 22 Feb 1752, Philipes Patent, New York; died 14 Jul 1836, Goshen, Connecticut.

While Roxalana was not born a Scoville, she was raised in the Scoville household from the age of two and used the surname Scoville until her marriage to Reuben Dean. It is important to list her here as her husband, Reuben Dean, had a close connection to my ancestor Ithamar Scoville (the stepbrother of Roxalana), and their lives intertwined.

There was another man named Reuben Dean who also resided in Cornwall during the time the Scovilles resided there, but he cannot be the same Reuben who married Roxalana for the following reasons:

1. Reuben Dean is listed on the Cornwall Grand List records, which began in 1742 (the Reuben Dean of *this* record was born ten years later).
2. The Cornwall census records show a Reuben Dean and a Reuben Dean, "Jr." This *could* be a father and son?
3. The name of Reuben Dean's father was Seth Dean, not Reuben.
4. Reuben Dean and Roxalana Scoville did not have any biological children that I am aware of, but they did "adopt" two children—a boy and a girl with the surname Scoville.
5. The age of the male child in the 1800 census for Reuben Dean may be Amasa Sco-

261 All dates of birth and Civil War records for the children of Rufus and Betsy Carrier comes from Ancestry.

ville, (one of the adopted children and probable son of Ithamar Scoville) or it could be some other child working in his household.

As I delved further into the Reuben Dean conundrum and reviewed the 1790 census, there were two Reuben Deans listed: Reuben Dean and Reuben Dean, 2nd. The first Reuben in Cornwall cannot be the Reuben Dean I am researching; however, the Reuben Dean listed as the "2nd" I believe *is*. Only two people are listed in this household: a male 16 and over, and a female 16 and over. This couple would fit nicely into the supposition that this *is* Reuben Dean and Roxalana Scoville Dean,[262] and the records show via the Cornwall Grand List that he (Reuben) was listed as a taxpayer in Cornwall from 1782–1792 and from 1795–1799.[263]

The Reuben[1] Dean mentioned in the earlier records *of Cornwall* may have been a relative of the Reuben Dean of this record, perhaps an uncle, or this man could be from a completely different Dean family.

The Reuben Dean who married Roxalana Scoville was born in Philipse Patent, New York.[264] His parents (Seth Dean and Sarah ______)[265] are said to have removed from Bristol Township, Schoharie County, New Yor,k to Salisbury, Litchfield, Connecticut, about 1764.

A *Seth Dean,* born September 15, 1723, in Lebanon, New London County, Connecticut, *could* be the father of Reuben, but I have no evidence at this time to support that claim.

In *Rudd's List of Freemen,* May 3, 1779, a Seth Dean is mentioned, and a Seth Dean took the "Oath of Fidelity" in September 1777.

In Church's *List of Revolutionary Soldiers, Connecticut Men* (page 583), a Seth Dean was in Colonel Canfield's militia and went to West Point in 1781.[266]

There is another mention of a Seth Dean having his taxes abated 1777–1782 and that he owned land "way up on Under Mountain Road, in Salisbury."

A mention of a Seth Dean and his family was found in a *History Collection,* Vol. 2, (page 60): "wife's name is Sarah." Their children (the last three baptized per the Canaan Congregational Church Records):

Ruth Dean, 28 Aug 1750, NY Gov't
Reuben Dean, 22 Feb 1752, Philipse Patent, NY
Anne Dean, 8 Jan 1754, Salisbury[267]

---

262 There is no one named Reuben Dean on the 1790 census for Norfolk. (There is a Reuben Dean in Cornwall.)

263 The *other* Reuben Dean is also listed as a taxpayer up until 1796; after that a singular Reuben Dean is listed until 1799.

264 Doherty, Frank J., *The Settlers of the Beekman Patent Dutchess County, New York; Patent; From Darbyshire and Everitt,* Vol: 4, 1997.

265 Some have given her maiden name as Scroggs, but I have not done any research to prove or disprove this.

266 If the Seth Dean born in 1723 is the same one who was mentioned as being in Col. Canfield's militia and at West Point in 1781, he would have been fifty-eight years old.

267 All birth dates in Salisbury come from *Connecticut Births and Christenings 1649–1906,* FamilySearch.

Sarah Dean, 28 Jul, 1757, Salisbury
Joel Dean, 3 Oct 1759, Salisbury
Lydia Dean, 21 Jan 1762, Salisbury
Jessie Dean, 3 Sep 1766, bap. 12 Oct Salisbury; d. June 1 or 18, 1790[268]
Seth Dean,[2] bap. 28 Aug 1764, Salisbury[269]
Benajah Dean, bap. 18 Nov 1764, Salisbury
Amasa Dean, born/bap. 8 Feb 1769, Salisbury (Salisbury records Vol.1, pg. 41)

I have been unsuccessful in locating any records on Seth Dean other than the ones already noted.

What *is* known is that the Dean family was living in an area of much dispute called Philipse Patent[270] in New York during the time that Ruth and Reuben Dean were born.

When the settlers were kicked off this strip of land, the Deans must have removed to Salisbury, Connecticut, and, according to the baptismal records of some of the children, they were in said town from 1754 to 1769. The town of Salisbury was incorporated in 1741. This area was rich in iron ore and mining was an early industry. Salisbury became well known for its use of this iron ore in the American Revolution.[271] Since the iron ore furnaces were a major employer of the area, it is possible that some of the Dean men took part in this industry, and this is what brought them to Salisbury.

≈

Prior to Reuben's marriage to Roxalana, he was a soldier in the Revolutionary War. He served with the company commanded by Captain Allen of the 7th Regiment commanded by Colonel Swift. Per his service records located in the National Archives in Washington, D.C., he served in the regiment for "fifteen months and nine days," and his pension was $51 per annum. The War Department Records from the Pension Office, June 1833:

War Dept Records—Pension Office June 1833

Enlisted 1775 for 5 months—private—Capt. Allen—marched through Ticonderoga
Enlisted 1776 for 1 month—private—Capt. Allen—St. John's
Enlisted 1777 [7 months? ] private—[ ]—Montreal

---

268 "died in his 24th year." Greenpasture.com.

269 "Mr. Lee (minister of the Congregational Church from 1744–1788 and "ruled his flock with an iron hand) once fined Seth Dean, Jr., five shillings for swimming in the twin lakes for "diversion" on June 11, 1784 . . . it was a Sunday." www.asd.1817.org.

270 The Philipse Patent was a British royal patent for a large tract of land on the east bank of the Hudson River about 50 miles north of New York City, belonging to the Philipse family, first purchased in 1697. It was a 250 square mile track of land. Tenants eventually lived on the land, but in the 1760s there was a tenant uprising. Perhaps this is the reason for the Deans to remove to Salisbury. Wikipedia Article.

271 Cannon and other munition manufacturers in Lakeville (once called Salisbury Furnace and afterword Furnace Village) and all other sundry iron products were made during the Revolutionary and Civil Wars. Many of the furnaces have been preserved and can still be seen today.

Enlisted 1779 for 2 months private—[ ]—Lawrence—New Jersey, Fishkill, Horse Neck

The handwriting of the Declaration is very poor, and it is very difficult to make out many of the words. The declaration was taken on June 7, 1832, in Norfolk, CT. The record is to prove that the soldier did indeed serve his country so that he could receive a pension.

Personally appeared in open court now sitting before me Michael F Miles esquire judge of probate having [ ] court room building Ruben Dean a resident of the town of Norfolk in Litchfield County of [ ] aged 80 years [ ]February. [ ] being first duly sworn [ ] [ ] doth in his oath make the following declarations in order to obtain the benefit of the act of Congress [ ] June 7, 1832. That he intends the service of the [ ] state in the month of August 1775 by enlistment for the term of five months in the company of captain Allen and Colonel Warner's regiment in March [ ] the northern army at or near Ticonderoga and that he went down the lake [ ] water and landed about two or 3 miles that he [ ]then left [ ] when he landed with some that [ ] [ ] for a month or two and then joined the company at [ ] on from there and a [ ] of the company of which he belong did not come back to St. John's until he [ ] [ ] his [ ] home after Saint johns near four of his company to which he was attached went down as far as Montreal and before his time and they came to a place by water to a place called [ ] paint? in from their/his? home town(?)

That in the year 1776 such that he cannot recall the month he was drafted as a volunteer [ ] in the town of Canaan I was at a place on the north [ ] in Peekskill and was about one month that [ ] [ ] the time the British [ ] came with the [ ] that he was under the [ ] [ ] [ ] state his name is Canfield(? ) And was John Ensign of Canaan.

The year 1777 on or about 1 May he again and listed as a substitute for Eli Dean that he left Kayden under captain Titus Watson and that he joined the Army at or near Peekskill the latter part of May in the Continental line in the regiment of Captain Heman Swift and that he [ ] had with [ ] regiment into the state of New Jersey near the [ ] Germantown had [ ] had [ ] quarters off [ ] [ ] but won (? ) Marched to Fishkill when he was discharged about the middle of January that as of the time, he entered the company it was for nine months though he did not serve quite the whole time.

That in the summer of 1779 he was drafted as a militia man from the town of Canaan in the state for the term of two months in the company of Captain Lawrence and Colonel Noah Phelps regiment and was stationed at Horse Neck the whole of his term of two months and was discharged. If he had any written discharge [papers] he lost them.

That he was born in the state of New York at a place then called Phillips Patent and that when about two years his father moved into the town of Salisbury, in the state of Connecticut that sometime before the revolution he came into the town of Canaan and said state when he resided at the time [ ] [ ] [ ] and that for the last 30 years he has resided in the town of Norfolk that he is well acquainted with [ ] Joseph [ ] Clergyman of said town of Norfolk and with Augustus Pettibone, Ensign, Joseph B___, Esquire(?) of said Norfolk and that there is credibility in their character.

And that he [the rest is completely illegible] signed Reuben Dean.

~

State of Connecticut Litchfield County Norfolk August 16, 1832 on this day persons [ ] being there Ruben dean of said Norfolk who after being duly cautioned and [ ] and sworn [ ] said that in the year 1777 in the month of May he enlisted into the [ ] of the [ ] state into the company of captain Titus Watson and Colonel Heman Swift's regiment and joined the Army in Peekskill in the state of New York and served(?) In said the new company (?) 2nd Regiment right until January 1778 that his term of service was nine months but was dismissed (?) Some days [ ] the time was (?) And that he then on [ ] has been acquainted with Joel Dean then of Danbury in said state but not of [Broom] in the state of New York that he [ ] remembers or knows that the same Joel Dean [ ] in the same Company and regiment with [ ] I at Fishkill with him and returned home with him that [ ] near this [ ] nine months though it was a few days short of nine months that [ ] Joel Dean served as a substitute for Isaac barber(?) of Canaan.

Ruben Dean sworn and who into the 16th day of August 1832 before me Michael J Mills justice of peace and I [ ] certify that above named Reuben Dean, who is of the town of Norfolk is well known to me is a credible person and that his statement is [ ]. Signed Michael J mills justice of peace.[272]

You will note from Reuben's declaration to receive a pension that he "came to the town of Canaan where he was residing at the time" to enlist. This statement does not contradict my supposition that he was "of Cornwall" around 1782 until 1796 (or 1799). His brother, Joel Dean, may have been living in Canaan at this time. As a matter of record, there were many Dean families living in Canaan during the 1800s per the cemetery records of that town.

~

The earliest land transaction I have come across for Reuben Dean is from 1795:

Ruben [sic] Dean of Benajah Douglas to all people to whom these presents shall come greeting. know ye that I Benajah Douglas of Canaan in Litchfield County and state of Connecticut. For the consideration of 40 pounds lawful money for satisfaction of Ruben Dean of Cornwall in the county and state aforesaid. To give Grant bargain sell and confirm unto the said Ruben Dean a lot of land in Norfolk lying westerly of the road landing from Norfolk meetinghouse to Goshen being by Number the 48th lot in the 3rd Division on the 2nd going over bounds east on lot [ ] and begins at the northeast corner of lot 47 [ ] 83 rods to a Beach marked then east 9° south 100 roads to a Beech Birch marked then to the first bounds and contains 50 acres with allowance for [ ] rod road through said lot east and west.
13th Day of October 1795.[273]

272 I have left the grammar, punctuation, etc. as it is in the original document.

273 Canaan Land Records, Vol. 6, 198. Paper copies from the Connecticut State Library in my

Witnesses: Signed
Benajah Douglas

William Douglas
[ ] Dou [ ]

This land was very close to the all-important Intervail Lot 43, originally purchased by Reuben's brother-in-law, Ira Scoville, in 1796—land which passed back and forth between the Scovilles.

Two other land records are of interest as they indicate what Reuben Dean was involved in as an occupation; the other is the area of Norfolk in which he lived.

Ruben Dean of Roger foot though all man by these presents that I Roger foot of Norfolk in Litchfield County and state of Connecticut in [ ] for the consideration of 7 pounds 10 shillings lawful money already received my full satisfaction of Ruben dean of Norfolk aforesaid do you let please and assign to him said we've been doing the spot of land and a place called Meekertown Brook in said Norfolk whereon a sawmill now stands belonging to said Ruben, Captain Pettibone and myself with land sufficient for log way and Hill (?) yard large enough to draw on logs for sawing and to pick up (?)? Boards of any quantity that the mill shall saw also at liberty to make a dam on said brook and also liberty to plow said meadow with any depth water said Rubin shall choose from the first day of October and keep the same plowed until the fifteenth day of May each year all which privileges [ ] and lease to the said Rubin for the term of time that the said Reubin or his assigns shall choose to keep the mill on said spot in suitable repair to saw boards and I the said Roger warrant that I have good right to lease and dispose of the same in manner and form as abovesaid and I do by these presents, even [ ] with said Rubin for myself and my heirs and assigns and warrant the peaceable? And said profession of the same to him Rubin his heirs and assigns that said Mill shall be continued thereon in repair to saw boards and when said mill shall be discontinued the same shall be delivered up to said Roger also I the said Roger do sell and deliver one quarter of the irons that belong to the said mill to said Rubin as his own proper estate on quarter of said mill and irons in witness is where of I have hereunto let my hand and seal this 7th day of April 1806.[274]

Signed Sealed and Delivered Signed
In the presence of Roger Foot
Samuel Foot
Roger Foot, Jr.

---

personal possession.

274 Norfolk Land Records, Vol. 7, 340. Paper copies in my personal possession from the Connecticut State Library.

Joseph Jones, Town Clerk.
Junia Beach to John Bradley and to all people to come these presents shall come greeting; Know Ye that we John Bradley and Ruben dean of Norfolk in the county of Litchfield and state of Connecticut for the consideration of $50 received to our full satisfaction of Junia Beach of Granville in the state of Massachusetts and by these presents [ ] release and forever quit-claim unto said Junia his heirs and assigns forever, all such right entitle and demand whatsoever as we have or ought to have in or to a dwelling house situated in said Norfolk in that part of town called Meekertown at the south east corner of the mill yard near the sawmill in said Meekertown built by Noah Frisbee.

To have and to hold the above prescribed premises unto him that said Junia to his only use and behoove his heirs and assigns forever, so that neither we [the]said John and Ruben nor our heirs nor any other person or persons for as or in our name and behoove shall, or will hereafter claim or demand any right or title to the premises nor any part thereof but they and every[ ] of them show by their presents be excluded in forever debarred(?).

In witness whereof we have hereunto set our hands and seals the fifth day of May 1814.[275]

Signed, Sealed & Delivered
In the presence of
Augoniah(?) Smith
William Pendleton—Justice of Peace

John Bradley seal
Reuben Dean seal

We see that Reuben Dean was engaged in a sawmill with his partners, at least until 1814. I have not come across any further land records that mention the sawmill once it had been sold to Junia Beach.

From reading these two land transactions you will note the mention of Meekertown Road and Meekertown. I traveled to this area and, while the town of Norfolk is still not heavily populated, this area was even less so during the time that Ithamar Scoville and Reuben Dean lived there. The road itself no longer continues through as it once did (see illustration).

The first record is a point of interest as it mentions a sawmill in this area:

There was for a time a sawmill and cheese box shop in Meekertown, a little distance below Dolphin* or Balcolm Pond, which is the source of the Naugatuck River. This mill long since disappeared. It was owned and operated by Joshua Beach, Amos Baldwin, Amos Gilbert, Myron Johnson, and others, at various times.

There was also a sawmill for some years a short distance below the outlet of Tobey Pond.

*Called Dolphin Pond after an Indian that had lived near there.[276]

275 *Ibid*, Vol. 9, 568

276 Eldridge, Rev. Joseph, D. D. (opening chapters) and Crissley, Theron Wilmot, L.L.B, (compiler) *1744 –1900 History of Norfolk, Litchfield County, Connecticut*: (1900) 256.

This had to have been the sawmill mentioned in the foregoing land records—Reuben being "one of the others . . ."

Specifically, regarding the people of this area, the following: in the early days of the town there was quite a settlement toward the southwest part, near the Canaan line, called Meekertown, from the principal settler in that region, Phineas Meeker, (who in 1764 married Sarah Brown).

Mr. Meeker seems to have immigrated circa 1820 and Deacon Noah Minor reported to the church that there was a settlement in Meekertown that he called a "hamlet of heathens, living in intellectual, moral and spiritual darkness, and recommended that some missionary work be done there."

"It was said at the time that not half of the people of Norfolk knew that there was such a place within its borders." Mr. E. Lyman Gaylord, a native of this town, now living at Rocky Hill, Connecticut, writes that, about 1820 or 1821, in company with Mr. Wilcox Phelps, he rode through Meekertown on horseback and from what he saw "we concluded that Deacon Minor's report was not overstated." There was a burial place in Meekertown, and a number of persons were buried there—their graves being marked only by a rough stone; no name being found or any inscription whatsoever. The place is now grown up into a forest again. One man named Meeker is said to have been buried there, but so far no monument was ever erected at his grave, and now the place even is unknown.

I find the above equally humorous and interesting. Humorous because of the description of the people who lived there (and perhaps therefore I can find very few records of the people who lived there, such as Ithamar Scoville and his unknown wife!). Interesting, because of the graves being marked only by "rough stone; with no names," as shown in photos of the Dean Lot.

The map on the next page shows the area in which Reuben Dean (and Ithamar Scoville) lived along Meekertown Road on the border of Canaan, Connecticut. Also note the area where the mill would have been (in the upper right where Joshua Beach and Amos Baldwin owned property).[277]

We now return to 1806, where the baptismal record shows the following:

Baptisms—A.D. 1806—August 31st—Amasa and Lodamia [sic]—adopted children of Reuben Dean & _________.[278]

While their surnames are not given in this record, we know that they are Scovilles by birth based on other extant records that exist.

After years of putting puzzle pieces together of the *life and times* of Ithamar Scoville, I concluded that Amasa and Lodema Scoville were *his* children and he let Reuben and Roxalana raise them as their own.

In all the years I have been plodding along with this family, I have *never* come across any record of birth or death of a child/children of Reuben and Roxalana. Of course, that does not mean that they didn't have a child/children born to them, but if there were, they must

---

277 This map was given to me by Richard Byrne of Norfolk the day he showed us Intervail Lot 43. I do not know the origin of the map.

278 *Baptisms, Marriages, Burials And List Of Members Taken From The Church Records Of The Reverend Ammi Ruhamah Robbins, First Minister Of Norfolk, Connecticut, 1761–1813. (1910).*

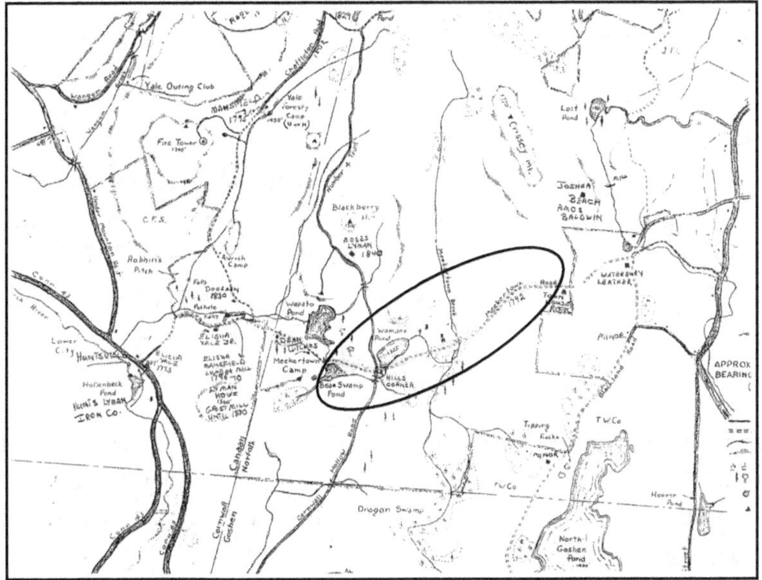


The circled portion is what is known as Meekertown Road in Norfolk, Connecticut.

have died at birth or soon thereafter, as no record exists of any such event. Remember, too, that they lived around Meekertown, an unknown place to all others of Norfolk and where a minister cast aspersions upon them as being "heathens," and there is also the matter of those unmarked, unadorned, rough stone graves that are in this area. The Meekertown area is certainly full of mysteries.

~

While it may seem "odd" to us that children would be essentially given to another family to raise as their own, it was not that uncommon, and keep in mind that Roxalana was technically the stepsister of Ithamar Scoville but raised in the same family, as a sister—Amasa and Lodema would not be going to strangers, but to perhaps a childless couple related to him. Many children went to work on farms, and they would board with that family for years, so, as I said, this was not an unusual situation.

We also must consider that, based on the census records for Ithamar, he had several mouths to feed, and I believe he was relatively poor, seeing that he and his family were trying to get support from the town of Cornwall in 1814 and 1815.

When Amasa and Lodema were baptized in 1806, they were fifteen and eleven years old respectively.[279] What year Amasa and Lodema were taken in by the Deans is unknown, and so-called "adoptions" as we know them today did not exist and rarely left a paper trail. If it wasn't for their baptismal record, there wouldn't be any record at all. What their relationship was with their biological parents is unknown, although, I imagine they would have seen them

279 I contend that these two children were baptized as older children, not infants. This is based on many factors, census records, ages at death for Lodemia and Amasa, etc.

regularly with Ithamar Scoville living "next door" to Reuben for many years.

~

The records are silent after 1814. This couple lived their daily lives from that point without leaving a trace of any documentation until 1832, when Reuben applied for his pension for his service during the Revolutionary War. The following documents come from the National Archives in Washington, D.C., and are declarations from several people who knew Reuben and attested to his service.

I have transcribed these records as they were written in the original.

> Ruben Dean sworn and who into the 16th day of August 1832 before me Michael J Mills justice of peace and I [ ] certify that above named Ruben Dean is who of the town of Norfolk is well known to me is a credible person and that his statement is [ ]. Signed Michael J mills justice of peace.
>
> DECLARATIONS:
> State of Connecticut Norfolk probate district on this [ ] day of September 1838 personally appeared before the court appropriate for the district of Norfolk Roxalana being a resident of said town of Norfolk age 80 years will be first duly sworn according to law as on her both make the following declaration in order to [ ] the benefit of the provisions made by the act of Congress [ ] July seventh 1838 entitled an act granting half-pay? and pensions and [ ] certain Widows that she is the widow of Ruben Dean late of said Norfolk deceased that her said husband Ruben Dean was a pensioner until the act of Congress in 1832. She has frequently heard him in his lifetime mention the towns and places he served but she cannot now state them she believes the evidence of his service is in the War office that after his discharge he forwarded his certificate to know the pay was due him at the time of his decease.
>
> She further says that she was married to said Reuben Dean on the 24th day of February in the year one thousand and seven hundred and eighty. That she does not know of any record [ ] of their marriage.
>
> That her husband the aforesaid Ruben Dean died at Norfolk aforesaid on the 24th day of December 1836. That she was not married to him prior to his leaving the service but that she was married to him [ ] the first day of January 1794[280] viz. at the time above states that she is now and has been a widow since the death of the said Reuben Dean.
>
> Signed Roxalana X Dean.

This declaration is the first time that we have a record of Roxalana's "voice."

280 This line in her declaration makes no sense. Once again, the handwriting is abysmal and very difficult to decipher.

Solomon Dean of Canaan in the county of Litchfield in the state of Connecticut aged 80 years being duly sworn according to law does testify and then say that he was always acquainted with Ruben Dean of said Norfolk deceased with Roxalana his wife and I further say that I was present at the marriage between said Ruben Dean and Roxalana and *that her name was Scoville before she was married* and I further say that the marriage *took place at the town of Cornwall* in the month of February I believe the 24th day but cannot be certain as to the day or the month it was in the year 1780.

Signed Solomon X Dean.

I Joel dean of the town of broom in the county of Bristol, Schoharie in state of New York now in Salisbury county of Litchfield in state of Connecticut depose and declare that I am well acquainted with Ruben dean of Norfolk said county of Litchfield and knowing that in the latter part of April 1777 he enlisted in the revolutionary war and joined the company of captain Titus Watson and Colonel Heman swift regiment at Peekskill on the north river on the first day of May after the deponent having enlisted and served in the army and regiment with the said Ruben Dean the terms of service was for nine months that his service with said company and regiment from said first day of May 1777 until the month of February 1778. He marched with the army into the state of New Jersey and had winter-quartered with the army at Valley Forge was in the battle of Germantown from Valley Forge he marched to Peekskill? And he said North River which he was discharged to part of January 1778 this deponent was with said Rubin throughout the whole of said time and served with him and is well knowing to the year above past.

Signed Joel Dean.

On the fourteenth day of July 1836, Reuben Dean died at the age of eighty-four. He died in Goshen, Litchfield, Connecticut. What brought Reuben to Goshen we will likely never know. The couple was still residing in Norfolk in 1830 according to the 1830 census for Norfolk. What sad news to bring home to his aged wife.

Reuben Dean did leave a will,[281] which was drawn up on May 29, 1836. I have dispensed with the usual preamble:

. . . I give and demise unto my beloved wife Roxalana dean do use an improvement of all the estate both real and personal that I shall own and possess at the time of my dicease, during her natural life and if the use of my property shall not be sufficient for

281 *Norfolk (CT) Probate Record, Litchfield County*; Connecticut State Library, Hartford, Connecticut.

the comfortable support of my said wife, that she has the right to dispose of so much of the personal and real estate which I show own at my decease so that, with her own industry she have a comfortable support during her natural life.

I give and demise after the decease of my wife to Calvin Dean the son of my brother Joel Dean and to Darius Dean the son of my brother Seth Dean deceased,, the sum of $25 apiece and all the remainder of my estate to Amasa Scovil whom I brought up as my son to him and to his heirs forever.

Lastly, I do make and constitute the said Amasa Scovil executor of this my last will and testament. In witness where of I have here on to set my hand and seal the 29th day of May A.D. 1836.

Signed
Reuben Dean

Signed, sealed, and published and pronounced by the said Ruben Dean as his last will and testament in the presence of each other have hereunto to subscribe our names; Augustus Roy's, Ruben Brown, J.M. Cowles.

At the same court: this court doth appoint Thomas Moses and Alden Minor, freeholders to appraise under oath all the estate of said deceased and make a correct inventory thereof.

At the same court—this court Does decree that six months be allowed the creditors of said estate to exhibit their claims against the same to said Executor who shall give public notice of this order by advertising the same in a newspaper published in Litchfield and by posting the same on a public signpost inside town of Norfolk.

Norfolk 4 February 1837. An inventory of the personal estate of Ruben Dean deceased, appraised by Thomas Moses and Alden minor:

| | | |
|---|---|---|
| Land and Building $600 | 1 Cow $20 | 2 tons of hay $16 |
| 1 plow $5.10 | 1 set plow irons .50 | 1 cart hook .50 |
| 1 sheep $5.00 | 1 crowbar $2.10 | 140 gal. iron kettle $8.00 |
| Iron kettle $3.00 | 1 small iron kettle $1.51 | 1 iron pot $1.25 |
| 1 small brass kettle $2.00 | 1 iron tea kettle .75 | 1 spider and 1 skillet .58 |
| 1 Ox yoke $1.50 | 1 small Ox yoke $1.00 | 1 chain .75 |
| 1 other chain .42 | 1 dog wedge .42 | 1 iron wedge $1.00 |
| 1 square .75 | 1 handsaw .42 | 1 crooked adz .75 |
| 1 carpenters adz .75 | 2 carpenter augers .50 | 1 brace & 1 bit .25 |
| 2 planes $1.00 | 6 chisels $1.37 | 1 draw shave .25 |
| 1 taper bit .13 | 1 broad axe .50 | 2 narrow axes .75 |
| 1 bush scythe & [ ] $1.00 | 1 tined fork .75 | 1 scythe srath? .50 |
| ½ barrel cider $2.50 | 1 pair sheepshearers .48 | 1 scythe srath? .50 |
| ½ bushel .25 | 1 chest $1.00 | 2 Bealls? .25 |
| 2 flannel shirts $1.00 | 1 coat & vest .75 | 1 great coat $1.00 |

1 cotton shirt .13
1 leather apron .39
1 pair of shoes .67
1 pair sat irons .50
1 pair pinchers .42
2 nail hammers .62
1 shoe hammer .25
1 stone hammer .49
1 sieve .25
1 hoe .25
1 flat hoe .34
1 flail? .25
1 scythe .50
1 piece black fulled[282] cloth $11.00
1 piece blue do. $13.75
1 shovel .13
1 card .13
1 neck yoke .25
1 chest of drawers $2.00
Total: $726.00

Signed by Thomas Moses and Alden Minor—appraisers under oath.
Received in the Probate Office, March 16, 1837.

Eleven days later Roxalana sold two parcels of land to Amos Baldwin:[283]

> To all people whom these presents shall come greeting: no ye that I Rocksalana [sic] Dean of the town of Norfolk in the county of Litchfield state of Connecticut for the consideration of $80 received to my full satisfaction of Amos Baldwin of Norfolk in county and state aforesaid. Do give grant bargain sell and confirm unto the said A. Baldwin—2 certain pieces or parcels of land lying in the 1st(?) part of said Norfolk near the land which said Baldwin bought of C.L. Norton—one piece bounded East [of] highway, South on Stephen Norton's land, West and North on said Baldwin's land and contains about 4 acres more or less –
>
> The other bounded West on said highway, North and East on said Baldwin's land and South on Stephen Norton's land and contains about 5 acres more or less.
>
> To have and to hold the above granted and bargained premises, with the appurtenances thereof unto him the said Amos, his heirs and assigns forever, to his and their own proper use and behoof. And also, I the said Rocksalana do for myself my heirs, executors and administers, covenant with the said A. Baldwin his heirs and assigns, that at and until the ensealing of these presents, I am well seized of the premises as good indefeasible estate in fee-simple, and have good right to bargain and sell the same in manner and form as is above written and that the same is free of all encumbrances whatsoever...
>
> In witness whereof I have hereunto set my hand and seal tis 21 day of March 1838.[284]

282 "Fulled" cloth is cloth that has gone through the cleaning of cloth (particularly wool) to eliminate oils and dirt, as well as making the cloth thicker.

283 Amos Baldwin, born about 1779; died May 9, 1847, Norfolk, Connecticut. His house still stands in Norfolk on 92 Goshen Road. The house was built about 1765 and was added to the National Register of Historic Places in 2016.

284 Norfolk Land Records, Vol. 13, 349.

Witnesses
Daniel Hotchkiss[285]—Justice of Peace  Rocksalanda [sic] X Dean
Amasa Schovel[286]

This is the last known record for Roxalana. Out of her eighty-one years of life we have only heard her "voice" two times: her statement to receive a pension from her deceased husband's service and the selling of land to Amos Baldwin.

Whether she stayed in Norfolk or went to live with her adopted son Amasa will never be known. The following year, on July 14, 1839, Roxalana died. She and her husband Reuben are buried in the South Norfolk Cemetery, Norfolk. Their headstones are still there, very weathered and barely legible.[287]

285 My Hotchkiss line also resided in Norfolk, having come originally from Danbury, Fairfield County, Connecticut. While my direct ancestor—Josiah Hotchkiss—had a son named Daniel, I do not know if this is the same individual who was the Justice of Peace who signed this land transaction.

286 The"'adopted" son of Reuben and Roxalana Dean.

287 Photos taken by the writer of this record in South Norfolk Cemetery, early 2000s.

# Fifth Generation

### *9. Philo Scovill*[5] *(Timothy,*[4] *Timothy,*[3] *Stephen,*[2] *Stephen,*[1] *Arthur)*

Born 30 November 1791,[288] in either Salisbury or Cornwall, Connecticut; died 3 June 1875, Cleveland, Cuyahoga, Ohio; married 16 February 1819, Canfield, Trumbull, Ohio,[289] Jemima Bixby; born 27 December 1800;[290] Lisbon, Columbiana, Ohio; died 4 April 1888,[291] Cleveland, Cuyahoga, Ohio; daughter of Benjamin Bixby and Margaret Walker.

Like many of his ancestors, Philo Scovill struck out on his own at the age of twenty-five[292] and headed to Ohio. The year was 1816 and when he arrived in Cleveland, he was ready to make a mark for himself. He first established himself as a merchant in the drug and grocery trade. Apparently, this was not quite the line of work he was happy with so he moved into the lumber business with a man named Thomas O. Young. These two men built a sawmill[293]—"Scovill & Young"—and began building and house contracting.

According to *The Pioneer Families of Cleveland, 1796–1840,*[294] Philo Scovill met his future wife, Jemima Bixby, while she was on a visit to the Merwins in their tavern at the foot of Superior Street. They married in 1819 and started a family soon after as their son, Edward A. Scovill, was born in 1819 (possibly November or sometime before). Philo was likely still involved with the sawmill and building. By 1825, Philo had built the Franklin House,[295] a tavern that he managed until 1848. Mrs. Scovill was quite keen on this venture, as in the book *The Pioneer Families of Cleveland* Mrs. Scovill is said to have "entered the tavern scheme with zeal, bringing into it all her New England habits of thrift, order, and neatness of the best culinary skill, and of executive ability, so that in time, it sustained an enviable reputation for clean beds and sumptuous fare."

During his career as an entrepreneur, Philo also had purchased over 110 acres in and around Cleveland. It is said that he was a very popular individual[296] and his entrepreneurial state helped him to gain a seat as the County Commissioner in 1827 and as a Whig Representative

---

288 Refer to Footnote #103.

289 *Ohio County Marriage Records, 1774–1993*, Ancestry.

290 Per headstone inscription.

291 *Ibid*

292 *Encyclopedia of Cleveland History;* Case Western Reserve University, case.edu.

293 Since Philo's father (Timothy[2]) was a millwright, it is not surprising that he learned all he knew about tools and general mechanical matters.

294 Gertrude Van Rensselaer Wickham, 1914.

295 A likeness of the original tavern can be found online at *Cleveland and Its Environs, The Heart of New Connecticut,* Elroy McKendree Avery, Vol. 1, 103. The tavern was torn down in 1938 to make way for a parking lot.

296 Because of his popularity, there are schooners and lighthouses that have been named after him in Cleveland.

to the State Legislature in 1835–36; he was also on the Cleveland City Council in 1841–42. He was content to serve only a single term in each office he held. Later in life, he became the director of the Cleveland & Pittsburg Railroad and the founder of the First National Bank (1863), and later became its president.

Jemima (Bixby) Scovill is said to have been born on December 27, 1800, in Cleveland, Ohio,[297] to Benjamin Bixby (1759–1829) and Margaret Walker (1762–1821), her parents having married in Granville, Hampton County, Massachusetts. Jemima was the eighth child of ten and named after her paternal grandmother. How and when the Bixbys removed to Cleveland, Ohio, is unknown.

Jemima Scovill was very involved in good works on behalf of the city. She was an early member of Trinity Church[298] and was the founder of the "Old Women's Home of Cleveland." Unfortunately, there is not much more written about Jemima, other than a few blurbs found in older books on the history of Cleveland.

Philo Scovill is on the Cuyahoga County tax lists from 1819–1868 via Ancestry and on the federal census records from 1820–1860. The couple and their family lived in the hotel along with their guests and on the 1850 and 1860 censuses, Philo's occupation is listed as a "gentleman," as is his son Edward's.

I have not been able to locate Philo on the 1870 census; I've tried alternate spellings, using his wife's name, and other family members' names, without success. From that point on, the records are silent on this family until 1875, when Philo died on June 3rd.

The will of Philo Scoville was filed on June 7, 1875[299] and reads as follows:

> Know all men by these presents then I Philo Scoville of the City of Cleveland in the County of Cuyahoga, and State of Ohio, being of sound and disposing mind, memory and understanding to hereby make, publish, and declare this to be my last will and testament as follow to wit.
>
> [First is the preamble on the executor's duties, etc.]
>
> *Second:* I give, devise, and bequeath to my beloved wife Jemima Scovill the entire use and control of my house and lot on Euclid Street on which we now reside together with all furnishings and fixtures thereunto belonging so long as she may live—and furthermore, I wish my beloved wife to have and to receive the entire net yearly income from all my bank stock, government bonds and all other personal assets in securities that I may be possessed of at this time of my decease for so long as she may live.
>
> *Third:* after the decease of my beloved wife, I give and devise to Catherine Wilkes,[300] the only daughter of George and Helen Wilkes of Brantford, Canada West now of Ontario the sum of $5000.

297 Per FamilySearch.

298 The first of Trinity Cathedral's forerunners was Trinity Parish, organized November 9, 1816. Clevelandhistorical.org.

299 Copy of the actual record in my possession. Recorded in Book: G; Page: 319; Number: 1254

300 I have not been able to discover who this young lady is and why she was left such a considerable sum. Perhaps her parents were friends of the Scovills.

*Fourth:* I give and devise to the Cleveland Orphan Asylum, the sum of $5000 to be paid by my Executor after the death of my wife Jemima Scoville.

*Fifth:* It is my will, and I do so order and direct my executor, after the death of my wife Jemima Scovill, to pay from the funds of my estate to the institution called the "Trinity Church Home" the sum of $5000 and a donation from my wife Jemima Scovill.

*Sixth:* After the death of my said wife Jemima Scovill, I order and direct my executor to sell and dispose of my house and lot on Euclid Street, in the City of Cleveland, Ohio, to make good in sufficient deed or deeds to the purchasers of the same, the sale and dispose of the furniture in or belonging to my said dwelling house on Euclid Street in the said City of Cleveland, and also to sell and dispose of all my bank stocks, government bonds, and all other securities belonging to my estate, to divide the net proceeds equally, share and share alike among the following named persons: my grandchildren viz. Alice Bemis, George Bemis, Mary F. Parsons, and Tracy Scovill, William S. Scovill, Caroline Gibson, Charles P. Scovill, Josephine Scovill and Catie Scovill.

*Seventh:* I give and devise to my son Edward A. Scovill during his natural life, my property known as the "Cleveland Tube Works" situated on Hamilton Street in the said City of Cleveland, together with all machinery and fixtures of said mill: and I further give to my son Edward A. Scovill during his natural life all such real estate as I may own or which stands in my name situated on Garden Street, and now on Brownell Street in said City of Cleveland and that on the decease of said son, Edward A. Scovill, it is [ ] that all of the above described property in which Edward A. Scovill has life estate is to pass to E. Tracy Scovill and William S. Scovill, sons of Edward A. Scoville share and share alike.

*Eighth:* I give and devise to my daughter, Caroline A. Bemis during her natural life, my Brick Block[301] on Frankfort Street said City of Cleveland, being sixty-nine feet front of said Frankfort Street and extending towards Superior Street in said City of Cleveland and 180 feet; I also gave my said daughter Caroline A. Bemis, a life estate in nineteen feet off the West end of my Brick Block on Superior Street in said City of Cleveland and which the First National Bank of Cleveland now stands, and said piece of nineteen feet to extend back towards Frankford Street to a point 180 feet from Franklin Street; and that on the decease of my daughter Caroline A. Bemis, said property of which a life estate is given to her shall pass to and [rest?] in her children forever, share and share alike.

*Ninth:* I give and devise to my son Oliver C. Scovill a life estate in Fifty-nine feet of the Easterly portion of my Brick Block on Superior Street in said City of Cleveland and extending back towards Frankfort Street to a point of 180 feet from Frankfort Street; and that on the decease of my son Oliver C. Scovill the said property of which a life estate is given to him shall pass to and [rest?]in his legal heirs forever.

---

301 Orth, Samuel Peter, *History of Cleveland, Ohio, Vol.1,* Cleveland, S.J. Clarke Publishing Company (1910). The "Brick Block" mentioned here can be found in further detail in the above-captioned book via Google Books, if you want to know more about Philo Scovill's "Brick Block."

*Tenth*: It is my will and desire that the alleyway leading to the rear of the side of Superior Street Brick Block from said Frankfort Street in which is situated at the Westerly end of the Brick Block on Frankfort Street give it to Caroline a Bemis as above stated shall be kept open and used for an alleyway and be held in common and use for the benefit of the owners of the Brick Block on Superior Street and a Brick Block on Frankfort Street.

*Eleventh:* I hereby constitute and appoint [ ] of the city of Cleveland, Ohio the Executor to see that this is carried into full effect. I hereby revoke all former wills prior to this date. In testimony hereto, I have hereunto set my hand and seal the 29th day of April? 1875

His estate of cash, bonds, shares, savings, etc. valued approximately $70,921.[302]

After the death of her husband, Jemima continued to live in their home on Euclid Street, as she is listed on the 1880 census as "Jamima," age seventy-nine, and her occupation is listed as "mother." Also living in the household were two servants: Rita Lehman, age nineteen, and Lise McQuade, age twenty-eight.

Eight years later, on April 4, 1888, Jemima Bixby Scovill died at the age of eighty-eight.

On April 10, 1888, in Cuyahoga County, Ohio, an application for probate was requested by her son, Edward A. Scovill. The will reads in part:

Last will of Jemima Scovill –

Be it remembered that heretofore to wit: at the January term A.D. 1888 of the Probate Court held at the courthouse in the city of Cleveland, within and for the County of Cuyahoga and State of Ohio by and before Hon. Henry C. White, Judge of said court and on April 7th, 1888, was presented and an application made by Edward A. Scovill for admission to probate of an instrument in writing . . .

Gives and bequeaths to son Edward, "silver tea service," whatever money I have on deposit at the time of my decease in the Society for Savings in the City of Cleveland.

$5000 to "Trinity Church Home for the Sick and Friendless" per request of her late husband.

The residue of the property went to her three children: Edward A., Caroline A. Bemis, and Oliver Scovill, share and share alike, and to their legal representatives.[303]

Philo Scovill left the home of his parents in the early settlement of Hector, Tompkins County, New York, and settled in Cleveland to become a man of means and of benevolence and good works along with his wife—to share and share alike.

Philo and Jemima Scovill are buried in Erie Street Cemetery, Cleveland, Ohio.

302 In today's market (taking inflation into consideration), this amount would be slightly over $1,631,598.

303 Original probate record in my possession, Vol. P—Q, 1887–1889.

**_Children of Philo Scovill and Jemima Bixby_**

i. Edward Alexander Scovill,[6] b. 22 Dec 1819, Cleveland, Cuyahoga, Ohio; d. 20 Apr 1890, Cleveland, Cuyahoga, Ohio; m. 22 Jun 1824, Danville, Livingstone, New York; Catherine Scholl; d. 29 Oct 1885, Cleveland, Cuyahoga; daughter of Jacob Scholl/Sholl and Sarah Hyland. This family lived in the Franklin Hotel as noted on the 1850 and 1860 censuses. Like the other members of this family, I cannot locate them in 1870. By 1880 they were living on Emilice(?)[304] Street, Cleveland.[305]

On January 3, 1862, in Parma, Ohio, Edward A. Scovill enlisted in Co. B. of the 128th Ohio Infantry Regiment; his rank was Lt. Colonel. In August of 1863 he was promoted to Full Major.[306] Edward was officially discharged on April 10, 1865. Like his father, Edward can be found in the various books of history for Cleveland, Ohio (although, not as often). Looking through some of the city directories for Cleveland, Edward is sometimes referred to as an "agent," or as having an office located on Euclid Avenue.[307] Based on his will, the one thing Edward was involved in was sporting clubs. He was a member of several of them, as was fitting for a "gentleman."

The children of Edward A. Scovill and Catherine Scholl were:

*a. i.* Edward Tracey Scovill,[7] b. 12 Aug 1846, Cleveland; d. 11 Jun 1926, France; m. 22 Jun 1896, Cleveland, Cuyahoga, Ohio, Florence Harriet Sholes.

*b. ii.* William Sholl Scovill,[7] b. 2 Aug 1850, Ohio; d. 17 Oct 1897.

The will of Edward Alexander Scovill:[308]

> In the name of the benevolent father of all I, Edward A. Scoville, do make and publish this my last will and testament in Mentor following:
>
> *First:* after the payment of my just debts and funeral expenses, I give, devise and bequeath to my beloved son, Edward Tracy Scoville all my right, title and interest in lots number 55 and 66 in the block [ ] of Coultons third addition to the town of Lisbon, County of Ransom and State of North Dakota, all my stock and interest in the Winous Point Sporting Club with all my hunting and fishing outfit of every nature or kind; belonging thereby. All my stock and interest in the Castralia Sporting Club with all of its incidental belongings, all my stock and interest in the Oneida Club, with all of the appurtenance they are by belonging, all my office furniture,

304 This is likely Euclid, but the copy is poor, and the address is hard to make out.

305 Jemima was counted twice on the 1880 census: once in her own home with her servants and once in her son's home.

306 *Official Roster of Soldiers of the State of the Union Blue: 1860–1865; History of MOLLUS.* Ancestry.

307 The Scovills lived at 48 Euclid Avenue in Cleveland. Euclid Avenue was known as "Millionaires Row." This area was a four-mile stretch. From the years 1870–1929, Euclid Avenue was a much sought-after address to live. From the addresses I have seen for these mansions, they are numbered much higher (i.e., 2605, 3813, etc.). I believe that while Philo Scovill was well-to-do, he wasn't in the same league as the Mathers, Stagers, and Rockefellers.

308 Estate Files, Docket 22, [Case#4043-4067], 1890–1891. Ancestry.

fixtures and belongings, including all letters, papers, all documents, keepsakes, and curiosities there and held or they are to belonging.

All my household furniture and appliances including all my crockery, dishes, tableware, table linen, cutlery, silverware, stoves, beds and bedding, carpets, rugs, pottery, pictures, statuary, bric-a-brac, mirrors, and all other personal effects not mentioned or otherwise disposed of.

*Second:* To my beloved son, William Scholl Scoville, I give devise and bequeath all my right title, and interest in the tract of set of land known as section 15 of Township 133, in range 55 County of Ransom and State of North Dakota, all my stock and interest in the Cold Creek Sporting Club together with all the belongings and appurtenances thereby all my stock and interest in the Adirondack Preserve Association, together with all of its incidental appurtenances and belongings, all my stock and interest in the K.D. Box Company of every nature and kind.

*Third:* All the rest, residue, and remainder all my estate, both real and personal, I give devise and bequeath to my two beloved sons Edward Tracy Scoville and William Shaw Scoville to be equally divided between them and their heirs share and share alike, and to hereby revoke any and all former wills made by me.

*Fourth:* I do hereby nominate and appoint my friend Charles C. Baldwin, the executor of this my last will and testament here by authorizing and empowering him to compromise, adjust, release and discharge in such manner that he may deem proper, the debts and claims due me. I do also authorize and empower him if it shall become necessary in order to pay my debts, to sell by private sale or in such a manner upon such terms of credit, or otherwise as he may think proper, all or any part of my real estate and deeds by. [ ]

[ ] execute, acknowledge, and deliver in fee simple.

I desire that no appraisal and no sale of my personal property be made, and that the court of probate direct the omission of the same, in the [ ] of the statute.

In witness whereof I have hereunto set my hand the 16th day of November A.D. 1889

Edward A. Scovil

ii. Caroline Amelia Scovill,[6] b. 12 May 1822, Cleveland, Cuyahoga, Ohio; d. 22 Sep 1897, Cleveland, Cuyahoga, Ohio; m. Elijah St. John Bemis, 1839, Buffalo, Erie, New York.[309] Elijah St. John Bemis was the son of Asaph S. Bemis and Margaret K. St. John[310] and the nephew of Dr. John R. St. John and Mrs. Skinner. He was a paper manufacturer and a book publisher, doing business under the name of "Penniman & Bemis" (his partner being Francis Penniman).[311]

---

309 *New York City, Compiled Marriage Index, 1600s–1800s.*

310 The records of Elijah's parents are confusing. His obituary gives his mother's name as Margaret, yet the census lists her as Amelia.

311 Foley, Thomas J., and Foley, Janet Wethy, *Early Settlers of New York State, Their Ancestors and Descendants, Extracts, Vol. 3, #12 (June 1937).* This publication began as a monthly magazine in 1934.

By all accounts, the marriage to Elijah St. John Bemis was not approved of by Mr. and Mrs. Philo Scovill and was considered an "unfortunate" match. Caroline was only seventeen at the time of her marriage; Elijah was eight years older. The marriage went on for almost forty years—but not happily.

I could not locate this couple on the 1840 census in Buffalo or Cleveland. By 1850 they are listed on the census as residing in Buffalo in the fifth ward of the city. By this time, the couple had five children.

Elijah is listed as a "merchant."

According to *Pioneer Families of Cleveland, 1796–1840,*[312] this couple separated after the birth of two daughters; however, they are still together up until 1870 and still residing in Buffalo. All their children were living in the household as well, the youngest, Mary, being twenty-one years of age.

It is not until 1880 that we see Caroline (Scovill) Bemis and her daughter, Mary Bemis, living in the household of her son, Philo S. Bemis, who, at the time, was living in Flushing, New York, with his family. I did not know if the marriage dissolved, or if she was only visiting, as her husband, Elijah, was still living. This question was answered when I read the 1880 census for Buffalo—Elijah St. John Bemis was living with his aged mother, Amelia, on 147 Franklin Street. This is the census that gives us the answer to the marriage situation—he was listed as "divorced."

I have not been able to go any further with Caroline after the 1880 census. I do not know if she remarried or removed to parts unknown. Her death date is given as occurring in 1897 in Buffalo, but I do not have primary evidence to support this, and I could not find any reference to a grave using *Find A Grave.*

Her former husband, Elijah St. John Bemis, died on October 14, 1892, at 147 Franklin Street. A brief obituary appeared in *The Buffalo Express,* Tuesday Morning edition, October 25, 1892. It reads:

***Death of Elijah St. John Bemis***

> Elijah St. John Bemis, one of the oldest residents of Buffalo and a man of large interests, formerly in the lake trade, died yesterday at his home at No. 147 Franklin Street, after quite a long illness. He was connected, on his mother's side, with the St. John family, whose houses were two of the few buildings left standing here at the time Buffalo burned. He was born on March 4, 1814, the son of Asaph S. Bemis and Margaret K. St. John Bemis, the second of their six children. His brother, Asaph S. Bemis, died in 1888, and the two naturally possessed a fund of interesting recollections of Buffalo in its youth.
>
> For some years Mr. Bemis was connected with the newspaper business in Cleveland. Afterward he came back to Buffalo and he and the brother just named

---

Heritage Books, Inc., reprinted Part One, Vols. I–III in book form.

312 Wickham, Gertrude Van Rensselaer, Under the Auspices of the Executive Committee of the Women's Department of the Cleveland Centennial Commission—1896; (1914) 177.

ran a ship-chandler store until the 60s. He also owned large vessel interests. For a number of years, he had lived in retirement. He leaves a son, Philo S., and a daughter Alice. The funeral will be held from the house at 2 o'clock this afternoon.

***Children of Elijah St. John Bemis and Caroline Amelia Scovill***[313]

*a.i.* Philo Scovill Bemis, b. 1840, Cleveland, Ohio; d. 24 Feb 1897, Flushing, Queens, New York; m. Katherine "Kate" Starkey (1843–1912) 26 May 1863, Cleveland, Cuyahoga, Ohio. The census report for 1860 shows this family still living in Buffalo and Philo is employed as a "ship-chandler." Their two children, Philo S. and Anna, are also listed. By 1880 the family is living in Queens, New York, and Philo S. is now employed as an agent for the railroad.[314]

There is now seven people in this household, including his mother, Caroline, and his sister, Alice. Caroline gives her marriage situation as "widowed," even though her ex-husband was still alive. This is not an unusual situation. Divorce was seen as shameful, particularly in the upper classes.[315]

In 1897 Philo died, and his will was probated on Feb. 17, 1898.[316] His wife, Kate, was made the executrix along with Morris K. King of Norfolk, Virginia. Philo S. Bemis left to his "beloved" wife, Kate S. Bemis, of Flushing, Long Island, New York, all his property of "every nature and kind—real and personal situated in Cleveland, Ohio." The will was signed by Philo on Dec. 31, 1885. There was no mention of his children. It's possible they had already received their portion of the estate while he was still alive. Philo is buried in Forest Lawn Cemetery, Buffalo, New York, with a simple marker. Regarding his widow, Kate, I've only been able to discover two other records for her. She was found in 1903 in the Portland, Oregon, City Directory as the widow of Philo S. Bemis and boarding at 714 Everett. The second record is her death record showing that she died on 28 February 1892 in the District of Columbia.[317] Her body was brought back to Buffalo for burial. The names of their children come from the census reports: Anna J.; Philo S.; and Edward.

*b. ii.* Helen Marion Bemis,[7] b. 16 Jun 1842, Cleveland, Cuyahoga, Ohio; d. 26 Dec 1866, Cleveland; m. George Henry Wilkes (1836–1929) Feb 1865.

*c. iii.* Alice Marie Bemis,[7] b. 8 May 1844, Cleveland, Cuyahoga, Ohio. A death date and place has not been discovered. She did apply for a U.S. passport on Oct. 10,

313 The information on the children of this couple comes from various sources on the internet. More time and research are needed for anyone interested in this family.

314 Philo S. Bemis is listed as a purchasing agent for the New York, West Shore, and Buffalo railroad. *The Official Railway List: A Complete Directory of the Presidents, Vice Presidents,* (1883), 85.

315 *Divorce in New York from the 1850s to the 1920s,* thesis by Di Long, 2013. "... divorce was difficult obtain because couples had to prove at least one of them was at fault to gain a divorce ... Consequently, couples and their attorneys tried every means to divorce in New York or out of the state ... wealthier couples would travel to another state or even a foreign country." 1–2.

316 *New York Wills and Probate Records 1659–1999.* Ancestry.

317 *District of Columbia Deaths, 1874–1961.* FamilySearch.com

1888, along with her sister, Mary. Alice is listed as age 44, 5′ 4″ tall, with dark brown eyes, dark brown/gray hair, and a dark complexion.

*d. iv.* Mary Townsend Bemis,[7] b. 18 Apr 1849,[318] Buffalo, Erie, New York; d. 1891 Ashtabula, Ohio; m. Samuel Holden Parsons (1852–1929) 21 Oct 1874, Geneva, New York.[319] Her husband, Samuel, was born in Ashtabula on 7 Nov 1852. Interestingly, he died in Washington, D.C., on 15 Jan 1929, as did his mother-in-law. He was the son of Henry Ethelbert Parsons and Abby Catherine Parsons. In 1880 Mary and Samuel were living with his parents in Ashtabula. In 1879 a passport application for Samuel is shown as intending to travel abroad with his wife, Mary B. Parsons. Samuel's attributes were grey eyes, light auburn hair, and a fair complexion, and he was 5′ 6 ½″ tall. His wife Mary's statistics were dark brown eyes, brown hair, and a dark complexion, and she was equal in height to her husband.

There is a marriage between a Samuel H. Parsons and Florence L. Spencer in Manhattan, New York, on Dec 23, 1891, and the couple is found on the 1920 census living in Manhattan. He may have remarried.

It doesn't appear that there were any children born to either spouse.

*e.v.* George A. Bemis,[7] b. 1847, Ohio; lived in Buffalo in 1860. Nothing more is known.

***The Children of Philo Scovill and Jemima Bixby continued . . .***

iii. Oliver Comstock Scovill,[6] b. 25 Jun 1823, Cleveland, Cuyahoga, Ohio; d. 9 Mar 1894, Peoria, Tazwell, Illinois; buried in Cleveland, Cuyahoga, Ohio;[320] m. 4 Jun 1847 Cuyahoga, Ohio, Adeline Clark(e); d. 27 Mar 1880, Cleveland, Cuyahoga, Ohio.

According to *The Pioneer Families of Cleveland, 1796–1840,*[321] Oliver C. was called "Crockett" and, at age seventeen, he went off on a whaling expedition and was gone for three years. It also states that when he returned home, he learned the printer's trade.

When gold was found in California, he got the fever and became a "forty-niner" and was gone for six years. When he came back he opened a cooper's shop on the flats.

While I haven't been able to find Oliver on the 1850 census, there are records of him on the tax records for Cleveland beginning in 1850. California had a state census in 1852 and Oliver, his wife, Adeline, and their daughter, Caroline, are listed in the town of San Francisco, with Oliver listed as a "merchant."

In 1860, this family is back in Cleveland, where Oliver is now listed as a "canal collector" living with his wife, his four children, and two domestics. A military draft registration record was found for Oliver for April 1865;[322] a notation of "p.g."[323] is in the margins. A few men have this notation, while others say "over age," "in service," "alien," etc. I could not find any other military records for him that he served in the Civil War.

318 Her birth information comes from an application for a U.S. Passport. Ancestry.

319 *New York, Episcopal Diocese of Rochester Church Records 1800–1970.* Ancestry.

320 *Ohio, Find A Grave Index, 1787–2012.* Ancestry.

321 See note 294.

322 The Civil War ended on April 9, 1865.

323 This could also read "p.d."

By the 1870 Cleveland census Oliver is now occupied in the "silver mining" business; his wife, children, and one domestic are also living in the household. Since Adeline died March of 1880, she is not listed on the census for that year, as it did not commence until June 1. Where was Oliver? He had lived another fourteen years, and at the time of his death he had been living in Peoria, Illinois.

Oliver Comstock and his wife, Adeline, had the following children:

***Children of Oliver Comstock Scovill and Adeline Clark(e)***

*a. i.* Caroline Amelia Scovill,[7] b. 18 Apr 1847, Cleveland, Cuyahoga, Ohio; d. 20 Feb 1933, Salt Lake City, Utah;[324] m. George J. Gibson. At the age of eighty she is listed as a passenger to Hawaii on 13 Nov 1928 and is listed as a "widow."[325]

*b.* ii. Charles Philo Scovill,[7] b. 24 Sep 1854, likely Cleveland, Cuyahoga, Ohio; he is listed on a roll of the United States Military Academy, admitted 1873.[326] He is also listed on a cadet record via the U.S. Military and Naval Academies, graduating West Point, Orange, New York, in 1877.

*c. iii.* Kate Scovill,[7] b. 6 Sep 1856, likely Cleveland, Cuyahoga, Ohio; d. 5 Jul 1918, Cook County, Illinois; m. Charles Solon Corning.[327] This family lived in Chicago—at least at the time of her death. The will mentions her children, Mildred Corning Hamilton and Warren Scovill Corning, as well as her husband. Additionally, she mentions the Scovill Block on Superior Street in Cleveland as subject to a ninety-nine-year lease, to be "divided equally between them, share and share alike."

*d. v.* Josephine Scovill,[7] b. 6 Sep 1856 (twin?), likely Cleveland, Cuyahoga, Ohio; d. 28 February 1876, Cleveland, Ohio.

## *10. Amasa Scoville[5] (Ithamar,[4] Timothy,[3] Stephen[2], Stephen[1], Arthur)*

Born 1791[328] in Norfolk, Litchfield, Connecticut; died 7 October 1842, Wolcottville, Litchfield, Connecticut; m. Lucy C. Foote prior to 1819 in Torrington, Connecticut; she born November 1795 in Torrington to Col. Samuel Foote and Lucy Lord; she died 5 October 1863, Chicago, Illinois.[329]

There is no primary evidence that proves Amasa Scoville is the son of Ithamar Scoville;[330]

324 *Utah Death Registers, 1847–1996,* and death certificate, Ancestry.

325 *Honolulu, Hawaii, Passenger and Crew Lists, 1900–1959.* Ancestry.

326 *School Catalogs, 1765–193.* Ancestry.

327 *Illinois, Wills and Probate Records, 1772–1999.* Ancestry.

328 Year of birth is based on his age and date of his death. His birth record has never been found; however, the records found online and *Survey of Scovels* by Brainard consistently give his birth as November 1791. Norfolk is his likely birthplace. Since Brainard did not cite his sources, it is unknown where this information came from.

329 *Cook County, Illinois, Marriage and Death Indexes, 1833–1889.*

330 An early correspondent regarding the parentage of Amasa Scoville stated that he "found" a reference that substantiated Ithamar Scoville being the father of Amasa at the LDS Library in Salt Lake

however, enough data exists that I am confident enough to place him with this family. As previously discussed, Ithamar and his unnamed wife had several children, and the only child who has been identified as the son of Ithamar is Franklin Scoville, via a death certificate. I will use a timeline for Amasa the same way I did for Ithamar.

### *TIMELINE AND NOTES FOR AMASA SCOVILLE*

1791—November—born in Norfolk, CT[331]

1800—census, Norfolk—Ithamar Scoville. 1 male and 1 female under 10 (likely Amasa and Lodema Scoville). A male and female under 10 were also counted in Reuben Dean's household. I suspect that these children were counted twice.

1806—Norfolk—Amasa Scoville and Lodema (also written as Lodemia) Scoville were baptized as "adopted children of Reuben Dean and ______." If Amasa, born 1791, is the same Amasa "adopted" by Reuben Dean, he would have been fifteen at his baptism and Lodema would have been eleven/twelve years of age. [*Baptisms, Marriages, Deaths*, by Rev. Ammi Robbins].

1806—16 June—Ira Scoville granted property to Amasa and Lodem[ia] Scoville—3rd Division 2nd going over.[332]

1815—Amasa receives two pieces of land he originally quit-claimed to Elisha Carrier and Lodemia (Scoville) Carrier in June 1806 (see above).

1817—Amasa Scoville "of Torrington" sold to Roxalana Dean (wife of Reuben Dean) nine acres of land in Norfolk, which "is land and all the land which Ira Scoville deed to myself and Lodemia in 1806."

1817—13 March—Samuel Foot [sic] deeded forty-three acres to Amasa Scovil [sic], Thomas Watson, Asa Wells, Charles Mather, Nehemiah Beach, Nathaniel Smith, John Gillette, Ransley Birge, and Fitch Bissell, " a piece of land lying in Torrington . . . together with dwelling house, and other buildings thereon and a joiners shop on the highway in front of said land, lying in common & undivided with the grantor under the encumbrance of a mortgage deed to Eliphat Eno for the sum of seventeen hundred & fifty dollars, each according to his proportion aforesaid." Amasa paid $214.45 for his portion.[333]

1818—Amasa Scoville made a freeman.[334]

---

City, but because he did not cite his source, he couldn't remember where he found the information—he believed it was the Torrington Cemetery Records. I have never found such a record.

331 Could not find a birth record in Barbour Vital Records, Connecticut State Library, Town Clerk's offices in various towns in Litchfield Co.

332 A professional researcher indicated that she doesn't understand how property was granted to Amasa and Lodema as they were under twenty-one years of age, yet the land records prove that it did occur.

333 Torrington Land Records, Vol. 10, 10:382—Warrantee Deed, 13 March 1817; [MF # LH 1218-19]; Roll # 1699.Connecticut State Library.

334 Orcutt, Samuel, *History of Torrington, Connecticut: From Its First Settlement in 1737, with Biographies and Genealogies*, (1878). A freeman owned land and had the right to vote.

1818–1820—Amasa Scoville marries Lucy C. Foote.

1819—Torrington—Charles Foote Scoville born to Amasa and Lucy Scoville.[335]

1819—3 December—Amasa Scoville of Torrington quit-claimed to Seth Coe two parcels of land in Torrington and New Hartford. The land in New Hartford was a farm of "about one hundred and fifteen acres and is the farm lately deeded by Samuel Foot[e] to Seth Coe, Nathaniel and others."[336]

1820—census, Torrington, Connecticut—1 male 20–30; 1 female 20–30. The census was taken on the first Monday in August (August 7th).

1822—Torrington—Mary Lord Scoville born to Amasa and Lucy Scoville. Approximate date.

1827—Torrington—Samuel D. Scoville born to Amasa and Lucy Scoville. Approximate date.

1830—census, Torrington, Connecticut—Amasa Scoville's household consisted of:

1 male <5 (perhaps son Samuel, born 1827)
1 male 5–10 (perhaps Charles Foote Scoville, b. 1819)
1 male 15–20 (born between 1810–1815)
1 male 20–30 (Franklin Scoville, brother of Amasa?)[337]
1 male 30–40 (Amasa Scoville, b. 1791)
1 female 10–15 (perhaps Mary Lord Scoville)
1 female 30–40 (Lucy Scoville, b. 1795)

1831—Torrington—Henry Scoville born to Amasa and Lucy Scoville. Approximate date.

1834—Torrington—George Scoville born to Amasa and Lucy Scoville. Approximate date.

1834—Lucy C. Scoville becomes a member of the church.[338]

1837—29 June—Amasa Scoville is made deacon of the Third Congregational Church.

1837—6 November—Amasa Schovel [sic] "of Torrington" for $500 of Charles F. Schovel [sic] "of Torrington" one piece of land in the south part of Norfolk containing 50 acres more or less with a dwelling house and all other buildings thereon . . . is the same land lately belonged to Reuben Dean deceased."[339]

---

335 His birth record has not been found.

336 Torrington Land Records, Vol. 10:306, QC, 14 May 1820; [MF# LH 1218-19, CSL Roll #1699].

337 Once again, we are left with speculations as to who is in the household other than the head and his wife. I've never been able to find Franklin Scoville on the 1830 census and I suggest that he was living with his brother Amasa until his marriage on October 6, 1830. He could also potentially fit the profile of the male listed as between 15–20, as Franklin would have turned 21 on August 9, 1830.

338 Likely the Third Congregational Church in Wolcottville. The village of Wolcottville later became the center of Torrington, Connecticut, and the Third Congregational Church is now known as *Center Congregational Church.*

339 Norfolk Land Records, Vol. 14:492, [MF# LH 1170-71], Roll #1215. CSL. This is the land that Ira Scoville originally purchased in 1796 and where Reuben Dean and Ithamar Scoville also lived, in the area known as "Meekertown."

1839—John Cook to Amasa Scovil [sic] sells "one piece of land lying in said Torrington." Amasa paid twenty-five dollars for this piece of land which was about "one mile North of the village of Wolcottville."[340]

1840—census, Torrington—Amasey Schovel [sic]:

1 male < 5 (b. about 1835)

2 males 5–10 (b. between 1830–1835—Henry & George 1831 & 1834?)

1 male 15–20 (b. between 1820–1825—Charles Foote Scoville?)

1 male 40–50 (b. between 1790–1800—Amasa Scoville)

1 female 20–30 (b. between 1810–1820—Mary Lord Scoville?)

1 female 30–40 (b. between 1790–1800—Lucy Scoville)

1841—2 June—Amasa Schovel [sic] to Harlow Roys of "Norfolk" quit-claims a "certain piece of land & buildings lying & being said Norfolk . . . contains about 15 acres . . . being a house and other buildings." The property was sold for $400.[341]

1842—29 May—Amasa Scoville grantor to Charles F. Scoville and Samuel D. Scoville, both of "Torrington" the rights and privileges of building a dam and taking water on a piece of land that was deeded to John Cook in 1839. Charles and Samuel could go on "said land at any time for the purpose of refining(?) said dam and ditch."[342]

1842—29 May—Grantor Amasa Scovill "of Torrington" sold to Theodosia M. Lord[343] "of said Torrington, a piece of land lying in said Torrington containing about ninety rods[344] of land, conveyed to me by deed from John Cook excepting the water privilege this day deeded to me by Charles F. and Samuel D. Scovill."[345]

1842—7 October—Amasa Scoville dies age 51, in Torrington, Connecticut,[346] and is buried in Center Cemetery, Torrington.

1842—Amasa's estate probated.

The estate record for Amasa is held in probate district of Litchfield, Connecticut, no. 5111.[347]

The estate record included:

1—Bond

340 Torrington Land Records, Vol. 14:258, Warrantee Deed 18 April 1842; [MF# LH 1220-21], Roll #1701; CSL.

341 Norfolk Land Records, Vol. 14:401, [MF# LH 1170-71], Roll #1215;CSL.

342 Torrington Land Records, Vol. 14:271, Water Rights, 21 May 1842, [MF# LH 1220-21], Roll#1701; CSL.

343 I have not been able to determine with any certainty who Theodosia M. Lord is and how she connected to this family. An Elisha Lord married Theodosia Wells; however, she died in 1792. The estate of Elisha Lord mentions Samuel Foot as his son-in-law. He may have been married to Elisha Lord's daughter, Theodosia Lord. Further research is needed.

344 Ninety rods equal 0.562 acres.

345 Torrington Land Records, Vol. 14:272, Warrantee Deed 21 May 1842, [MF# LH 1220-21], Roll #1701; CSL.

346 *Connecticut, Deaths and Burials Index, 1650–1934.*

347 Copy of will in my possession and it is quite difficult to decipher.

1—Application & Petitions
1—Inventory
3—Returns to Court
2—Account of Admin.

Since the handwriting is so poor, I have only transcribed the inventory. The packet did not include the usual will or any codicils.

| 5 Vol. Scott's[348] Family Bible | 1 book Life of The Apostles | A lot of old books |
|---|---|---|
| 1 overcoat | 1 great coat | 1 straight-body coat |
| 1 vest | 1 pair pantaloons | 3 beds with underbeds and pillows |
| 3 bedsteads and ropes | 2 pair flannel sheets | 2 pair linen sheets |
| 9 pair cotton sheets | 10 pair cotton pillowcases | 5 tablecloths, brown towel |
| 6 white towels | 5 blankets | 4 bed quilts, [ ] comforters |
| 4 shirts | 5 pair of stockings | 4 candlesticks, 1 clock |
| 1 table | 12 chairs | 5 chests, 1 case of drawers |
| 1 cooking stove | shovel and tongs | 1 stand, 1 iron pot |
| 2 brass kettles | 1 iron kettle | 1 tea kettle, 1 frying pan |
| A lot of crockery | also of tin | a lot of earthen ware, 4 jugs |
| A lot of old barrels | 30 bushels potatoes | [ ] lb. pork |
| 8 gallons molasses | [ ] wheat flour | 1 [ ] salt |
| 1 wood saw | 3 axes | buckle(?) [ ] wedges |
| 6 rakes | 3 hay forks | 4 chains, 1 yoke |
| 3 grindstones | lot of lumber | a lot of old iron |
| 1 old stove | chest of tools | 3 [ ] |
| 1 yoke of cattle | 2 cows | 1 yearling, 1 calf |
| 1 sap pan | 90 sap quarts | 3 sap tubs, 1 sled |
| 1 [ ] knife | 2 tine forks | 6 ½ tons of hay |

About 80/84 cords of hemlock dark
About 50 acres of land and house called the Dean [ ]

The rest of the record is illegible.

Based on the inventory, we know that Amasa (and perhaps his wife) were literate (based on the number of books in the household), and that the home was well equipped with bedding, household items, and some livestock. Where their home was situated in Torrington is unknown.

348 Thomas Scott (1747–1821), an influential English preacher and author. His best-selling works *A Commentary On The Whole Bible.*

1843—12 January—Charles F. Schovel[sic] "of Torrington" sold to Alden Miner "of Norfolk land situated in Norfolk . . . contains 50 acres more or less."[349]

1844—Advertisement in the *Litchfield Enquirer*[350] regarding the estate of Amasa Scoville for public Auction; "the land is lying in the town of Norfolk . . . continuing about one-hundred and twenty acres more or less. The same being called the Sterling farm . . . also, fifty-acres more or less called the Dean lot . . . sold to Charles Scoville of Torrington for $480.00."

1847—26 April—"Lucy C. Scoville, William Leach, Julia Leach, William S. Foot, Thomas Matthews, Clarissa Matthews all 'of Torrington.' . . . Elias Hatch and Cornelia M. Hatch 'of Winchester' for the consideration of $100 received of Lucius H. Foote, 'of Torrington' quit-claim unto said Lucius H. Foote . . . a piece of land lying in said Wolcottville . . . bounded northeast and west on land owned in common by Lucius Foot and the other children of Samuel Foot—reserving the right the use of the stairs in the upright aforesaid house and chambers under and above passing and repassing to and from the cellar and chambers above that part of the house not herein described and conveyed also the right to pass to and from the cellar through by the ga[te?] on the north-end of the upright part of said dwelling house.

"Witness: Samuel Foot."[351]

What is known about Amasa's life is encapsulated in the timeline. There are no records of his birth, marriage, or even dates of birth of his children. We do know that he was about fifteen years of age when he came into the Reuben and Roxalana Dean household and was raised by them as a "son." I have speculated that Amasa was, in fact, the son of Ithamar Scoville and his unnamed wife. As already discussed, Ithamar was the brother-in-law of Reuben Dean and lived near Reuben, and the land that they lived on was the original parcel purchased by Ithamar's brother, Ira, in 1796 (Intervail Lot 43). No other person named Amasa Scoville fits into any other Scoville family but that of Ithamar, and unless proof can be found that calls for a different conclusion, my theory stands as proposed.

Amasa, having been raised in Norfolk, Connecticut, made his way to Torrington—a town about fifteen miles south. According to *The History of Torrington, Connecticut . . .* by

349 Norfolk Land Records, Vol.14:221; [MF# LH 1170-71]; Roll #1215. CSL. Charles F. Scoville sold the Intervail Lot 43 for $500.

350 *Litchfield Enquirer*, September 5, 1844, Vol. XIX, No. 15, Whole Number 951. Torrington Historical Society. "Estate of Amasa Scovill, late of Torrington, in said district, will be sold at public auction, to the highest bidder, on the 20th day of September 1844 at 2 o'clock, in the afternoon, if not previously disposed of, so much of the real estate of said deceased as will raise the sum of $628.38, with incident charges of sale. Sale will take place on the premises in Norfolk, in Litchfield County." William Leach, Administer. William Leach was the brother-in-law of Lucy Foote Scoville.

351 Torrington Land Records, Vol. 15:210 Quit-Claim, [MF# LH 1221]; Roll #1702. CSL. Not being an expert on matters of land deeds and such, it appears that this property was held in common by the siblings of Lucius Foot and that said property was sold to him, whereby he had rights to a certain portion of the home.

Rev. Samuel Orcutt, many families from Windsor, Hartford County, Connecticut, settled in Torrington. The General Assembly Act of 1732 pronounced it a town and as the years went on, Torrington became the city "hub" of Litchfield County as it consisted of various mills, shops, and factories. These activities may have been what drew Amasa to remove to a larger town. Perhaps he saw what a hard-scrabble life it was trying to make it in farming, and living in poverty with his father and mother for several years may have driven him to a better life.

Amasa attended the Congregational Church (now Center Church) in Wolcottville.[352] This church was first organized on December 3, 1819, at the house of Captain Taylor, and Amasa became a member. This church became the focal point of his life as he was also made a deacon of this church in 1837.

Lucy, like her husband, also became a member of the Congregational Church. Again, nothing is known of Lucy outside the fact that she was born to Col. Samuel Foote and Lucy Lord about 1795, that she married, and that she died.

As of the 1850 census Lucy Scoville was still living in Torrington with sons Henry, Samuel, and George. Amasa and Lucy's daughter Mary had married and left Connecticut and was living in New York, and their son Charles F. Scoville had removed to Chicago, Illinois.[353]

Sometime after the 1850 census Lucy removed to Chicago and she was living in her son's household at that time. On October 7, 1863, Lucy C. Foote Scoville died at the age of sixty-eight.[354,355]

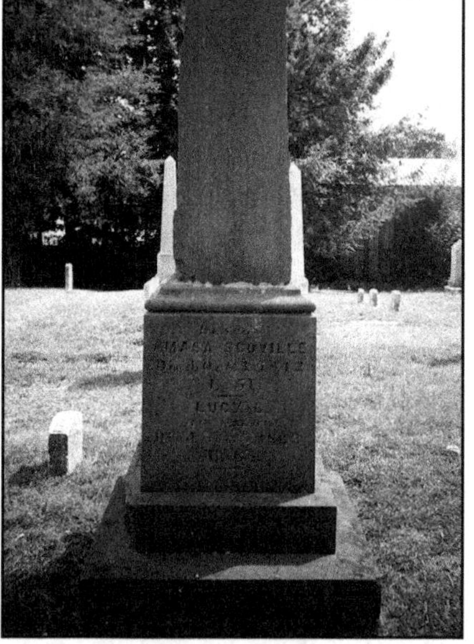

***Children of Amasa Scoville and Lucy C. Foote***

14. i. Charles Foote Scoville,[6] b. circa 1819, probably Torrington, Litchfield, Connecticut; d. 4 Feb 1890, Chicago, Cook, Illinois; m. (1) Clarissa Spencer; m. (2) Sarah Baird.
15. ii. Mary Lord Scoville,[6] b. circa 1822, probably Torrington, Litchfield, Connecticut; d. 29 Dec 1893, Yorkville, Oneida, New York; m. Abner Wilson.

352 Wolcottville was a village within the town of Torrington. The original purchaser was one Amos Wilson, who had a mill by March 1751. He then opened a store and shoe shop.

353 Amasa and Lucy also had a son named James, born about 1839. He was living with his brother Charles F. Scoville in Derby, New Haven, Connecticut, prior to the removal to Chicago. This is shown in the 1850 census for Derby, Connecticut.

354 *Cook County, Illinois, Marriage and Death Indexes, 1833–1889.* Ancestry. (Original data is from Sam Fink's Chicago Marriage and Death Index). There are two death places for Lucy—Chicago and Torrington, Connecticut. I believe this error is because Lucy Scoville was returned to Torrington to be buried with her husband, Amasa. Her headstone gives her age as "68." Amasa and Lucy are buried in Center Cemetery, Torrington, Connecticut.

355 Photo from the author's collection.

iii. Samuel D. Scoville,[6] b. circa 1827, probably Torrington, Litchfield, Connecticut. Other than being mentioned in the Water Rights deed with his brother Charles, he is listed as a "merchant" on the 1850 census. Nothing more is known about him.

iv. Henry C. Scoville,[6] born circa 1827 in Torrington, Litchfield, Connecticut; died 25 Dec 1893,[356] probably Colorado; buried in Glenwood Cemetery, Madison, New York, with his sister and her husband.

Henry C. Scoville is first mentioned on the 1850 census for Torrington with his mother and brothers. It is not until 1862 that another record is located for him. On September 1, 1862, in Denver, Colorado, he enlisted in the 3rd Infantry Regiment, Company E[357] and was mustered out (transferred) October 1, 1863. He is then found as serving with the 2nd Colorado Calvary as a private in Company M[358] and then with the 3rd Colorado Calvary Infantry as a private in Company E.[359] All of the above-mentioned units were part of the Union Army. According to an article on *Wikipedia*, the 2nd Colorado Calvary was organized in St. Louis, Missouri, by consolidating the 2nd Colorado Infantry and the 3rd Colorado Infantry from October 1863. The unit was under the command of Col. James Hobart Ford. A detailed record of the unit and their battles and skirmishes can be found in the online article.

From 1865 (when the war ended) until 1871 it is unknown where Henry Scoville was; however, a brief mention in the *Rocky Mountain Directory, County Gazetteer* for 1871 indicates that Henry was involved with mining.

Mining in Colorado was "the most significant industry from the nineteenth—and early twentieth century."[360] The first gold rush took place in Colorado between 1858 and 1859 with men, women, and whole families going to Colorado to make their dreamed-of fortunes. There were various types of mines: hardrock—which included shaft mines and tunnel mines; ore-concentrated mills; smelters; and coal mines. Around the mines were the mining settlements and residences that housed the miners and provided equipment and other sundry items.

With Henry's involvement with mining, he could have been anywhere during the 1870 census, although there are two land records found for 1876. The first is dated August 15, 1876 for a mine called "Cecil Lode" of 1.75 acres.[361]

Another purchase occurred on December 12, 1876, for "Twin Lode," which was 2.89 acres.[362] Both of these mines are in Clear Creek County, Colorado. Unfortunately, there were

---

356 Death date comes from the headstone located in Glenwood Cemetery, Madison, New York.

357 *U.S. Civil War Soldiers, 1861–1865*; Film Number: M534; Roll: 3; Original data: National Park Service, Civil Soldiers and Sailors System, http://www.itd.nps.gov/cwss/ acquired by Ancestry 2007.

358 *Ibid*

359 *American Civil War Research Database*; Historical Data Systems, Inc.; Duxbury, MA 02331; Source Information: Historical Data Systems, comp. *U.S. Civil War Soldier Records and Profiles, 1861–1865*; Ancestry.

360 *History of Colorado—Colorado Archives/* www.historycolorado.org.

361 *U. S. Department of the Interior, Bureau of Land Management (BLM); Doc#1905; BLM Serial# COCOAA 056024. www.glorecords.blm.gov.*

362 *Ibid*, Doc# 2057; BLM Serial# COCOAA 019568.

no images of the actual land records on the Bureau of Land Management site to view. How long he worked these mines and whether they produced anything of note, again, remains a question mark.

Mining towns sprung up like mushrooms all across Colorado for the thousands of people who came. The miners' accommodations were roughly and hastily built—not warm in the winter or cool in the summer. While some men brought their families with them, many of the men were single. Some had mining partners. But all in all, mining was backbreaking work and, I imagine, often very lonely.

Occasionally, the miner would come back to "civilization," as is shown in this brief article found in the *Denver Rocky Mountain News:*[363] *Henry Scoville of the Big Thompson came into town yesterday and is stopping at the American.*

The Big Thompson is a river that flows through Big Thompson Canyon in Larimer County, Colorado. Whether Henry was mining there is unknown. There are no other records for him on the Bureau of Land Management website.

The American was [the] American House, on Blake and the corner of Sixteenth Street. The proprietor was Col. George Brand.[364] It was a three-story building built in 1868 by John Wesley Smith. It was considered for the time "one of the most luxurious early hotels" and was called the "Old Reliable." It had 200 "First Class" rooms, suites, and apartments.[365] Henry may have been well-off enough from his mining to be able to afford such a classy hotel.

I did find Henry on the 1880 census living in Idaho Springs, Clear Creek, Colorado. It is difficult to tell if he is living on his own or not. He is listed as family #233; age "48," "single," and occupied in "mining." Idaho Springs is where the Gold Rush began in 1859 when a fellow by the name of George A. Jackson discovered gold at the junction of Chicago Creek and Clear Creek.[366] People from all over the United States came to Colorado to find their fortunes.

It is said that in March 1848, 157,000 people left their homes and former livelihoods for California.[367] However, ten years later in "just one part of Colorado, the Cripple Creek and Victor Mining District, produced over 500 mines and 21 million ounces of gold—or more."

Colorado elected to have a census taken in 1885, however, Henry Scoville could not be located for this particular year (using variable spellings of the last name). It is not until 1889 that another record is located, when Henry applied for his pension for his years of Civil War Service.[368] The date of this record is March 25, 1899. This online record does not indicate *where* Henry was living at the time of his request.

The last record for Henry C. Scoville is his death, which occurred on December 25, 1893; he was sixty-two years old. He is buried with his sister and her husband in Glenwood

---

363 Wednesday, March 9, 1881, issue; Denver, Colorado, 2; www.genealogybank.com (herein GenealogyBank)

364 See www.digital.denverlibrary.org.

365 See www.historical.ha.com. The hotel was torn down in 1933.

366 Text is from *Tailing Tracks and Tommyknockers: History of Clear Creek County;* Historical Society of Idaho Springs; www.historicalidahosprings.com.

367 Text from The History Channel online; www.history.com

368 *U.S. Civil War and Later Pension Index, 1861–1917;* Ancestry.

Cemetery, Madison, New York.

He never married and left no descendants.

v. George E. Scoville[6][369] born circa 1834 Torrington, Litchfield, Connecticut; died 15 April 1872;[370] buried in Oakwoods Cemetery, Chicago, Cook, Illinois.

There are only two censuses that George can be found on—in 1850 in Torrington, Connecticut, and 1860 in Chicago when he was living in the Edwards household with his brothers Charles and Albert and Charles' wife and children. The only other record for him is his last will and testament as transcribed here:

> I, George E. Scoville of the city of Denver in the County of Arapaho and Territory of Colorado, of the age of thirty-eight years and being of sound mind and memory, do make, publish, and declare this my last will and testament in the manner following, that is to say
>
> *First* - . . . It is my will that funeral expenses and all my just debts be fully paid.
>
> *Second* - . . . I do hereby give, grant, devise and bequeath unto my sister Mary L. Wilson, now of the Village of Cleveland in the County of Oswego and State of New York, ten bonds of the County of Marshall in the state of Kansas, said bonds being numbered fifteen to twenty-four inclusive and each being the denomination of one-thousand dollars to be used and enjoyed by her and she to have sole right, use and benefit the accruing interest thereon for and during the terms of her natural life and from and immediately after her decease said bonds or their representative proceeds shall revert to [ ] in and be equally between the children of Charles F. Scoville and in the event that any of his said children should die before my said sister and should leave behind them [ ] than in that event such children shall be entitled to the share of said bonds to be equally divided among them that their parent would been entitled to had he or she have lived, said bonds to be by my said executor to be hereafter named placed in the possession of my said brother Charles F. Scoville . . . the rest of the account goes on to say how the money is to be distributed and when, and that both parties must be in agreement.
>
> *Third* - . . . to said brother Charles F. Scoville, now of the city of Chicago . . . ten bonds of the County of Marshall and State of Kansas . . . bonds are numbered twenty-five to thirty- four . . . one-thousand dollars each.

The record goes on to say that his brother Henry C. Scoville would receive the same amount of bonds (one thousand each), as well as his niece Mary Jane Scoville. Sarah (Baird) Scoville received two bonds for Marshall, Kansas (same denomination), as well as a bond for

369 This George Scoville is not to be confused with the *other* George Scoville (also of Chicago) who represented his brother-in-law, Charles Guiteau. Charles Guiteau assassinated President James A. Garfield. Both George Scovilles were living in Chicago at the same time.

370 The date of death is based on the information from the gravesite on www.findagrave.com (herein Find A Grave). He may have died in Missouri as that is where his will and probate record were drawn up.

the County of Knox, Missouri.

In addition, George E. Scoville left his nephew Frank Scoville of "Knox County, of Iron, Missouri" twenty bonds as well as 132 shares of stock in the Pacific & Atlantic Telegraph Company.

He bequeathed $500 to a Mrs. Samuel Dean of Junction City, Kansas; to his cousin, Mrs. Mary Beach, "now of said Chicago," $500 cash; "to the infant child of my co-partner in business Mr. W. Axtell, of [ ] in the County of Loraine, State of Ohio"—the above-referenced bequests were made upon the condition if there was money left to comply with George's desires.

Everything else (real or personal property) was left to his nephew Frank Scoville.

The executors of the will were his business partners, W. Axtell, and Frank White "now of Marysville, in the County of Marshall, Kansas." It was signed:

Signed Geo. E. Scoville

Like his brothers Henry, James, and Albert, George did not marry and left no descendants.

vi. Albert (possibly "M") Scoville,[6] b. circ 1837, perhaps Torrington, Litchfield, Connecticut. Albert is listed with his brother Charles Foote Scoville and his family on the 1860 census in Chicago, Illinois, where it states his occupation is a "printer." Nothing more is known.

vii. James A. Scoville,[6] b. circa 1838, probably Torrington, Litchfield, Connecticut; died 17 June 1862 aboard the ironclad *Mound City* (see narrative for his brother Charles F. Scoville).

### *11. Lodema[5, 371] Scoville (Ithamar,[4] Timothy,[3] Stephen,[2] Stephen,[1] Arthur)*

Born circa 1794, probably Norfolk, Litchfield, Connecticut; died 1873 Brimfield, Portage, Ohio; married 29 May 1813 in Goshen, Litchfield County, Connecticut, to Elisha Carrier; born circa 1768, Connecticut; died August 1845, Brimfield, Portage County, Ohio.

If you recall, Elisha Carrier was first married to Triphene Scoville (sister of Ithamar Scoville). After her death in March 1813, he remarried to Lodema Scoville, the conjectured daughter of Ithamar.

If we conclude that Lodema's birth year was about 1794, she would have been approximately nineteen years of age at her marriage and Elisha was already forty-five years old. This couple remained in Goshen for a time as they are living there as of the 1820 census.

1 male <10 (born between 1810–1820)
1 male 45+ (Elisha Carrier)
1 female 16–26 (born between 1794–1804)
1 female 26–45 (born between 1775–1794)

371 For the sake of consistency, I am using the spelling as "Lodema" unless an actual record spelled it in an alternative way.

Lodema could fit in either of the last two categories of this census as she would have been approximately twenty-six in 1820; either way, it brings up the question as to who the other female was. Could it be the daughter born to Elisha and his first wife, Triphene, who was listed on the census as being under age ten in 1800? It is impossible to know as we do not have a name for this child or how she is related—if at all.

This "other" female does not show up in this household in 1830 when the Carriers were living in Warren, Litchfield, Connecticut:

1 male 10–14 (born between 1816–1820—Lucius)
1 male 40–49 (Elisha)
1 female <5 (born between 1825–1829)(unknown daughter?)
1 female 30–39 (Lodema)

This family was still residing in Warren, Connecticut, in 1831 as they (Elisha, Lodema, and their son Lucius) are listed as having been baptized "on profession of faith," on 25 September.[372]

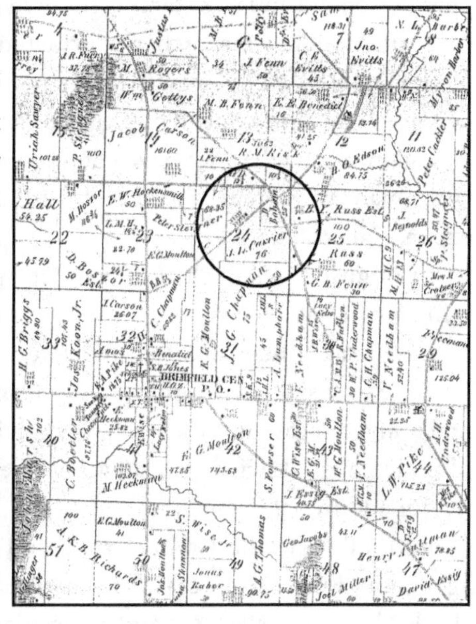


In 1833, Lodema Carrier purchased fifty-one acres in Brimfield Township, Portage, Ohio,[373] and the deed was recorded in Portage County on 15 November. Whether this family left Connecticut prior to the purchase of property in Ohio or after is unknown. Note that the deed was in Lodema's name and *not* in her husband's. Elisha may have decided to do this because of their age difference and did not want his wife to have to go through the expense of probating his estate after his death.

Brimfield Township was part of the Connecticut Western Reserve. The Carriers were just another family who made the trek out "west" to acquire better land and (hopefully) become more prosperous. After the Revolutionary War, Ohio became the primary destination of westward-bound pioneers. The land was very fertile in the farmland of the Ohio River Valley. The Firelands of Ohio were reserved for Connecticut to help compensate losses when some of the towns were ravaged during the Revolutionary War.[374]

The Carrier family must have gone to Ohio as a family group that included Rufus Carrier and his family, as he died in Brimfield, Ohio, at the age of thirty in 1838 (if you recall, my

372 *Connecticut Church Records Abstracts, 1630–1920,* Vol. 119, Warren, Connecticut.

373 A professional genealogical researcher provided this data for me. *Letter 'C', Portage County General Index to Deeds, 1795—31 December 1916, page 44, Portage County Reporter, 449 South Meridian St., Ravenna, Ohio.* Date of deed, 15 November 1833.

374 See *United States Migration to Ohio, Northwest Territory Southwest 1785 to 1840,* online via FamilySearch Wiki.

belief is that Rufus is the son of Elisha Carrier and his first wife, Triphene Scoville Carrier).

A map of Brimfield Township landowners of record, circa 1857, shows "L. Carrier" as owner of fifty-one acres, and an adjoining landowner identified only as "Carrier" as owner of twenty-five acres in lot 24.[375]

The family of Elisha and Lodema are on the 1840 census in Brimfield:

1 male <5 (Joseph L.)
1 male 20–30 (Lucius)
1 male 50–60 (Elisha)
1 female 20–30 (Orilla)
1 female 50–60 (Lodema)

I believe this to be the combined households of Elisha, Lodema, Lucius, his wife Orilla, and their son Joseph L. In the same year, Lucius purchased twenty-five acres of land adjacent to his parents in Brimfield Township.[376]

Two years after the 1840 census, Lucius died at the age of twenty-two. He had just purchased land and was starting his own family. The cause of his death is unknown.

A professional researcher speculated that after his son's death, Elisha may have felt compelled to have his widow (Lodema) have control of the real estate rather than leave his daughter-in-law in control of the property.

Again, Elisha may not have felt there was any reason for him to leave a will, since Lodema was already the owner of record of the real estate and there would have been no reason for the expense of probate.

In August 1845, Elisha Carrier died at the age of seventy-seven. It is said that he "lost his mind" in his later years.[377]

Lodema and her daughter-in-law were now widows and running a farm. By 1850, Lodema, now age fifty-six, her daughter-in-law Orilla, age thirty-nine (written "Amelia" in the record) and grandson Joseph L., age ten, were living together in one household. Since the properties of Lodema and Lucius were adjacent to each other, one of the parcels may have been rented out for additional income.

In 1860,[378] Orilla (written as "Aurelia") was now listed as the head-of-household and age forty-nine, son "Lucas"[379] is now twenty-one and is listed as a "farmer," and "Ludena" (Lodema) is age sixty-six and is listed as being "retired." Two years later, Orilla died.[380]

---

375 P. J. Brown, surveyor, *Map of Portage County, Ohio from Actual Surveys,* (Philiada: Matthews & Taintor Publishers, 1857) K.6. [Doc. 1].

376 Card File Index to Probate Court Estate Records, Portage County Probate Court. Elizabeth A. Walters, comp., *Portage County, Ohio Wills and Estates 1811–1874,* Apollo, PA: Clossen Press (1993) 18 and 19. Betty Widger, comp., *Portage County, Ohio Estate Index* (Ravenna, Ohio: n. pub., n.d.) no page numbers.

377 *History of Portage County, Ohio;* Warner, Beers & Co., Chicago (1885).

378 1860 census, *Brimfield, Portage, Ohio;* Roll: M653_1025; Page: 265; FHL: 805025. Ancestry.

379 I believe that this is a reference to Joseph Lucius Carrier.

380 Find A Grave—only the year of death is listed. I have not been able to find the month and day.

Lodema and her grandson, Joseph L., were the only ones left of this family. This would only last for a short time as the 1870[381] census shows Lodema once again listed as the head-of-household at age seventy-six. The family unit consisted of the following:

Lodema Carrier, age 76, born Connecticut
Joseph L. Carrier, age 30, farmer, real estate $4,300; personal estate $600, born Ohio
Mary M. Carrier, "wife," age 32, born Ohio
Arthur W. Carrier, "son," age 8, at school (all children born in Ohio)
Emma E. Carrier, "daughter," age 6, at school
Joseph L. Carrier, "son," age 4, at school
Frederick Carrier, "son," age 10/12 (born August 1869 as the census was taken on 28 June 1870)
Dearsam, Elizabeth, age 14, b. Ohio (relationship unknown)

As with Lodema's birth, we only have the year of death for Lodema (1873). No record of her death was located at the Portage County Probate Court and there are no estate records for either Lodema or Elisha. The headstones in Restland Cemetery (Brimfield) are the only evidence we have of their deaths.

Additionally, there is no legal record of her land (51 acres) transferring to her grandson Joseph;[382] however, there is a deed selling the fifty-one acres out of the family by the heirs of Joseph, and there are no records of the twenty-five acres purchased by Lucius being transferred out of the family.

The map of Brimfield Township from 1874 indicated that Joseph Carrier was the owner of seventy-six acres, which would be the entire acreage purchased by his grandmother and his father. Clearly by 1874 Joseph was the owner of record for the purpose of taxation. It remains unclear when and by what means the land transferred into Joseph's name as far as the deed records are concerned.

Lodema, like her husband, apparently died without a will. More research would be needed via tax records to determine exactly when ownership of the two parcels of land was put into Joseph's name. They also may indicate how much personal property Elisha had at the time of his death—if any.

The Carrier family are buried in Restland Cemetery, Brimfield, Portage County, Ohio, Lot 45 of the north addition, the west part of plot 17.[383]

### *Children of Elisha Carrier and Lodema Scoville*

i. Lucius Carrier,[6] b. 1820, likely Goshen, Litchfield, Connecticut; d. 1842 Brimfield, Portage, Ohio; m. 10 February 1839, Portage County, Ohio,[384] to Orilla Emerson; b.

381 1870 census, *Brimfield, Portage, Ohio;* Roll: M653_1258; Page: 293B. Ancestry.

382 *Portage County General Index to Deeds*, 44.

383 Ragan, R.L., and Ragan, L.M., compiled *Portage County Cemeteries Vo. VIII, Brimfield Township and Suffield Township, 18–8—199* (Ravenna, Ohio: Portage County Historical Society, 1992), 116.

384 *Portage County Ohio Marriages 1808–1850, Vol. 1, 1990.*

1811, New York; d. 1862, Brimfield, daughter of Joseph Emerson and _____.

When Lucius married Orilla he was just nineteen and she was twenty-nine.

Other than the land that Lucius and his mother had lived on, he had also purchased land in Mercer County, Ohio, which was recorded in the Lima Land Office. According to *U.S. General Land Office Records—1776–2015,* Lucius Carrier "of Portage County, Ohio," whereby, "full payment has been made by said Lucius Carrier according to the Act of Congress of the 24th of April 1820, entitled 'An Act making further provisions for the sale of Public Lands.'" The date of this transaction was October 10, 1840 and it contained forty acres. Nothing more of Lucius' short life is known.

This couple were married for three short years until an illness or accident claimed the life of Lucius. One child was born to this couple:

*a. i.* Joseph L. Carrier,[7] b. 24 Nov 1839, Brimfield, Portage, Ohio; d. 30 Sep 1896, Brimfield, Portage, Ohio; m. 11 Jun 1861,[385] Brimfield, to Mary M. Edson; b. 5 June 1836, Ohio; d. 5 Sept 1899,[386] Brimfield, Portage, Ohio; daughter of Benjamin O. Edson and Catherine Caris of Rootstown, Portage County.[387]

Joseph was born on the farm that his father and grandmother had purchased. While Joseph was a farmer, he also served six terms as the justice of the peace and was the town clerk and held other minor offices in Brimfield. According to *Portage County, Ohio, Portage Biographies,* Joseph was a prominent member of the Masonic fraternity and involved in politics as a Democrat. Joseph was also on a list of those who took part in a school program, "in an evening of displaying the oratorical powers." Joseph was eighth on the list and his speech was on "The studies that should be pursued in school, opinion given by J. L. Carrier."[388]

Draft registration records show that Joseph was drafted at the age of twenty-three.[389] He is listed as a "farmer" and "married," and born in Ohio. The remarks also indicate that he had no prior military service and was "drafted in October 18, but [he] got a substitute." In other words, he paid someone to go in his stead. This is something that also occurred during the Revolutionary War.

The Enrollment Act of 1863 provided that a draftee could pay a substitute enrollee the sum of $300 (equivalent to approximately $5,000 in today's market) to enlist in his place.

There were different categories for a man who wanted to pay a substitute. One of these was the "only son of a widower;" such were exempt from being drafted.[390] I believe this was the case of Joseph. He was the only male in a household with an elderly grandmother, a wife, and children to run a large farm.

---

385 *Ohio County Marriage Records, 1774–1993.* Ancestry.

386 Dates of birth and death are from the headstone.

387 A B.O. Edson purchased Lot 12 in Brimfield. This property bordered the land owned by Joseph L. Carrier.

388 McCormick, Edgar L., *Brimfield and Its People, Life in a Western Reserve Township, 1816–1941* Thompson and Ruttner, Inc., (1998) 70.

389 *Draft Registration Records, 1863–1865;* National Archives and Record Administration. Image 136 or 336.

390 National Archives and Record Administration.

The 1880 Non-Population Federal Census for Brimfield[391] shows Joseph L. owning forty acres of land, although thirty-four and a half acres were woodland. An earlier non-population agricultural schedule[392] shows him with forty-eight acres, with twenty-seven of those being unimproved.

The 1880 Federal Census shows Joseph L. Carrier still living in Brimfield with wife, Mary, and their children: Arthur W., Elmer A., Milton I (?), Fredrick L., Ethel I (?), and cousin Mary Emerson.

In 1896 Joseph Lucius Carrier died at the age of fifty-seven, and his wife Mary followed him three years later, age sixty-three. They are buried in Restland Cemetery with the other members of their family.

### *Children of Joseph Lucius Carrier and Mary Edson*

*aa .i.* Arthur W. Carrier,[8] b. 1862[393] Brimfield, Portage, Ohio; d. 24 Aug 1908,[394] Ohio; buried Alliance, Stark, Ohio; m. 5 Jun 1888, Stark County, Ohio, Lola E. Cook;[395]she died 4 Aug 1927 in Cleveland, Cuyahoga, Ohio.[396]

Arthur and two of his brothers were teachers in the Brimfield school system. Arthur can be found in the *American Antiquarian Society U.S. School Catalogs, 1765–1935* having attended college in Twinsburg, Ohio, in 1886. He belonged to a college fraternity (Sigma). According to *Brimfield and Its People,*[397] Arthur and his brother Elmer attended Mt. Union College in Alliance, Ohio, and while they grew up on a farm on Edson Road, Joseph and Mary Carrier "gave their sons the best educational advantages." All four sons began their careers as teachers in the township's schools.

The 1900 census shows this family living in Twinsburg, where Arthur is teaching school. After Arthur's death in 1908, Lola is found on the 1910 census as "Lula," living in Cleveland, Ohio, with children Harry, Lucile, and Harold, and her sister, Lillian Cook.

Lola is listed on the Cleveland City Directories up until 1925 where she is consistently listed as the widow of Arthur. Her sons also are living in Cleveland in their own households. The children of Arthur W. Carrier and Lola (Laura J.) Cook are Harry E., Harold R., and Lucille M.

---

391 Brimfield, Portage County, Ohio, T1159; Roll: 87; Page 9; Line: 4; Schedule Type: Agricultural. Ancestry.

392 This schedule appears to be an earlier one, but I have not been able to determine its date, although I suspect it is probably from 1850.

393 The 1900 Federal Census gives his month of birth as "January" and born in "1864." His wife Lola's month of birth is listed as "March" and she was born in "1868." Ancestry.

394 Probate Court Record, 11 November 1909, *Ohio Wills and Probate Records, 1786–1998.* Ancestry.

395 *Ohio County Marriages Records, 1774–1993.* Ancestry.

396 Per headstone she is listed as "Laura J. 1869–1927," Mount Union Cemetery, Alliance, Stark County, Ohio. Memorial ID# 76437490. Also buried in this plot is Kenneth Cook 1802–1908 (?). Find A Grave.

397 Chapter: Mind and Soul, p. 151

*bb. ii.* Elmer Edson Carrier,[8] b. Nov 1863, probably Brimfield, Portage, Ohio; d. 1921, Brimfield, Ohio;[398] buried in Restland Cemetery, Brimfield; m. 3 Jul 1896 to Jennie Koon;[399] she born 1874 in Ohio to Charles Koon and Ettie MacKee; d. 1939 and buried in Restland Cemetery.

Like his brother Arthur, Elmer went on to become a teacher. By 1900 he and his family are listed as living in Kent, Franklin Township, Portage County, Ohio, and by this time he had become the superintendent of the Navarrre, Ohio, school system. He had a career change in 1910 (although he was still working in the school system) and was the principal of South School in Franklin Township.[400]

Curiously, by 1920 Elmer is listed as a "clerk" in a steel works. I double-checked all entries for men named Elmer Carrier and this is the only one that names the same wife and daughter as in previous census entries. At that time, he was fifty-six years of age. None of the Carrier men were long-lived and by 1921 Elmer was dead.

Elmer and his wife, Jennie, had one child, a daughter, Edna B. Carrier, who is listed on the 1900 census as having been born in October 1897. In 1920 she is still living in her parents' household and does not have an occupation.

*cc. iii.* Frederick L. Carrier,[8] b. 31 Aug 1869, Brimfield, Portage, Ohio;[401] d. 3 July 1947, Orange, California;[402] m. 4 Mar 1902, Haverhill, New Hampshire, S. Gertrude Little;[403] b. 8 January 1870, Monroe, Grafton, New Hampshire, to John Little and Maria/Mary Susan M. Chase; d. 28 July 1926, Orange, California.[404]

Like his brothers before him, Frederick L. Carrier started his career as a teacher and was also a Universalist minister. His wife was listed as a "dressmaker" on the marriage record.

On the 1900 census for Frederick, he is living in Haverhill, New Hampshire,[405] in the Charles B. Griswold household on Elm Street. Frederick is a boarder and makes his living as a "clergyman." In this same household is a servant by the name of Luna Little.

On the next street (Smith Street) lives Gertrude Little, and she is a boarder in the Clarence Randall family. Frederick and S. Gertrude could have met through church, or perhaps through Luna Little, who was the sister of Gertrude.

This couple moved around but they were easily found via the various census records, as well as military and birth/death records.

The *United States Veterans Administration Master Index, 1917–1940* through FamilySearch shows that Frederick L. Carrier served in the War with Spain on July 22, 1898. While he

---

398 The year of death is from his headstone in Restland Cemetery in Brimfield, Ohio. The year of his birth coincides with the year of birth given on the 1900 census.

399 *Ohio County Marriage Records, 1774–1993*. Ancestry.

400 Elmer is said to have loved literature and his schoolmaster's desk is housed in the Kelso Museum in Brimfield.

401 *Ohio, Births and Christenings Index, 1774–1973*, Ancestry.

402 *California Death Index, 1940–1947*, FamilySearch.

403 *New Hampshire, Marriage and Divorce Records, 1659–1947*, Ancestry.

404 *California Death Index, 1905–1939*, Ancestry.

405 1900 Federal Census, FamilySearch.

stated he was living in Santa Ana, Orange, California, he enlisted in the infantry as a chaplin with Company 26, the 1st New Hampshire.[406]

The 1910 census shows the family residing in Riverside Township, California. The household includes his wife, Gertrude, and son, Stuart. Frederick's occupation is a "minister" in the Universalist Church.

In 1920 they are living at 901 S. Birch Street in Santa Ana, California, where Frederick is now a high school physics teacher. By 1923, he is listed as a teacher and a pastor of All Souls Universalist Church on 657 Lemon Street in Riverside.[407]

In 1930 Frederick is now a widower, his wife, Gertrude, having died in 1926. The census does not list any occupation for him, and he may have retired.

On June 17, 1933, Frederick and his son, Stuart, are listed on the *New York Passenger and Crew Lists, 1909, 1925–1957.*[408] The ship, *President McKinley,* sailed from Los Angeles and arrived in New York on July 1, 1933. The reason for this trip is unknown, but perhaps it was just to take some time away.

Other than voter registration records (Frederick was a Republican and his son, Stuart, a Democrat), nothing more is known concerning Frederick until his death.

This couple had three children, but only one survived to adulthood. They are:

*aaa .i.* Edson Stuart/Stuart Edson Carrier,[9] b. 4 Oct 1905, Mason, Warren, Ohio; d. 18 Mar 1974, Riverside, California. Stuart followed in the Carrier footsteps and became a teacher. After his mother's death, Stuart lived with his father in the home at 901 S. Birch Street in Santa Ana. The 1940 census shows that Frederick's sister, Ethel (Bissell), is also living in the household. Stuart is a high school teacher during this time.

At the age of thirty-seven, he was required to register for the draft. The registration card shows he worked for the Santa Ana School Board, in Orange, California. His physical description was given as "5'6"" tall; "150 pounds;" with blue eyes, red hair, and a ruddy complexion.[409] Photos of Stuart Carrier can be found through Ancestry via the U.S. School Yearbooks, 1900–1990. Stuart Carrier remained a bachelor.

*bbb. ii.* Frederick Emerson Carrier,[9] b. 28 Sep 1907, Mason, Warren County, Ohio; d. 4 Nov 1909, Mason, Warren County, Ohio. This child died from convulsions and is buried in Cincinnati, Ohio.

*ccc. iii.* Unnamed Child; b. 26 Feb 1912,[9] Aberdeen, Brown, South Dakota; died and buried the same day in Olivewood Cemetery. The child was stillborn.[410]

---

406 According to a Wikipedia article, this unit was assigned to the Third Brigade, Third Division, First Army Corp. There were 952 enlisted men.

407 This church was built in 1891–1892 and still stands today. The church is listed on the National Register of Historic Places and is now called Universalist Unitarian Church of Riverside and the address is now 3657 Lemon Street.

408 Information via FamilySearch.

409 *U.S. WWII Draft Cards Young Men, 1940–1947,* National Archives and Records Administration.

410 Records for bbb. ii. and ccc. iii. are from FamilySearch.

***The Children of Joseph Lucius Carrier and Mary Edson continued...***

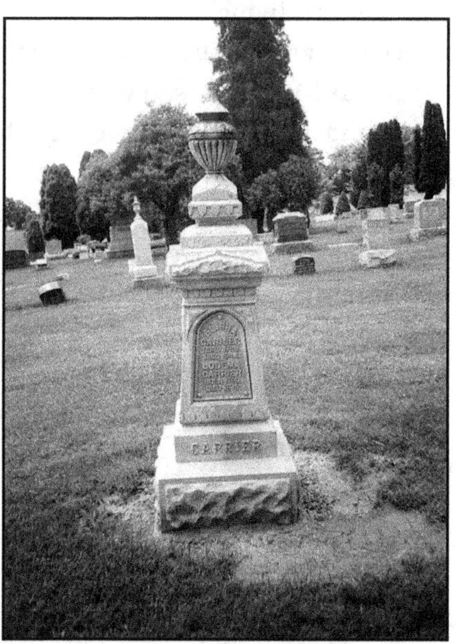

*aa. iv.* Ethel June Carrier,[8] b. 23 Jan 1872, Brimfield, Portage, Ohio;[411] d. 23 Nov 1956, Riverside, California;[412] buried Aurora Cemetery, Aurora, Portage, Ohio;[413] m. 19 Sep 1900, Portage, Portage, Ohio, Sylvester Loy Bissell; he b. 7 May 1876, Ohio; d. 2 February 1938, Portage, Ohio.[414] Ethel was a teacher on the 1900 census, but on consecutive census reports she is listed at home. Her husband was a salesman for Standard Oil. They had one child, Herman Bissell, b. 19 Apr 1907, Kent, Ohio: d. 30 Dec 1977, Ravenna, Portage, Ohio. He married Grace McClintock.[415, 416]

## *12. Almira Scoville[5] (Ithamar,[4] Timothy,[3] Stephen,[2] Stephen,[1] Arthur)*

Born circa 1796 in either Cornwall or Norfolk, Litchfield, Connecticut;[417] died 31 Jan 1868, Maine, Broome, New York; buried Maine Town Cemetery;[418] married Horace Kelsey circa 1820, perhaps in Austerlitz, Columbia, New York; born 21 April 1798, New Marlborough, Berkshire, Massachusetts.[419] His parentage has not been verified.[420]

A clue that Almira is the daughter of Ithamar comes from two people. One is a descendant of William H. Scoville (the great-grandson of Ithamar), and the other is a descendant of Almira Scoville. These two people, who had knowledge of one another, had the same exact

---

411 *Ohio, County Marriage Records, 1774–1993,* Ancestry.

412 *California, Death Index, 1940–1997,* Ancestry; Find-A-Grave website.

413 Find-A-Grave, Sec A Row 24.

414 Find-A-Grave, Sec A Row 24.

415 All vital records comes from Ancestry.

416 This photo was sent to me many years ago. Unfortunately, I no longer have the sender's information.

417 Since Ithamar Scoville is not on the *Grand Lists* for Cornwall in 1796, it is likely he was in Norfolk by this time. Since Almira died at the age of 72, her year of birth would be about 1796.

418 Find-A-Grave website.

419 Birth information provided by the obituary notice in the *Owego Gazette,* published October 30, 1890.

420 Some online family trees have speculated that Daniel Kelsey "of Killingworth, Middlesex County, Connecticut," and Abigail Hurd are his parents, as there are many Kelseys from the Killingworth area, however, there is no proof that Horace comes from this couple.

photos of Horace Kelsey and Almira Scoville. The person who is the descendant of William H. Scoville never shared her photos on any online platform. I believe that this is more than a mere coincidence and certainly serendipity.

Almira Scoville would "fit" nicely as a daughter of Ithamar (age under ten) on the 1800 census, as well as a daughter (age between ten and sixteen) on the 1810 census.

While this information in and of itself is not conclusive proof, the theory that Almira is the daughter of Ithamar is plausible.

Almira spent a good portion of her young life between Cornwall and Norfolk. Her young life must have been filled with uncertainty as her parents had been warned out of Cornwall on two recorded occasions because they were considered paupers and Cornwall did not want to pay for their upkeep (even though Ithamar was born in Cornwall and had resided there). Whatever the reason, the powers in Cornwall wanted them out to return to Norfolk.

In 1820, Almira married a man named Horace Kelsey. Horace is said to have been born in New Marlborough, Massachusetts. Almira may have met Horace while her family was living in Norfolk. The distance between Norfolk, Connecticut, and New Marlborough, Massachusetts, is approximately ten miles. Granted, the roadways would have been much rougher during that time, but it would have been easy enough for a man to go courting; going back and forth between northern Connecticut and southern Massachusetts would not be unusual.

Unlike his wife, Almira, we have bits and pieces of Horace's young life revealed in his obituary. Horace had been "bound out at the age of six years." Being bound out meant that a child (or children) could be removed from their homes by local authorities[421] to work as servants for "more respectable" families. They had to work for their master for a certain number of years (usually until the age of twenty-one) in exchange for food, shelter, and some sort of education.

In the summer of 1813 (when Horace was fifteen years old), he received such "usage he could not bear it and ran away and was gone until November 1815." Where was he for those two years? If he went back to his family, I believe that is the first place the authorities would have looked for him. *If* he had a family to go back to.

Horace finally returned to his "master" and remained with the man until February 1818, when "by consent of both parties he left for good." Horace was twenty years old at this time and still would have had one year left on his "contract." It is unfortunate that we do not know where his servitude took place or who he was bound out to. Searching old newspaper articles for a "runaway" servant has proved to be fruitless.

When reviewing the 1800 census for New Marlborough, Massachusetts, only one family by the name of Kelsey resides in said town—David Kelsey. There is one male child under the age of ten in the household. Of course, this could be a male from age one through nine and it doesn't necessarily mean it was a son of David's. But let's look at the "facts" of this family as we can ascertain from the available records. David Kelsey is said to have been born on August

421 For much of the 1800s, orphans and children of families who were too poor to care for them were apprenticed or bound out to learn a trade. These matters would often be brought up in the town or county court.

17, 1763, in Alford, Berkshire County, Massachusetts, and died May 12, *1806*.[422] He married on December 11, 1788, in Killingworth, Middlesex County, Connecticut, to Olive Parmalee. She was born in 1759 and died in *1803*.

If Horace was six years old when he went into servitude, the year in which his servitude began was about 1804—only a year after his speculative mother had died. David Kelsey is said to have died two years later, so none of the children had parents to raise them. It is also possible that Horace was sent to a near relative, but that relative could not afford another mouth to feed and had him "bound out."

As tantalizing as this information may seem, the *Kelsey Genealogy* published in 1928 does not include any information on David and Olive Kelsey as having lived in New Marlborough, Massachusetts. Since the bulk of the information (for the Kelsey book) was submitted by various descendants, it is difficult to know what sources the author used to verify the data—if any.

Another *Public Tree* submitter via Ancestry has David Kelsey being the son of Daniel Kelsey (1739–1810) and Jemima Bronson (1732–1806) with a spouse of Olive Parmalee (1759–1803). Since none of the submitters provided any sources, we can presume that they "grabbed" information willy-nilly and placed it in their trees.

What *is* known, however, is that there *was* a David Kelsey family living in New Marlborough in 1800. Delving into the court records in and around New Marlborough may be the only way to prove Horace's parentage.[423]

Without knowing who Horace's "master" was, searching the 1810 census for Horace is futile.

Horace is found on the 1820 census in Austerlitz. The 1820 federal census was begun on Monday, August 7th. Since Horace is listed as the head of the household and between the ages of 16–26, we can presume the woman also listed as between the ages of 16–26 is Almira, and that this couple married prior to the date of the census. I question whether this couple married in Austerlitz for the simple fact that a young woman on her own would not have traveled with a man who was neither her husband nor a relative.

It is more likely that this couple married in or around her "hometown" where family members could be present, or a family member traveled as a chaperone to Austerlitz.

What was their desire to strike out to Austerlitz? The town was established on March 28, 1818, by the act of the New York legislature (even though it had been settled some sixty years earlier). It was new land . . . and fertile new land, with many "watered powered mills and other industries."[424] How long this couple remained in Austerlitz I cannot say without delving deeply into whatever records are available for this town.

While Horace's early years were fraught with unkindness and hard usage, his life went in the opposite direction as one of mercy. On May 26, 1826, Horace was ordained a Baptist

422 Other records indicate that David Kelsey died 7 March 1832, Killingworth, Connecticut, and his wife, Olive, died in 1830. Ancestry Public Tree.

423 The New Marlborough, Massachusetts, town clerk's office, as well as the Historical Society in said town, could not provide any birth information on Horace Kelsey.

424 Tom Moreland, Town Historian, *A Short History of Austerlitz*, austerlitzny.com.

minister in Columbus, Chenango County, New York, "having done most of his work in Ostego, Chenango, Tompkins, Broome, and Tioga counties."[425]

They likely had moved from Austerlitz to Columbus prior to 1826. Whether he was a circuit rider[426] or had a church of his own is debatable. His obituary notes that "he preached as a regular minister for 51 years and for four years on supply or in school h [ ] making 55 years in the ministry." While he was considered an exemplary man, his "labors were not attended with great revivals, yet he would pave the way that a revival would generally follow."[427]

What was the call to Horace's being ordained? History tells us that the Second Great Awakening was a "Protestant Revival" movement. This movement began around 1790 and gained momentum by 1800; after 1820, membership rose rapidly among Baptist and Methodist congregations, whose preachers led the movement.[428] By 1870, however, the movement began to decline.

The movement began in Kentucky and Tennessee, especially among the Baptists, Methodists, and Presbyterians. Eventually, the fervor moved east, where it also had a profound effect. Perhaps Horace, too, was caught up in this movement.

In 1830, Horace and family are living in Edmeston, Ostego, New York (this information coincides with his obituary notice). Edmeston's early settlers were primarily from New England, and it was used as a "stop-over"[429] on their way west. It is said that in this town was a "strong Baptist influence."[430] It would be of no surprise, then, that Horace settled here. The household at the time of the 1830 census shows the following inhabitants:

1 male 10–14 (Silas)
1 male 30–39 (Horace)
1 female <5 (unidentified)
1 female 5–9 (Clarissa)
1 female 30–39 (Almira)

Ten years later this family is now counted on the 1840 census as living in Greene, Chenango, New York. The first Baptist church was organized there in 1795 and was known as the *Baptist Society of East Greene*, pastored by Elder Nathaniel Kellogg.

The second Baptist church was formed in 1807 by Elder Jeduthan Gray.[431] I have not found any mention of Horace in either of these churches in the various annuals of history of the Baptist churches where he may have preached.

---

425 *Owego Gazette,* October 30, 1890.

426 Circuit riders were clergy in the Methodist Episcopal Church and related denominations. Similar itinerant preachers could be found in other faiths as well, particularly among minority faith groups. Wikipedia.

427 *Owego Gazette,* October 30, 190.

428 From *The Second Great Awakening,* courses.lumenlearning.com.

429 Robert Nonenmacher, *Town of Edmeston—History,* edmestonny.org.

430 *Ibid*

431 *History of Greene, New York, Gazetteer and Business Directory of Chenango County, N.Y. For 1869–70.* Compiled and published by Hamilton Child, Syracuse, NY

The enumerator counted the following people in Horace's household:

1 male <5 (Philo)
1 male 15–20 (Silas)
1 male 40–50 (Horace)
1 female 5–9 (Melissa)
1 female 10–15 (unidentified)
1 female 30–40 (Almira)

In addition, Horace's son-in-law, William Benson, and wife Clarissa are listed on the same page, living a couple of houses up from Horace.[432]

On June 25, 1841, Horace buys one-half acre of land from Esck H. and Amy Eddy in Pittsfield, Otsego County, New York.[433] The land in Pittsfield was bounded "on the north by two acres of Land formerly owned by Calvin Eddy and owned by Benjamin Hall on the west by Reuloff Ten Broeck on the south land's land [sic] to Henry Randall and on the East by the centre of the highway." This land was sold by Horace and Almira on April 25, 1844: "2 ½ acres in Pittsfield part of subdivision No. three in Great Lot No. Nine in Wharton Creek tract in Butters Patent. The land was sold by Jacob Ten Broeck to William Cooper, the Cayuga turnpike road, adjoining landowner Reoloff Ten Broeck and Henry Randall. Sale subject to the payment of $100 mortgage and interest executed by Horace Kelsey to Josiah G. [-? Bluey?] in Dec 1843. Land subject to conditions of Letters Patent whereby the lands were originally granted."[434]

J. H. French, the author and compiler of *Gazetteer of the State of New York,*[435] states that Pittsfield was formed from Burlington on March 24, 1797: ". . . It is centrally situated upon the W. line of the county. Its surface is hilly upland, terminating in abrupt declivities upon Undadilla River, which forms its W. boundary. Wharton Creek flows across the N.W. corner, and several small tributaries of Butternut Creek flow through the S. part. The soil is generally a slaty and gravelly loam . . . The first church (Bap.) was formed at an early period, in the S.E. part of the town."

Sometime after the sale of their property in Pittsfield, the family was living in Barker, Broome County, New York, in 1847. According to *French's Gazetteer,* there were no Baptist churches in Barker (circa 1860); however, there existed Baptist churches in neighboring towns and it's conceivable that Horace had to travel to do his preaching. Interestingly, their next move brought them to Colesville—a neighboring town to Barker—and this town (Colesville) had two Baptist churches. Perhaps Horace had hopes of starting a Baptist church in Barker, but it didn't pan out, and he subsequently removed to Colesville.

---

432 1840 census, Greene, Chenango, New York; Roll: 273; Page: 89; FHL: 0017183. Ancestry.

433 Otsego County, New York, Otsego County Deeds, 67: 458–459, Warranty deed, Horace Kelsey grantee.

434 *Ibid,* 76: 282–283, Warranty deed, Horace, and Almira Kelsey grantors, Zenas Bryant grantee, 25 April 1845.

435 John Homer French (1824–1888) was an author and compiler of gazetteers for the various counties in New York. The Gazetteer referenced here was published by R. Pearsall Smith, Syracuse, NY, 1860.

As previously mentioned, 1850 brought the Kelsey family to Colesville, Broome County, New York, where they were enumerated.

The date of the census is July 21, 1850—just a little over a month from when the census commenced on June 1st. I point this out as it is said that Horace also resided in Maine (Broome County) as he served as a minister there in 1850.[436] Since this family frequently moved, it is very possible that the enumerator recorded them before or after they are said to have been in Maine of the same year.

With the 1850 census came the listing of each person by name living in the household, along with their ages and occupations and where they were born:[437]

Horrac Helsey [sic][438](age 51, Clergyman B., b. MA)
Almira (age 54, b. CT)
Malissa (age 17, b. NY, attended school within the year)
Philo (age 14, b. NY, attended school within the year)
Real Estate: $600

In 1852, Horace and his son, Silas, show up on the Broome County, Maine, tax rolls.[439] We can conclude that they both owned land during this time and were being taxed for it.

So far, we have been able to capture this couple's movements every decade, with some exceptions of extant records; that is not to say they remained in each place for ten years only to move again for the next census. This is where the New York State Census becomes a great tool to see where your ancestors were in five-year intervals. Did they remain in the same town and county, or did they move again?

The 1855 census shows that, yes indeed, the Kelsey family had moved from Colesville to Candor, a town in Tioga County. This census was taken on June 9, 1855, and apparently the couple had just moved to Candor as they are listed as only having lived there "one month out of twelve."[440] Horace is listed as a "landowner" with a "frame-house" valued at $250.

This couple is perpetually on the move, likely following Horace's assignments with the Baptist church.

We now come to the 1860 federal census, which shows Horace and Almira living in Barton, Tioga County, New York, with their mail delivery going to a post office box in Waverly—a town approximately six and a half miles from their domicile. Living with them is their son, Philo Kelsey (age 24, engaged in farming), and his wife, Elizabeth (age 26, born in New York). Horace is still making his living as a Baptist clergyman and his real estate value has increased to $700 with a personal estate of $300.

---

436 This information was provided to me by a descendant of Horace Kelsey and comes from the "Moak-Hardy-Flint-Kelsey research notes," from Mrs. Gordon H. Woodward to Blanche Monnier. Hereafter cited as Moak-Hardy-Flint-Kelsey research notes.

437 Even with this information, it should still be verified as the ages and places of birth are not always correct. 1850 census, *Colesville, Broome, New York;* Roll: 477; Page:154b. Ancestry.

438 The enumerator's handwriting has the "K" look like an "H."

439 Moak-Hardy-Flint-Kelsey research notes.

440 1855 New York State Census, Sheet: 6; Line: 6; Dwelling: 46; Family: 55. Ancestry.

By 1865 Horace and Almira are back in Maine, New York. Horace is an owner of land (a frame house valued at $150), and he was still preaching the Gospel. This census indicates that Almira was the mother of ten children. We only know the names of six of those children; some of the children may have died young and no name was ascribed to them, or the records are lost to time.

Three years later, while still living in Maine, Broome County, Almira died on January 31, 1868. She was approximately seventy-two years of age and was buried in the Maine Cemetery in Broome, New York. While the stone is very faded, it does give her year of birth as "1796."[441]

Unlike her husband, Horace, there is no obituary for Almira that tells of her life or her attributes. There are no diaries or letters showing her struggles to raise a family, the loss of children, her times of contentment and joy, who perhaps was alone much of the time while Horace was busy getting ready for sermons or revivals—and being on the "ready" to move to a new town at any time (as we have seen from the available census records, and they may have moved many more times than what has been found in the available records). As with many women of her time, her joys were having heathy children, keeping a nice home, and supporting her husband in his vocation. Unfortunately, we rarely get a glimpse of the woman behind all of that.

After the death of Almira, Horace married a second time to Celinda Bachelor.[442] Celinda was the daughter of Jeremiah Bachelor and Artemisia Heath.[443] A Jeremiah Bachelor is on the 1840 census for Barton, Tioga County, New York. He is not listed after this time on any census, and we will have to presume that he died (unless further documentation is provided). However, his wife shows up on the census reports as the head of the family in 1850, 1855, 1860, and 1865—still living in Barton, New York, with her daughter, Celinda, and sons Nelson and Lyman. It would seem likely that Jeremiah died sometime after the 1840 census.

Celinda's first marriage was to Horace at the age of forty-five (*if* her birth year of 1824 is correct). Since the Bachelor family had lived in Barton since 1840, it is likely this is how she met Horace and his family, as the Kelsey family were living in Barton per the 1860 census. According to the census, the Kelsey and Bachelor families were not neighbors and the population of the town of Barton during that year was 4,234. Horace and Celinda may have met through mutual friends or Celinda Bachelor attended the Baptist Church where Horace preached. They married sometime after Almira's death in 1868 and before the 1870 census was taken (June 1st of said year).

The 1870, 1875, and 1880 state and federal censuses (and up until Horace's death in 1890) show the Kelseys living in Barton—this is the longest time that Horace had lived anywhere in his life. While Horace may not go down in the annals of history as a powerful preacher, he was steadfast and true to his faith and continued ministering to those in need until the end of

441 Find-A-Grave website.

442 While it is known that Horace's second wife's first name was Celinda, from the census records from 1870 on her surname was unknown until recently. (As of this writing, she was the daughter of Jeremiah Bachelor and Artemesia Heath of Tompkins County, New York, and northern Connecticut. In 1900, Celinda Kelsey is living next door to "brother" Nelson Bachelor.)

443 Jeremiah Bachelor is said to have been born 1790/91 and died sometime in 1840. His wife's vitals are 1801–1869. None of this has been confirmed as of this writing.

his life at the age of ninety-two. His difficult early life led him to a calling that would last fifty-five years, moving from town to town, spreading the Gospel. While we know next to nothing about his two wives, I'd like to believe that they assisted him in his endeavors.

There are two obituaries for Horace Kelsey, which I have recorded here.

> BARTON.
> Oak Hill, Oct. 27—Horace Kelsey died on Wednesday, October 22nd. The funeral was held at the Oak Hill Church on Friday at 2 P.M. Reverend F. J. Salmon officiating. The deceased was born at New Marlboro [sic], Berkshire County Mass., April 21, 1798. At the age of six years, he was bound out. In the summer of 1813, he received such usage that he could not bear it, and ran away and was gone until November1815, when he returned and remained with the man until February 1818, and by consent of both parties left for good. He was ordained a Baptist minister May 26, 1825, at Columbus, Chenango County, New York, and has done most of his work in Ostego, Chenango, Tompkins, Broome, and Tioga Counties.
>
> He preached as a regular minister for 51 years and for four years and supply or in school h [ ] making 55 years in the ministry, and during all that time no man as far as I can learn can say that he ever brought reproach and God's cause. He was looked upon as being an exemplary man.
>
> While his labors were not attended with any great revivals, yet he would pave the way for the revival that would generally follow. He leaves a wife and two daughters, one living, I believe at Triangle, N. Y., and the other at Maine, N. Y., and his wife at the old homestead on Oak Hill.[444]

The second obituary is very brief:

> The Rev. Horace Kelsey a superannuated clergyman of the Baptist denomination died in Barton, New York on Sunday, aged 92 years. For a number of years and since his retirement from active work, he has lived on his farm, near the village of Barton. He leaves several children who are well advanced in years.[445]

The copy of the will is in my possession for Horace Kelsey from the Tioga, New York, Surrogate Court. The transcription of the will is not verbatim. I will only include the parts with the most interest:

> . . . to my wife Celinda Kelsy, my house and lot now owned and occupied by me situated in the town of Barton . . . to have and hold for her own use or disposal as she choose[s].
>
> . . . to my wife Celinda Kelsey, my cow and my entire household furniture, and all the use of all other property that I may possess at the time of my decease, said

444 *Owego Gazette*, Tioga County, New York, 30 October 1890.

445 The *Sun and New York Press.*, November 7, 1890 edition; Vol: 58- 4.

> property to be converted into money by my executrix at her option . . . the interest to be paid her annually to my wife Celinda Kelsey (this is interest secured by Bond and Mortgage).
>
> . . . excepting and reserving from the above-mentioned property in the sum of one hundred dollars which I hereby give and bequeath to my daughter-in-law Betsey Kelsey to be paid [from the executrix after all debts are paid].
>
> . . . that my wife Celinda Kelsey that she shall use so much of the principal as may be necessary.
>
> . . . I do further order that whatever amount shall be left or remain of my estate at the death of my wife Celinda, shall be given to my two daughters, Clarissa Benson and Melissa Flint, and my daughter-in-law Betsey Kelsey to be divided equally with the three.

Horace appointed his wife, Celinda Kelsey, as his sole executrix of his *last will and testament, hereby revoking all former wills by me made.*

On the 14th day of March 1891, the will was approved.[446]

New York had a state census taken in 1892, where we see that Selinda [sic] Kelsey is living alone in Barton, sixty-five years of age. By 1900 she has removed to Van Etten, Chemung County, New York, living next door to her brother, Nelson Bachelor, who is now widowed and living with his son and daughter-in-law. Nelson Bachelor died April 13, 1903, in Van Etten and is buried with his wife in Westbrook Cemetery, Van Etten.

An undocumented source indicates that Celinda Kelsey died July 6, 1901, likely in Van Etten. She is not listed on the 1905 New York census, and she is not listed in the household of her nephew, Llewellyn/Lovelling Bachelor (son of Nelson and Roxena Bachelor). The presumption was that she died sometime between 1900–1905, with the date of 1901 a possibility; however, two newspaper articles were found in *Valley Breeze,* a newspaper in Van Ettenville, New York. The first article was published July 5, 1901: "Miss Selinda Bachelor is seriously ill at her home on Barnes Hill."

The second article was published in the same newspaper on July 12, 1901:

> Miss Selinda Batchelor aged 80 years died at her home on Barnes Hill, Wednesday, July 3. The funeral was held from the home of her brother, Nelson Batchelor, Saturday, July 6, and was attended by a large concourse of relatives and friends. She was a consistent Christian lady and death was a welcome relief from her terrible suffering.[447]

What is curious in both articles is the use of her maiden name (Batchelor) instead of the name Kelsey. The reason for this would be purely speculative.

---

446 Since the will was sent to me by another party, I do not have the proper source to site here, but Ancestry does have this on record under *New York Wills and Probate Records, 1659–1999.*

447 Articles provided by Deborah L. Horzen.

~

The two photos of Horace Kelsey as shown were taken at different times. The photo on the left is courtesy of Deborah Horzen, a descendant of Horace. The photo on the right is courtesy of Sandra Amador, a descendant of William H. Scoville (a distant cousin of this author).[448] The photo was labeled "Horace Selsey, 4/18/1876, sister's husband." We had no idea why he was in her collection of Scoville photos until Deborah and I made contact and shared the photos.

Horace Kelsey (courtesy of Deborah L. Horzen)

Horace Kelsey (courtesy of Sandra Amador)

Almira Scoville Kelsey (courtesy of Sandra Amador and Deborah L. Horzen)

448 Deborah L. Horzen is also in possession of the Sandra Amador photo as well.

The photo of Almira Kelsey is one that is in the collection of Deborah Horzen and Sandra Amador.

The photos from Sandra Amador are labeled "Almira Selsey, age 71 on 9/24/1866, sister of William Harrison Scoville." This information is incorrect as to who the brother was—it was, in fact, Franklin Scoville, *father* of William H. Scoville, who was the brother of Almira. While the name was recorded as "Selsey" on the Amador photos, they are certainly the same people. These photos give further credence that Almira *was* the daughter of Ithamar Scoville and sister to Franklin Scoville.

**_Children of Horace Kelsey and Almira Scoville_**

i. Lyle Kelsey,[6] b. between 1820–1825. Nothing more is known.

16. Silas Kelsey,[6] b. Apr 1816; d. 10 Sept 1861, age 45 years, 5 months; m. (1) Patsy/Patty M.; m. (2) Flavia ______ after 1848 and before 1850.

17. Clarissa Kelsey,[6] b. 1822; d. Oct 1890; m. about 1840, New York, William Benson; b. about 1816, Lewis Co., New York.

ii. A daughter, b. between 1825–1830, New York. Nothing more is known.

18. Melissa Kelsey,[6] b. 13 Feb 1833, Ostego Co., New York; d. 21 Jun 1910, Madison Township, Hancock Co., Iowa; buried 23 Jun 1910, Concord Cemetery, Garner, Hancock Co.; m. (1) Abner Flint, Jr.; (2 ) Lester Buck; (3) John W. Garlow.

19. Philo Kelsey,[6] b. 1836, Danby, Tompkins Co., New York; d. 15 Aug 1864 in the General Hospital number 1, Chattanooga, Tennessee; m. 5 Apr 1858, West Danby, Tompkins, New York; Elizabeth "Betsy" Cowles, b. 29 Nov 1834, Spencer, Tioga, New York; d. 20 Jul 1891, Spencer, Tioga, New York; daughter of Elon Cowles (1795–1872) and Lucinda Case (1799–1894).

## *13. **Franklin Scoville,**[5] (Ithamar,[4] Timothy,[3] Stephen,[2] Stephen,[1] Arthur)*

Born 29 August 1809, Cornwall, Litchfield, Connecticut;[449] died 11 July 1901,[450] Pine Meadow, Litchfield, Connecticut; married 6 Oct 1830,[451] Norfolk, Amarilla Hotchkiss; she born 17 January 1810,[452] Norfolk; died 6 June 1882; Pine Meadow, Litchfield, Connecticut; daughter of Oliver Hotchkiss and Rebecca Sturdevant.

---

449 A personal diary of 1896 states, "Father Scoville, died August 29, 1809;" (see Ancestry). The owner/writer of this diary was Elmina Smith (1826–1905), daughter of Carlo Smith and Amanda Goodwin. Franklin Scoville's daughter, Irene Scoville, married Merritt Ellsworth Smith, brother of Elmina. Photo of the diary available for review. *Hale Collection of Cemetery Inscriptions and Newspaper Notices 1662–1934;* Find-A-Grave and my own personal visit to Pine Grove Cemetery in Pine Meadow; obituary notice.

450 *Ibid—Hale Collection,* Find-A-Grave, visit to cemetery.

451 *Connecticut Marriage Index 1620–1929,* Barbour Collection. Ancestry.

452 Personal visit to Pine Grove Cemetery, Pine Meadow; Find-A-Grave and Nellie Cowdell's, *The Hotchkiss Family First Six Generations Descendants of Samuel Hotchkiss (ca. 1662–1663) of New Haven Connecticut,* Vol.1:277, (1985).

Every time I look at the photo of my third great-grandfather, he seems to have an openness, friendliness about him. Of course, I may be projecting my own feelings on a photo, but based on an obituary notice, he had all those qualities and more—but more on that later.

As with most of our early ancestors it is difficult to paint a portrait of their early lives. What do we know?

Franklin was born in a very sparsely populated town, perhaps around Meekertown Road in Norfolk, and lived with his parents. We know that times were tough for this Scoville family (based on the "warnings out" records for Ithamar), but Franklin seems to have overcome all of that. He was a lover of reading and had many friends. His marriage lasted fifty-two years and they had six loving children.

Franklin spent his life in the County of Litchfield in the towns of Norfolk, Barkhamsted, North Canaan, Colebrook, and, finally, in Pine Meadow (a village of New Hartford), and in two towns in Hartford County: Canton and Hartland.

As I proposed in the section of Amasa Scoville (conjectured brother of Franklin), I believe that the male listed as aged between twenty and thirty on the 1830 census for Torrington, Connecticut, is Franklin, as he cannot be found listed as a head of his own household. The 1830 census commenced on June 1, and Franklin married on October 6, 1830. Regrettably, prior to 1850, the enumerators did not record when they made their entries on any particular day. Despite this, it is plausible that Franklin lived with his brother prior to his marriage and then made a way for himself and his wife.

This couple's first child is recorded in 1832 in New Marlborough, Berkshire County, Massachusetts. Whether another child was born prior to this time has not been found in any records that I've been able to review. The same can be said as to why they were in New Marlborough; this town borders Litchfield County, Connecticut, and is not far from North Canaan and Norfolk. Whether Franklin was working in the town, visiting, or had resided there is a question I have not been able to answer.[453]

After Franklin's marriage in 1830 and the registered birth of his first child in 1832 there are no further records to be found until 1836, when he bought and sold land apparently on the same day in Colebrook, Connecticut:

> I Levi Bolls of Colebrook in consideration of $150 of Franklin Scovil of Canton one certain piece on parcel of land lying inside Colebrook containing about 20 rods of ground more or less with a dwelling house standing on the same and bounded as follows: East on highway, South on Allen Greens land, West and North on Erastus Seymour's land.[454] September 21, 1836.
>
> I Franklin Scovil of Canton in the County of Hartford to Wyllis Bunnell of Barkhamsted in consideration of $96 a certain piece of land lying in Colebrook in the County of Litchfield and State of Connecticut containing about 20 rods of

453 The 1830 census was read page by page for New Marlborough, Berkshire, Massachusetts, and Franklin was not listed.

454 Colebrook Land Records, Vol: 10:60. Paper copies in my possession via the Connecticut State Library.

ground more or less with a dwelling house standing on the same bounded East on highway South on Allen Greens land West and North on Erastus Seymours land.[455] September 21, 1836.

I Franklin Scovil of Canton for $54 of Levi Bolls a certain piece of land lying in Colebrook aforesaid containing about twenty rods of ground more or less with a dwelling house standing on the same bounded East on highway South on Allen Greens land West and North on Erastus Seymours land subject however to a mortgage this day given to Wyllis Bunnell.[456] September 21, 1836.

Two years later, in 1838, Franklin was of "Hartland" and for "$96 to Wyllis Bunnell of New Hartford" bought "a certain piece of land lying in Colebrook in the County of Litchfield and State of Connecticut containing twenty rods of ground more or less with a dwelling house standing on the same bounded East on highway South on Allen Greens land West on Erastus Seymours land. Also, a cooking stove belonging to said house."[457] The date of this document is January 2, 1838.

These transactions all concern a piece of property that is in Colebrook, Connecticut. From all appearances, Franklin bought this property for $150 from Levi Bolls. One the same day, Wyllis Bunnell pays to Franklin $96.00 for the same piece of property. Franklin then receives $54 from Levi Bolls (this would be the balance due for the property).

The mortgage was now satisfied, and the final transaction transfers the property to Wyllis Bunnell.

It appears that Franklin re-purchased this property for $96 in 1838 from Wyllis Bunnell.

By the time the 1840 census rolled around the Franklin Scoville family were living in Barkhamsted in district twenty-eight. Barkhamsted is in northeastern Litchfield County where the Farmington River flows through it. The town was once allocated to Windsor (Connecticut) in 1732 and the early proprietors used the land for farming and raising livestock. The General Assembly renamed the town Berkhamsted. The town was not officially recognized until 1779 and it wasn't until 1795 that the present spelling of Barkhamsted was used.

The population or Barkhamsted at the time of the census was 1,571.[458] One of its main employers was Hitchcock Chair Factory, built circa 1825–1826 by Lambert Hitchcock in the Riverton section of Barkhamsted.[459] It is plausible that Franklin may have worked in this factory during the time he was living in the town. Since the census records from 1790–1840 do not provide any additional information other than who is in the household, I can only speculate who the residents are:

The Scoville (listed as Franklin Scovel) family is as follows:

2 males <5 born between 1835–1840 (Charles and William)
1 male 5–9 born between 1831–1835 (Charles? He born circa 1835.)
1 male 30–39 born between 1801–1810 (Franklin)

---

455 *Ibid*, Vol. 10:70.

456 *Ibid*, Vol. 10:71.

457 *Ibid*, Vol. 10:422

458 *Population of Connecticut Towns 1830–1890*, portal.ct.gov.

459 *Historic Buildings of Connecticut*, historicbuidingsct.com.

1 female <5 born between 1835–1840 (Julia)
1 female 5–9 born between 1831–1935 (Irene)
1 female 30–39 born between 1801–1810 (Amarilla)

All the children born prior to 1840 are known to me except the "extra" male who is listed on this census. The son Charles can fit into either category as he was born circa 1835, but it still leaves a question mark as to who the other male is.

During the1840s two more sons were born: Albert Franklin, born in Colebrook, August 1, 1846, and Lucius Edwin, born in Winchester, June 31, 1848.[460]

By 1850 the family is living in New Hartford. The census for this family was taken on October 12. The reason for highlighting this date will become clear further on in this account.

New Hartford was settled around 1733 by the Hartford patentees (and subsequently named New Hartford). The town is a hilly and mountainous[461] area. It is bounded north by Barkhamsted, east by Canton, west by Torrington, and south by Burlington and Harwinton.

To return to the census, we now have the names, ages, and occupations of the members of the household:

Dwelling #171; Family #191

Francis Scoville, 40, male, sawyer,[462] (born) CT
Amarilla Scoville, 40, female, CT
Chat Scoville, 15, male, CT
Julia Scoville, 12, female, CT
Wm Scoville, 11, male, CT
Albert Scoville, 5, male, CT
Lucius Scoville, 2, male CT

You will notice the age gap between William and Albert—I suspect that Amarilla may have had one to two more children during that gap, but they did not survive.

Additionally, you will note that daughter Irene is absent from the household. In checking the 1850 census for her, I found an "Irene Scovil," age 18, in the Zenas Dyer household in Canton, Hartford County, Connecticut. This census was taken on August 30, 1850—forty-two days prior to the enumerator visiting the Scoville residence. In addition, "Charles Scovil," age 16, was also in the Zenas Dyer household working as a "laborer." These two are not listed as any relation to the Dyer family, and there are three others of various names also working for the Dyers.

Zenas Dyer was an innkeeper[463] and lived with his wife and a son and daughter (relationship

460 All birth dates and places for the children of Franklin and Amarilla Scoville are supported by vital records.

461 "Mountainous" is a loosely used term for Connecticut hills, which are certainly nothing like the mountains out west.

462 A sawyer is someone who cuts trees and/or works in a sawmill.

463 Dyer's Tavern, built in 1789, still stands today as a historic building in Canton, Connecticut, at 1 Dyer Cemetery Road, off Route 44. The former name was Dyer's Inn and Tavern. Zenas's father, Daniel, gave the house to his son as a wedding present. Unfortunately, it is no longer a tavern or an

based on their surnames). While I cannot prove with documentary evidence that the Irene and Charles Scovil listed with the Dyers are the same children belonging with the Scoville family, my instinct tells me that they are—simply based on their ages and the proximity from New Hartford to Canton, these are indeed Franklin's children.

As previously stated via the 1850 census, Franklin's occupation was that of a sawyer. There is an article in Wikipedia entitled *Gillette's Gristmill.* The article is about a grist mill in New Hartford that is on the National Register of Historic Places.[464] I mention this because the owner of the gristmill (Joseph Gillette) also operated a series of industries in the nineteenth century . . . including two sawmills. It's possible that Franklin worked at one of those two sawmills during his time in New Hartford.

The 1860 and 1870 censuses shows the Scovilles are now living in North Canaan,[465] Connecticut. The history of this town is rather complicated, and I would suggest reading further regarding Canaan's history for those who are interested.

The main industry in and around this area was iron ore. A monument to the history of the blast furnace, which makes the products from the ore, is in East Canaan: the Beckley Blast Furnace, located on the Blackberry River. It was built in 1847 by John Adam Beckley and the furnace produced large quantities of pig iron, which is refined to produce steel or wrought iron.[466] Charcoal also had to be made to feed the furnace. If you recall, Franklin's father, Ithamar, lived in an area where there were many remnants of charcoal pits. Working around the blast furnace and making charcoal were very hazardous occupations.

According to the 1860 census, Franklin's occupation was a "mechanic." Agriculture was still a robust enterprise in New England. Connecticut had small workshops and factories well before the 1840s.[467] According to *Gazetteer of the Manufactures and Manufacturing Towns Of The United States—Connecticut,* North Canaan "contains one iron foundry and a sash and blind company, besides several country stores."[468] It's likely that Franklin worked in the foundry as a mechanic during this time.

In addition, the Scoville household became smaller in 1860, with only his wife, Amarilla, and two of their sons, William and Albert, still living at home. The older children had married, and some had moved to other towns.

On December 17, 1865, Amarilla's mother died in Norfolk. Her father followed three years later on November 29, 1868, also in Norfolk. They are both buried in Center Cemetery in said town.

---

inn and has been divided into six apartments.

464 "National Register Information System," *National Register of Historic Places.* National Park Service. July 9, 2010.

465 "The town of North Canaan, known locally as Canaan, did not separate from the parent town of Canaan until 1858. The Town of Canaan, known by many today as Falls Village, kept the original name, and confusion over the two municipal entities has plagued visitors and state officials ever since." northcanaan.org.

466 Connecticuthistory.org.

467 Brown University, David R. Meyer, *The Roots of American Industrialization, 1790–1860, The Puzzle of Industrialization. Eh.net*

468 Publisher: J.M. Bradstreet & Son. books.google.com.

The 1870 census for North Canaan was taken on the tenth day of June. The family is comprised of Franklin, Amarilla, and their youngest son, Lucius. Included in the family dynamic is their grandson, Albert, age thirteen, who is attending school.

Albert was the child of Franklin's late son Charles Scoville and his wife Catherine, who was now living in New Britain, Connecticut. Whether Albert was visiting or living with his grandparents for a time is unknown. Albert's mother, Catherine, had remarried two years after her husband's death. It's possible the transition of having a stepfather was difficult for Albert and he was sent to his grandparents' home for a time.

Franklin is once again listed as a "farmer" and is now sixty-one years old and no longer working in the foundry. At least his son Lucius would be able to assist his father with the farming.

I've often wondered whether, while Franklin was living in North Canaan, he lived anywhere near where his father, Ithamar, had lived in Falls Village (Canaan) at a place he called "Ithamar's Garden." While this may be a fanciful idea, it speaks of quiet and rest and the joy of nature. Perhaps Ithamar Scoville was a fanciful individual to have named such a place. I am certain such a place existed, but it is doubtful any land record would ever be found for such a place called "Ithamar's Garden."

Sometime after 1870, the couple had removed to Pine Meadow, a village within New Hartford, Connecticut.

The 1880 census shows the elderly Scovilles were now living with their eldest daughter, Irene, and their son-in-law, Merritt E. Smith, along with Merritt's mother, Amanda (Goodwin) Smith. Merritt's mother is listed as "infirm," and Irene's mother, Amarilla, is occupied with housekeeping. The Smiths did have a "servant" in the household by the name of William Thorp, "age 32," who is also listed as a "laborer." Merritt Smith is listed as a "farmer" and [ ][469] maker.

According to a land ownership map of 1874,[470] the Smiths were living on Wicket Street on a reasonably sized property with the Farmington River flowing nearby.

On June 6, 1882, Franklin's wife, Amarilla, died. She was seventy-two years old and had been married to Franklin for fifty-two years. She bore seven children—at least one or two who did not survive infancy.

Amarilla was the daughter of Oliver Hotchkiss (*Josiah,[5] James,[4] Samuel,[3] Samuel,[2] Samuel,[1] John*) and Rebecca Sturdevant (*James,[4] James,[3] John,[2] John,[1] William*). The immigrant ancestor, Samuel,[1] came from England and settled in what was New Haven Colony, which was settled 1637/38. At some point James[2] Hotchkiss either was in Norfolk, Litchfield County, Connecticut, or resided there for a time, as his son Josiah was born there in 1755, and

469 I have not been able to decipher this word, comparing the first letter to others on the page without success.

470 See *U.S. Indexed County Land Ownership Maps, 1860–1918,* 1874, Pine Meadow, Town of New Hartford via Ancestry.com or through the Library of Congress, Washington, D.C.

this is where the family remained.[471] Amarilla's maternal line has a similar history. William Sturdevant was born in Norwalk, Fairfield County, Connecticut, in 1650. The Sturdevant line is a little "muddier," as it is unknown when William came to Connecticut, or even if he came from England.

Since this is not a genealogy on the Sturdevant line, suffice it to say that William Sturdevant's great-grandson, James[3] Sturdevant, made his way to Norfolk and settled there for a time.

Amarilla was one of ten children (Rebecca, Merritt, Oliver Lucius, William, Martin Luther, Betsy, Matilda, Lavinia, and Lucy) and many of her own children would share some of these names as their second (or middle) name. By the time her children were born, the naming patterns had changed. The Biblical names of the Scovilles from a generation or two back were no longer used.

After the death of his wife, Franklin continued to live with his daughter Irene and son-in-law Merritt in Pine Meadow. We have a snapshot of Franklin over the years from a few articles printed in a North Canaan newspaper called *Connecticut Western News*.[472]

*March 25, 1915—Gossip of Days Gone By* (originally published in 1883)

—Franklin Scoville, formerly of Canaan, now of Pine Meadow, was a guest of Canaan relatives.

*April 18, 1891—North Canaan*

—Franklin Scoville of Pine Meadow, is visiting his son, L. E. Scoville.

*August 31, 1893—North Canaan*

—Franklin Scoville of Pine Meadow is visiting his son, L. E. Scoville.

*June 14, 1894—North Canaan*

—Franklin Scoville of Pine Meadow arrived last Thursday to visit his son Lucius for an indefinite time.

*August 27, 1894—North Canaan*

—Franklin Scoville of Pine Meadow, is visiting his son, L. E. Scoville, and calling on his old friends in town.

*September 2, 1897—North Canaan*

—Lucius Scoville and his wife went to New Hartford and spent Sunday with Mr. Franklin Scoville, it being his 88th birthday.

*June 1, 1899—North Canaan*

—Franklin Scoville of Pine Meadow is visiting his son Lucius, and family in this place.

*September 21, 1899—North Canaan*

—Franklin Scoville of Pine Meadow reached the age of 90 years on August 29 and he celebrated his birthday by walking several miles visiting his acquaintances. He

471 For a full account of the Hotchkiss line, see Nellie Cowdell's *The Hotchkiss Family First Six Generations Samuel Hotchkiss (ca. 1622–1663) Vol.1.* Gateway Press, Inc. (1985).

472 The *Connecticut Western News* was founded in Salisbury, Connecticut, in 1871, by editor and owner Joseph L. Pease. In 1876 the print shop was moved to the nearby village of Canaan and the paper was published in North Canaan. All articles come from Genealogy Bank.

formerly resided in Canaan. His son still resides here.

The last news article on Franklin was his obituary notice. As I mentioned earlier, there were two obituaries and one death notice. Both are from the *New Hartford Tribune*:

*New Hartford Tribune 19 July 1901:*
Deaths: In Pine Meadow, July 11, Franklin Scoville, aged 92 years.[473]

The second notice is a news column: "Mr. Franklin Scoville died very suddenly last Thursday afternoon at five o'clock at the age of 92 years. The funeral was held from the house of J. C. Smith Saturday afternoon at two o'clock, Reverend Henry Tarrant officiating. Relatives were present from Winsted, New Britain, Bristol, Canaan, Westboro, and other places. His son Albert Scoville and wife remained over Sunday with his sister, Mrs. Merritt Smith, who is Scoville's daughter."

The second obituary came from the Thursday edition of the *Connecticut Western News*, published July 18, 1901:

**Death of Franklin Scoville**
Most of the following sketch of the late Franklin Scoville, who was for a number of years resided in Canaan is copied from the Winsted Citizen, but some corrections and additions were made by the News after interviewing Lucius E. Scoville who resides here in Canaan.

Franklin Scoville, the oldest in very highly respected resident of Pine Meadow, died there on Thursday, July 11 at 5:30 p.m. He was born in the town of Cornwall, August 29, 1809, and was married to Amarilla Hotchkiss, October 6, 1830. Seven children were born to them, one dying in infancy.

One son, Charles M., a member of the 14th Connecticut Volunteers in the late Civil War, died in Alexandria in 1864. Five children survive him, Mrs. Irene Smith of Pine Meadow, Mrs. Julia Raidart of Robertsville, William of Noroton, Connecticut: Albert of Worcester, Mass., and Lucius of Canaan, Conn.

He relocated in Pine Meadow about sixty-five years ago. Removing from there to Canaan, he returned in 1875, since which he has made his residence in Pine Meadow. His wife died June 6, 1882. Since then, he has resided with is daughter, Mrs. Irene Smith who has made a very pleasant home for him in his old age.

Mr. Scoville was of commanding stature, very industrious, a great reader and kept himself well posted on the general topics of the day, of kindly disposition and sociable. He followed the occupation of a farmer nearly all his life and will be missed by a large circle of friends.

Since Mr. Scoville returned to Pine Meadow in 1875, he frequently visited his relatives and friends in Canaan, and he will be missed by many persons in Canaan.

His funeral took place Saturday afternoon at 2 o'clock from the residence of his daughter, Mrs. Smith. Internment in Pine Meadow.

473 Receipt of a letter from Roger W. Jones of New Hartford, Connecticut, 9 November 1982.

Franklin Scoville—photo courtesy of Sandra Amador.

Amarilla Hotchkiss Scoville—photo courtesy of Sandra Amador

Franklin and Amarilla are buried together in Pine Grove Cemetery, New Hartford, Connecticut.

***Children of Franklin Scoville and Amarilla Hotchkiss***

20. i. Irene Scoville,[6] b. 22 Sep 1832, New Marlborough, Berkshire, Massachusetts; d. 9 Feb 1927, Pine Meadow, Litchfield, Connecticut; m. sometime after 1850, marriage place unknown; Merritt Ellsworth Smith, b. 31 Mar 1828, Pine Meadow, Litchfield, Connecticut; d. 18 Mar 1892, Pine Meadow, Litchfield, Connecticut; son of Carlo Smith (1796–1852) and Amanda Goodwin (1803–1890).
21. ii. Charles Martin Scoville,[6] b. circa 1834/35,[474] probably Colebrook, Litchfield, Connecticut; d. 14 Jul 1864; buried Alexandria National Cemetery, Alexandria, Virginia; m. 20 August 1855, Colebrook, Litchfield, Connecticut, to Catherine Schneider (Snyder, Snider), b. 17 May 1838, Newark, Essex Co., New Jersey; d. 17 Dec 1908, New Britain, Hartford, Connecticut. She m. (2) 3 July 1866, New Britain, Hartford, Connecticut, Gotlieb Christian Gammerdinger; b. 6 Dec 1827, Unterjesingen, Wurttemberg, Deutschland (Germany), son of Gottfried Gammerdinger and Marie Agnes _______; d. 8 March 1888, New Britain, Hartford, Connecticut.
22. iii. Julia Rebecca Scoville,[6] b. 9 May 1837, Colebrook, Litchfield, Connecticut; d. 16 Jan 1918, Winchester, Litchfield, Connecticut; m. 19 Feb 1854 to William Henry Raidart, b. 29 Feb 1832, Worstadt, Grand Duchy of Hesse, Darmstadt, Hesse, Germany; d. 27 May 1898, Winchester, Litchfield, Connecticut.

474 According to the Town Clerk's Office, Colebrook Records of 1835/36 are missing.

23. iv. William Harrison Scoville,[6] b. 4 Dec 1839, Barkhamsted, Litchfield, Connecticut; d. 10 Sep 1911, Noroton Heights (part of Darien), Fairfield, Connecticut; m. 9 Sep 1861, North Canaan, Connecticut, Mary Catherine Dunn; b. 2 Feb 1844, New York; d. 23 Nov 1930, Tacoma, Pierce, Washington.

v. A child. Died in infancy.

24. vi. Albert Franklin Scoville,[6] b. 1 Aug 1846, Colebrook, Litchfield, Connecticut; d. 9 May 1915, Worcester, Worcester, Massachusetts; m. (1) 29 Sep 1863, Hannah E. Hall, North Canaan; she died before 1880, possibly in Massachusetts; m. (2) 20 Oct 1882, M. Estella Apperson, Worcester, Worcester, Massachusetts; b. about 1856; d. 11 Aug 1893, Worcester, Worcester, Massachusetts; m. (3) 30 Aug 1894, M. Viola Moore, Worcester, Worcester, Massachusetts; b. 12 Dec 1855, Presque Isle, Aroostook, Maine; d. 18 Oct. 1933, Springvale, York, Maine.

25. vii. Lucius Edwin Scoville,[6] b. 13 Jun 1848, Winchester, Litchfield, Connecticut; d. 14 May 1917, Torrington, Litchfield, Connecticut; m. 8 Nov 1871, either North Canaan or Sheffield, Massachusetts, Ellen (Nellie) Amanda Sullivan, b. circa 1851, Canaan, Litchfield Co., Connecticut; d. 1924, Connecticut; daughter of Sally Doolittle and John Sullivan.

# Sixth Generation

### 14. i. Charles Foote Scoville[6] (Amasa,[5] Ithamar,[4] Timothy,[3] Stephen,[2] Stephen,[1] Arthur)

Born 10 August 1821,[475] probably in Torrington,[476] Litchfield, Connecticut; died 1 January 1890,[477] Chicago, Cook, Illinois; buried in Oak Woods Cemetery,[478] Chicago, Cook, Illinois; married (1) 1 January 1846,[479] Clarissa Spencer,[480] Wolcottville, Litchfield, Connecticut; she died 5 January 1855,[481] Chicago, Cook, Illinois; buried likely in Center Cemetery,[482] Torrington, Litchfield, Connecticut; married (2) Sarah Baird, born circa 1831,[483] Scotland; died 20 November, 1891,[484] Chicago, Cook, Illinois; likely buried in the same cemetery as her husband.

Charles grew up in the town of Torrington, which, by the time of Charles' birth, was increasing, not only in population, but in industry as well. Torrington was originally called Mast Swamp, simply because of the pines that were harvested for the use in ship masts and that had other uses as well.[485] The town also became the hub of an "industrial center for the manufacture of brass needles, tacks, woolen cloth and millwork."[486]

As with so many early ancestors, we know very little about Charles' life while he lived in Torrington. The first record where his name appears is on the land deed between Amasa Scoville, "grantor" to Charles F. Scoville and Samuel D. Scoville, on May 29, 1842. This is the record previously mentioned in the narrative of Amasa Scoville, where he (Amasa) granted "rights and privileges" to his two sons.

---

475 This date comes from the headstone of Charles F. Scoville. Since his wife was still living, the date is probably accurate.

476 Charles' parents lived in Torrington and/or the village of Wolcottville at the time he was born.

477 Find-A-Grave and *Cook County, Illinois, Death Index, 1878–1922; Illinois Wills and Probate Records, 1772–1999.*

478 Find-A-Grave.

479 *Connecticut, Town Marriage Records, pre-1870 (Barbour Collection);* [Image 52 of 65; page 132]. Ancestry.

480 Clarissa Spencer, the daughter of Ebenezer Spencer (1801–1840) and Hannah Merrill (?–1873).

481 Find-A-Grave; *U.S. Newspaper Extractions from the Northeast, 1704–1930;* January 20, 1855, "age 30."

482 *Hale Collection of Cemetery Inscriptions and Newspaper Notices, 1629–1934.* The Charles R. Hale Collection. Ancestry.

483 Birth year and place is based on the various census reports and age given at death.

484 *Illinois, Select Deaths Index, 1877–1916; Illinois Statewide Death Index, pre-1916.* Ancestry.

485 Torrington, www.connecticuthistory.org; Connecticut Humanities Series.

486 *Ibid*

The next record that came to light was the marriage record between Charles F. Scoville "of Wolcottville" and Clarissa Spencer of Litchfield, who were married on January 1, 1846, in Wolcottville by the Rev. Henry Zell.[487] In addition, a newspaper article in the *Morning News* (New London, Connecticut) on January 8, 1846,[488] under the heading *Matrimony Notice,* reads, "In Wolcottville, in Trinity Church on the 1st inst, by Rev. Henry Zell, Charles F. Scoville of Wolcottville [and] Clarissa Spencer, of Litchfield . . ."

By the 1850 census, this couple were no longer living in Torrington/Wolcottville. They are found residing in Derby, New Haven, Connecticut, a town some thirty-seven miles south of Torrington.

The town of Derby is in the southwest part of Connecticut where the Housatonic and Naugatuck Rivers converge. What these towns had in common was that both were involved with various types of manufacturing, particularly the manufacturing of brass.

In 1834, three men partnered to open a brass mill in Wolcottville, which would eventually become Wolcott Brass Company. One man in particular, Anson Green Phelps, was the co-founder of Phelps-Dodge Company; the copper mines that Phelps-Dodge owned supplied the factories that made brass products in Wolcottville and "other valley companies,"[489] of which Derby, Ansonia, and Waterbury were a part.[490]

It is quite possible that Charles F. Scoville was working in such a factory in Wolcottville when the decision was made to remove to Derby. The enumerator showed up to count the Scoville family on October 9, 1850.[491] They are listed as: Dwelling #133 and Family #138.

Chas. Scoville, 27, m., millwright, b. Conn.
Clarissa Scoville, 27, f., b. Conn.
Franklin Scoville, 8/12, m., b. Conn.
James A. Scoville, 11, m., b. Conn.

At the time of reviewing this census, I did not know who this "James A. Scoville" was. He couldn't be the son of this couple as they didn't marry until 1846. It was highly doubtful that he would have been a son from a previous marriage as Charles would have been only sixteen years old at the time of James' birth. It only came to light recently that James A. (possibly James Albert) was the brother of Charles.

This family were not enumerated in Connecticut in 1860 as the family had removed to Chicago, Cook, Illinois. When checking the 1860 census, the record states that Charles was now working for the Illinois Central Railroad. Backtracking I learned he was in the service

487 *Connecticut, Town Marriage Records, pre-1870 (Barbour Collection)*; Image 52 of 65, page 132; Ancestry.

488 *Genealogy Bank, Newspaper Archives*; GenealogyBank.

489 CTHistory.org. Derby—Connecticut Humanities online article.

490 Waterbury, Connecticut, was known as the "Brass City." Ironically, the company that made Waterbury into what it became was the Scovill Manufacturing Company, which previously had been Abel Porter & Co., in 1802. James and William H. Scovill formed the company in 1850 and had a successful brass button operation. James and William H. Scoville were the descendants of the immigrant, John Scovill.

491 1850 census, *Derby, New Haven, Connecticut*; Roll:46; Page 279b. Ancestry.

of the ICR (Illinois Central Railroad) since 1851,[492] and Charles is listed in the Chicago City Directory as early as 1843—this would imply that he was in Chicago in 1842.[493] This information also makes me question whether Charles was actually in Derby, Connecticut, during the 1850 census—unless he made frequent trips back to Connecticut to see his family.[494]

~

The Scoville family had been living in Chicago for a short time when Charles' wife, Clarissa, died on January 5, 1855, at the age of thirty. There are two records that state she died in Chicago; however, there is one record that claims she died in Torrington. I believe this record is in error and it is possible that this "mix-up" is because Clarissa is buried in Center Cemetery in Torrington, Connecticut. Here is a list of the of records available online:

Clarissa Spencer, age, 30
Died: January 5, 1855
Torrington, Connecticut
Married: Charles F. Scoville[495]

Death Record—*New Haven Columbian Register*
Publication date: January 20, 1855, Connecticut
Claims death occurred in Chicago.[496]

Clarissa Scoville, age, 30
Born: about 1825
Died: January 5, 1855
Death Place: Chicago
Father: E. Spencer
Spouse: Charles F.[497]

It is my supposition that Clarissa was in Chicago when she died and was brought back to Connecticut to be buried in Center Cemetery in Torrington, Connecticut, with Charles' parents, Amasa and Lucy (Foote) Scoville.

---

492 Alison Hinderliter, Project Archivist, Illinois Central Railroad Archives, The Newberry Library, Chicago, IL. Letter received Feb. 14, 2003.

493 *Chicago, Cook County, Illinois City Directory, 1843,*Ancestry. Note that Charles is listed as *Charles Foot Scoville.* Only his name is entered—no occupation or residence. Unfortunately, the online City Directories for Chicago do not run in consecutive years and it is impossible to follow his trail until we get to 1851.

494 His daughter Mary Jane was born in Ansonia, Connecticut in 1852.

495 *Connecticut, Deaths and Burials Index, 1650–1934*; Ancestry and Find-A-Grave.

496 *U.S. Newspaper Extractions from the Northeast, 1704–1930*; Ancestry.

497 *Connecticut, Hale Collection of Cemetery Inscriptions and Newspaper Notices, 1629–1934;* Connecticut State Library, Hartford, Connecticut.

The death of his wife left Charles with two young children to raise: Franklin, aged five, and Mary Jane, aged three. While Charles' mother could have cared for them for a time, it wasn't a long-term solution.

Charles married for a second time to Sarah Baird. A marriage record has not been located for them, but they were married sometime after 1855 and prior to the 1860 census as she is listed as "Sarah Scoville" in Charles' household at that time.

Sarah Baird was born in Scotland (per all available census records). Her parents were Andrew Baird and Jane _____.

There is an Andrew Baird family living in Paterson, New Jersey, in 1840 with six people in the household. There is one female whose age is given as "5–9." This female *could* be Sarah.

The 1850 census provides a further clue that the Baird family was living in Paterson, New Jersey, in 1840, and is the same family who was now living in New Haven, New Haven, Connecticut.

1850[498] census for New Haven, New Haven County, Connecticut:

Andrew Beard [sic], 47, b. Scotland, Blacksmith
Ann Beard, 49, b. Scotland
Sarah Beard, 20, b. Scotland
Margaret A. Beard, 9, b. NJ
Sarah Marter, 8, b. NJ
Alexander Esber, 19, b. NJ, Machinist

The probate record (as we will see later in this record) for Sarah provides information on her family:

The children of Andrew Baird and Jane are:
Jeanette Baird—husband Augustus Dickinson
Sarah Baird—husband Charles F. Scoville
Jane Baird—husband William Fuller
Andrew Baird—died age 5 years
Child with 2nd wife Annie Anderson
Margaret A. Baird—husband Frank H. Wightman

As we've seen, the Baird family were living in New Haven, Connecticut, in 1850.

It is my theory that the two families (Scoville and Baird) were acquainted. Andrew Baird's occupation was a blacksmith and it is probable that he worked with Charles at American Car Company. American Car Company was in Humphreysville, Connecticut (now known as Seymour), and this company was in operation circa 1850–1857.[499] Seymour, Connecticut, is in New Haven County, with Ansonia and Derby located to the southeast. If you recall, Charles and Clarissa Scoville were living in Derby during this timeframe (1850–1852). The available records provide information that Andrew Baird was working as a blacksmith in Chicago at

498 1850 census, *New Haven, New Haven, Connecticut*; Roll:47; Page: 241a. Dwelling #1694; Family# 2295; Ancestry.

499 See www.midcontinent.org for information on old railway companies.

ICR in 1852 and Charles Scoville was his foreman in the machinery department. This is too much of a coincidence for them not to have known one another prior to their moves to Chicago.

After the death of a wife, men would often marry as soon as possible (especially if there were children involved) and it was often someone they already knew.

According to statistics, the average age for a first-time marriage for women to marry in the nineteenth century was between the ages of 20 and 22.[500] Sarah—being of the age of twenty-six or so—was on her way to spinsterhood, an unenviable position for most women during that time. Most women did not have the means to support themselves, although some did have their own businesses, but that was not the norm. Many women ended up living with their aged parents or in a sibling's household; or they may go to work as a domestic servant, farm worker, washerwoman, or housekeeper for other people.

It wasn't until the 1900s when women started to work outside the home in various acceptable occupations. Still, the woman's place was in the position of wife and mother, the caretaker of hearth and home, morals, and right behavior.

Since Charles' situation was dire, he needed to find a wife, and who better than an unmarried daughter of Andrew Baird? Many marriages during those times were not always "love matches" but ones of necessity. Love would often come later—if not a deep abiding respect and friendship. The children (who were very young at the time of their mother's death) now had a mother figure to help them, and Charles could work without worry and provide for his family.

Without knowing when the marriage between Sarah and Charles took place, and while there isn't an exact timeframe of how long they had been married, by the time of Charles' death in 1890, they had been married for at least thirty-four years.

The Chicago City Directories[501] have been helpful in tracking Charles through his life. He can be found during the 1850s:

1852 Scoville, Charles, Foreman American Car Works
1853–54 Scoville, C. F. American Car Works, foreman
1855 Scoville, C. F. Foreman IC freight Depot, boards 24 Michigan

While Charles was a "railroad" man, he didn't operate the trains but took part in the building of the machinery. Since he was a foreman, he had people working under him whom he oversaw, making sure everything was going smoothly. An interesting article was found in the *Press and Tribune*, a Chicago newspaper:

> **Illinois Central Rail-Road Car Works—For the Press and the Tribune**
> Passing by the car works of the Illinois central railroad we thought we would stop and see the modus operandi of keeping the rolling stock of such a large railroad in repair. We inquired at the office for the necessary permit to examine the works, but instead of receiving it, we were taken round by the polite Superintendent, C. F.

500 April Sanders, *Age of Marriage in the U.S. in the 1800s;* updated March 3, 2019; www.theclassroom.com

501 *Chicago City Directories,* various years provided by Ancestry.com.

> Scoville from whom we learned many interesting facts connected with the history and management of the concern, since it first went into operation.

Charles must have loved his job to take time out of his busy day to give a tour and history lesson on the ICR to these newspapermen.

The family is listed on the 1860 census[502] as living in Ward 1, Chicago, with another family, the Edwardses. While reading this census it appeared that this was one household, not two (unless the enumerator made an error):

Frank Edwards, 42, tailor, born England[503]
Hannah Edwards, 54, born England
Clarissa Edwards, 16, born England
Jas. M. Edwards, 14, born Lake Michigan
George Marshall, 35, machinist, birthplace unknown
*M. S. [sic] Scoville, 40, Superintendent Car Works, born Connecticut, personal estate, $1500 (Charles M. Scoville)*[504]
*Sarah Scoville, 28, born Scotland (wife)*
*Frank Scoville, 10, born Connecticut (son)*
*Mary Scoville, 8, born Connecticut (daughter)*
*Lucy Scoville, 65, born Connecticut (mother)*
*Albert Scoville, 22, Printer, born Connecticut (brother)*
*George Scoville, 27, P[attern?] Maker, born Connecticut (brother)*

It's unfortunate that the earlier censuses did not include the streets that the citizens lived on; however, since a general location had to be noted in larger cities, we know that the family was living in Ward 1.

This area of Chicago was in the "South Division."[505] According to a map for 1863, Ward 1 was bordered "North on the Chicago River; South on Monroe Street; East on Lake Michigan and West on Chicago River." Sometime later, this family moved further west to the Oak Park section of Chicago.

~

In 1862, tragedy struck the Scoville family. James A. Scoville, brother of Charles, was killed while on board the gunboat *USS Mound City*[506] on June 17, 1862. The *USS Mound City* was an

502 1860 Census; *Chicago, Cook County, Illinois;* Dwelling 1462; Family #1290.Roll: M653_164; Page 256; FHL:803164.

503 The house where the Edwardses and Scovilles lived is long gone—if not by the "Great Chicago Fire," then by urban revitalization. I have not spent any time on researching who the Edwardses were, or if there is any relation between the two families.

504 I have indicated the relationship in parentheses.

505 The foregoing information on Ward 1in Chicago comes from the website chicagology.com.

506 Named after Mound City, Illinois, where the river gunboat was built. civilwar.com.

ironclad gunboat built for service on the Mississippi River and its tributaries in the American Civil War. The gunboat was originally commissioned as part of the Union Army's Western Gunboat Flotilla and remained in service until October 1862.[507]

James had enlisted in the Navy[508] on October 10, 1861. The enlistment record states that he was "born in Connecticut, "33"[509] years of age, and a sailor. He stood "5'6"" and had "gray eyes" and "light brown hair." James was assigned to the *USS Mound City.* Prior to his enlistment he was a timekeeper at I. C. Car Works (in 1861).[510]

On this fateful day, James was the Acting Master[511] of the gunboat. The *USS Mound City* had just returned to action in June. During a bombardment at St. Clare, Arkansas, the gunboat was seriously damaged. Many men drowned trying to save themselves from being scalded to death.

The newspapers were flooded with articles about this tragedy, such as the one from the *Chicago Daily Tribune,* Monday, June 23, 1862, Chicago, Illinois, page 5:

> **The Mound City Catastrophe**
> The terrible catastrophe to the U.S. gunboat Mound City, announced on Saturday by telegraph, caused a shudder of horror and a thrill through the city, and has cast a gloom upon many households, a sickening suspense, for many of our "gallant" boys were upon that ill-fated craft . . . thus far but two names of Chicago men have come among the many victims . . . [The] two names are John H. Kinzie, Jr., Second Master, and James A. Scoville, Fourth Master, both of this city . . . James A. Scoville was about 22 years of age and a brother of the present superintendent of the Illinois Central Rail-Road Car Works. He was formerly of Connecticut, his parents now residing in the southern part of the city . . .
>
> In all respects, he was an upright, active, gallant, and pious young man . . .

During the Civil War there was no official way to notify the next of kin. If the military member was of a high rank, a telegram may be sent; maybe a fellow soldier wrote a letter to the next of kin, but mostly people found out through the newspaper.

It wasn't until a month later that services for James A. Scoville were held. Again, from the *Chicago Daily Tribune,* Saturday, July 26, 1862, Chicago, Illinois, page 5:

> The Rev. J.H. Dill will preach a sermon commemorative of the death of James A. Scoville, late Fourth Master of the gunboat, Mound City, in the South Congregational Church, corner of Rio Grande St., and Calamet Ave., Sabbath morning. Services commencing at 10 ½ o'clock.

---

507 *USS Mound City (1861);* Wikipedia; en.m.wikipedia.org.

508 *Naval Enlistment Rendezvous 1855–1891;* NARA, M1953; Roll: 17; Film: 2381634. Ancestry.

509 The age is incorrect. James was 23 years old in 1861.

510 *Chicago, Illinois City Directory,* 1861; Ancestry.

511 Information comes from the military website Fold3.com.

James' remains are buried in Oakwoods Cemetery, Chicago, Illinois. James never married and did not leave any descendants.

While the papers were filled for days with the horrible news, one last article I will note here from the *Chicago Daily Tribune*, Monday, September 1, 1862, Chicago, Illinois: (page 2):

> [Special Dispatch to the Chicago Daily Tribune—Cairo, August 30, 1862]
> Lt. Commander Fry, the rebel who ordered his men to fire upon the drowning sailors of the gunboat Mound City, was yesterday taken from the hospital and confined in the guard house.

A brief article was written by Sam Dickinson for the *Arkansas Times* in 1984:

> The Curse of the St. Charles—Captain Joseph Fry's cannon fired the single most disastrous shot of the Civil War. Several years later, he became its last casualty.[512]

After he had recuperated, he was exchanged[513] and went on to command another ship during the war. He died during the Ten Years War with Cuba in 1873.[514]

After James' death, life went on in the Scoville household, as it must.

We have a snippet of Charles' life through the 1860s from the Chicago City Directories. Based on what I have seen in the census records, Charles never owned a home and they moved often. I find this surprising considering the amount of his estate after his death.

The online city directories for Chicago are available for the years 1862, 1863, 1864, 1865, and 1869.

All the addresses are on the south side of Chicago. This family remained in this area until their deaths.

1862[515]—East Dodge Ave., between Rio Grande and Buena Vista
1863—House corner of Cottage Grove and Kankakee
1864—House corner of Cottage Grove and 26th Ave., master mechanic
1865—House on 187 Kaukakee Ave
1869—187 Kaukakee Ave., Superintendent I.C.R.R.

Most, if not all, of the addresses given above have been overtaken by urban sprawl.

The 1870[516] census shows that this family was now living in Ward 4 of Chicago. This area is located where the Museum Campus, Kenwood, and the lakefront area from Grant

---

512 November 1984 issue, 101; The Arkansas in the Civil War Message Board; www.history-sites.com.

513 The exchange of prisoners was a common occurrence during the Civil War.

514 Joseph Fry, CSN; https://sites.google.com/site/290foundation/290-standing-orders/joseph-fry-csn

515 *U.S. City Directories 1822–1995*; Chicago, Illinois, 1862, 1863, 1864, and 1865; Ancestry.

516 1870 census, *Chicago, Cook County, Illinois*; Roll: M593_200; Page:141A; Image: 74957; FHL: 545699.

Park to Hyde Park now stand. The enumerator arrived at their doorstep on July 29, 1870. I am envisioning a very hot day in Chicago when Mr. Sherman knocked on the door, probably mopping his head when the door was opened, likely by Josephine Holm, who was the domestic servant in the household. If Mrs. Scoville was home, it is likely she who provided the information. Mr. Sherman began to record the entry as Dwelling #1769; Family #2015:

> Scoville, Charles F., age 49, m, w, Supt of Car Works, value of personal estate: $5000,[517] b. Conn.
> Scoville, Sarah B., age 39, f, w, Keeping house, b. Scotland.
> Scoville, Mary J., age 18, f, w, at home, b. Conn.
> Holm, Josephine, age 21, f, w, Domestic Servant, b. Sweden.

Their neighbors are blacksmiths, laborers, candlemakers, and the like. Only two people in that neighborhood owned a house: Mr. Eugene Schneider, a candle manufacturer who hailed from France, and a Mr. E. Wheeler, whose occupation was a railroad superintendent and who had been born in New York.

~

Sometime in the month of June 1871,[518] rain had become scarce. This was the catalyst of what was to come.

It had been a long, hot summer. Summer turned into fall without any relief. On the evening of Saturday, October 7, a fire started at 209 South Canal Street.[519] The Scovilles were living at 1215 Prairie Avenue (according to the 1872 city directory).[520] From a current map this area is a little over one and a half miles from where the fire began. The houses were made of wood and, with having only an inch of rain in the previous months, went up like a tinderbox as the strong winds helped in fanning the flames.

It didn't take much for the fire to get out of control. It is said the fire "jumped" the river, causing more destruction. Many people ran to Lake Michigan, jumping into the water thinking that they would be saved, but the fire found them there as well.

From various accounts, there were nine separate fires that spread out. The fire departments throughout the city couldn't keep up. By the time the fire ended, approximately four square miles of the city were destroyed, three hundred people were dead, and at least 100,000 were homeless.

---

517 Based on the current inflation rate (2021) $5,000 in 1870 is now worth $106,421.98.

518 Some records suggest the drought was six weeks long (Wikipedia article), while Neil Gale, Ph.D., in his blog on December 28, 2016 (https://drloihjournal.blogspot.com), wrote that the drought was fourteen weeks, and it is his estimation of the drought that I am using.

519 209 South Canal became 558 W. DeKoven Street in 1909. The spot where the O'Leary's house stood is now occupied by the Chicago Fire Academy.

520 Keep in mind the city directories report where the citizens lived in the year prior, i.e., 1872 directory is reporting on where the citizens and businesses were in 1871.

Whether the Scovilles home was damaged or destroyed is unknown. According to a map of the path of the fire,[521] it doesn't appear that the fire went in the direction of Prairie Avenue.

≈

The 1870s were a time of rebuilding the south side of Chicago. It was at this time (1871) when Charles is listed as employed as a superintendent of "bridgeworks." The family is given as still living at 1215 Prairie Avenue.

It is unknown if their home had been damaged in the fire; however, by 1873[522] the city directory states that the family had moved to 1211 Prairie Avenue[523] and Charles was now working for Wells, French and Company as their superintendent.

Wells, French and Company is listed in the Chicago City Directory in 1874/75 under the heading "Bridge Builders." From an online record, "Sources disagree on whether Wells, French and Company entered the car building field in 1871 or 1874." The date of 1871 seems more likely as an 1873 publication about Chicago Industry refers to the firm as a "bridge and car works," where it says: "The bridge and car works of Wells, French & Co.—C.F. Scoville, Superintendent..."[524]

The article goes on to explain when the company was established, the number employed (300), and its financial information with a description of the type of business ("the manufacture of building cars and building bridges").[525]

When Wells, French and Company went into the car building busines they wanted Charles F. Scoville to be the superintendent of the plant. At the time of his hire, Charles was then in the car department of the Illinois Central Railroad and had been an experienced millwright before—in 1852—being employed by the American Car Company of Seymour Connecticut for a short time."[526]

The online article goes on to list some of their employees. It states in part:

> Charles F. Scoville (1821–1890) was born at Torringsford,[527] [sic] Connecticut. He learned the trade of millwright (machine builder) and apparently practiced that trade for several years. In 1852 he went to work for the American Car Company at Seymour, Connecticut, but shortly thereafter moved to Chicago [possibly drawn by the success of his uncle Hiram Scoville, and his cousins James, William, and Ives[528]

521 See bostonraremaps.com.

522 *U.S. City Directories, 1822–1995*, Chicago, Cook County, Illinois, 1873.

523 1211 Prairie Avenue is now 1211 S. Prairie Avenue, where One Museum Park Condos stand.

524 *Building of Wooden Railway Cars—and some other stuff*; 11 April 2006, midcontinent.org.

525 *Ibid*

526 *Ibid*

527 Torringford is a section of Torrington, Connecticut.

528 This is erroneous information. Charles did not have an uncle Hiram or cousins James, William, and Ives. This is a different Scoville line and, while they may share a common ancestor, they

> incorporating their business as the Chicago Locomotive Company, and possibly participating in that enterprise]. He eventually went to work for the Illinois Central Railroad in their car department [possibly after the Scovilles sold out their interests in the Chicago Locomotive Company in 1855].
>
> In 1871, Wells & French hired him to set up their freight car plant and he became its superintendent, a position he held for all but a few months before his death.[529]

Charles continues to be included in the various years of the city directory throughout the 1870s. By 1880[530] the family has moved again, now living at 2013 Michigan Avenue. This is perhaps a couple of blocks from where they formerly resided. The Scoville family are listed as "boarders" and many people on the census page are also boarders for the same address. This was likely an apartment building to which they may have moved since both children were out of the household.

I am not sure who gave the information (perhaps the landlord or a neighbor?) as most of the data is incorrect; however, *it is* the same family based on Charles' occupation.

> Scovill, Chas, w, m, 55, boarder, bridge builder, b. NY; father b. NY; mother b. NY
> Scovill, Mary(?), 45, w, f, boarder, at home, b. NY (same for father and mother)
> Haney, George, 28, w, m, boarder, bookkeeper, b. NY

In 1881 an article appeared in the *Chicago Daily Tribune*[531] regarding Sarah's father:

> **Presentation:**
> Mr. Andrew Baird was presented with a handsome gold headed cane and silver tobacco box, by the employees of the I.C.R.R, Car-Works blacksmith shop, where he had been a foreman for over twenty-seven years. He came to Chicago when the road was in its infancy. He has retired at the age of 79, much esteemed and respected by all who know him. Mrs. Baird was also presented with a fine French clock.

One year after his retirement, Andrew Baird died on October 5, 1882, in Chicago, Cook, Illinois.[532] According to the record, Andrew was born about 1802 in Ayrshire, Scotland; he was age eighty at the time of his death and was a "blacksmith" by trade. He is buried in Graceland Cemetery[533] in Chicago.

Five years later, Sarah's stepmother died, and a short death notice was posted:

---

were not closely related. I requested that this error in lineage be corrected, and it has been.

529 Charles began to work for Wells & French in/about 1872 according to the Chicago City Directory. The information regarding only working there for a "few months" is also incorrect.

530 1880 census, *Chicago, Cook County, Illinois,* Roll: 185; Page: 398D; Enumeration District: 015; Dwelling #162; Family #216

531 *Chicago Daily Tribune,* Sunday, April 10, 1881; 9.

532 *Cook County, Illinois Death Index, 1878–1922S*; FHL: 1031443. Ancestry.

533 Section G; Lot: 911S ½. Wife Anna is buried in the same plot.

**Baird**—February 25, Anna, relict of Andrew Baird, aged 86 years. Funeral services at her late residence number 2642 Calumet Avenue. February 27 at 2 PM.[534]

The family continued to move. In 1885 they lived at 1604 Michigan Ave. In 1888 they moved to 1616 Indiana Avenue,[535] and this is where they lived out the rest of their lives. Two years later, on February 4, 1890, Charles died at the age of sixty-eight. Following are the various notices that were published:

*Chicago Daily Tribune*
February 5, 1890
C.F. Scoville
The funeral of Charles F Scoville was held yesterday at number 1616 Indiana Ave.; Bishop Cheney officiating. Mr. Scoville was one of the early settlers of Chicago having come here about 1852 from Connecticut. He was with the Illinois Central Railroad for many years as master mechanic at the car works. 19 years ago, he became connected with the Wells-French Company continuing with this firm until last October when ill health obliged him to retire. Mr. Scoville was always ready to assist the needy. In politics he was a staunch Republican. A widow, son, and daughter survive him.

*Chicago Daily Tribune*
February 2, 1890
Deaths
In the evening of February 1, Charles F. Scoville, aged 68 years. Notice of funeral hereafter.

*Chicago Daily Tribune*
February 3, 1890
Saturday evening funeral at residence 1616 Indiana Avenue, Tuesday, February 4 at 1:30 p.m. Internment at Oakwoods.

*Chicago Daily Tribune*
February 8, 1890, page 3
Judge Kohisaat granted letters of administration to Mrs. Sarah Scoville on the estate of her husband Charles F. Scoville, who left property worth $45,000, which goes to the widow, son, and daughter.

534 *Daily Inter Ocean*, Saturday February 26, 1887 edition, Chicago, IL/Vol: XV; Issue:339; Page: 8.

535 Also at this address were Mr. and Mrs. Augustus Dickinson, Curtis Dickinson, and William Loomis. These were family members of Sarah Scoville's. See *1890 Chicago Blue Book*; www.livinghistoryofIllinois.com.

Charles left a substantial estate[536]—too lengthy to go into here, but an Administrator's Bond—Probate Court of Cook County dated February 7, 1890, states in part, "Know all Men by these Presents, That we Sarah Scoville, Edward T. Cushing and Christopher B. Bouton of the County of Cook and State of Illinois, are held and firmly bound until the people of the State of Illinois, the penal sum[537] of ninety thousand dollars,[538] current money of the United States . . ."

Sarah Scoville was the "Administratrix" of Charles' estate. A copy of the receipts and disbursements were submitted to the Cook County Probate Court in January 1891. In the disbursements there are several doctors listed (Dr. E.C. Dudley; Dr. M.G. Hart; Dr. F.W. Mercer; Dr. F. S. Johnson; Dr. E.W. Andrews). This would imply that Charles did not die suddenly, but had been ill, as the February 5, 1890, *Chicago Daily Tribune* conveyed.

Other items (labeled *Receipts)* included cash on hand from C. National Bank, cash from Wells & French Company, shares of stock, and sale of stock that totaled $28,998.56.

On February 20, 1890, the appraiser valued the property allowed to the widow:

> Family pictures, wearing apparel, Jewelry, ornaments of the widow and minor children; school books and family library; one sewing machine; necessary beds, bedsteads, bedding for widow and family; stoves; pipes used in the family, necessary cooking utensils, household in kitchen furniture; one milch cow; two sheep and fleeces; one horse, saddle and bridal; provision for the widow and family for one year; food and stock above specified for six months; fuel for the widow and family three months. The total of these items was $2,410.00.

<u>Stocks Owned</u>

Union Horse and Nail Company (located in Connecticut)
Big Laramie Land, cattle improvement company (Wyoming Territory)
Rodger and Ballast Car Company
Wells & French Company

Charles Foote Scoville was buried in Oakwoods Cemetery, not far from his home on Indiana Avenue.

≈

One year and nine months later on November 20, 1891, Sarah Baird Scoville died. According to the headstone, she was sixty-one years, nine months, and twenty-six days old at her death, which suggests she was born January 1, 1830.[539]

---

536 All mentioned probate records come from *Probate Court Cook County, 2/4650; Doc. 18; various pages; Box 2/4650.* See also *Illinois, Wills and Probate Records, 1772–1999* via Ancestry—this online record is only a synopsis—not the full record.

537 Penal Sum is based on the value of the estate.

538 The current exchange rate for $90,000 in 2021 is $2,679,924.

539 Sarah's date of birth was calculated using the Birthdate Calculator developed by Mac Timus

Sarah Scoville also left a will and subsequent probate record. A brief synopsis:

Sarah left her sister Jane Baird Fuller 12 silver forks and six silver spoons, wearing apparel and household goods. Natalie Cushing received a piece of statuary and Frank Scoville a bronze clock.[540] Her estate and appraisal:

Three cloaks, one piece of statuary; one bed stead and bedding; one dresser; one washstand; five chairs; three stools; one table; one mirror; one lounge; six picture frames; one bookcase; 20 miscellaneous books; one silver tea set; one china tea set; one lot of underwear; four dresses; two dresses; one seal skin cloak; one seal skin muff; one seal skin wrap (old;) two shawls; one camels hair shawl; one wrap; two bonnets; one lot of handkerchiefs; one lot of gloves; one satchel; one traveling wrap; 12 silver forks; six silver spoons; one set of cluster diamond pin and two earrings; one set solitaire diamond; one stick pin; one cameo pin; one silver tobacco box.

In addition, Edward T. Cushing, the executor of Sarah Scoville's will, petitioned the court to pay the "respective bequests" as stipulated:

Frank Scoville, bequest of $5,000; $1,500 in cash and the note secured by trust deed
Jennette Dickinson, bequest of $5,000
Natalie Cushing, daughter of said petitioner, $5,000

***Children of Charles Foote Scoville and Clarissa Spencer***

26. i. Franklin "Frank" Scoville,[7] b. Dec (January?) 1850, Ansonia, New Haven, Connecticut; d. 30 Oct 1922, California; m. 1872, Ironton, Missouri, Kate Shepard, b. 29 Mar 1852, Ohio; d. 2 Mar 1908, Corona, Riverside, California; daughter of Bilbe Shepard and Lydia Gobel Truesdale.
27. ii. Mary Jane Scoville,[7] b. 6 Nov 1852, Ansonia, New Haven, Connecticut; d. 6 Nov 1933, Chicago, Cook, Illinois; m. 6 Jan 1875, Edward T. Cushing, Chicago, Cook, Illinois; b. Sep 1845, Illinois; d. 6 Apr 1909, Cook County, Illinois.

## *15. ii. Mary Lord Scoville[6] (Amasa,[5] Ithamar,[4] Timothy,[3] Stephen,[2] Stephen,[1] Arthur)*

Born circa 1822 in Torrington, Litchfield, Connecticut;[541] died 29 December 1893, Yorkville, Oneida, New York;[542] married 4 April 1847 Wolcottville, Connecticut, to Abner Marshall Wilson;[543] born circa 1821, perhaps in/around Torrington, Litchfield, Connecticut, or

---

for Long Island Genealogy, www.longislandgenealogy.com. This is by no means primary proof of her birth month and day, but a guide in searching for a possible date of birth.

540 Note that Frank's sister, Mary Jane Scoville Cushing, is not named at all in her stepmother's will. She (Sarah) may have preferred her granddaughter Natalie Cushing to receive any bequests in her stead.

541 A birth record for Mary Lord Scoville has not been discovered as of the date of this writing. Since the family lived in Torrington (or one of its villages of Torringsford and Wolcottville) I am confident that this is the place of her birth.

542 *New York Death Index, 1852–1956*, Ancestry.

543 *Connecticut Town Marriage Records, pre-1870 Barbour Collection*; Vol:1; 126; Connecticut

Oneida, New York;[544] his parents possibly Roger Wilson and Hannah Marshall;[545] died 29 December 1894, Oneida, Madison, New York.[546] Mary Lord Scoville Wilson and Abner Marshall Wilson are buried in Glenwood Cemetery, Oneida, Madison, New York.[547]

The first record we find of Mary as an adult is through her marriage to Abner Wilson. The Rev. Henry Zell, rector of Trinity Church in Wolcottville, performed the service at the home of Col. Samuel Foote in Wolcottville: ". . . united in the holy estate of matrimony according to Gods ordinance [ ]form of the Protestant Episcopal Church the laws of the State of Connecticut . . ." Samuel Foote (1771–1848) was the grandfather of Mary Lord Scoville and was a descendant of the early settler Nathaniel Foote of Wethersfield, Connecticut.[548] Samuel died a year after his daughter's marriage at the age of seventy-seven.

The young couple were living in Vienna, Oneida, New York, by the 1850[549] census and likely removed there soon after their marriage. Abner was an "innkeeper" and was occupied in this vocation for many years, as we will see on subsequent census reports.

An article published in a local newspaper in 1850 provides a brief description of this area:

> Vienna lies west of Rome and is divided from it by Fish Creek, Camden north and Oneida Lake West. Fish Creek Landing, where a large amount of lumber is shipped by the Side Cut Canal, connecting its waters with the Erie Canal at Higginsville in Verona.
>
> There are five Post Offices in the town, the Plank Road from Rome to Oswego, the Rome and Watertown Rail Road, the Plank Road from Fulton by the shore of Oneida Lake to Rome, the Fish Creek and McConnellsville, the New London and Pine Plank Roads all pass through this town in various directions, giving an easy communication to other towns in its neighborhood, and water navigation by Lake, Creek and Canal such as but few towns can boast of.[550]

---

State Library, Hartford, Connecticut.

544 Roger Wilson, b. 2 August 1756, in Torrington, Litchfield, Connecticut; d. 19 March 1839 Oneida County, New York. He is buried in Blackmer Cemetery in Westmoreland, Oneida, New York; spouse: Hannah *Marshall* Wilson. This information is found on Find A Grave. It is unknown how accurate the information is; however, Roger Wilson was in Oneida at least before his death. Another sticking point to Abner's parentage is the fact that Roger Wilson and Hannah Wilson married in 1780. This would mean that Hannah was 62 years old at the time of Abner's birth, which seems highly unlikely.

545 As noted above, more research is required to determine the various Wilson families. Abner's middle name is "Marshall." Does this mean Hannah Marshall, wife of Roger Wilson, *was* the mother of Abner?

546 *New York, Death Index, 1852–1956,* Ancestry. *New York Wills and Probate Records,* copies in my possession.

547 Findagrave.com.

548 Godwin, Nathaniel, *The Foote Family; or the Descendants of Nathaniel Foote, One of The First Settlers of Wethersfield, Connecticut; 427;* Hartford: Press of Case, Tiffany, and Company, (1849).

549 1850 census, *Vienna, Oneida, New York*; Roll: 565; Page: 225A, Ancestry.

550 Article from: *Rome Citizen,* Wednesday, October 30, 1850; submitter: Barbara Anderson to

While this brief description does not mention a specific named inn, there were "two Public houses and two taverns" in nearby villages[551] and Abner could have been managing one of them.

The family was still living in Vienna for the New York State census of 1855.[552] The enumerator visited the household on the "nineteenth day of June 1855."

Dwelling #64; Frame dwelling; value $800; Family #68

A.M. Wilson, 34, m, b. Madison (N.Y.), married, resided in town 5 years, Tavern keeper, native

Mary L. Wilson, 33, f, wife, b. Conn.; " "

Lucy C. Scoville, 59, f, wife's mother, b. Conn., " 8/12[553]

Frank Scoville, 5, m, boarder, b. Conn., 7/12

Mary J. Scoville, 3, f, boarder, b. Conn., 7/12

This is a curious scenario. Lucy C. Scoville had arrived sometime in October 1854 and her grandchildren in November of the same year (this is a rough guess if the dates of being a resident in the town are correct). Was it common to visit for such a length of time, or was it because the children's mother was ill? A train journey from Chicago to Vienna, New York, per current calculations, would take approximately "14 hours and 3 minutes" via Amtrak.[554] In 1854/55 this journey would have taken approximately two days.[555, 556]

Eventually, Lucy C. Scoville, Frank, and Mary went back to Chicago as they were living with the Edwardses in 1860.

By 1860 the Wilsons were living in Lenox, Madison, New York. Lenox lies south of Vienna and is in the north-eastern section of the county of Madison. Abner Wilson may have found another opportunity in Lenox. The population in Lenox at this time was 8,024 persons.[557] By contrast, Vienna's population at the same time was 3,460[558] and, by 1870, Vienna's population dwindled even more.

The town of Lenox boasted six hotels: Oneida Valley Hotel, The Railroad Eating House,

---

www.oneida.nygenweb.net.

551 *Ibid.*

552 *New York State Census, 1855;* Ancestry; Original data: Census of the state of New York, for 1855. Microfilm. Various County Clerk Offices, New York. Household: 68; Line: 10; Sheet: 8; E.D: 2.

553 According to this particular census, Lucy C. Scoville had been living in Vienna eight months out of twelve with the Wilsons, and the children seven months out of twelve.

554 This information comes via www.wander.com.

555 I have assumed that this trip was made by rail, since Lucy Scoville's son was the superintendent of the I.C.R.

556 The amount of time to reach New York by train from Chicago comes from *United States Department of the Interior National Park Service; Railroad Development in Minnesota, 1862–1956; 5–6;* www. dot.state.mn.us.

557 Historical population tabulation according to the 1860 census for Lenox, NY; www. en.m.wikidpedia.org.

558 *Ibid*

The Eagle, Madison House, Allen Hotel, and Globe Hotel.[559] Abner Wilson is named as a proprietor of the Oneida Valley Hotel[560] in the 1868–9 business directory.

An 1859 map of Oneida Valley pinpointing where the Oneida Valley Hotel was located:[561]

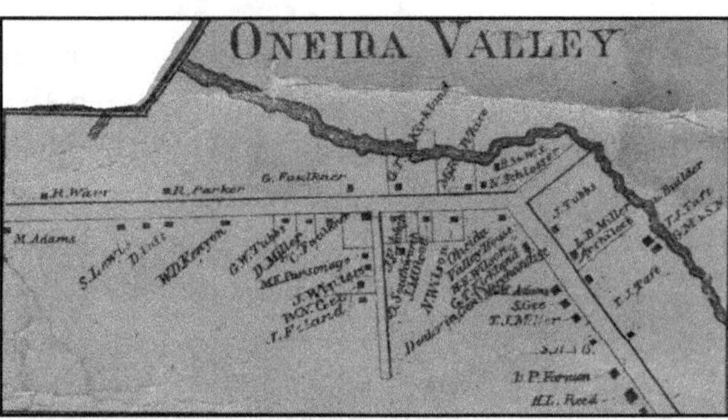

Note the reference of "N. Wilson"—to the right of that is the Oneida Valley House Hotel.

The 1860[562] census for Lenox shows the family on the twenty-first day of June listed as Dwelling 219; Family 218:

A. M. Wilson, 39, m., b. New York, Hotel Keeper
Mary L. Wilson, 35, f., b. New York
Margaret Mulholland, f., 19, b. New York, "deaf and dumb"

Depending upon which census you read, Margaret Mulholland is listed as either having been born in New York or Ireland. Because of her disability of being a non-hearing person, she may have had a special way to communicate with her employers, Abner and Mary.[563]

The New York state census for 1865 has the family still residing in Lenox. Abner's occupation is listed as a "landlord," and on this census he is born in "Madison (NY);" his wife Mary is listed as being born in "Connecticut." Margaret is now twenty-two, a "servant," and was born in "Ireland."

The other household member is Parliman Wilson, who is sixty-eight and a "boarder," born in "Connecticut" and occupied as a "carpenter." Who is Parliman Wilson? According to the *Barbour Collection*[564] Parliman was the son of Roger Wilson and Hannah _______, born August 15, 1797, in Torrington, Connecticut. Could he be the older brother of Abner? If that is the case, why is he listed as a boarder and not as a brother or some other relation? (perhaps the enumerator meant to write brother instead of "boarder?")[565] A death record shows that Parliman Wilson died May 10, 1875, in Bloomfield, Oakland, Michigan.

A copy of the original entries can be found online in *Michigan Death and Burials Index, 1867–1995.*[566] He was seventy-seven at the time of his death and the cause of said death was "suicide."

559 Smith, James H., *History of Chenango and Madison Counties; History of Lenox;* Chapter 55, 716; published by D. Mason & Co., Syracuse, NY—(1880) www.madison.nygenweb.com.

560 Childs, *Gazetteer and Business Directory of Madison County, N.Y., for 1868–9;* 190.

561 French, J. H. Gillette, *Map of Madison County, New York;* from actual surveys under the direction of J. H. French, Syracuse Philadelphia: Jno. E. Gillette, 1859.

562 1860 census; *Lenox, Madison, New York;* Page: 626; FHL: 803781.

563 Margaret Mulholland was employed as a domestic servant up until the time of Mary's and Abner's deaths.

564 *Connecticut Town Birth Records, pre-1870.* Ancestry.

565 *If* Parliman Wilson is the brother of Abner, there is a twenty-four-year age gap. More research on this family is needed.

566 Record #96; Page: 266; Ancestry; Original data: Death Records, Michigan Department of

~

This family is still living in Lenox in 1870.[567] The only difference in the household is that a new boarder by the name of John Bowman is now residing with the family. Mr. Bowman's occupation is listed as a "hostler"[568] for the Wilsons.

In 1872, Mary's brother, George E. Scoville, died in Chicago. In his will he left Mary five bonds from the "County of Marshall in the State of Kansas." Each bond was worth one-thousand dollars and was to be "used and enjoyed by her."[569]

In 1875[570] the Wilsons, with their servant, Margaret, were now residing in Cleveland Village, Constantia, Oswego, New York. Cleveland Village is located on the shores of Oneida Lake and is the largest village in Constantia with the New York, Ontario and Western (Midland) Railroad located in the southeast corner of the town.[571]

The lake itself is the largest body of water in the state of New York, with a surface area of 79.8 square miles.[572] The well known Finger Lakes are close by, and Oneida Lake is sometimes referred to as the "thumb" (of the Finger Lakes) even though it does not resemble any of the other lakes.

Two of the known hotels in Cleveland Village were Lakeside House[573] and Weldon House. Again, the proprietors are named but there is no mention of Abner Wilson as being a proprietor of an inn or hotel; however, he is still employed as a "hotel keeper," as the census report reveals.

The New York census for Cleveland Village shows there are multiple boarders in this household and Aber's wife, Mary, and servant, Margaret Mulholland, are still part of the household dynamic.

Enumerated on June 1,1875:

---

Community Health, Division for Vital Records and Health Statistics, Lansing, Michigan.

567 1870 Census; *Lenox, Madison, New York;* Roll: M593_968; Page: 376B; FHL: 552467. Ancestry.

568 "Hostler—a man employed to look after the horses of people staying at an inn." In current times this word has acquired additional meanings, most notably in the railroad industry. Merriam-Webster Dictionary https://merriamwebster.com/dictionary/hostler.

569 *Missouri Wills and Probate Records, Buchanan, 1766–1988,* Ancestry.

570 1875, New York State Census; Original Data: Census of the State of New York for 1875; New York State Archives, Albany; E.D. 01; Household: 15; Line:29; Sheet:2. Ancestry.

571 Bannister, Gaylene Kerr, transcribed the *1895 Landmark Book, Oswego County, New York, Chapter XXI—Constantia,* for Oswego County, New York Genweb online site, August 22, 2004; www.sites.rootsweb.com.

572 Ausobel, Seth (Sep. 10, 2008) "Section 319 Nonpoint Source Success Stories: New York: Oneida Lake; Projects reduce Phosphorus in Lake;" Environmental Protection Agency Meeting. Archived from the original on 28 August 2009. en.wikipedia.org.

573 Ira P. Brown was the proprietor of Lakeside House (date unknown); Churchill, John C., LLD, assisted by Wilson, H. Perry and Child, W. Stanley, *Landmarks of Oswego County, New York;* (Syracuse, New York, D. Mason & Co. Publisher, 1895), 507.

Dwelling Type: Frame; Value: $5,000

H. Marshall [sic] Willson, 56, Hotel Keeper

Mary L. Willson, 54

John Bowman, 61, hostler, Margaret Mulholland, 30, servant, Alvira Stanton, 30, servant

Peter Vanderberg, 71, tin smith, Israel S. Morse, 35, storekeeper

William W. Morse, 28, storekeeper, Alice Morse, 22

George Albert Morse, 0 (infant)

Joel Morse, 37, merchant clerk

Dillon Williams, 70, clergyman

Ella I. Williams, 30

Rebecca T. Williams, 24

Elizabeth A. Williams, 21

Jane Truman, 59 (wife's sister)

The Wilsons had added an additional servant to help with the running of the hotel, and there are two families who are making the hotel their home.

There are only ten pages to the 1875 census for Cleveland Village. One the same page as Abner Marshall is another hotel keeper by the name of Cyrus Marble. According to *Landmarks of Oswego County, New York,*[574] Cyrus Marble had come to Cleveland Village in 1834 and kept the "famous" Marble House for "over forty years," it being one of the "most widely known and popular hostelries in the State." The Marble Hotel was only a few dwellings away from Abner Wilson's.

Some of the trades in which people were employed in this town were glass blowers and glass cutters;[575] carpenters; wood cutters; railroad workers; physicians; tailoresses; blacksmiths; boatmen; well diggers; farm laborers; bookkeepers; telegraphers; masons; storekeepers; and butchers.

When it was time for the 1880 census, the Wilsons were still living in Cleveland Village, but Abner is no longer listed as a "hotel keeper;" in fact, there is no occupation for him at all. The family consists of his wife, Mary, and their servant, Margaret Mulholland. Abner (at this time) was now sixty years old. Perhaps he was financially sound and no longer had to work for his livelihood, as so many men had to, well into their late seventies.

You will also note that John Bowman, the Wilson's hostler, is no longer listed with this family. He may have moved on or died by 1880 as I haven't located a record of him on the 1880 census.

The few records left for this family are concerning two land assessment records for Abner. The first was on June 10, 1884, Madison County, New York, with grantor Milo E. Lewis to

574 Edited by Churchill, John C., LL. D. D. Mason & Company, Publishers, Syracuse, N.Y. 1895; www.genealogy.trails.com.

575 Anthony Landgraff was a "prominent" settler and the originator of the glass industry in the town of Constantia.

grantee Abner M. Wilson.[576] Unfortunately, beyond the name of the grantor/grantee and the date of this assessment, there is no further information (at least online) to expand on this.

The second land assessment is for grantor the Oneida Cemetery Association to grantee Abner M. Wilson. The date of this record is March 26, 1894, Madison, New York.[577] I suspect that this is the purchase of a family plot in said cemetery.

On the fourth day of February 1890, Mary's brother Charles F. Scoville died. After her brother George's death in 1872, whereby George's will left bonds to his sister Mary, George had appointed Charles to be the trustee of those estate proceeds. Even though George wrote that Mary could use the bonds "as she wished," she would have had to go through Charles to get any of the money coming to her. This is how things were handled during this timeframe where woman rarely handled their own monetary affairs. Mary agreed with this arrangement. After Charles' death a new trustee would have to be appointed and to do this, Mary was required to go through the Court of Equity for a legally binding document.

> In Circuit Court of Chicago, Cook County, Mary L. Wilson brought petition against Frank Scoville and Mary Cushing. Mary L Wilson of Oneida, Madison County, New York, states that on March 22, 1872, George E Scoville "a brother" made and executed his will.

The wording as it relates to Mary L. Wilson is as follows*:*

> I do hereby give, grant, devise and bequeath to "my sister," Mary L. Wilson, now of the Village of Cortland in the County of Owego and State of New York, ten bonds of the County of Marshall, in the State of Kansas. These bonds were numbered from fifteen to twenty-four and were each one-thousand dollars to be used and enjoyed by her and that she had the sole right use and benefit of the accruing interest for the term of her natural life. After her decease, the bonds or their representative proceeds should revert to be vested between all the children of "my brother Charles F Scoville.

The deposition goes on to say that "should her brother Charles and she decide to change the bonds into 'other property' as long as they both agree to the terms of the change."

George E. Scoville died 15 April 1872. His will was probated in the Probate Court of the County of Buchanan, State of Missouri, on the second day of May 1872. His will in part states that the executor of George E. Scoville deceased, to the said Charles F. Scoville, the following number bonds: "viz. to Mary L Wilson ten bonds in Marshall County, Kansas bonds of one-thousand each."

Because Charles died on 1 February 1890, leaving only his children, who were made defendants, the trustee cannot be appointed in the stead of Charles F. Scoville without the aid of the Court of Equity.

---

576 *United States Land Records, 1630–1974, 524*. Ancestry.

577 *Ibid,* 164.

The sheriff of Cook County was commanded to:

> . . . summon the defendants [ ] Scoville, Frank Scoville and Mary Cushing to appear in court the "first day of the next term thereof."
>
> Signed Mary L. Wilson

> On the [ ] May 1890, a complaint for the appointment of a trustee as a successor to Charles F Scoville, deceased, for the bonds in question of Marshall County, Kansas, face value ten-thousand dollars, was requested.

Edward T. Cushing was appointed the new trustee without bond instead of Charles F Scoville. The court ordered that after the decease of Mary L. Wilson, the defendants will each be delivered five thousand each, "face value." Mary Wilson consented to the appointment of Edward Cushing as trustee, as did Frank Scoville and Mary Cushing.[578]

It's difficult to determine what type of relationship Mary had with her niece and nephew. They had come to stay with her and Uncle Abner in 1854/55, but they were very young at that time. The court case may have just been a legal technicality to appoint a new trustee upon the death of her brother Charles F. Scoville and there was no family discord at all.

Since most of the 1890 population schedules (that were held at the Commerce Department Building) were destroyed by a fire in 1921, it leaves a ten- to twenty-year gap without a census for researchers.[579]

New York State mandated a census to be taken in 1892[580] because of the destruction of the censuses previously mentioned. This is the last census on which Abner M. Wilson appears. This census page that records Abner Wilson's information is barely legible; he is living in Oswego, Oswego, New York; he is 70 years old, born in 1822, and is a citizen of the United States. Because of the poor copy, it is impossible to tell whether Mary Wilson is listed.

Oswego is located on Lake Ontario and is now a city of some 18,142 citizens according to the 2010 census. This is the place that Abner and Mary Wilson would live out the remainder of their lives.

One year later, on the 23rd day of December 1893,[581] Mary Lord (Scoville) Wilson died.

---

578 The court case is in my possession. Regrettably, I did not cite the volume or page numbers. The case was before the Circuit Court of Cook County, Illinois; State of Illinois Cook County, Mary L. Wilson vs. Frank Scoville and Mary Cushing; Bill Appointment of Successor in Trust.

579 Some states did take a census every five years, but most were every ten years. If you were a "ten-year" state, that meant the last census available to you is the 1880, until the next census in 1900. There were some special censuses taken, such as the 1890 census for veterans of the Union side of the Civil War, *i.e., United States Census of Union Veterans and Widows of the Civil War,* and New York completed one for 1892.

580 *New York State Census, 1892,* original found at the New York State Library, Albany, New York; copies online at Ancestry and FamilySearch; E.D. 02.

581 *New York State Death Index, 1880–1956—Oneida, New York;* Entry Number: 53561; Record Number: 15; FamilySearch database.

She was approximately seventy-one years of age and had been married to Abner for forty-six years.

While the New York Death Index indicates that her death took place in Oneida, I believe that both Mary and Abner died in Oswego, New York. If you recall, Abner had purchased a plot in Oneida, Madison County, in March of 1894—this purchase occurred nine months prior to Abner's death on December 29, 1894—one year and six days after his wife, Mary.[582] Abner and Mary are buried in Glenwood Cemetery (Onieda), along with Mary's brother, Henry C. Scoville.

Abner Marshall left a will,[583] which was probated on January 5, 1895 in the Village of Oneida.

The Last Will and Testament of Aber M. Wilson

Hiram Wilson, executor of Abner M. Wilson of Lenox—Almira [ ] whose married name and place of residence was unknown and could not after reasonable diligence be ascertained, who if living was a sister of said testator; if dead her heirs at law, next of kin and descendants, if any, whose respective names, ages, and residences were unknown could not after reasonable diligence be ascertained.

[ I have left out the common preamble]

First . . . to Margaret Mulholland, now my housekeeper, the sum of $200.00 in money, also one bedstead with bedding for the same. One set of plates, knives, and forks; one set of silver teaspoons; one willow rocking chair; one cane seated rocking chair; one bureau and all my deceased wives' dresses.

Second . . . to Mrs. Antonelle Davis of Augusta, New York, the sum of $100.00.

Third . . . to my cousin, Hiram C. Wilson[584] of Oneida, New York, the sum of $200.00.

Fourth . . . to my cousin, Barnes Davis[585] of Oneida, New York, the sum of $100.00.

Fifth . . . to my cousin Mrs. Malvina Davis, the sum of $100.00.

Sixth . . . to my cousin Wilson Frisbie of Rome, New York, the sum of $100.00.

Seventh . . . to my cousin, Henry T. Frisbie[586] of Cape Vincent, New York, the sum of $100.00

582 *New York State Death Index, 1852–1956, Oneida, New York; Original data: New York State Death Index, New York Department of Health, Albany, New York;* Certificate Number: 51323; FamilySearch.

583 *New York Wills and Probate Records, 1659–1999—Madison Wills;* Vol: 41–42; 1894–1896; copy in my possession.

584 Hiram C. Wilson, b. Sept. 1819 Connecticut; d. 23 Jan. 1903 Oneida, New York; m. Adelia ______; According to various census reports Hiram was a hotel keeper, boatbuilder, and carpenter. He died intestate. *New York Death Index, 1852–1956, Oneida, New York; New York Wills and Probate Records, 1659–1999, 485; Letters: Vol: 006; 1898–1903; 1900 Federal Census for Oneida, New York,* shows that his birth month was September.

585 Barnes Davis (1820–1898), buried Oneida Castle Cemetery.

586 Henry T. Frisbie, d. 22 March 1897, Cape Vincent, New York; Original Record: *New York Dept. of Health, Albany, New York; New York Death Index, 1852–1956;* Certificate Number: 12525.

Eighth . . . to Mary E. Beach, Rockford, Illinois, the sum of $50.00.

Lastly, if anything remains after the foregoing bequests are divided equally between Mary E. Cushing of Chicago, Illinois and Frank Scoville of South Riverside, California.

Hiram C. Wilson nominated executor, November 12, 1894.

Signed A.M. Wilson

On March 2, 1895, Hiram C. Wilson was back at the Surrogate Court with J (or F?) Devereaux, Esq. appointed the special guardian of "such the unknown descendants of Almira Wilson (if she be dead) as may be minors for the protection of their respective interests in this proceeding."

What became of Almira Wilson (the sister of Abner), who she may have married, or what, if any, descendants she may have had, I have been unable to ascertain.

### *16. i. Silas Kelsey[6] (Almira,[5] Ithamar,[4] Timothy,[3] Stephen,[2] Stephen,[1] Arthur)*

Speculative birth date 10 April 1821,[587] either in Connecticut or New York; died 10 September 1861,[588] Maine, Broome, New York; burial Maine Town Cemetery; married (1) Patty M. ________ about 1847;[589] died 2 March 1848, Maine, Broome, New York;[590] married (2) Flavia C. ______; she born circa 1823, perhaps Tioga, New York.[591]

Researching these early families has been difficult. They were not prominent people, and no diaries or journals are available to assist us in building a three-dimensional narrative of their lives. As you have seen from this work, most of these gleanings come from the census records to track where they were at any given time—granted, there are often five- to ten-year gaps between the census records, but we can harness some of that information to build a "picture" of our ancestors' lives. Of course, we will never truly *know* them, but we can get a glimpse of how they lived.

The Horace Kelsey and Ithamar Scoville families have been difficult subjects because of the lack of vital records and the fact that some of them were not long-lived, such as Silas Kelsey, who did not live long enough to provide us with much information.

---

587 Much of the documentation on the Kelsey family comes from a descendant—Deborah L. Horzen—and I thank her for graciously providing this information to me. This date is an estimate from the age at his death, which is given as "aged 40 yrs. 5 mos." as is inscribed on his headstone.

588 The death date comes from the Silas Kelsey headstone marker.

589 This information was provided by Mrs. Gordon H. Woodward, Endicott, New York, through the Moak-Hardy-Flint-Kelsey research notes; hereinafter cited as "Moak-Hardy-Flint-Kelsey research notes."

590 Her death date comes from *U.S. Find A Grave.*

591 Census reports 1850, 1855, and 1860. The 1855 state census provides information on the county of birth.

What we *do* know is that Silas Kelsey was born in 1821, perhaps in Connecticut or New York. Since his parents are said to have married in Austerlitz, New York, in 1820, it is more likely that Silas was born in New York.

Silas is enumerated with his parents on the 1830 and 1840 censuses. The family is living in Greene Township, Chenango, New York, in 1840 and by 1842/43 Silas has moved to Maine, Broome, New York.[592] Sometime around 1847, Silas married a woman only known as Patty M_______.[593] The name Patty *could* be a diminutive of Martha, Patience, or Patricia; however, without a surname it would be a futile attempt to try to locate her as only male heads of households are listed on the census prior to 1850.

Patty Kelsey died shortly after giving birth to twins. The boy child died at birth February 14, (1848) and his sister survived less than six weeks.[594] *If* Patty brought the twins to full-term this would mean that her marriage to Silas occurred early in 1847 and she would have been pregnant by May of the same year.

Sometime after the death of Silas's first wife, Patty, and before the 1850 census, he remarries a woman by the name of Flavia C._______. Once again, we do not have her maiden surname. Whether the "C" denotes her maiden name or a middle name is unknown. The 1855 census indicates that she was born in Tioga County, and she had lived in Broome County for eight years; that would mean she was in Broome County in 1847 and was likely in the town of Maine during this time.

The reasoning here is that, after the death of Patty, Silas would have looked for a wife locally and Flavia C. ______ could have been known to the Kelsey family prior to Patty's death.

The 1850 census[595] for Maine, Broome, New York, shows a family of three individuals:

> Silas Kelsey, 29, farmer, born Connecticut, real estate value: $700
> Flavia Kelsey, 27, born New York
> Philo Kelsey, 14, born New York

Silas' brother Philo may have been living with his brother and his wife during this time, helping out on the farm, or was simply visiting when the enumerator came to call. The fact that Silas has real estate valued at $700 would suggest that he owned the farm and was paying taxes as Silas and his father (Horace) were on the Maine tax rolls for 1852.[596]

On April 26, 1854, Abner Flint, Jr., and his wife, Melissa (Kelsey), deeded some property to Horace Kelsey. Silas Kelsey is an adjoining landowner,[597] however, by the time the New

592 The timeframe is based on the 1855 census where, for the question of how long the person resided in said town, Silas (or whomever answered) responded "13 years."

593 Moak-Hardy-Flint-Kelsey research notes.

594 Based on notes from Deborah L. Horzen, Silas Kelsey is buried near his first wife, Patty, "their twins," daughter Ella, and Mother Almira. Herein "DLH research notes."

595 1850 census, *Maine, Broome County, New York*; Sheet: 404; Dwelling:16; Family: 16. DLH research notes.

596 Maine Tax Rolls; DLH research notes; Moak-Hardy-Flint-Kelsey research notes.

597 A township map for Maine 1855 shows Abner Flint, Jr's property located in section 116 of the town of Maine. Other family connections owned nearby land (Moak, Hardy and Emerson).

York State census for 1855[598] was done, Silas is no longer a landowner. The census copy is very poor but what can be made out is the following:

> Frame house, Value $75; Silas Kelsey, 34, b. Connecticut, farmer, married, resided (Maine) 12 yrs.
> Flavia Kelsey, 32, b. Tioga Co., married, resident 8 yrs.
> Ella M. Kelsey, 4, b. Broome Co.
> Nathan E. Kelsey, 11/12, b. Broome Co.

Whether Silas Kelsey had financial difficulties during this time period, causing him to have to sell his land, is unknown, but his fortunes must have changed by the time of the 1860[599] census. The family is still living in Maine, Broome County, on August 16, 1860, when the enumerator recorded their information.

The real estate was valued at $600 and personal estate at $100. So, it would seem Silas was back on track as far as owning land to farm; however, his wife, Flavia, is listed as "insane" on the census. The reason for this designation is unknown. Their children, Ellen and Nathan, age eight and five respectively, are attending school.

The Kelsey family is enumerated for the second time in 1860 on October 29 in Union, Broome County. They are now living with James and Harriet Emerson. Both James and Silas are listed as farmers. James Emerson's real estate value is $800 with a personal estate of $150; Silas' real estate and personal estate values were the same as they were in Maine, Broome County.

On this second census, Flavia Kelsey is still listed as "insane." Also enumerated is a George Kelsey, age four. Why isn't George listed on the census in the town of Maine in August?[600]

| | | | Name | Age | Sex | Occupation | Real estate | Personal estate | | Remarks | |
|---|---|---|---|---|---|---|---|---|---|---|---|
| 33 | 1830 | 1829 | James Emerson | 28 | M | Farmer | 800 | 150 | — | | 33 |
| 34 | | | Harriet | 31 | F | | | | — | | 34 |
| 35 | 1831 | — | Silas Kelsey | 41 | M | Farmer | 600 | 100 | — | | 35 |
| 36 | | | Flavia | 37 | F | | | | — | Insane | 36 |
| 37 | | | Ella | 10 | F | | | | — | | 37 |
| 38 | | | Nathan | 6 | M | | | | — | | 38 |
| 39 | [illegible] | | George | 4 | M | | | | — | | 39 |
| 40 | [illegible] | | Wm | | | | | | | | 40 |
| | | | No. white males, 23; No. white females, 16; No. colored males, ; No. colored females, ; No. foreign born, ; No. deaf and dumb, ; No. blind, ; No. insane, | | | | 10,925 | 4,000 | No. idiotic, ; No. paupers, | No. convicts, | |

Were the households combined because Silas couldn't work the farm anymore due to illness? Why was Flavia listed as "insane?"

Many women were placed in institutions for depression, epilepsy, suppressed menstruation, childbirth, overwork, domestic troubles, and what we now call post-partum depression, and many other reasons a woman could be labeled as "insane." Women's "issues" were little understood, and women in general had few rights during the timeframe being discussed here.

598 1855 *State Census, Maine Broome, County, New York*; Dwelling: 67; Family: 16; Original data: Census of the state of New York, for 1855. Microfilm. Various County Clerk Offices, New York. Ancestry.

599 This family is enumerated twice—once in Maine, Broome, New York, and the second time in Union, Broome, New York, 1860 census—Maine—Sheet: 189; Dwelling: 2102-02; Family:1152-3; 1860 census—Union—Sheet: 286-7; Dwelling:1928-3; Family:1828-29. DLH research notes.

600 Image of the 1860, *Union, Broome, New York*. Ancestry.

Perhaps their son George was very ill during this time. All we know about George is that he was born approximately in 1856 (from census records) and that he died before 1861.[601] Flavia's husband, Silas, made out his will in June 1861 and died in September of the same year at the age of forty—these two deaths would be a plausible reason for Flavia to be grief stricken (and termed "insane") but again, this is only speculation on my part.

**The Will of Silas Kelsey**

In the name of God amen. I Silas Kelsey of the Town of Maine in the County of Broome and State of New York of the age of forty years and being of sound mind and memory do make publisher and declare this is my last will and Testament in [ ] following that is to say.

First

After paying my debts I bequeath to my wife Flavia C. Kelsey for her support and the support of my two children Ella Kelsey and Nathan E Kelsey all the property of whatever name and nature I may be possessed of at the time of my death.[602]

Second

And I do hereby dispose of commit the tuition(?) and custody of my children Ella Kelsey and Nathan E. Kelsey and each (? ) of them for such time as they or any of them [ ] continue unmarried or under the age of twenty-one years to my wife Flavia C. Kelsey provided she remains my widow but is she should die or marry during the [ ] life or marriage? of my said children. I hereby dispose of and commit there to tuition? in custody to my executor here in after nominated and appointed. And lastly, I do hereby nominate and appoint my friend Robert Hogg[603] the executor of this my last will and testament hereby revoking all former wills by me made. In witness whereof I have heretofore set my hand and seal the 12th day of June in the year of our Lord 1861.

Signed: Silas Kelsey

Witnessed by William Hogg & Martin J. Swift

There is an additional record in regards to the deposition of one William Hogg. Mr. Hogg gave his deposition in the courthouse in Broome County, indicating that he had seen the deceased (Silas Kelsey) sign the last will and testament on the "12th day of June 1861," and that he (William Hogg) had witnessed said document. A similar record for witness A. J. Swift was also submitted for the record.

The will, which was devised on June 12, 1861, was proved on November 2, 1861, in the Surrogate Court.

601 DLH research notes.

602 George Kelsey is not mentioned in Silas' will; this would seem to indicate that George had already died.

603 Robert Hogg, along with Squire William Hogg and James Hogg, were from Scotland and settled in Maine, Broome County, New York, at a place once known as Mt. Ettrick as they were from Ettrick, Selkirkshire, Scotland; www.history.rays-place.com and www.brydondale.com.

The will and probate do not provide any details on the estate itself (whether real or personal). Where Flavia may have lived after the death of her husband is a mystery. She may have stayed with the Emersons for a time until she could make plans for the future for her and her two children.

But death came to call again on July 11, 1863,[604] when their daughter, Ella M. Kelsey, died. She is buried with her father, grandmother, and half-siblings in Maine Town Cemetery, Maine, Broome, New York.

In 1865,[605] Flavia C. Kelsey is living as a boarder in the Lewis Tyrell household. The household consisted of Lewis Tyrell, age 61, born Columbia County; his wife, Caroline, age 45, born Broome County; Lewis' sister, Cynthia T. Loomis, age 60, born Columbia County; and Flavia Kelsey, age 42, a border, born Tioga County. There is no occupation listed for Flavia. How did she end up of living with the Tyrell family? Were they friends, neighbors at one time, or relatives? Where is her son, Nathan Kelsey? He would have been approximately eleven years of age at this time. No further record has been located on Nathan Kelsey after the 1860 census. He either died prior to 1865, or he may have been "adopted" by another family and took their last name as his, or was put in an orphan's home if Flavia could not care for him.

The last record we have for Flavia is the 1870 census.[606] She is still residing in Maine, Broome County, but is now living with the Miner Pier family. Miner is listed as the head-of-household and is age 26, a farmer with a real estate value of $4,000 and a personal estate of $600. His wife, Lidia, age 27, and a daughter, Marcia, age nine months are also listed. Included in this household is George Davis, age 32, also a farmer with real estate worth $1,500, his wife, Mary, age 22, their daughter, Viola, age 2, and an infant (no name), age two months. Flavia Kelsey is listed as age forty-seven and "teaches school;" she has a personal estate of $200.

It is curious that after being listed as "insane" on the 1860 census, she is now, ten years later, teaching school. Was her so-called "insanity" in 1860 an aberration—a temporary condition?

After 1870, Flavia "disappears" from all census records (1875, 1880, and 1892) for New York. While the name Flavia is not that common, and using other variants of her name, she is not found as having removed from New York to another state. A marriage record has not been discovered to indicate she remarried after the 1870 census. All known genealogical resources available to me have been checked and rechecked. Without her maiden surname, all efforts in locating her with family members have been stymied.

The following death notice appeared in [the] *Broome Republican* on June 6, 1897:

> Mrs. Flavia Kelsey died at St. Lawrence County, New York a few weeks ago. Formerly of Maine, New York.

---

604 DLH research notes.

605 1865 Census—*Maine, Broome, New York;* Original data: Census of the state of New York; Microfilm New York State Archives, Albany, New York; District: 1; Line: 19; Page: 31; Ancestry.

606 1870 Census—*Maine, Broome, New York;* Roll: M593_907; Page: 387B; FHL: 552406; Dwelling: 454; Family: 462; Original data: NARA microfilm. Ancestry.

Her death would have occurred either the second or third week of May 1897. Her burial location is unknown. Flavia C. Kelsey was seventy-four years old at the time of her death.

***Children of Silas Kelsey and Patty M.*_______**

i. boy Kelsey (twin), b. 14 Feb 1848, Maine, Broome, New York; died same day.

ii. girl Kelsey (twin), b. 14 Feb 1848, Maine, Broome, New York; d. perhaps Feb/Mar 1848.

***Children of Silas Kelsey and Flavia C.* ______**

iii. Ella Kelsey, b. circa 1851, Broome County, New York; d. 11 Jul 1863, Broome, New York.

iv. Nathan E. Kelsey, b. circa 1854, Broome County, New York; nothing more is known.

v. George Kelsey, b. circa 1856, New York; d. before 1861, New York.

### *17. II. CLARISSA KELSEY[6] (ALMIRA,[5] ITHAMAR,[4] TIMOTHY,[3] STEPHEN,[2] STEPHEN,[1] ARTHUR)*

Born circa 1822/23, probably in New York;[607] died 31 October 1911, Triangle, Broome, New York;[608] buried South Street Cemetery, Triangle, New York; married circa 1839, William Benson, born 5 July 1814, Denmark,[609] Lewis, New York; died 16 October 1893, Triangle, Broome, New York; buried South Street Cemetery, Triangle, New York; son of Isaac Benson and Jane Bowker.[610]

Clarissa Kelsey was the second child born to Horace and Almira (Scoville) Kelsey. Some of the census records indicate that she was born in Ostego County, New York. As we've seen in the record of her father, Horace, this family moved frequently. There is also a town within Ostego County that is also called Ostego; whether she was born in the town or the county remains unknown.

Clarissa's mother and father are listed on the 1840[611] census for Greene, Chenango County. I theorize that they lived there for a time and that this is where Clarissa met and then married William Benson on November 10, 1839. Clarissa would have been sixteen or seventeen at this marriage and William approximately twenty-three years old. The marriage was officiated by Clarissa's father, the Rev. Horace Kelsey.

---

607 Some of the censuses indicate she was born in Connecticut; however, it doesn't seem probable as the Kelsey family were in Austerlitz, Columbia County, New York, in 1820. Horace Kelsey's obituary mentions the various towns he preached in—Connecticut is never mentioned.

608 Headstone states that she was "88 yrs." at her death on 31 October 1911. Grave memorial #74994657; Find A Grave.

609 *Town Clerk's Register of Men Who Served in the Civil War, 1861–1865*; Collection# (N-Ar) 13774; Box: 4; Roll: 3; New York State Archives, Albany, New York.

610 *Ibid.*

611 1840 census, *Greene, Chenango, New York*; Roll: 274; Sheet: 89; FHL: 0017183. Original data: Sixth Census of the United States, 1840 (NARA microfilm publication M704, 580 rolls). Records of the Bureau of the Census, Record Group, 29. National Archives, Washington, D.C.

This newly married couple is listed on the 1840 census for Greene Township, with Clarissa's mother and father living three dwellings away from them.

The Town of Greene was incorporated April 12, 1842, and is situated on the Chenango River (which roughly runs north-south in the eastern part of town). During this period there were approximately 850 inhabitants. The town boasted that it had four churches (Baptist, Congregational, Episcopalian, and Methodist), two banks, two hotels, a grist mill, a foundry, a machine shop, two plaster mills, several stores and mechanic shops, and the Union School.[612] How long this couple remained in Greene Township has not been revealed through a range of records that have been checked. Their trail can only be followed through the various census records.

They may have moved a few times prior to the next census to be taken (1850). Clarissa's parents had purchased land in Pittsfield, Ostego County, New York; whether Clarissa and William went with them cannot be ascertained at this time.

By the time of the 1850[613] census this couple were now living in Barker, Broome County, New York (the counties of Chenango and Broome border one another). William Benson is listed as a "farmer" with a real estate value of $200.00, and he was now the father of four children: Susan J. (10), Niles (8), Isaac (6), and Juliette (1); wife Clarissa "keeps house."

When the next census was taken in 1855[614] this family had removed to Maine, Broome, New York. The census indicates that they had been there for one year. At this time, Clarissa's parents were living in Candor in Tioga County, New York, some twenty-six miles distant.[615] However, next door to the Bensons were Clarissa's sister, Melissa, her husband, Abner Flint, and their family, as well as brother Silas Kelsey, who also resided there.

During this time frame, the Benson family was living in a log home that had a value of one hundred dollars. William is still listed as a "farmer," but he did not own the land that he worked. William and Abner (Flint) likely labored side-by-side to provide for their families, and the sisters would be doing the same in sharing the labor in their daily chores and child-rearing.

The Benson family had not grown between the 1850 and the 1855 censuses. The family still consisted of William (39), born Lewis Co., NY; Clarissa (33), born Ostego, NY; Susan P. (14), born Chenango Co., NY; Niles H. (13), born Chenango Co., NY; Isaac (11), born Broome Co., NY; and Juliette (5), born Broome Co., NY.

Time moved on and the wind of war soon stirred the country. William was between forty-

---

612 Child, Hamilton, *History of Greene, New York, Gazetteer and Business Directory of Chenango County, New York for 1869–70*; compiled and published, Syracuse, New York (1869).

613 1850 census; *Barker, Broome County, New York*; Dwelling: 187; Family: 197; Sheet: 243A. Ancestry.

614 1855 *New York State Census, Maine, Broome County*; Dwelling: 394; Line: 33; Original data: Various Clerk's Offices, New York. Ancestry.

615 This figure is based on current roadways.

three and forty-seven years old when he enlisted[616] on September 9, 1861, at Whitney Point,[617] Broome, New York. He enlisted for three years with the 89th Infantry Regiment, Company F.[618] His rank was a private and he was assigned as a "wagoner."[619] He was mustered into service on October 4, 1861, at Elmira, New York.

The only battle that William may have been involved in was the Battle of South Mills, North Carolina, on April 19, 1862. Not long after, William Benson was discharged from service on May 25, 1862, from Camp Dickinson, Roanoke Island, North Carolina, due to disability.

The Battle of South Mills[620] had been commanded by General Jesse L. Reno on the Union side. Reno was given this assignment by Union Army Major General Ambrose E. Burnside and the battle was part of the "Burnside Expedition" to reclaim the northeastern portion of North Carolina for the Union. The Confederate Army was commanded by Ambrose R. Wright. On the morning of April 19, 1862, Reno marched north to the road to South Mills (the Union Army had 3,000 soldiers to the Confederates' 1,000).[621] Unfortunately, one group of Union soldiers took the wrong road, which led to an unplanned ten-mile march, and by the time they met up with the larger force, they found their fellow soldiers "hotly engaged by entrenched Confederates."[622] The goal of the Union was to destroy the locks on the Dismal Swamp Canal; however, confusion prevented the Union troops from reaching the locks. General Reno abandoned this expedition and both sides claimed victory. The Confederates were really the victors here as the locks remained intact and their casualties were much less than the Union side.

The Union suffered "13 killed; 101 wounded and 13 missing; the Confederates had 6 killed; 19 wounded and 3 captured."[623]

Without William Benson's military records at hand, I am uncertain if William Benson was wounded during this particular battle. His discharge papers state that he had "chronic rheumatism," while his wife claims her husband had "chronic diarrhea and received an injury with the back leading to his death."[624] The back injury *may* have occurred during the Battle of South Mills.

---

616 These figures are assumptions based on ages given at various census times (born between 1814–1818).

617 His service muster roll. The muster roll also states his age is "44," however, if he was indeed born in 1814, he actually would have been forty-seven years old.

618 *Town Clerk's Register of Men Who Served in the Civil War, 1861–1865*; Collection# (N-Ar) 13774; Box: 4; Roll: 3; New York State Archives, Albany, New York.

619 Also known as a teamster—one who provides supplies for the troops and follows them through each battle and skirmish.

620 The Confederates referred to this battle as the Battle of Camden (Camden, N.C.).

621 These figures vary depending upon which article is online.

622 See www.ncdr.gov.

623 See www.ncpedia.org.

624 DLH research notes. According to the discharge papers William was 44 years old, 5′ 5 ½″ tall, with light complexion, gray eyes, and brown hair.

While William was away serving in the Civil War, Clarissa Benson was likely managing the land that they were living on, along with all the other duties she had, like so many other women during this time. Since this family has not been located on the 1860[625] census it is difficult to know if there were any relatives nearby to assist her. The Bensons are no longer living next door to the Flints as they had been in 1855. Regardless, for seven months Clarissa was virtually on her own.

Congress authorized a bounty of one hundred dollars to be paid to those men who had enlisted for three years in July 1861. However, this would not be a "lump sum" payment, but paid in monthly installments with the soldiers' regular compensation. The soldier would have sent most of that money home.

Other than the usual work that had to be done, women also took time to sew uniforms, make bandages, and knit socks for the men. Women also became independent while their husbands were away, making daily decisions on finances and operating the farm. When their husbands came back from the war, the men were often suffering from life-long disabilities—not only of body, but of spirit. The wife may have had to continue with the farming until the husband was well enough to assist in the labor; or they may have decided to hire out help if there were no sons to assist. The women who had become independent during the war, now had to navigate the *new* household dynamic with their husbands' return.

Two years after being discharged from service, the Benson family is now living in Triangle, Broome, New York. The 1865[626] census reveals that William is now a landowner. Perhaps he was able to purchase a farm with money that may have been owed to him for his service in the Civil War. The family consists of the following:

William Benson, 50, b. Jefferson Co.; farmer; owns land, formerly in army
Clarissa Benson, 43, b. Osteo Co.; 6 children, 1 married
Horace N. Benson, 23, b. Chenango Co., single, laborer, now in army
Juliet Benson, 16, b. Broome Co.
Carrie Benson, 6, b. Broome Co.
The value of the frame house is $800.00

The town of Triangle was formed from the town of Lisle in 1831 by an Act of Legislature. The town was previously known as "Chenango Triangle," having been first settled in 1791.[627] Whitney Point (where William Benson enlisted) is a village within Triangle. Like many of the towns in upper New York State, they are sparsely populated, even to this day.

625 I've read the whole of the 1860 censuses for Triangle, Maine, and Barker, New York. It is possible their name has been misspelled or this family was missed all together. In addition, there is only one Clarissa Benson in Collins, Erie, New York, age 35, in the Jacob Van Ostrand household. Family: 115; Dwelling: 118; Page: 105. Ancestry.

626 1865 *New York State Census, Triangle, Broome County, New York;* Sheet: 14; Dwelling: 116; Family: 120; Line: 37; Page: 14; Original data: Census of the state of New York, for 1865, microfilm, New York State Archives, Albany, New York.

627 See www.wikipedia.org "Triangle, New York."

By 1870[628] William had increased not only his personal estate ($1,560), but his real estate was now valued at $6,000.00—this does not mean the couple was wealthy; as the old saying goes when speaking of farmers, they were "land rich [and] cash poor." While farmers may have had many acres of land to make them "land rich" their daily living was often a struggle and so, "cash poor." The growing season is short in this part of the country (depending on what type of crop is grown), with August being the typical harvesting time. Many farmers may have also planted root vegetables to be harvested as late as December. However, as with all farmers, they never knew from year to year what their income would be due to fluctuations in the weather and market.

The aforementioned census (1870) lists only three people now living in the household: William (56), Clarissa (50), and daughter Carrie (12).

In addition to the 1870 Federal census as noted above, William is also enumerated on the 1870[629] Non-Population Schedule. This information provides information on the amount of acreage, how many farm animals he owned, as well as the amount of grain he may have.

William at this time has 140 acres of land—120 acres improved and 20 acres of woodland. As noted in the federal census his land is valued at $6,000 and the following:

Farming implements: $200.00.Total amount of wages paid during the year, excluding board: $100

| | | |
|---|---|---|
| Horses: 4 | Milk Cows: 19 | Other Cattle: 1 |
| Sheep: 5 | Swine: 5 | Value of all livestock: $1,460. |
| Spring Wheat: 17 (bushels) | Indian Corn: 50 (bushels) | Corn: 200 (bushels) |

As with the 1860 census, this family has not been located for the 1875 New York State census. This family would likely still be living in Triangle as that is where they are living in 1880.[630] Again, the household is made up of William (67), Clarissa (57), Carrie (21), and Frank Barber (22), who has been hired on as a "laborer." The 1880 census does not provide any information regarding the value of real or personal estate for William.

In 1890[631] a special census was taken for veterans of the Civil War as well as the widows of the veterans.

> William Benson, private, Co. F, 89 NY Infantry; 4 October 1861—25 May 1862; length of service: 7 mo. 21 days.
>
> Notes: *chronic diarrhea and injury to back and general disability.*

---

628 1870 *New York Census, Triangle, Broome County, New York*; Roll: M593_907; Page: 463A; FHL Film#: 552406; Dwelling: 328; Family: 356. Ancestry.

629 1870 *Agricultural Census, Triangle, Broome County, New York;* Line: A20; Roll: 20 Line: 24; Page: 7. Ancestry.

630 1880 *Census, Triangle, Broome County, New York;* Roll: 811; Page: 441C; Enumeration District: 056; Sheet: 9; Dwelling: 28; Family: 28; Original data: Tenth Census of the U.S. 1880 (NARA Film, pub. T9, 1,454 rolls); Records of Bureau of the Census, Rec. Group 29; National Archives, Washington, D.C. Ancestry.

631 1890 *Special Census—Surviving Soldiers, Sailors and Marines, and Widows, etc.* (NARA) microfilm M123; Page:1; S. District: 9; E. District: 77; Line: 49: Home#: 74; Family#: 77; Triangle Township.

Regarding the New York census for 1892[632]—I cannot find where William was enumerated during this time.

On August 7, 1893, William made out his will. He had turned seventy-nine the previous month and, like many soldiers before him, suffered much from the effects of the war throughout his life, and that life was nearing its end.

> In the Name of God, Amen, I, William Benson, of the town of Triangle in the County a Broome and State of New York, being of sound mind and memory, and considering its uncertainty of this life, do therefore make, ordain, publish and declare, this to be my last Will and Testament: that is to say, first, after all my lawful debts are paid and discharged, I give, and bequeath to my wife Clarissa Benson, all my property and estate real and personal of what name or kind sorrow to have and to hold my said property to herself and her heirs forever. Likewise, I make, constitute, and appoint my said wife Clarissa Benson and my son-in-law Charles E, ADAMS to be executor of this my last Will and Testament, hereby revoking all former Wills by me made. In Witness Whereof, I have hereunto subscribed my name and affixed my seal, the Seventh day of August in the year of one thousand eight hundred and ninety-three.
>
> Signed: William Benson (L.S.)

The above instrument consisting of one sheet, was at the date thereof, subscribed by "William Benson the Testator named in the foregoing Will, in the presence of each of us, and at the time of making such subscription the above instrument was declared by the said Testator to be his last Will and Testament and each of us at the request of said Testator and in his presence, and in the presence of each other, sign our names as witness thereto, as the end of the Will."

E. W. Simmons, Residing at Triangle, Broome Co., NY

C.H. Pickering, Residing at Triangle, Broome, Co. NY[633]

The will was probated at the Surrogate Court in Binghamton, Broome, New York, on March 19, 1894, and on May 18, 1894, since there was no one to oppose the last Will and Testament of William Benson, and since all witnesses were interviewed and evidence proven sufficient, the probate was granted. At this time, Clarissa Benson and Charles Adams would have to collect William's assets and take steps to pay any debts or taxes that may be owed as well as funeral expenses, doctors' bills, etc.

William Benson is buried in the South Street Cemetery in Triangle with his son Isaac, who had died in the Civil War.

≈

After the death of her husband, it is unknown where Clarissa Benson was living. It is not until 1910[634] when she is listed on the census in Triangle Village, living next door to her daughter

---

632 Both FamilySearch.org and Ancestry.com were checked for William Benson.

633 Transcription of will provided by Deborah L. Horzen. The will can also be found on Ancestry.

634 1910 census *Triangle, Broome County, New York;* Dwelling: 158; Family: 169; Roll:

Carrie and her husband, Charles (Adams). She is now eighty-six years old, a widow, having born six children—four of which were alive.

Going back over the 1900 census, I find Carrie and Charles Adams living in Triangle, but Clarissa is not listed living with them or even in the neighborhood.[635] The mystery of where she was living remains.

Clarissa Benson died on October 31, 1911, in Triangle, Broome County, New York, a town she has resided in for forty-six years. She is buried with her husband, William, and son Isaac in South Street Cemetery in Triangle.

### *Children of William Benson and Clarissa Kelsey*

28. i. Susan Jane Benson,[7] b. 9 Oct 1840,[636] perhaps Greene, Chenango, New York; d. 26 Mar 1937,[637] Ventura, Ventura, California; m. circa 1861, Henry Newton Elliott, b. 21 June 1837,[638] Greene, Chenango, New York; s.o. John Elliott (1799–1846) and Jane Blake (1800–1869); d. 21 Mar 1918, Los Angeles, California.[639]

29. ii. Niles Horace Benson[7] (aka Horace Benson, Henry N. Benson), b. 28 Sep 1841, Greene, Chenango, New York;[640] d. 4 Sep 1930, York, York, Nebraska; buried Greenwood Cemetery;[641] m. circa 1866 to Olive I. Stowell.

iii. Isaac Benson,[7] b. 1 Mar 1844,[642] Maine, Broome, New York; d. 31 Oct 1864 Fortress Monroe, Virginia. Like his father and brother, Isaac Benson heeded the call to serve in the Civil War. He enlisted for the first time on September 1, 1861, in the 27th Infantry Regiment, Co. C as a private. He was only seventeen years old at that time. He had been in the Battle of Gaines Mill, which occurred on June 27, 1862, and was wounded in the arm. He was discharged on May 31, 1863. Isaac went back home to Triangle and continued to work on the farm; however, on January 30, 1864, Isaac went to Cortlandville (N.Y.) to re-enlist. Isaac must have been set on doing this as Cortlandville is twenty-six miles from Triangle.

He enlisted for three years and was mustered in on February 1, 1864, as a private in the 16th Regiment Independent Light Artillery. The records show his age as "20 years old" with "blue eyes, light hair, light complexion and stood 5′10″ tall."[643]

---

T624_926; Page: 6A; E.D: 005; FHL: 1374939; Original data: NARA T624—1,178 rolls.

635 I read the 1900 census line by line for Whitney Point and Triangle. I did not find Clarissa in either town.

636 The date of birth is based on her age given in her obituary, "96 yrs., 6 mos. 16 days."

637 Sources: *Social Security Death Index;* obituary notice, *The Los Angeles Times,* Saturday, March 27 edition, 1937; 34.

638 This information comes from a descendant of this family; however, it has not been verified.

639 *California Death Index, 1905–1930*; original data: California Department of Health & Welfare; herein CA Vital Records. Ancestry.

640 Date of birth comes from *Records of Soldiers & Officers In Military Service.* Ancestry.

641 Death information comes from Find A Grave.

642 Date of birth comes from *New York Civil War Muster Roll Abstracts, 1861–1900;* 270; (Herein: Muster Roll). Ancestry.

643 Muster Roll.

On April 16, 1865, Isaac was involved in the Battle of West Point in Georgia and, at some point, he was admitted to the field hospital and died of disease[644] at Fortress Monroe, Virginia, on October 31, 1864.[645] His remains were brought back to Triangle, New York, where he is buried with his mother and father.

The irony of this battle is that General Robert E. Lee surrendered at Appomattox Court House nine days earlier. The news of Lee's surrender traveled slowly, and many lives were needlessly lost. It wasn't until May 13, 1865, that the Civil War officially ended.

Isaac Benson never married and had no issue.

iv. Juliette Benson,[7] b. circa 1849, likely in Broome County, New York; d. unknown; m. prior to the 1870 New York census, Abram Young(s) (aka Abram F. Young/Abram T. Young), b. 7 Apr 1849, Broome, New York, son of Henry Young(s) and Catherine Taft;[646] d. about 1898.

In 1864, at the age of eighteen, Abram Young enlisted in the 64$^{th}$ Infantry Regiment, Co. E in Goshen, New York. His registration record states that he was born in Triangle, New York, and this record also gives his parents' names as noted above. Abram was mustered out of the service on July 14, 1865. Sometime prior to 1870,[647] Abram Young and Juliette Benson married, as they are listed on that census . Abram is listed as a "farmer" and the value of their personal estate is $400.00.

By 1875, the couple had moved to Binghamton, Ward 2, Broome, New York. The 1880 census shows that they have moved again, this time to DeWitt, Onondaga, New York. Abram is now employed as a bookkeeper. They also have a two-year-old daughter named Mary Young, who had been born in 1878. Sadly, their daughter Mary died at age eleven months in February 1880.[648]

Abram is listed on the *1890 Veterans Census Schedule* as "Abraham F. Young."[649] There is a notation that he had been "shot in the arm" but, apparently, he had no disability of any kind.

In 1892 the couple is enumerated in Syracuse, Onondaga, New York (now listed as "Abram F. Young and Julia E. Young"). Both are aged forty-three and Abram continues to work as a bookkeeper. This couple begins to show up in the city directories in 1885–1891 in Syracuse. Even though the city directories go beyond 1891, I could not locate Abram any further.

Julia Young filed for Abram's pension[650] in/about January 1899, so Abram must have died sometime after 1892 and prior to 1899.

---

644 The predominant illnesses that took the lives of many soldiers were: pneumonia, typhoid, diarrhea/dysentery, and malaria. Approximately two-thirds of deaths of Civil War soldiers were caused by uncontrolled infectious diseases.

645 All information on Isaac Benson's service comes from Muster Rolls.

646 *Ibid*

647 1870 census, *Triangle, Broome, New York;* Roll: M593_967; Page: 463A. Ancestry.

648 *U.S. Mortality Schedules, 18850–1885.* Ancestry.

649 The day of his enlistment and day of mustering out is the same as the Abram Young who enlisted in 1864, so I will conclude that this is the same person.

650 *U.S. Civil War Pension Index. General Index to Pension Files 1861–1934.* 64$^{th}$ Infantry Regiment, Co. E. Ancestry.

Lastly, a Julia Young is enumerated in 1925 in Syracuse, age seventy-five. Because there are some other women with the same name in Syracuse at the same time, I am uncertain if this is the woman who had married Abram Young.

In addition, I have not been able to find out where this couple with their infant daughter are buried.

### *18. iii. Melissa Kelsey*[6] *(Almira,*[5] *Ithamar,*[4] *Timothy,*[3] *Stephen,*[2] *Stephen,*[1] *Arthur)*

Born 13 February 1833, Pittsfield, Ostego, New York;[651] died 21 June 1910, Madison Township, Hancock, Iowa;[652] buried Concord Cemetery, Garner, Hancock, Iowa;[653] married (1) 25 December 1850, Abner Flint, Jr., born 23 June 1826, Rensselaer County, New York;[654] died 14 July 1878, Maine, Broome, New York;[655] son of Abner Flint (1783–1866) and Anna West (1791–1870);[656] married (2) 8 June 1891, Lester W. Buck, New York; born circa 1832, place unknown; died 29 November 1892,[657] Broome County, New York; married (3) 30 October 1893,[658] Garner, Hancock, Iowa, John W. Garlow, born circa 1820, Cazenovia, Madison, New York; died 11 September 1897, Humbolt County, Iowa; buried Union Cemetery.

At the time of Melissa Kelsey's birth in 1833, her parents resided in Edmeston, New York, per the 1830 census—a trek of about six miles north of Pittsfield. Whether they were living in Pittsfield or just visiting during this time is a question that can't successfully be answered here. There *was* a Baptist church in Pittsfield, so the Kelsey family living in this town is a possibility as the first record of Pittsfield's First Baptist Church dates back to 1823. It would be no surprise then if Horace Kelsey preached there for a time.

Since the Kelseys left no paper trail (that anyone is aware of), any information must come from imagination and the facts that are available. Unfortunately, anecdotal evidence is rare to come by for your everyday, average ancestor. While it has been mentioned several times previously in this narrative on the Scoville family and their relations, we can presume that Melissa—as with many females during this time—learned the skills from her mother (or another female relative). It was a hard life. According to some reports, the average agricultural individual worked from "first light to dark," sometimes as many as seventy hours per week, particularly in the first half of the nineteenth century.[659]

---

651 Melissa Kelsey's birth/birthplace information comes from varying sources: the Garlow family Bible; death certificate; Flint Bible records; obituary notice; letter from Lena Flint Remy to Althia Flint Steward, 26 Feb. 1963; DLH records.

652 *Ibid* death certificate; obituary notice.

653 DLH records; Find A Grave.

654 DLH records via Flint Bible Records; Macri's *Early Families of Broome Co. New York,* online: www.freepages.rootsweb.com.

655 *Ibid.*

656 *Ibid*

657 *Broome County, New York Wills,* 20–21; 127–128; Ancestry.

658 Marriage notice, *Hancock Democrat,* November 2, 1893, edition.

659 From "Hours of Work in U.S. History;" *Economic History Association,* www.eh.net.

There is some disagreement on how many hours a person worked during this time; nevertheless, work was all-encompassing, except for Sunday.

Most people observed Sunday as a day of "rest;" no work was performed and going to church was all important for much of the population, and I would imagine especially for the Kelsey family. A fine example of how Sundays were spent comes from the diary kept by Joshua Hempstead of New London, Connecticut. An entry example: "Sund 2d it began to rain about Sunrise & held it till near night. Mr. adams pr all day."[660] While Mr. Hempstead accounted for his life during the eighteenth century, and attending church was by far stricter in his time, it was still an important part of life for many people during the time frame discussed here.

In February of 1850, Melissa had turned seventeen and was living with her parents and brother Philo in Colesville, Broome, New York, as noted on the census. At the same time, Abner Flint, Jr. was living in Conklin, a town about eighteen miles south of Colesville. Abner was living in the household of Hoyt Boughton, a young man of twenty-nine years. Mr. Boughton was by trade a carpenter and joiner and was living with his wife and two small children, as well as Abner (a carpenter) and William Harsing (?) (carpenter). Perhaps these men were in business together for a time.

In December of the same year, Abner Flint, Jr. married Melissa Kelsey in the county of Broome.[661]

Whether this young couple had set up housekeeping in their own household or lived with the Flints or Kelseys shortly after marriage is unknown; however, they were living in their own household by the 1855 census[662] in the town of Maine. Living next to the Flints were sister and brother-in-law William and Clarissa Benson and family. The Flint home was a frame dwelling with a value of $200.00[663] of which Abner is marked as "owner."

Dwellings during this period were simple, usually rectangular, where additions could be added as needed. The exterior was typically clapboard or shingle siding and had a center chimney. Many of these homes were one story with post and beam construction and had very little ornamentation.[664]

While Abner was working as a carpenter, Melissa—like all farm wives—was constantly busy and had very little idle time. She would have had a kitchen garden, from which she would preserve the fruit and vegetables by "canning" for the hard winters that were inevitable in this part of New York. The other part of her day was filled with caring for livestock and poultry, making the family garments, cooking, and being part of the labor force during planting and harvest times. The above-mentioned duties do not touch upon the fact that the children in the

---

660 Diary entry copied as written. pr = preached. Hempstead, Joshua, *Diary of Joshua Hempstead of New London, Connecticut, Covering A Period of Forty-Seven Years from September, 1711, to November, 1758*. 403.

661 Flint Bible.

662 1855 census *New York State, Broome County, New York*; ED 1–2, Family 394 & 395. Ancestry.

663 Using an online inflation calculator, $200.00 in 1855 would be approximately $5,985.93 in 2020. www.officialdata.org.

664 Craven, House, *Style Guide to the American Home*, updated September 25, 2019; www.thoughtco.com.

family needed guidance and direction, which was the providence of the mother.

By the 1855 census Abner and Melissa had one child, Leroy, who was three years old, which wasn't too young to start helping his mother with easy chores such as feeding the poultry, collecting eggs, or pulling weeds in the garden. Farm life was a family endeavor, and everyone had to pitch in.

In 1860 two censuses were taken: the Federal Population census and the "Federal Non-Population Schedule." The purpose of the latter was to "determine the types of resources that the government needed, how to allocate them, as well as looking at public health issues."[665]

There were six types of non-population schedules: Agriculture; Manufacturing; Defective, Dependent and Delinquent; Mortality; Slave; and Social Statistics. Not *all* states desired to use any or all the above-mentioned schedules.[666]

The Maine, Broome, New York, census shows the Flint family as a family of four:

Abner Flint, 34, carpenter, real estate: $1300; personal estate: $400; b. NY[667]
Melissa Flint, 27, b. NY
Leroy Flint, 8, b. NY, attending school
Frank Flint, 3, b. NY

Leroy Flint likely attended the one-room schoolhouse that is located at 2819 Rte. 26 in the Hamlet of Maine. An online photo shows a small frame building with two sets of doors (one door was for the girls and the other for boys to enter and exit). The school was built in 1845, and whether the school had a specific name I have not discovered. This schoolhouse is now part of the Janet W. Bowers Museum.[668] Children walked to and from school in all kinds of weather, often walking four or five miles to get to school. All grade levels were in one room, separated by age. The school year was shorter as well. Many children were absent during harvest time to help their families with the crops. Farm children (during the time that Leroy would have been attending) usually went as far as the eighth grade and had to take an exam to graduate. Of course, there were children who never got that far in school as their families were too poor and needed the children at home to be part of the workforce.[669]

---

665 Lisson, *Is Your Ancestor In The Often Overlooked U.S. Federal Non-Population Schedules of 1850–1880?* www.lisalisson.com.

666 New York State has the following Non-Population Schedules: Agriculture, 1850, 1860, 1870, & 1800; Defective, Dependent and Delinquent Classes: 1880; Industry/Manufacturing: 1850, 1860, 1870, & 1880; Social Statistics: 1850, 1860, & 1870. National Archives, www.archives.gov.

667 1860 census, *Maine, Broome, New York*; Page: 143; FHL: 803724; Dwelling: 1130; Family: 1086.

668 To see a photo of the schoolhouse, go to Naticoke Historical Society, www.nebula.wsimg.com.

669 An excellent article on attending school during the nineteenth century can be found at www.mentalfloss.com; *11 Ways School Was Different in the 1800s*; Erin McCarthy, January 7, 2016 (updated September 7, 2020).

While the 1860 Non-Population Schedule[670] may appear to be "dry" reading for some, it is a meaningful snapshot of how the family supported itself during the previous year.

| Improved Land: 40 acres | Unimproved: 18 acres | Cash Value of Farm: $1,300 |
|---|---|---|
| Value of Farming Implement: $50 | Horses: 2 | Milch Cows: 2 |
| Other cattle: 2 | Sheep: 13 | Swine: 1 |
| Livestock value: $170 | Wheat: 8 bushels | Rye: 5 bushels |
| Indian Corn: 30 bushels | Oats: 109 bushels | Wool: 20 lbs. |
| Irish Potatoes: 50 bushels | Buckwheat: 9 bushels | Value orchard products: $5 |
| Butter: 350 lbs. | Hay: 12 tons | Maple Sugar: 60 lbs. |
| Molasses: 3 gallons (maple) | Value of animals slaughtered: $50 | |

The first thing that strikes me is the number of pounds of butter that was churned and produced in 1859—a little over twenty-nine pounds per month. These products of their labor were then sold to the markets, and some kept for themselves.

Reviewing this list speaks to how hard people of this time worked, especially with only two adults in the household. Even with their young children helping with these labors, it is conceivable that they had to hire help periodically, but all in all it was Abner and Melissa who provided for most of the labor on their farm.

Abner Flint is listed in *Consolidated List of all persons of Class II subject to military duty in the Twenty Sixth Congressional District* (Schuyler, Tompkins, Broome, and Tioga Counties) and he was "enumerated during the month of June 1863 under the direction of E. C. Kartell, Provost Marshall."

Maine, Flint, Abner, Jr., 38, white, carpenter, NY

According to *Union Draft Records,* the records were divided into three parts, or classes: Class I—men 20–35 subject to military duty and unmarried men 36–44 subject to military duty; Class II—married men 36–44, and Class III—volunteers.[671]

As far as I have been able to ascertain, Abner was never called up to duty and Melissa never collected a pension from his service, and he is not listed as having served in the army on the 1865 census.

On the 1865 census Abner and his family are still residing in Maine (Broome), where he is still employed with carpentry work. The frame house is valued at $150.00, and he is marked as a landowner. Did the Flints move? The Kelsey, Gray, and Knapp families are not neighbors of the Flints on the 1860 census, but five years later they are. With the absence of land records, I will have to presume that they did move to another location.[672]

Melissa states that she is the mother of three children, one being married in the prior year. To date, the censuses have only noted two children (Leroy and Frank); however, the Flints

---

670 1860 Non-Population Schedule, Maine, Broome, New York; Post Office District: Killawog; Page: 225; Line: 4; Ancestry.

671 Explanation of classes from FamilySearch and *Consolidated Lists of Civil War Draft Registrations, 1863–1865;* Ancestry.

672 Note that, five months after this census was taken, Horace and Almira Kelsey deeded back to Abner Flint property that Abner had deeded to them in 1854. The date of this record is 3 November 1865.

did have another son named Floyd, born in July 1859, and died December 1859,[673] who is included on the 1860 census.

According to the 1859 Mortality Schedule, Floyd Flint was two and a half (months?) old and died of Scarlet Fever. He had been ill for twelve days before he succumbed to the illness. What a terrible time this must have been for the family. The death of a child was an all too common occurrence for most families.

Floyd Flint is buried in Allentown Cemetery, Glen Aubrey, Broome, New York.[674]

~

In 1870[675] the family is still in Maine. Melissa's parents are now living in Barton; her sister Clarissa is in Triangle (her brothers Silas and Philo by this time were deceased).

Abner Flint, 49, farmer, real estate: $4,000; personal estate: $1,358, b. NY
Melissa Flint, 37, keeps house, b. NY
Leroy Flint, 18, at home, b. NY, attended school within the year
Frank Flint, 12, at home, b. NY, attended school within the year
Ira Flint, 4, at home
Phoebe J. Hicks, 6, b. Pennsylvania, works in the house

The changes in this family are apparent. Abner is no longer listed as a carpenter and is now working full-time on his land, of which the value has now increased, along with his personal property. Another son has been born to this couple and they have a young girl working in the house. While the two older sons are attending school, she is not. Who was Phoebe J. Hicks and how did she come to be working in the Flint household?

In Nancy Grey Osterund's book *Bonds of Community, The Lives of Farm Women in Nineteenth Century New York,* she states, "Households readily expanded to include relatives who had no families of their own.

"Between 1855 and 1900, five percent of households included siblings of the heads; half that many included descendant relatives. Orphaned children were commonly adopted by aunts and uncles or brought up by older siblings."[676] Was Phoebe J. Hicks a relation of some sort? After doing a typical search for any vital records, nothing more was discovered regarding Phoebe other the 1870 census.

~

In 1872 Abner is listed as being a resident of Castle Creek, lot 114, G.D., farmer.[677] Castle

---

673 Birth and death dates: Garlow Bible; *U.S. Federal Census Mortality Schedules, 1850–1885;* Archive Roll Number: M2; Census Year: 1859; Census Place: *Maine, Broome, New York.*

674 Find A Grave Memorial # 76802203; Allentown Cemetery is located at Rte. 26 & Flint Rd.

675 1870 census; *Maine, Broome, New York;* Roll: M593_907; Page: 371B; Ancestry.

676 Osterud, *Chapter Two: The Power of Kindship.* 1991, 59.

677 Child, 1872–3 *Gazetteer and Business Directory of Broome and Tioga Counties (NY)* Syracuse,

Creek is a hamlet within Broome County and approximately fourteen miles east of Maine, New York. While the record states he was a "resident," was this just another piece of property that he owned or were the Flints living in Castle Creek in 1872?

Castle Creek was part of "The Grand Division of Boston Purchase" ("Boston Ten Townships") and refers to an area of 230,400 acres in Tioga and Broome Counties, New York, between the Chenango River (to Chenango Forks) and Tioughnioga River on the eastern boundary, and the west branch of Owego Creek (western boundary) from the Susquehanna River—about twenty-five miles northward. It includes the northern half of the town of Owego, and the towns of Newark Valley, Berkshire, and Richford in Tioga County, and a portion of the Broome County towns of Lisle and Nanticoke, with Maine east of these. These towns are bounded on the west by the Watkins and Flint Purchase. The Watkins and Flint Purchase is a tract of land of approximately 300,000 acres in the southern tier of New York State and was granted by John Watkins and Royal Flint and Associates of New York City.[678] Land purchasing companies were common throughout the early history of our country. The well-to-do would form such land companies as an investment and then sell the land for a profit. Many of the men who purchased such great tracts of land rarely lived in the new settlements that were to come—theirs was purely a business venture—unlike the purchaser of said land. Farmers purchased land not only for their own livelihoods. They were not "in the game" of purchasing tracts of land for the short-term. They did engage in purchasing and selling land, but the purpose of these transactions was for "familial ends," by "subdividing their own land," and where they "bought and/or helped their children buy land from neighbors," and selling land to nonrelatives to furnish their children with cash.[679]

Throughout this narrative and in various chapters, we have seen fathers and sons living next door to one another. Farming families wanted the assurance that their children (and heirs) were provided for in subsequent generations.

In 1874, when Abner was forty-eight years old, he drew up his will.

Dated October 23, 1874:[680]

> In the Name of God Amen. I Abner Flint of the town of Maine in the County of Broome and State of New York being of sound mind and memory, and considering the uncertainty of this frail and transitory life do therefore make, ordain, publish and declare this to be my last will and testament, that is to say:
>
> First. After all my lawful debts are paid and discharged, I give and bequeath to my beloved wife Melissa all my personal estate which I have or may have at the time of my death.
>
> Second. I give and bequeath to my beloved wife Melissa the sole use, occupation and control during the term of her natural life of all the real estate which I have or

---

New York, 1872, 259. "G.D." is an abbreviation for "Grand Division."

678 From a Wikipedia article "*Grand Division of Boston*." The foregoing content of the article is "shareable" under CCBY-SA 3.0. www.en.m.wikipedia.org.

679 Osterud, *Chapter Two: The Power of Kinship*. 1991, 63.

680 *New York, U.S., Wills and Probate Records, 1659–1999. New York Surrogate's Court (Broome County);* Vol: 008; 1878–1879. Ancestry.

may have at the time of my death.

Third. After the death of my said wife, I give and bequeath my said real estate to my beloved children, LeRoy, Frank & Ira and to their heirs and assigns forever the same to be divided equally between them.

Likewise, I make, constitute and appoint my said wife Melissa to be executrix of this my last will and testament revoking all former wills by me made.

In witness whereof, I hereunto subscribed my name and affixed my seal on the twenty-third day of October in the year of our Lord one thousand eight hundred and seventy-four.

The above written instrument was subscribed by the said Abner Flint in our presence and acknowledged by him to each of us and he at this same time declared the above instrument so subscribed to be his last will and testament and we at his request have signed our names a witness hereto in his presence and in the presence of each other and written our respective places of residence.

Aaron DeLano, residing in Maine, N York
Ellen DeLano, residing in Maine, N York

Executed: 23 October 1874
Probated: 10 August 1878

Whether LeRoy, Frank, and Ira had been given any tracts of land prior to Abner's death has, as of this writing, not been ascertained. Once again, I refer to Osterud's book *Bonds of Community*, where she states, "Wills were only one instrument for the passage of property from one generation to another. Deeds were equally important; older children generally received the bulk of their portions while their parents were still alive. Wills might simply confirm or tidy up arrangements made years before."[681]

By the year 1875 the Flint household had changed. Eldest son LeRoy was now married and living in Nanticoke (Broome), New York, and raising a family of his own. Abner Flint is marked as owning land, living in a frame dwelling with a real estate value of $600, with farming as his livelihood. Frank and Melissa are now in their mid- to late forties and raising two boys: Frank (17) and Ira (8).

Now that Abner and Melissa were grandparents, LeRoy and his wife may have come periodically to visit with their children. This would have most assuredly occurred on a Sunday as, while the distance between Nanticoke and Maine is "only" six miles, going to visit with a horse and wagon may have taken two hours or more, depending on the time of year and difficulty of the roadway (as opposed to eight minutes by automobile). Being with family, friends, and neighbors was essential to the people of this time.

A community was only as "healthy" as its citizens were; this was all important. Being part of something greater than yourself (even while maintaining your own individuality) kept a community on an even keel.

It was not all work and drudgery for our ancestors. Many farmers belonged to agricultural

681 Osterud, *Bonds of Community,* Chapter Two, *The Power of Kinship: The Inheritance of Land,* 62.

societies and a short article was found in an edition of the Broome *Republican, 1871–1874* entitled "Agricultural Reading." The article concerns drains and drainage for the farmer: "... this Spring the water came to the surface, ran a few yards above ground and was received or sucked into the drain again. Now if a practical demonstration is wanted, enquire[sic] of Mr. Abner Flint of the town of Maine."

The agricultural societies were important to the farmers to hear of new techniques in better planting methods, machinery, and drainage problems on the farm.

Women belonged to their own societies and spent time with other women quilting and engaged in church activities, entering their handiwork or culinary skills into the agricultural fairs—but the old adage of "a man works from sun to sun, but a woman's work is never done"[682] was certainly a truism.

~

Life went on as usual for the Flint family[683] until July 14, 1878, when Abner Flint, Jr. died. He was fifty-two years old. According to one piece of anecdotal information "Dad Flint had a parletic [sic] shock."[684] There are two possible definitions of "parletic shock." The first is what was called Apoplexy,[685] what we know as a stroke in modern parlance. The second "paralytic shock" is an "obstruction of the bowel from paralysis of the bowel wall, usually because of localized or generalized peritonitis or shock."[686]

Since New York State didn't mandate death certificates until 1880, it is unlikely we will know Abner's cause of death with any certainty.

At the time of Abner's death, Melissa Flint was forty-six years old with two sons in the household. Her life was now transformed from a wife to widowhood. Since her son Frank was the eldest in the household at the time, he likely took over the running of the farm. Unlike most wills left by husbands, Abner Flint, Jr.'s specified clearly that Melissa would own the property until her death, at which time the property would be divided equally among the sons:

682 Think of all the chores a woman had to do without any conveniences: washing, scrubbing, mending, making clothes, hanging clothes in all kinds of whether, preparing food from scratch for the family and hired hands, taking care of the children, caring for sick and elderly parents or other relatives or neighbors—and this doesn't account for the outside work of the kitchen garden, taking care of the livestock, and helping during times of planting and harvesting. This is not to say that the man of the household didn't pitch in and care for the sick, etc.; however, it was mostly the woman who handled these duties.

683 I can only presume that this was the case since there is no evidence to state otherwise.

684 DLH records. "Don't know when he died but Dad Flint always said he died quit[e] young. He had a parletic shock." It is unknown if "Dad Flint" was Ira Flint, as the information may have come from Ira's daughter.

685 Thornber, Craig, *History of Medicine Glossary Of Medical Terms Used In The 18th And 19th Centuries*, www.thornber.net/

686 Definition of Paralytic ileus, www.dictionary.com.

> ... bequeath to my beloved wife Melissa the sole use, occupation and control during the term of her natural life of all the real estate which I have or may have at the time of my death.
>
> Third. After the death of my said wife, I give and bequeath my said real estate to my beloved children, LeRoy, Frank & Ira and to their heirs and assigns forever the same to be divided equally between them.

In addition, there is nothing in this version of the will that specifies what happens to the property if Melissa should remarry. This is unusual. Many wills specify that the widow would get one-third of the estate after her spouse died, or if she remarried, the estate would revert to a son.

Perhaps Abner Flint had confidence in his wife that she could handle the daily affairs of running a farm and so wrote the will the way that he did.

In 1880 New York, there were two censuses taken—the Population Census and the Non-Population Census. The population census was taken on June 4, 1880, in the "town of Maine." While Melissa (47) is the "head" of the household, she is not listed as such; that section is left blank.[687] She is listed as "keeping house," while her son Frank (22) is a "farmer" and Ira (14) is a "farm laborer."

Now let's review the agricultural census for 1880:[688]

| Tilled Land | Other[689] | Fences, land, buildings |
|---|---|---|
| 75 acres | 25 acres | $2,500 |
| Farming Implements: $200 | Livestock: $350 | Building/Repairs: $10 |
| Cost fertilizers 1879: $2 | Wages Paid: $30[690] | Weeks of hired labor: 4 |
| Value of productions: $575 | | |
| Acreage 1879 | | |
| Mown: 25 | Not Mown: 18 | Hay: 25 |

| | | |
|---|---|---|
| Horses of all ages June 1, 1880: 2 | | |
| Milch Cows: 3 | Other: 8 | Calves dropped: 7 |
| Calves Purchased: 1 | Slaughtered: 1 | |

| | | |
|---|---|---|
| Butter made on farm—1879: 400 lbs. | Swine on hand June 1, 1880: 1 | Poultry: 20 |
| Egg Production 1875: 75 | | |

687 The enumerator, P.J. Casey, left the relationship section blank for all heads of households, whether male or female. 1880 census, *Maine, Broome, New York,* Dwelling: 39; Family: 39; E.D. 9; Ancestry.

688 1880 *U.S. Census Non-Population Schedule New York 1850–1880*; 4 June 1880; Maine, Broome, *Agriculture Archive Collection#* A33; Roll: 33; Page: 4; Line: 4; Original Data: *New York State Library, Albany, New York.* Ancestry.

689 Meadows, pastures, orchards, and vineyards.

690 The figures regarding wages paid, hired labor, and value of all farm productions are for 1879.

Buckwheat 1879/ 6 acres/ 100 bushels
Indian Corn/3 acres/ 25 bushels
Oats/ 15 acres/ 550 bushels
Beans: 1 bushel
Sugar (Maple): 200 lbs.
Molasses: 10 lbs.
Irish Potatoes/1 acre/40 bushels
Apples/8 acres
Bearing Trees: 150
Bushels 1879: 20
Total Value of orchard products sold or consumed: $10.00

In comparison to the 1860 non-population census, the 1880 non-population census shows the Flints had acquired more property (now owed 100 acres), and the production of grains was also greater, as well as the production of other products.

We now come to a period of silence in the records. The State of New York began recording its citizens not only through the federal census, but also the state census, which began in 1825.[691] However, what we have available to us online begins in 1855. Unfortunately, because of the number of political and bureaucratic conflicts, an 1885 census was not taken (and a future 1895 census that would have also been taken). However, New York did take a census in 1892, but there is a gap of twelve years of Melissa Flint's life of which we have no record. What we do know is that Melissa's father, Horace Kelsey, died in October 1890, and his obituary lists his daughter as "Melissa Flint." She still had not remarried by that time; however, sometime after her father's death and before the 1892 census, Melissa did remarry to Lester W. Buck. While the copy of the 1892 census is barely legible, Melissa's last name is given as "Buck," and gives the couple as living in Maine during this time, with Lester's age given as "60" and Melissa as "61."

Who was Lester W. Buck? According to unsourced records,[692] Lester W. Buck was born February 28, 1834, in Pennsylvania and was the son of Anson Buck (1788–1839) and Esther Springsteen (1788–1875). Anson is said to have been born August 29, 1788, in Pennsylvania* and died 8 April 1839 and is buried in Coopers Plains, Steuben, New York.[693]

*If* these are indeed the parents of Lester W. Buck, the family (minus the father) was living in Woodhull, Steuben, New York, in 1840.[694]

In the New York censuses of 1850 and 1855 the family is still living in Woodhull. The family (1850) consisted of David Buck and Jane Buck as the projected siblings of Lester. The places of birth for Lester suggest he was born in Pennsylvania or New York. Ironically, the 1880 census lists his birthplace (as well as his family) as being born "NY/Penn."[695] More

691 The Federal census runs from 1790–1940 at ten-year intervals; the NY State census includes 1825, 1835, 1845, 1855, 1865, 1875, and then 1905, 1915, and 1925. Another special census was taken in 1892 in New York because of the destruction of the 1890 census by fire. Note: the state censuses beginning in 1825–1845 are not online.

692 The unsourced data comes from Public Trees on Ancestry. None of the "trees" viewed had any citations of where the information came from. I have placed an asterisk * next to all information that is not sourced.

693 There is a headstone for Anson Buck in this cemetery located on Find-a-Grave.

694 1840 census; *Woodhull, Steuben, New York*; Roll: 340; Page: 77; FHL: 0017207.

695 Woodhull, Steuben, New York, is not far from the Pennsylvania border and could be the

research by a descendant of Lester W. Buck would need to be done for clarification on his birthplace.

Sometime between 1855 and 1860, Lester W. Buck married Amanda Hoyt, who was born circa 1838—again, the census records state her birthplace as either Connecticut, New York, or New York/Pennsylvania.

In 1860 this couple was living in Lake City, Wabasha, Minnesota.[696] The household consisted of:

L.W. Buck, 28, farmer, real estate value: 1,000; personal estate: 100, b. NY
Amanda Buck, 23, b. NY
Charles Buck, 2, b. NY
Ben Buck,[697] 1/12, b. MN

According to an article on Lake City, Minnesota (via *Wikipedia*), the first [white] settler was Jacob Boody, who arrived in 1853, and the town was platted in 1855. Based on this information, the Buck family were in Lake City not long after it was first settled. The area was still considered a territory of the United States and didn't become a state until 1858.

Immigrants and settlers from other parts of the U. S. began pouring into Minnesota in the 1850s, but especially after 1854 with the creation of the combined river–rail transportation route between Minnesota and the East Coast via Chicago.

Many of the new residents were farmers, but there was also a glut of land speculators. The speculation bubble burst in August of 1857 when a large New York finance office failed, and panic ensued in Minnesota. Creditors called in their loans, and everyone was in debt. The railroad-building halted, and immigration stopped. Those who farmed suffered rough times.[698]

Because of these rough times I surmise that the Bucks left Minnesota and returned to Steuben County, New York, as they were counted in the town of Addison when the 1865[699] state census was taken.

L.W. Buck, 32, dentist, b. Pennsylvania
A.M. Buck, 28, (wife) b. Connecticut; 3 children born; 1 child married
Charlie Buck, 7, (child), b. Steuben (NY)
Nelly Buck, 3, (child), b. Illinois

We can see from this census snapshot that Lester W. Buck had a complete reversal of occupations. How did he go from laboring as a farmer to his current occupation as a dentist? I find this intriguing; however, I haven't discovered any records that would help to explain this sudden reversal of his livelihood.

---

possible reason for the confusion.

696 1860 census, *Lake City, Wabasha, Minnesota*: Page: 248; FHL: 803575.

697 This child does not show up on any subsequent census report and must have died young.

698 *Minnesota Historic Farm Study; Early Settlement, 1820–1870: 1850 Developmental Periods:* 6; www.dot.state.mn.us.

699 1865 census, *Addison, Steuben County, New York*; Microfilm, New York State Archive, Albany, New York. Ancestry.

There is a Lester Buck listed in *The Western New York Gazetteer and Business Directory for 1880*[700] under *Business Directory: Buck, L. dentist.* I could not find any advertising broadsides for him. Lester Buck must have become a dentist sometime between 1862 and 1865. Where/how he learned this profession is a mystery, but he practiced dentistry right up until his death.

There was a child (Nelly) who was born in Illinois around 1862, and her brother, Charlie, was born in Steuben County circa 1858. This would suggest that Lester W. Buck and Amanda Hoyt married sometime between 1856 and 1857. Since they were in Lake City, Minnesota, in 1860, they may have left New York shortly after Charlie Buck's birth.[701] The question is whether the Buck family was *residing* in Illinois or were they on their way back to New York when Nelly was born (they would have had to travel through Illinois to get back to New York)?

~

The Buck family remained in Addison, New York, throughout the 1870s and 1880s (although I have not located the Buck family in 1875). Lester W. Buck was still practicing dentistry and his real estate was valued at $3,000, with a personal estate of $1,000. There were now three children in the household: Charles (12), Nellie (8), and Rosey (1),[702] as well as John Breman (41), who was born in Ireland and worked in a sash factory. Mr. Breman's real estate value was $500 and his personal estate was $200.00.

Per the 1880 census the family now included children: Charles (22),[703] "without imploy[sic]; Nellie (18); Harry (11),[704] "at school;" and Jesse (8). Lester's wife, Amanda, is age 44 and is listed as having "consumption."[705] Based on this census record, we don't know how long Amanda was ill with this disease.[706] The life expectancy of someone with tuberculosis (TB) from onset was one to three years. Many tuberculosis victims went into special sanitoriums as it was thought that clean, fresh air and sunlight would cure the disease.[707] Unfortunately,

---

700 Online, through the Monroe County (New York) Library; libraryweb.org.

701 Ben Buck must have died, as there is no mention of him in 1860.

702 No further record of this daughter.

703 Unsourced data for Charles "H" Buck; b. circa 1857, NY; d. 1921 Oneonta, Ostego, NY; m. Jane Cecilia Carson (1867–1946). On the 1910 census he is listed as the "proprietor of a furniture shop" in Binghamton, NY.

704 A Harry Buck was found as born 24 July 1869, New York; he served in the military (likely the Spanish–American War) on 15 April 1899 and resided in Binghamton, New York; d. 7 August 1929 and is buried with his wife, Nina M.____ (1879–1958), in Floral Park Cemetery, Johnson City, Broome, New York. The headstone gives his name as "E. Harry Buck."

705 Tuberculosis—a contagious disease that killed countless people over the centuries. Also called "phthisis" or "white plague."

706 Amanda Buck may have been bedridden by this time or had the appearance of someone who had consumption.

707 The first sanitorium in New York was the Adirondack Cottage Sanitarium established on Saranac Lake in 1885 by Dr. Edward Livingston Trudeau (who also suffered from the disease).

the circumstances of Amanda Buck's case, along with a death date for her, have not been discovered as of this writing.[708]

≈

During the 1880s, there were a number of land transactions, beginning in 1885, for various members of the Buck family in Allegheny, New York.[709] While I only have the dates of these transactions and who the grantor/grantees were (and not the actual copy of said transactions), I wasn't able to reconcile how Amanda Buck is listed as the "grantor" of land in 1889 and 1892 when it's conjectured that she had died sometime after the 1880 census.[710] However, this was answered by someone familiar with these types of documents who found that the land was transferred per her will.[711]

Some examples of the transactions are as follows:

1889

| Grantor | Grantee | Vol. | Page |
|---|---|---|---|
| Amanda Buck | Amy Buck[712] | 125 | 294 |
| Amanda Buck | David | " | " |
| Amanda Buck | Lester Buck | " | " |

1892

| Grantor | Grantee | Vol. | Page |
|---|---|---|---|
| Amanda Buck | Willie Buck | 159 | 38 |
| Amanda Buck | Nellie Buck | " | " |
| Amanda Buck | Harry Buck | " | " |
| Amanda Buck | Lester Buck | " | " |
| Amanda Buck | Jesse Buck | " | " |

In 1889 there is also a land transaction between the grantor David Buck and grantee Lester W. Buck (David Buck is believed to be Lester's brother).

Despite the fact that Amanda Buck transferred land per a will, there is still another conundrum regarding the marriage between Lester W. Buck and Amanda Hoyt. The following newspaper article from the *Hornellsville Weekly Tribune*[713] leaves us with more questions than answers:

708 The usual sources, i.e., Ancestry and Family Search, have been searched, along with records of cemeteries in Addison, Steuben, NY (Addison Rural, Maple, and Baldwin cemeteries), and have not provided any further information.

709 *Land Assessment, New York Land Records, 1630–1975*, FamilySearch.

710 One unsourced reference indicates she died in 1881.

711 The will is not in my possession and I do not know its contents.

712 Amy and David Buck are Amanda's in-laws.

713 Hornellsville, New York, Friday, January 11, 1889, edition; 8. Newspapers.com. (herein: Newspapers).

**TROUBLE AT ALMOND**

A Terribly Mixed-Up Family—A History of the Proceedings.

About three years ago[714] Lester Buck, a dentist, came here and purchased a house and lot on Chapel Street and moved into it with his family, which consisted of his wife and five children.

It was understood that he and Mrs. Buck had been married about four years before moving here, she being a widow with three children, and he a widower with two.

Everything appeared agreeable in the family, she treating his children as kindly as her own. Buck was away most of the time, supposed to be working at his trade, but occasionally came home and settled up bills she was obliged to make at the stores.

Once he sent a quantity of butter, more than she could use without it spoiling, so she sold a part of it. When he returned he was angered because she had done so, although she had used the money to purchase other family necessaries, and on a slight provocation at the dinner table, it is reported, [he] threw a goblet at her, inflicting a serious wound near the eye, and struck her a severe blow across the back with a caster. He then left, and for about a year has been living in Addison.

Mrs. Buck learned not long since that he had married another woman, and was coming here to get what he claimed was his part of the household goods.

On Thursday he arrived and proceeded to load up. She protesting, he threatening. He succeeded however, in getting away with them except some bedding.

She went before Esq. Stebbins, swore out a peace warrant and he was arrested and gave bail. She next swore out a warrant for bigamy against him, but as the offense charged was committed in Steuben County it had to be dropped here.

He then went to the house and took the bedding, demoralizing things generally. She then swore out a warrant for the assault and battery before spoken of, and he was again arrested. She also had instituted proceedings in the other county for his arrest on the charge of bigamy.

By this time Mrs. Buck, who is a small woman, but has enough grit for a dozen big ones, had made it so warm for his Buckship that he became exceedingly anxious to settle, and has agreed to give a deed of this house and lot if she would cease further proceedings against him, which she has consented to do if he fulfills.

Mrs. Buck is a lady highly respected by her neighbors and much sympathy is had for her.

O.D.W.

Based on this article we know:

1. The couple married in 1885.
2. They had both been previously married as they are referred to as "widow and widower."
3. Mrs. Buck brought three children into the marriage and Mr. Buck two.
4. The couple moved to Almond, NY, in 1886.

---

714 "About three years ago" would be sometime in 1886.

5. Mr. Buck was "away most of the time."
6. Mr. Buck remarried another woman while still married to the current Mrs. Buck.
7. A Lester W. Buck married 15 Oct 1888 in Lindley, NY, to Edith M. Hoop, aka Edith M. Griggs.[715] Lindley is in Steuben County, New York.

If Lester Buck married in 1885 and called himself a "widower," does that mean Amanda Buck had died from the "consumption" prior to 1885?[716]

The article indicates that Mrs. Buck had three children and Mr. Buck two. The various census reports for Lester W. Buck shows he had at least four living children and two who had died likely as infants.[717] Either the reporter (O.D.W.) received incorrect information or Mr. Buck wasn't forthcoming with the facts.

Lastly, it is stated that he was "away most of the time." Lester W. Buck was a dentist in Addison, Steuben, New York, as per the 1880 city directory; Almond, New York, to Addison, New York, is quite a distance (approximately 40 miles), and it would stand to reason that he would not be going back and forth daily. This would also give him a lot of "free time" to see other women if he were so inclined.

Mrs. Buck infers that she found out that Mr. Buck had married another woman and swore out a warrant against him for bigamy. Was the other woman Edith M. Hoop/Griggs as appears in the 1888 marriage records? Keep in mind the newspaper article was published in 1889, so Edith may have been the proverbial "other woman."

According to the Melissa Flint Garlow Bible, she had married Lester W. Buck on June 8, 1891, in Lacona, Oswego, New York.[718]

The 1892 New York State census shows Lester W. Buck and Melissa (Flint) Buck listed together, along with Lester's daughter, Jesse Buck. While the census is barely legible on Ancestry, Melissa is recorded with the surname "Buck" in this record. If Melissa was aware of Lester's previous difficulties with the law and past wives, there are no records from descendants to illuminate us.

The 1892 census that began on February 16, 1892, would suggest that this couple married in 1891 as the aforementioned Bible indicates.

Their marriage was short-lived as Lester W. Buck died in 1892—the exact date has not been discovered. He signed his will the 17th day of October 1891 and it was proved on 7 December 1892.

715 *New York State Marriage Index, 1881–1967.* Ancestry.

716 A death record for Amanda Buck has not been located. Marriage records between Amanda Hoyt and Lester Buck and Lester Buck and the second "Mrs. Buck" have also not been located.

717 Charles Buck (Mar 1858–Jun 1921) and daughter Jesse Buck are mentioned in Lester Buck's probate record in 1893 and on the 1892 census for Maine, Broome, NY. She married H.A. Martin and died 4 Sep. 1917. Harry Buck is also listed on the 1892 census in Binghamton, Broome, NY. There is an "E. Harry Buck" born in 1869 and died in 1929 and who is buried in Floral Park Cemetery in Johnson City, Broome, NY. Nelly Buck died in 1883 in Hornellsville, NY, at the age of 21. Death information comes from *Press and Sun Bulletin,* Binghamton, NY, Newspapers.

718 DLH records.

In the name of God Amen, I Lester W. Buck of the town of Maine, Broome County, New York, being of sound mind and memory, and considering the uncertainty of this life, I do, therefore make, ordain, publish and declare, this my last will and testament. That is to say:

First—after all my lawful debts are paid and discharged, I give and bequeath and devise to my wife Melissa Buck for her and her natural life all of the estate both real and personal of which I may die seized and on her decease, I give and divise all of my said estate to such of her children and my children as shall be then living. Likewise, I make, constitute and appoint Charles H. Green of the town of Maine aforesaid, with full power to sell and convey real estate to be executor of this my last will and testament here by revoking all former wills by me made. In witness whereof, I have hereunto subscribed my name and I affixed my seal the 17th day of October in the year 1891.

Lester W. Buck (L.S.)

The above instrument consisting of one sheet, was on the date thereof subscribed by Lester W. Buck the Testator named in the forgoing Will in the presence of us and each of us, and at the time of making such subscription the above instrument was declared by the above Testator to be his last Will and Testament, and each of us, at the request of the said Testator and in his presence, and in the presence of each other, sign our names as witnesses thereto, as the end of the Will.

F. W. Downs Residing at Binghamton, N.Y.[719]
B. F. Smith Residing at Binghamton, N.Y.

Eight days later, Melissa Buck appeared in the Surrogate Court to have her late husband's will proved:

Be it Remembered, that heretofore, to wit: on the *7th day of December* in the year of our Lord one thousand eight hundred ninety-two, Melissa Buck, the widow, devisee and legatee named in the Last Will and Testament of *Lester W. Buck* late of the town of *Maine* in the County of Broome deceased, appeared in open Court, before the Surrogate of the County of Broome, and made application to have the said Last Will and Testament which relates to both Real and Personal Estate, proved: and on such application the said Surrogate did ascertain satisfactory evidence who were the widow, devisees & legatees & all the heirs at law and next of kin of the said testator and their respective residences, . . . [ ] and said Surrogate did thereupon issue a Citation in due form of Law, directed to the said devisee, legatee, heirs at law and next of kin of said decedent, by their respective names, . . . [ ] . . . requiring them to appear before said Surrogate at his office in the Court House in the City of Binghamton, in said County on the *27th day of January 1893*, to attend the Probate of said Will.

719 The witnesses are the attorneys for Lester W. Buck and Melissa Buck.

> And in appearing from such application that *Jessie Buck* heir at law and next of kin of said decedent was an infant, a notice was duly issued to her requiring her to appear by guardian is she had one and if she had none that she appear and apply for one to be appointed or show cause why she should not be appointed, and that upon failure or neglect so the Court would appoint a guardian to represent and act for her in this proceeding.
>
> . . . no one appearing to oppose the probate of said Will, and said *Jessie Buck*, having in the interim arrived at the age of 21 years, no guardian was appointed for her: And said matter having been duly adjourned from time to time to this 20th day of February 1893; and on this said 20th day of February 1893, said Melissa Buck . . . adjudged the said Will to be valid.

The Surrogate Court documents make no mention of sons Charles Buck or Harry Buck. Perhaps they had already received their portions while their father was still alive.

~

On October 30, 1893, Melissa Buck married Mr. John W. Garlow in Garner, Hancock, Iowa.[720] Melissa Buck was now sixty years old. Many women went to live with their son or daughter when they became a widow, but, apparently, Melissa was not ready for that just yet. When, how, or where Melissa met John Garlow remains a mystery, as does the fact that they married in Iowa instead of New York. Let's start from the beginning with the marriage record between these two parties.

The marriage record states that John W. Garlow was the son of John Garlow and Elizabeth Whitaker and was born "about 1819"[721] in Cazenovia, Madison, New York.[722]

His parents removed to Sherman, Scott Township, Pennsylvania, when he was a "young man." However, I have not found a census record in Pennsylvania for a John Garlow.

It is possible they went to Sherman in between census years and returned to New York, as a John and Elizabeth Garlow are living in Sanford, Broome, New York, in 1850.[723]

Because of the number of men named John W. Garlow and John Garlow, it is difficult to differentiate between them; however, I theorize that John W. Garlow was married three times—once as a suspected bigamous marriage. Let's follow the trail of John W. Garlow.

The earliest census record I can find for John Garlow,[1] father of John W.[2, 724] is the 1840[725] census for Tompkins, Delaware, New York. There are six persons in the household, including

720 DLH records—Melissa (Flint) Garlow Bible, date of marriage only; *Early Families of Broome County, New York;* Buck-Garlow marriage record; *Iowa Marriage Records 1880–1922*, Department of Public Health, Des Moines, Iowa.

721 Various records give his birth year between 1818–1822.

722 His place of birth comes from his obituary and military records.

723 1850 census, *Sanford, Broome County, New York;* Roll: 477; Page: 180A. Ancestry.

724 To differentiate between father and son, I numbered them "1" and "2."

725 All census records for *John Garlow* can be found through Ancestry.

two males who would "fit" John W. since we do not have an exact date of his birth: 1 male 15–19 and 1 male 20–29.

If we continue with this theme, the 1850 census shows the John Garlow family living in Sanford, Broome, New York. In this record John Garlow is also referenced as *John W. Garlow,* born circa 1785,[726] NY; Elizabeth (his wife) b. circa 1798, NY; Stephen F., b. circa 1838, NY; Elizabeth, b. circa 1843, NY.

But where is son John W. Garlow?[2]

He is found living in Sanford, Broome, New York, next door to his parents. John[2] is listed as age "30," born in NY, and his occupation is "sawyer." His wife, Sarah, is "28," also born in NY, as are all the children:Phebe (8), Darcus [sic] (7), Mary (3), and William (5).

In the 1855 census for John[2] the family is still in Sanford, Broome, NY; however, his wife, Sarah, is not listed. The family now consists of John,[2] "sawyer" b. Schoharie, NY; Elizabeth (14), b. Broome; Dorcas (10), b. PA; William (8), b. Broome; Polly[727] (this is likely Mary) (7), and Clarasa [sic] (4).

Sarah A.(Sally) had died July 12, 1852,[728] and John[2] was now raising the children on his own. It is possible she died in childbirth or from the effects of childbirth as the last child, Clarasa [sic], was born 1851/52.

By 1860[729] John W. Garlow[2] was living in Scott, Wayne, Pennsylvania,[730] with a new family:

John Garlow, 37, farmer, real estate: $700; personal estate: $600; b. NY
Hannah Garlow, 35, b. NY
Polly Garlow, 12, b. PA (c. 1848) d.o. Sally & John Garlow
Olivia Garlow, 10, b. PA (c. 1850) d.o. Sally & John Garlow
Medisa [sic] 8, b. PA (c.1852, this is likely Clarasa/Clarissa) d.o. of Sally & John Garlow
Almeda Garlow, 6, b. PA (c. 1854) d.o. Hannah & John Garlow?
Alveretta Garlow, 4, b. PA (c.1856) d.o. of Hannah & John Garlow
Almissa Garlow, 2, b. PA (c. 1858) d.o. of Hannah & John Garlow
Albert Boardman, 23, b. PA (c. 1857), no occupation given

My contention is that the first three children are from Sally and John Garlow's marriage (John's first wife, Sarah/Sally, died in 1852). As we can see, a child was born circa 1854—yet the 1855 census for John W. Garlow[2] shows the absence of a wife.

---

726 The following information on John[1] (W) Garlow comes from the *War of 1812 Military Pension Record,* Roll: 35; Archive Publication #M313: *John Garlow, b. circa 1783; m. 9 Jan. 1817, Sanford, Broome, NY, Elizabeth Whitaker; d. 6 Feb. 1864, Scott Center, Wayne, PA. He enlisted 13 May 1811; discharged: 1815. He is buried in Hale Eddy Cemetery, Deposit, Broome, NY.*

727 "Polly" is often the nickname for Mary.

728 See www.findagrave.com; member id#88891065; Sarah A (Sally) Garlow, b. 12 Dec. 1820, NY; d. 12 July 1852 in Sanford, Broome Co., NY; burial Hale Eddy Cemetery, Deposit, Broome, NY. Sarah's (Sally) maiden name is *Glendenning,* per the marriage records of her children.

729 1860 census, *Scott, Wayne County, Pennsylvania;* Dwelling #589; Family #596; Page: 646; FHL:805194.

730 I have not located John[1] Garlow in PA or NY in 1860.

It is also noteworthy that the children—Phoebe, Elizabeth, Dorcas, William, and "Clarasa"—are not living with their father and stepmother in 1860. Where were they? It is possible that Elizabeth may have married, but what about the other children, where were they? Were other family members raising them in New York?[731]

While a marriage record has not been located (online) for John W. Garlow and Hannah ______, I was able to locate a reference to Hannah's surname prior to her marriage to John W. Garlow—it was "Wheeler." This was borne out in a marriage record for their daughter Alveretta G. Nelson, who on September 28, 1921, and married one Burt Davidson in Binghamton, New York. She names her parents as "John Garlow and Hanna [sic] Wheeler."[732]

Hannah Wheeler Garlow is buried in Floral Park Cemetery.[733] Her headstone reads 1833–1913[734] and she died in Johnson City, Broome, New York. Her short obituary notice notes that she was living at "24 Dickenson Street" (her daughter Alveretta and her new husband were living at 23 Dickenson Street at the time of their marriage).

The *U.S. Civil War Records and Profiles 1861–1865* show that John W. Garlow enlisted on August 13, 1862, in Tompkins County, New York, as a private and was mustered in on September 27, 1862, with Company A of the 144th Infantry Regiment, and was mustered out on December 12, 1863. John Garlow must have cut a striking figure at 6′ 1″ tall, with blue eyes, black hair, and a dark complexion.[735]

John's son William,[736] at the age of eighteen, also joined up with his father in the same company and regiment and served until the end of the war. The special 1890 census for *Union Veterans and Widows*, Binghamton, Broome, New York, does not provide any notes as to his discharge or if he was invalided in any way.

John W. Garlow's service in the Civil War is what caught him in the act of bigamy, but more on that later.

---

731 There has been difficulty tracking down the children of Sally and John W. Garlow (except William), especially the females. Naturally, some of these children may have died young. Much more research would need to be done to round out this family.

732 *New York U.S., County Marriage Records, 1847–1849, 1907–1936.* Ancestry: note the marriage record gives her name as "Retta" G. Nelson. This was her third marriage. Her first husband died, and she divorced the second.

733 There is another Hannah Wheeler, but she does not have "Garlow" as her surname; she is listed as "Hannah *Wheeler*" (1830–1912) former name *Decker.* She is buried in Rock Ridge Cemetery, Monticello, Sullivan, NY. It is a coincidence that her death date is the same as Hannah Wheeler, wife of John[1] W. Garlow.

734 Her death date is 1912. *Binghamton Press,* Monday, December 2, 1912, 2. www.FultonHistory.com.

735 The average height for males during the 1860s was 5′ 7″—this was considered tall by world height standards. *Civil War Talk, Average height during the Civil War; Civil War History Discussion.* www.civilwartalk.com.

736 William Garlow, b. 23 June 1844, NY; discharged from service in 1865. He entered the "old soldier's home" in Bath, Steuben, NY, in 1931 at the age of 91. *U.S. National Homes for Disabled Volunteer Soldiers, 1866–1938,* (NARA M1749).

As we move to through the years, the 1870 census for Scott Township, Wayne, Pennsylvania, has John Garlon [sic] (50), Hannah Garlon (40), Gertrude (14), Almin [sic] (12), Henry (10), and Alvin (3). Gertrude Garlow would have been born about 1856, as was Alveretta—are they one in the same, or two separate children? Without accurate birth dates it is impossible to tell.

The Garlows were still in Wayne County by the time the next census was taken (1880). John W. is occupied as a farmer and is now sixty years old. The other members of the household include: wife, Hannah, (50); Henry (18); Alvin (12); Emily (9); and Elizabeth, John's mother (83).[737]

Time passes and a curious event occurs—on October 30, 1893,[738] John W. Garlow marries the widow Melissa (Kelsey) Flint Buck in Garner, Hancock, Iowa. At this time, John W. Garlow is still married to Hannah Wheeler Garlow[739] and John's mother is still alive. An article in the *Hancock Democrat* states, "Married—In Garner, Iowa, October 30, 1893, John W. Garlow, Esquire, and Malissa [sic] Buck, both of Garner. Rev. F.L. Fisk officiating. The wedded couple are nicely settled in Mrs. Sheckler's house."[740] Note the use of the word "esquire" after John W. Garlow's name. While the term is often associated with someone in the legal profession, this does not mean that John Garlow was an attorney. It could also apply to someone who was well esteemed in the community, and I believe that is how it is used in this instance.

How did these events transpire? Did John and Hannah separate? Why Garner, Iowa? There are so many questions that cannot be answered by this writer. The Iowa marriage record states the following: "John W. Garlow, age 74, born NY; married to Melissa Buck, age 61, she born 'Pittsfield,' NY."

In 1895,[741] Iowa conducted a census and John W. and Melissa Garlow are listed as "74" and "61" respectively and residing in Garner Corporation, Hancock, Iowa. By 1897 they were living in Humboldt, Humboldt, Iowa. On September 15, 1897, John W. Garlow died. A number of obituaries are represented in various newspapers regarding his death. From *The Garner Signal:*[742]

> The report has just reached us of the sudden death from heart disease of Mr. John Garlow at his home in Humboldt, Iowa. Mr. Garlow was a former resident of Garner and a man highly esteemed by all who knew him. He was a veteran of the War of the Rebellion serving in a New York Regiment. He was quite aged being nearly 80 years

737 Elizabeth Whitaker Garlow is living in 1860 with her presumed son, George (30), and his family. Elizabeth's husband is not listed with the family.

738 *Iowa Marriage Records, 1880–1940*, Ancestry.

739 Hannah Wheeler Garlow was still living in 1893. To date, a divorce record has not been located and it must be presumed that this couple were still legally married. John's mother, Elizabeth, was still alive (she died in 1895). Did she remain living with her daughter-in-law?

740 November 2, 1893, edition; Page: 8; Column: 1.

741 *Iowa, U.S. State Census, 1895;* Original Data: Iowa 1895 State Census, Des Moines, IA, State Historical Society. An image is not available online. Ancestry.

742 September 15, 1897, edition, Page: 5; Column: 2.

of age at the time of his death. Thus, one by one are the "old boys:" answering the last bugle call on earth and being marshalled on the other side of the river, with their old commander and comrades-in-arms, gone before.[743]

From *The Humboldt Independent:*[744]

Headquarters Albert Rowley Post No. 193, G.A.R.

Whereas: Our beloved comrade John W. Garlow has heard the Great Commander's command to "Come up higher," and has answered the summons by passing over the death-line of imprisonment into the great beyond and answered, "I'm here" to the roll call of the Great Captain," therefore:

Resolved: That with sincere sorrow we mourn the loss of one who was a faithful to his comrades as he was loyal to his Creator –

That in the life of our late comrade in arms we recognize that type of manhood blending citizen and soldier. –

That our Post has lost a fraternal comrade, our town an exemplary citizen, his church a consistent member and his wife a devoted and loving husband, and to her we extend the fraternal hand, and sympathetic voice as we bow our heads in sorrow.

Resolved: That our charter and altar be appropriately draped for the period of thirty days, and that these resolutions be recorded, and a copy forwarded to the wife of our departed comrade.

F. F. French, Com.

~

On September 20, 1897 (just five days after John Garlow's death), the legal widow, Hannah, filed the paperwork to collect his military pension. It wasn't until two months later (November 23, 1897) that Melissa also filed for his pension. Whether Melissa was unaware of her husband's marital status prior to her marriage to John W. Garlow will remain a mystery; however, the facts became crystal clear (to Melissa) when her application for the pension was denied and the said pension was awarded to his *legal* wife, Hannah Garlow. The United States Civil War Pension Office referred to Melissa in the records as a "relative" under Hannah Garlow's name.

How had Hannah Garlow known about her husband's death? Did the obituary from the *Humboldt Republican* get dispatched to a newspaper in New York? Did one of their children relay this information?

The obituary that was placed in the newspaper (probably by Melissa ) for John W. Garlow, only mentions two of his wives; his first wife, Sally A. Glendening, "with whom he had six children, three boys and three girls;" and his third wife, "Mrs. Melissa Flint, whom he married in Garner, Hancock, Iowa, having moved to Humbolt, Iowa in the fall of 1895."

743 Newspaper notices during this timeframe could often be very "poetic" and glowing, especially if the person served in the military.

744 September 30, 1897, edition; Page: 4

Another notice also appears in the newspaper on September 18, 1897, to alert anyone interested that she (Melissa Garlow) is the administratrix of her late husband's estate.

John W. Garlow is buried in Union Cemetery, Humboldt, Humboldt, Iowa. What the "real" story is of what occurred between these families will never be known. We can only surmise and conjecture what truly transpired. Melissa Kelsey Flint Buck Garlow had outlived all her husbands and sadly was the recipient of a bigamous marriage.[745]

Two notices appeared in the *Humboldt Republican* in the Thursday, 7 October 1897, edition of the paper.[746] The first is the notice in the matter of the estate of John W. Garlow (deceased). The interested parties were William Garlow, Henry Garlow, Alvin Garlow, Lena Nyes, Emma Clark, and Elizabeth Juycax. The second notice was to tell everyone that "Mrs. Garlow left for Garner, where she will live with relatives. Her sale of household goods was fairly successful." I wonder how Melissa dealt with all this turmoil in her life.

In 1900, Melissa is living with her son and his family in Ell Township. The household consisted of Frank Flint, his wife, Aletha, and their six children. In 1910 the family is now in Madison Township, Hancock, Iowa. The census for that year began on April 15 and two months later on June 21,1910, Melissa Kelsey Flint Buck Garlow died at the age of "77 years, 4 months and 8 days."[747] The obituary mentions that she belonged to the Methodist Episcopal Church—which was a departure from her Baptist faith as a child.

The second obituary comes from *The Klemme Times*[748]indicating that "she resided with her son Frank Flint in Ellington Township." She is interred in Concord Cemetery, Garner, Iowa.

What became of Hannah M. Wheeler Garlow? She died on November 28, 1912, in or around Binghamton and is buried in Floral Park Cemetery.[749] Her headstone reads 1833–1913[750] and that she had died in Johnson City, Broome, New York. Her short obituary notice notes that she was living at "24 Dickenson Street" at the time of her death (her daughter Alveretta and her new husband were living at 23 Dickenson Street at the time of their marriage in 1921).[751]

745 The marital status of Melissa's second husband, Lester Buck (at the time of *their* marriage), has not yet been revealed.

746 Page 5.

747 *Garner Signal,* June 21, 1910, edition. Newspapers.

748 June 30, 1910, edition, Page: 5. Newspapers.

749 There is another Hannah Wheeler, but she does not have "Garlow" as her surname; she is listed as "Hannah *Wheeler"* (1830–1912) former name *Decker.* She is buried in Rock Ridge Cemetery, Monticello, Sullivan, NY. It is a coincidence that her death date is the same as Hannah Wheeler, wife of John[1] W. Garlow.

750 Her death date is 1912. *Binghamton Press,* Monday, December 2, 1912, 2. www.FultonHistory.com.

751 Hannah M. Garlow is on the 1910 census in Sidney, Delaware, New York. She is listed as a "widow," age "77," born "New York," with "7 children born," "5 living." 1910 census, *Sidney, Delaware, New York;* Roll: T624_935; Page: 9B; ED: 0032; FHL:1374948.

### *The Children of Abner Flint, Jr., and Melissa Kelsey*[752]

i. Leroy Flint,[7] b. 16 Oct 1851, Maine, Broome, NY; d. 24 Jan 1918, Maine, Broome, NY; burial, Glen Aubrey, Broome, NY; m. (1) 7 Jul 1872, Mary Ann Dunham, b. 4 Jun 1851, Broome Co., NY; d. 31 July 1880, Broome Co., NY; m. (2 ) 25 Aug 1881, Martha M. Holmes, b. circa 1853, NY; death unknown. Children between Leroy Flint and Mary Ann Dunham: Irvin J. Flint (1873–1911); Hettie Arvilla Flint (1874–1966) who had married Abram Green (1873–1939).

30. ii. Frank Flint,[7] b. 11 Aug 1857, Maine, Broome, NY; d. 4 Aug 1931, Spink, South Dakota; m. 1882, Althia Almeda Hardy, b. 27 Aug 1865, Broome Co., NY; d. 16 Aug 1929, Redfield, Spink, SD; d.o. John Augustus Hardy (1836–1918) and Elizabeth Amy Moak (1843–1911). Their children: Laura Edna Flint (1884–1918); Elizabeth Amy Flint (1886–); Ida May Flint (1889–1932); Nettie Melissa Flint (1895–); Fred Abner Flint (1898–1994); Susie Camilla Flint (1900–); Althia Almeda Flint (1903–1989).

iii. Floyd Flint,[7] b. 31 Jul 1859, Maine, Broome, NY; d. 19 Dec 1859, Maine, Broome, NY; burial, Allentown Cemetery, Glen Aubrey, Broome, NY.

iv. Ira Flint,[7] b. 20 Mar 1866, Maine, Broome, NY; d. 9 Jan 1950,[753] Endwell, Broome, NY; burial 11 Jan 1950, Riverside Cemetery, Windsor, Broome, NY; m. 25 Oct 1885, Broome, NY, Flora Grace Knowlton (1867–1951). Ira was a charter member of the Endwell Methodist Church.[754] Their Children: Lena M. Flint (1889–1970), m. A. J.

Melissa Kelsey Flint Buck Garlow

Abner Flint, Jr.

752 All details (census and vitals) on the children of Abner Flint, Jr., and Melissa Kelsey comes from DLH records.

753 Died at his home at 307 Hooper Road, Endwell, Broome, NY.

754 Obituary notice from *Binghamton Press and Sun Bulletin*, Binghamton, NY, 9 January 1950, 17. Newspapers.

Remy; Floyd Flint (1892–1905); Harold K. Flint (1904–1920).[755]

There were no children born between Melissa Flint and Lester Buck or John W. Garlow.[756]

### *19. iv. Philo Kelsey[6] (Almira,[5] Ithamar,[4] Timothy,[3] Stephen,[2] Stephen,[1] Arthur)*

Born 12 October 1836;[757] died 15 August 1864, Chattanooga, Hamilton, Tennessee; buried Chattanooga National Cemetery, Chattanooga, Hamilton, Tennessee;[758] married 5 April 1858 West Danby, Tompkins, New York,[759] to Elizabeth "Betsey" Cowles,[760] born 29 November 1834, Spencer, Tioga, New York; died 20 July 1891, Spencer, Tioga, New York; daughter of Elon Cowles (1795–1872) and Lucinda Case (1799–1894).[761]

Philo Kelsey was the last child born to Horace and Almira Kelsey, perhaps in Danby, Tompkins County, New York. Philo's parents moved frequently due to his father being a Baptist preacher. We know that Horace Kelsey was in Tompkins County, but whether the family was in Danby at the time of Philo's birth has yet to be uncovered.[762]

In 1855 Philo Kelsey is living in Chenango, Broome County, in the Abner Flynn household as a "servant." For the same census year, Elizabeth Cowles is living with her brother Jason Cowles in Spencer, Tioga, New York. The household consisted of her parents (Elon and Lucinda Cowles) her uncle, Henry, nieces and nephews, and an eleven-year-old servant.

On 5 April 1858 in West Danby, Tompkins County, New York, the marriage between Philo Kelsey and Elizabeth Cowles was performed by Philo's father, Horace Kelsey.[763] The couple does not appear to have set up housekeeping on their own as they were living with Philo's parents in Barton, Tioga, New York, per the 1860 census. At the time of the 1860 census, Betsey Cowles was four months pregnant with their first child.[764] However, by the time of the birth of their first child (in November of that year), the couple were perhaps living in Broome, New York, as that is where the birth is recorded.[765]

---

755 Obituary notice from *Binghamton Press and Sun Bulletin, Endicott News* states that he was "16 years old and died at his home on Hooper Road; No cause of death given." January 26, 1920, 13. Newspapers.

756 Photos courtesy of Deborah L. Horzen.

757 This is an estimated year of birth and comes from various sources (i.e., 1855 and 1860 censuses, pension files).

758 *U.S. National Cemetery Internment; U.S. Burial Registers, Military Posts; U.S. Civil War Pension Index;* all records from Ancestry.

759 *Ibid*...Widow's Pension claim; Certificate, Kelsey-Cowles marriage.

760 This name is pronounced "Coles."

761 Birth and death dates come from Find A Grave.

762 The 1855 census (NY) states he was born in "Broome County."

763 The date of marriage is confirmed by the certificate of marriage and from the deposition of Elizabeth "Betsey" Kelsey in her application for a pension from her husband's service.

764 Charles Franklin Kelsey, born 2 November 1860, Broome, NY.

765 It is also possible that the couple went to stay with family members who could assist in the birth of their first child.

According to the pension records and depositions from Cornelia Knapp[766] and Melissa Flint, they are the ones who assisted in the birth of both of Betsey's children. It was common for the female relatives, neighbors, and midwives to assist in the birth of children, as did the husband of the woman giving birth.[767]

As with the male population before him, Philo Kelsey enlisted in the Civil War. He joined Company E of the 137th New York Infantry Regiment Volunteers on August 21, 1862, in the town of Binghamton (NY) as a private.[768] He was mustered into the service on September 3, 1862. Philo had signed up for a three-year stint with a bounty of $37.71.

When Philo left, his wife, Betsey, was six months pregnant with their second child. Many women of that period were left behind as so many of their husbands, brothers, or sons had also enlisted. Many women were left to care for their children and themselves without any assistance. Betsey was fortunate in that she had family nearby to assist her.

On December 22, 1862, Betsey gave birth to a son, Philo Lewis Kelsey.[769] Philo Lewis either was born with a deformity or it developed as he grew: a humpback and a sunken chest. How difficult this must have been for his mother. Did she write her husband and tell him this news?

~

The 137th New York were involved in several battles; the first was the Battle of Chancellorsville in April–May 1863, and then they moved on to Gettysburg. Philo Kelsey is listed on the Muster Roll of Mower USA General Hospital at Chestnut Hill, Philadelphia, in Ward 39, and was present for May and June 1863 roll call (this date is just prior to the Battle of Gettysburg). He is also listed as being in the General Hospital, Aquia Creek (VA) in June 1864; many soldiers suffered with various illnesses during their time in the service—the most common cause was dysentery. One month later Philo was wounded at the Battle of Peachtree Creek in Atlanta, Georgia, and died either on August 15 or 16, 1864[770] at the military hospital in Chattanooga, Tennessee. The wound had been to his hip and a brief mention of Philo Kelsey and another soldier appeared in *Fields of Fame & Glory: Col. David Ireland and the 137th New York Volunteers*:[771] "Pvt. Philo Kelsey, Co. E., and Sgt. Robert Evelyn, Co. H., were severely wounded in the legs. Surgeons amputated. Both died."

---

766 Could Cornelia Knapp be the unknown child of Horace Kelsey and Almira Scoville born between 1825–1830 in NY? The 1880 census shows her living in Maine a few houses down from Melissa Kelsey Flint. Her age given (53) on this census record would put her birth year as 1827 in "NY." This Cornelia is the wife of Peter Knapp. They are next-door neighbors on the 1865 NY census for Maine, Broome, NY. More research would be required to prove or disprove this hypothesis.

767 See Osterud's *Bonds of Community—Rural Women's Lives—Childbearing;* Chapter 4, 109–119.

768 Military and pension records. Ancestry.

769 His name is sometimes written in the records as "Lewis Philo Kelsey" and he went by the name of "Lew."

770 His cousin, Charles M. Scoville, also died in a military hospital on July 14, 1864, Alexandria, Virginia.

771 Cluetz, David; published 2010, 330.

Philo Kelsey is buried in the Chattanooga National Cemetery, Hamilton County, Tennessee, grave marker #128.

Elizabeth "Betsey" (Cowles) Kelsey never remarried. She lived out her life in Spencer, Tioga County, New York, where she can be found on the 1865–1880 censuses. After her husband's death, she moved back with her parents, along with her sons Charles and Philo, in 1865. From 1870 to her death she lived next door to her brother Jason Cowles and cared for her mother, Lucinda Cowles,[772] up until the 1880 census.

Elizabeth Kelsey died July 20, 1891, in Spencer, Tioga, New York, at the age of fifty-seven. She is buried in North Spencer Cemetery, Spencer, Tioga, New York.

### *The Children of Philo Kelsey and Elizabeth Cowles*

31. i. Charles Franklin Kelsey,[7] b. 2 Nov 1860, Broome County, New York; d. 19 Feb 1919, perhaps Spencer, Tioga, New York; m. (1) Dora Seeley, 30 April 1882; m. (2) Isabel Cowell, circa 1898.
32. ii. Philo Lewis Kelsey,[7] b. 22 Dec 1862, Broome County, New York; d. 14 Nov 1934, Van Etten, Chemung, New York; m. Rose M. Hobson, circa 1892.

## *20. I. IRENE SCOVILLE[6] (FRANKLIN,[5] ITHAMAR,[4] TIMOTHY,[3] STEPHEN,[2] STEPHEN,[1] ARTHUR)*

Born 22 September 1832, New Marlborough, Berkshire, Massachusetts;[773] died 9 February 1927, Pine Meadow, Litchfield, Connecticut; burial: Pine Grove Cemetery, New Hartford, Litchfield, Connecticut; married 19 October 1851 in South Canaan, Litchfield, Connecticut, to Merritt Ellsworth Smith,[774] born 31 March 1828, Pine Meadow to Carlo Smith (1796–1852) and Amanda Goodwin (1803–1890); he died 18 March 1892 in Pine Meadow.

The first "independent" record we have regarding Irene Scoville is the 1850 census for Canton, Connecticut.[775] An "Irene Scovil" is in the household of Zenas Dyer—a hotelkeeper.[776] I believe that this is the same Irene Scoville who was the daughter of Franklin

772 Lucinda Cowles outlived her daughter Elizabeth. She is listed as age "92" on the 1892 census and died 2 February 1894 in Spencer, New York. *New York, U.S., Death Index, 1852–1956; Certificate#5447;* New York Dept. of Health; Albany, NY; Ancestry.

773 While I have never seen an official vital record of Irene Scoville's birth, this date has been consistent since the time of Holley's book: *Arthur Scovel and His Descendants*. In addition, Irene lived until 1927 and it must have been common knowledge of her family members when her birthday was and one of them must have relayed this to Mrs. Holley through correspondence.

774 Obituary notice. The marriage date is of unknown origin as the source was not cited by this writer.

775 See Fifth Generation, Franklin Scoville regarding the 1850 census. Canton, Connecticut, is a part of Hartford County and was incorporated in 1806 when it separated from the parent town of Simsbury, Connecticut.

776 Zenas Dyer owned a tavern called the "Dyer Tavern" in Canton, Connecticut. From *Reminiscences by Sylvester Barbour, a Native of Canton, Conn. Fifty Years a Lawyer,* (1908) comes the

and Amarilla Scoville. The enumerator did not record her occupation, however, she is likely working as a domestic servant in this household.

Her husband-to-be was still living with his parents in New Hartford, Connecticut, and was working as a butcher in 1850. The Smith family lived in the same neighborhood as the Scovilles as is shown on the 1850 census for New Hartford. The Smiths are enumerated as Dwelling: 168; Family: 188 and the Scoville family is listed as Dwelling: 171; Family: 191, so it is easy to see how Irene and Merritt met.

Merritt Ellsworth Smith was the son of Carlo (Carlos, Carlow) Smith who had been born in 1796 in Sheffield, Berkshire, Massachusetts, and was residing in New Hartford as early as 1830.[777] The Smiths remained in New Hartford/Pine Meadow throughout their lives.

The 1860 census shows the family enumerated in New Hartford:

> Merritt E. Smith, 31, mechanic, b. New York
> Irene Smith, 27, b. Connecticut
> John Smith, 9, real estate $1,500; personal estate $300; attending school

Who is John Smith?[778] According to his age, he would have been born circa 1851. There is no designation on the census of how he is related to the head of the household—is he a son, nephew, or other?

No record that I reviewed provided a month and day for his birth or who his parents were.

Merritt E. Smith had five sisters and one brother (Horatio Nelson). Since I could not find a reference to Horatio having a son named "John," I speculate that one of his sisters may have had a child out-of-wedlock since the surname "Smith" was retained. A partial answer came

---

following:

"Mr. Zenas Dyer, grandfather of Daniel T. Dyer, was another man who took part in Canton's setting-off proceedings. In 1812 he built the house in which the grandson lives, situated on the north side of the old Albany turnpike, near Farmington River, on an elevation commanding a fine view of varying scenery. Mr. Dyer used the house for a time as a tavern, sharing with nearby Hosford's tavern the entertainment of the extensive traveling public. I well remember him and his son Daniel, who many years owned and occupied that house, both highly respected men. Daniel T., the only child of Daniel, succeeded to the ownership of that house, and resides there. He is the owner of some 500 acres of land, and is an honored member of the democratic party, to which party, if I mistake not, Zenas and Daniel belonged. The present Mr. Dyer and his estimable wife, to whom I have already referred, are royal entertainers. Numerically, and in winsome manners, 'their children would delight the heart of President Roosevelt, and they help to make up a very happy family. Mr. Dyer's exhibition at the centennial of his grandfather's old tin lantern, which was a guide to travelers seeking a good inn to tarry at, attracted much attention."

777 I have not been able to locate him prior to the 1830 census in either Connecticut or Massachusetts; however, his father, Medad Smith, and family are living in Granby, Hampshire, Massachusetts, during that time with a son between the ages of 16–24, which would fit Carlo Smith's age at the time of the census.

778 There is also a "John C. Smith" living in New Hartford, Connecticut, at the same time as John Smith with the same year of birth (1851). Is he one and the same?

(as far as the relationship) between Merritt E. Smith and John Smith via the obituary notice[779] for John Smith: "John Smith, a nephew of Merritt Smith, he was born in Norfolk [Connecticut] and came to Pine Meadow to live with his uncle Merritt Smith when he was a boy. He lived here most of the time since." Now we know that he was a nephew, but who were his parents?

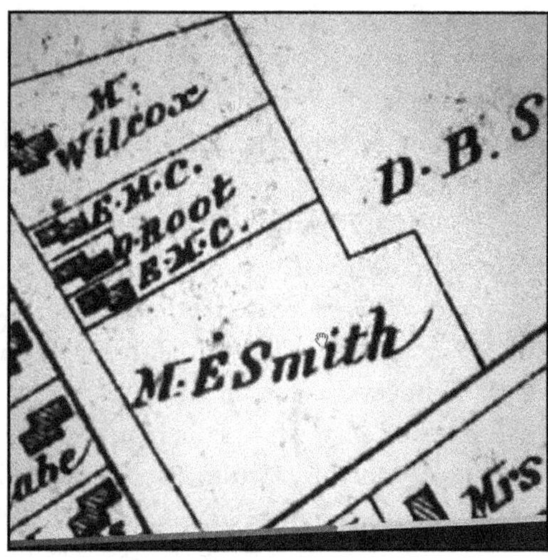


Another curious factor is that the enumerator listed John Smith as having real and personal property. This must have been an error on the part of the enumerator as a nine-year-old child would have been unlikely to have real estate. This entry may have been meant to go on the line for Merritt E. Smith.

By 1870, Merritt E. Smith is listed as a farmer. His nephew John is still in the household.

The 1874 landownership map[780] shows the property owned by M.E. Smith.

The Farmington River flows behind the property on Wicket Street where the Smiths lived.[781]

13 Wicket Street, Merritt E. and Irene Smith homestead in Pine Meadow.

The 1870 agricultural census shows that the couple owned ninety acres of land—sixty of which was developed. The farm was valued at $8,000, farming implements at $500, and wage paid for the prior year at $600.00. They had a horse, five milch cows, two working oxen, and one other labeled as "cattle." There were also five swine. The value of all the livestock was $800.00. There were also bushels of rye, Indian corn, and oats, as were typical of a farm.

779 The obituary was received from the New Hartford Historical Society, New Hartford, Connecticut. There isn't a date on the letter, but I surmise it was sent to me in the 1990s.

780 *U.S. Indexed Ownership Maps, 1860–1918; New Hartford, Connecticut;* Ancestry.

781 Photo is courtesy of Sandra Amador, a descendant of William Harrison Scoville (William Harrison,[6] Franklin,[5] Ithamar,[4] Timothy,[3] Stephen,[2] Stephen,[1] Arthur). William H. was a brother to my great-great-grandfather, Charles M. Scoville.

Based on the same type of census ten years later, the Smith's property had dwindled to twenty acres of tilled land with thirty acres of meadows, pastures, and orchards and thirty-five acres of woodland. The value of the farm was the same, but the farming implements value went down to $300.00.

There could be a few reasons for this, one being age. Farming was a tough business; your health and stamina took a beating. It may have been too much for him to handle and his nephew, John Smith, was now out of the household.

~

While the Smiths were childless (and I believe they raised Merritt's nephew, John, as their own) they had many nieces and nephews who visited them.

Irene Smith was very involved with her church (St. John's Episcopal[782]) in Pine Meadow where she taught Sunday School for many years and was a member of the choir.

In the population census for 1880, Merritt and Irene are caring for their aged parents: Amanda Smith, and Franklin and Amarilla Scoville. This is what was done. You took care of your family and neighbors.

On March 18, 1892, Merritt Ellsworth Smith died in Pine Meadow. He was sixty-four years old. The cause of his death is unknown. His wife, Irene, and her father, Franklin, were the only two left, and Irene cared for her father until 1901 when he, too, passed away. Irene Scoville Smith lived for another twenty-six years.

In 1910 she is living on Wicket Street in Pine Meadow in Dwelling: 85; Family: 90. Next door is John C. Smith with his wife, Emma, and her father, Elmer Moses. The home on Wicket Street is the same farm that she had lived on with her husband, Merritt.[783] While the census

---

782 While Connecticut may have started with a Congregationalist population in the early settlement of the state a sea change occurred, according to *Episcopal Church in Connecticut (episcopalct.org):*

"The growth of the Anglican Church in a heavily Congregationalist colony was enhanced on September 13, 1722, when Dr. Timothy Cutler, president of Yale College, Samuel Johnson, Daniel Brown and James Wetmore announced their conversion to the Church of England and departed for Great Britain for ordination by the Bishop of London. By the close of the American War of Independence there were 44 parishes in Connecticut. Connecticut." I have recognized that many of the ancestors who are part of this work were once Congregationalists or Baptists who turned to the Episcopalian Church for their religious nourishment.

783 According to *Pine Meadow Historic District,* the Smith family lived at 13 Wicket Street. The following comes from the website www.livingplaces.com: "Among the best-preserved of the 18 examples on Wicket Street are those at 27, 32, 35, and 39 Wicket Street. All have a more pronounced and taller doorway surround and a slightly higher plate height for the main block. Two nearly identical houses on the north end of Wicket Street have the typical form and massing but no other Greek Revival features (69 and 71 Wicket Street). Their entrances are in the side elevation rather than the facade. Another one at the south end of the street, **the M.E. Smith House (13 Wicket Street), has a metal-shingled roof, as well as an exceptionally large barn at the rear. The barn is**

stated she lived "alone," the house could have been partitioned off for her sole use until her death.

We find her living with John C. Smith and his wife on the 1920 census as well—still living on Wicket Street.[784]

On February 9, 1927, Irene Scoville Smith died at the age of ninety-five, and she is buried with her husband, Merritt, in Pine Grove Cemetery. Irene left a will and, while I do not have a copy of the *actual* will, I do have the Inventory and Appraisal[785] of her estate.

Irene Smith's niece's son, George H. Raidart, was the administrator of the estate, and John C. Smith was one of two appraisers (the other was Charles H. Pflueger). The following is the "true and complete inventory of all the property, real and personal . . ." of Irene Smith:

Book No. 4712 Mechanics Savings Bank—$344.47
Book No. 6231 Farmington Savings Bank—$315.88
Book No. 93835 Society for Savings—$302.22
Wearing Apparel—$40.00
Household Furniture—$69.75
Three Shawls—$35.06
One gold eye glass frame—$1.25
One pair of spectacles—.25

============
$1108.88

The probate judge (Frank L. Whitney) signed off on the 1st day of October 1927.

This document also names the "heirs at law and distributes of said estate . . . under the last will and testament."

| | |
|---|---|
| George H. Raidart, Winstead, Conn. | (nephew)[786] |
| Mrs. William Carr, 7 Ball St., Worcester, Mass. | (niece) |
| Mrs. George Prince, 28 Putnam St., New Haven, Conn. | (niece) |
| Mrs. Frank Van Deusen, 40 Barber St., Torrington, Conn. | (niece) |
| Mrs. Agnes Billion[sic], 16 Pine St., New Britain, Conn. | (niece) |
| Mrs. Edmond Roys, Stockbridge, Mass. | (niece) |
| Harry Scoville, Ashley Falls, Mass. | (nephew) |
| Albert Scoville, 14 Spring St., Hartford, Conn. | (nephew) |
| Frank Scoville, Paragould, Arkansas | (nephew) |
| Mrs. Howard Ashley, c/o Mrs. M.C. Lindberg, Gig Harbor, Washington | (niece) |
| Charles M. Scoville, P.O. Box 3507, Tampa, Fla. | (nephew) |

---

**one of four from this period on this street.**"

784 John C. Smith lived on Wicket Street up until his death on 7 May 1943.

785 From the Probate Court for the District of New Hartford; 59-611.

786 While the probate record lists the "heirs at law" as nieces and nephews, they are the children of her nieces and nephews. In addition, there is one "nephew" who is not listed here (even though he was still living), and that is Wilbur H. Raidart, son of George H. Raidart. More on Wilbur later in this work.

| | |
|---|---|
| Mrs. Anna Durick,[sp?] 85 [ ] St., Astoria, L.I. (NY) | (niece) |
| Mrs. Grace Claflin Nash, 94 Bradford St., Everett, Mass. | (niece) |
| Grove M. Deming, Mount Herman, Mass. | (nephew) |
| Earl Deming, Windsor Locks, Conn. | (nephew) |
| Ralph Deming, Colebrook, Conn. | (nephew) |

The fact that John C. Smith is not named as an "heir-at-law" seems to confirm that he had received the house and farm on Wicket Street likely upon the death of his uncle, Merritt E. Smith. As Merritt and Irene took care of him, he, in turn, took care of his "aunt" Irene until her death.[787]

Photo at "Aunt Irene's." Kneeling: George H. Raidart; Sitting: Irene Scoville Smith Standing Rear: Elizabeth Sears; Grace Claflin Nash; Far Right: Florence Scoville Carr. The young girl behind Irene S. Smith could be Marjorie Nash, daughter of Grace C. Nash. 13 Wicket Street, Pine Meadow, Connecticut.

### *21. ii.* ***Charles Martin Scoville***[6] *(Franklin,[5] Ithamar,[4] Timothy,[3] Stephen,[2] Stephen,[1] Arthur)*

Born circa 1834/35[788] possibly in Colebrook, Litchfield, Connecticut; died 14 July 1864, Alexandria, Virginia; buried 15 July 1864, Alexandria National Cemetery;[789] married 20 August

787 Photo courtesy of either Sandra Amador or Ken Sears, descendants of Franklin Scoville and Amarilla Hotchkiss. Notice the dog peeking around the corner.

788 A birthdate for my great-great-grandfather has never been discovered. The Town Clerk's Office in Colebrook has stated that their records from 1834/1835 are missing. The Connecticut State Library in Hartford does not have his birth recorded or his pension papers. I have birth records for all his siblings as well as photographs for all, except for Charles.

789 All information on Charles' military service comes from his military and pension papers provided by the NARA.

1855,[790] Colebrook, Litchfield, Connecticut, to Catherine Schneider; born 17 May 1838,[791] Newark, Essex, New Jersey; died 17 December 1908, New Britain, Hartford, Connecticut. She married (2) Gottlieb Christian Gammerdinger, 3 July 1866, New Britain, Hartford, Connecticut;[792] died 8 March 1888, New Britain, Hartford, Connecticut.[793]

Discovering the birthdate for Charles M. Scoville has been difficult. Franklin had land in Colebrook that he sold in September of 1836. The deed states that Franklin Scoville was of "Canton" (Connecticut). The question is whether the Scovilles were there when Charles was born.

They certainly were in Colebrook by 1837 when Charles' mother gave birth to his sister Julia. Unless other data becomes available my theory is that Charles was born in Colebrook sometime between 1834/1835.

Charles was working for the Zenas Dyer family in 1850 (like his sister Irene) in Canton, Connecticut. By the time he was eighteen, Charles was working in a furniture factory.[794] The factory was likely the Union Chair Company, which was in Colebrook.

The Union Chair Company had been inherited by Samuel Roberts, who ran it until 1840 when he and his partner sold out to their competitor, Hitchcock and Alvord in Riverton, Connecticut.[795]

Prior to Charles' employment in the furniture factory, he met a young girl who was to become his wife. Her name was Catherine Schneider and she met Charles when she was fourteen and he seventeen. Catherine had been born in Newark, Essex, New Jersey, on 17 May 1838 to German immigrants, John and Barbara (Fischer) Schneider.[796] It hasn't been determined when John Schneider came to the United States but it was before his first daughter was born in 1838.

John Schneider's arrival in the United States was considered part of the "old immigration."[797] Germany had experienced devastating crop failures in the 1830s and this could be the reason that John Schneider left Germany.

All the Schneider children were born in Newark and were baptized in St. John Catholic

790 Town Clerk's Office, Colebrook, Connecticut; pension records.

791 Death Certificate; Baptismal Record; Pension Record.

792 Marriage Certificate, New Britain, Connecticut, Town Clerk's Office.

793 Death Certificate; newspaper article.

794 Pension papers in my possession.

795 Vining, Henry Hart, *Lure of the Litchfield Hills,* Colebrook Historical Society (www.colebrookhistoricalsociety.com).

796 For the sake of consistency, I am using the spelling "Schneider" unless a specific record spelled it in an alternate way.

797 The immigrants that arrived in the U.S. between 1830–1880 were considered part of the "old immigration," those who came from England, Sweden, Ireland, and Germany.

Church[798] in Newark. This family shows up on the 1840 and 1850 censuses in Newark, but sometime after 1850, this family is in Colebrook, at least by 1852.

The 1850 census reveals the occupation of John Schneider as a "razor grinder" and he must have worked in one of the many factories that were in Newark.

My curiosity asks why a family living in Newark, New Jersey, where the population is said to have been 38,894 in 1850, would travel some 140 miles to a small, rural town in western Connecticut with a population of 1,317? Why would you leave a place with many other Germans who spoke your language, were part of the same German clubs, and were of the same religion (Catholic) to go to a town that was primarily Protestant, rural, and only one other known German immigrant[799] was living in the town of Colebrook? I haven't adequately been able to answer this question.

Other than the pension record for Catherine Schneider Scoville, where her deposition indicates she met her future husband when she was fourteen (1852), nothing more is known about the Schneiders in Colebrook.

≈

Charles and Catherine courted for three years until she reached the age of seventeen. At that time, her parents finally gave their permission for her to marry. The couple was wed on Wednesday, August 20, 1855, by Reverend Luther H. Barber. The couple may have lived with either the Scovilles or Schneiders during the early part of their marriage.

The first child born to them was a son, Albert A. Scoville, on April 7, 1857, in Colebrook.[800]

It is debatable how long Charles and Catherine remained in Colebrook after Albert's birth as by 1859 the couple was living in the "big city" of New Britain, Hartford, Connecticut.

Charles' father and mother had departed from Colebrook and were now residing in North Canaan, Connecticut, by 1860. The young couple likely felt it was time to strike out on their own and they chose New Britain as their new home.

The city of New Britain is centrally located in Connecticut and is part of the County of Hartford. It was once known as the "Great Swamp" in the Berlin section of Farmington. In 1754 the colony received approval of this new parish, which was named "New Briton." By the nineteenth century New Britain was becoming a booming industrial village and was known as the "Hardware City" and home to P.F. Corbin's and the Stanley Works Company and many other manufacturing companies.

When Charles, Catherine, and Albert left Colebrook for New Britain, Catherine's parents went with them. Catherine's parents likely felt more at home in New Britain as there were many German immigrants already living in the city (New Britain has had a wide and diverse immigration population throughout its history).

---

798 Copies of baptismal records are in my possession. Catherine Snyder bap. 14 Oct 1838; Anthony Snyder bap. 2 Aug 1840; Mary Ann Snyder bap. 14 Nov 1841. Another daughter, Agnes, was born to this family, but no baptismal record was received for her.

799 William H. Raidart also immigrated in 1839 to the U.S. from Hesse, Darmstadt, Germany.

800 Date of birth is from the pension records of his father. I speculate that Albert's middle name may have been Anthony, after Catherine's brother, but I do not have proof of this.

In March 1859,[801] Catherine's father died from consumption of which he suffered for six months. He is likely buried in an unmarked grave in Fairview Cemetery (or a pauper's grave). That July Catherine gave birth to a girl on the eleventh day with the help of a physician, B.M. Comings, M.D.[802]

The family was living in the South Division of New Britain in 1860[803] when the census was taken. The family consisted of:

Charles Scoville, 23, teamster,[804] b. Conn.
Catherine Scoville, 22, b. Conn.
Albert Scoville, 2, b. Conn.
Margaret Snyder, 50, b. Germany

The Scovilles must have been renting an apartment as there isn't any real or personal estate listed on the census form. And where was daughter Agnes? Why isn't she listed with the family? Reviewing the census, she is located five dwellings down with the Ebenezer Burrill family.[805] Why is she there and not with her own family? The Ebenezer Burrill household has a strange mixture of people living there. Since the 1860 census[806] doesn't indicate what relationship each individual had to the head of the household, much more research would have to be done to find out if these various people are related in any way.

Let's look at the Burrill household as it was in 1860:

Ebenezer Burrill, 53, mechanic, real estate $2,000, b. Conn.
Adelia Brainard, 27, b. Conn.
Hannah Burrill, 25, b. Conn.
Villeroy Burrill, 16, b. Conn.

---

801 *U.S. Federal Census* for those who died during the year ending 1 June 1860. John Snider is listed as a "mechanic," age "50." Shepard, James 1838–1926 *History of St. Mark's Church, New Britain, Connecticut and of its predecessor Christ Church, Wethersfield, Berlin: From the First Church of England Service in America to Nineteen Hundred and Seven. (1907) (herein History of St. Mark's)*. Lists the burial of John Snider as April 2, 1859; burial in New Britain; 623.

802 This information comes from the doctor's deposition for the pension application.

803 1860 census, *New Britain, Hartford, Connecticut*; Dwelling #205; Family #227; South Division of the town of New Britain, Hartford, Connecticut; page 28; enumerated on the 7th day of June 1860. Ancestry. An 1858 map of New Britain shows "E. Burrill" living on Kensington Street. Since the 1860 census shows both Burrill and Scoville living in the same neighborhood, I theorize that this is where the Scovilles were living during that time.

804 A teamster was a person who drove a team—usually oxen, horses, or mules—pulling a wagon. They were responsible for delivering goods. During the Civil War the teamster was responsible for bringing supplies to his unit. A teamster's job was very dirty and dangerous and he was generally "under the thumb of the quartermaster." www.wikipedia.org; www.civilwar.mrdonn.org; www.historynet.com has a more in-depth article on the life of teamsters during the Civil War.

805 Dwelling: 210; Family: 232; page 28.

806 The 1850, 1860, and 1870 censuses list names of people in each household. It wasn't until the 1880 census that the relationship between people was recorded.

Frank Little, 7, b. Mass.
**Agnes Scoville, 10/12, b. Conn.**
Mary Little, 13, b. N. J.
Lillian Brainard, 7, b. Conn.

The adult women may be married/widowed daughters and/or daughters-in-law of Ebenezer Burrill with their children living in his household; although it doesn't answer the question as to who Frank and Mary Little belong to.[807]

In 1861 Catherine Scoville gave birth to a girl whom they named Margaret. Sadly, this child did not live long. There is contradicting information regarding the birth date of this child.[808] However, the baptismal record at St. Mark's Episcopal Church states that she was baptized on October 12,1861, to "Charles and ______ Scoville." She died the following day (October 13) aged three months and is interred in New Britain.[809] If this information is correct, Margaret would have been born in July 1861.

On June 27, 1862, a son by the name of Joseph was born to this couple. He was baptized on September 26, 1862, the son of "Mr. and Mrs. Charles Scoville," aged three months, and died September 29, 1862, and was interred in New Britain.[810]

While Catherine was baptized a Catholic in New Jersey with the rest of her siblings, apparently by the time she and Charles married and settled in New Britain, Connecticut, she and her parents were parishioners of St. Mark's Episcopal Church. It doesn't appear that Charles Scoville was ever a member.

≈

The winds of war had come and, like so many of his brethren, Charles M. Scoville enlisted on July 31, 1862,[811] in New Britain. Samuel A. Moore (who would become Charles' commander) was also a resident of New Britain and had signed Charles up for a three-year term in Com-

807 *Massachusetts, Compiled Birth, Marriage, and Death records, 1700–1850* documents two children born to an Ebenezer Burrell and Samantha Burrell in Chester, Hampden County: Delia, born 25 June 1832, and Hannah, 12 September 1834. A death record for Adelia Burrill Armstrong for 9 Jul 1871 shows her death recorded in New Britain. She was the spouse of William B. Armstrong. Her birthdate matches the Delia born in Chester, Mass. I speculate that Hannah, Villeroy, and Adelia are all children of Ebenezer Burrill. The daughter listed as "Adelia Brainard" on the 1860 census is shown on the 1870 census as being the "wife" of "Wm. B. Armstrong" with "daughter" Lillie Armstrong" (formerly Brainard) in the household.

808 There was no birth or death certificate for this child, only a notation at the town clerk's office in New Britain.

809 *History of St. Mark's*, 492; 623

810 *Ibid*; 494, 623

811 Charles' brother William enlisted a couple of weeks after his brother, and they served in the same company.

pany F of the 14th Regiment Infantry Volunteers.[812]

How did Catherine react to this news that her husband had enlisted? Some men may have discussed with their wives their intentions ahead of time. I also suspect that many men enlisted on the spur of the moment with the idea of patriotism and serving their country, but they also enlisted for economic purposes.

There may have been many tears and arguments regarding the husband's enlistment; however, many women eventually reconciled with the fact that they were going to be left on the home front. During this time many women expanded their horizons while their husbands were away. Some got involved with nursing or factory jobs and many formed soldiers aid societies to provide any kind of support that they could, such as food and clothing. Many women knitted socks (as did William Scoville's wife, Mary Catherine).

How did the Scoville family react when they learned both of their sons (Charles and William) were going off to war? Their reactions could have been a full spectrum of emotions, from being proud, to trepidation, to plain outright fear.

Since I have no photo of Charles, I can only give his physical attributes when he enlisted. He is said to have been "5′ 10 ½″ tall, with a dark complexion, black eyes, and black hair." His coloring is completely different than all his siblings and is quite a contrast to their lighter hair, eyes, and complexions. He was a teamster by trade, age "27," and was born in "New Hartford, Connecticut."[813]

The raw recruits were sent to Camp Foote in Hartford, Connecticut, to learn the "art of war," which meant they did a lot of marching and drilling.[814] This particular regiment had 1,015 men.[815] All companies (except companies A and B) were armed with Springfield rifles, while companies A and B had Sharps.[816]

Each company was represented by different towns. Company F, under Jarvis E. Blinn, had sixty-five men from New Britain, fifteen from Bloomfield, thirteen from Berlin, three from Wolcott, and two from Wethersfield. The towns of Bridgeport, Hartford, Norwich, New

812 Charles' enlistment came on the heels of two of their children dying in a short span of time. Did his patriotic duty and their need for economic help weigh heavily on him after the loss of two children and having to leave his wife to mourn their loss on her own?

813 All foregoing information relating to Charles M. Scoville's military service is provided by his military and pension papers, unless otherwise noted. Charles may have given New Hartford as his place of birth as he had lived there for some time. He may not have known where he was born.

814 Page, Charles D., *History of the Fourteenth Regiment, Connecticut Volunteer Infantry*; herein Page's History; Meriden, Conn.: The Horton Printing Company, (1906). Herein *History of the Fourteenth.*

815 *History of the Fourteenth.*

816 There is some dispute as to whether the green recruits were issued weapons. One opinion is that the men were not issued weapons until they were on enemy soil in Arlington, Virginia. See 14th Connecticut, www.kbacon.com.

Haven, New London, Barkhamsted, and Vernon had one man each.[817]

In the chapter *Birth of the Regiment*[818] it states: "No member of the Regiment will forget those closing days at 'Camp Foote,' the hurried bustle of preparation for departure, the throngs of people who came to say farewell to father, brother, husband and friend." I would like to think that Charles' wife, children, family, and friends were present to bid their farewells to him and William.

On the 25th day of August the regiment broke camp to start for Washington, D.C. All along the way the men marched in columns of four and the citizens of each town they marched through came to see them off with bands playing. There were six companies that boarded the vessel *City of Hartford*. The same type of crowds greeted them when they reached Middletown (Connecticut) where baskets of fruit and food were presented to the men. Hearty greetings were made. The new recruits were on their way to New York, and it wasn't long until they would become battle tested.

It is not clear how Catherine supported herself and their children after Charles left. Men who had volunteered were rewarded a bounty of one hundred dollars. Most of this money was deferred until the soldier was honorably discharged, although it is possible Charles may have received a portion of this money in advance, which he would have turned over to his wife. Many men from poorer families volunteered because of the lure of the bounty.[819]

Did Catherine join any ladies aid societies? Women in the northern states spent time baking, canning goods for the soldiers, and knitting socks and blankets (as her sister-in-law Mary Catherine Dunn Scoville had done). Some women became nurses. This still does not tell us how Catherine supported herself. She may have taken in a boarder to help make ends meet.[820]

Without going into the details of each battle that Charles Scoville was involved in, I will list them here. There are numerous articles and books on Civil War battles:

Antietam, September 17, 1862 (Maryland)
Fredericksburg, December 13, 1862 (Virginia)
Chancellorsville, May 1, 2, & 3, 1863 (Virginia)
Gettysburg, July 2 & 3, 1863 (Pennsylvania)
Falling Waters, July 14, 1863 (Virginia)
Auburn, October 14, 1863 (Virginia)
Bristow Station, October 14, 1863 (Virginia)
Blackburn's Ford, October 17, 1863 (Virginia)
Mine Run, November 29, 1863(Virginia)
Morton's Ford, February 6, 1864 (Virginia)
Wilderness, May 5 & 6, 1864 (Virginia)

817 *History of the Fourteenth;* 18.

818 *History of the Fourteenth,* Chapter 19.

819 Later in the war (1863 and onward) the bounties were increased to \$300, then \$1,200, then \$1,500. This is when the more "affluent" men decided to join the ranks. See Nat'lParkService.gov for more information.

820 She did take on boarders later in life.

Laurel Hill, May 10, 1864 (Virginia)
Spotsylvania Courthouse, May 12, 1864 (Virginia)[821]

Charles had enlisted as a private and, after the Battle of Blackburn's Ford, he was promoted to corporal in November of 1863. Three months later, on February 6, 1864, Charles was wounded in the groin during the Battle of Morton's Ford in Virginia. His wound was not severe, and he was returned to the ranks. On February 17, 1864, Charles was promoted to sergeant.

On May 5–6, 1864, began the Battle of the Wilderness—an apt name. According to one account by Major Hincks he presumed that they were on their way to Spotsylvania Courthouse ". . . so thick were the trees it was difficult for the men to advance in-line and we could seldom see more than a few rods ahead . . .

St. Paul's Church, Alexandria Virginia

"Bullets cut through the air and 'the men' fell from the ranks like autumn leaves in a November gale."[822]

Charles was still working his team, bringing supplies to his company, and on the 9th of May the company marched to Spotsylvania Courthouse. Sometime during the battle on May 12th, Charles was wounded severely in the hips with a conical ball. He was removed from the battlefield to St. Paul's Church.[823] The Second Division had taken over the church to be used as a hospital.[824]

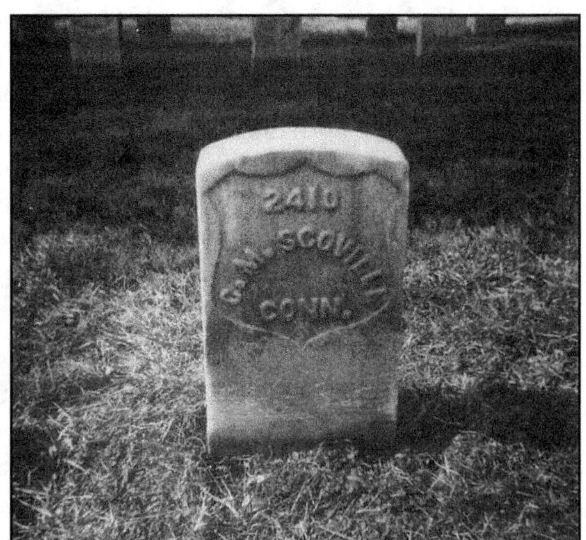



Headstone of Charles M. Scoville. Photo taken by the author.

There he languished for two months until, on 14 July 1864, he succumbed to his injuries and died. His military records do not specify whether his death was caused by infection, but it is probable. Infections such as gangrene were rampant. Internal organs were also damaged. Many extremities (such as

821 This battle went on from the 13th, 14th, 18th, & 22nd

822 *History of the Fourteenth*, 236

823 Image of St. Paul's Church is in the public domain.

824 Virginia Department of Historic Resources (Wikipedia), Virginia Landmarks Register (retrieved May 10, 2021).

arms and legs) were removed. However, since Charles' wounds were to the hips, it is unlikely any amputations were performed. How he must have suffered.

The following day, on 15 July 1864, Charles M. Scoville was laid to rest in grave number 2410 in Alexandria National Cemetery, Alexandria, Virginia.

I keep coming back to how families were notified of their loved one's death. Since Charles' brother, William, was in the same company, word may have been passed to him and he got word to the family. William's wife, Mary Catherine, was in New Britain during this time, and she may have been the one to notify Charles' wife, Catherine. According to all census records for Catherine, she could neither read nor write. It is difficult to imagine not being able to keep in contact with your husband for two years.

This is the news that all families dreaded and now it had come to Catherine's door. Her in-laws were living in North Canaan during this time and most of his siblings were scattered across Litchfield County. Other than Mary Catherine Scoville, Catherine Scoville only had her mother, Barbara Snider, to look to for emotional support.

When Charles left for the war, his son Albert was seven years of age, and his daughter Agnes was five. Memories of their father must have been very vague.

In 1866, Catherine applied for a widow's pension. She was to receive eight dollars[825] per month" commencing on "July 4, 1866," and ending on "July 10, 1875." Each child received two dollars per month.[826] Catherine was appointed guardian of her own children on August 16, 1866, "having no father, guardian or master."[827]

Another event occurred on July 3, 1866, when Catherine Scoville married a man named Gottlieb Gammerdinger (also spelled Gamerdinger).[828] The marriage was performed by the Rev. L. B. Baldwin of St. Mark's Episcopal Church in New Britain, Connecticut.[829]

The Record is in the words and figures following, viz:

| Date. | Names. | Age. | Color. | Birth place. | Residence. | Name of person officiating. |
|---|---|---|---|---|---|---|
| July 3 | Gottlieb Gammerdinger | 38 | White | Germany | New Britain | L. B. Baldwin |
| 1866 | Catharine Scovill | 28 | " | " " | " " | Clergyman |

And I further certify, that I have no interest in the object sought for by this document.

Rich. S. Porter Registrar

825 Eight dollars would be equivalent to $131.06 in 2021 inflation rate.

826 Many depositions were taken prior to a widow receiving a pension. Depositions were taken from former military leaders, doctors, neighbors, friends, and relatives. The children (Albert and Agnes) would receive a pension up until the age of sixteen.

827 Pension records for Charles M. Scoville.

828 *Ibid*

829 For widows, eligibility rules focused on date of marriage and if they had remarried. Early pensions required that the service member must have died in service, the widow had to have been married to him at the time of his death, and she could not have remarried. Catherine may have applied for pension earlier in the year and it was awarded to her and to commence on July 4,

Gottlieb was ten years older than Catherine (whom he called "Kate or Katie"). It is unknown how or when they met. There were several German societies in New Britain, and it is possible they met through one of these clubs.

Gottlieb Gammerdinger was a recent immigrant to the United States from Wurttemberg, Germany, having arrived in the U.S. with his brother John in 1857, and they settled in New Britain.[830, 831]

~

The Gottlieb Gammerdinger family is listed on the 1870[832] census. I believe at this time the family were living at 49 Pleasant Street[833] and they (Catherine and Gottlieb) remained there until their deaths.

The people living in the household are as follows:

Gottlieb Gammerdinger, 42, works in cutlery shop, real estate $2,200, Germany
Catherine Gammerdinger, 33, keeping house, New Jersey
Agnes Scoville, 10, at home, Connecticut
Margaret Snider, 61, at home, Bavaria
John Gammerdinger, 30, works in hardware shop, Wurttemberg

A month prior to the census, Catherine was confirmed at St. Mark's Church on June 19, 1870, by the Right Reverend John Williams, D.D.[834] There is no mention of Gottlieb Gammerdinger becoming a member of this church.

Gottlieb (like many other Germans in the United States) joined German societies and clubs. According to his obituary, he belonged to the Turner, Schwaben, and Harugari societies. These societies helped to promote and preserve the German culture and tradition through song, schuhplattler dance, and good food.

Catherine as well was involved with the various German societies. After Charles' death and she remarried a German man, she (being a first-generation German) may have become more involved than she was previously.

---

1866—a day after she remarried. It is doubtful that she received the pension she had been awarded. essentialcivilwarcurriculum.com.

830 Gottlieb and John Gammerdinger became citizens of the United States; Gottlieb on 29 March 1864 (Vol. II, 98, Superior Court Records, Hartford, Connecticut). John became a citizen on 27 March 1863—(Vol. II, 57, Superior Court Records, Hartford, Connecticut).

831 Marriage record of Catherine Scovill[sic] and Gotlieb Gammerdinger. Copy in my possession.

832 Note that Albert Scoville was living or visiting his Scoville grandparents in North Canaan, Connecticut, during the time of the 1870 census. The enumerator was at the Scoville residence on the 10th day in June. The enumerator didn't visit the Gammerdinger household until the 7th of July.

833 This home still stands today but in a different configuration. The original home was a two-family old-style home.

834 *History of St. Mark's*, 597.

In the year 1875, a marriage occurred between Catherine's daughter Agnes Scoville and a recent German immigrant by the name of Ferdinand Billian. Agnes had just turned sixteen years old on July 11th and the marriage took place on the twenty-fourth of that month.[835] I suspect that they met during one of the many German gatherings that took place in the city.

There are no records for the interval years until the 1880 census.[836] The family group consists of:

Gotlieb Gammerdinger, 52, works hardware shop, born Germany
Catherine Gammerdinger, wife, 41, keeps house, born New Jersey
Albert Scoville, 20, stepson, works hardware shop, born New Jersey[837]
Barbara Schneider, 70, mother-in-law, at home, born Germany

The hardware shop mentioned in the 1880 census was "P.F. Corbin Company."[838] This company was a mainstay in New Britain for many years. Philip Corbin began to work for the Matteson, Russell & Erwin Company (latter Russell Erwin). He acquired the necessary skills to advance in the hardware industry. From there he went to work for Henry Andrews where Corbin apprenticed and learned the art of lock making. Philip's brother Frank Corbin had joined him and soon after P&F Corbin Company was formed.

~

Two events occurred in the early to middle part of the 1880s: Albert Scoville married, and Catherine's mother, Barbara, died on August 28, 1885. She is buried in Fairview Cemetery in New Britain, Connecticut. She was seventy-five years old. The Schneider family has been difficult to research.

John and Barbara Schneider seemingly were born somewhere in "Bavaria," Germany, and immigrated to the United States, I suspect sometime in the 1830s. The couple settled in Newark, Essex, New Jersey. All the children were born in Newark and baptized at St. John Catholic Church. I have never been able to follow the trail of Catherine's sisters, Agnes and Mary Ann.[839] It is possible that they died young. Catherine's brother Anthony left somewhat of a trail, but any records pertaining to him are incomplete. Whether Anthony Schneider kept in touch with his family or ever visited them in Connecticut is a mystery.

---

835 As far as I am aware, this was not a "rushed" marriage as their first child was born in August 1876.

836 1880 census, New Britain, Hartford County, Connecticut; *U.S. Federal Population Census, 1880* (NARA microfilm series T1132); House #49, Dwelling: 236; Family: 411. Ancestry.

837 Albert A. Scoville was born in Connecticut, *not* New Jersey.

838 City directories for New Britain show Gotlieb being employed by "P. F. Corbin Company" during the 1880s. P & F Corbin Company eventually merged with other local manufacturers and became the American Hardware Corporation. Black and Decker purchased the company in 1989. In 2010, the Stanley Works, also of New Britain, purchased Black and Decker, now called Stanley Black & Decker. www. connecticuthistory.org.

839 The children of John Schneider and Mary Margaret Barbara Fischer were Catherine (1838–1908), Anthony (1839–1899), Mary Ann (1841–), and Agnes (1844–), all born in Newark, New Jersey.

In February 1888 tragedy struck the family. The newspaper account gives the details:

**New Britain: An Elevator Accident**

About 8 a.m., Monday, two men Gottlich[sic] Gammerdinger and William Farrelly, were going up an elevator at P&F Corbin's and reached the fourth story when something gave way. Farrelly jumped to a landing and escaped with a bruised foot. Gammerdinger tried to work the brake rope, but in doing so had four fingers cut off. He fell with the elevator, sustaining severe bruises and having a leg broken. Dr. Styles was called and later in the day the leg was amputated, leaving the patient in a dangerous condition. The elevator was in temporary charge of Gammerdinger and had been working all right. There was not [a] heavy load upon it and no negligence seems to attach to anyone. It was first thought that the wire rope carrying the elevator had broken, but an examination of the whole apparatus showed that there was nothing broken. What caused the accident remains a mystery, though it is conjectured that from some unknown cause the big drum on which the rope winds must have slipped letting the rope run out.[840]

An addendum to the above article appeared in *The Hartford Courant* March 10th issue:[841]

Gottlieb Gammerdinger the man who was injured by the falling of an elevator at P&F Corbin's recently, died Thursday morning. He was nearly 60 years old, was born in Wurttemberg [sic] and had been in this country about 20 years. He was a member of the Turner, Swabian and Harugari societies,[842] who with the city band, will attend his funeral which will be held on Saturday at 2 p.m." His funeral was well attended by all the people he knew from the German societies, associates, and family. Ironically, the following day (March 11th) the Great Blizzard of 1888 dumped at least fifty inches of snow in some areas of Connecticut. Everything was shut down in New Britain. Perhaps Catherine stayed with her daughter Agnes and her husband after the funeral. Otherwise, she would have been completely isolated after her husband's death since the storm didn't abate for three days.

Now that Catherine was a widow, she had to find a way to obtain an income. I believe it was during this time that she began to take in boarders.[843] At the time of Gottlieb's death, Catherine was fifty years old, and she never married again. Her meager income sustained her,

840 *The Hartford Courant*, February 28, 1888, issue, 4; Proquest: 1887–1922; document: 795232102; CSL, Hartford, CT.

841 *Ibid.* Death caused by peritonitis per death certificate.

842 The Turner Societies was founded in Meriden, Connecticut, in 1866 and was dedicated to the promotion and preservation of German culture and tradition. Chapters of these societies sprang up wherever Germans had emigrated through good food, music, and schuhplatter dance.

843 This information comes via the pension records of her first husband, Charles M. Scoville.

and she continued to live at 49 Pleasant Street until her death in 1908.[844]

Little is known about Catherine's personality except what was told to me by my grandmother.[845] Catherine was a "very nice person" and she used to make raspberry juice (or cordial) to bring to her daughter's house when someone was sick.

Catherine (Kate) Schneider Scoville Gammerdinger died on December 17, 1908, in New Britain, Connecticut, at the age of seventy. Her will is as follows:

**Estate of Katherine Gammerdinger**[846]

Last Will and Testament

I, Katherine Gammerdinger of the town of New Britain, County of Hartford, and State of Connecticut, do hereby make, publish, and declare this to be my last will and testament, hereby revoking all former wills by me made.

First, I direct that my just debts and funeral expenses be paid out of my Estate by my executor hereafter named.

Second I give, devise and bequeath all my estate both real and personal to be divided equally between my two children, Albert A. Scoville and Agnes R. Billian to them and their heirs forever. Third If my said son Albert A. Scoville should not survive me then in that event I give, devise and bequeath the share he would receive if alive to Jennie L. Scoville to her and her heirs forever. Fourth I constitute and appoint my son Albert A. Scoville executor of this my last will and testament. In witness whereof I have hereunto set my hand and seal this 18th day of May 1900.

Katherine X Gammerdinger

Her obituary appeared in the *New Britain Daily Herald* on December 18, 1908:

Mrs. Gottlieb Gammerdinger, 71 years, 8 months old, widow of the late Gottlieb Gammerdinger, died last night at her home, 49 Pleasant Street where she lived many years. She was a member of several German societies and has lived in this city for many years, she—being one of the most well-known German ladies in the city. She leaves two children. Albert Scoville and Mrs. Ferdinand Billian; three grandchildren, Ernest and Fred Billian, Mrs. George Kumm; two great-grandchildren, Raymond Billian, Clarence Kumm. The funeral services will be held Sunday afternoon at 2 o'clock and 2:30 from St. John's German Lutheran Church."

Even though Catherine was baptized Catholic, she had attended St. Mark's Episcopal Church for a time—even getting married there; however, by the time of her death she was

844 City Directories for New Britain, Connecticut, shows her consistently living at this address in 1890, 1891, 1893, 1906, and 1907 (some years missing on the Ancestry website). Crosschecked census for her daughter and her husband and she was not in their household during those times.

845 Caroline Halldin Billian (my grandmother) was the daughter-in-law of Agnes Scoville Billian, and relayed some anecdotal information on Catherine Scoville Gammerdinger.

846 *Connecticut Wills and Probate Records, 1609–1999.* Ancestry.

attending St. John's Lutheran Church.

Catherine and Gottlieb Gammerdinger are buried in Section 15 of Fairview Cemetery, New Britain.

***Children of Charles Martin Scoville and Catherine Schneider***

33. i. Albert A.[847] Scoville,[7] b. 7 Apr 1857, Colebrook, Litchfield, Connecticut; d. 31 Oct 1944, Hartford, Hartford, Connecticut; m. Laura Jennie Steele, circa 1882; b. 23 Jan 1861, Simsbury, Hartford, Connecticut; d. 22 Mar 1939, North Newington, Hartford, Connecticut; she the daughter of Thomas Steele and Sarah Cornish.

34. ii. Agnes R.[848] Scoville,[7] b. 11 Jul 1859, New Britain, Hartford, Connecticut; d. 13 Apr 1948, New Britain, Hartford, Connecticut; m. 21 Jul 1875, New Britain, Hartford, Connecticut, Ferdinand Billian; born 1 June 1851 Schabenhausen, Wurttemberg, Germany; d. 2 Jul 1921, New Britain, Hartford, Connecticut; son of Ferdinand Billian and Katharina Geiger.

iii. Margaret Scoville,[7] b. Jul 1861, New Britain, Hartford, Connecticut; d. 13 Oct 1861; New Britain, Hartford, Connecticut.

iv. Joseph Scoville,[7] b. 27 Jun 1862, New Britain, Hartford, Connecticut; d. 28 Sep 1862, New Britain, Hartford, Connecticut.

## *22. JULIA REBECCA SCOVILLE[6] (FRANKLIN,[5] ITHAMAR,[4] TIMOTHY,[3] STEPHEN,[2] STEPHEN,[1] ARTHUR),*

Born 9 May 1837, Colebrook, Litchfield, Connecticut;[849] died 16 January 1918,[850] Winchester, Litchfield, Connecticut; married 19 February 1854;[851] William Henry Raidart; born 29 February 1832, Worstadt, Grand Duchy of Hesse, Darmstadt, Germany;[852] died 27 May 1898,[853] Winchester, Litchfield, Connecticut. His parents' names are unknown.[854]

As you would expect, records for Julia Scoville are non-existent except for those where she is connected to her husband. Julia was born in Colebrook—a very rural area in Litchfield

847 The middle initial (A) could possibly stand for "Anthony"—named after Catherine's brother.

848 Some records indicate her middle initial as "R." It would seem plausible that the "M" would stand for Mary or Margaret after her mother's name.

849 Birth information comes from Julia's death certificate. The informant was her son, George H. Raidart.

850 *Ibid.* Death caused by arteriosclerosis and cerebral apoplexy (stroke).

851 *Hale Collection*—newspaper *Christian Secretary,* published March 3, 1854, call number: 486549. GenealogyBank.

852 Birthdate comes from Taylor, William Harrison, *Taylor's Souvenir of the Capitol 1897–98 Portraits and Autographs,* published 1897, 249, herein *Taylor's Souvenir.* The headstone inscription coincides with the information found in said article.

853 Death information comes from various online sources such as Find-A-Grave; *Hall Collection of Cemetery Inscriptions and Newspaper Notices, 1629–1934;* obituary notice.

854 Photo courtesy of Sandra Amador.

County—in 1837. Julia's mother (Amarilla Hotchkiss Scoville) used her own siblings' names either for first or middle names of her own children. Rebecca Sturdevant was the mother of Amarilla, and so Rebecca became the middle name for Julia. During this timeframe, naming patterns were still used to some degree.

In 1850, Julia is living in New Hartford, Connecticut, with her parents and her siblings; she is listed as twelve years old.[855] Four years later, at the age of sixteen, she was married to William Henry Raidart, who was six years older than Julia.

William Henry Raidart arrived in the United States on November 6, 1848.[856]He was sixteen years old.[857] His embarkation was from Antwerp, Belgium, on the ship *Lady Arabella*, which landed in New York.[858] The voyage lasted thirty-seven days.[859] The ship's manifest gives his name as *Wilhelm Raitard* and he was a "native of Worstadt,[860] Grand Duchy of Hesse Darmstadt, Germany in the Rhine Valley;"[861] his occupation is listed as a "turner."[862]

According to an article, many immigrants sailed to America or back to their homelands in packet ships, vessels that carried mail, cargo, and people. Most crossed in steerage, which was below decks. Conditions varied from ship to ship, but steerage was normally crowded, dark, damp, and rats, insects, and disease were common problems.[863] After landing in New York it's impossible to know whether he remained in the city for a time before coming to Connecticut. Often, a relative who had immigrated previously wrote to their relatives still living in the homeland to tell them of the opportunities in America. While I have not found such a relative for William, it is a plausible explanation for why William ended up in such a rural area other than a big city. If you recall, I raised the same question with John Schneider and why he removed to Colebrook from Newark, New Jersey. It's not as if this area of Litchfield was a

855 She would have turned 13 on 9 May 1850. The 1850 census for this family was taken on 13 October.

856 *Connecticut Naturalization Records 1795–1942;* FHL:105279785; 1853; NARA—*Index to New England Naturalization Petitions 1791–1906;* M1299; microfilm serial: M1299; microfilm roll: 31.Ancestry.

857 The ship's manifest states he was 17.

858 Information comes from the actual manifest provided by *Immigrant Ships Transcribers Guild;* https://www.immigrantships.net.

859 *Taylor's Souvenirs, 249.*

860 Wörrstadt is a town in the Alzey-Worms district of Rheinland-Palatinate, Germany.

861 *Ibid.* Since William Raidart was still alive when this book was published, it is likely the information was accurate.

862 This occupation may refer to a lathe operator.

863 "Aboard A Packet," www.americanhistory.si.edu.

hotbed of German immigrants at that time (1848–1850).[864] According to a *Wikipedia* article, "the largest wave [of German immigrants] arrived after the Revolutions of 1848, in which thirty-nine German states sought democracy and increased political freedoms." This reason, and possibly others, could be why a young lad of sixteen years would travel such a distance to come to the United States.

The next record for William was found in the 1850 census in the town of Barkhamsted. He is living in the household of Pelatiah Ransom:

William Reidant, 18, Germany, chair maker.

According to Taylor's *Souvenirs*, William had worked for one year at Alford's Chair Factory[865] in Riverton (a district of Barkhamsted), before joining Union Chair Factory in Robertsville, a village in the southern part of Colebrook. It's possible that William (known as "Billy") met his future wife through Julia's brother Charles.[866]

In 1853 William H. Raidart petitioned the court to become a citizen of the United States. The document image can be found on FamilySearch and reads as follows:

> To the Honorable County Court, Now in Session at Litchfield, within and for the County of Litchfield.
>
> The Petition of William H. Raidart of Colebrook in said County humbly showeth, that he is a foreigner, a subject of the United Kingdom of Great Britain and Ireland. That he landed in the United States on the 4th day November 1848 and was at that time sixteen years and a half year old and has resided in the Country ever since 1848 and has sustained a good moral character.
>
> Dated 3rd day of January 1853
>
> William H. Raidart and his atty H.B. Gr______(?)

It's curious that William is referred to as a "subject of Great Britain and Ireland." Why isn't he referred to as a subject of Germany? Did he land in England first, then journey to the United States? On January 3, 1855, William became a naturalized citizen of the United States.

By the time of the 1860 census,[867] the Raidart family had grown to four and were living in Colebrook:

Dwelling: 252; Family: 259
William Raydent [sic], 28, mechanic, born Germany
Julia Raydent, 25, Connecticut
Alice Raydent, 5, Connecticut

864 The 1870s in Litchfield County, Connecticut, showed an influx of German, Irish, and French immigrants to this area.

865 Alba Alford was a partner of Lambert Hitchcock of Hitchcock Chair factory and at one time it was called Hitchcock, Alford & Co.

866 If you recall, Julia's brother Charles also worked in a chair factory in Colebrook (Robertsville).

867 The census reports for 1850, 1860, 1870, and 1880 for this family come from Ancestry.

George Raydent, 3, Connecticut

Note that now William is occupied as a "mechanic." Whether he is a mechanic in the chair factory or some other enterprise is unknown.

You may notice from this point on that many of the families were made up of fewer children (as with the Raidarts). Since many of our early ancestors were farmers from colonial times through the early part of the nineteenth century, families had many children as it was a matter of survival for the whole family; however, by the middle to latter part of the nineteenth century, many couples were having fewer children. Some reasons were that many women were marrying sometimes in their late twenties and early thirties, which meant there was less time to have children. Alternatively, couples were also consciously trying to limit the number of children that they had, which was a revolutionary practice in the nineteenth century.

~

On August 5, 1870, the census taker came once again to the Raidart household. It was likely a hot day, as are most days in August in Connecticut. The family was composed of:

Dwelling: 139; Family: 135, page 15:
Raidart, William H., 38, chair maker, value of real estate $2,000; born Darmstadt
Raidart, Julia, 33, Keeps house; born Connecticut
Raidart, Alice, 15, born Connecticut
Raidart, George, 12, born Connecticut

We see that William is once again listed as a "chair maker" in this census. He continues his occupation at the Union Chair Factory and has raised his position to superintendent of said company.

The children are not marked as having attended school in the previous year. If a child did complete their schooling it would have been by the age of fourteen, as that is when public school ended, and they would have to pass a final exam. So, while the 1870 census does not record them as attending school, they did attend at various times.

Fortunately, the Colebrook Historical Society has records on the various school districts, as well as names of students who attended. Here are some examples:

**Forge School District**

**1869** a plain piece of paper is a list of fifty-four student names, each followed by a number, their ages, no doubt, but several have two numbers separated by a hyphen. There does not seem to be a ready explanation for these second numbers.

Francis Jenings 13, Ellen Fleming 15, Jenny Fleming 10, Effie Osborn 9, Wallace Osborn 7, **Alice Reardart** 13–6, **George Reardart** 11–6, Anna Leitzback 8, Augustus Leitzback 6.

1872, Sept. 5
Mr. Wm H. Raidart Sir

I received a line from you requesting a statement of the school affairs as they were when I left. 1st The number of scholars as I numbered them was thirty 30.

2nd The money I received from Town $66.40.

The wages I paid the teacher was $56.00 pr month including board, which was $4.00 per week.

Borrowed of George D. Felton the sum of $18.00 to pay for insurance and gave him the note of the district for the same. Regarding how much the district is in debt, I have no means of knowing, as I do not know how much money was to come from the Town, nor how much the district was in debt before.

I will give you the items of the act as it stands on my book and, I will send you the statement Mr. Viets gave me when school was out.

I agreed to pay the teacher for the summer $5.00 per week to board around and find herself out of school time or over Sunday.

Forge School District To: P.B. Osborn Dr.

Oct. 25 to stove cover $1.00 Nov 4 to 3 glass .70

- "15 to one broom .40
- "20 to box blackboard pencils .30 Feb. 26-to-16-week board of teacher @ $4.00 64.00 66.40

  Received payment by order on Town"

I find credited on book to Joseph Demming [sic] for wood 9 nine cords $2.50 per $22.20 cord. My debt Teacher's wages 66.40 160.00 248.90

If there is anything more, I will let you know anytime you like if you will let me know what you want. My regards to all inquiring friends.

Yours respectfully.\, P.B. Osborn

~

The letter from P.B. Osborn (possibly the treasurer for the Forge School District) is giving William Raidart an accounting of expenses and debits for the beginning of the school year.

From the transcribed records[868] William H. Raidart was involved with the Forge School Committe as early as 1863. In a letter written to him on July 10, 1863, he is addressed as "W.H. Raidart, Esq.,[869] Clerk of Forge School District, Colebrook."

~

The dynamic of the family changed circa 1877 when William and Julia's daughter, Alice B. Raidart, married John Allen Deming. The couple lived in Colebrook and were able to visit

868 *Colebrook Historical Society*, records transcribed and submitted by Bob Deming. www.colebrookhistoricalsociety.org.

869 In this instance, the use of the word "esquire" does not denote an attorney but refers to a title of office.

their parents without traveling too far.

The 1880 census for Colebrook was taken on the tenth day of June and the family is listed as dwelling: 153; family: 167:

Raidart, William H., 48, superintendent chair shop, Hesse
Raidart, Julia R., 43, keeping house, Connecticut
Raidart, George H., 23, works in chair shop

During the 1880s, William became more involved with serving the town of Colebrook. In 1888, he was a Justice of the Peace,[870] and in 1897 he is listed as a member of the General Assembly as a Republican.[871] It is possible that he held other positions during the earlier years in Colebrook, but those records have not been discovered.

On May 27, 1898, William Raidart died at the age of sixty-six in Winchester, Litchfield, Connecticut. A very brief obituary was published in *The New Hartford Tribune:*[872]

> William H. Raidart of Robertsville, father of George H. Raidart of Winsted, died May 27, age 66. He was the republican representative from Colebrook to the last General Assembly.[873]

William H. Raidart is buried in Forest View Cemetery in Winsted, Connecticut. William came to this country as a teenager and made a good life for himself and his family, becoming involved with his community and rising through the ranks at the Union Chair Company to become its superintendent.

Because of the lack of the 1890 census for Connecticut, we don't know anything about Julia until 1900, when Julia is found still residing in Colebrook.[874]

She was sixty-three, widowed, and her occupation is a "farmer." Living with her is her daughter, Alice Deming, age forty-five, and grandson, Grove W. Deming, 18—a laborer.

Unfortunately, I have not been able to find Julia, Alice, or Grove on the 1910 census. I read the whole of the Colebrook census and they are not listed there. Either they are no longer in Colebrook, or they were missed by the enumerator.

In 1911 William and Julia's daughter, Alice, dies at the age of fifty-six. She is buried with her parents (not her husband).

The next records for Julia are found in the city directory for Winsted Connecticut in 1912,

870 Hubbard, Everett M., Secretary of State, *Regulations and Manual—State of Connecticut Secretary of State,* published 1888.

871 *Journal of the House of Representatives of the State of Connecticut, January Session;* (1897); 7.

872 Friday June 3, 1898, edition; no page recorded; Newspapers.

873 For some reason, his daughter, Alice B. Deming, is not mentioned in this notice and it's possible someone other than a family member submitted the death notice.

874 Dwelling: 82; Family: 83.

Julia R. Scoville Raidart

Julia R. Scoville Raidart

1916, and 1918 as boarding with her son, George, at 195 North Main Street.[875]

On January 16, 1918, Julia Rebecca Scoville Raidart died of arteriosclerosis and cerebral apoplexy (stroke).[876] As stated previously, Julia is buried with her husband and daughter in Fair View Cemetery in Winsted.[877]

***Children of William H. Raidart and Julia R. Scoville***

i. Alice B. Raidart,[7] b. 6 May 1855, Colebrook, Litchfield, Connecticut; d. 9 March 1911, Colebrook; buried Fair View Cemetery, Winsted; married about 1877 to John Allen Deming; b. 30 April 1854, Colebrook, Litchfield, Connecticut; d. 29 May 1938, Colebrook, Litchfield, Connecticut; said to be the son of Harvey Deming (1827–1876) and Amaret Spencer (1830–1914).

This couple is listed on the 1880 census in Colebrook. There were no children listed at that time. However, they did have four children born to them:

a. i. Grove Walter Deming—1882–1966
b. ii. Earl Lewis Deming—1884–1948

875 City Directories for Winsted, CT; 1912, p. 82; 1916, p. 104; 1918, p. 97; via www.ancestry.com; 195 North Main Street, Winsted, still stands; Ancestry.

876 Cause of death per the death certificate in my possession.

877 This "unidentified" photo is courtesy of Ken Sears (a descendant of William and Julia Scoville Raidart), who generously entrusted me with all his old photos. While Ken Sears doesn't believe the older woman is also Julia, I disagree. Based on the shape of her face, ears, nose, mouth, eyes, and her hairline, I believe this is a photo of Julia towards the end of her life.

c. iii. Ralph Spencer Deming—1887–1938
d. iv. Grace E. Deming—1896–1992

At some point this couple may have separated or divorced. In the 1900 census Alice and their son Grove were in her mother's (Julia's) household. Where were the other children? The 1900 census for Colebrook shows John A. Deming, age 46, laborer, daughter Grace E., age four, and Lucy Schuman, age 24, listed as the housekeeper. John is listed as being married for twenty-three years.[878]

John Deming can be found on the 1910 census still living in Colebrook with the housekeeper, Lucy Schuman, and daughter, Grace, now age thirteen. John is renting his home and works as a general laborer. He has been married for "thirty-three years." His wife, Alice, is not in the household.

There was an Alice Deming found living in New Britain, Connecticut, at the "Erwin Home for Worthy and Indigent Women"[879] in 1910.[880] This Alice is listed age 68 and a "widow."[881] She indicates that she has three children and three are living. The main question is whether this woman in the Erwin Home is the same Alice Deming who was married to John Deming, and the answer is no, it is not. While these two women have the same name, and were approximately the same age, the Alice Deming who was living in the Erwin Home was still living in 1917 (see footnote 882).

Grace Deming was born approximately nine years after Ralph Deming, the last child of John and Alice. Is it possible that Grace Deming's mother was actually the housekeeper—Lucy Schumann? Is this the catalyst that drove a wedge between John and Alice? This scenario would explain why Grace was living with her father and the "housekeeper" and not her "mother."[882]

It is doubtful that Alice and John Deming ever reconciled. Alice died at the age of fifty-five in 1911 and she is buried with her parents, William and Julia Raidart (not her husband).

John Allen Deming continued to live out his life in Colebrook with his housekeeper, Lucy Schuman. Nothing more is known about John Deming's life. He died May 29, 1938, in Cole-

---

878 To reiterate, since divorce carried a stigma—especially for a woman—oftentimes they would refer to themselves as "married" or "widowed" to a census taker.

879 The Erwin Home for Worthy and Indigent Women at 140 Bassett Street was founded in 1885, funded by a bequest from Cornelius Erwin. The home was to provide a place for "worthy women of limited means." The building now encompasses an entire city block on Edson, Bassett, and Ellis Streets. The home is still in operation and the Queen Anne style architecture is on the U. S. National Register of Historic Places. www.wikipedia.org.

880 1910 census, *New Britain Ward 1, Hartford, Connecticut;* Roll: T624_134; Page: 3A; ED: 0216; FHL: 1374147.

881 The age for this Alice Deming is off. The Alice Deming who died in 1911 was fifty-six and an article in 1917 notes a "Mrs. Alice Deming of Bassett Street" entertaining a guest. While the name and the number of children of this Alice Deming coincides with the Alice Deming of this record, it is likely that they are two separate women.

882 While my hypothesis is that Lucy Schumann is the mother of Grace, DNA is the only way to determine if she is the natural daughter of Alice and John Deming.

brook and is buried in Hemlock Cemetery, also in Colebrook. His marker is a flat stone and covered in lichen and he seems to be buried alone. His housekeeper, Lucy Schuman, died two months prior on March 12, 1938. She is buried in the same cemetery as John Deming, but she is buried with her father, Jacob Schuman.

***Children of John Allen Deming and Alice B. Raidart***[883]

i. Grove Walter Deming,[8] b. 15 Apr 1882, Colebrook, Litchfield, Connecticut; d. 9 Jan 1966, Daytona Beach, Volusia, Florida; m. 17 Aug 1910, Colebrook, Litchfield, Connecticut, to Marilla Irene Moore (1881–1937). Three children (Irene, Grove, Jr., Faith).

ii. Earl Lewis,[8] b. 22 Jul 1884, Colebrook, Litchfield, Connecticut; d. 28 Jun 1948, Colebrook, Litchfield, Connecticut; m. Marion G. Waite (1890–1964).

iii. Ralph Spencer Deming,[8] b. 6 Nov 1887, Colebrook, Litchfield, Connecticut; d. 28 May 1938,[884] Colebrook, Litchfield, Connecticut; m. 12 Jun 1910, Colebrook, Litchfield, Connecticut, to Bessie A. White (1888–1977). One child: Spencer Deming (1911–1995).

Alice and George Raidart

35. ii. George Henry Raidart,[7] b. 2 Aug 1857, Colebrook, Litchfield, Connecticut; d. 28 Sep 1937, Winsted, Litchfield, Connecticut; m. 6 Apr 1885, Alice Maude Deming, b. 30 Jul 1863, Riverton, Connecticut; d. 28 Sep 1937, Winsted, Litchfield, Connecticut.[885]

### 23. iv. William Harrison Scoville[6] (Franklin,[5] Ithamar,[4] Timothy,[3] Stephen,[2] Stephen,[1] Arthur)

Born 4 December 1839, Barkhamsted, Litchfield, Connecticut;[886]died 10 September 1911, Noroton Heights (Darien), Fairfield, Connecticut;[887]buried Fitch's Home Cemetery, Noroton Heights, Fairfield, Connecticut; married 9 September 1861, North Canaan,[888] Litchfield,

883 Vitals for the children comes from Ancestry Public Tree with corresponding sources.

884 Ralph Deming committed suicide on May 28, 1938. A day later his father, John Deming, died.

885 Photo courtesy of Sandra Amador: sister and brother, Alice and George H. Raidart.

886 Birth information comes from William's military and pension records (in my possession).

887 Death record/pension records (in my possession).

888 North Canaan, Connecticut, Vital Records.

Connecticut, to Mary Catherine Dunn; born 2 February 1844, New York;[889] died 23 November 1930, Tacoma, Pierce, Washington.[890]

William was the fourth child to be born to Franklin and Amarilla Scoville in the town of Barkhamsted, which is in the northwest corner of Litchfield County and is located on the Farmington River. The town contains six villages: West Hill, Mallory, Center Hill, Washington Hill, Pleasant Valley, and Riverton.[891]

It is impossible to say how long William's parents remained in Barkhamsted. As we've seen, the family moved from town to town per the census reports and they could have easily lived in other areas that are not known to me.

From the census records of his parents, we know that the family was in New Hartford by the 1850 census. William is marked on this census as having "attended school within the past year," as did his brother Charles and sister Julia.

By 1860 the family was living in North Canaan and William is now age twenty. The census does not provide an occupation for William; however, later census reports consistently show him to be a carpenter. During the 1860 census he may have been apprenticing to learn the trade but, for whatever reason, his occupation was not listed.

On the ninth day of September 1861 William Harrison Scoville married Mary Catherine Dunn in North Canaan, Connecticut.[892]

I have had no success in finding Mary Catherine in the 1850 and 1860 censuses, whether

William Harrison Scoville

Mary Catherine Dunn

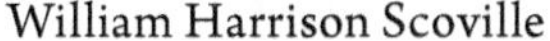

889 All census reports indicate that Mary Catherine Dunn was born in New York. I have not found her or her parents on any of those records.

890 Washington, Select Death Certificates 1907–1960. FamilySearch.

891 FamilySearch.

892 Photos of William Harrison Scoville and Mary Catherine Dunn courtesy of descendant Sandra Amador.

in Litchfield County or anywhere else in Connecticut. Her birthplace is consistently given as "New York," with parents born in Ireland. I have read the censuses page by page for New Hartford, North Canaan, and Canaan without locating her. I can only surmise she arrived in North Canaan after the census was taken or was not counted. Where and how this couple met remains an unknown. Her parentage is also a mystery—although her obituary states that her widowed mother took her to Saint Paul (Minnesota) when she was young. However, no name was given for the mother. Mary Catherine did have two sisters that I *am* aware of: Lizzie Dunn Clough and Nellie Dunn Morin.[893] But, like Mary Catherine, it is like trying to find a needle in the proverbial haystack due to the commonness of the surnames.

I surmise that once the couple was married they lived in North Canaan for a time while William supported his wife doing carpentry work. As mentioned earlier, a carpenter would have had to learn the trade and know mathematics. Whether William was taught by his father or was in an apprenticeship, the records are silent. He may also have worked in the chair factory, as did his brother Charles, to learn the basics.

The couple were married less than a year when their first child was born, Frank Ellsworth Scoville, on July 14, 1862.

One month later, on August 9, 1862, William enlisted, like his brother Charles, in the 14th Connecticut Infantry Regiment, Company F.[894] William may have "battled" with himself about whether to serve, especially since his wife just had their first child, but his older brother had enlisted a little over a week prior and William made the choice to join his brother. Since there are no letters or journals or other anecdotal evidence, the reason for his going off to war is not known to us. Was it for patriotism? For the bounty? Or both?

On August 23, 1862, William was mustered into the service and left Connecticut with all the other "boys" on the *City of Hartford*—destination: the south.

Like brother Charles, William was assigned to the wagons bringing essential equipment to the men at the front.

William had made it through the Battle of Antietam (September 17, 1862). There are no reports of his being wounded during this battle; October and November go by without much event. In the soldiers' downtime at camp the men would often play cards to help with the boredom. Many found camp life to be monotonous.

In November of 1862, the Fourteenth began marching toward Fredericksburg.[895] The weather began to get cold, and the rain was relentless for a time, causing their camps to become swamp-like.

Fredericksburg, Virginia, is a city on the Rappahannock River just south of Washington, D.C. When the Fourteenth arrived, they had to cross this river. When the regiment reached

893 Photos sent by Sandra Amador have identified Lizzie and Nellie Dunn each as "mother's sister."

894 *Connecticut: Record of Service of Men During the War of Rebellion*; report of Colonel Ward, 8th Connecticut Infantry; May 6, 1863; also, Page, Charles D., *14th Regiment, Connecticut;* The Horton Printing Co., Meriden, Connecticut (1906). All information regarding William's Civil War service comes from his pension/military records via his pension records and the above-captioned books.

895 The soldiers had no knowledge of a place called Fredericksburg until after the battle.

the other side, they found the town eerily quiet. When they first arrived, they believed the rebels had retreated, but the longer they were there the more uneasy they became.

On the morning of December 13, they woke to a very thick fog. Neither the enemy nor their own guns on the opposite side of the river could be seen. Eventually, the fighting ensued, and this is where William Scoville was wounded. The records indicate that he was wounded "slightly," however, he was not involved in any further battles throughout the war. This did not mean he was able to go home. He went to the division hospital and subsequently remained to assist in the care of other wounded soldiers.

William would no longer be able to watch over his brother Charles and vice versa. It was two years later when Charles was wounded severely enough to die of his wounds.

Many women during this time spent time knitting and sewing for the soldiers at the front. Mary Catherine was no different. Throughout the ages women have always risen to the call of service, especially for our soldiers.[896]

During William's convalescence he was transferred to New Haven, Connecticut, to the Knight Hospital,[897] which was built in 1862 to provide medical care for wounded soldiers who had been invalided after being wounded in battle. The hospital remained open until the close of the war in 1865. Some of the patients were returned to their units; others, like William, remained as he had lost use of his wrist.

Since her husband was now in Connecticut, Mary Catherine could visit him. One of those visits had to have occurred in April 1864, because on January 1, 1865, a daughter, Minne Irene Scoville, was born to them.

Mary Catherine was living in New Britain, Connecticut, during that time.[898] The couple likely removed from North Canaan to New Britain sometime after their marriage, perhaps for better job opportunities for William, and of course, his brother Charles and his family were living there as well.

On May 23, 1865, William was officially discharged from his Civil War service. How long they remained in New Britain is not known. The city directories for this time are not available either online or in the various libraries that were checked.[899] By 1870, the family was back in North Canaan, Litchfield, Connecticut:[900]

> Dwelling: 118; Family: 129—census taken on the 11th day of June 1870
> Scoville, William, 30, carpenter, born Connecticut

---

896 Much of this information comes from Mary Catherine's obituary. She was a member of Women's Relief Corps, as well as holding an honorary life membership in Miriam Chapter, O.E.S. (a masonic order).

897 To commemorate the hospital, a monument was placed in Evergreen Cemetery in New Haven, Connecticut. Those who died while in the hospital are buried in this cemetery around the monument. The book by Spar, Ira, M.D., *New Haven's Civil War Hospital: A History of Knight U.S. General Hospital, 1862–1865,* goes into greater detail than what has been outlined here.

898 Pension/military papers.

899 The libraries include New Britain Public Library, Godfrey Library-Middletown, CT, and the Connecticut State Library.

900 1870 census, *North Canaan, Litchfield, Connecticut*; Roll:M593_06; Page: 311A. Ancestry..

Scoville, Mary, 27, keeping house, born New York
Scoville, Frank E., 7, born Connecticut
Scoville, Minnie I., 5, born Massachusetts
Sickerman,[901] Eli, 30, works at furnace, born Connecticut

Since there is no real estate value given, it will have to be presumed that William didn't own the property. Additionally, Eli Sickerman was likely a boarder in their home as he is no relation to the Scoville family.

William's parents had been enumerated the day prior and lived in dwelling number 88, family 96. I suspect that they visited each other on a regular basis with the grandkids in tow.

Another ten years have would have to pass before we know where this couple was—they have removed to Winchester, Litchfield, Connecticut, as per the 1880 census.

Dwelling: 271; Family: 358
Scovill, William H., 40, carpenter, born Connecticut, parents Connecticut
Scovill, Mary C., 37, wife, keeping house, born New York, parents Ireland
Scovill, Frank E., 17, son, works in coffin factory, born Connecticut/parents Connecticut and New York
Scovill, Minnie, 15, daughter, born Connecticut, Connecticut and New York

As we've seen through the 1870 and 1880 censuses, William is still occupied as a carpenter. He managed somehow with a damaged wrist during this time.

From 1880–1900 are what I call the "blank" years. Unfortunately, there are no city directories online for some of the towns in Litchfield County to follow William and his family, and of course, the 1890 census was destroyed by fire. Despite this, William does show up back in New Britain in 1892—this would mean the family was there in 1891. William and Mary Catherine were living at 141 Main Street (this house is no longer in existence). According to the directory of 1893 (1892) the couple was living at 42 Church Street. William's health was in decline and he likely could not make his living as a carpenter anymore, as the city directory for 1894 states, "removed to Noroton Heights."

Noroton Heights is a neighborhood of Darien, Fairfield, Connecticut, which lies on Long Island Sound, some sixty-nine miles away. Noroton Heights is where Fitch's Home for Soldiers was located (photo next page).[902]

Essentially, this was the "first veteran's hospital and was dedicated on July 4, 1864, on Noroton Avenue. The building was financed by Benjamin Fitch, who dedicated more than $100,000 to the project."[903] By 1910, the home had grown to 547 soldiers. The soldiers' home even had its own newspaper, *Knight Hospital Record,* with L. J. Merchant as its editor.[904,905]

---

901 I have written the name as it is on the census report. An "Ely Seckman" is found on the 1860 census in North Canaan.

902 Vintage postcard of the Fitch's Home courtesy of Sandra Amador.

903 Gordon, Maggie, *The Darien Times* article, February 9, 2010.

904 Photos courtesy of Sandra Amador.

905 You can see from these photos of William that he was a large man (look at the size of his

At the time of the 1900 census, William is counted with his other comrades at Fitch's, but his wife, Mary Catherine Scoville, was counted in Kalispell Township, Flathead, Montana. What was she doing there? She is listed as a "boarder" in the Channing Smith household. The house was on "3rd Avenue East." This is certainly Mary Catherine, as all vital particulars coincide with what we know (born Feb. 1844; married 38 years; two children born, two alive; birthplace: New York; parents: Ireland). In reviewing the 1900 census for her daughter Minnie Irene Scoville Ashley, we see that Minnie, her husband, and three children were living in Jocko Township, Flathead, Montana. However, Kalispell to Jocko Valley[906] is eighty-eight miles. Because of the lack of anecdotal information, the reasons for Mary Catherine to be in Kalispell Township remain unclear.

In 1910, William is still residing in Fitch's, but his wife, Mary Catherine, I have not been able to locate. I've checked each family member from children to grandchildren without a result.

On September 10, 1911, William Harrison Scoville died aged seventy-two years. The primary cause of his death was Bright's disease. "Bright's disease is an historical classification of kidney diseases that are described in modern medicine as acute or chronic nephritis. It was characterized by swelling and the presence of albumin in the urine and was frequently accompanied by high blood pressure and heart disease."[907] The following comes from a book on the Fitch's Home and their residents; unfortunately, I did not cite the source at the time and have not been able to find it on the web.

> William H. Scovill [sic] of F. Company, died at the Soldier's home, Noroton, Connecticut, from Bright's disease on September 10, 1911, aged seventy-two years. Comrade Scovill was born December 4, 1839, in Barkhamsted, but early in life drifted to New Britain and learned the carpenter's trade successfully for several years but received a bad fall from which he never recovered, although making several unsuccessful attempts to work. He was obliged to give up finally and entered the Soldier's Home February 13, 1894 and was made very comfortable to the end. His

---

hands). According to his military enlistment records, William was six feet four inches in height with gray eyes, light hair, and dark complexion

906 Jocko Township no longer exists. The Jocko Valley in western Montana is land where the Flathead Indians have their Reservation.

907 Wikipedia article on *Bright's Disease.*

William H. Scoville and brother Albert F. Scoville—Fitches Homes for Soldiers

William H. Scoville and niece Florence Scoville (daughter of Albert F. Scoville)

William Scoville, Mary Catherine Scoville, Florence Scoville, Frank E. Scoville (son of William and Mary Catherine). This photo was taken on a different day than the one above (re: Florence's clothing is different).

> Comrades at the home speak highly of his character. He was a fine figure standing over six feet tall.

William was buried in Spring Grove Cemetery in Darien, Connecticut. A simple stone displays his name, date of death, and the Civil War regiment that he served in. The photo was taken by one of his family members.[908] After William's death, Mary Catherine spent her time

908 Photo courtesy of Sandra Amador. This photo must have been taken not too long after William's death as the cemetery is relatively empty.

Headstone of William Harrison Scoville

Photo of Mary Catherine Dunn Scoville in her later years.

living with her children. Sometimes she was in Texas with her son Frank and his wife. She lived in Montana, Minnesota, the state of Washington, and Alaska.

The 1920 census shows Mary Catherine living with her granddaughter Rhoda Miller in Tacoma, Washington, and in 1930 she is still in Tacoma but now living with her daughter Minnie's household. On the 23rd of November that same year, Mary Catherine Dunn Scoville died.[909] At the time she was residing at 948 South Sheridan Avenue in Tacoma. She was 86 years, 8 months, and 27 days old. The cause of her death was cardiac infarction. Her resting place is in the Tacoma Cemetery.[910]

***Children of William Harrison Scoville and Mary Catherine Dunn***

36. i. Frank Ellsworth Scoville,[7] b. 14 Jul 1862, Canaan, Litchfield, Connecticut; d. 30 Oct 1952, Paragould, Greene, Arkansas; m. (1) Jesse Jane Joslyn, 11 July 1888, Connecticut; b. 8 Aug 1856, Manchester, Hartford, Connecticut; d. 26 Apr 1910, Laredo, Texas; m. (2) Eugenia Philipe Schaeffer, b. 20 Mar 1908, San Antonio, Texas; d. 4 Oct 1952, Paragould, Greene, Arkansas.

37. ii. Minnie Irene Ashley Scoville,[7] b. 1 Jan 1865; New Britain, Hartford, Connecticut; d. 14 Apr 1951, Seattle, King, Washington; m. (1) Howard Ashley, Nov 1884, Massachusetts; b.19 Mar 1862, Massachusetts; d. 2 Jun 1939. Seattle, King, Washington; m. (2) Paul Michael Lindberg, (date unknown); b. 6 Oct 1886, Småland, Sweden; d. Dec 1951, Seattle, King, Washington.

909 Death Certificate, Washington State Board of Health. Ancestry.

910 Photos of Mary Catherine Dunn Scoville, Hannah Hall, and Albert Franklin Scoville courtesy of Sandra Amador.

≈

24. Albert Franklin Scoville[6] (*Franklin,[5] Ithamar,[4] Timothy,[3] Stephen,[2] Stephen,[1] Arthur*) born 1 August 1846, Colebrook, Litchfield, Connecticut;[911] died 9 May 1915, Worcester, Worcester, Massachusetts;[912] married (1) 29 September 1863, East Canaan, Litchfield, Connecticut, Hannah E. Hall,[913] she perhaps born in North Canaan, Litchfield, Connecticut; died before 1880 in either Connecticut or Massachusetts; married (2) 20 October 1882, Margaret Estella Apperson;[914] born circa 1856, Worcester County, Massachusetts; died 11 August 1893, Worcester County, Massachusetts; married (3) 30 August 1894, Worcester, Worcester, Massachusetts, Melissa Viola Moore;[915] born 12 December 1855, Presque Isle, Aroostook, Maine; died 18 October 1933, Springvale, York, Maine.

In 1860, when the Scoville family was living in North Canaan and Albert was fifteen, their neighbor was James Root, and in his household was a young lady by the name of Hannah E. Hall, aged sixteen. The enumerator does not refer to her as a "servant" and what her relationship to the Root family was is not clear. However, based on this data, we can safely conclude that this is how Albert F. Scoville met his first wife, Hannah E. Hall. Hannah is listed as having been born in Connecticut and had attended school "within the year." It seems rather late for a young lady of that age still to be attending school, but that is what the record indicates.

Based on what I have been able to find through online records, Hannah E. Hall may have

Hannah Hall

Albert Franklin Scoville

911 Albert's birth date and place come from the consistency of data from his marriage records.

912 Death certificate, will, and obituary notice.

913 North Canaan, Connecticut, marriage record.

914 *Massachusetts Town and Vital Records, 1620–1988*. Ancestry.

915 *New England Selected United Methodist Church Records, 1787–1922*. Ancestry.

been the daughter of David Hall and Mary Ann Cotterill. This family is listed on the 1850 census for Canaan, Litchfield, Connecticut. There are four people in the household: David Hall, Mary Ann Hall, Hannah Hall, and Lucy Hall (who was two years younger than Hannah). I have not located any other records that would confirm her parentage.

The young couple courted for approximately three years before they married on September 19, 1863, in North Canaan.

Unlike his brothers William and Charles, Albert did not enlist in the Civil War. It was not mandatory at that time to join up (the draft didn't come until later). Perhaps his parents did not want him to go, or he already felt that two sons of his parents were enough to be called up to the war. There may have also been letters describing the horrors of war that put him off from enlisting.[916]

The young couple started out their lives in North Canaan. The town of North Canaan is in the northwest corner of the state in Litchfield County and shares its northern border with Massachusetts. The town of Canaan is often referred to by the locals as Falls Village, which was a principal settlement and is the town center. The towns of Canaan and North Canaan informally divided with the formation of the Second Ecclesiastical Society in 1769.[917] The population of Canaan in 1860 was 1,426. Today the population is a little over 3,000 residents—as you can see from these numbers, the area is still very rural.

We find the family still in North Canaan in the 1870 census. The household now contains two small children:

Dwelling: 139; Family: 151
Scoville, Albert, 24, carpenter, real estate value: $1,000, born Connecticut
Scoville, Hannah, 23, keeping house, born Connecticut
Scoville, Cora I., 4, born Connecticut
Scoville, Charlie,[918] 2, born Connecticut

Albert, like his brother William, was a carpenter; it is possible that they worked together. In the March 1873 issue of the newspaper *Connecticut Western News,* there is an article regarding Albert Scoville and Horace E. Holt who had been in partnership but it had been dissolved.

**Reminisces of By Gone Days**
Albert F. Scoville and Horace E. Holt, East Canaan, dissolved partnership.[919]

No other newspaper article was found regarding when the partnership began or why it was dissolved. Horace E. Holt was born January 1850 and died in North Canaan in 1926. The 1900 census records his occupation as a "carpenter and builder." This would suggest that the partnership between Albert and Horace had to do with the building trade.

916 Albert Franklin Scoville is not found on any draft, enlistment, or service records via Ancestry.

917 From www.connecticuthistory.org.

918 Undoubtedly named after his late uncle Charles. Charles and Catherine Scoville also named their first child "Albert."

919 Thursday edition, March 31, 1910, North Canaan, Vol: XXXIX, 2.

Sometime between the censuses of 1870 and 1880, Albert's wife, Hannah, dies. A death record for her has not been located.[920] Hannah's birth date and death date are currently unknown; however, the death record for her daughter Cora gives Hannah's birthplace as "Housatonic." Since Connecticut did not (and does not) have a town with this name,[921] I decided to check Massachusetts, as North Canaan is very close to their border. There *is* a community in Berkshire County with the name "Housatonic," which is part of Great Barrington. This may be where Hannah was born.

In 1880, Albert and his two children are living in Meriden, New Haven, Connecticut. Albert is marked off as "widowed" and "carpenter," and the children, Frank and Cora, are attending school.[922]

According to the Meriden City Directories, Albert is listed as living in said town in 1876, 1877, 1878, and 1879;[923] once again, he is listed as a carpenter. We can presume that Albert was in Meriden at least by 1875. Opportunities for work would have increased as the population (of the town) was 15,540 in 1880.[924]

By 1882, Albert and his children were in Worcester, Worcester, Massachusetts, as he married there on October 20, 1882, to Margaret Estella Apperson.[925, 926]

Margaret Estella Apperson was the daughter of James Apperson (1823–1862), born in Ireland, and Jane McCausland (1815–1892), born in Tyrone County, Ireland.[927] Margaret was born in Worcester about 1856 and her marriage to Albert was her first.

We are now in a time period when the records become few and far between. Thankfully, the city directories for Worcester gives us a yearly account of where the Scovilles were living. The directories also show how Albert F. Scoville moved from a "carpenter" to "builder/architect." More on this later.

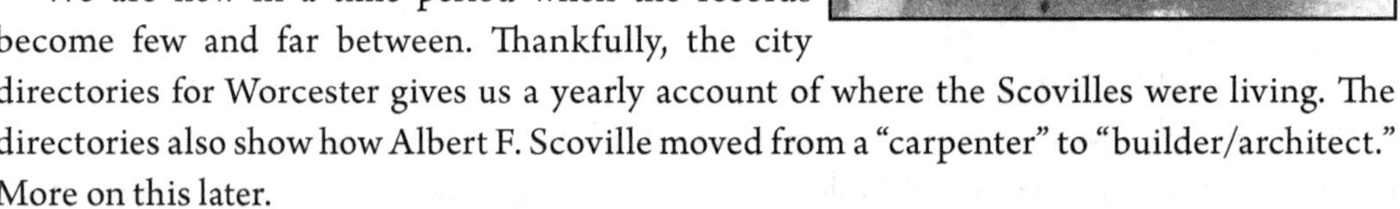

920 North Canaan and Meriden, Connecticut, town clerks stated that they did not have a death record for Hannah Hall Scoville.

921 Confirmed via Connecticut State Library, Hartford, Connecticut.

922 1880 census, *Meriden, New Haven, Connecticut;* Roll: 104; Page: 372C; ED:052. Ancestry.

923 *Price, Lee & Co.'s;* Meriden Directory, 1878; 117.

924 Meriden, Connecticut, was nicknamed "Silver City" due to the large number of silver manufactures. www.wikipedia.org.

925 *Massachusetts Marriage Records, 1840–1915;* Ancestry.

926 Possibly the wedding photo of Albert F. Scoville and Margaret Estella Apperson. Photo courtesy of Sandra Amador.

927 Parentage per the 1860 census and marriage record.

In 1886 their first child was born,[928] a daughter named Florence Mabel Scoville.[929] Two other daughters were born in 1889 and 1893. At the birth of the third child, Margaret Estella Scoville died due to septicemia on August 11, 1893,[930] and the child (a female) was stillborn; there is no record of this child being given a name, at least not any that I've been able to find.

Once again, Albert is left a widower, now with three children to raise. On August 31, 1894,[931] Albert married for the third and last time in Lynn, Massachusetts, to Melissa Viola Moore. At the time of the marriage, Melissa was thirty-seven years old (Albert was forty-nine). Prior to her marriage, Melissa Moore was a teacher who had been born in Presque Isle, Aroostook, Maine, on December 12, 1855, to William Moore and Orilla Hatch. At the time of this marriage, Florence was eight years old, and the only child left in the home. (Charles and Cora Scoville had already married and lived elsewhere.)

In 1895 Albert is on the list of "Valuation of Taxes" as a non-resident:[932]

> 1895 Schoville, Elbert [sic] F. & Edward W. Wheeler, 518 Main Street, Worcester
> House at 31 Church St., value: $1800., land 18 rods, value: $350; land, 33 Church St., 22 rods $400. Total tax: $26.70.

What we see here is that Albert was in partnership with one Edward W. Wheeler. An advertisement in a 1902 issue of the city directory for Worcester:

The following information on Edward W. Wheeler was found in the book *History of Worcester County, Massachusetts, Geographical and Personal Memoirs:*[933]

> Edward William Wheeler, son of Edwin Wallace Wheeler... he studied architecture and remained with Fuller and Delano for five years. He was with Webb Granite & Construction Company for six months. He went into business with Albert E [sic]

928 It is possible another child was born prior to 1886, but I have not found anything to confirm or deny.

929 *Massachusetts Birth Records, 1840–1915;* Ancestry.

930 *Massachusetts Death Records 1841–1915* for both mother and child. Ancestry.

931 *Massachusetts Marriage Records, 1840–1915; New England Select United Methodist Church Records, 1787–1922.* Ancestry.

932 Westborough, Massachusetts Historical Society. I am not sure why he is referred to as a "non-resident."

933 Crane, Ellery Bicknell, Vol:1; 153; (1907).

Scoville in the contracting and building business. The firm named is Scoville & Wheeler. They have offices in the Knowles Building 518 Main Street. The have a large variety of contracts and have been successful. It is one of the most promising firm of builders in Worcester. Some of their work as follows:

1. Howe Memorial Library—Shrewsbury
2. Women/Men's Wards for State Colony for the Insane—Gardner
3. Two modern schoolhouses—Gardner
4. Builders/additions to Haywood Brothers & Wakefield Co.—Gardner
5. Residence of John S. Gould, German Street, Worcester

≈

In 1895 the family suffered another loss as Albert's daughter (from his first marriage), Cora Irene, died in childbirth. She was thirty years old. Cora's daughter, Grace Claflin, had gone to live with her grandfather, as is shown on the 1900 census.[934] The family was living at 7 Ball Street, Worcester, Massachusetts. The house still stands today:

According to Zillow,[935] the home at 7 Ball Street was built in 1892 and had four bedrooms and two baths. The interior also shows several stained-glass windows and intricate wood moldings.

The household consisted of Albert Scoville, now a "contractor and builder," his wife, Melissa V. Scoville, daughter, Florence Scoville, and granddaughter, Grace Claflin, who was ten years old. The home was owned and free of mortgage.

The only other records for Albert F. Scoville are from the 1910 census and the city directories for Worcester, Massachusetts, beginning in 1893 up until his death. The other records are tax records for his business and a house that he owned at 31 Church Street in Westborough, Mass., as well as a factory, land, a house at 33 Summer Street, a barn and another piece of land

934 1900 census, *Worcester Ward 6, Worcester, Massachusetts*; Page: 5; ED: 1766; FHL: 1240697; Dwelling: 75; Family: 49.Ancestry.

935 www.Zillow.com.

that is not specified as to where it is located.[936] Since the census records never show this family living in Westborough, I will have to presume that the houses on Church and Summer Streets were rental properties.

The last census for Albert is the 1910 for Worcester. The family consists of Albert, Melissa, and Florence Scoville. Grace Claflin is no longer in the household as she subsequently married in 1907.

On the ninth day of May 1915, Albert Franklin Scoville died at 1:32 pm from "organic dementia arteriosclerotic type with contributing factors of cerebral hemorrhage and hyperstatic pneumonia." He was "68 years, 9 months and 8 days" old.[937] According to the death certificate, he died at the Worcester State Hospital.

Albert's obituary notice[938] is very brief:

> **Albert F. Scoville**
> Albert F. Scoville, aged 68 years, 9 months, and 8 days, died yesterday afternoon at his home, 7 Ball Street, from cerebral hemorrhage. He was native of Colebrook, Ct., and was son of Franklin and Aurilla [sic] (Hotchkiss) Scoville. He leaves his widow and one daughter, Miss Florence M. Scoville. The funeral will be held tomorrow afternoon at 2:30 o'clock from the home.

Albert did leave a will, which names his third wife, Melissa Viola Scoville, as the executrix. He disposes $2,000 in his wife and left some bequests to his children ($120 each to his two daughters and son).[939]

Albert is buried in Hope Cemetery, Worcester, Worcester, Massachusetts. The burial took place on 11 May 1915. He is buried with his second wife and his daughter Olive Jane.

***Children of Albert F. Scoville and Hannah Hall***

38. i. Cora Irene Scoville,[7] b. 29 Oct 1865, Canaan, Litchfield, Connecticut; d. 11 Nov 1895, Worcester, Worcester, Massachusetts; m. 22 Jul 1882, Worcester, Worcester, Massachusetts, Charles Ripley Burnett Claflin, Jr., b. 3 May 1860, Massachusetts; d. 15 Mar 1935, Astoria, Queens, New York; son of Charles R. B. Claflin, Sr. and Emma Locke.
39. ii. Charles Merritt Scoville,[7] b. 17 Sep 1867, North Canaan, Litchfield, Connecticut; d. 14 Jul 1938, Richmond, Ontario, New York; m. (1) 19 June 1888, Mary Elizabeth Johnson; b. 26 Apr 1861 Hodgdon, Aroostook, Maine; d. 28 Jul 1949, Los Angeles, Los Angeles, California; m. (2) Eudora Marian Steele; b. 30 May 1873, Addison, Washington, Maine; d. 6 Jan 1927, Syracuse, Onondaga, New York.

---

936 Information comes from Westborough Town Clerk's office, local history room at the Westborough Public Library.

937 Certificate of Death, the Commonwealth of Massachusetts.

938 *Worcester Evening Gazette*, Monday edition, May 10, 1915, page 11, column 5. Worcester Public Library, Worcester, Massachusetts.

939 Based on the inflation rate, $2,000 in 1915 would be approximately $53,305 in today's (2021) money. As far as his bequests of $120.00, each child would have received a little over $3,000.

**_Children of Albert F. Scoville and Margaret Estella Apperson_**

40. iii. Florence Mabel Scoville,[7] b. 11 Apr 1886, Worcester, Worcester, Massachusetts; d. 29 Oct 1964, Worcester, Worcester, Massachusetts; m. 20 Oct 1915, Worcester, Worcester, Massachusetts William Louis Carr; b. 21 Apr 1880, Presque Isle, Aroostook, Maine; d. 12 Mar 1959, Worcester, Worcester, Massachusetts.

iv. Olive Jane Scoville, b. 8 Apr 1889, Worcester, Worcester, Massachusetts; d. 29 Aug 1890, Worcester, Worcester, Massachusetts.[940] Death caused by Cholera Infantum (summer diarrhea of infants and children).

v. Baby Girl Scoville, b. 8 Aug 1890, Worcester, Worcester, Massachusetts; d. 8 Aug 1890, Worcester, Massachusetts. Child stillborn.[941]

No children were born between Albert F. Scoville and Melissa Viola Moore.

## *25. vi. Lucius Edwin Scoville[6] (Franklin,[5] Ithamar,[4] Timothy,[3] Stephen,[2] Stephen,[1] Arthur)*

Born 13 June 1848, Winchester, Litchfield, Connecticut;[942] died 14 May 1917, Torrington, Litchfield, Connecticut; married 8 November 1871, Sheffield, Berkshire, Massachusetts, Ellen "Nellie" Amanda Sullivan; born September 1851,[943] Canaan, Litchfield, Connecticut; died 1924,[944] buried Lower Cemetery,[945] North Canaan, Litchfield, Connecticut. Daughter of John Sullivan and Sally Doolittle.

Lucius Edwin Scoville was the last child born to Franklin and Amarilla Scoville and, according to his death certificate, his birth occurred in Winchester, Connecticut.[946]

Lucius Scoville was a farm laborer and teamster. He likely helped his father, Franklin, who is listed on the 1870 census as a "farmer." All the children were out of the household by this time and Lucius was twenty-two years old. The following year, Lucius entered into marriage with Ellen "Nellie" Amanda Sullivan.

Ellen Sullivan is listed on the 1870 census also in North Canaan. She is a domestic servant in the William Adam household, as is her mother, Sally Doolittle. The Adams family is listed as dwelling 34 and family 39, while Lucius

940 *Massachusetts Birth Records, 1840–1915*. Ancestry.

941 *Ibid* (birth and death record).

942 Dates of birth and death come from death certificate.

943 Month and year of birth come from the 1900 census. I have surmised that she was born in Canaan as that is where her parents were in 1850.

944 *Connecticut Deaths and Burials Index, 1650–1934*, Ancestry.

945 *Connecticut Hale Collection of Cemetery Inscriptions and Newspapers*, 615–1 (14), *Ibid.*

946 Lucius Edwin Scoville, photo courtesy of Sandra Amador.

and his family are in dwelling 88 and family 96. The distance between these two residences is not that great and they (Lucius and Nellie) may have known one another for some time.

William Adam was a very well known citizen of North Canaan. On the 1870 census his real estate value is $10,000 and the personal estate is $15,000.

The following article comes from the Connecticut Humanities Project, written by Sara VanDeusen, entitled "The Land of Nod Farm, East Canaan, Connecticut." The focus is on the Adam farm—a farm that is said to have "fed the people of Canaan." William Adam was the grandson of the couple who settled in Canaan and began the farm around 1787.

The article mentions William Adam as follows:

> William Adam, a grandson of John and Abigail Adam, continued the family legacy in Canaan when, in the late 1830s, the idea of building a railroad track alongside the Adam property arose.
>
> Afraid that the sparks from passing steam engines might set his farm on fire, William Adam proposed that the track run through the center of Canaan instead, and in exchange, he build a hotel for the town. After acceptance of this plan, the tracks were built, as was as a combination hotel and railroad station (known as the "Canfield Hotel") that proved quite lucrative for the town. Thirty years later, as Adam feared, sparks from a passing steam engine set fire to the Canfield Hotel.

The 1850 census for William Adam shows Sally Doolittle, age twenty-nine,[947] and John Sullivan, age twenty-eight (laborer), as members of his household. This census was taken on the twenty-fifth day of September. The following September, Ellen Sullivan was born, and we can presume that sometime in January 1851, John Sullivan and Sally Doolittle had intimate relations. I have yet to find a marriage record between these two individuals, however, on two census reports (1880 and 1900) Sally is listed as "D" (divorced) and then in 1900, she is designated as a "widow." A marriage must have taken place, but a record has not been located.

All census records refer to Sally with the surname "Doolittle." The only place that I have found where her married name is used is in the *Connecticut Death Records, 1897–1968,*[948] where she is referred to as "Sally Sullivan." Ironically, her headstone also reads "Sally Doolittle." Somehow, I get the feeling that Sally and John (Sullivan) did not part amicably, as Sally continued to use her maiden name whenever possible.

Sally Doolittle remained in the Adam household until her death in 1903. She had worked faithfully for this family for fifty-three years. John Sullivan's whereabouts after 1850 remain a mystery.[949]

By 1880, the Scoville family was now living in New Marlborough, Berkshire, Massachusetts. New Marlborough is a "hop, skip, and a jump" over the border from North Canaan.[950]

---

947 Sally Doolittle, born 17 January 1821, Canaan, Connecticut; daughter of Henry Doolittle (1790–1869) and Mary Richards (1791–1832).

948 Connecticut State Library, http://ctstatelibrary.org/death-records/.

949 This photo was taken by P. Welch, a member of Find-A-Grave.

950 On today's roads it is 10.5 miles between the two towns. Lucius's sister, Irene, was also born

Lucius Scoville is making his living as a teamster. It is possible that he was employed by one of the many manufacturers[951] in New Marlborough, as well as laboring in ploughing farmland.

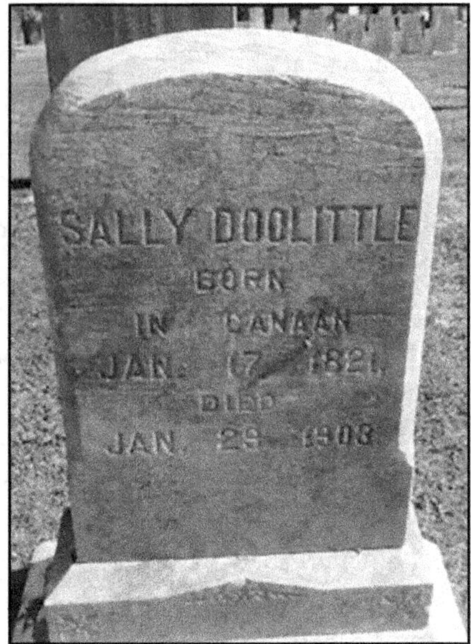


An article appeared in the *Connecticut Western News*[952] entitled "Fall and Winter Ploughing," which was written by William Sardam of Canaan Valley, on January 2, 1885. He states in part:

> . . . Lucius Scoville ploughed for me, with my team, on the 15th and the 16th of Dec., last, and the last day of the same month and New Year's Day, doing me two good days' work. He ploughed the old year out and the new year in, and that I call good for Canaan Valley and a good start to 1885.

Another brief snippet from the same paper contained the headline for East Canaan: "Grove Dunham and Lucius Scoville of Canaan Valley ploughed all day January 1st."[953]

≈

Based on the birthplaces of Lucius and Ellen's four children, we can see where the family was residing during those times: 1874—Connecticut; 1876—Sheffield, Massachusetts; 1880—New Marlborough, Massachusetts; and 1883—Canaan, Connecticut.

Now, once again we come to the "lost" years; in other words, the time from 1881–1900. Where the family was living during those twenty years is speculative, however, I believe that they were back in North Canaan shortly before 1885.[954]

On June 19, 1900,[955] the enumerator counted their household as Dwelling: 278; Family: 294. The family consists of Lucius Scoville, "day laborer," his wife, "Nellie," and their three daughters, Lucy, Irene, and Mary. Son Harry was in Sheffield, Berkshire, Massachusetts, and was employed as a servant in the William Dunham household.

That same year, Lucius and Nellie's daughter, Julia Irene, married in September and, two years later, Lucy Scoville married. By 1910, all the children (except Harry) had found spouses

---

in New Marlborough and I have wondered whether there is some connection to this town, but I have not found anything that would confirm a connection to this town.

951 By 1890, New Marlborough had several paper mills, carriage makers, and whip makers as well as 261 farms. Lucius may have been employed by any one of these entities.

952 Canaan, Connecticut, Wednesday, Jan. 7, 1885, edition.

953 *Ibid.*

954 *Ibid.*

955 1900 census; *North Canaan, Litchfield, Connecticut*; Page:13; ED:0247; FHL:1240140. Ancestry.

and had set up their own households.

In 1910, the Scovilles are once again living in Massachusetts—Ashley Plain Road, Sheffield.[956] Their son Harry and his wife, Jessie, along with Nellie, are living together. Father and son are "working out" as farm laborers.

It is doubtful that Lucius Scoville owned his own home and likely worked the farm for someone else. As he was getting older (he was sixty-two years old in 1910) he likely required the help of his son and they had determined to live together to help one another.

A farm laborer's life was a tough one. I suspect that Lucius Scoville and his son Harry were working for other farmers plowing *their* land (as noted in the article from 1885), walking behind the plow, forking hay, and all other sundry duties of a farmer. Looking at the occupations of his neighbors, most were laborers, farm laborers "working out," odd jobbers, and the like.

By 1914[957] Lucius and Nellie Scoville were living in Torrington, Litchfield, Connecticut, at 74 Calhoun Street,[958] with their daughter Lucy and her husband, Frank VanDeusen. Laboring on a farm for most of his life took its toll and Lucius could no longer do such work to support his family. An article about their move appeared in *Connecticut Western News:*

> **Ashley Falls** (Massachusetts)
> Mr. and Mrs. Lucius Scoville moved to Torrington Thursday and will make their home with their daughter, Mrs. Frank VanDeusen.[959]

Lucius Edwin Scoville died on May 14, 1917, in Torrington, Connecticut.[960] The family was still living on Calhoun Street at this time. The cause of death was chronic interstitial nephritis[961] and an arthritic condition. His obituary was published in *The Hartford Daily Courant:*[962]

> **L. E. SCOVILLE DIES IN TORRINGTON**
> Lucius E. Scoville, 69 years old, died this morning at the home of his daughter, Mrs. Lucy Van Deusen on Calhoun Street after fifteen years of ill health. He was born in Winsted and had lived in Torrington about three years. He leaves a wife, one son, Harry Scoville of Ashley Falls, Mass.: three daughters, Mrs. Van Deusen of this

956 1910 census; *Sheffield, Berkshire, Massachusetts;* Roll: T624_572; Page:10B; ED:0086; FHL:1374585; Dwelling: 227; Family: 238. Ashly Plain was the previous name for what is now Polikoff Road. It runs from the Connecticut state line to Hewins Street. Hewins ends at County Road, which takes you to New Marlborough.

957 *1914 City Directory Torrington, Litchfield, Connecticut,* 142. Ancestry

958 The house at 74 Calhoun Street still stands today, a small A-frame colonial.

959 Thursday, May 21, 1914, edition, North Canaan, 4.

960 Certified Death Certificate. Town Clerk, Torrington, Connecticut.

961 According to an online definition, this condition is due to a kidney injury.

962 Tuesday, May 15, 1917, edition.

town, Mrs. Irene Prince of New Haven and Mrs. Mary Roys of Stockbridge, Mass., and two sisters, Mrs. Irene Smith of Pine Meadow and Mrs. Julia Raidart of Winsted. The funeral will be held at 11 o'clock Wednesday morning. Rev. W. E. Aiken of the Calvary Baptist Church will officiate. The body will be taken to Canaan for burial.

Lucius E. Scoville is buried in North Canaan, Lower Cemetery.

Ellen "Nellie" Scoville continued to live with her daughter Lucy and son-in-law Frank Van Deusen. They had moved from Calhoun Street to 123 Winthrop Street.[963] In 1920 Nellie was still living with her daughter and son-in-law on Winthrop; four years later, Ellen "Nellie" Amanda (Doolittle) Scoville died on June 22, 1924.[964] She is buried with her husband and mother in Lower Cemetery.[965]

***Children of Lucius Edwin Scoville and Ellen "Nellie" Amanda Doolittle***

i. Lucy A. Scoville,[7] b. Nov 1874,[966] either Connecticut or Massachusetts; d. 25 Mar 1938, Torrington, Litchfield, Connecticut; m. 31 December 1902, North Canaan, Litchfield, Connecticut;[967] Frank H. Van Deusen; b. April 1862, Massachusetts;[968]d. after 1940, Winchester, Litchfield, Connecticut; his parentage has not been proven, but is likely Egbert Van Deusen and Martha C. Reed.[969]

This couple lived in Torrington all their married lives. Frank Van Deusen was employed at a brass mill in 1900, as a laborer. The couple rented an apartment at 57 Workman Avenue.[970] By 1920 they had moved to 123 Winthrop Street and Frank was listed as a teamster in a coal yard at T. Coal & Oil Company. Finally, in 1930, the couple was living at 40 Barber Street. The rent was $25.00 per month. The residents of the household were head Frank Van Deusen, wife, Lucy, Burtrand [sic] Reed, cousin, and Raymond Bennett, a lodger.

Frank and Lucy Van Deusen continued to live on Barber Street throughout the 1930s.[971]

963 This home was built in 1910 and still stands today as a single-family home.

964 *Connecticut Death Records, 1897–1968*. Ancestry.

965 *Hale Collection of Cemetery Inscriptions and Newspapers;* 615-1 Lower Cemetery; 14. Ancestry.

966 The month and year of her birth come from the 1900 census for North Canaan, Litchfield, Connecticut. I have been unsuccessful at finding her actual day of birth. She is consistently listed as having been born in Massachusetts.

967 *Connecticut Marriage Records, 1897–1968;* Connecticut State Library. The names are written as "Frank Vandewsen and Lucy Scorillo."

968 The month and year of his birth comes from the 1900 census for Goshen, Litchfield, Connecticut, living in the household of Lyman Hall.

969 The 1930 census for Torrington shows "Burtrand Reed" in the Van Deusen household, who is listed as a "cousin."

970 This multi-dwelling home still stands today.

971 Per Torrington City Directories. Ancestry.

Lucy (Scoville) Van Deusen died on March 25, 1938,[972] in Torrington at the age of sixty-four. An obituary has not been located for her, nor a place of burial.

By 1940, Frank Van Deusen is living in Winchester, Litchfield, Connecticut, in the household of Frank Oles as a "lodger" at 78 Moore Avenue. By this time he is seventy-eight years old. This is the last information that can be found on Frank H. Van Deusen. His date of death and place of burial are a mystery as of this writing. This couple did not have children.

ii. Harry Oliver Scoville,[7] b. 27 Nov 1876, Sheffield, Berkshire, Massachusetts;[973]d. 27 Apr 1961, Sheffield, Berkshire, Massachusetts; m. 3 Nov 1909, Sheffield, Berkshire, Massachusetts;[974] Jessie Maud Ball; b. 2 Jun 1892, New Marlborough, Berkshire, Massachusetts;[975]d. 29 Dec 1973, North Canaan, Litchfield, Connecticut;[976]daughter of Sylvester Ball (1854–1918) and Esther J. Hall (1856–1929).

Harry O. Scoville married Jessie Maud Ball when he was thirty-three years old, and she was just seventeen. We have seen through the census that this couple was living with Harry's parents in the early days of their marriage.

In 1917, like all men, Harry registered for the draft for WWI. His attributes were given as "of medium build, medium height with blue eyes and brown hair."[977] Though he registered, he was never called up to serve in active duty.

The couple's first child was born in 1918—nine years after they married.[978] In 1920, the family is living on School Street in Sheffield, Massachusetts, and Harry is working as a teamster for a mill.[979] The 1929 city directory[980] for Sheffield has the family living in Ashley Falls on Clayton Road. Harry is employed as a clerk at Red Mill.[981]

In 1930 the family still resided in Ashley Falls.[982] The Scovilles now own their own home with a value of $1,000, and they also owned a radio set. I believe we've all seen old photos or art pieces (think Norman Rockwell) of families sitting around the radio intently listening to the radio programs. I imagine this family did the same thing.[983] Perhaps after a long day at work

972 *Connecticut Death Records, 1897–1968,* Connecticut State Library, Hartford, Connecticut.

973 *Massachusetts Town and Vital Records, 1620–1988,* Ancestry.

974 *Massachusetts Marriage Records, 1840–1915.* Ancestry.

975 *Massachusetts Birth Index, 1860–1970.* Ancestry.

976 *Massachusetts Death Index, 1901–1980; The Berkshire Eagle;* Find A Grave.

977 *WWI Draft Registration Cards, 1917–1918,* NARA, Ancestry.

978 There may have been other pregnancies, miscarriages, or births, but there are no records of such.

979 There were a number of mills in Sheffield, Mass., one being the "Old" Red Mill. Harry worked for the Durham Feed Mill, as is noted in his obituary.

980 *Sheffield, Berkshire, Massachusetts,* city directory, 1929, 393. Ancestry.

981 This mill was built in the early 1800s and no longer exists.

982 1930 census, *Ashley Falls, Berkshire County, Massachusetts;* Page:10B; ED:0086; FHL: 1374585;Dwelling: 79; Family: 79. Ancestry.

983 According to *The History of the Radio Industry in the United States to 1940,* "its popularity grew

Harry may have listened to the news or a ball game; Jessie perhaps liked music, cooking shows, and health or fashion programs, and Esther likely listened to the serials that were popular for children.

The family continued to live in Ashley Falls throughout the rest of their lives. Their daughter Esther had married, and she and her husband were living with the Scovilles in 1940.

Harry spent his adult working life in various grist mills in Massachusetts, as is mentioned in his obituary that was published on Friday, April 28, 1961:[984]

> Harry O. Scoville
> Sheffield—Harry O. Scoville, 84 of Clayton Road, Ashley Falls, died at Fairview Hospital late last night. Born in Ashley Falls, the son of Lucius and Nellie Doolittle Scoville. He lived there all his life and was employed as a miller at Dunham Feed Mill for fifty years. He retired nineteen years ago. A member of the Ashley Falls Methodist Church, he is survived by his wife, the former Jessie Gall [sic], one daughter, Mrs. P. C. Kradel of Ashley Falls: two grandsons and several nieces and nephews.

He is buried in Sackett Cemetery in Ashley Falls.

Harry's wife, Jessie, lived until 1973. At the time of her death, she was in Greer Memorial Extended Care Facility in Canaan, Connecticut. Her home was still on Clayton Road in Ashley Falls. Jessie was eighty-one at the time of her death. Her obituary states in part ". . . Mrs. Scoville was born June 2, 1892, the daughter of Sylvester and Esther Hall Ball. She had lived in this area all her life. She leaves one daughter, Mrs. Plummer C. Kradel of Ashley Falls; two grandsons and three great-grandchildren."

She is buried in Ashley Falls Cemetery.[985]

### *Children of Harry Olive Scoville and Jessie Maude Ball*

a.i. Esther Vaughn Scoville,[8] b. 19 Nov 1918, Ashley Falls, Berkshire, Massachusetts; d. 26 Nov 1999, Great Barrington, Berkshire, Massachusetts; m. 10 July 1938, Sheffield, Berkshire, Massachusetts, Plummer Charles "Hap" Kradel; b. 4 Jul 1912, Butler, Butler, Pennsylvania; d. 4 Jan 1999, Sheffield, Berkshire, Massachusetts; son of Theodore Kradel and Alice J. McCl [ ] g.

Two sons were born to this couple: Thomas H. Kradel (1940–2005) and Richard L. Kradel (1946–1995).[986]

~

rapidly in the late 1920s and early 1930s." www.eh.net.

984 *The Berkshire Eagle,* 15; Newspapers.

985 *Ibid,* Monday, December 31, 1973, edition; 11.

986 Information on this family comes from Find-A-Grave and *Massachusetts Marriage Records, 1620–1988,* Ancestry.

***Children of Lucius Edwin Scoville and Ellen "Nellie" Amanda Doolittle continued . . .***

iii. Julia Irene Scoville,[7] b. 18 Feb 1880,[987] New Marlborough, Berkshire, Massachusetts; d. 23 Apr 1959, New Haven, New Haven, Connecticut; m. 30 Sep 1900,[988] Millerton, Duchess, New York, George James Prince; b. 16 Apr 1880,[989] Salisbury, Litchfield, Connecticut; d. 22 Dec 1939,[990] in either Hamden or New Haven, Connecticut.

According to their marriage record, George J. Prince was an electrician. In 1910 the family was still living in New Haven on Putnam Street and George was a conductor for the railroad. During this time there were three children (Donald, Jennie, and Stanley) in the household.

Living in a city must have been quite a change for Julia Irene,[991] having come from such a rural upbringing. After the 1910 census was completed, there was an estimated population of 133,605 souls living in New Haven.

By the time of the 1930 census the family was living in Hamden, New Haven, Connecticut, at 90 North Street[992] and George was working as a brakeman for the NY NH & H Railroad.[993] On December 22, 1939, George James Prince died and was buried in Evergreen Cemetery. Per the *New Haven City Directory* for 1939, the couple was listed as living at 11 Lambert Street.

The following year (1940), Julia Irene Prince is still living at 11 Lambert Street with her son John. Julia Irene was not employed and was paying twenty-five dollars per month for rent. Her son John was working as an "attendant" in a retail gas(?) station.[994]

Because the 1950 census will not be available until 2022, we can only track Julia Irene in the subsequent years via the city directories.

1941/42—250 Bassett Street
1951/53—housekeeper, 1752 Whitney Avenue
1954—removed to Warren[995]
1957/59—28 Howard Avenue

Julia Irene Scoville Prince died April 23, 1959, in New Haven, New Haven, Connecticut, at the age of seventy-nine.

Their children were Donald Scoville Prince (1902–1966), Jennie Thorpe Prince (1904–1991), Stanley Prince (1909–1988), and John Lucius Prince (1914–1979).

987 *Massachusetts Birth Records, 1840–1915; New Marlborough.* Ancestry.

988 *Massachusetts Town and Vital Records, 1620–1988.* Ancestry.

989 *U.S. World War 1 Draft Registration Cards, 1917–1918; U.S. Social Security Applications and Claims Index, 1936–2007.* Ancestry.

990 Find-A-Grave.

991 Most census records have her recorded as "Irene."

992 This multi-family home still stands today in Hamden.

993 New York, New Haven, Hartford Railroad.

994 I am not certain this is what it says on the census "retail [?] sta."

995 Julia Irene Prince is not in the 1955/56 editions of the city directories for New Haven.

iv. Mary Doolittle Scoville,[7] b 2 Jun 1883, Canaan, Litchfield, Connecticut; d. 5 Jan 1945, Lee, Berkshire, Massachusetts;[996] m. 4 Aug 1907, Sheffield, Berkshire, Massachusetts,[997] Edmond Davis (or David) Roys; b. 19 Jul 1880, New Marlborough, Berkshire, Massachusetts;[998] d. 1963, Pittsfield, Berkshire, Massachusetts;[999] son of John M. Roys and Rhoda D. Huggins.

Prior to his marriage to Mary D. Scoville, Edmond Roys had previously been married to Maud Bowen on October 31, 1900, in Millerton, Duchess, New York.[1000] Maud Bowen was only fourteen years old when they married (Edmond was twenty). Prior to his first marriage to Maud, Edmond Roys is listed on the 1900 census in Sheffield, Berkshire, Massachusetts, living in the household of Ralph Hurlburt. Edmond is listed as a "servant" and "farm laborer." This couple did have one son, Eugene Edmond Roys, born October 3, 1901,[1001] but the child died February 6, 1902, in Sheffield.[1002] The record indicates that he died at "4 months, 15 days" from "suffocation." I haven't been able to find any news articles relating to this incident. The death may have been caused by what we know now as "sudden infant death syndrome."

Edmond Roys divorced Maud Roys, however, a date for the divorce is not in any online records I could find. The marriage record requests information on what your marital status was prior to the current marriage and Edmond is recorded as "D" for divorced. Mary Scoville is listed as having been "single" prior to her marriage to Edmond.

Like all of men of his time Edmond was required to register for the draft in 1917–1918. He gives his present occupation as a teamster for the J. B. Hull Co., of Stockbridge. At that time, Edmond was already thirty-eight years old; however, "by the guidelines set down by the Selective Service Act, all males aged 21 to 30 were required to register to potentially be selected for military service." At the request of the War Department, Congress amended the law in August 1918 to expand the age range to 18 to 45 and bar further volunteers.[1003]

This couple lived in Stockbridge per the 1910 and 1920 censuses. Edmond was employed as a teamster/in trucking.

The 1929–31 Stockbridge directory[1004] mentions that this couple removed to South Lee, Massachusetts, and this is where we find them on the 1930 census. Edmond is still a teamster for a coal company. The couple were renting a two-family home on Main Street at eight dollars a month.

They are in Lee in 1940. Edmond's occupation has changed from a teamster to cleaning (rivers?).[1005]

---

996 *Massachusetts Town and Vital Records, 1620–1988*. Ancestry.

997 *Massachusetts Marriage Records, 1840–1915*. Ancestry.

998 "Massachusetts, Birth Records, 1840–1915," Ancestry.

999 Find-A-Grave.

1000 *Massachusetts Marriage Records, 1840–1915*. Ancestry.

1001 *Massachusetts U.S. Birth Records, 1840–1915*. Ancestry.

1002 *Massachusetts U.S. Death Records, 1840–1915*; Vol: 528; Page: 131; Index Vol: 50; Ancestry.

1003 *Selective Service Act of 1917*—Wikipedia.org.

1004 *U.S. City Directories, 1822–1995*; Stockbridge; 436. Ancestry.

1005 The second word for his occupation is illegible.

In 1942, the United States was involved in another war and Edmond, once again, had to register, which was accomplished on April 27, 1942, at the local registration board. He is now sixty-one years old and is employed by Robert Turner, the Superintendent State Highway [Department]. They are residing on Pine Street in South Lee. Three years later, Mary D. Scoville Roys died at the age of sixty-two. *The Berkshire County Eagle* published her obituary in the Wednesday edition on January 10, 1945:

> **Mrs. Mary Roys, 62, Dies at Home**
> Lee—Mrs. Mary D. Roys, 62, wife of Edmond Roys, died at midnight at her home in South Lee. A native of Canaan, Conn., Mrs. Roys had lived in South Lee for 20 years. Besides her husband, she is survived by a sister, Mrs. A. J. Prince of Mill River and a brother, Harry Scoville of Ashley Falls.[1006]

Mary D. Roys is buried in Fairmont Cemetery, Lee, Berkshire, Massachusetts.

There are few records to track Edmond Roys' movements after Mary's death. There are no city directories (online) available for Edmond until 1952, where he is living in Berkshire and employed by the town of Lee. The next available record is the 1957[1007] city directory where it states he is employed by the town and resides at City Farm.[1008]

Nothing more is known about Edmond Roys. He died in 1963, although the day and month of his death are not known. He is buried in Fairmont Cemetery, Pittsfield, Berkshire, Massachusetts.

This couple had no children.

---

1006 Newspapers; 4.

1007 Edmond is seventy-seven years old by this time.

1008 I have not been able to determine the location of "City Farm."

# Seventh Generation

### *26. i. Franklin "Frank" Scoville*[7] *(Charles Foote,*[6] *Amasa,*[5] *Ithamar,*[4] *Timothy,*[3] *Stephen,*[2] *Stephen,*[1] *Arthur)*

Born December 1850,[1009] Ansonia, New Haven, Connecticut; died 22 October 1922, San Diego County, California;[1010]burial: Sunnyslope Cemetery, Corona, Riverside, California;[1011] m. 1872, Ironton, Iron, Missouri, Kate Shepard; born 29 March 1852, Hamilton, Ohio; died 2 March 1908, Corona, Riverside, California.

Frank Scoville was born in Ansonia, New Haven, Connecticut, after his parents removed there from Torrington. Sometime prior to the 1860 census, the family had removed to Chicago where Frank's father (Charles) worked for the various railroad companies. At the age of five, Frank's mother, Clarissa, had died and he and his sister, Mary Jane, were raised by Charles' second wife, Sarah Baird. As they were so young when their mother died, memories of her must have been murky, and they likely looked upon Sarah as their mother. Based on the narrative for his father (Charles), the Scovilles lived a relatively comfortable existence.

As previously seen regarding his father, Charles, the family has not been discovered on the 1870 census; however, by 1872,[1012] Frank Scoville had married in Ironton Township, Iron, Missouri, to Kate Shepard.

Kate Shepard was the daughter of Bilbe Shepard (1817–1901) and Lydia Gobel Truesdale (1815–1882) and was born in Hamilton, Butler, Ohio, on March 29, 1852.[1013] Whether they met in Ohio or Missouri is impossible to say. Kate Shepard's father (Bilbe) was born in Pennsylvania and removed to Butler County, Ohio, sometime prior to 1843 as he married Lydia Truesdale in said county on April 25, 1843.[1014] By the 1860 census the Shepard family was living in Iron Township, Missouri.

---

1009 The actual date of birth for Franklin Scoville has not been ascertained, although the year of birth (1850) is consistent. The 1850 census (which commenced on the first day of June) gives his age as 8/12. The actual date when the enumerator visited the Scoville family was on 9 October 1850. If he was truly eight months old, he would have been born sometime in March 1850. However, on the 1900 census his birth is given as "December" 1850. Neither his obituary notice nor his headstone reveals the month and day that he was born.

1010 Obituary notice *Iron County Register, Ironton, Missouri,* 16 November 1922 edition, 1; Newspapers, and Find A Grave.

1011 *Ibid*

1012 Obituary for Franklin Scoville, *Iron County Register, Ironton, Missouri;* 16 November 1922 edition; Vol: LVI; Number: 25. Newspapers.

1013 Kate Shepard's birthdate comes from two sources: grave marker (Find A Grave) and her obituary notice (*Iron County Register;* 12 March 1908; 5.Newspapers).

1014 Marriage date comes from *Ohio, U.S. County Marriage Records, 1884–1993;* Ancestry, and census records for 1850 and 1860.

During their time in Iron, Missouri, Frank Scoville worked as a train dispatcher in St. Louis for the Iron Mountain Southern Railroad (reminiscent of his father's livelihood). The StLIMSR[1015] is a historic railroad and was operated during the nineteenth and twentieth centuries from St. Louis, Missouri, to Texarkana, Arkansas, and was used to transport iron ore from Iron Mountain to St. Louis.

Depending upon what record you read, Frank Scoville and family had removed to Bellevue, Illinois, or Chicago.[1016]

Frank Scoville left the railway for a time and became involved with the milling and lumber business, as well as operating a general merchandise store for "three years and moved back to Chicago where he was associated with the Wells & French Car Company and Bridge Builders until 1891."

The editor of the *Iron County Register* printed an article of his "old friend" Frank Scoville, that he (the editor) was in receipt of a postal card "... lately of Chicago" that he (Frank Scoville) was on a train heading for California and that "in future my address will be South Riverside, Cal., all well; regards to all." The editor goes on to say that "Mr. Scoville was for many years a resident of Ironton, and everybody remembers him as a genial, jolly, and whole-souled gentleman," and that "He purchased an orange grove in the Golden State and will make that his future home. All his friends here joins us in wishing him and his health, happiness and prosperity in their new home."[1017]

The family did move to South Riverside, California, in 1894, a few years after the settlement began in the area.[1018] Frank likely purchased the orange and lemon grove prior to their removal to the new settlement.

Frank Scoville entered a partnership with two early settlers of Corona—Tom Drinkwater and George Brown—and with them founded the first packing house in town, the Sunset Fruit Company.[1019]

In the book *History of Riverside County, California,*[1020] the author writes, "From the beginning Frank Scoville has been a manager of the Sunset Packing House and is well known in the fruit world and is held in the highest esteem by the people of his hometown," and, "Frank Scoville also started the erection of a fine residence on the corner of Ontario Avenue and Main Street."[1021]

---

1015 StLIMSR is still in operation for train rides through the countryside.

1016 The *U.S. City Directories* for Chicago show a "Frank Scoville" as a "Superintendent of Bridge Works" for 1889 and there is an "F. Scoville" listed in 1872 as an "Assistant Superintendent." These very well could be the Frank Scoville of this record. I have not located any records in Bellevue, Illinois, for this family.

1017 Published Thursday, 19 October 1893; 5. Newspapers.

1018 See Kate Shepard Scoville, www.gatheringleaves.org/cgs/sunnyslope/Kate_Shepard_Scoville.htm. A historical reenactment put on by the Corona Genealogical Society, April 2014.

1019 *Corona California: The Queen Colony Fruit Exchange,* "Mr. Frank Scoville is the Secretary and General Manager of the Exchange in Corona." Corona Publishing Company, (1902).

1020 Pages 271 & 273 of the "History of Riverside County, California."

1021 Photo courtesy of Kathleen Dever, the Corona (California) Historical Society.

The Scoville home that once stood on the corner of Ontario Avenue and Main Street in Corona, California.

The population of Corona in 1894 was 1,200 and it was founded at the height of the citrus boom in California in 1886. Corona was incorporated in 1896 and it is situated at the upper end of the Santa Anna River Canyon.

When Frank Scoville removed to Corona, he had a fine home built, which was completed in 1895.[1022]

The home was "quite grand" as it had a winding staircase, seven bedrooms, two parlors, a dining hall large enough to hold dances, and two bathrooms.[1023]

The property had 8.64 acres with trees such as olive, pepper, California palm, and pine. There were also orange and lemon trees on the property that had been planted by the local doctor, Dr. Rio De los Barbar.

The 1900 census shows the family in Corona with a full household.
Dwelling: 40; Family: 40
Scoville, Frank, b. Dec 1850, 49, m. 28 yrs., b. Connecticut, fruit broker
Scoville, Kate F., wife, Jan 1854, m. 28 yrs., 8 children born/6 living; b. Ohio
Scoville, Harry F., son, May 1880, 20, b. Missouri, student
Scoville, Gilbert L., son, Jul 1882, 17, b. Missouri, at school
Scoville, Mabel M., daughter, Aug 1887, 12, b. Illinois, at school
Scoville, Ethel M., daughter, Dec 1890, 9, b. Illinois, at school

1022 The house was burnt to the ground in the 1980s by tenants who were barbequing. The property was a vacant lot through the 1980s and 1990s. The area was subsequently built up as a shopping center.

1023 See article on Kate Shepard Scoville, www.gatheringleaves.org/cgs/sunnyslope/Kate_Shepard_Scoville.htm. Herein Kate Shepard Scoville article.

Shepard, Bilbe, father-in-law, b. Aug 1813, 84, widowed, m. 58 yrs., b. Pennsylvania[1024]

Dickenson, Janette,[1025] Aunt, b. Mar 1829, 71, widowed, m. 45 yrs., 1 child born/0 living, b. Scotland

The following year on February 22, 1901, Kate Scoville's father, Bilbe, died at the age of eighty-three from an apparent self-inflicted gunshot, but it was then determined that he died from a heart attack. Mr. Shepard was found at this daughter's home by A. F. Le Gaye, who had been walking passed the Scoville homestead. Mr. Le Gaye noticed the "old man" lying on his face in front of the barn. There was a large pool of blood nearby. A shotgun was found in between the legs and an investigation ensued. They initially thought that he had committed suicide, but investigation revealed he had heart disease, which had caused his demise.

When the authorities interviewed Mrs. Scoville, she stated that her father got his gun to "shoot some cats." The opinion was that after killing his game, "the excitement and shock of the discharge" caused his heart failure. The article continues to state the "old man was very feeble and had not fired a gun for a number of years." He was eighty-four years of age and was "well-known in the vicinity." Apparently, Mr. Shepard was sitting in a chair when he took his aim and fell after the discharge, cutting his head quite severely, and the conclusion was that was where the blood came from.[1026]

Mr. Shepard is buried in Corona Sunnyslope Cemetery.

In 1902 another article on Mr. Frank Scoville was printed in the *Iron County Register.* Frank Scoville and the editor of the newspaper were good friends and, even though they lived many miles apart, they kept in touch:

> . . . the editor is in receipt of an invitation to attend the thirtieth anniversary of the marriage of Mr. and Mrs. Frank Scoville at South Riverside, California on Friday evening, October 17th. We tender Mr. and Mrs. Scoville with the best wishes, and may they enjoy many happy returns of the day.[1027]

I imagine the anniversary party may have taken place in their "grand" home with the winding staircase all decorated to celebrate their special day.

≈

On the first day of March 1908, Kate Scoville decided it was time to clean out the attic. While finding "treasures" was fun for the two Scoville girls when they were young, it was time to dis-

---

1024 Find A Grave record suggests he was born 10 August 1817 based on the dates on the headstone.

1025 Frank Scoville's "aunt" (not biological) from his father's second marriage.

1026 *Riverside Daily Press,* Tuesday Evening edition, 26 February 1901; 4. Newspapers. Article was found on Find A Grave website posted by Ann Gilmore.

1027 Thursday, October 16, 1902, edition; 5. Newspapers.

pose of some of the items in the attic. Kate made a good sized trash pile of items that were no longer needed. Trash service was not available during the early part of the twentieth century, and everyone burned their own rubbish. After Kate started the fire, somehow her clothes also caught fire. You can imagine her crying for help. Frank Scoville is said to have fought heroically to put out the fire, but it was too late. She died the following day at four in the morning.

Her obituary mentions that she was a member of the Order of the Eastern Star and attended the Episcopalian church. The funeral was delayed as the rest of the family was waiting for their son George to make his way to California from Elyria, Ohio. She was fifty-four years old[1028] and is buried in Sunnyslope Cemetery.

Her death shook the family to the core, not just from the death itself but the manner of her death. Sixteen days later a short notice appeared in the *Los Angeles Times*: "Frank Scoville, the fruit man, is ill at his home on Upper Main Street, suffering from a nervous collapse, following the tragic death of his wife."[1029]

This was a tight-knit family and his family gathered around and helped each other in their grief.

Later that year, on Christmas Eve, Frank traveled to Oakland, California, to be with his son George, as well as his daughters Mabel and Ethel; Christmas was very likely a lively affair at the Scoville household prior to Kate's death.

~

By 1910, Frank is still living in his home in Corona City with his son Harry and daughters Mabel and Ethel. Frank is a farmer on his lemon ranch. Harry Scoville is employed as an attorney, while his daughters do not have any occupations. They are certainly taking care of the home and their father.

There are no further newspaper articles found for Frank Scoville. The last two records are the 1920 census, where Frank is now living in Monrovia with his son Harry, Harry's wife, Mariah, and their daughter, Elinor.[1030] Prior to his death, Frank was living with his daughter Mabel Thayer and her family in San Diego, California.

Franklin Scoville died at the age of seventy-two on October 30, 1922. His old friends in Ironton, Missouri, published his obituary, which appeared in the *Iron County Register* on the sixteenth of November. The services for Franklin Scoville were private and were held at his "former home in Corona." His son George A. Scoville, who lived in Rochester, New York, could not be there for his father's funeral. The Rev. Harian Bailey "read an impressive Episcopal burial service." Franklin was cremated and was buried alongside his wife in the family plot in Sunnyslope Cemetery in Corona.

The obituary in the *Iron County Register* is one that all genealogists hope for. It tells where he was born, where he went to school, when and where and to whom he married, as well as his

1028 Kate Shepard Scoville article. Corona Historical Society.

1029 Wednesday, March 18, 1908, edition; 25. Newspapers.

1030 According to Franklin's obituary, he moved in with his son Harry in 1917. Once his health began to fail, he moved in with his daughter Mabel, sometime after the 1920 census was taken.

employment history, the civic organizations he belonged to, and the names of his children. Surprisingly, the obituary in the California newspaper *Monrovia Daily News*[1031] only printed a brief snippet.

From the *Iron County Register:*

> . . . Mr. Scoville, with Mr. George Brown, deceased, and Mr. T. P. Drinkwater, built the first packing house in Corona and packed the fruit for the settlers whose groves were coming into bearing. In later years his company sold their interests to an association of growers, and he served as their manager until 1916 when he retired from active business . . . Mr. Scoville was one of the early presidents of the Citizens Bank of Corona and served on its board of directors for several years. He was also one of the early directors of the Temescal Water Company and served them for many years. He was a member of the Knight Templar Commandery, Council of Royal and Select Masters, Royal Arch Chapter of Masons, Temescal Lodge No. 314. F. & A. M., Corona, and Crown Chapter No. 162, Order of Eastern Star. He was regarded by those with whom he was associated, and his many friends, as a man of very high ideals and character and unquestionable integrity.

***Children of Franklin Scoville and Kate Shepard***

41. i. Charles Mittean Scoville,[8] b. 5 Jan 1874, Ironton, Iron, Missouri; d 28 May 1947, Riverside, Riverside, California; m. 12 Jul 1893, St. Joseph, Berrian, Michigan, Sarah "Sadie" L. Jackson; b. 10 May 1871, Illinois; d. 10 Jan 1962, San Diego, San Diego, California; d.o. Daniel Jackson and Mary Philbrick.

42. ii. George Albert Scoville,[8] b. 21 Dec 1876, Ironton, Iron, Missouri; d. 14 Jan 1940, Rochester, Monroe, New York; m. 10 May 1905, Riverside, Riverside, California, Mary Josephine Dyer; b. 29 Jul 1877, Illinois; d. 24 Apr 1957, Orange, Orange, California; her parents are unknown.

43. iii. Harry Franklin Scoville,[8] b. 10 May 1880, Ironton, Iron, Missouri; d. 30 Aug 1963, Pomona, Los Angeles, California; m. 1910, Los Angeles, Los Angeles, California, Clara Marian Bennett; b. 20 May 1885, Missouri; d. 30 Sep 1976, Los Angeles, Los Angeles, California.

44. iv. Gilbert Lafayette Scoville,[8] b. 26 Jul 1882, Ironton, Iron, Missouri; d. 17 Jan 1940, San Gabriel, Los Angeles, California; m. 29 June 1910, Petaluma, Sonoma, California, Lulu A. McMahon; b. Oct 1884, Michigan; d. 17 Jan 1980, San Gabriel, Los Angeles, California; d.o. Joseph McMahon and Harriet ______.

45. v. Mabel M. Scoville,[8] 3 Aug 1887, Illinois; d. 20 Sep 1944, San Diego, San Diego, California; m. 20 May 1913, Seattle, King, Washington, Earl Levi Thayer; b. 25 Oct 1855, Luther, Lake, Michigan; d. 24 Jun 1939, San Diego, San Diego, California; s.o. Thomas Thayer and Cora Ferguson.

46. vi. Ethel May Scoville,[8] b. 15 Dec 1890, Illinois; d. 17 Mar 1941, Riverside, Riverside, California; m. 5 Jan 1914, Frederick W. Kuster, California; b. 14 May 1884,

1031 November 10, 1922, issue, page 1. Newspapers.

Williamsburg, Franklin, Kansas; d. 15 Jun 1949, Orange, Orange, California; son of Jacob Kuster and A.B. Kuster.

### *27. ii. Mary Jane Scoville*[7] *(Charles Foote,*[6] *Amasa,*[5] *Ithamar,*[4] *Timothy,*[3] *Stephen,*[2] *Stephen,*[1] *Arthur)*

Born either September 1851 or 6 November 1852,[1032] Ansonia, New Haven, Connecticut; died 6 November 1933,[1033] Chicago, Cook, Illinois; married 6 January 1875,[1034] Cook County, Illinois, to Edward Theodore Cushing; born September 1845, Illinois; d. 6 April 1909,[1035] Cook County, Illinois; parents possibly Nathan Cushing and Martha ______.[1036]

Not much is known about Mary Jane Scoville and her husband, Edward T. Cushing. While they were well-to-do, I have not found many articles to help paint a picture of what their lives were like. What we do know comes from the censuses and city directories. In 1900, the family was living in the township of Hyde Park, Chicago, Cook, Illinois. Hyde Park is where many "captains of industry" built and lived in their large estates. The Cushing family lived at 4820 Greenwood Avenue (and would continue to live there throughout their lives).[1037] The home had five bedrooms and three baths. Mr. and Mrs. Cushing, their daughter, Natalie, and two servants were counted on this census.

Edward T. Cushing is listed as an assistant secretary and treasurer for the Union Foundry Works, which was located on Fifteenth and Dearborn Streets.[1038] Edward would remain there until his death, which occurred in 1909. The year prior, Edward made out his will.[1039] He was sixty-four old at that time and whether he made out a will because of his age or because he was ill is not known. The will in part states:

> . . . Second, I give, devise and bequeath to my friend Anna H. Wagner, the sum of $5,000.00[1040] for faithful service in our home for many years.

1032 The birth information is not cited, and I am uncertain as to where this information comes from; the 1900 census gives her birth month and year as "September 1851."

1033 *Cook County, Illinois, Deaths Index, 1908–1988.* Ancestry.

1034 *Cook County, Illinois, Marriages Index, 1871–1920.* Ancestry.

1035 *Cook County, Illinois, Deaths Index, 1878–1922.* Ancestry.

1036 The 1850, 1860, 1870, and 1880 censuses have a Nathan Cushing and wife, Martha, with a child, Edward Cushing, whose age would "fit" the Edward Cushing of this record.

1037 Based on Google Maps, Greenwood Avenue is now South Greenwood Avenue; 4820 Greenwood no longer exists. I also checked ChicagoAncestors.org for the street addresses and received the same results.

1038 *Chicago, Illinois City Directories,* 1888, 1889; Ancestry.

1039 *United States Wills and Probate Records, 1772–1999;* Record of Wills, Book: 62, 1908–1909, Book: 63, 1909. Ancestry.

1040 Anna H. Wagner is on the census with this family through 1910; she may have married or went off on her own. $5,000.00 is the equivalent in purchasing power to approximately $160,235.12 today.

> . . . the rest of the estate, real and personal, to my wife Mary Scoville Cushing and my daughter Natalie Scoville Cushing to be divided between them on the basis of three-quarter (3/4) to Mary Scoville Cushing and one-quarter (1/4) to Natalie Scoville Cushing.[1041]

The last part of the will states that his friend Walter Tod will hold the monies for Natalie as trustee. If Mr. Tod dies before Edward, the trustee will be Christopher Bouton, both friends of Edward Cushing. And if Mr. Bouton should die, then Erastus Foote will be the trustee.

Natalie was not allowed to handle the money on her own as her father intimated "knowing as I do how little experience she has had in handling money how quickly it would go if not wisely handled."[1042] If Natalie needed funds from "time to time" she would need to request it from the trustee.

On April 6, 1909, Edward Cushing died in Chicago. His obituary is very brief:

> Cushing—Edward Theodore Cushing, April 6, aged 63 years—funeral services at late residence, 4820 Greenwood Avenue Friday afternoon at 2 o'clock; burial at Oakwoods.

Mary S. Cushing continued to live in the home on Greenwood Avenue with her daughter, Natalie. On the 1920 census they had one "private family maid" by the name of Nora Shannon. However, by the 1930 census Mary S. Cushing no longer employed a maid. The home's value is given as $40,000 and the family owned a radio set. Natalie, now aged forty-nin, still lives with her mother.

Mary S. Cushing died on November 6, 1933, in Chicago. Her obituary is just as brief as her late husband's:

> Cushing—Mary Scoville Cushing, Nov. 6, 1933, widow of Edward T. and mother of Natalie S. Cushing. Funeral Thursday at 2 p.m. at her late residence, 4820 Greenwood Av. Interment Oakwoods.

### *Child of Edward Theodore Cushing and Mary Jane Scoville*

a. i. Natalie Scoville Cushing,[8] b. 22 Sep 1885,[1043] Chicago, Cook, Illinois; d. 9 Jul 1965, Cook County, Illinois.[1044]

Natalie remained single her entire life, although she was engaged in 1904 per a notice in the *Chicago Sunday Tribune:*

> The engagement is announced of Miss Natalie S. Cushing daughter of Mr. and Mrs.

1041 This was based on the event that "the decease of my said wife or daughter shall occur before or contemporaneously with my death, in that event, the survivor of them shall take the whole."

1042 This was the typical opinion of most fathers, brothers, and husbands for centuries.

1043 Natalie's birth information comes from a passport application.

1044 *Cook County, Illinois Death Index, 1908–1988.* Ancestry.

> Edward T. Cushing, 4820 Greenwood Avenue, to Dr. Andrew J. Berry of New York City.[1045]

Records are scarce for Natalie. Other than the census reports and an announcement of her engagement, we are left with her passport application and her obituary.

She left the United States on May 14, 1910, to "sojourn in Florence, Italy" for "two years" for the purpose of "traveling." Without any known photographs of Natalie, the only "picture" we have for her is the description on the passport: she is thirty-two years old with a high forehead, blue eyes, a round nose, small mouth, round chin, brown hair, fair complexion, and a full face.

The passport is stamped "Feb. 18, 1913." I presume this is when she returned to the U.S.[1046]

The years pass by and the last census that is available to us is the 1940. Natalie is now living at 4556 South Greenwood Avenue, dwelling: 229. She is now renting for $125.00 per month and is living with Saima A. Nylund, a widow. Natalie is listed as the head of the household and Saima is listed as "partner." They were not involved in a business (as a business partner) but rather as roommates. While it is not common to see this designation (partner), it is sometimes used for a roommate. Neither Natalie nor Saima are employed. If Natalie sold her home at 4820 Greenwood Avenue, she would have been able to live well from those proceeds.

Nothing more is known of Natalie until her death in 1965. Lastly, the obituary for Natalie comes from *The Chicago Daily News:*[1047]

> Natalie Scoville Cushing, beloved daughter of the late Edward T. and Mary Cushing, dear friend of Mrs. Saima A. Nyland. Funeral service Monday 11 a.m. at Donellen Funeral Home, Jefferson Blvd at 77th Street. Interment Oakwoods Cemetery.

### *28. i. Susan Jane Benson[7] (Clarissa Kelsey,[6] Almira Scoville Kelsey,[5] Ithamar,[4] Timothy,[3] Stephen,[2] Stephen,[1] Arthur)*

Born 9 October 1840,[1048] perhaps Greene, Chenango, New York; died 26 March 1937,[1049] Ventura, Ventura, California; married circa 1861, Henry Newton Elliott, b. 21 June 1837,[1050] Greene, Chenango, New York; s.o. John Elliott (1799–1846) and Jane Blake (1800–1869); d. 21 March 1918, Los Angeles, California.[1051]

---

1045 Published February 14, 1904, 31. Apparently, the engagement was called off as Natalie remained single.

1046 Note that the 1910 census began April 1st of that year and Natalie is still listed on that census.

1047 Monday, July 12th edition; 7. Newspapers.

1048 The date of birth is based on her age given in her obituary, "96 yrs., 6 mos. 16 days."

1049 Sources: Social Security; Obituary notice, *The Los Angeles Times*, edition: Saturday, March 27, 1937; Page: 34. Newspapers.

1050 This information comes from a descendant of this family; however, it has not been verified. The 1900 census indicates he was born "June 1837" in New York.

1051 Obituary notice and the *California Death Index, 1905–1939* (Ancestry).

There is only an index for the 1860 census for New York, in which Henry N. Elliott is listed for Greene, Chenango.[1052] Henry is also found on the *U.S. Naval Enlistment Rendezvous* for June 1863. He enlisted for one year and was age "25" with a "fair" complexion and estimated birth year of "1838 in Greene, New York."[1053]

The first we find Susan Benson Elliott is on the 1870 census, living in Kansas. She is not with her parents on the 1865 census, and probably married Henry N. Elliott prior to the state (1865) census for New York.[1054] There is a "Henry Elliot" on the 1865 agricultural statistical census for Greene, Chenango, New York, whereby it states he had "80 acres of improved land and 15 unimproved," with a value of $2,000. He also had "$800 in stock; tools and implements were valued at $100."[1055]

As mentioned previously, this couple was enumerated in Manhattan City, Riley, Kansas, in 1870. What drew the couple to Kansas is unknown. Manhattan City sits on the Kansas and Big Blue Rivers and was originally settled in 1855 by New England Free-Staters. These were men who traveled to the Territory of Kansas in opposition of the Nebraska–Kansas Act, which would allow the population of the Territory of Kansas to decide whether slavery would be legal. The Free-Staters were opposed to this act and Manhattan City would remain a "free state."

Since New York is not part of New England, it is doubtful he removed his family there as a member of the coalition of "Free-Staters," but rather as an opportunity to be part of the land boom.

As we can see from the census for 1870, Henry N. Elliott went from farming to being employed as a real estate agent:

> Elliott, H. Newton, 33, real estate agent, real estate value, $1,800; personal estate, $350.00, b. New York
> Elliott, Susan, 29, Keeping house, b. New York
> Elliott, Clara, 8, at school, b. New York
> Elliott, Mary, 1, b. Kansas

I have not been able to locate any newspaper articles regarding his time in Manhattan City or surrounding areas. However, by 1875, the Elliott family were back in Greene, Chenango, New York.[1056] Whether Henry's aspirations didn't quite "pan-out" in his career as a real estate agent, or whether he was successful, again, has not been discovered. Henry Elliott is back to farming and the family has grown to include a son, Howard B. Elliott, who was born during their time in Kansas.

In 1880 they are still in Greene, New York, and the family has grown to include Clara (18), Mary H. (11), Howard B. (8), Susie E. (5), and Elsie G. (2).

---

1052 *New York U.S. Census Substitutes Index 1790–1890;* 434. Ancestry.

1053 Vol: 26; Affiliate Publication Number: M1953; GS Film Number: 20; Record Number: 7834. Ancestry.

1054 I have not been able to locate the Benson family in 1860.

1055 District: 2; Line: 2; New York State Census 1865. Ancestry.

1056 1875 *New York State Census*, Greene, Chenango, New York; ED: 01; Sheet: 21; Household: 214. New York State Archives.

As it has been stated before, the 1890 census is not available, and the 1892 special census for New York does not list the family of Henry N. Elliott. The reason that the family cannot be found is that they are now living in Los Angeles, California. The earliest record is from the *California Great Registers, 1850–1920.*[1057] The earliest record found is for May 4, 1888. Henry's age is given as "fifty-one," born "New York," living at 3 Myrtle Street, and he is an "insurance agent."

On September 11,1890, he is living on Reservoir Street and is employed as an "agent," and the last record found is for August 2,1892, 2 Reservoir Street, age 55, 5′ 11 ½″, light complexion, blue eyes, and light brown hair; born in New York, employed as a land agent.

Based on the voting registration records, Henry was trying his hand at selling insurance as well as selling land. Many immigrants began to move to California and towns began to "spring up;" from January 1887–July 1889 there were over sixty towns that were "plotted."[1058]

By the 1900 census the family is now living at 2136 Reservoir Street in Los Angeles:[1059]

Elliott, Henry N., b. June 1837, 62, m. 69 yrs., carpenter, b. New York
Elliott, Susan J., wife, Sep. 1840, 59, 5 children b., 5 children living, b. New York
Elliott, Mary H., daughter, b. Oct. 1869, 30, stenographer, b. Kansas
Gates, Albert C., son-in-law, b. Feb. 1875, 25, m. 2 yrs., b. Indiana
Gates, Susie E., daughter, b. Nov. 1874, 25, 1 child born, 1 living, b. Illinois
Gates, Ruth E., granddaughter, b. Feb. 1899, 1, b. California

Once again, Henry's occupation has changed. Perhaps he was now building houses during the boom.

In 1910 their daughter Elsie and her husband, Oliver Charlton, were living with her parents on Reservoir Street. The young couple had been married for ten years at the time of the census and they had no children.[1060]

There are no records for the Elliotts until 1918 when Henry Newton Elliott died on March 23rd at the age of "80 years." While there is no explanation of the cause of his death in this very brief mention in the newspaper notice, it is possible his death was due to the Spanish Flu epidemic. His obituary and funeral notice appeared in the *Los Angeles Evening Express:*

> Elliott. H. N., 2144 Reservoir Street, on March 21, H. N. Elliott, aged 80 years, beloved husband of Susan J. Elliott, father of Mrs. B. W. Peirce [sic] and Mrs. S. G. Bailie of Los Angeles, H. B. Elliott of San Diego, Mrs. A. C. Gates of Santa Barbara, and Mrs. O.A. Charlton of Berkeley. Funeral services Saturday. 1:30 p.m. at chapel of Bresee Brothers.

---

1057 FamilySearch. Each registration is recorded as Henry N. Elliott having been born in New York.

1058 This reference may also have meant "platted," whereby the property is developed and divided into parcels.

1059 1900 *Los Angles, Los Angeles, California*; Page: 8; ED: 8; 2nd Ward; Precinct: Los Angeles Township; Dwelling: 120; Family: 120. Ancestry.

1060 1910 census: ED: 74; Page: 2A; 29th Precinct; Dwelling: 37; Family: 38; Ancestry.

**Henry N. Elliott**

Elliott—The funeral of Henry N. Elliott will be held at the chapel of Bresee Brothers, 855, Figueroa, Saturday at 1:30.

**Elliott.** At N. 2144 Reservoir Street

Susan J. Elliott appears on the 1920 and 1930 censuses as living alone at 2142 ½ Reservoir Street. She owns her own home and is listed as a "widow." On March 27, 1937, an obituary appeared in the *Los Angeles Times*[1061] for Susan:

**Elliott.** Mrs. Susan Jane Elliott, beloved mother of Mrs. Clara Pierce and Mrs. Mary Bailie of Los Angeles, Mrs. Susie Gates, and Mrs. Earl Charlton of Ventura; aged 96 yrs., 6 months, and 16 days. Services 10 a.m. Monday at Pierce Brothers.

***Children of Henry Newton Elliott and Susan Jane Benson***

i. Mary Harford Elliott,[8] b. 13 Oct 1868,[1062] New York; d. 1 Dec 1953,[1063] Orange, Orange, California; m. 6 Sep 1901,[1064] Los Angeles, Los Angeles, California, Samuel Girven Bailie; b. 1872, Canada; d. 14 Jun 1947,[1065] Phoenix, Maricopa, Arizona. This couple divorced. Mary is listed as "divorced" on the 1920 census. Samuel Bailie was naturalized on May 26, 1894, per the *California Voter Registers, 1866–1898.*[1066] According to his obituary, he was an organizer of the Phoenix of the American Automobile Association and had remarried to a woman named Freda ______. However, while he calls himself a "widower" on the 1940 census, his wife (Freda) is apparently still alive, as the obituary states "survived by his wife Freda."

Samuel G. Bailie and Mary H. Elliott had two children: Everett G. Bailie (1903–1984) and Edward E. Bailie (1907–1944).

According to Mary's obituary[1067] she arrived in Los Angeles in 1887 and went to work for the "old law firm" of Jackson A. Graves, Henry O. Melveny, and James H. Shankland in the "Baker Block" on North Main Street and she remained with them until 1901. In 1915, she went to work for the Farmers and Merchants National Bank as J. A. Graves' secretary. She retired from that position in 1943. She had made her home with her son Everett Graves Bailie. She died at the age of eighty-five at the Santa Ana Sanitarium.

Mary is buried in Melrose Abbey Memorial Park, Anaheim, Orange, California. Samuel is buried in Greenwood Memorial Lawn Cemetery in Phoenix, Maricopa, Arizona.

ii. Howard Benson Elliott,[8] b. 27 May 1872,[1068] Manhattan, Riley, Kansas; d.p. unk.; m.

---

1061 Saturday morning edition, 16. Newspapers.

1062 *California Death Index.* Ancestry.

1063 *Ibid*

1064 *California, County Birth, Marriage and Death Records, 1849–1980.* Ancestry.

1065 Find-A-Grave.

1066 Los Angeles Precinct No 8, Ward 2; page 1. California State Library. Ancestry.

1067 *Los Angeles Times,* Thursday, December 3, 1953, edition; page 88. Newspapers.

1068 *U.S. Passport Applications, 1795–1925.* Ancestry.

Mercedes _______.[1069] Howard registered for the draft, where he gave his birthdate as May 27, **1876**, which would make him four years younger.[1070] He was employed as a clerk for the San Diego and Arizona Railway and was living at 4180 Conklin East, San Diego. He is not found on the 1900 or 1910 censuses. The reason comes to light in his passport application. Howard B. Elliott was living in Mexico from 1896–1914 and from 1915–1916 in lower California, Sonora, Sinalco, Tepic, and Jalisco (Mexico). He states that he is living at 4180 Conklin Avenue in East San Diego and is employed as a railroad clerk.

In his physical attributes he was 5′ 7 ½″ tall, had blue eyes and blonde hair; he had a scar high on his forehead; his right wrist was enlarged, and his left leg injured.

I have been unsuccessful in locating any further information on Howard Elliott.

iii. Susie E. Elliott,[8] b. 23 Nov 1874,[1071] Illinois; d. 17 Apr 1967, Ventura, Ventura, California;[1072]m. on/about 20 April 1898, Los Angeles, California, Albert Cassius Gates;[1073] b. 26 Feb 1874, Centerville, Wayne, Indiana;[1074] d. 31 Oct 1937, Ventura, Ventura, California;[1075] son of Laborious Gates and Maria _______.[1076]

Susie and Albert lived for a time with Susie's parents in 1900 in Los Angeles with their daughter, Ruth. By 1910 the couple was living in Ventura and owned their own home. By this time, Albert was involved in the real estate business as an agent, and each consecutive census after 1910 he is listed as a title examiner, and lastly a manager of the abstract office in 1930. The 1930 census indicates that their home is worth $15,000, which was a considerable sum, especially during the Depression.

Like most men, Albert Gates registered for the draft and was a registered voter. According to the voter registration records (and the draft record) he was dark complected, had brown hair and eyes, and was of "medium" height.

Albert died after an abdominal operation that was performed at Foster Memorial Hospital in Ventura. He had undergone a similar procedure the year prior and had never completely recovered.

According to the obituary[1077] he had come to California from Centerville, Indiana, "42 years ago and had been in the title business for 40 years."

He was a manager of the Ventura Abstract Company until it merged with the Title Insurance & Trust. Albert was also a member of the Rotary Club. He was cremated and was buried at Ivy Lawn Memorial Park.

---

1069 *U.S. WWI Draft Registration Cards, 1917–1918.* Ancestry.

1070 All males were subject to duty between the ages of 18–45 during WWI.

1071 Date of birth comes from the *U.S. Social Security Death Index, 1935–2014;* Ancestry; place of birth from the census—town and county unknown.

1072 *Ibid (SSDI).*

1073 *The Evening Express: Los Angeles, Cal., Wednesday, April 20, 1898,* edition; 8. Newspapers.

1074 Date of birth comes from *U.S. World War I Draft Registration, 1917–18.* Ancestry.

1075 Obituary notice and California Death Index, 1905–1939.

1076 1880 census for *Center Township, Wayne, Indiana;* Roll: 322; Page: 200B; ED: 066. Ancestry.

1077 *Ventura County, Star Free Press,* Monday edition, November 1, 1937; front page. Newspapers.

Susie E. Gates is found on the 1940[1078] census living at 953 E. Main Street, San Buenaventura. Her rent was $40.00 per month. The home she had lived in with her husband, Albert, was likely sold and the monies from that sale may have gone into her estate. For the prior year (1939) her income was $450.00 per annum. This income may have been from an annuity as the census indicates it came from another source (other than "wages").

From the city directories of Ventura County 1957–1961, Susie was living at 445 Coronado in Ventura. No other records could be found.

Susie E. Elliott Gates died April 17, 1967, and is buried with her husband, Albert, in Ivy Lawn Memorial Park in Ventura. She was ninety-three years old. Their children were Ruth E., Richard A., Marjorie, and Oliver P. (1908–1981).

iv. Elsie Gertrude Elliott,[8] b. 25 Apr 1878, Greene, Chenango, New York;[1079] d. 1 Dec 1974, Ventura, Ventura, California;[1080] m. July __ 1899, Los Angeles, Los Angeles, California, Oliver Adair Charlton;[1081] b. Mar 1874, Iowa;[1082] d. 25 Aug 1942, Ventura, Ventura, California; son of George B. Charlton and Mary E. ______.

Prior to his marriage to Elsie Elliott, Oliver Adair Charlton enlisted in the Spanish–American War, and he was a corporal in Company D, 7th California Infantry Volunteers. From the original documents posted online, this regiment was never called up to serve in the Philippines and the men were sorely disappointed. The regiment remained inactive in San Francisco until "October 13, 1898," when they "were ordered to Los Angeles and were stationed at Camp Pratt until December 2, 1898, when they were mustered out of the United States Service."[1083]

The following year (in July) Oliver and Elsie were married. They likely moved in with Oliver's parents as on the 9th day of June 1900, the Charlton family were enumerated in San Jose Township, Los Angeles, California.[1084] The census also states that Elsie had one child, but none were living. By 1910,[1085] this couple were living with Elsie's parents in Los Angeles. There is not much information on this couple in the intervening years beyond the census reports. As was required, Oliver registered for the draft in 1917 and at that time they were living at 2121 Woolsey Street, Berkeley, Alameda, California.[1086] He was employed as a supervisor of railroad signals for the Southern Pacific Railroad.

---

1078 1940 Census, San Buenaventura, Ventura, California; Roll: M-t0627-00365; Page: 2A; ED: 56–44. Ancestry.

1079 *U.S. Social Security Applications and Claims Index, 1936–2007.* Ancestry.

1080 *California, Death Index, 1940–1997; Ibid.*

1081 *Los Angeles Daily Times,* Thursday, July 6, 1899 edition; 14; the date of marriage record that is available via Ancestry for California is illegible, although it appears to read July 6.

1082 *U.S. World War I Draft Registration Cards, 1917–1918.* NARA via Ancestry.

1083 www.militarymuseum.org.

1084 1900 census, *San Jose, Los Angeles, California.* ED:0126; FHL Microfilm: 1240092; Sheet: 3; Dwelling: 52; Family: 52. George Charlton is listed as a fruit grower. Ancestry.

1085 1910 census, *Los Angeles Assembly District: 74, Los Angeles, California;* Roll: T624_84; Sheet: 2A; ED: 0074; FHL: 1374097; Dwelling: 57; Family: 38. Ancestry.

1086 This home still stands today and recently sold for $2,450,000. Original features of this home are not evident, other than perhaps the exterior.

They continued to live on Woolsey Street as that is where they were enumerated in 1920, with a boarder by the name of Crittenden L. Woolsey, age 29. He was also a railroad worker in "railroad supplies."

The couple moved again, this time to Tulare City, Tulare, California. They were living on Southern Pacific Tracks in 1930. This may have been housing near the railroad depot in Tulare. Oliver Charlton was now sixty-five and still employed as a signal supervisor. Elsie is employed as a substitute teacher.

The *U.S. City Directories, 1822–1995* for California continues to show that the family is residing in Tulare, Visalia, and Ventura throughout the 1930s.

Throughout most of their marriage this couple rented the homes in which they lived, but by 1940[1087] they were living at 71 Laurel Street, Ventura, and are listed as owning their own home. The home was valued at $3,500. Oliver is age "66" and employed as a "trainman." Elsie is not designated with an occupation.

On 25 August 1942 Oliver Charlton died at the age of sixty-eight. His obituary appeared in the Ventura County *Star Free Press:*[1088]

> **Oliver Charlton Dies At Local Hospital**
> Oliver Adair Charlton, 68, died this morning at a local hospital following a brief illness. A veteran of the Spanish-American war, he had lived in Ventura for six and a half years. The family residence is at 71 N. Laurel Street. Mr. Charlton was a former signal supervisor, for the Southern Pacific railway at Tulare. He leaves his widow Elsie G. Charlton of Ventura, and a brother Robert Charlton of New York. Private funeral services will be conducted from Pierce Brothers mortuary, Los Angeles by internment at Rosedale cemetery.

As has been mentioned on several occasions in this work, finding anything that would give a clearer picture on the personality of our female ancestors is difficult, however, I happened upon a letter that Elsie wrote to the *Tulare Advance-Register* (next page).[1089]

Her letter is bright and cheery, and from it we learn that she was involved with the Girl Scouts but also was a member of a church that she was quite involved in, as well as preferring the "small-town" news and values.

After Oliver's death, Elsie lived at various locations; in 1956–1962 she lived at 85 S. Santa Cruz Street in Ventura; in 1965 and 1966 she lived at H115 S. Santa Rosa Street in Ojai.[1090]

Elsie Gertrude (Elliott) Charlton died December 1, 1974, and is buried with her husband in the Charlton family plot in the Angelus Rosedale Cemetery. An obituary has not been located.

There were no children from this marriage.

---

1087 1940 census; *San Buenaventura, Ventura, California;* Roll: M-t0627-00365; Sheet: 1B; ED: 56-44. Ancestry.

1088 Tuesday, August 25, 1942, edition. Newspapers.

1089 Saturday, March 9, 1935, edition; page 1. Newspapers. Article now in the public domain.

1090 *U.S. City Directories, California, 1822–1995*. Ancestry.

**Why I Prefer My Home Newspaper**

Letters From Our Readers

I came to Tulare fourteen years ago from a large city, where all I had ever known was a city daily paper. You can imagine my surprise when I, as Captain of Girl Scout Troop No. 1, went to the office of the "Register" and asked for some publicity for our Troop. I naturally supposed that I would have to pay to get our notices printed in the paper but, instead, I found that the office force made me feel that we were welcome to bring in anything to be printed that would be of help to the Troop.

Later, when I became engaged in Church activities, I found the same courteous treatment was accorded me whenever we needed any publicity. I know that it is not to any one church or organization that this help is given, but that all are treated alike. Can you think of any better way for a paper to serve a community than to help them to learn of the better things of life? When there are better things to be read one can always count on reading them in the Tulare Times and Advance-Register.

There are many other reasons too numerous to mention as to why I prefer my "Home Newspaper," but I must mention one or two. The lack of sensational headlines or the featuring of the things which are not conducive to better living is one most important reason. I also appreciate the local advertising, for by consistent reading of the advertisements I am enabled to buy to better advantage. Last but not least I am now able to find much amusement in "10 years." If I live long enough I expect to be equally amused with the "20-30 years."

Long may the Tulare Times and Advance-Register live!

Yours very truly,

ELSIE G. CHARLTON, 245 North J St., Tulare, Cal.

### *29. ii. Henry N. Benson*[7][1091] *(aka Horace Benson, Niles Horace Benson) (Clarissa Kelsey,*[6] *Almira Scoville,*[5] *Ithamar,*[4] *Timothy,*[3] *Stephen,*[2] *Stephen,*[1] *Arthur)*

Born 28 September 1841, Greene, Chenango, New York;[1092] died 4 September 1930, York, York, Nebraska; buried Greenwood Cemetery;[1093] married circa 1866, Olive I. Stowell; born 22 July 1844, New York; died 9 March 1925, York, York, Nebraska; daughter of Sherman Stowell and Miranda Woodruff.[1094]

Henry enlisted to serve in the Civil War, as his father and brother Isaac had done. His enlisted record from the *New York Town Clerk's Registers of Men who Served in the Civil War ca. 1861–1865* records his name as "Henry N. Benson." He enlisted at Triangle, Broome, New York, as a private in the 27th Regiment, Company C. During his time with this regiment, he was involved in the battles of Bull Run, Gaines Hill, South Mountain, and two battles at Fredericksburg. He was discharged from service May 31, 1863.[1095]

Henry must have gone back home to his family and continued farming. However, Henry re-enlisted on August 16, 1864, at Binghamton in the 1st Veterans Calvary, Company M as a

1091 I will use the name Henry N. unless a specific record states otherwise.

1092 Date of birth comes from *Records of Soldiers & Officers in Military Service*. Ancestry.

1093 Death information comes from: Find A Grave.

1094 Birth, death, and parents' names comes from Find A Grave. Note that Henry and Olive's son's name is "Sherman."

1095 Collection: (N-AR) 13774; Box: Number 4; Roll: 3. Ancestry.

quartermaster. In September he was promoted to sergeant and was discharged from service on June 8, 1865.[1096] Henry's physical attributes are given as 5′ 8″ tall with blue eyes, light hair, and fair complexion.

After the war, Henry goes back to his parents' home in Triangle. He appears on the 1865 state census as "Horace N. Benson."[1097] Between 1865–1866 Henry married a hometown girl by the name of Olive Stowell.[1098] This couple did not remain in New York long as by the 1870 census they are living in Waverly, Bremer, Iowa.

When the Bensons removed to Waverly, the population was approximately 2,300 people. The town had first been settled in 1850 and, because of the exceptional waterpower, the town grew to importance with many flour mills and sawmills. Waverly was chosen as the county seat because of its commercial position and the railroad facilities.[1099]

The profile of the family for the 1870[1100] census reads as follows:

> Benson, Henry M.[sic], 27, Produce Broker, personal estate: $500, b. New York
> Benson, Olive, 24, keeping house, b. New York
> Benson, Sherman, 3, b. New York
> Stowell, Jerry W., 28, cooper, b. New York.

There were four wards in Waverly—Ward one being the smallest with eighty-eight families. Within this ward were two men occupied as produce brokers, one being Henry Benson and the other a Mr. Sprague. Ward three had a produce buyer and a produce dealer. Whether Henry Benson was successful in this endeavor is unknown.

By 1880 the family was living in Nebraska. We find the answer to when they arrived there in Henry's obituary. It states that the family "left Iowa and settled in Nebraska in 1871." According to the Bureau of Land Management Henry applied for a homestead in York County in 1879.[1101]

> Land office of Lincoln Nebraska Act of Congress approved May 20, 1862, to secure Homesteads to actual settlers as the public domain and the acts supplemental thereto the claim of Henry N. Benson northeast quarter of section thirty in township, eleven north of range, three west in the district of lands subject to sale at Lincoln Nebraska containing one-hundred and sixty acres.

The census for 1880 shows that Henry Benson is now occupied as a farmer. In the household is his wife, Olive, son, Sherman, age 13 and who is attending school, and daughter, Alice, 7, who was born in Nebraska.

---

1096 *Ibid.*

1097 *N.Y. U.S. State Census, 1865*—Triangle. Line: 39; Page: 14.

1098 *Ibid*, Line: 34; Page: 31.

1099 https://www.Bremercountyiowa.gov.

1100 1870 census, *Waverly, Ward 1, Bremer, Iowa;* Roll: M593_378; Page: 333B; Dwelling: 45; Family: 45; Line: 12. Ancestry.

1101 Homestead Certificate: 78071; Application: 7376. The location of the homestead is listed as 011N-003W. glorecords.blm.gov.

The 1890 *Veterans Schedules*[1102] indicate Henry N. Benson as living in Lockridge Township, York, Nebraska. He served for "2 years, 11 months, 22 days." The record also indicates that he had a "chronic inability(?)."[1103] It is not explained in the document what this means. Almost no soldier came away from the war unscathed in some shape or form.

I have not been able to locate Henry or Olive Benson in 1900. Their son, Sherman, and his family are living in Bradshaw, Nebraska, but the parents are not living with them. Neither are they in Lockridge or anywhere else in Nebraska that I can find. However, they are in Bradshaw in 1910[1104] living on their own. At this point, the couple had been married for forty-four years and owned their home "free and clear." Henry is not employed but living on his "own income."

The 1920 census records them in "Bradshaw Village," and all information is the same as the prior census.

Olive Benson died March 9, 1925, in York, Nebraska. The following obituary comes from *The Bradshaw Monitor:*[1105]

> **Mrs. H. N. Benson**
> Many people in this vicinity were saddened Monday morning when word reached that Mrs. HN Benson, a former resident of this place, passed away at the home with her daughter, Mrs. C.H. Kolling [of] York. Because of failing health, the deceased with her husband moved from here to York last fall, and while the change seemed beneficial for a time, yet it did not prove permanent, and for a few weeks she suffered considerable the final summons coming to her at 4 o'clock Monday morning at the advanced age of more than 80 years. Besides her husband, she leaves to mourn, one son Sherman, and one daughter Mrs. Chris Kolling both of York, besides other relatives, and many friends. Burial took place in York, Tuesday.

She is buried in Greenwood Cemetery in York.

Henry lived long enough to be enumerated on the 1930[1106] census (taken on April 4th) and was recorded in York. Living with him was an R. E. Stevens, age 70—a widow. She is listed as a lodger and housekeeper. Henry's address was 815 East Avenue.

On September 4, 1930, Henry N. Benson died at the age of eighty-nine. Once again, *The Bradshaw Monitor* published the obituary:

---

1102 The National Archives at Washington, D.C.; Washington, D.C.; *Special Schedules of the Eleventh Census (1890) Enumerating Union Veterans and Widows of Union Veterans of the Civil War*; Series Number: *M123*; Record Group Title: *Records of the Department of Veterans Affairs*; Record Group Number: *15*; Census Year: *1890*; Page: 1; ED: 92. Ancestry.

1103 The notation for the veteran above Henry states: "chronic dissabillety[sic], yet for Henry the word appears to be "inabillety" [sic].

1104 1910 census, *Bradshaw, York, Nebraska;* Roll: T624_857; Page: 4A; ED: 0195; FHL microfilm: 1374870; Dwelling: 77; Family: 77.

1105 Thursday, March 12, 1925, edition, 1. Newspapers.

1106 *1930*; Census Place: *York, York, Nebraska*; Page: 3B; Enumeration District: 0027; FHL microfilm: 2341030. Dwelling: 76; Family: 86. Ancestry.

**Henry N. Benson Passes Away at His Home Today**

Henry N. Benson, 89, one of the earliest pioneers of York County and a veteran of the Civil War, died at his home, 815 East Ave., this morning at 8:30 o'clock following an illness of several days. He had been in failing health for several years.

Mr. Benson was born in the state of New York and enlisted with the 27th New York Volunteers at the outbreak of the Civil War. At the end of his two-year term, he reenlisted with the 1st Calvary Regiment and served the unit until the close of the War.

In 1871, Mr. Benson and his family moved to York County and settle on one of the early homesteads near Bradshaw. Later he retired and moved to York, but soon moved back to the village of Bradshaw to be nearer his land interests. A few years ago, Mr. and Mrs. Benson returned to York to make their home. Mrs. Benson died about five years ago. He is survived by one daughter, Mr. C. H. Kolling and one son, Sherman Benson, both of York and four grandchildren.

Burial will be at Greenwood Cemetery Friday morning at ten o'clock—*York Daily News Times,* Thursday, September 4, 1930.

***The Children of Henry N. Benson and Olive I. Stowell***

a.i. Sherman S. Benson,[8] b. 29 Jun 1867, New York; d. 6 Oct 1940, York, York, Nebraska; m. 11 Dec 1895, Sophie Kolling, York County, Nebraska; b. 13 Feb 1871, Germany; d. 13 Jul 1962, York, York, Nebraska; daughter of Christian Kolling and Sophie Bremer.[1107] They had a daughter, Olive, b. Nov 1896 and a son, Howard, b. Mar 1899.[1108]

b. ii. Alice M. Benson,[8] b. 7 Feb 1873, York, York, Nebraska; d. 24 Aug 1949, York, York, Nebraska; m. 27 Apr 1898, Christian H. Kolling, York County, Nebraska; b. 26 Apr 1868, Hanover, Region Hanover, Lower Saxony, Germany; d. 9 Aug 1949, York, York, Nebraska; son of Christian Kolling and Sophie Bremer. They had three children: Gretta Kolling (1899–), Henry B. Kolling (1902–1994), and Delia H. Kolling (1908–1984).[1109]

## *30. ii. Frank Flint [7](Melissa Kelsey,[6] Almira Scoville Kelsey,[5] Ithamar,[4] Timothy,[3] Stephen,[2] Stephen,[1] Arthur)*

Born 11 August 1857, Maine, Broome, New York;[1110] died 4 August 1931, Mead Farm, Jefferson Township, Spink, South Dakota; buried Athol Cemetery, Spink, South Dakota;[1111] married 2 December 1882, Choconut Center, Broome, New York, Althia Almeda Hardy,[1112]

1107 Information on Sherman Benson and Sophie Kolling comes from Find A Grave; *Nebraska Marriage Records, 1855–1908;* Ancestry.

1108 Months and year of births come from the 1900 census. Ancestry.

1109 See footnote 1102.

1110 Melissa Flint Bible (herein Flint Bible). DLH records.

1111 Death Certificate and cemetery records.

1112 Flint Bible.

born 27 August 1863 (or 1865), Broome, New York;[1113] died 16 August 1929, Redfield, Spink, South Dakota;[1114] daughter of John Augustus Hardy (1836–1918) and Elizabeth Amy Moak (1843–1911).

This couple removed to Iowa sometime after the birth of their first daughter (Laura) in 1884 as their second child (Elizabeth) was born in Garner, Iowa, on 24 September 1886.[1115]

They were in Hancock, Iowa, by the time of the 1895 census.[1116] At the time of this census, they were residing in Garner Corporation, Hancock, Iowa.

While the family was in Iowa, they moved several times per the census reports. In 1900[1117] they were living in Ell Township,[1118] in the county of Hancock. Frank Flint owned the farm, although he was still paying the mortgage on it. The household was a large one, which we can see here:

Flint, Frank, head, b. Aug. 1860, 40, b. NY, farmer, owns
Flint, Althia, wife, b. Aug. 1866, 33, m. 18 yrs., 7 children born, 6 living, b. NY
Flint, Laura, daughter, b. Apr 1884, 16, single, b. NY, at school
Flint, Lizzie, daughter, b. Sep 1886, 13, single, b. Iowa, at school
Flint, May, daughter, b. May 1899, 11, single, b. Iowa, at school
Flint, Nettie, daughter, b. Nov. 1895, 4, single, b. Iowa, at school
Flint, Fred, son, b. May 1898, 2, single, b. Iowa
Flint, Carrie,[1119] daughter, b. June 1900, b. Iowa
Garlow, Melissa, mother, b. Feb. 1833, widow, b. NY

The family was in Hancock, Iowa, on the 1905 census, however, there are no images available on Ancestry. By 1910 they were in Madison Township, Hancock, Iowa.[1120] At this time Frank Flint is renting the house that they live in and is still listed as a farmer. The only one who is not in the household is daughter Laura Flint, who had married and set up housekeeping with her husband.

In 1911 the family was in Forest City, Winnebago, Iowa.[1121]

After some thirty-one years in Iowa, the Flints removed to Athol,[1122] Spink, South Dakota,

1113 *Ibid*, the date is illegible—could be 1863 or 1865.

1114 Monnier, Blanche, compiler, *The Flint Family History* (self-published, 1987).

1115 The family is not listed on the 1885 Iowa state census, so it is likely there were still in New York.

1116 *Iowa, U.S., State Census, 1895*. Ancestry.

1117 1900 Census Place: *Ell, Hancock, Iowa*; Page: 13; ED: 0116; FHL: 1240434; Dwelling: 233; Family: 232. Ancestry.

1118 Ell Township was organized in 1879 and was named after a pioneer settler, Sebastian Ell. https://en.wikipedia.org/wiki/Ell_Township,_Hancock_County,_Iowa

1119 Carrie—is this a nickname for Susie Camilla Flint?

1120 1910; Census Place: *Madison, Hancock, Iowa*; Roll: T624_393; Page: 16B; Enumeration District: 0135; FHL microfilm: 1374406. Ancestry

1121 Forest City is in both Hancock and Winnebago counties, Iowa.

1122 As of 2018, Athol had a population of 67 persons.

in the winter of 1915.[1123] Athol was originally called Myrtle City for Myrtle Taylor, the child of an early settler. In 1881 the name was changed when the Chicago and Northwestern Railroad came through the area and it was named after Athol, Massachusetts.[1124] Athol was and is an extremely rural area.

The following year, tragic news came to the family that their eldest child, Laura Edna Gilbert, had died four days after giving birth to a son, Russell, on November 20, 1918. The child died a day after the mother and they are buried together in Ell, Iowa. Whether the Flint family were able to attend the funeral is unknown but it is doubtful as the trip would be approximately 400 miles one way. Farmers couldn't just drop everything and make a journey such as that.

In 1920[1125] the census shows us that the Flints had moved again, this time to Pioneer Township, Faulk, South Dakota. Faulk County is "located on the east side of the divide between the waters of James and Missouri Rivers."[1126] The family lived in what was known as "Section 11" of Pioneer Township. The household consisted of Frank and Althia, May, Nettie (a teacher at a rural school), Fred, Susie C., and Althia. Fred Flint is also listed as a farmer and was likely assisting his father with the farm.

South Dakota had a state census for 1925, but it does not indicate where they were living during this time. Fred and Althia's information indicates that their marriage year was 1885 and that they were "Congregationalists."

Althia Flint's health began to decline sometime between 1924 and 1929.[1127] Her obituary appeared in the *Forest City* (Iowa) newspaper:[1128]

**MRS. FRANK FLINT PASSES AWAY HERE THURSDAY**

Many homes were saddened when Mrs. Frank Flint of Athol suddenly passed away at the home of her daughter, Mrs. Earl Prindle, of Redfield, where she had been visiting for a few days. The end came very unexpectedly at 1:15 o'clock Friday morning, Aug. 16, caused by an embolism.

Funeral services were conducted Sunday afternoon, Aug. 18, at the Congregational church at Athol, and were in charge of the Rev. R.E. Rich of Oelrichs, S.D., friend of the family. Floral offerings were numerous and beautiful. Special music was furnished by a quartette, Mr. and Mrs. A.D. Coleman, Mrs. John Knapton and Rev. R.E. Rich. She was borne to her last resting place by her son and five sons-in-law, and tenderly laid to rest in the Athol cemetery.

Althia Almeda Hardy, a daughter of Mr. and Mrs. J.A. Hardy, was born Aug. 17, 1865, in Broome County, New York, where she grew to womanhood. She had

1123 *Garner Signal (Iowa). Forest City* obituary for Althia Flint. DLH records.

1124 https://en.wikipedia.org/wiki/Athol,_South_Dakota.

1125 1920; Census Place: *Pioneer Township, Faulk, South Dakota;* Roll: T625_1719; Page: 1A; ED: 141; Image: 74; Dwelling: 9; Family: 9, Ancestry.

1126 Ellis, Captain C. H., *History of Faulk County, South Dakota,* 23; (1909).

1127 DLH records.

1128 *Ibid.* The obituary is copied as it originally appeared.

attained the age of 63 years, 11 months, and 20 days at the time of her death.

On December 2, 1882, she was united in marriage with Frank Flint. In 1885 they moved to Garner, Iowa, later moving to Forest City, Iowa. In the winter of 1915, the family moved to South Dakota and located on a farm near Athol. Mr. and Mrs. Flint had eight children, two having preceded their mother in death, an infant son, and one daughter, Mrs. Laura Gilbert, who passed away in 1918.

Mrs. Flint was a member of the Methodist Episcopal church of Garner, Iowa. She was a wonderful Christian character, a kind, faithful, loving wife, a devoted mother, and a true friend, ministering to the needs of many. Surviving to mourn her departure are her grieving husband, five daughters, Mrs. Frank Mead, Mrs. Roy Brown, Mrs. Douglas Steward and Miss Nettie Flint, all of Athol, and Mrs. Earl Prindle of this city: and one son, Fred Flint, also of Redfield. There are 15 grandchildren, two sisters, and one brother, Mrs. Stephen Boyer of Sandgrudo, Alberta, Canada, Mrs. Hattie Brigham and Fred Hardy of Binghamton, New York and an aged uncle, James Moak of Perham, Minn., besides many other relatives and a host of friends.

Those from away who attended the funeral were James Gilbert and two sons, Dean and Raymond of Algona, Iowa. The bereaved family have the sympathy of their friends here in their sorrow.

After Althia's death, Frank Flint is living with his daughter Elizabeth "Lizzie" and his son-in-law, Frank Mead, in 1930[1129] in Athol, as well as Nettie Flint—daughter of Frank and the sister of Elizabeth.

On August 4, 1931, Frank Flint suffered a stroke and died. Frank was found in the barn by his family. His obituary:[1130]

**Mr. Frank Flint Dies At Athol**

*Was Found in Barn Suffering Stroke of Paralysis—Was Native of New York*

Friends were pained to learn of the sudden death of Frank Flint well known in and about Athol. Mr. Flint was stricken with paralysis while he was out in the barn and was found by the members of his family. Dr. Potter of Redfield was immediately summoned, but advancing years were to claim their toll and death came.

Frank Flint, son of Mr. and Mrs. Abner Flint, was born August 11, 1857, in New York State and grew to manhood and passed away, August 4, 1931, at the home of his daughter, Mrs. Frank Mead near Athol, at the age of seventy-four years. On December 2, 1882, he was united in marriage to Aletha Hardy, also of New York state. In 1885 they moved to Garner, Iowa, later living in Forest City. In the winter of 1915, they moved to South Dakota locating on a farm near Athol.

1129 1930 census, *Athol, Spink, South Dakota*; Page: 2A; ED: 0003; FHL: 2341964; Dwelling: 19; Family: 19. Ancestry.

1130 DLH records. Source unknown.

Mr. Flint leaves to cherish his memory five daughters, Mrs. Frank Mead, Mrs. Roy Brown and Miss Nettie Flint of Athol, Mrs. Earl Prindle of Redfield, and Mrs. Douglas Stewart of Chelsea, and one son Fred Flint of Redfield.

Mr. Flint was a devoted father and a kindly neighbor. He will be missed by a large circle of his friends and neighbors.

Frank Flint is buried in Athol Cemetery, Athol, Spink, South Dakota.

While there hasn't been much in the way of newspaper articles or historical information on the towns where the Flint family lived, they were certainly well thought of by family, friends, and neighbors.[1131]

L-R: Melissa Flint Garlow, Frank Flint, Laura Flint Gilbert, and grandchild?

Althia Hardy Flint

### *Children of Frank Flint and Althia Hardy*

i. Laura Edna Flint,[8] b. 10 Apr 1884, Broome, New York; d. 24 Nov 1918, Ell Township, Hancock, Iowa; m. 21 Feb 1906, Cummins Farm, Hancock, Iowa, James Alfred Gilbert;[1132] b. 5 Nov 1881, Monroe, Green, Wisconsin; d. 10 Nov 1956, Bethany, Harrison, Missouri;[1133] son of Peter Gilbert and Amy

Laura Flint Gilbert and family. Photo courtesy of Ryan Bridges.

1131 Photos courtesy of Deborah L. Horzen.

1132 *Iowa Marriage Records, 1880–1940.* Ancestry.

1133 Find A Grave.

Kelly.[1134] He m. (2) Emma Marie Badker. Children of Laura Flint and James Gilbert: Eva, Dean, Raymond, Russell.

ii. Elizabeth (Lizzie) Amy Flint,[8] b. 24 Sep 1886, Garner, Hancock, Iowa; d. 8 Apr 1975, Colonial Acres Nursing Home, Rock Falls, Whiteside, Illinois; bur. Elm Lawn Cemetery, Princeton, Bureaus, Illinois; m. 10 Jun 1912, Forest City, Winnebago, Iowa, Frank Monroe Mead; b. 31 Dec 1885, Ohio, Bureau, Illinois; d. Jun 1970, Bureau, Illinois; son of Chester Benton Mead and Anna Rachel Hubbard.[1135] Children of Elizabeth Flint and Frank Mead: Blanche R. Mead Monnier, Morris, Lorran, Velma, Warren.

iii. Ida May Flint,[8] b. 27 May 1889, Garner, Hancock, Iowa; d. 19 Jan 1932, "at home northwest of Athol,"[1136] Spink, South Dakota; m. 12 Feb 1924, Aberdeen, Brown, South Dakota, Roy William Brown; b. 1 Mar 1888, Athol, Spink, South Dakota;[1137] d. 24 Aug 1972, Athol, Spink, South Dakota;[1138] son of Elias Brown and Emma Hudson.[1139] Children of Ida May Flint and Roy Brown: Laura Katherine Brown Christianson, Frank Elias Brown.

iv. Baby Boy Flint,[8] b. 20 Jul 1893, Hancock, Iowa; d. 30 Jul 1893 Garner, Hancock, Iowa; bur. Concord Cemetery, Garner, Hancock, Iowa.[1140]

v. Nettie Melissa Flint,[8] b. 20 Nov 1894, near Garner, Ell Township, Hancock, Iowa;[1141] d. 1 Oct 1985, Nora Springs, Floyd, Iowa, bur. Park Cemetery, Nora Springs, Floyd, Iowa; m. 3 Mar 1951, Wesleyan Methodist parsonage, Redfield, Spink, South Dakota, Paul Fuller; b. 16 Oct 1897; d. 1 Aug 1966;[1142] probable son of Eugene Fuller and Elizabeth Fuller.[1143] Nettie had been a teacher and she was fifty-seven years old at her first marriage. She was also an active member of the Wesleyan Church in Rudd, Iowa. This was a second marriage for Paul Fuller—his first wife was Ocea May Piper. No issue from this marriage.

vi. Fred Abner Flint,[8] b. 28 May 1898,[1144] Ell Township, Hancock, Iowa; d. 20 Jan 1994, James Valley Healthcare Center, Redfield, Spink, South Dakota;[1145] bur. Greenlawn

---

1134 *Missouri Death Certificates, 1910–1962.* Ancestry.

1135 Find A Grave and DLH records.

1136 DLH records.

1137 *South Dakota Birth Index, 1856–1918;* Ancestry.

1138 Find A Grave.

1139 *Ibid.*

1140 Slingerland, Margaret and Moak, Grace, compilers, *Jacob Moak of New Scotland and His Descendants 1720–1991,* Albany, New York, (1990), 26, date of birth only. Melissa (Flint) Garlow Bible, month and year of death only. DLH records.

1141 Melissa (Flint) Garlow Bible. *Ibid.*

1142 Find A Grave.

1143 1900 census for Ulster, Floyd, Iowa; ED: 0098; FHL: 1240431. Ancestry.

1144 Melissa (Flint) Garlow Bible. DLH records: *U.S. WWII Draft Cards Young Men, 1940–1947.* Ancestry.

1145 Find A Grave and DLH records.

Cemetery, Redfield, Spink, South Dakota; m. 19 Aug 1922, South Dakota, Beryl Dorothy Kegler; b. 28 May 1901, Faulk, South Dakota; d. 21 Nov 2002, Redfield, Spink, South Dakota; bur. Greenlawn Cemetery, Redfield, Spink, South Dakota; daughter of George Kegler and Meeta Janes.[1146]

Fred was a member of the United Methodist Church in Redfield and was the secretary-treasurer for many years. Known children of Fred Flint and Beryl Kegler: Keith Flint and Marlin Flint.

vii. Susie Camilla Flint,[8] b. 4 Jun 1900, Ell Township, Hancock, Iowa; d. 15 Aug 1975, James Valley Nursing Home, Redfield, Spink, South Dakota; m. 6 Sep 1924 Aberdeen, Brown, South Dakota,[1147] Earl William Prindle, b. 1897, Iowa; d. 1980, place unknown. Children of Earl William Prindle and Susie Camilla Flint: Dayle Prindle (female), Dwayne Prindle, Doris Prindle, Dorinne Prindle.[1148]

viii. Althia Almeda Flint,[8] b. 29 Sep 1903, Ell Township, Hancock, Iowa;[1149] d. 8 Aug 1989, Americana Healthcare Center, Aberdeen, Brown, South Dakota; bur. Richland Wesleyan Church Cemetery, Mina, Edmonds, South Dakota; m. 23 Jun 1926, Aberdeen, Brown, South Dakota,[1150] Orville A. Douglas Steward, b. 11 Sep 1900, Cedar County, Missouri; d. 30 Mar 1980, Chelsea, Faulk, South Dakota; son of Walter Steward and Ella Leedy.[1151] Althia Flint Steward was a member of the Northville Wesleyan Church for thirty-eight years until its closing. She also taught in rural schools in Faulk County, South Dakota.[1152]

## *31. Charles Franklin Kelsey[7] (Philo Kelsey,[6] Almira Scoville,[5] Ithamar,[4] Timothy,[3] Stephen,[2] Stephen,[1] Arthur)*

Born 2 November 1860, Broome, New York; died 19 February 1919, New York; bur. Evergreen Cemetery, Spencer, Tioga, New York; married (1) 30 April 1882, Dora Seeley; (2) about 1898, Isabel Cowell.[1153]

It has been difficult to provide any anecdotal information here regarding Charles Franklin Kelsey;

1146 *Ibid.*

1147 *South Dakota Marriages, 1905–2017.* Ancestry.

1148 1940 census, *Redfield City, Spink, South Dakota.* Ancestry.

1149 Melissa (Flint) Garlow Bible.

1150 *South Dakota Marriages, 1905–2017.* Ancestry.

1151 Obituary notice for Walter Steward; *The Eldorado Springs Sun. Newspapers; Obituary Index 1940–1955.* Ancestry.

1152 DLH records.

1153 Photo courtesy of Amanda Crocker.

basically, all we have are names, dates, and places. I could not find any newspaper articles other than one real estate transfer between Charles and his wife Belle in 1901.

What we *do* know is that Charles was only four years old when his father, Philo, died during the Civil War. His memories of his father must have been very slim (other than what he was told by his mother or other relatives).

Charles was born in Spencer, New York, in 1860. At that time, the town of Spencer had 1,881 inhabitants and the downtown area (known as "The Corners") was bustling with stores and businesses.[1154] Growing up without a father must have been difficult for Charles and his brother Lew as their mother never remarried. He and his brother had to help wherever they could. In 1870 both boys are attending school and, as with most children of that time, they had to complete chores before and after school.

By 1880,[1155] the household included mother, Betsy, age 44; Charles, 19, farmer; Lewis, 17, farm hand; and Betsy's mother, Lucinda Cowles, 81.

Charles began courting a young woman by the name of Dora Seeley. Her birthplace is unknown, but per the various census records, she was living in Newfield, Tompkins, New York. One thing that Dora had in common with Charles was that she too had been raised by her mother, as her father (Charles Barber Seeley) had died (in 1864) in Andersonville Prison during the Civil War.

The couple exchanged vows on April 30, 1882. The following year, on April 18,1883, a daughter was born to them by the name of Eula Carrie Kelsey.[1156]

I am not aware of any other children born to Charles and Dora. This family was together until Dora died on August 28, 1890, in Spencer, New York. There is no record found of her cause of death.

The following year (July 20, 1891) Charles' mother, Betsey, died at the age of "56 yrs. 7 months(?) 21 days."[1157]

In the intervening years after Dora's and Betsey's deaths, we only have the 1892 *New York U.S. State census* for Spencer, New York. All this census tells us is that Charles' age is thirty-three and that he is a citizen, but it doesn't list an occupation for him. His daughter, Eula, is no longer living with him; she is now living with her maternal grandmother, Priscilla Seely, in Spencer, New York.[1158] Eula remained living with her grandmother (1900 and 1905 censuses) until her marriage to William Phillip Eaton on November 6, 1907.[1159]

Sometime in 1898, Charles remarried a woman by the name of Isabel Cowell.[1160] No official record has been located for their marriage. Isobel (who went by the name "Belle") was

---

1154 Alve, Jean, Town/Village Historian. https://tiogahistory.org.

1155 1880 census; *Spencer, Tioga, New York;* Roll: 70; Page: 23C; ED: 128; Dwelling: 92. Ancestry.

1156 This information comes from Find A Grave as well as a photo of daughter Eula and her father Charles that can be found on Ancestry.

1157 Find A Grave.

1158 *New York, U.S., State Census, 1892;* Newfield, New York; ED:03. Her name is written as "Prescilla Seely."

1159 *New York State Marriage Index, 1881–1967.* Ancestry:

1160 The projected year of marriage is based on the birth of their first child as a couple. Margaret E. Kelsey was born in 1899.

the daughter of Edward and Margaret Cowell, of Spencer, New York, and is said to have been born March 22, 1860.[1161]

The Edward Cowell family is found on the *1892 New York U.S. State Census* (page 13) in Spencer. Belle was single and thirty-two years old.

The couple shows up on the 1900[1162] census as living on Park Street. Charles is a farm laborer and owns his own property free of a mortgage. Belle and Margaret are the other members of the household.

In 1910,[1163] Charles has a change of occupation. He is now the owner of a general store in Spencer. At this point the family had grown to four—a son, Edward Charles Kelsey, was born in 1902 in Spencer.

Nothing more is known about this family until the death of Charles F. Kelsey on February 19, 1919. There is no obituary that I've been able to locate in any of the online newspaper sites.

Charles is buried in the Evergreen Cemetery in Spencer.

Belle Kelsey lived until 1935. She remained in Spencer, living with her children until they went off and married. The 1930 census shows her still living on Park Street as the head of household and she owns the home, valued at $2,000.

On July 15, 1935, Belle Kelsey passed away and was buried in Evergreen Cemetery with her husband, Charles. The Find-A-Grave website had an interesting note attached to Isabel (Belle) Cowell Kelsey. Her rug loom, on display in the Spencer Museum, was gifted to the museum by her daughter-in-law, Isabelle Zimmer Kelsey.

### *Children of Charles Franklin Kelsey and Dora Seeley*

i. Eula Carrie Kelsey,[8] b. 18 Apr 1883; d. 1 Oct 1982; bur. North Spencer Cemetery, Tioga, New York; m. 6 Nov 1907, Newfield, Tompkins, New York, William Philip Eaton (1884–1961). Children: Dora (1908), Gertrude (1910), Carl (1916), Francis (1920), and Maurice (1923).[1164]

### *Children of Charles Franklin Kelsey and Isabel (Belle) Cowell*

ii. Margaret Elizabeth Kelsey,[8] b. 23 Aug 1899, Spencer, Tioga, New York; d. 1974, Spencer, Tioga, New York; bur. North Spencer Cemetery, Tioga, New York; m. 30 Jun 1923, Spencer, Tioga, New York,[1165] James J. Swartout; b. 22 May 1898, Lopez, Sullivan, Pennsylvania; d. 25 Jul 1989; bur. North Spencer Cemetery. Margaret was a teacher and her husband, James, held various positions from farming to operating

1161 Her birth date comes from the Find A Grave website.

1162 1900 census; *Spencer, Tioga, New York;* ED: 0135; Sheet: 9; Dwelling: 2241; Family: 225; FHL:1241168. Ancestry. Note that the length of marriage (18 years) on this census is erroneous.

1163 Note: This family is also listed on the 1905 and 1915 state censuses for Spencer, New York, but I have decided not to list it here as it does not provide any additional information. 1900 census; *Spencer, Tioga, New York;* Roll: T624_1084; Page: 1B; ED: 0163; FHL: 1375097. Ancestry.

1164 All information from Find A Grave.

1165 Marriage notice; *Ithaca Journal News,* Tuesday Evening, 3 July 1923; 5; Newspapers; *Marriage Index 1800s–1999.* Ancestry. All other information comes from Find A Grave.

the Spencer Hardware store, as well as a second-hand store. He was a past master of the Spencer Grange and was a life member of the Spencer Historical Society.[1166] James and Margaret did not have any children.

iii. Charles Edward Kelsey,[8] b. 27 Feb 1902, Spencer, Tioga, New York; d. 31 Oct 1983, Spencer, Tioga, New York; bur. Evergreen Cemetery, Spencer, Tioga, New York; m. 24 Oct 1925, Spencer, Tioga, New York, Isabelle Sarah Zimmer;[1167] b. 12 Oct 1907, West Candor, Tioga, New York; d. 14 Sep 1981; Spencer, Tioga, New York; bur. Evergreen Cemetery, Spencer, Tioga, New York;[1168] daughter of George Zimmer and Sadie Foster (per marriage record).

Early in Edward Kelsey's life he was working as a farm laborer, however, by the 1930 census[1169] he is listed as a mechanic in a garage. The family were living at 129 Academy Street in Spencer Village, and they owned their own home. The family consisted of Charles Edward, Isabelle, and their daughters Helen M. and Ruth M. In 1940[1170] the family was living on Park Street in Spencer. Charles is listed as "Edward" and he is now a truck driver for the town highway department. There are now three daughters: Helen, Ruth, and Alice.

At the time of Isabelle's death in 1981, they were living on Michigan Hollow Road in Spencer. Their children: Helen Margaret Kelsey Cotton (1926–1998), Ruth Marie Kelsey Anderson (1928–1965), and Alice Marion Kelsey Vergason (1933–2019).[1171]

### 32. *Philo Lewis Kelsey*[7] *(a.k.a. Lew or Lewis) (Philo Kelsey,*[6] *Almira Scoville,*[5] *Ithamar,*[4] *Timothy,*[3] *Stephen,*[2] *Stephen,*[1] *Arthur)*

Born 22 December 1862, Broome, New York; died 14 November 1934, Van Etten, Chemung, New York; buried Canfield Cemetery, Van Etten, Chemung, New York; married 23 March 1892, Spencer, Tioga, New York, Rose Hobson, born December 1872/73, New York;[1172] died 14 July 1955, Horseheads, Chemung, New York;[1173] buried Canfield Cemetery, Van Etten, Chemung, New York; daughter of Jesse Hobson (1846–1927)[1174] and Mariah/Marie/Moira

---

1166 From James' obituary notice, *The Ithaca Journal*, Friday, July 29, 1989, edition. His date of birth comes from: *U.S. World War I Draft Registration Cards, 1917–1918*. Ancestry.

1167 *New York, County Marriage Records, 1847–1894, 1907–1936*. Ancestry.

1168 Birth, death, burial come from Find A Grave.

1169 *Spencer, Tioga, New York;* ED: 0021; FHL: 2341387; Family: 135. Ancestry.

1170 *Spencer, Tioga, New York;* Roll: m-t0627-02791; Page 8B; ED: 54-32. Ancestry.

1171 Information on the children of Charles Edward and Isabelle Kelsey comes from Find A Grave.

1172 Headstone is inscribed "1872" as the date of birth; the 1900 census states she was born "December 1873."

1173 Find A Grave and obituary notice.

1174 Jesse Hobson was born 14 June 1846 in Coleby, Lincolnshire, England; father: Thomas Hobson; Mother: Mary_____. Jesse Hobson was a Quaker. He emigrated to New York and likely settled in Van Etten. He died in Sayer, Pennsylvania, on 27 June 1927. His wife's name is given as Moriah, Moira, and Maria in the records. Her maiden name was "Westbrook." Information on Jessie and Moriah comes from 1851 census, *Lincolnshire, England; U.S. Quaker Index to Quaker Obituary*

Westbrook (1849–1940).

Philo Lewis went by the name of "Lew" or "Lewis" during his life and most records refer to him as such.

Lew was born with a deformity,[1175] as noted in the pension records for his father, Philo. A deposition from Daniel J. Bryant states in 1909 that he was "acquainted with him [Lew] ever since he was a small boy," as he lived only "a mile and a half from him." He goes on to say that "he was always deformed from the first, bad humpback and [a] very narrow chest. He could never stand any hard work, if he could work . . . he was never lazy; his ambition was too great for his constitution. I knew he drew a pension until he was sixteen years of age." I believe that this deposition was taken as Lewis was seeking funds from his father's pension to assist with his financial situation. Children of Civil War veterans killed in action were provided a separate pension (from the widow's) up to the age of sixteen years.

Mr. Bryant went on to say, "He [Lew] seems to get worse as years roll by and for part of the year, he has not been able to do his chores. He has been under the care of [a] doctor most of the summer." Because Mr. Bryant lived very near Lewis, he helped him over the summer and the most I've known him to do "is to sit on a reaper and reap about two acres of oats." The last thing that Mr. Daniel Bryant wanted to add is that he knew "Lewis Philo Kelsey to be an honest, reliable and truthful man, absolutely temperate."

Lewis spoke at his own deposition on the first of August 1909:

> . . . I drew a pension also my brother Charles Kelsey, until we were sixteen years of age. That my mother Betsey Kelsey drew a pension as a widow of said Philo Kelsey. That after my pension ceased and until my mother's death, I stayed home with her and work as best I could and done all I could until about six months ago I became so disabled that I cannot do anything and have been advised by my doctor not to work if I ever expect to be any better. I never was a robust child or man, I am what is called a humpback and was always so from a child, but it seems to get worse of late years and causes great pain from my back into my shoulder, and causes me to catch my breath . . .

The pension board reviewed his request, and the request for additional funds was denied on November 23, 1909. What a blow this must have been. How could he continue to support himself and his wife? Getting help from the town was considered charity, which was an embarrassment for the person claiming help and most hesitated in doing so.

When Lew was seventeen, he was listed on the 1880 census as a farm hand. He was still living in Spencer at this time with his mother and brother Charles, and the 1892[1176] census shows him enumerated alone, age 30 years, and a farmer.

This census was taken on February 16, 1892. Rose Hobson was enumerated with her family

---

*Notices 1822–2012;* and *Pennsylvania U.S. Death Certificates, 1906–1967.* Ancestry.

1175 This "deformity" I believe to be "congenital Kyphosis," where the spine does not develop properly in the womb. See: https://www.hopkinsmedicine.org.

1176 *New York, State Census, 1892, Spencer, Tioga;* Page: 12. Ancestry.

in Van Etten, Chemung, New York, the same year.[1177] On March 23, 1892, Lewis married Rose Hobson in Spencer. I wonder how this marriage was perceived by her family, friends, and the town? Lewis Kelsey was well known in Spencer, and I suspect very well thought of by his neighbors. Despite his "deformity," he was an "honest, reliable, truthful and temperate man" who did his best despite his limitations.

The 1905 census shows Rose Kelsey and "Louis P. Kelsey" living on Front Street in her parents' household in Van Etten. By 1910, they are back in Spencer. They had been married eighteen years at this point and no children were born to them. Lewis owned the property that he farmed.

In 1920 and 1930 the couple lived on a farm on Langford Creek Road in Van Etten. This is where Philo Lewis Kelsey died on November 14, 1934, at the age of 72. His obituary in the *Star-Gazette* indicates that he had had an "extended illness and had been a farmer and a life-long resident of rural Van Etten."[1178] While the obituary indicates he was buried in Mount Hope Cemetery, he is actually buried in Canfield Cemetery in Van Etten.

After Lewis' death, Rose's brother, Charles J. Hobson, wrote to the Pension Department on behalf of his sister Rose to petition for support.[1179] He writes, "She has no income for her support. I shall appreciate some statement as to what proof prefer [sic] in showing the death of Mr. Kelsey."

A response was received from an E. L. Bailey on December 19, 1934 (Director Widows and Dependents Claim Service). His letter explains the conditions of receiving payment, but the underlying tone (of his letter) does not appear to be positive; however, "a certified copy of the public record of the death of the pensioner is required as well as filing an application Form 5036."

A handwritten reply was sent back to Mr. E. L. Bailey from Mr. Hobson with a question on Form 5036 where it states, "Not to be used if the deceased pension left a widow & etc.—he did leave a widow, but no children." He requested that Mr. Bailey forward blanks for mailing an application to the Veterans Administration for "burial allowance."[1180]

A letter from January 14, 1935, from Mr. Bailey to Mr. Hobson explains that "the accrued pension is only payable to a widow in the case of a deceased soldier—not the widow of the pensioner."

This was the last letter that C. J. Hobson wrote for his sister Rose.

Not to be denied (and in desperation) the next letter was written by Mrs. Philo Lewis Kelsey on February 14, 1935, to the Department of Interior, Bureau of Pensions. She states that since "Mr. Kelsey's pensions have been stopped, I am left without means of support and will have to apply to Public [ ].[1181] If it is possible to get any help through your department as Mr. Kelsey did not leave property to support me."

---

1177 *New York, State Census, 1892, Spencer, Tioga;* Page: 2. Ancestry.

1178 Friday, November 1934 edition; Page: 25; Newspapers.

1179 Type-written letter to Pension Department, Washington, D.C., by Charles J. Hobson on "November 21, 1934."

1180 This is the reply that Mr. Hobson sent to Mr. Bailey. The letter was dated "December 26, 1934."

1181 The word is illegible, but it would appear to be what we know as "Public Assistance."

A response dated March 8, 1935, to Mrs. Philo L. Kelsey from Mr. E. L. Bailey: "This is a reply to your letter of February 14, 1935. Pension is not payable to a daughter-in-law of a Civil War Veteran. It is regretted that a more favorable reply cannot be made."

Rose Kelsey wrote another letter dated March 6, prior to receiving the one dated March 8, 1935:

> Dear Sir –
>
> I am the widow of Philo Lewis Kelsey who died Nov. 15th, and I am asking for information in the matter of my getting the pension as I have lived with him and done for him for 43 years the best I could and as I have no other means of support myself it seems I ought to have the same as if he was a soldier. I ask the poor (pay?) master to write you and could not bear the thought of being on the town, but I have had to ask for one Bill of groceries, he said he had written you concerning the matter as I ask [sic] weeks ago but last I spoke to him about it he said probably you would not be in any hurry to answer so I thought I will do my own writing. My Husband and myself helped to elect the Democrats & my father was a strong Democrat and now if you can assist me in any way so I can be relieved as to my future maintenance I will appreciate it greatly.
>
> Yours sincerely,
> Mrs. Philo Lewis Kelsey
> RD#1, Van Etten, N.Y.[1182]

This is the last letter in the pension file. Rose would have received the letter dated March 8, 1935, shortly after she sent her additional letter. She received her answer—she did not qualify for any funds. What a blow this must have been to her.

Rose must have had to remain on public assistance of some sort to be able to feed herself. Perhaps family members also helped her out.

During all the requests for funds from the Veterans Administration, the government passed the Social Security Act, which was signed by FDR on August 14, 1935. In January 1937 the first one-time lump-sum payments were made. Three years later, in January 1940, regular monthly benefits were made. These benefits would help Rose to some degree.

≈

The 1940 census for Van Etten[1183] shows Rose Kelsey living at 94 Briggs Hill; she is renting for $5.00 per month and she answered "yes" to the question of "Other Income Source." I suspect this was the social security benefits that she began to receive as of January 1940.

---

1182 This letter was transcribed exactly how it was written without grammatical or punctuation corrections.

1183 1940 census, *Van Etten, Chemung, New York;* Roll: m-t0627-02514; Page: 5B; ED: 8-81. Ancestry.

Since the city directories for Van Etten do not exist online and the 1950 census is not yet available, there are fifteen years missing from her life that cannot be recreated here. The last record we have for Rose Kelsey is her obituary notice, which was published in the *Elmira Advertiser*:[1184]

> Mrs. Rose M. Kelsey of Van Etten, Thursday, July 14, 1955. She was the widow of Lewis P. Kelsey. Survived by brother C. J. Hobson of Van Etten; sister, Mrs. Floyd P. Drake of Waverly; several cousins. Body at Arnold Funeral Home, Van Etten, where friends may call there Saturday at 2:30 p.m., the Rev. Ernest Warren, Canfield Memorial Cemetery, Van Etten.

Philo Lewis Kelsey and Rose Hobson did not have any children.

### *33. Albert A.[1185] Scoville[7] (Charles Martin,[6] Franklin,[5] Ithamar,[4] Timothy,[3] Stephen,[2] Stephen,[1] Arthur)*

Born 7 April 1857, Colebrook, Litchfield, Connecticut;[1186] died 31 October 1944, Hartford, Hartford, Connecticut;[1187] married circa 1882, Laura Jennie Steele, place unknown;[1188] born 23 January 1861, Simsbury, Hartford, Connecticut;[1189] died 22 March 1939, North Newington, Hartford, Connecticut; daughter of Thomas Steele and Sarah Cornish.

Albert was the first child born to Charles and Catherine Scoville in Colebrook after two years of marriage. They moved shortly after to New Britain, Connecticut, where Albert would grow up into manhood. In 1880 he was listed with his mother, his stepfather, and his German grandmother at 49 Pleasant Street. At that time, he and his stepfather, Gottlieb, were working in a P. F. Corbin's hardware company.

According to the 1881 city directory for New Britain,[1190] Albert A. Scoville was a mechanic and living at 132 Kensington Avenue, also in New Britain. Since the date of this directory is before automobiles came on the scene, I presume that Albert was a mechanic at P. F. Corbin's or another hardware manufacturer, as the 1888/1889 directory states that Albert was a mechanic for Stanley Rule and Level Company. For approximately eleven years this was Albert's occupation and he continued to live at 132 Kensington Avenue.

---

1184 Second Section Pages 11–18; Elmira, N.Y., Friday Morning, July 15, 1955. Newspapers.

1185 My belief is that his middle initial, "A," may stand for Anthony after his mother's brother—however, this is only my opinion.

1186 Albert's birthdate comes from the pension records, where his mother (Catherine) had to provide dates of birth for each child.

1187 Obituary notice that is no longer in my possession. Also, *Connecticut Vital Records—Index of Deaths 1897–2001*, Connecticut State Library, https://ctstatelibrarydata.org. (herein: CSL)

1188 The year of marriage is a complete guess on my part. I have not found a record of marriage online.

1189 Birth, death, and parents' names come from her obituary.

1190 *U.S. City Directories, 1822–1995* (Herein City Directories). Ancestry.

Albert Scoville did a complete change in his employment, as in 1890 he was now a bartender and roomed at 141 Main Street in New Britain. For the next twelve years he held the same position and was living at 90 Church Street. Many of places that he lived are no longer there due to sprawl and "revitalization."

According to Laura Jennie Scoville's obituary, the couple removed to Hartford in 1903, however, even while the city directories are a year behind, the couple is still listed as being in New Britain up until 1905.

In 1906 they are listed as living in Hartford. He was still bartending, but that changed too.

There were not many newspaper articles regarding either Albert or Jennie, however, I did find a few tidbits. *The Hartford Dailey Courant* ran an article in the Thursday edition of the paper on April 25, 1907. From Minnie Martin Schroeder's will:

> . . . solitaire pearl ring to Mrs. Albert A. Scoville if living at the time of testatrix's death and if not to Mrs. Scoville's husband; paintings designated to Mr. and Mrs. Albert A. Scoville of Hartford.

In the 1908 issue of *The Hartford Courant:*[1191]

> The will of Catherine Gammerdinger was filed for probate yesterday She left her property to her two children, Albert A. Scoville and Agnes R. Billian, share and share alike. Mr. Scoville named executor.

In 1911 they are living at 14 Spring Street in Hartford. At some point, he became a clerk and eventually the owner of the lodging house at 14 Spring Street. Again, the building is no longer there, but viewing the other buildings in this area, it was likely a large brick building with multiple rooms to be rented.

There is a rather humorous anecdote about Albert that my paternal grandmother told me many years ago when I was asking her questions about the family history. She told me that Albert was very tall and had to duck to get into doorways and he always wore a stocking cap with a tassel at the end. Keep in mind that my grandmother was *perhaps* five feet tall. Unfortunately, there are no known photos of Albert to see if she was correct in her assessment.[1192] However, Albert did have to file a form for the *1917 Connecticut Military Census.* At the time Albert completed the form he was sixty years old. My jaw dropped though when he wrote that he was "5′ 4″" tall and "170" pounds. I can't believe my grandmother was *that* wrong on his height, and my contention is that Albert mis-wrote his own statistics![1193]

---

1191 Thursday, December 24, 1908, edition; Part Two; pages 15–20. ProQuest Newspapers (CSL).

1192 I've also asked the last living relatives of my grandmother—her daughter and son (my aunt and uncle)—to confirm Albert's height, but they do not recall ever meeting him.

1193 A woman who is barely five feet tall could hardly mistake a man of five feet four for someone who had to "duck" into doorways. I believe Albert Scoville mistakenly wrote "5′ 4″" instead of "6′ 4″" on his draft registration record.

Albert also suffered from "rheumatism" and had served with the National Guard for five years as a private in the First Regiment. Albert also wrote "**No**" to the following questions on the military census: ride a horse; handle a team; drive an automobile; ride a motorcycle; understand telegraphy; operate a wireless; any experience with a steam engine; any experience with electrical machinery; handle a boat, power, or sail; any experience in simple coastwise navigation; any experience with high-speed marine gasoline engines; are you a good swimmer.

The 1930 census for Hartford shows the Scovilles living at 14 Spring Street and the value of the real property is $16,000. By this time, Albert is seventy-two years old, and his wife is sixty-seven. There are ten lodgers—all males—renting rooms from the Scovilles. Their ages range from twenty-nine to sixty-eight, all working at various jobs.

Two years later in the real estate section we find this notice:

> **Warrantee Deed**[1194]
> Albert A. Scoville to Hattie M. Nelligan, etal., land and building, 14 Spring Street.[1195]

The Scovilles continued to live at 14 Spring Street until sometime in 1937 or 1938. The couple moved to 101 Francis Avenue in North Newington, which was the home of Mr. and Mrs. Simon Kaplan. I do not know how they knew this couple, but they let them move into their small home.[1196]

At some point, Laura Jenny's health deteriorated as she was placed in Municipal Hospital in Hartford, where she died on March 24, 1939. She was seventy-eight years old at her death and is buried in Fairview Cemetery in New Britain.

Not long after, Albert A. Scoville was admitted to the Municipal Home on 2 Holcomb Street in Hartford. He is on the 1940 census as one of the "inmates" and his age is given as "84." He stayed at the Municipal Home until his death on October 31, 1944.

I have not been able to find an obituary for Albert and don't know if he was buried with his wife or not.

This couple did not have any children.

## *34. **Agnes R.**[1197] **Scoville**[7] (Charles Martin,[6] Franklin,[5] Ithamar,[4] Timothy,[3] Stephen,[2] Stephen,[1] Arthur)*

1194 The definition of a warranty deed: "a type of deed where the grantor guarantees that he or she holds clear title to the piece of real estate and has a right to sell it to the grantee, in contrast to a quitclaim deed, where the seller does not guarantee that he or she holds title to a piece of real estate." Wikipedia.

1195 *The Hartford Daily Courant,* Wednesday, May 18, 1932, edition; 20. Newspapers.

1196 The house still stands today and, according to Trulia, was built in 1925.

1197 Some references give her middle initial as "M." It is unknown what the initials may represent.

Born 11 July 1859, New Britain, Hartford, Connecticut;[1198] died 13 April 1948, New Britain, Hartford, Connecticut; buried Walnut Grove Cemetery, Meriden, New Haven, Connecticut; married 22 July 1875, New Britain, Hartford, Connecticut, Ferdinand Billian, born 2 June 1851, Schabenhausen, Württemberg,[1199] Germany; died 2 July 1921, New Britain, Hartford, Connecticut; buried Walnut Grove Cemetery, Meriden, New Haven, Connecticut; son of Ferdinand[1] Billian and Catherina Geiger.

I never knew my great-grandmother, but I have been able to glean some personal accounts from two people who knew her: my grandmother, who was the daughter-in-law of Agnes, and a grandson of Agnes. Even so, these are personal opinions of two people. Her character cannot be rounded out by these observations. This is the difficulty of writing about people not known personally by the writer. My grandmother stated that Agnes was a "very proud" woman. One of her grandsons (George Kumm) stated she was "very friendly" and would "always wave to them when they went by her house," and Agnes herself told my grandmother that she was "one-quarter Mohegan Indian." Two different perceptions of her character and a statement (of being one-quarter Mohegan) that has not been proven through DNA.[1200] Such is family oral lore.

Agnes was five years old when her father died. Her memories of her father must have been very dim, and any recall of memories are likely things her mother told her. As an example, the oral history was that her father was in the calvary during the Civil War. This may have been something her mother told her, either by design or deliberate misinformation; or perhaps it was a romantic notion from Agnes herself. Her father *was* a teamster—not as fascinating as a calvary officer—but again, there's that grain of truth—her father did have horses, he just wasn't riding them.

Agnes lived with her mother and stepfather until 1875 when, at the age of sixteen, she married a recent German immigrant by the name of Ferdinand Billian (Agnes had just turned sixteen ten days prior to her marriage on July 11, 1875).

**Marriage License.**

Registrars issuing a License where one of the parties is a minor, without the written consent of the parents or guardian, subject themselves a fine of sixty-seven dollars.

This Certifies, That Mr. Ferdinand Billiand, of New Britain nd Miss Aggie Schofield, of New Britain, have eclared their intention of marriage, and have complied with the provisions of the laws of the tate of Connecticut relating to Registration of Births, Marriages, and Deaths.

Attest, John Walsh Registrar.

Dated at New Britain this 21 day of July, A. D. 1875

1198 Pension file and death certificate.

1199 Now part of Baden-Württemberg, Germany. Birth records from parish registers in Germany provided.

1200 The reason Native American DNA doesn't always show up is due to the fact that this DNA may have been "washed" out over the generations, especially if only one person of Native blood long ago married a Caucasian and there had been no other marriages between a white person and an Indigenous person. It wasn't "fashionable" during my great-grandmother's time to state that you were part "Indian." While we must take this information with a grain of salt, there may be a particle of truth to it.

Ferdinand's mother and his siblings had come to the United States in 1873 and settled in Meriden, New Haven, Connecticut. Ferdinand followed in 1874. The family "legend" is that Ferdinand was in the German (or Prussian) army when one of the officers spat in the face of one of his friends—this type of cruel treatment that was endured made him want to leave—which he did. It is said that he slipped out of the country through Switzerland, where he had relatives.[1201] It was also stated that he was a "stow-away" on the ship. If this story is true, he likely had to go to France to take a ship out. Personally, I have not been able to locate a manifest with his name on it[1202] and he may have used an alias to get to the United States.

Ferdinand did live in Meriden for a while, but then removed to New Britain. There he would have met many German immigrants through the various clubs and civic organizations. It was also a place where many jobs were available for a "master machinist," which Ferdinand was.

Ferdinand became a naturalized citizen of the United States on October 20, 1880.[1203] This must have been a proud day for him and his family. Becoming a citizen of the United States had changed over the years. By 1880 a person who wanted to become a citizen had to have been in the United States for at least five years. That individual had to file a number of requests before he/she could become a naturalized citizen. The first would be the *Declaration of Intention,* then *Petition the Court,* and, finally, the person would receive a certificate of naturalization. It wasn't always a quick process as they (the court) wanted to make sure the person was of good moral character and that they would take the oath of allegiance to the Constitution of the United States.

The census was also taken in 1880 and the family consisted of: Ferdinand, 28, works hardware shop; Agnes,[1] wife, 20, keeps house; Agnes[2], daughter, age 3; and Frederick, son, age 2.

Without the 1890 census the only way to capture where a particular person was is through the city directories. For these "lost" years (1890–1899) we can follow where Ferdinand and Agnes were during this time.

In the 1889/90 city directory for New Britain[1204] the family was living at 49 Pleasant Street (this is where Agnes' mother, Catherine Schneider Scoville, was also living at that time).

Ferdinand was employed by the National Mattress Company, where they made brass and iron bedsteads and cribs. By 1891 (while still living on Pleasant Street) he was working for Stanley Rule and Level Company.

The couple had moved to a three-family home (which still stands today) at 78 Winthrop Street in 1892/93 and Ferdinand was still working at Stanley Rule and Level Company.

In 1896 the couple had moved again. Ferdinand was an "extract peddler." This line of work only lasted a year or so as he was back working at Stanley Rule in 1898.

---

1201 It has been confirmed that Ferdinand did have cousins living in Switzerland during this timeframe.

1202 The ship passenger list where Ferdinand's mother and siblings are recorded was provided to me by a professional genealogical researcher in Germany.

1203 *Connecticut, Federal Naturalization Records, 1790–1996;* Certificate No: 1875–1903 Page: 88; City Court New Britain. Ancestry.

1204 *City Directories—New Britain,* Ancestry.

In 1900[1205] the family is living at 417 Church Street, New Britain. They own their own home at this point.

Daughter Agnes and son Frederick are no longer in the household; however, a son, Ernest C., age 3, is listed, as well as a boarder, John Zeiner.

Ernest Clarence Billian was born May 22, 1897, twenty years after Ferdinand and Agnes' son Frederick was born. From what I learned about this situation from my grandmother, Agnes thought that her child-rearing years were behind her, and she wasn't happy about having to go through it again.[1206]

Another issue arose when Father Ferdinand spoiled his son Ernest, treating him more like a grandchild than his own child. This treatment brought tension between husband and wife.[1207]

The Billian family; left–right: Agnes,[2] Agnes,[1] Ferdinand, Ernest, and Frederick.

The family continued to live on Church Street when, in 1901, a civil suit was brought against Ferdinand and Agnes to "recover $100." The suit was filed by Edward Bergman and T. B. Wilcox to recover the same amount against the "property belonging to the Billian's on Church Street has been attached."[1208]

Without obtaining the actual Civil Suit document it would seem self-evident that the Billians owed money to both complainants. According to *Investopedia* an attachment "is a legal process referring to the action of seizing property in anticipation of a favorable ruling for a plaintiff who claims to be owed money by the defendant. At the request of a creditor, a court of law may transfer specific property owned by the debtor to the creditor (or sell the property for the benefit of the creditor)."[1209] The debt owed must have been rectified as the Billian family continued to live at 417 Church Street until 1912.

In reading the 1910[1210] census Ferdinand is a "laborer in a church factory."[1211] The family

1205 1900; Census Place: *New Britain, Hartford, Connecticut*; Page: 10; Enumeration District: 0209; FHL: 1240139.

1206 The relationship between mother and son was fraught with tension and there were many times that they did not speak to one another.

1207 Photo courtesy of this writer and is only one of two photos that exist of Agnes.[1] Photo taken approximately 1900/1901. New Britain, Connecticut.

1208 *The Hartford Courant*, Tuesday, November 5, 1901, 12. Newspapers.

1209 See https://Investopedia.com.

1210 1910 census, *New Britain, Hartford, Connecticut;* Ward 4; Roll: T624_134; Page: 8B; ED: 0226; FHL:1374147.

1211 The writing on this page of the census is faint and the transcriber indicates that Ferdinand works in a church factory. Several other men listed on the same page also work at this factory. The

consists of Ferdinand, Agnes,[1,] and Ernest. Sometime in 1912 the family moved to 198 Maple Street (a three-family home) and resided there until 1916/17.

Ferdinand Billian changed his employer and his residence[1212] around 1913/1914. Ferdinand went to work for P. & F. Corbin, a very well known hardware company that manufactured keys, locks, and many other products throughout their history.

On August 14, 1914, England declared war with Germany and the other Central Powers. The United States at that time (under President Woodrow Wilson) did not want to get involved in another war. However, when the United States entered the war in 1917, the citizens of the United States were hypervigilant. There were outbreaks of violence against those who were seen as disloyal to the U.S. The people who suffered the most were the German Americans.[1213] One of those people who was harassed was Ferdinand Billian.

The following is a complete report of the FBI investigation as to whether Ferdinand Billian was a German sympathizer.[1214]

> Mr. Charles H. Lane, Jr., Hartford, Connecticut, May 14, 1917
> In RE Fred Billian[1215]—European Neutrality
>
> Pursuant to instructions I proceeded to New Britain today, relative information from C.H. Sawyer, to effect that one Fred Billian, of 158 Maple Street New Britain, was an active German sympathizer. At Corbin Lock Company, of New Britain, I ascertained that Billian has been employed as a machinist in their concern as follows—
>
> from November 30th, 1911, to Sept. 24, 1917.
> From December 16th, 1912, to Oct. 14, 1914.
> From November 23, 1914, to present time.
>
> Superintendent Fletcher, of this company, informed me that Billian had always been a very reliable worker, and most trustworthy. I then questioned Billian's foreman, Charles Brummer; he stated that he had not heard Billian say very much about the War for the past couple of months, but prior to the United States entering the War, Billian had oft times expressed the wish that Germany would be victorious. He also stated that Billian was German born, and spoke with a decided accent, and that when heckled by other fellow workers he would become very aggressive in his stand for Germany; Bremmer assured me however, that Billian was very harmless and that to his mind a very good citizen.
>
> I then proceeded to the home of Mr. Billian, at 158 Maple Street, he informed me

---

name of the business is unknown.

1212 The family at that time were living at 156 Maple Street, another three-family home.

1213 *America in World War I, Facts, Worksheets and Consequences.* https://schoolhousehistory.co.uk.

1214 *FBI Case Files; Old German Files 1909–1921;* Case Number: 8000-15524; European Neutrality: Page: 1; M1085; Investigative Case Files Bureau of Investigation 1900–1922; Roll: boi_german 257-850_0086; https//www.Fold3.com. Investigative report transcribed as it was written.

1215 "Fred" was the name Ferdinand was called by family and friends.

> that he had been in the United States, for over 40 years and had been an American Citizen, since 1884; that he spent 5 years in the Connecticut National Guards, and never had any difficulty of any kind with the authorities.
>
> From a neighbor I learned that Mr. Billian and another tenant had an argument over the War question, but that Billian did not say anything which in any way reflected on the United States.

This is the end of the report. I can only presume that Mr. C.H. Sawyer's suspicions were found to be baseless and without merit. While I would like to make Mr. Sawyer the "bad guy" here, I don't know what type of man he was. Did he think he was doing his duty or was he someone who didn't like Germans? Or, perhaps he had a son or other relative serving in the war or who had been wounded or killed and that made him suspect Fred Billian.

We've seen these actions throughout history—people casting aspersions on others. It is a complex issue and one that I will not get into here.[1216]

Ferdinand Billian

I do not know how long Ferdinand remained at P. & F. Corbin. In 1917 he was already sixty-six years old at the time of the FBI report.

Agnes Billian is mentioned in three land transfers that occurred between 1918 and 1919. The first was between Agnes R. Billian and her son, Ernest C. Billian, where the property on Maple Street was transferred to him. The date of this transfer is "January 3, 1918."[1217]

Again, on January 5, 1918, under "Transfers of the Week," "Agnes R. Billian and others to Earnest C. Billian land and buildings on Maple Street."[1218]

Between 1918 and 1919 the family had removed to the Westfield[1219] section of Middletown, Middlesex, Connecticut.[1220]Ferdinand and Agnes' youngest son, Ernest, had bought a house in this area. I suspect that Ernest sold the property in New Britain not long after having it transferred to him to buy the farm in Westfield.

---

1216 Photo courtesy of this writer. Date unknown but probably taken around the same time as the family photo. I am uncertain what the medals designate, but they are likely from fraternal organizations he belonged to. Even when enlarging the photo, the words on the medals are not legible.

1217 *New Britain Daily Herald;* Saturday, January 3, 1918. Page number unknown as it is torn; GenealogyBank.com. Agnes must have owned these properties outright as her husband is not named in any of the transactions.

1218 *Ibid*

1219 This area is now known as *Highlands National Historic District*—Atkins and Country Club Road area in Middletown. There was a train/trolley station there and the MW&CR Railroad line ran through this section of the town that was used to get to Meriden, Connecticut.

1220 My uncle Howard (Billian) kept a record of all the places the family had lived throughout his life.

The family is listed on the 1920 census[1221] in the Westfield section of Middletown.

West Road Highland Station
Dwelling: 172; Family: 191 & 192
Billian, Ernest, head, owns, 22, born Connecticut, farmer, general farm
Billian, Carolina, wife, 22, born Connecticut
Billian, Howard, son, 1 11/12, born Connecticut
Billian, Fred, head, 68, arrived 1874, naturalized, 1890, born Germany, machinist, music co.
Billian, Agnes, wife, 60, born Connecticut

The family's time in Middletown was short-lived. In 1921 Ferdinand and Agnes were back in New Britain living at 96 Pleasant Street. Ferdinand was suffering from stomach cancer and succumbed to this disease on July 2, 1921. According to the death certificate the duration of the disease was "90 days."[1222]

He was buried in the family plot in Walnut Grove Cemetery, Meriden, Connecticut.

Ferdinand's obituary appeared in the *New Britain Daily Herald:*[1223]

> **Ferdinand Billian**
> Ferdinand Billian of 96 Pleasant Street, 70 years of age, died this morning. He was a native of Germany, but had lived here many years, and had been employed as a machinist. Besides his wife, he leaves a daughter Mrs. Agnes Cafferty, and two sons, Ernest, and Frederick J. Billian. He also leaves two brothers, Andrew and Benjamin, and a sister, Mrs. Mary Hoffman.
>
> The funeral will be held at Pleasant Street residence at 2 o'clock and interment will be made in Meriden.[1224]

After Ferdinand's death, Agnes continued to live in New Britain at various locations (8 Locust St., 83 Hart St., and 16 Pine St.). By 1930 she is living with her son Frederick at 559 Arch Street. Frederick did not own this home and was renting it for twenty-eight dollars per month. A lodger by the name of Harry Steele was living with them as well.

From 1938–1943,[1225] Agnes was living at 545 Arch Street. On the 1940 census Agnes is now eighty years old and Harry Steele, a lodger, is seventy-four.

Agnes was getting older, and she was hoping she could move in with one of her children. Frederick went knocking on his brother's and sister's doors to see if they could take her in, but none of them seemed to have the room.

---

1221 1920 census; *Middletown, Middlesex, Connecticut;* Roll: T625_188; Page: 9B; ED: 224; Image: 173. Ancestry.

1222 Medical Certificate of Death, Town Clerk's office, New Britain, Connecticut.

1223 Saturday, July 2, 1921, edition, 3.

1224 According to my grandmother (Ferdinand's daughter-in-law) he (Ferdinand) was a "very nice man."

1225 *U.S. City Directories, 1822–1995,* New Britain, Connecticut; Ancestry.

In 1946, Agnes entered the New Britain Town Home, which was located at 150 Rocky Hill Avenue in New Britain.

On April 13, 1948, Agnes Scoville Billian died at the age of "88 years, 9 months, 2 days." She was buried with her husband in Walnut Grove Cemetery, Meriden, Connecticut. No obituary has been found.

### *Children of Frederick Billian and Agnes[1] Scoville*

47. Agnes Mary Billian,[8, 1226] b. 2 Aug 1876, New Britain, Hartford, Connecticut; d. 12 Oct 1960, New Britain, Hartford, Connecticut; bur. Fairview Cemetery, New Britain, Hartford, Connecticut; m. (1) 15 Jul 1898, George C. Kumm, New Britain; (2) 5 Apr 1919, Charles C. Cafferty, New Britain; (3) 24 Jan 1925, Bert Sanborn, New Britain.
48. Frederick Joe Billian[8] (aka Fred Joe), b. 31 Dec 1878, New Britain, Hartford, Connecticut; d. 11 Sep 1963, New Britain, Hartford, Connecticut; bur. Maple Cemetery, Berlin, Hartford, Connecticut; m. (1) 27 Oct 1897, Ada L. Church, Berlin, Hartford, Connecticut; (2) prior to 1940, Agnes L. Case.
49. **Ernest Clarence Billian,**[8] b. 22 May 1897, New Britain, Hartford, Connecticut; d. 24 Oct 1980, Middletown, Middlesex, Connecticut; m. 17 Apr 1917, Caroline Linnea Halldin, b. 2 Jul 1897, New Britain, Hartford, Connecticut; d. 13 Jan 1982, Middletown, Middlesex, Connecticut; d.o. Johan Anders Halldin and Carolina Charlotta Carlsdotter.

## 35. *George Henry Raidart*[7] *(Julia Rebecca,*[6] *Franklin,*[5] *Ithamar,*[4] *Timothy,*[3] *Stephen,*[2] *Stephen,*[1] *Arthur)*

Born 2 August 1857, Colebrook, Litchfield, Connecticut; died 28 September 1937, Winchester, Litchfield, Connecticut;[1227] buried Forest View Cemetery, Winsted, Litchfield, Connecticut; married 6 April 1885,[1228] Riverton, Litchfield, Connecticut, Alice Maude Deming; born 30 July 1863, Riverton, Litchfield, Connecticut; died 18 February 1944, Winsted, Litchfield, Connecticut;[1229] daughter of George Gilbert Deming, Jr. (1831–1913) and Jenette Woodward (1842–1927).

As did his father, George Henry Raidart began his working life in a chair

1226 I have seen her middle name as Mary or May. On some census reports she is referred to as "Agnes M. J."

1227 The birth and death data comes from the headstone via Find A Grave.com. The *U.S. Find-A-Grave Index, 1600s–Current,* states that he died in "Colebrook;" however, *WEB: Connecticut Death Records, 1897–1968* (CSL) states he died in Winchester, Litchfield, Connecticut.

1228 I do not have the source of the month and day of marriage as I did not record it. The 1900 census states that they had been married for "15 years," which would bring the marriage year to 1885.

1229 The birth and death data comes from the headstone in Forest View Cemetery, Winsted, Litchfield, Connecticut.

factory;[1230]however, by 1884, he was appointed Postmaster for Robertsville.[1231] The following year he married Alice Maud Deming in Riverton (a section of Colebrook, Litchfield, Connecticut). Alice Deming was a descendant of the progenitor of the Deming line, John Deming (1615–1705), who had come from Shalford, Essex, England, to New England during the Great Migration. He originally settled in Watertown, Massachusetts, then removed to the Connecticut River Valley in 1636 and helped to found Wethersfield, Connecticut;[1232] *his* descendant, Daniel Deming (1753–1828), was born in Wethersfield and eventually removed to Colebrook.

The city directories for Winsted for 1889 through 1893 list George Raidart as employed as a bookkeeper for Clark & Hart, which was located at 363 Main Street in said town. Clark & Hart was a dry goods establishment that sold carpets, wallpaper, groceries, crockery, and other sundry items. George remained there for a few years but by the 1893–1894 directory he was a bookkeeper for Winsted Manufacturing Company, which was involved with the manufacturing of scythes and corn and hay knives.

In 1900[1233] the George Raidart family is living at 240 Holabird Avenue[1234] in Winchester Town (a borough of Winsted). The family consists of George, Alice, son Wilbur, daughter Olive, and a servant by the name of Emma Jones. George does not own this home but is renting and he is still employed as a bookkeeper.

From 1901–1909[1235] George Raidart and his family were still living in Winsted but had moved from Holabird Avenue to, first, 142 Main Street, and then to 36 Main Street. He was still working for the Winsted Manufacturing Company and had been promoted to "secretary" of the company.

In 1910[1236] the family is back living on Holabird Avenue (number 34), Winchester:

Raidart, George H., head, 53, m. 25 yrs., b. Connecticut, bookkeeper—office, rents
Raidart, Alice M., wife, 47, m. 25 yrs., b. Connecticut
Raidart, Wilbur H., son, 18, b. Connecticut, Assistant Accountant—office
Raidart, Olive M., daughter, 9, b. Connecticut

Note that George's occupation is listed as "bookkeeper" on the census. There isn't an enumerator's mark on this census to indicate who gave the information. Could "bookkeeper" and "secretary" be synonymous with one another? Nevertheless, it is likely that George is still

1230 1880 census, *Colebrook, Litchfield, Connecticut,* Sheet: 18. Ancestry.

1231 *U.S. Appointments of U.S. Postmasters, 1832–1971; Vol: 47; Volume Year: 1876–1892.* Ancestry.

1232 Deming, Judson Keith. *Genealogy of the Descendants of John Deming of Wethersfield, Connecticut* with historical notes, University of Wisconsin, Madison: Publisher Press of Mathis-Mets Co., (1904).

1233 1900 census; *Winchester, Litchfield, Connecticut;* Roll: 141; Page: 5AA; ED: 0267; FHL: 1240141. Ancestry.

1234 This home was built in 1890 (per real estate records) and as of this writing is still occupied.

1235 *U.S. City Directories, 1822–1995;* Ancestry.

1236 1910 census; *Winchester Town, Borough of Winsted, Litchfield, Connecticut;* Roll: T624_135; Page: 9A; ED: 0287; FHL: 1374148; Dwelling: 189; Family: 200. Ancestry.

employed at Winsted Manufacturing and his son, Wilbur, may be working alongside his father.

For a time, the family was back living at 195 North Main Street with George's mother, Julia Raidart. George's son, Wilbur, also lived with his grandmother in 1914 and is listed as being a superintendent for W E T Works, but by 1918 it doesn't appear Wilbur was employed.

George H. Raidart continued to move up in the ranks of his employer and is recorded as an "assistant manager" on the 1919 city directory for Winsted.

In 1920[1237] the family is living at 78 South Main Street, Winsted. George and his wife are finally homeowners.[1238] George is now a superintendent of the company that he works for. His wife, Alice, and daughter, Olive, are still residing with him in the household.

Throughout the Depression years, George Raidart continued to be employed and had reached the position of "General Manager" at the scythe factory. They must have counted themselves fortunate to continue to own their home and have a steady income. Both children were out of the home and on their own with their families. Their son, Wilbur, had removed to Chicago and daughter, Olive, had married.

George H. Raidart retired from the Winsted Scythe firm after forty-two years of service.[1239]

Two years later, George Henry Raidart died on September 28, 1937. The website *U.S. Find A Grave Index, 1600s–Current* states that he died in Colebrook, Litchfield, Connecticut. Since I have been unsuccessful in locating an obituary, I cannot say for certain this is where he died. At the time of his death, he was eighty years old.[1240]

George H. Raidart and grandchild?

George's wife, Alice, continued to live in the family home at 78 South Main Street and is the sole occupant as per the 1940 census. She died at the age of eighty-one on February 18, 1944, in Winsted.[1241]

Alice Maud Deming Raidart left a will. Although it is not in my possession, the grandson of George and Alice Raidart stated that she left her son, Wilbur, $1.00 "for reasons known to him."

They are both buried in Forest View Cemetery, Winsted, Connecticut.

1237 1920 census; *Winchester, Litchfield, Connecticut;* Roll: T625_187; Page: 13B; ED: 234; Image: 158; Dwelling: 260; Family: 384.

1238 Looking at Google Maps for this address, the homes in this area are now quite run-down and ramshackle. I believe 78 South Main has been torn down.

1239 The year that George retired would have been around 1935 when he was approximately seventy-eight years old.

1240 Original owner of this photo is Ken Sears. He is a descendant of Olive Raidart Sears.

1241 *WEB: Connecticut Death Records,* 1897–1968; CSL.

### *Children of George Henry Raidart and Alice Maud Deming*

50\. i. Wilbur Henry Raidart,[8] b. 12 Aug 1891, Riverton, Litchfield, Connecticut; d. aft. 1942, perhaps Chicago, Cook, Illinois; m.? (1) Mary Armead(a) Stacy, b. 1891; m. (2) 19 April 1929, Zion City, Illinois, Esther Mae Hedges; b. 24 Apr 1909, Zion City, Illinois; d. unknown; daughter of Paul Hedges and Rosetta Berfield.

ii. Olive Mildred Raidart,[8] b. 1 May 1900, Winsted, Litchfield, Connecticut;[1242] d. 17 Feb 1981, Winsted, Litchfield, Connecticut; m. 15 May 1923, Winchester, Litchfield, Connecticut, Ralph Edwin Sears; b. 6 Mar 1899, Barkhamsted, Litchfield, Connecticut;[1243] d. 12 Jan 1995, Winchester, Litchfield, Connecticut.[1244, 1245]

Olive Raidart

Alice, Olive, and George Raidart

Ralph Sears was an electrical engineer for a number of companies. The Sears family lived at 66 Main Street in Winstead, and they had two children: Elizabeth Raidart Sears (1924–2002) and Ralph Edwin Sears (1929–1993).

After the death of Olive's mother, she inherited part of the estate.

## 36. *Frank Ellsworth Scovill*[7, 1246] *(William Harrison,*[6] *Franklin,*[5] *Ithamar,*[4] *Timothy,*[3] *Stephen,*[2] *Stephen,*[1] *Arthur)*

Born 14 July 1862, Canaan, Litchfield, Connecticut; died 30 October 1952, Paragould, Greene, Arkansas;[1247] buried Linwood Cemetery, Paragould, Greene, Arkansas; married (1) 11 July 1888, Hartford, Hartford, Connecticut, Jessie Jayne Joslyn, born 8 August 1856, Man-

1242 *Connecticut Death Index, 1949–2012.* Ancestry.

1243 *U.S., World War I Draft Registration Cards, 1917–1918.* Ancestry.

1244 *U.S., Social Security Death Index, 1935–2014.* Ancestry.

1245 Original photos in possession of Ken Sears.

1246 From all records observed, Frank Ellsworth spelled his last name without the "e" at the end.

1247 Birth and death information comes from Frank Scovill's death certificate as well as the information on Find A Grave.com.

chester, Hartford, Connecticut; died 26 April 1910, Laredo, Webb, Texas;[1248] burial South Manchester Cemetery, Hartford, Connecticut; daughter of Richard Joslyn (1825–1879) and Sarah French (1823–1881); married (2) 25 October 1910, Wichita Falls, Wichita, Texas, Eugenie Phillipe Schaeffer, born 29 July 1869, Austin, Texas; died 17 June 1934, Paragould, Greene, Arkansas; buried Linwood Cemetery, Paragould, Arkansas.[1249]

In 1865,[1250] Frank Ellsworth Scovill is found listed on the Massachusetts State Census with his mother, Mary Catherine, and his sister (Minnie Irene) in the household of Cecelia McGrath.[1251] They are likely visiting until Frank's father returned from the war.

In 1880 Frank was seventeen and living with his parents in Winchester, Connecticut, and is employed as someone who "works at coffin trimmings."

He was likely employed at the Strong Manufacturing Company located on Main Street; handles, hardware and metalware, and other items were attached to the coffin. In 1882 Frank E. Scovill is listed as employed as a telephone operator in New Britain (CT) and rooming at 227 Main Street. In 1883 the city directory states that he "removed to Meriden (CT)."[1252] Frank's uncle Albert (Scoville) was living in Meriden at that time with his two children. Frank may have lived with or near his uncle.

Jessie J. Joslyn was born in Manchester, Connecticut, in 1856 to Richard Joslyn and Sarah French. Her parents had married in Canaan, Connecticut, on November 16, 1846.[1253] Her father was a sash-blind manufacturer, and the family was fairly well-off for that time. The how and when Frank and Jessie met remains unknown, but interestingly, the 1888 *U.S. City Directory* shows Jessie J. Joslyn living at 136 Seymour Street, Harford, Connecticut, and it also states the following: "m. July 11, Frank E. Scoville of St. Paul Minnesota."

Going back to the *Arthur Scovell* book by Holley, she states the following:

> Frank Ellsworth Scovill left home early and served various telephone companies as electrical engineer in Hartford and New Britain, Conn. In 1894 he was sent to St. Paul, Minn., to die of consumption, but he did not. Remained there ten years and recovered his health. He then went to Austin, Texas, on a contract as electrical engineer for the city of Austin. After completing the contract, he was for more than eight years manager of the Street Railway Company at Austin; later accepted a position at Laredo, Texas.[1254]

---

1248 Information on birth, death, and marriage comes from the obituary notice, *Hale Collection of Cemetery Inscriptions and Newspaper Notices;* Ancestry and Find A Grave.

1249 *Ibid.*

1250 1865 census, *Great Barrington, Berkshire, Massachusetts;* household: 491; Reel: 2; Volume: 3. Ancestry.

1251 Cecelia is either a sister of Mary Catherine Dunn Scoville or a cousin. A number of photos of the McGraths are in the Scoville collection of Sandra Amador.

1252 *U.S. City Directories* (New Britain and Meriden, Connecticut). Ancestry.

1253 *Barbour Collection.* Ancestry.

1254 Holley, *Arthur Scovell and His Descendants; 218–219.*

Much of Holley's information came from correspondence with descendants of the Arthur Scovel line and it would be interesting to learn who submitted this information to Mrs. Holley. Ironically, Frank E. Scoville's sister, Minnie Irene Scoville Ashley, was living in St. Paul in 1894, as *her* son, Howard, was born there the same year.

To return to the excerpt in the Holley book—we can see that the dates of Frank Scovill's imminent death by consumption were incorrect, as he must have made a full recovery to marry Jessie J. Joslyn in 1888.

In searching the city directories for St. Paul, I only found one reference in 1895 (which would be for the year 1894): *Scovill, Mrs. Mary C., bds 237 Nelson Avenue; Scoville, Frankie, bds 458. St. Peter.*

I cannot confirm that the "Frankie Scoville" mentioned in the city directory for St. Paul, Minnesota, is the same as Frank Scovill of this record; however, Mrs. Mary C. Scovill *is* the mother of Frank E. Scovill and had followed her daughter and her husband to the various states that they had lived in.[1255]

I was not able to locate Frank E. Scovill in St. Paul through the "ten years" he is said to have lived in St. Paul; however, if he *had* been receiving care from a hospital or sanitarium, it would have been unlikely he would have been listed in a city directory.[1256]

The information that Frank E. Scovill was in St. Paul in 1894 is that "grain of salt" that may or not be factual, but it must be noted that there are no other "Frankie Scovilles" listed in the city directory after 1895. However, "Frank E. Scoville, electrical engineer, board of public works, office 109 W. 8th, boards [at] Mrs. Lizzie Phillips" *is* listed in the 1895 city directory for Austin, Texas.

In 1900[1257] Frank and his wife, Jessie, are living at 1609 Congress Avenue in Austin. Frank was a superintendent of Street Dealers. The couple had two black servants, Lula Smith and Lawrence Watson.

The article on the following page is from the monthly edition of *Street Railway Review,* which reports on the activities of Frank E. Scovill as the general manager of the Rapid Transit Railway Company. It is unknown when this article was written, but it was likely sometime in the early 1900s.[1258]

Newspapers often had what was referred to as "gossip" columns, and in 1905 one such article appeared:

> Mr. and Mrs. Frank Scoville after a pleasant, but short visit to old friends in our city, have returned to their new home in Laredo.[1259]

---

1255 Minnie Irene Scoville Ashley (daughter of Mary C. Dunn Scoville) and her husband, Howard Ashley, had removed from St. Paul, Minnesota, to Troy, Montana, sometime in 1894. *U.S. City Directory, St. Paul, Minnesota,* "Ashley, Howard, removed to Troy, Montana," 265.

1256 This is my opinion only.

1257 1900, *Austin Ward 7, Travis, Texas;* Page: 10; ED: 0093; FHL: 1241673. Ancestry.

1258 This article was sent to me in 1985 by Mr. George Rowland of Paragould, Arkansas.

1259 *Austin-American Statesman,* Sunday, April 2, 1905, edition.

Below is a group photo of the family while they were in Austin, Texas. Perhaps taken circa 1895/96.[1260]

While living in Laredo, Jessie Scovill became quite ill and died on April 24, 1910. An article appeared in the *Austin American Statesman* regarding Jessie's health:

> Word was received this morning from Mrs. Brenizer, who has been at the bedside of Mrs. Jessie Scoville of Laredo for the past three weeks, that Mrs. Scoville's death is expected at any hour.[1261]

Jessie Jane Joslyn Scovill did die that very same day. Her body was transported by train to where she was born and raised in South Manchester, Connecticut. An article appeared in one of the newspapers in Texas (next page):[1262]

WINDSOR & KENFIELD PUBLISHING COMPANY,

MONON BUILDING, - - CHICAGO.

TELEPHONE, HARRISON 754.

**Published on the 15th of each month.**

SUBSCRIPTION, - - THREE DOLLARS.

FOREIGN SUBSCRIPTION, - FOUR DOLLARS AMERICAN MONEY.

*Address all Communications, and Remittances to Windsor & Kenfield Publishing Company, Monon Building, Chicago.*

H. H. WINDSOR, Editor. F. S. KENFIELD, Business Manager.

**The following clipping is cut from our issue of this month:**

STEAM PLANT FOR AUSTIN, TEX.

Mr. Frank E. Scovill, general manager of the Austin, (Tex.) Rapid Transit Railway Co., spent last week in Chicago, combining business with calls upon his many acquaintances. Mr. Scovill returns to erect a power house and install the machinery for a steam plant to operate his lines, which have been dependent on mules since the loss of the big dam. Mr. Scovill has been in electric work from the start, and is one of 23 men who at one time constituted the entire manufacturing force of what is now the General Electric Co.

The Austin company will now abandon its use of water power, as it is doubtful when the big dam will be rebuilt. The new steam plant will run condensing direct connected engines, working one unit, with one always in reserve. At present the cars are being drawn by three mules each, requiring 18 mules per car per day.

Water for condensing will be carried in an 8-in. pipe 1,500 ft. from the river to the new structure, and the laying of the pipe involves some difficulty, as it must be laid 38 ft. below the surface and all the distance through loose sand.

Left to Right: Mary C. Scoville, Frank Scovill, Rhoda Ashley, Jessie Jayne Joslyn Scovill

1260 Photo courtesy of Sandra Amador.

1261 Wednesday, April 24, 1910, edition; 12.

1262 Mr. George Rowland of Paragould, Arkansas, sent me the clipping of the obituary, however, he did not provide details on the newspaper the article appeared in.

**FUNERAL YESTERDAY**

**Remains of Mrs. Scovill Shipped This Morning to Her Old Home South Manchester, Conn.**

The funeral service over the remains of Mrs. F. E. Scovill was had yesterday afternoon at the family residence on the Heights, Rev. G. W. Plack of the Presbyterian church officiating.

During the service a chorus composed of Mesdames T. A. Austin, Paul Huberich, J. R. Moore, George W. Woodman, and J. C. Seymour sang several song [sic] one of which was "One Sweetly Solemn Thought."

This morning at 5:40 two cars left International and Great Northern Station for the convenience of friends of the deceased who wished to accompany the funeral party to the train. Many took advantage of the early service and went to the Scovill home and from their [sic] to the north bound I. & G. N. train which the remains were shipped to Connecticut.

Following are the pallbearers who assisted in the removal of the casket from the house to the depot: Messrs. C. E. H. Glazbrook, O. H. Rowland, J. R. Moore, John Coleman, Sam Mackin and W. P. May.

Mrs. N. O. Brenizer[1263] who was a great friend of Mrs. Scovill's accompanied Mr. Scovill as far as Austin.

Mr. Scovill who is accompanying his wife's remains to the east is due to arrive in South Manchester, Conn. Sunday afternoon and plans have been made to hold short funeral services at the grave Monday when Mrs. Scovill will be buried in the family plot in the South Manchester cemetery.

What a long and sad journey for Frank E. Scovill. It is likely that some of Jessie's family were waiting for Frank at the train station to accompany their sister back home. Another funeral took place on Sunday afternoon. Jessie Joslyn Scovill left a brother, Clarence R. Joslyn "of Hartford," and two sisters, Mrs. H. H. Smith of Syracuse, New York, and Miss Carrie Joslyn of Shelton, Connecticut.[1264] Another sister, Miss Bessie Joslyn, died shortly before her sister Jessie.[1265]

Frank Scovill returned home to Laredo and continued on with his life.

He was enumerated on the fourth day of May for the 1910[1266] census in Laredo:

Scovill, F. E., head, 48, widower, manager electric and railway co., b. Connecticut

---

1263 Mrs. N. O. Brenzier was born Annie Clime, 2 November 1859 in Ohio; she died 6 September 1941 in Austin, Texas, and is buried in Oakwood Cemetery, Austin. She married Dr. Nelson Orlando Brenzier in 1880 in Ohio. This brief information comes from Find A Grave; Annie's death certificate and marriage record were found on Ancestry.com.

1264 This information from *The Hartford Daily Courant,* Saturday, April 30, 1910, 8.

1265 Bessie Joslyn died 14 February 1910. Death Records, CSL.

1266 1910 census; *Laredo Ward 1, Texas,* Roll: T624_1599; Page: 18A; ED: 0143; FHL microfilm: 1375612. Ancestry.

Farnum, J. H., nephew,[1267] 23, superintendent BMT, b. Connecticut
Neiste, Manuela, servant, 22, housekeeper, b. Mexico

Six months after his wife's death, Frank Scovill remarried on October 25, 1910. An article appeared in *Laredo Weekly Times* announcing this event:

> Scovill—Schaeffer
> On a trip to North Texas recently, Mr. Frank E. Scovill, Manager of the Laredo Electric & Railway Company of this City, prepared a surprise for his friends. While at Wichita Falls, October 25th at the residence of the Rev. R. R. Hamlin pastor of the Christian Church, of that City, he was united in marriage to Mrs. Eugenie Philipe Shaeffer of Lampasas, Texas. Mrs. Scovill was a native of Austin, Texas, having lived there the greater part of her life until a few years ago. She is now at Lampasas closing up her home preparing to return with Mr. Scovill after the Shriner's Reception which will be at Austin in the Senate Chamber at the Capitol on the 21st.
>
> Mr. and Mrs. Scovill will be at Home after December 1st.

Eugenie Shaeffer was born Eugenie Philipe/Phillipe in Austin, Texas, to parents who had immigrated from France. Per the 1910 census, Eugenie Shaeffer is listed as age "40, divorced and is a partner in the Hotel business." Eugenie's mother, Claudia "Philipi," is also living in this hotel in Lampasas.

It would seem that Eugenie would have had to have been in Wichita Falls at the same time as Frank to meet him (unless they knew one another prior to his visit there).

Frank and Eugenia remained in Laredo for approximately ten years, at which time they removed to Camden, Ouachita, Arkansas, a town with a population of 3,238 in 1920.[1268] Their time in Camden was short lived as Frank's talents were required in Paragould, Arkansas. An article appeared in *The Camden Daily News:*[1269]

> Frank E. Scovill, for the past 15 months manager of the Camden branch of the Arkansas Power and Light Company, and general "big time" booster for anything and everything that is for the betterment of Camden, has been transferred to the management of the plant for the same company in Paragould. The plant at Paragould is larger than the local plant, and is given Mr. Scovill as a recognition of the splendid work he has performed in administering the affairs of the Camden office.
>
> During the short time Mr. Scovill has been in charge of the local light and water plant, the city has been furnished with the best services it has ever had, and by the installation of more business-like methods by Mr. Scovill, the income of the Camden

1267 I am unfamiliar with this name. This person could be related to the Dunn side of the family.

1268 Town population per the 1920 census. https://en.wikipedia.org/wiki/Camden,_Arkansas Arkansas.

1269 Article sent to me in the late 1980s by George Rowland of Paragould, Arkansas. The date is perhaps 13 September 1920. Article copied as written in the newspaper.

plant has been increased several thousand dollars, which puts the Camden plant near a paying basis for the first time since the increase in the cost of living.

Mr. Scovill, who is a Mason, past potentate of the Shrine of Austin, Texas; past exalted ruler of the Elks, and past commander of the Knights Templar, has been actively engaged in the church, civic and fraternal life in the city. He has been a most dependable worker on committees in the Chamber of commerce organization, and as superintendent of the Sunday School of St. John's Episcopal church. As a member of St. John's church, Mr. Scovill has been an important factor in the campaign that is being put on to obtain rector for full time.

Mr. Scoville has been in the electrical business since 1882, spending ten years in the plant at Laredo, Texas, and ten years in Austin. He will be succeeded by W. B. Goldsberry of Atlanta, Texas, who is just entering the employment of the Arkansas Light and Power Company.

Mr. Scovill will leave the latter part of this week for his new work at Paragould. His family will continue to reside in Camden until arrangements are made to find suitable quarters in Paragould.

An article appeared on the front page of the *Paragould Soliphone* in the October 4, 1920, issue. The headline reads: SCOVILL SAYS PARAGOULD IS SPLENDID CITY.

Frank E. Scovill wrote to C. A. Doak, secretary of the Camden Chamber of Commerce to tell him his first impressions of the city of Paragould.

I wish a few of the workers on the Camden Chamber of Commerce could drop into this little town and see what has been accomplished here, not only the few good workers, but it would be wonderful to turn the majority of members of the Camden Chamber of Commerce loose in Paragould for about three hours. I have always found wonderfully nice people there, but they are so self-satisfied that they never have been able to accomplish much that so many of you wish to do. With few workers you have, there are more than enough of the satisfied ones who hold back any civic improvements.

Paragould has forty-nine blocks of paved streets, and the greater portion of the people own their own homes. The streets and lawns are beautifully kept, there are no fences to mar the beauty of the lawns, everything is clean and mowed. You will see such uniformity of cleaning that you would think it was one big park. They have a dandy hotel (the Vandervoort—parentheses are the author's) and a great progressive bunch of business men. There are not men of great wealth here, but everyone seems progressive and wants to do something to help beautify the town. Even on the side of the town where people of smaller means live (east of the railroad tracks - - parentheses are the author's) the lawns are wonderfully well kept, the streets the same way. I would love to have the Chamber of Commerce of Camden drop in and take a few lessons from Paragould. They have a white way here that is six blocks long on one street (Pruett) and four block long on a cross streets four blocks wide (Court) and it extends two blocks either side of these streets four blocks wide. The white way consists of posts on every corner with five lamps to the post with two posts on every corner with five lamps to the post with two posts of the same kind set in between blocks and it is a beautiful sight coming in as I did at 11 o'clock at night and finding the streets beautifully lighted, and a great big sign right at the depot all in electric lights, 'You'll like Paragould.'

I wrote my wife immediately on my arrival that this was what greeted me, and I did like Paragould and the longer I stay the more I am impressed with Paragould as a progressive, up-to-date little city.[1270]

(I wonder how the people of Camden felt about Frank Scovill's glowing report of Paragould? It would seem Camden was a little "backward" per Frank Scovill's opinion).

I have been unsuccessful in locating Frank and his wife Eugenia on the 1920 census. They may have been in between Camden and Paragould when the census was taken. However, they *are* on the 1930[1271] census living in Paragould on North 68th Street:

Scovill, F. E., head, 67, owns home, \$3,500, 26 yrs. of age at first marriage, b. Connecticut, manager Light Plant
Scovill, Eugenia P., wife, 60, 17 yrs. at first marriage, b. Texas
Scovill, Eunice G., daughter, 22, born France (American citizen)

Eunice G. "Scovill" was born March 20, 1908, supposedly in France.[1272] Frank E. Scovill and Eugenia Philipe did not marry until 1910. Eunice is likely the child from Eugenia's first marriage to a man named "Shaeffer."[1273]

Frank's wife, Eugenia, died at the age of sixty-four of "carcinoma of the liver" on June 17, 1934, in Paragould.[1274] She was the daughter of Eugene Philipe "of Paris" and Claudia Le Senes of "France."

A brief obituary appears in the *Paragould Daily Press:*[1275]

Eugenia Phillipe Scovill died at 332 North Sixth St.—wife of former manager of Arkansas Utilities of Paragould who retired March 1, 1933. She was a native of Austin, Texas—marriage at Wichita Falls, Texas on Oct. 25, 1910—moved to Paragould Sept. 1920 when Mr. Scoville became manager of Arkansas Utilities. Funeral at First Methodist Church. Survived by husband, a daughter Mrs. E. L. Conley of Florence, Alabama; two brothers, Gaston Phillipe of San Antonio and Louis Phillipe of Austin, Texas.

---

1270 Article provided to me by George Rowland, Paragould, Arkansas.

1271 1930 census; *Paragould, Greene, Arkansas;* Page: 3A; ED:0007; FHL microfilm: 2339811; Dwelling: 332. Ancestry.

1272 1940 census states she was born in Texas. (1940 census, *Marked Tree, Poinsett, Arkansas;* Roll: m-to627-00162; Page: 21A; ED: 56-9.) Ancestry.

1273 Since Eunice was two years old at her mother's marriage it is possible that she thought of Frank as her father as he is listed as her father on her death certificate.

1274 *Arkansas Death Certificates, 1914–1969.* Ancestry.

1275 June 18, 1934, issue. Provided by George Rowland, Paragould, Arkansas.

Eugenia Scovill is buried in Linwood Cemetery in Paragould.

Frank was once again a widower. There is no record of him after his wife's death and as with the 1920 census, I have not been able to locate him on the 1940 census. He may have been traveling or was simply missed. A clue to his whereabouts circa 1943 comes from his own death certificate where he had entered the *Home for Aged Masons* in Arlington, Texas, nine years prior to his death.

Frank E. Scovill's office in Laredo, Texas

One October 30, 1952, Frank E. Scovill died of "senility" at the age of "90 years, 4 months and 16 days."

The obituary appeared in *Paragould Daily Press* on November 1, 1952:

> Frank E. Scovill, aged 89, former manager of the Arkansas Utilities Company in this city for about fifteen years died at 5:30 yesterday afternoon at the Masonic Home at Arlington, Texas. He was a native of Connecticut and came to this city from Austin, Texas. He retired in 1933.
>
> Mr. Scovill was a charter member of the Paragould Rotary Club and served as president of the club in 1928 and 1929. He was an active member of the Masonic Lodge and the Shriners while he was in this city.
>
> The body will arrive tonight over the Cotton Belt (railroad). Funeral Services will be held at two Sunday afternoon at the Verlyn Heath Funeral Home and burial will be in Linwood Cemetery. The Rev. S. B. Wilford, pastor of the First Methodist Church, will officiate.
>
> He had no known immediate survivors.[1276]

≈

Eunice "Scovill" Conley died three weeks before Frank on October 4, 1952, perhaps in Alabama. She was born March 20, 1908, in Texas and married Ernest L. Conley on August 9, 1930, in Paragould, Greene, Arkansas.[1277] Eunice is buried with her mother and "father" in Linwood Cemetery.

There were no children born between Frank E. Scovill and Jessie Jayne Joslyn.[1278]

---

1276 Frank's sister, Minnie Irene Scoville Ashley Lindberg, was still living when Frank's obituary was written.

1277 *Arkansas, County Marriages Index, 1837–1957.* Ancestry.

1278 Photo courtesy of Sandra Amador.

## 37. *Minnie Irene Scoville[7] (William Harrison,[6] Franklin,[5] Ithamar,[4] Timothy,[3] Stephen,[2] Stephen,[1] Arthur)*

Born 1 January 1865, Great Barrington, Berkshire, Massachusetts;[1279] died 7 January 1960, University Place, Pierce, Washington;[1280] buried New Tacoma Cemetery, Pierce, Washington; married (1) 18 November 1885, Winsted, Litchfield, Connecticut,[1281] Howard Ashley, born 19 March 1862, Colebrook, Litchfield, Connecticut; died 2 June 1939, Seattle, King, Washington;[1282] buried Pioneer Cemetery, Skagway, Skagway Borough, Alaska; son of James Ashley and Mary Moore;[1283] married (2) 17 January 1921, Seattle, King, Washington, Michael O. Linberg;[1284] born 8 February 1875, Fardal, Norway;[1285] died 18 February 1970, Gig Harbor, Pierce, Washington; burial Cromwell Cemetery, Gig Harbor, Pierce, Washington.[1286]

It was suggested by the 1865 state census for Great Barrington, Massachusetts, that Minnie Irene was given the name of "Mary I. Scoville;" however, a direct descendant states that "she never knew her in life as anything but Minnie Irene."[1287]

While Minnie Irene had been born in Massachusetts, her early life was spent in North Canaan, Winchester, and New Britain, Connecticut.

According to Minnie Irene's great-granddaughter, Minnie Irene loved writing poetry and likely started at a young age. Even when she had debilitating arthritis in her later years, she always found a way to write poems. She (Minnie Irene) was also a very "strong and spirited person" as well as a "loving and caring person." As Minnie aged, she became very thin and walked with a cane, however, Minnie Irene was always well dressed, even in her nineties.

Minnie Irene is on the 1880 census living in Winchester, Litchfield, Connecticut, age fifteen. She had attended school the prior year. The age of leaving school during the 1800s was fourteen. Since she had completed her schooling, she spent her time helping her mother, Mary

---

1279 According to most census records, Minnie Irene's birthplace is given as "Massachusetts." The 1865 State Census for Great Barrington, Berkshire County, shows her, her mother, and brother Frank living with Cecelia McGrath. Minnie's age at this time is given as "4 months." Minnie's father, William, had not been discharged from the war at the time of Minnie's birth. He was in New Haven, Connecticut, convalescing and helping out with the other soldiers who had been more seriously wounded. Minnie's mother, Mary Catherine, likely went to a family member to give birth. Cecelia McGrath could be one of her sisters as there are photos of McGraths in Sandra Amador's photo collection.

1280 Find A Grave.

1281 *The New Hartford Tribune,* Friday, November 27, 1885; 3. GenealogyBank.

1282 Obituary notice; Find A Grave.

1283 1870 and 1880 censuses. Ancestry.

1284 *Washington County Marriages, 1855–2008.* FamilySearch.

1285 *U. S. Naturalization Records, 1840–1957;* Ancestry.

1286 *Washington Death Index, 1940–2014;* Obituary; Find A Grave.

1287 I am fortunate to have first-person accounts of Minnie Irene's life, which come from a great-granddaughter who knew Minnie personally. Much of the anecdotal information in this record comes from her.

Minnie Irene Scoville approximately seventeen years of age.

Catherine, calling on friends, and perhaps becoming involved with the church and its activities.

Minnie may also have attended a function in 1882 where the New Hartford Harmony Society was giving a concert, and where a young man by the name of Howard Ashley was a member and performed in the concert on February 17th.[1288, 1289]

In 1870 Howard Ashley was age nine and working in a cotton mill along with his sisters and brother (Iola, 14, Elizabeth, 13, and Albert, 11). Howard's father, James Ashley, was a house painter by trade. The Ashley family were living in Pine Meadow (a village of New Hartford), Connecticut. There was a cotton mill in the town named Greenwoods Mill Company. This company began in 1845 and they made cotton dock, sail cloth, paper felts, twine, cotton belting, and other heavy cotton fabric.[1290] When Howard Ashley was eighteen, he was employed in a caster shop. I have not been successful in locating a name of this factory; however, Howard was manufacturing caster wheels, which were used in a variety of ways from furniture to equipment.

Howard Ashley had been born in Colebrook, Litchfield, Connecticut, and lived his early life there before his family removed to Pine Meadow. Howard's father, James Ashley, is on the 1860[1291] census living in the residence of Harvey De Wolf, who is the "landlord." James Ashley appears to be a single man of forty-two years of age who was born in New York. Howard's mother (Mary Moore) didn't begin having children until she was thirty-two years of age. It is unknown whether she is the first or second wife of James Ashley.

A marriage notice appeared in *Connecticut Western News* on November 27, 1885:[1292]

> **Marriages**
> At West Winsted, November 18 at the residence of the bride's parents, Howard Ashley and Miss Minnie Scoville, both of Winsted.

On the same date another article was published in *The New Hartford Tribune:*[1293]

> Mr. and Mrs. Howard Ashley of Winsted were in town Saturday calling upon friends . . .

1288 *The New Hartford Tribune,* Saturday, February 17, 1882, edition; 3. GenealogyBank.
1289 Photo courtesy of Sandra Amador, the great-granddaughter of Minnie Irene.
1290 New Hartford Historical Society (https//www.newhartfordhistory.org).
1291 1860 census, *Colebrook, Litchfield, Connecticut;* Page: 847. Ancestry.
1292 Friday edition, 3. GenealogyBank.
1293 *Ibid* (same date, page, and edition. Just a different newspaper).

The newlywed couple did not remain in Connecticut very long. *The New Hartford Tribune*[1294] published in the section "Visiting News" the following:

> . . . Mrs. Howard Ashley, who as Miss Minnie Scoville was well known in town, now of Aurora, Illinois, is visiting her parents in Winsted.

Regrettably, city directories are not available (online) for Aurora, Illinois, and I haven't found online historical societies to be of much help. Suffice it to say, the couple did not remain long in Aurora as they had moved on to St. Paul, Ramsey, Minnesota. This is where their first child, Rhoda, was born on December 11, 1889, as well as her brother, Howard B., in 1894.[1295]

Howard Ashley is only listed in the city directory for St. Paul from 1889–1895. Unfortunately, these particular directories did not list the wives' names—I can only presume this is *the* Howard Ashley of this record. He is consistently listed as a "machinist" throughout this period, and they had lived at 618 E. 5th Street, 401 Charles, 395 Eichenwald, and 853 Frances. The only house that still stands today is 395 Eichenwald.

The family moved again—this time to Kalispell,[1296] Flathead, Montana. The population of Kalispell in 1900 was approximately 2,500 persons and it began as a railroad town.[1297]

Far left: Howard Ashley, Rhoda Ashley, unknown child, Mary C. Scoville sitting on steps. Child at right nearrailings is Burnett Ashley. Kalispell, Flathead, Montana.

---

1294 Friday, May 27, 1887, edition; 3. Newspapers.

1295 The home in St. Paul, Minnesota, is not included here as the original is of a poor quality; however, the home was very large in the Italianate style, which included a wrap-around veranda.

1296 From the Salish Indian language meaning "flat land (prairie) above the lake." Wikipedia.org.

1297 Photo courtesy of Sandra Amador.

The town was platted in the spring of 1891 in order to serve as the division point of the Great Northern Railway from St. Paul, Minnesota, to Seattle, Washington.[1298] The clue as to why the Ashleys kept moving westward is that Howard was working in his capacity as a mechanic/machinist for the railroad system.

The 1900 census[1299] has the family in Jocko Township, Flathead, Montana. The Jocko Indian Reservation was the original name of the Flathead Indian Reservation, which is between Missoula and Kalispell.

Ashley, Howard, head, March 1862, 38, m. 14 yrs., b. Connecticut, no occupation given

Ashley, Minnie I., wife, Jan. 1865, 35, m. 14 yrs., 3 children born, 3 living, b. Connecticut

Ashley, Rhoda E., daughter, Dec. 1889, 10, b. Minnesota

Ashley, Howard B., son, Jan. 1894, 6, Minnesota

Ashley, Frank V. C., son, July 1899, 10/12, Montana

In my research, I have not found a town with the name of "Jocko" or "Jocko Township." The only information comes from a Wikipedia article: "The **Jocko Valley** is located in western Montana in the northwestern United States. It is located on land of the Flathead Indian Reservation. The valley was named for Jacques Raphael Finlay, a trapper and fur trader in the area during 1806–1809."

By September 1901, the family had moved again, this time to Skagway, Alaska. An article appeared in *The Daily Morning Alaskan*[1300] heralding the arrival of the Ashleys to Skagway:

> Howard Ashley, General Foreman at the W. P.& Y Ry[1301] shops, and family have moved into W. H. Hooper's elegant residence at the corner of Sixteenth and State Street.

The W. P. & Y. Railway was built in 1898 during the Klondike Gold Rush, which started in 1896. Gold was discovered by George Carmack and two men from First Nations—Skookum Jim and (Tagish) Dawson Charlie—at Rabbit Creek.[1302] There are many tales regarding the discovery of gold and how it came about (and who discovered it); many have tried to separate fact from fiction, and I will leave that to the historians of the Klondike Gold Rush to discern.

While Howard Ashley was employed by the W. P. & Y Railway, it doesn't appear he had any interest in prospecting—at least there are no articles regarding such an interest.

There are many newspaper articles of the Ashelys while they were in Skagway. Howard was involved with many aspects of the community; he was on the schoolboard, church

1298 *Historical Walking Tours of Kalispell, Montana Flathead County,* Montana Historical Society. https://www.mhs.mt.gov.

1299 1900 census, *Jocko township, Flathead, Montana;* ED: 34; Sheet: 2; FHL: 1240911; Dwelling: 34; Family: 34. Ancestry.

1300 September 8, 1901, 1. Newspapers.

1301 White Pass & Yukon Railway.

1302 University of Alaska, https://www.canadianmysteries.ca.

committee, White Pass Employee's Club, elected Councilman, and became the Mayor of Skagway. Minnie Irene belonged to the Ladies Guild of the Episcopal Church, had sewing bees, and the like.

Many of the articles come from the "Visiting and Gossip" columns that were common during that time. Here are some examples:

> 1903, Tuesday, August 11—Misses Pomeroy and Shaffer, who have been visiting Mr. and Mrs. Howard Ashley, leave for Seattle on the Dolphin.[1303, 1304]

> 1908, Saturday, March 21—Mr. and Mrs. Howard Ashley have taken what is known as the Winslow residence on Second Street near Main, Mrs. Ashley with young son Frank, having returned from the south today. Mr. Ashley has been living at the Fifth Avenue hotel during the winter while Mrs. Ashley was away. Their daughter, Mrs. E. L. Miller returned also on the Jefferson from a visit to Seattle.[1305]

Possibly W. H. Hooper's home that the Ashleys moved into when the family first arrived in Skagway.

A number of articles appeared in February's *Daily Alaskan* in 1909 where Minnie Irene was in the hospital for "severe heart trouble," as well as suffering from a "severe cold." She spent time in the White Pass Hospital.

> 1909, Wednesday, April 7—People Show Confidence Electing Five Councilmen—Howard Ashley Gets Highest Poll![1306]

> 1909, Monday, December 27—Mr. Howard Ashley returned on the Jefferson from a vacation visit to Tacoma where he visited with relatives and friends. Mr. Ashley will make his home at the Pullen house for the winter.[1307]

1303 *The Daily Morning Alaskan,* Newspapers.

1304 Photo courtesy of Sandra Amador.

1305 *Daily Alaskan,* Vol: 10; Page: 5, GenealogyBank.

1306 *Ibid,* Vol: 11; Page: 2.

1307 *Ibid,* Vol: 12; Page: 4.

In 1910 the family was living on Sixth Street in Skagway. The enumerator visited the household on January 20th of that year:[1308]

Ashley, Howard, b. March 1862, 47, m. 24 yrs., b. Connecticut, railway master mechanic

Ashley, Minnie I., wife, b. Jan. 1865, 44, m. 24 yrs., 3 children born/3 living, b. Connecticut

Ashley, Howard B, son, b. Jan. 1894, 16, b. Minnesota

Ashely, Frank V., son, b. July 1899, 10, b. Minnesota

An article appeared in the Saturday edition of the *Daily Alaskan* on January 22, 1910:[1309]

> Mrs. E. L. Miller writes that she and Margaret[1310] reached Tacoma in due time, and they are now at University Place visiting with Mrs. Miller's mother, Mrs. Howard Ashley. Mrs. M. C. Schoville of Texas, mother of Mrs. Ashley, grandmother of Mrs. Miller and great-grandmother of Margaret is also visiting at University Place.
>
> Mrs. Ashley is very much improved in health and expects to return to Skagway in the spring. University Place[1311] at Lemon Beach and is gaining a reputation as an "open air" health resort.

Based on the various newspaper articles, Minnie Irene did not spend the winters in Skagway. She would go "south," usually around October, and spend her time in Washington. Minnie had suffered from debilitating arthritis in her later years and the extreme cold in the Alaskan winters would have been difficult.

There are a few articles from the *Daily Alaskan* from 1911 regarding the celebration of the twenty-eighth anniversary of "Mr. and Mrs. Howard Ashley."[1312] Another article from October 1911 described how Minnie was "confined to her home due to an illness."[1313]

After 1911, there is no mention of "Mr. and Mrs. Howard Ashley" or "Mrs. Howard (Minnie) Ashley." It appears that this couple had separated as Howard Ashley remained in Skagway.

In 1916, Howard Ashley was elected mayor of Skagway. An article in the *Daily Alaskan* has his win in the April 5th edition of the newspaper:[1314]

> **Ashley Chosen Mayor**
>
> Howard Ashley received the heavy support of the votes for the pivotal position of the mayor of the city. Mr. Ashley has been mayor of Skagway for the past year. As

1308 1910 census, *Alaska Territory, Division 1;* Roll: T624_1748; Page: 45A; ED: 0006; FHL: 1375761. Ancestry.

1309 Vol: 12; Page 4; GenealogyBank.

1310 Mrs. E. L. Miller is Rhoda Ashley Miller and Margaret is her daughter.

1311 This is likely referring to University Place and Lemon Beach in Pierce County, Washington.

1312 Saturday, November 25th edition; Vol: 11; Page: 4. GenealogyBank.

1313 *Ibid,* Saturday, October 28th edition; Vol: 11; Page: 4.

1314 *Ibid,* Wednesday, April 5th edition; Page: 2.

> head of the council, he has endeavored to be fair, honest and render an efficient administration. The people have voiced their sentiment by [ ] one hundred and sixty votes for him.

Many articles and notices appeared in the *Daily Alaskan* regarding Howard Ashley's comings and goings, illnesses, travel, and the like up until his death.

On the 1920[1315] census for Washington we find Minnie Irene Ashley living alone in Hales Pass, Pierce County. At this time, she was fifty-five years old and was occupied in farming. She indicates that she is "married;" as we've seen from past instances of divorce, stating that you were "married" instead of "divorced" was a common occurrence.[1316]

Six houses away was Michael Linberg, age forty-four. He was the companion of Edward Iverson, along with Andrew Wang (also a "companion"). Michael Linberg was a logger and had come from Norway (the reason for mentioning Michael Lindberg will become clearer later on in this narrative).

Howard Ashley was in Skagway in 1920[1317] living alone in the Pullen House Hotel. He also lists himself as "married," and even though he was the mayor of Skagway, he is listed as a "master mechanic" for the "WP & YRR."

"On January 17, 1921, (Minnie) Irene Scoville Ashley married in Seattle Michael Linborg [sic].[1318] The witnesses were Mrs. Rhoda Miller and Mrs. Addie L. Vanderboget."[1319]

Michael Linberg was born on February 8, 1875, in Fardal, Norway, and immigrated to the United States in June 1881. He entered the U.S. from Liverpool, England, and arrived in Philadelphia.[1320]

In 1895, Michael is listed on the Minnesota State Census as living in Fremont, Winona, Minnesota. He is listed as "20 years old, born about 1875 in Norway and a farmer." He is also listed as being "5′ 11″ tall with brown eyes and hair and weighing 185 lbs."[1321] According to Michael's obituary, he arrived in Gig Harbor, Washington, in 1921.[1322]

---

1315 1920 census, *Hales Pass, Pierce, Washington;* Roll: T625_1935; Page: 3B; ED: 192; Image: 525; Dwelling: 66; Family: 67. The enumerator visited the household between the 12th and 13th of January.

1316 I have not found a divorce decree; however, the marriage license between Howard Ashley and Agnes C. Moffatt clearly states in the question section of whether Howard had been married prior—"once" was his answer. It also states that the previous marriage or marriages dissolved in "divorce;" *Alaska, Vital Records, 1816–2005;* Film: 106481818; FamilySearch.

1317 1920 census, *Skagway, First Judicial District, Alaska Territory;* Roll: T625_2030; Page: 2A; ED: 2. Ancestry.

1318 His surname is alternately spelled "Linberg, Linborg."

1319 *Washington County Marriages, 1855–2008;* Certificate No. 73511. Ancestry.

1320 *U. S. Naturalization Records, 1840–1957; Washington District Court and Petition Records, 1924, #2050-2149;* NARA Roll: 141; microfilm serial#: M1542. Ancestry.

1321 1895 state census; *Minnesota, U.S. Territorial, and State Census, 1849–1905;* Line: 12; Roll: V290-104. Ancestry.

1322 The date of his arrival in Gig Harbor is likely incorrect as Minnie Irene Ashley and Michael

In Alaska, another marriage took place two months prior to Minnie's on November 24, 1920, when Howard Ashley married Agnes C. Moffatt:[1323]

> The wedding of Miss Agnes C. Moffatt and Mr. Howard Ashley was solemnized on Thanksgiving Eve at the Pullen House, the Rev. E. L. Winterberger officiating. Mr. and Mrs. Eric Telfer stood with the bride and groom and were witnesses to the certificate of marriage . . . the bride came to Skagway several years ago and was one of the successful teachers in the public school system. She became assistant postmistress in Ketchikan and later Skagway . . . The groom has lived in Skagway for years and is the trusted master mechanic for the White Pass and Yukon route. He has always been active in civil, social, and political life and enjoys the confidence and esteem of all his acquaintances. Mrs. and Mrs. Ashley will make their home at the Pullen House for the present.

Each set of couples built new lives with their respective spouses. For Minnie Irene and Michael Linberg, it was living on the farm. Minnie had purchased eight acres where they raised apples, strawberries, vegetables, and all kinds of tulips, daffodils, and tuberose begonias. It is also said that Minnie Irene had a "beautiful rose arbor."[1324] In spite of her debilitating arthritis, she found a way to continue writing poetry.

Minnie Irene also took on the State of Washington when she wanted a road built to get to the ferry. The road was built just as she wanted. Mike Linberg was interviewed in 1970 for an article that appeared in one of the Washington newspapers regarding his ninety-fifth birthday party that was held for him by friends. Mike stated that, "At that time there was no road down the hill to Hales Passage." Mike said that:

> Mrs. Linberg took the matter in hand. Assisted by Mrs. Andrew Severtsen, they served the county commissioners a fine chicken dinner in order to secure that road. The commissioners were so impressed by their hospitality that shortly afterward the much-needed road was put in with the assistance of the men in the neighborhood.[1325]

Mike Linberg had been a saw filer by trade, having worked in the logging industry. Saw filing was done by hand and it is now considered a lost art. Mike also loved gardening and spent many pleasant hours working the farm.

≈

---

Linberg married in January, 1921.

1323 *Whitehorse Daily Star* (Whitehorse, Yukon, Canada); Friday, December 3, 1920, edition; *Canada, Newspapers* and *Marriage Index, 1800s–1999,* Ancestry.

1324 Recollections of great-granddaughter, Sandra Amador.

1325 A copy of the newspaper article was sent to me many years ago: "Old-Timer Celebrates 95th Birthday." The name of this newspaper is unknown.

Howard Ashley and his new wife, Agnes, had a different type of life in Skagway. Howard continued to be involved with the social activities and clubs in Skagway while still working for the WP & Y RR as a master mechanic. He was still the mayor of the town through the 1920s.

Howard's new wife, Agnes C. Moffatt , had been born in Canada (perhaps Huntingdon, Quebec) circa 1884.[1326] She had gone first to Ketchikan as an assistant postmistress and then onto Skagway, where she taught school for a time. She then returned to her former profession as an assistant postmistress in Skagway. Her mother, Emily Moffatt, had emigrated to Alaska with her daughter when Agnes removed to Ketchikan.

Emily Moffatt was born the same year as Howard Ashley and was a widow. She can be found on ship manifests from Canada to Alaska from 1926–1930.

The 1930 census[1327] for Howard Ashley:

Ashley, Howard, 67, married, b. Connecticut, master mechanic, WP & Y RR
Ashley, Agnes M., wife, 43, b. Canada, immigrated 1904, naturalized
Moffatt, Emily, mother-in-law, 66, widowed, b. Canada, immigrated 1889, not naturalized

The 1930 census[1328] for Minnie Irene Linberg:

Linberg, Michael O., head, 55, b. Norway, logger, logging company
Linberg, M. Irene, wife, 65, b. Massachusetts
Miller, Marjorie, granddaughter, 15, b. California
Scovill, Mary C., mother-in-law, 86, widow, b. New York

At the time of this census the Linberg family was living at 2048 Sixth Street in Tacoma, Washington. Michael Linberg was still employed at this time, and they were not living in Hales Pass on a permanent basis during this timeframe.

Throughout the 1920s many snippets of news articles appeared in the *Daily Alaskan* regarding the comings and goings of Howard Ashley, from entertaining dinner guests to being the guest at other people's homes; various nominations for offices; leaving on business to Juneau and returning. Mrs. Ashley also had card parties, a birthday party for her husband, and she made improvements on their home on the corner of 8th Avenue and State Street.

Howard Ashley was the Mayor of Skagway from 1915–1925, and continued to be busy in the town's affairs.

Sometime in the mid 1930s, the Ashleys returned to Washington (Seattle) and were living at 1236 E. 95th Street (this house still stands today).[1329] Howard must have retired as there is no entry for any type of occupation.

---

1326 The 1930 census gives her age as "43" while the 1940 indicates "56." The *Alaskan U. S. Arriving and Departing Passengers & Crew Manifests 1906–1963,* states that she was from "Huntingdon." Ancestry.

1327 1930 census, *Skagway Town (incorporated) First Judicial District, Alaska Territory;* ED: 0030; Page: 9A; FHL: 2342360; Dwelling: 116; Family: 116. Ancestry.

1328 1930 census; *Tacoma, Pierce, Washington;* Ward: 7; ED: 0185; Page: 1B; FHL: 2342246; Dwelling: 15; Family: 15. Ancestry.

1329 *U.S. City Directories, 1822–1995;* 77; Ancestry.

On the second day of June, 1939, Howard Ashley died at the age of seventy-seven in the home he shared with Agnes in Seattle. Large headlines appeared in the *Seattle Daily Times:*[1330]

> ASHLEY, SKAGWAY EX-MAYOR, DIES

The obituary tells of how he worked as a master mechanic for the railroads in Minnesota, Montana, and Alaska for "forty years," and returned to Seattle "four years ago." He was a member of the Elks in Skagway and left his widow, Agnes (Seattle), a daughter, Mrs. Rhoda Holmes (Los Angeles), two sons, H.B. (Howard Burnett) Longview (Washington) and Frank Ashley (Tacoma), and three grandchildren and one great-grandchild.

Howard was cremated and buried in Pioneer Cemetery in Skagway.

His widow, Agnes, is found on the 1940 census still living in the same dwelling. The information reveals that she owns the home and is age fifty-six. Her occupation states that she is a "practical nurse and went to four years of college."

Very little is known of Agnes C. (Moffatt) Ashley. She is listed on the 1905 state census for Minnesota living in the village of Nashwauk.[1331] She is "21," born in "Ontario," father born "South America," mother born "Canada." Agnes had lived there for "3 years" and was a "teacher." Nothing more is known of her until her marriage to Howard Ashley in 1920.

Agnes appears in the city directories from 1941–1960.[1332] She was employed during these years involved with various activities such as being a house mother for the Sigma Tau Alpha Society in 1942. In 1948 she was a page for SPL,[1333] and in 1951 Elk KCHS.[1334]

On December 30, 1962, Agnes C. Moffatt Ashley died in Seattle, Washington. A very brief obituary appeared in the *Seattle Daily Times:*[1335]

> Adams Forkner Funeral Home
> Ashley, Agnes Moffatt,[1336] of 1236 NE 95th cousin of Marian Reid, Victoria, B.C., and Mary Alvarez of Mechanic Village, N.Y. Member of Alaska Friends. At her request no services will be held.
>
> Cremated remains will be interred in Skagway, Alaska. Arrangements by Johnson and Hamilton.

---

1330 Saturday, June 3rd edition; 8. Newspapers.

1331 1905 state census, *Minnesota Territorial and State Census, 1849–1905; Nashwauk, Itasca County;* ED: 22; Roll: MNSC_129; 19 June 1905. Ancestry

1332 Years 1945–1948, 1950, and 1952, are missing from Ancestry's database. The 1960 directory is the last one that is available on Ancestry.

1333 I believe "SPL" may stand for "Seattle Public Library."

1334 Based on current information, the Elks have a scholarship for students. Whether this is the same as noted in 1951, I am not sure. Agnes' husband, Howard, had been very involved with the Elks Club during his time in Skagway.

1335 The obituary notice comes from *GenealogyBank* on December 30, 1962.

1336 She was born 22 October 1883, Canada. Social Security documents. Ancestry.

Her burial is alongside her husband, Howard Ashely, in the Pioneer Cemetery in Skagway. Current photos of the cemetery show it to be virtually in the forest. Lichen and moss cover most of the stones there.

~

In 1940[1337] Minnie Irene and Mike Linberg are listed as living in Hales Pass. Mike was sixty-five and Minnie Irene was seventy-five. They owned their own home, which was worth $2,000. Both had the necessary education at that time: Mike had completed the eighth grade and Minnie Irene had one year of high school. Mike was working as a carpenter.

To refer back to the newspaper article for Mike Linberg's birthday celebration, he reminisced on how (when he came to Gig Harbor in 1902) he worked as a logger and an "expert saw filer." There was only a wagon trail (no roads) and the town had one store, a school, and a post office. If you wanted to leave Gig Harbor you had to either go by rowboat or take the steamboat to Tacoma. In spite of some of the hardships, it must have been quite idyllic.[1338]

Minnie Irene Linberg's great-granddaughter relates how Mike would make flower boxes to put along the outside of the windows where she (Minnie) sat near the fire. He liked doing special things for her.

Mike and Minnie's home in Gig Harbor. It is unknown who the two girls are. You can just make out a dog to the right of the tallest girl. Mike called this property "Worlds End."

Minnie Irene's health slowly deteriorated and, in 1959, she was placed in a nursing home because Mike could no longer care for her. Minnie's great-granddaughter related that the nursing home "was awful," but there was no one who could care for her in the condition that she was in. Mike Linberg continued to care for their property that they had loved so much.

On Thursday, January 7, 1960, Minnie Irene Scoville Ashley Linberg died at the age of ninety-five. Her obituary appeared in the *Tacoma News Tribune* the following day. In spite of her debilitating arthritis, she lived a long and interesting life. Born in Massachusetts, she lived in Connecticut, Illinois, Minnesota, Montana, Seattle, Alaska, and, finally, landed at "Worlds End" in Gig Harbor. Minnie's funeral service was held at the C. C. Mellinger Memorial Funeral Church.

---

1337 1940 census, *Hales Pass, Pierce, Washington*; Roll: m-t0627-04355; Page: 4B; ED: 27-39; Dwelling: 96. Ancestry.

1338 Photo courtesy of Sandra Amador.

The funeral program includes a poem by Alfred, Lord Tennyson entitled "Crossing the Bar." So appropriate for one who loved poetry. Below is one of Minnie's poems:

If all the rhymes and "jingles"
That go flying through my Head
*Would only light on paper*
*I'd be famous when I'm Dead.*
*M.I.L.*[1339]

Minnie was laid to rest at the New Tacoma Cemetery.

Mike Linberg continued to live at "World's End" for the next ten years. An article appeared in *The News Tribune*[1340] in 1964 regarding the various people who lived on Fox Island, Kopachick Park, Cromwell, Horsehead Bay, and Gig Harbor, which was called "the Riviera of Pierce County." The article is entitled "Woodcutter: Mike Linberg."

> ... [Mike Linberg] who dwells on Hales Passage and gets his exercise from chopping wood. "I've been out here for 62 years" said Wisconsin-born Mike,[1341] "been up and down this Washington, and I've never seen any better country then where I stand.

On February 8, 1970, a 95th birthday party was held for Mike Linberg, hosted by Mr. and Mrs. Paul Kruegar. The article states that he still lives at East Cromwell, lived alone doing his housework, having a fine garden, and was happy to share everything with his neighbors. It was noted that Mr. Linberg was still able to care for himself and that neighbors took him shopping and to church. He also loves reading his Norwegian Bible and finds that earnest prayer is a great factor in his life.

Ten days after his birthday celebration, Michael Linberg died. He obituary appeared in *The News Tribune.*[1342] His survivors included his grandson, Howard W. Ashley, "of Tacoma." There was an addendum to the obituary that appeared the next day:

> His additional survivors are two sisters, Mrs. Mary Johnson, and Mrs. Ida Ferden, both Peterson, Minnesota.[1343]

Michael Linberg is buried in Haven of Rest in Gig Harbor, Pierce, Washington.

***Children of Howard Ashley and Minnie Irene Scoville***

i. Rhoda Ellsworth Ashley,[8] b. 11 Jan 1890, St. Paul, Ramsey, Minnesota;[1344] d. 9 Mar 1972, Anaheim, Orange, California;[1345] bur. Forest Lawn Memorial Park, Los

1339 Poem courtesy of Sandra Amador.

1340 Sunday, March 22, 1964, edition; 16. Newspapers.

1341 This is erroneous information.

1342 Friday, February 20, 1970, edition; 25. Newspapers.

1343 *The News Tribune,* Saturday, February 21, 1970, edition; 2. Newspapers.

1344 *Minnesota, Births and Christenings Index, 1840–1980;* Ancestry.

1345 Find A Grave. Plot: Columbarium of Purity and Vigilance, Lot 0, Space 62505.

Angeles, Los Angeles, California; m. (1) circa 1908,[1346] Eugene Lawrence Miller, b. 18 Nov 1880, Napoleon, Henry, Ohio; d. 13 Oct 1918, Denver, Denver, Colorado; bur. St. Augustine Cemetery, Napoleon, Henry, Ohio; son of Conrad Miller and Margaret Carroll; Eugene's father was born in Germany; m. (2) Robert W. Holmes; b. 1888; d. 28 Sep 1921 at age thirty-three;[1347] bur. Forest Lawn Memorial Park, Glendale, Los Angeles, California.

Eugene L. Miller is found on the 1900 census[1348] in Napoleon, Henry, Ohio, living with his parents and siblings, Nellie, Frances, and Carl. Eugene was employed as a school teacher. Eugene, who went by the nickname "Heine" (pronounced "hi-nuh"), left Ohio perhaps sometime in 1904 or earlier, as he was in Skagway in 1906 according to a newspaper article. Eugene left teaching and was working on the White Pass line. He likely met Rhoda while living in Skagway.

Little is known about Eugene and Rhoda. The 1917 draft registration records[1349] indicate that he was living at the Brown Palace Hotel on 17th and Tremont Street in Denver, Colorado, and worked for an oil and sulphur company. The draft registration was dated September 12, 1918.

One month (and a day) later, on October 13, 1918, Eugene died from the Spanish Flu, which turned into pneumonia. The following article appeared on Monday, October 21, 1918:[1350]

**Heine Miller Victim of Pneumonia**

Howard Ashley received the sad news this morning of the death of his son-in-law, E. H. Miller.

The advice [?] stated that death occurred on Oct. 14, at St. Joseph's Hospital, Denver, Colorado and was the result of an attack of influenza followed by pneumonia.

E. H. Miller,[1351] or "Heine" as he was known to many of his friends in Skagway was born in Napoleon, Ohio 33 years ago. He came to Alaska fourteen years ago and entered the employ of the White Pass Route. He was married to Mr. and Mrs. Howard Ashley's daughter, Rhoda, who survives her husband together with two small children.

The deceased was a member of the Skagway Lodge No. 431, B.P.O Elks, and although he left here several years ago to engage in business on his own account in the states, he has retained his membership here. Mrs. Miller and the two children are living with Mrs. Miller's mother in Tacoma.

Eugene was buried in his hometown of Napoleon, Henry, Ohio, near his parents.

---

1346 The year is based on the 1910 census for Skagway, Alaska, where the question is asked "how long married"? The answer was "2 years."

1347 The marriage must have occurred sometime after the 1920 census was taken, as Rhoda is listed as "Rhoda Miller, widow" in Tacoma, Washington.

1348 1900 census, *Napoleon, Henry, Ohio;* Page: 10; ED: 0031; FHL:1241286. Ancestry.

1349 *U.S. World War I Draft Registration Cards, 1917–1918.* Ancestry.

1350 *Daily Alaskan;* 2. Newspapers.

1351 The journalist may have thought "Heine" was Eugene's middle name and so used the initials, "E. H." instead of "E. L."

Rhoda Miller is listed on the 1920 census[1352] as the "head" of the family and is living at 212 South Tacoma Avenue, Tacoma, with her daughters, Catherine and Marjorie, her grandmother, Mary C. Scoville, and her brothers, H. Burnett Ashley and Frank Van C. Ashley.

Sometime after the census was taken in January 1920, Rhoda remarried a man named Robert W. Holmes. This was a short-lived marriage, as Robert died on September 28, 1921. I have not been able to find any information on Robert other than what is in the cemetery information and the *California Death Index, 1905–1939.*

The 1924 city directory for Los Angeles has Rhoda living on Hollister opposite San Francisco Cannery, where she was working at the time.

In 1930[1353] Rhoda was an apartment manager for the Modern Hotel Apartments, which was located at 3504 West Third Street. This building still stands today with a mix of apartments on the second floor and various businesses on the first floor.

Her daughters, Catherine (18) and Marjorie (15), were living with their mother.

By 1940,[1354] Rhoda Holmes was living with her son-in-law William Shaffer, daughter, Kay (Catherine), grandchild, Sandra, and daughter, Marjorie Brady, at 6071 Selma Avenue, Los Angeles.

Since the 1950 census has not been released as of this writing, we cannot track Rhoda any further. Deaths of family members occurred, with the first being her brother Frank in 1959; her mother, Minnie, in 1960, and her daughter Kay (Catherine), who died in 1971.

On March 20, 1972,[1355] Rhoda Ellsworth Ashley Miller Holmes died in Anaheim, Orange, California. She is buried in Forest Lawn Memorial Park, Los Angles, California.[1356]

***Children of Eugene L. Miller and Rhoda E. Ashley***

a. i. Margaret Eugenia Miller, b. 23 Oct 1908,[1357] Skagway, Alaska Territory; d. 17 Feb 1911, Laredo, Webb, Texas, bur. Elk's section of the city cemetery. An obituary appeared in *Laredo Weekly Times:*[1358]

**Sad Death**

Margaret Eugenia Miller aged two years and four months, little daughter of Mr. and Mrs. E. L. Miller, died at the residence of Mr. Frank E. Scovill, on the Heights, at 6:40 o'clock yesterday afternoon after an illness of about ten days. Funeral services will be

---

1352 1920 census; *Tacoma, Pierce, Washington;* Roll: T625_1936; Sheet: 2B; ED: 258. Ancestry.

1353 1930 census, *Los Angeles, Los Angeles, California;* Sheet: 1A; ED: 0186; FHL: 2339875. Ancestry.

1354 1940 census, *Los Angeles, Los Angeles, California;* Ward: 2; Block: 27; Sheet: 9B; ED: 60-127. Ancestry.

1355 *California Death Index, 1940–1997;* Find A Grave; Ancestry and FamilySearch.

1356 Plot: Columbarium of Purity and Vigilance; Space: 62505.

1357 Birth date comes from Find A Grave website.

1358 Sunday, February 19, 1911, edition; 12. Newspapers.

conducted from the residence of Mr. Scovill at 4 o'clock this afternoon. Interment will be made in the Elk's plot in the city cemetery.

Little Margaret Eugenia was the only child of Mr. and Mrs. E. L. Miller. She had been a favorite with all who knew her and was a lovely child in every way.

Mrs. E. L. Miller formerly lived in Laredo before her marriage and was known as Miss Rhoda Ashley. She is the niece of Mr. Frank Scovill of this city. Mr. and Mrs. Miller have only been in the city since the Christmas holidays, coming here at that time from Alaska where they lived sometime after their marriage.

b. ii. Catherine Irene Miller[8] (aka "Kay"), b. 15 May 1911, Laredo, Webb, Texas;[1359] d. 11 Jan 1971, Anaheim, Orange, California; m. (1) 27 Jul 1931, William S. Shaffer;[1360] b. 11 Mar 1906, Tipton, Cedar, Iowa;[1361] d. 16 Mar 2003, Sun City, Riverside, California;[1362] son of Charles Shaffer and Charlotte B. Piatt; m. (2) Don Bartelli, b. 4 June 1916, Denver, Denver, Colorado; d. 31 Dec 1993; bur. Forest Lawn Memorial Park, Los Angeles, California; son of Alexander Bartelli and Gertrude _____.

Kay worked for CBS for a time and then at Rocket Pictures. She was in charge of clerical, but did fill in occasionally for photo shoots. Kay's daughter, Sandra, relayed to me how her (Sandra's) class had a movie on the West and there her mother was riding in a covered wagon! All the kids in her class knew her mother and they had so much fun. She also mentioned how her mother would bring her to the movie lots and she had a lot of fun riding the horses and playing on the sets.

Bill Shaffer was an electrician by trade and had attended the University of Chicago. He is in a yearbook photo from 1927 of the freshman basketball team for the university.[1363]

Bill and Kay divorced and each remarried. Kay's second husband was Donald D. Bartelli. He had attended the University of Southern California and worked for Technicolor Motion Picture Corporation and Rocket Pictures. After Kay's death in 1971, he remarried Frouwina H. Polensky on January 29, 1972, in Los Angeles.

Bill remarried Helen Clare Rink Williams in Nevada on December 31, 1986.[1364]

Bill Shaffer and Kay Miller had one daughter, Sandra.[1365]

---

1359 *Texas Birth Certificates, 1903–1932*. Ancestry.

1360 *California, County Birth, Marriage, and Death Records, 1849–1980*. Ancestry.

1361 *Iowa, U.S. Birth Records, 1856–1944*. Ancestry.

1362 Find A Grave.

1363 *U.S. School Yearbooks, 1900–1999;* Ancestry.

1364 *Nevada Marriage Index, 1956–2005*. Ancestry.

1365 Sandra is the descendant of William Harrison Scoville, brother to my second great-grandfather, Charles M. Scoville. I am greatly indebted to her for her generosity in sharing not only the family photos, but her memories of them as well.

c. iii. Marjorie Miller,[8] b. 19 Jan 1915, Los Angeles, Los Angeles, California;[1366] d. 30 Nov 1988, Encinitas, San Diego, California; m. 20 May 1951, Humboldt, California,[1367] Robert A. Dickey; b. 6 Jun 1912, possibly Pennsylvania; d. Jul 1962.[1368] Nothing more is known about this family.

***Children of Howard Ashley and Minnie Irene Scoville continued . . .***

ii. Howard Burnett Ashley[8] (aka "Burnett") b. 27 Jan 1894, St. Paul, Dakota, Minnesota; d. 4 Dec 1989, Bainbridge Island, Kitsap, Washington; bur. Kane Cemetery, Bainbridge Island, Kitsap, Washington; m. 5 Aug 1920, Tacoma, Pierce, Washington, Laura G. Kilpatrick; b. circa 1897, Washington; d. 1 May 1990, Kitsap, Washington; bur. Kane Cemetery, Bainbridge Island, Kitsap, Washington.

At the age of twenty-three, Howard Burnett Ashley duly completed the draft registration card that all men of a certain age were required to do. The date written on his registration card is June 5, 1917 .

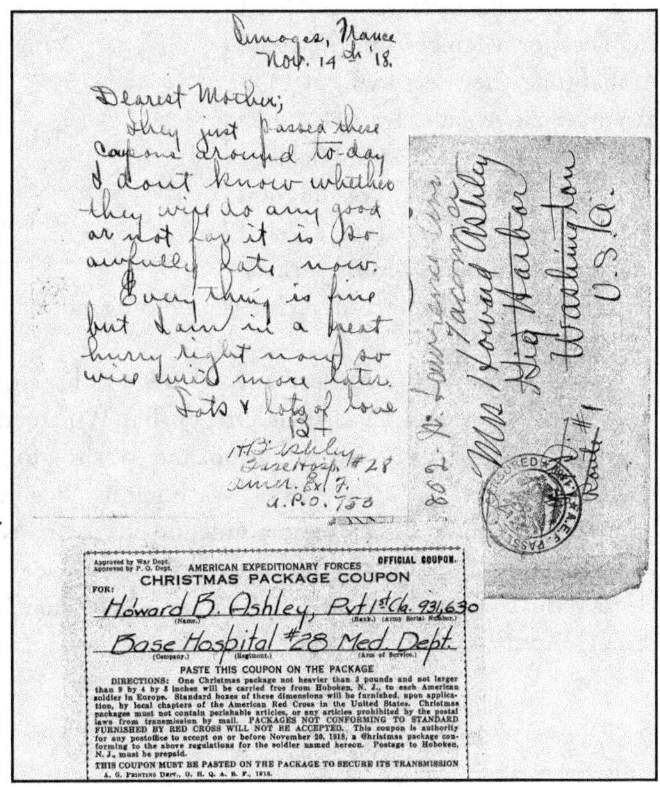
Limoges, France
Nov. 14th '18.

Dearest Mother;
They just passed these coupons around to-day I dont know whether they will do any good or not for it is so awfully late now.
Everything is fine but I am in a great hurry right now so will write more later.
Lots & lots of love
B+
H.B. Ashley
Base Hosp. #28
Amer. Ex. F.
A.P.O. 758

Mrs. Howard Ashley
Tacoma
Washington
U.S.A.

Approved by War Dept.
Approved by P. O. Dept.
AMERICAN EXPEDITIONARY FORCES
OFFICIAL COUPON.
CHRISTMAS PACKAGE COUPON
FOR:
Howard B. Ashley, Pvt 1st Cl. 931,630
(Name.) (Rank.) (Army Serial Number.)
Base Hospital #28 Med. Dept.
(Company.) (Regiment.) (Arm of Service.)
PASTE THIS COUPON ON THE PACKAGE
DIRECTIONS: One Christmas package not heavier than 3 pounds and not larger than 9 by 4 by 3 inches will be carried free from Hoboken, N. J., to each American soldier in Europe. Standard boxes of these dimensions will be furnished, upon application, by local chapters of the American Red Cross in the United States. Christmas packages must not contain perishable articles, or any articles prohibited by the postal laws from transmission by mail. PACKAGES NOT CONFORMING TO STANDARD FURNISHED BY RED CROSS WILL NOT BE ACCEPTED. This coupon is authority for any postoffice to accept on or before November 20, 1918, a Christmas package conforming to the above regulations for the soldier named hereon. Postage to Hoboken, N. J., must be prepaid.
THIS COUPON MUST BE PASTED ON THE PACKAGE TO SECURE ITS TRANSMISSION
A. G. PRINTING DEPT., G. H. Q. A. E. F., 1918.

Two months prior to his registration date the United States had declared war on Germany.

Burnett's card states that he is "single" and is employed as a "construction engineer" working for Tacoma Smelting Company.

Although, the details are sketchy as to where and when he was sent overseas, he wrote a letter to his mother (Rhoda Ashley) from Limoges, France, on November 14, 1918. A copy of that letter is provided at right.[1369]

Another letter arrived by post from the American Red Cross on May 2, 1919 (next page).[1370]

It is not recorded as to what his injury or illness was, but he did return home, as on

1366 *California Birth Index, 1905–1995*. Ancestry.

1367 This is a second marriage as she is listed on the marriage certificate as "Marjorie Gillies." Nothing is known about her first marriage. *California, U.S., Marriage Index, 1949–1959*. Ancestry.

1368 *Social Security Death Index*. Ancestry.

1369 Copy Howard Burnett Ashley's letter courtesy of Sandra Amador.

1370 *Ibid*

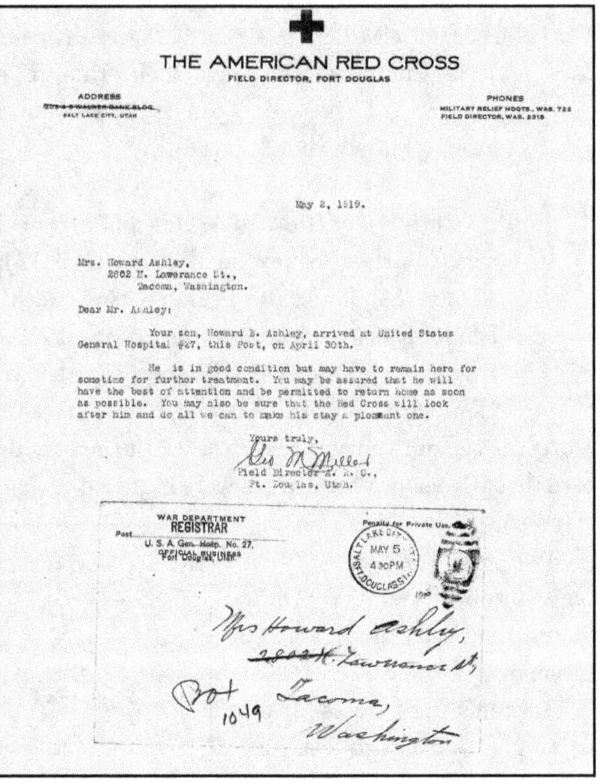

THE AMERICAN RED CROSS
FIELD DIRECTOR, FORT DOUGLAS

ADDRESS
~~203-4-5 WALKER BANK BLDG.~~
SALT LAKE CITY, UTAH

PHONES
MILITARY RELIEF HDQTS., WAS. 722
FIELD DIRECTOR, WAS. 2318

May 2, 1919.

Mrs. Howard Ashley,
2802 N. Lawerance St.,
Tacoma, Washington.

Dear Mr. Ashley:

Your son, Howard B. Ashley, arrived at United States General Hospital #27, this Post, on April 30th.

He is in good condition but may have to remain here for sometime for further treatment. You may be assured that he will have the best of attention and be permitted to return home as soon as possible. You may also be sure that the Red Cross will look after him and do all we can to make his stay a pleasant one.

Yours truly,
Geo M Millet
Field Director A. R. C.,
Ft. Douglas, Utah.

WAR DEPARTMENT
REGISTRAR
Post
U. S. A. Gen. Hosp. No. 27,
Fort Douglas, Utah.
OFFICIAL BUSINESS

Penalty for Private Use,

SALT LAKE CITY
MAY 5
4 30PM
FT. DOUGLAS STA.

Mrs Howard Ashley,
~~2802 N.~~ Lawrence St,
Tacoma,
Washington

August 5, 1920, he was married to Laurie G. Kilpatrick[1371] in Tacoma, Washington, by a clergyman. The witness were T. W. Gilpatrick and Bonnie A. Kirkpatrick.

She may be the daughter of Harry A. Kirkpatrick and Amy____. On the 1920 census a Laurie Kilpatrick is living with this family, with a sister named "Bonnie." Based on the name of the second witness to the marriage, I would surmise that this is her family.

The couple was living in Longview City, where Burnett was the head engineer for a lumber mill in 1930. At that time, they were living at 1338 Twenty-First Avenue. By 1940, they had moved to 2557 Pacific Highway in Longview, Cowlitz, Washington. Burnett was now listed as a "civil engineer" for a lumber mill. Because of the lack of any other records after 1940, nothing more is known about this couple. They did not have any children.

iii. Frank Van Cleve Ashley,[8] b. 2 Jul 1899, Kalispell, Flathead, Montana;[1372] d. 24 Jan 1959, Portland, Clackamas, Oregon; bur. Willamette National Cemetery, Oregon;[1373] m. 28 May 1927, Spokane, Spokane, Washington, Ruth Dover;[1374] b. 18 Jun 1903, Missouri; d. 18 Nov 1943, Washington;[1375] bur. Riverside Park;[1376] daughter of Solomon Wesley Dover and Emeline Elizabeth Penn.[1377]

Like his brother, Howard Burnett, Frank Van Cleve Ashley also served in World War I. He served as a private in Co. H, 340 Infantry, 85 Division. He served from September 7, 1917, through April 24, 1919.

---

1371 The records have her name as "Kilpatrick," but it may have been misspelled and should be "Kirkpatrick."

1372 *Montana County Births and Deaths, 1830–2011.* Montana Historical Society, Ancestry. The middle name of Frank, "Van Cleve," comes from someone whom his father knew in Skagway, Alaska.

1373 *U.S. National Cemetery Interment Control Forms, 1928–1962.* Ancestry.

1374 *Washington Marriage Records, 1854–2003.* Ancestry.

1375 *Washington Death Index, 1940–2014.* Ancestry.

1376 Obituary notice.

1377 Parents' names come from the marriage record.

F.V. Ashley France
Co. F 1st V.S. Engis' Oct. 22, 1918
Amer. E. F.
Dear Mother.

Don't suppose you will get this in time to mail the box but don't feel bad if you don't as I can easily get along without it. Have been in the hospital fourteen days now, that is why I have not sent it sooner nothing serious the trouble mostly my stomach and Rheumatism. Also I suppose because my system was rather run down, my heart went on the bum, but am fine now. I suppose you imagine I have been to the front line well I have seven of them and spent the last part of 10 months up there and am none the worse for it and I think there are a couple of square heads that are.

Don't suppose I will see Burnett but may be [ ] will all be together again.

Lots of love
Frank[1378]

Minnie Irene and Frank Ashley must have worried daily about their sons' welfare and must have breathed a sigh of relief when they both came home. Frank V. Ashley returned home aboard the *USS Leviathan*. The ship left Brest, France, on March 26, 1919.[1379]

When Frank returned home, he was a clerk, as it is noted on the 1920 census. At that time, he was living with his sister, brother Burnett, nieces, and grandmother in Tacoma.

In May of 1927, Frank married Ruth Dover in Spokane, Washington. Ruth was a "school teacher" and Frank a "salesman."

Their son, Howard Wesley Ashley, was born on August 10, 1929, in Venice, Los Angeles, California.[1380]

The family remained in California, as they appear living in Los Angeles on the 1930[1381] census at 2841 West Eighth Street, Wilerest Apartments.

Four Generations: Rhoda Ashley Miller (rear), Mary C. Dunn Scoville, Margaret Miller, & Minnie Irene Scoville Ashley Linberg

Frank and Ruth were paying $35 per month for rent. Ruth was no longer working as she was caring for their seven-month-old son, Howard. Frank was still making

1378 The letter has been transcribed as it was originally written.

1379 *U.S. Army Transport Service, Passenger Lists, 1910–1939*. Ancestry.

1380 *California County Birth and Death Records, 1800–1994;* FamilySearch. Mr. Ashley is still living as of this writing.

1381 1930 census, *Los Angeles, Los Angeles, California;* Block 3; Sheet 7A; ED: 19-328. Ancestry.

his living as a salesman, this time for a leather company.

After the crash of 1929, the Great Depression was affecting everyone's lives. I can only surmise that is why Frank Ashley became a forger. There is a saying that goes, "desperate men will do desperate things," and certainly the Great Depression was a desperate time. Frank V. Ashley did commit forgery on three occasions using various aliases.[1382]

The aliases that Frank used were John A. Gordon, Harold J. Holmes, Roy Miller, and William B. Peters.

It is unknowable when Frank decided to go into the forging business, but he was arrested in 1934 in Walla Walla, Washington, for grand larceny and was given a sixteen-month sentence.

Frank was caught again in 1938 for forgery in Shasta, California, using the alias John A. Gordon. This time his sentence was for one to fourteen years in San Quentin.

Left to right: Rhoda, Howard B., and Frank V. Ashley. Photo courtesy of Sandra Amador.

In 1940 he received an additional sixty days for "Contempt of Court" and was sent to Terminal Island, Los Angeles County.[1383]

Was this part of Frank's life an aberration due to the hard times of the Depression? Or something else?

Where was his wife, Ruth Ashley, during this time? Ruth is on the 1940 census living at 3305 North Ferdinand, where she is renting an apartment for thirteen dollars a month. She is working as a clerk in a public school. Son Howard is now ten years old. It is unknown how much he may have known about his father's situation during his early years.

Sadly, Ruth Dover Ashley died at the young age of thirty-nine years on November 18, 1943. Howard went to live with his grandmother, Minnie Irene, and she raised him. What of Frank?

He was paroled, I believe, in 1944. His wife was dead, and his son was being raised by his grandmother. I have not

Catherine Irene (Kay) Miller, age about eighteen

1382 *California Prison and Correctional Records, 1851–1950.* Ancestry.

1383 "A largely artificial island located in Los Angeles County . . . land use on the island is largely industrial and port-related except for [the] Federal Correctional Institution, Terminal Island." https://en.wikipedia.org/wiki/Terminal_Island.

found a "paper" trail for him through city directories or the newspapers. The only record available is his death and burial record from *U.S. National Cemetery Interment Control Forms, 1928–1962.*[1384]

He died in Portland, Multnomah, Oregon, and is buried in the veteran's cemetery. He was fifty-nine years old.

### *38. CORA IRENE SCOVILLE*[7] *(ALBERT FRANKLIN,*[6] *FRANKLIN,*[5] *ITHAMAR,*[4] *TIMOTHY,*[3] *STEPHEN,*[2] *STEPHEN,*[1] *ARTHUR)*

Born 29 October 1865, Canaan or North Canaan, Litchfield, Connecticut;[1385] died 11 November 1895, Worcester, Worcester, Massachusetts;[1386] burial place unknown; m. 22 July 1882, Worcester, Worcester, Massachusetts,[1387] Charles Ripley Burnett Claflin, Jr.; born 3 May 1860, Charlton, Worcester, Massachusetts;[1388] died 15 March 1935, Astoria, Queens, New York;[1389] son of Charles R. B. Claflin and Emma G. H. Locke.

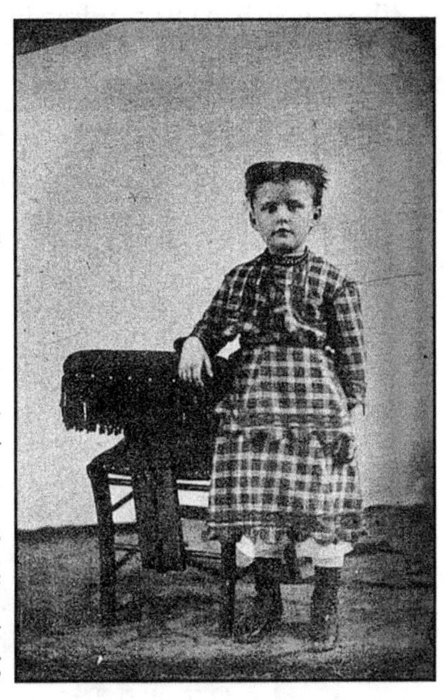

While Cora Scoville was born in the area of Canaan, Litchfield, Connecticut, in 1865, she did not spend much time there as her father[1390] removed to Meriden, New Haven, Connecticut, sometime prior to the 1870 census.[1391]

When the 1880 census was taken, Cora Scoville was listed twice—once in the household of George W. Sprague on June 2nd, where she was employed as a "servant," and then on July 8th she was counted in her father's household as "going to school." I believe these two Coras are one and the same.

At the age of sixteen, Cora married Charles Ripley Burnett Claflin of Worcester, Massachusetts (who was twenty-two years old at the time of his marriage). How these two met is curious seeing that there is approximately eighty-one miles between Meriden, Connecticut, and Worcester, Massachusetts. An easy explanation would be that Cora's father, Albert, had left Meriden, Connecticut, for Worcester sometime after the 1880 census was taken because

1384 Ancestry.

1385 Regrettably, the documentation for Cora's birthdate cannot be located.

1386 Death certificate in my possession, received from the Commonwealth of Massachusetts, Office of the Secretary of State William Francis Galvin, Secretary Archives Division; Vol: 456; Page: 8146; No.: 1696.

1387 *New England Select United Methodist Church Records, 1787–1922,* Ancestry.

1388 *Massachusetts Birth Records, 1840–1915.* Ancestry.

1389 *New York, New York, U.S. Index to Death Certificates, 1862–1948;* Certificate: 1903, Ancestry.

1390 There isn't a death record for Cora's mother, Hannah, in Meriden, Connecticut. It is unknown where or when Hannah Hall Scoville died, but it was before 1870.

1391 Cora Scoville Claflin, age about four/five years. Photo courtesy of Sandra Amador.

he, too, remarried in October 1882 in Worcester.

In 1870 and 1880, Charles R. B. Claflin was living with his parents—Charles R. B. Claflin, a photographer,[1392] and Emma—and their daughter, Josie. The family had a domestic servant by the name of Mary McNully and a boarder, Frances Baker, a teacher. The family home had a real estate value of $18,000 and they had $5,000 in personal property. In other words, the family was very financially secure.

In the 1880 census, the family is living at 22 Oread Street in Worcester. Charles is employed as a "crockery importer." After his marriage to Cora Scoville, Charles Claflin was involved in the manufacturer of dental equipment from 1882–1901,[1393]as an agent and then as a manager.

The couple had five children in quick succession beginning in 1883. One son, Walter, died at the age of six from drowning in 1893. Cora died two years later on November 11, 1885, in Worcester from eclampsia. The child that she was carrying also succumbed.

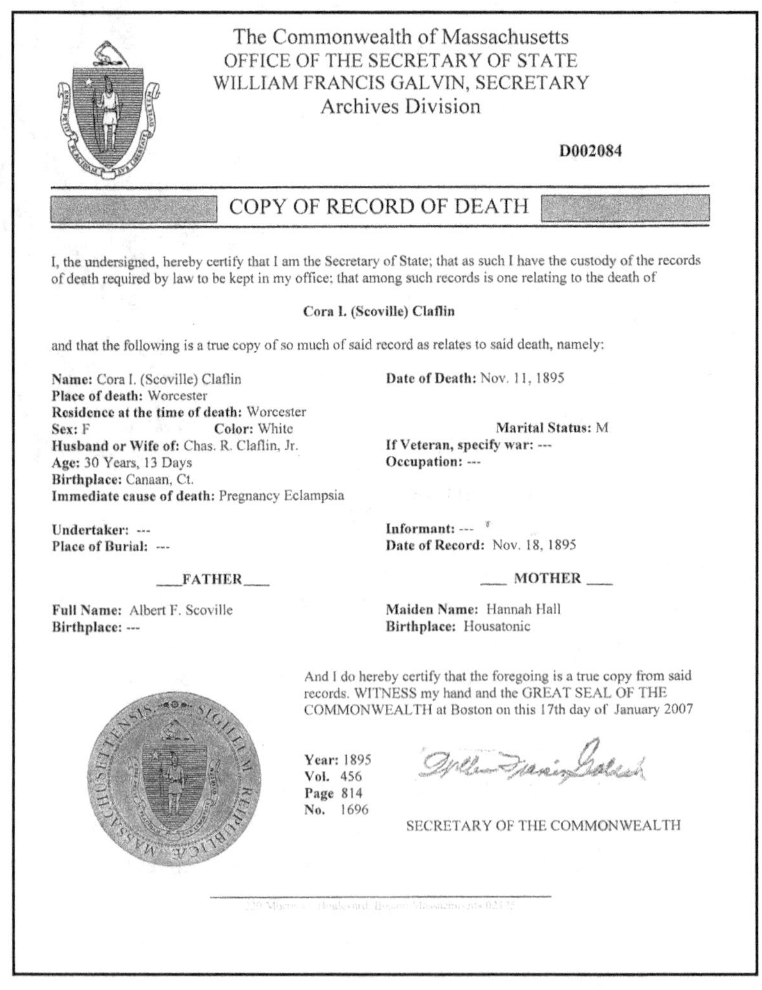

The Commonwealth of Massachusetts
OFFICE OF THE SECRETARY OF STATE
WILLIAM FRANCIS GALVIN, SECRETARY
Archives Division

D002084

COPY OF RECORD OF DEATH

I, the undersigned, hereby certify that I am the Secretary of State; that as such I have the custody of the records of death required by law to be kept in my office; that among such records is one relating to the death of

**Cora I. (Scoville) Claflin**

and that the following is a true copy of so much of said record as relates to said death, namely:

**Name:** Cora I. (Scoville) Claflin
**Date of Death:** Nov. 11, 1895
**Place of death:** Worcester
**Residence at the time of death:** Worcester
**Sex:** F **Color:** White
**Marital Status:** M
**Husband or Wife of:** Chas. R. Claflin, Jr.
**If Veteran, specify war:** ---
**Age:** 30 Years, 13 Days
**Occupation:** ---
**Birthplace:** Canaan, Ct.
**Immediate cause of death:** Pregnancy Eclampsia

**Undertaker:** ---
**Informant:** ---
**Place of Burial:** ---
**Date of Record:** Nov. 18, 1895

**FATHER**

**Full Name:** Albert F. Scoville
**Birthplace:** ---

**MOTHER**

**Maiden Name:** Hannah Hall
**Birthplace:** Housatonic

And I do hereby certify that the foregoing is a true copy from said records. WITNESS my hand and the GREAT SEAL OF THE COMMONWEALTH at Boston on this 17th day of January 2007

**Year:** 1895
**Vol.** 456
**Page** 814
**No.** 1696

SECRETARY OF THE COMMONWEALTH

1392 Charles R. B. Claflin (Sr.) had his photography studio at 229 Main Street, Worcester through 1872; around 1872/3 his studio was at 377 Main Street, Worcester; www.langdonroad.com.

1393 *U.S. City Directories, 1822–1995*; Ancestry.

After the death of Cora, Charles R. B. Claflin married four more times prior to his death in 1935.

His second wife was Minnie M. Rockwood Usher[1394] on June 10, 1897.[1395] Her death certificate gives her date of birth as December 16, 1865, and she died December 27, 1914.

She and Charles must have divorced as he married wife number three about 1903/1904: Marie Gertrude Moore.[1396] Marie Gertrude Moore was born November 5, 1891, in Hingham, Plymouth, Massachusetts, to Joanne Joseph Moore and Maria Agnete Maguire.[1397]

A newspaper article was printed in the *Boston Journal* with the following headline:

> **Claflin Held Under $800 for Grand Jury**
> Charles R. B. Claflin, who under arrest on charge of stealing 25,000 shares of stock from his former wife, Marie Gertrude Moore of Winthrop, was arraigned before Judge Parmenter in the municipal court yesterday, after a brief hearing was held in $800 bond for the next grand jury sitting.
>
> Claflin's marriage was annulled in the Superior Court in May last, and it is since that time. It is alleged he went to her safety deposit vault in the International Trust Company and removed the securities.

Marie Gertrude Moore

The outcome of the court case is not known, but in 1905 the city directory for Michigan shows that Charles R. B. Claflin was living in Lansing and was employed as a salesman.

His next marriage was to Ella Mary Tinker (or Ella Mary Tinker Craig). I have two marriage dates, one for January 26, 1906, Waltham, Middlesex, Massachusetts, but no citation accompanies this information. The other date of marriage is given as June 2, 1915. This marriage took place at Bromfield Street Methodist Episcopal Church.[1398] The marriage record indicates that this was the third marriage for both of them. Charles was fifty and Ella was thirty-five years old.

1394 The marriage information for Minnie Rockwood Usher states her father was James Rockwood Usher. In another record she states her parents are James and Jane Walker; Walker is the maiden name of her mother. Her death certificate states she is "widowed," and her husband was William H. Usher.

1395 *Massachusetts, U.S. Marriage Records, 1840–1915*. Ancestry.

1396 Regrettably, I do not know how I obtained this photo. Marie G. Moore remarried in 1914 to Valentine S. Duff (1887–1938).

1397 *Massachusetts, Boston Archdiocese Roman Catholic Sacramental Records, 1789–1900*. Ancestry.

1398 *Massachusetts, U.S. Marriage Records, 1840–1915*. Ancestry.

In 1920,[1399] Charles and Ella Claflin are now living in Hartford, Hartford, Connecticut, at 5 Kennedy Street. Charles was still managing the Derrick Oil Company at this time.

It is unknown whether Ella Mary Tinker Craig Claflin divorced Charles (or vice versa) or had died, as Charles married again on August 23, 1924, to Caroline Elizabeth Morgan in Harford, Hartford, Connecticut.[1400]

Caroline had been born in Portsmouth, New Hampshire, on March 10, 1875, to John Morgan and Carrie E. Hoyt.[1401]

The following year an article appeared in the *Hartford Courant* regarding Charles buying Whitmore Farm in East Hartford. The article mentions that "Charles R. B. Claflin, general manager of the Claflin Oil Derrick and Supply Company" purchased the farm from Hiram Fairman, who was returning to Massachusetts. The farm was sixty acres, of which "twenty acres will be used for tobacco."[1402]

There were other articles in the *Hartford Courant* where Charles did not pay his bills. A Kate L. Danehy "of Hartford" brought suit against the property of Caroline and Charles R. B. Claflin for $3,000. She sued to recover on a $2,700 note, installments on "which are overdue."[1403] Again, the results of this suit are not known.

When the 1930 census[1404] was taken, the couple were living in West Hartford at 103 Thomas Street. They owned the home, which was valued at $9,000. Caroline's son (Kenneth Burbrer [sic]) from a previous marriage was living with them.

Around 1930, the couple removed to Meriden, New Haven, Connecticut, and lived at 304 Center Street. Charles is listed as employed as "Illuminating Engineer and General Superintendent."

In 1933 the city directory (for Meriden) states that they "removed to New Jersey." Was Charles running from his debts? Or was it a simple matter of other job opportunities?

I've had no success locating him in New Jersey; however, they were living in Astoria, Queens, New York, in 1935 at the time of his death on March 15th. According to the death certificate[1405] the couple were living at 34–15 31st Street. Charles R. B. Claflin died from "coronary occlusion and secondary arteriosclerosis." His cremated remains are located in Fresh Pond Crematory and Columbarium in Queens, New York.[1406]

Prior to her marriage to Charles, Caroline had been married to Frank Breed Bubier (1864–1918) and had three sons with him: Sylvester Bubier (1895–1947), Francis Kennard (Kenneth?) Bubier (1902–1983), and Paul Morgan Bubier (1908–).

---

1399 1920 census; *Hartford Ward 2, Hartford, Connecticut;* Roll: T625_182; Page: 6B; ED: 54; Image: 657. Ancestry.

1400 *Connecticut Marriage Records, 1897–1968.* Ancestry.

1401 *New Hampshire, Births and Christenings Index, 1714–1904.* Ancestry.

1402 Saturday, March 19, 1921, edition; 3. Newspapers.

1403 Wednesday, January 16, 1929, edition; 3. Newspapers.

1404 1930 census, *West Hartford, Hartford, Connecticut;* Dwelling: 194; Family: 242; ED: 0231; Page: 12A; FHL: 2340004.

1405 *New York, New York, U.S. Index to Death Certificates, 1862–1948;* Certificate No.: 1903. Ancestry.

1406 Charles R. B. Claflin is not listed on the Find A Grave website.

A newspaper article regarding Mrs. Caroline E. Claflin was printed in the *Hartford Courant* regarding a bequest that she had received. Note that Charles R. B. Claflin is mentioned as the "inventor of the non-glare lightbulb."[1407]

**MRS. CLAFLIN, LEFT $25,000, LARGEST LEGACY, SHE SAYS**

**"Someone Is Always Leaving Me Money," Declares East Hartford Woman, Announcing Latest Bequest.**

"Someone is always leaving me money," said Mrs. Caroline Elizabeth Claflin of No. 369 Burnside avenue, East Hartford last night. Mrs. Claflin said she had just received word that she had been left a legacy of $25,000. "This is the fourth time I have had bequests," she declared. "But this is the largest one that has been left to me outright."

Mrs. Claflin is the wife of C. R. B. Claflin, inventor of a non-glare bulb which was recently put on the market by the Claflin Laboratories of Hartford. Before her marriage to Mr. Claflin she was a Mrs. Bubier of Lynn, Mass. Her first husband was a member of an old Massachusetts family.

The latest legacy to be received by Mrs. Claflin is a bequest of $25,000 which she is to receive under the final accounting of the Edward T. George fund, left by the late Mrs. Anna (George) Sawyer, of Worcester, Mass. and Oakland, Cal. Mrs. Claflin is a niece of Mrs. Sawyer.

**ANNOUNCES WORD OF FOURTH LEGACY**

MRS. CAROLINE E. CLAFLIN.

Caroline E. Claflin remarried on December 25, 1938, to Ira B. Davis in Dade, Florida.[1408]

At the time of her death in 1957, Caroline was living at 15949 Ludlow Street, Granada Hills, California. Her obituary does not mention her husband and I suspect that they divorced.[1409] The obituary appeared in *The Van Nuys News*.[1410]

> **Death Takes Carrie Davis**
>
> Mrs. Carrie Elizabeth Davis 82, of 15949 Ludlow Street, Granada Hills, passed away Saturday.
>
> She was a native of New Hampshire, and is survived by two sons, Kennard F.,

1407 Sunday, September 13, 1925, edition; Newspapers. Per Tony Dudek, Senior Account Executive, Tribune Content Agency. "This article was published in 1925, it is considered Public Domain. No need for permission or license."

1408 "Caroline Monrgan [sic] Claflin to Ira B. Davis." Names of Caroline's parents coincide with the information known. *Florida, U.S. County Marriage Records, 1823–1982;* Vol: 466; Certificate: 23347. Florida Heath Department. Ancestry.

1409 I cannot locate this couple on the 1940 census, either together or separately.

1410 Tuesday, October 1st edition, 7. Newspapers.

and Paul Bubier. Three grandchildren and three great-grandchildren. Services and committal are private. It is announced by Pierce Brothers, Van Nuys.

**_Children of Charles R. B. Claflin and Cora Irene Scoville_**

i. Maud Claflin, b. 12 Apr 1883, Worcester, Worcester, Massachusetts; d. 21 Aug 1883, Worcester, Worcester, Massachusetts;[1411] died from "cholera infantum."[1412]

ii. Anna J. Claflin[8] (aka Percy Judah), b. 21 May 1884, Worcester, Worcester, Massachusetts;[1413] d. Jan 1968, Woburn, Middlesex, Massachusetts; bur. Pepperell, Middlesex, Massachusetts;[1414] m. (1) 22 Jan 1905, New York, New York, St. Andrews Church, Charles Henry Hillman;[1415] b. 1876; (2) 28 Sep 1925, Manhattan, New York, Theodore Roosevelt Quick; b. 1899, d. 1945.[1416]

Anna's mother died when she was eleven. As we've seen, her father (Charles) was a businessman and was likely "a very busy man," and had married four more women after her mother died. It is unknowable what kind of relationship she had with her father. It is doubtful that Charles raised his daughter. Anna likely went to live with her paternal grandmother, Emma Claflin, soon after her mother's death.[1417]

Anna's path in life was very different than that of most women of that time, and it was one that would have had a stigma attached to it.[1418] Anna J. Claflin became Percy Judah—an actress.

The first evidence that I've been able to locate is a marriage notice that appeared in the *Evening Star*, a newspaper out of Washington, D.C.:

> Miss Percy Judah, a member of Mr. Nelson E. Roberts company, soon to open in "His Majesty" was married Friday to Mr. Charles Hillman, one of the officials of the Cleveland Street Railroad Company of Cleveland, Ohio.[1419]

The article appeared in the Sunday, January 28, 1906, issue of the paper (page 23). However, a marriage notice from *New York Episcopal Diocese of New York Church Records, 1767–1970,*[1420] has their marriage occurring on January 22, 1905, New York, New York, at St.

1411 Birth and death records come from *Massachusetts, Birth Records, 1840–1915* and *Massachusetts, Death Records, 1841–1915,* Ancestry.

1412 "Cholera infantum was the name Benjamin Rush gave to the so-called summer diarrhea of infants and children. This disease was known as 'the vomiting and purging of children' or 'the disease of the season' because of its regularity in appearing during the summer months." https://pediatrics.aappublications.org.

1413 *Massachusetts, Town and Vital Records, 1620–1988;* Ancestry.

1414 Find A Grave.

1415 *New York Episcopal Diocese of New York Church Records, 1767–1970;* Ancestry.

1416 *New York, New York, Extracted Marriage Index, 1866–1937.* Ancestry.

1417 Anna J. Claflin was living with her grandmother, Emma, in 1900. Anna was sixteen at that time.

1418 The thinking at that time was the belief that women on the stage were impure and improper.

1419 Newspaper.com.

1420 Ancestry.

Anna J. Claflin, aka Percy Judah. This photo was sent to me by a descendant of Anna J. Claflin in 2006.

One of the many advertisements that appeared in newspapers around the country during "Percy Judah's" career. This advert appeared in *The Philadelphia Inquirer,* Sunday, April 24, 1921, edition, 69. Newspapers.

Andrews Church. The *New York, New York U.S. Extracted Marriage Index, 1866–1937* also states that this couple married on January 22, 1906, as opposed to 1905.[1421]

Charles Henry Hillman was born in Birmingham, England, circa 1886. He was twenty years old at the time of his marriage to "Percy Judah." This marriage did not last, unfortunately. When it dissolved is unknown and Charles Henry Hillman remains a mystery.

There are various news articles available from 1912–1922 that mention various burlesque shows from New Jersey, Boston, Brooklyn, Indianapolis, Minneapolis, Pittsburg, Philadelphia, and Buffalo in which Anna was involved as Percy Judah.

In 1915 a woman named "Anna J. Pierce" appears on the New York State census in the town of Utica, Oneida.[1422] She is a boarder in the home of Mannie A. Owens. This woman gives her occupation as "stenographer." It's odd that Anna would have been in Utica, New York, at this time and it is likely it is not the Anna of this record.

In 1920,[1423] Anna is living with her sister Grace (Claflin) Nash and her husband in Chelsea, Suffolk, Massachusetts, on Beach Parkway. Anna is listed as "Judah, Percie [sic]" age "35" and

> **Percy Judah,** the prima **donna,** has
> **fascinating** manner, **wonderfully**
> ich **contralto** voice **and displays** one
> f **the** most **fetching wardrobes seen**
> ere **this season.**

1421 It is the aforementioned newspaper article that stated the marriage took place in 1905.

1422 New York State census, 1915, New York State Archives; Ward 7; ED: 4; Page: 11. Ancestry.

1423 1920 census, *Massachusetts, Suffolk, Chelsea City;* Ward 5; Roll: T625_743; ED: 651; Page: 4A. Ancestry.

is employed as an "actress." Later that year a brief article appeared in *The Washington Times* (previous page).[1424]

In 1921 Anna met Theodore R. Quick, who was a musician and was part of the cast in the Lew Talbot burlesque comedy "The Tempters," which was playing at the Stone Opera House in Binghamton.[1425] After 1922, I have not been able to locate any articles regarding Percy Judah. Perhaps by this time she had retired from the stage, or the theatrical parts for her had dried up.

On September 28, 1925, in Manhattan, New York, Anna J. Claflin and Theodore Roosevelt Quick were married. In 1930 the couple is living in Queens, Queens, New York, at 2426 29th Singer Street. Theodore Quick is the sole breadwinner working as a theater musician. In addition to the married couple, Theodore's mother, Josephine Quick, "a widow," was also living with them.

At some point, the couple removed to Dade County, Florida. Nothing more is known of their time there, except that Theodore R. Quick filed for divorce from Anna J. Quick, which was printed in *The Miami News* on Friday, January 29, 1937.[1426] The divorce was finalized.

On December 21, 1937, Theodore remarried to Christine H. Daniel in Broward County, Florida.[1427] They are listed on the 1940 census with Christine's two children in Miami. Theodore is still employed as a musician during this time.

Theodore R. Quick died at the age of forty-seven a day or two before August 22, 1945, when his obituary was published in the *Miami Daily News.*[1428]

The obituary accounts that he died in "the hospital Monday." He was survived by his "wife Christine, and a daughter, Gloria Quick, both of Miami Beach, and a son J.W. Quick, navy."

Nothing more is known of Anna J. Claflin/Percy Judah, and I have not found her on the 1940 census using a number of name combinations. Her death occurred in January 1968[1429] in Woburn, Middlesex, Massachusetts, and she is buried in Pepperell Cemetery. An obituary notice has not been located for her.

As far as the records reveal, no children were born to Anna J. Claflin with either husband.[1430]

Anna J. Claflin/Percy Judah

1424 Tuesday, November 2, 1920, edition; 10. Newspapers.

1425 *Press and Sun Bulletin,* February 21, 1921. Newspapers.

1426 Page: 4; Newspapers.

1427 *Florida, County Marriage Records, 1823–1982.* Ancestry.

1428 Wednesday's edition, 7. Newspapers.

1429 *U.S., Social Security Death Index, 1935–2014.* Ancestry.

1430 A public photo from Ancestry of Anna J. Claflin. Permission to use photo by original owner and shared on Ancestry, Username: kim13599.

iii. Walter M. Claflin,[8] b. 16 Apr 1887, Worcester, Worcester, Massachusetts;[1431] d. 21 Jul 1893, Worcester, Worcester, Massachusetts. Died from accidental drowning.

iv. Baby boy Claflin, b. 22 Jul 1888, Worcester, Worcester, Massachusetts; d. Jul 1888, Worcester, Massachusetts.[1432]

v. Grace H. Claflin,[8] b. 22 Aug 1888/89, Worcester, Worcester, Massachusetts;[1433] d. 6 Feb 1929, Everett, Middlesex, Massachusetts;[1434] m. 27 Mar 1907, Pepperell, Middlesex, Massachusetts, Ernest O. Nash;[1435] b. 11 Jul 1886, Westbrook, Cumberland, Maine;[1436] d. 23 Jul 1967, Woburn, Middlesex, Massachusetts;[1437] son of Oliver M. Nash and Myra B. Wyre.

I have not found proof of Grace Claflin's birth date. I have seen August 22, 18**88** and August 22, 18**89**. It *is* possible that Grace was a twin to Baby boy Claflin. While rare, twins can be born days, weeks, or even a month apart.

The 1900 census gives Grace's birth month and year as "August 1888" and the headstone states she was born in 1888 (her husband would have provided that information). The date of birth of August 22, 1889, comes from projected birth year based on age at marriage (eighteen in March 1907) and ages provided on the 1910 and 1920 census.

However, an obituary for Grace gives her age at death as "40 years, 6 months, and 15 days." Using the birth date calculator proved by Long Island Genealogy (longislandgenealogy.com) her birthdate is *23 July 1888*. This would mean that Grace H. Claflin *was* the twin of Baby boy Claflin (*if* the years, months, and days of death are also correct) It's possible that the family celebrated her birth in August for reasons unknown to us.

In 1910,[1438] the couple was living in Lawrence, Essex, Massachusetts, at 163 East Haverhill Street. Ernest was the foreman in a coating mill.[1439] The 1913 city directory[1440] for Lawrence, Massachusetts, indicates that they removed to Chelsea, Massachusetts. The couple remained there until at least 1925, where, once again, Ernest O. Nash is listed in the city directory as working for F. L. Manufacturing Company.

An article regarding Grace H. Nash appeared in *The Boston Globe* on Thursday, January 31, 1929:[1441]

---

1431 *Massachusetts, Birth Records, 1840–1915; Massachusetts, Death Records, 1841–1915*. Ancestry.

1432 *Ibid.*

1433 A birth record has not been discovered.

1434 Newspaper article; Thursday, January 31, 1929, 4; Find A Grave; Newspapers.

1435 *Massachusetts Marriage Records, 1840–1915*. Ancestry.

1436 *U.S., World War I Draft Registration Cards, 1917–1918*. Ancestry.

1437 *Massachusetts, Death Index, 1901–1980*. Ancestry.

1438 1910 census; *Lawrence Ward 1, Essex, Massachusetts;* Roll: T624_582; Page: 11B; ED: 0333; FHL: 1374595. Ancestry.

1439 Lawrence, Massachusetts, has a long history of textile and other mills as being the major employer. Many people removed to Lawrence to find jobs. Working in these mills was dangerous and unhealthy.

1440 *U.S. City Directories, 1822–1995*. Ancestry.

1441 Page: 4, Newspapers.

> Mrs. Grace H. Nash, 94 Bradford Street, is seriously sick at her home with pneumonia. She is being attended by Dr. Jackson.

Her condition worsened and she died on February 6, 1929, in Everett, Middlesex, Massachusetts. An obituary appeared in the *Evening Gazette*:[1442]

> **Mrs. Ernest O. Nash**
> The funeral of Grace H. (Claflin) aged 40 years, 6 months and 15 days, wife of Ernest O. Nash, who died last night in her home, 94 Bradford Street, Everett, will be at 2 p.m. tomorrow in the First Universalist Church. The body will be cremated in Mt. Auburn Crematory, Cambridge and the ashes will be buried in Pepperell, where she was married. She was born in Worcester, daughter of Charles R. B. Claflin and Cora (Scoville) Claflin. She leaves her husband, her father; a daughter, Marjorie, wife of Harold E. Brown; as sister, Anna P.J., wife of Ted R. Quick, Astoria, Long Island and an aunt, Florence S. wife of William L. Carr, 7 Ball Street, Worcester.

Ernest O. Nash never remarried. After his wife's death he lived for a while on Beach Highway in Chelsea with his daughter and his sister-in-law, Anna J. Claflin; however, he removed to West Springfield, Hampden, Massachusetts, and was living with his father, Oliver Nash, on Riverdale Street. Ernest continued working as a "color man" foreman for a paper coating company.

The following year (1941) his father, Oliver Nash, died in Agawam, Hampden, Massachusetts.

In 1942, Ernest Nash completed a registration card (as he had done for World War I) as was required for all men born "on or after April 28, 1877 and on or before February 16, 1887."[1443] He was still residing at 1067 Riverdale Street in West Springfield, Massachusetts, and was employed by the New England Card and Paper Company that was located at 20 Hanover Street in Springfield.

On July 23, 1967, Ernest Orville Nash died in Woburn, Massachusetts. His daughter, Marjorie, was also living in Woburn, and he may have lived with her. Services were held at the North Congregational Church.[1444]

### *Children of Ernest O. Nash and Grace H. Claflin*

a. i. Marjorie L. Nash,[9] b. 12 Jan 1908, Pepperell, Middlesex, Massachusetts;[1445] d. 19 Nov 1987 Hartford, Windsor, Vermont;[1446] m. 1926, Everett, Middlesex, Massachusetts,[1447] Harold Edward Brown, b. 3 Nov 1904, Everett, Middlesex,

---

1442 Friday, February 8, 1929, issue; page: 18. GenealogyBank.

1443 *U. S., World War II Draft Registration Cards, 1942.* NARA via Ancestry.

1444 *The Boston Globe,* Monday, July 24, 1967, edition; 28. Newspapers.

1445 *Massachusetts, Birth Records, 1840–1915.* Ancestry.

1446 *Vermont, Death Records, 1909–2008.* Ancestry.

1447 *Massachusetts, Marriage Index, 1901–1955 and 1966–1970.* This record only provides the

Massachusetts;[1448] d. 6 Apr 1976, Palmerton, Carbon, Pennsylvania; son of Joseph Winslow Brown and Elizabeth Winnek.[1449]

Harold E. Brown worked for a telephone company throughout his working life as a repair/maintenance man. The couple may have retired to Palmerton, Pennsylvania, as a son lived in Macungie at the time of his father's death in 1976. After Harold's death, Marjorie must have removed to Vermont to be closer to her daughter, Barbara, who was living there at the time of her father's death.[1450]

Harold and Marjorie had four children: Barbara Winslow Baker (1928–2018), Richard Nash Brown (1929–2019), Donald Claflin Brown (1932–2014), and Elizabeth Ann Smith (1937–2013).[1451, 1452]

Grace H. Claflin, Ernest O. Nash, Marjorie Nash

### 39. *Charles Merritt Scoville*[7] (*Albert Franklin,*[6] *Franklin,*[5] *Ithamar,*[4] *Timothy,*[3] *Stephen,*[2] *Stephen,*[1] *Arthur*)

Born 17 September 1867, East Canaan, Litchfield, Connecticut; died 14 July 1938, Richmond, Ontario, New York;[1453] buried Kenisco Cemetery, Valhalla, Westchester, New York;[1454] married (1) 19 June 1888, Everett, Middlesex, Massachusetts, Mary Elizabeth Johnson;[1455] born 26 April 1861, Hodgdon, Aroostook, Maine; died 28 July 1949, Los Angeles, Los Angeles, California; daughter of John Edgerly Johnson and Ellen Maria Cummings;[1456] married (2) circa 1894, Eudora Steel;[1457]born 30 May 1873, Addison, Washington, Maine; died 6 January 1927, Syracuse, Onondaga, New York; buried Oakwood Cemetery, Syracuse, Onondaga, New York.[1458]

---

year of marriage, not the day and month. Ancestry.

1448 *Massachusetts, Birth Records, 1840–1915*. Ancestry.

1449 Obituary—*The Morning Call,* Friday, April 7, 1976, edition; 20. Newspapers.

1450 This is speculation on my part based on where the children were living at the time of the parents' deaths.

1451 Children's vital information comes from various sources on Ancestry.

1452 Image comes from Ancestry, permission to use courtesy of kim13599.

1453 *New York, New York, U.S., Index to Death Certificates, 1862–1948*. Ancestry.

1454 Find A Grave.

1455 *Massachusetts Marriage Records, 1840–1915*. Ancestry.

1456 The birth and death information comes from my copy of her death certificate.

1457 An actual marriage record has not been located.

1458 Eudora's birth/death comes from the information on Find A Grave, as well as *New York, Death Index, 1852–1956*. Ancestry.

Charles M. Scoville was somewhat of a mystery for me early on in my research. I was able to locate him in some city directories for Worcester, Massachusetts, the marriage record in 1888, and the 1900 census for Everett City—but Charles M. Scoville just seemed to disappear after that census was taken. I was, however, able to follow his wife, Mary Elizabeth (Johnson) Scoville until the time of her death.

My theory is that Charles M. Scoville divorced Mary Elizabeth and remarried Eudora Steel. While I don't have proof of this, I believe my theory is plausible.

Charles Merritt Scoville met Mary Elizabeth Johnson and courted her. They eventually married on June 19, 1888, in Everett, Massachusetts. Mary Elizabeth was twenty-seven at the time of her marriage and Charles was twenty-one. After their marriage they lived in Everett and then removed to Worcester, Massachusetts, where they lived from 1889–1894. The 1895 city directory states that they removed to Quincy, Massachusetts.[1459]

Charles M. and Mary Elizabeth Scoville were back in Everett City in 1900.[1460] The couple was living at 7 School Street Place and the household consisted of:

Scoville, Charles M., head, b. Sept. 1866, 33, b. Connecticut, carpenter
Scoville, Mary E., wife, b. Apr. 1861, 39, no children born to her, b. Maine
Johnson, Ellen M, mother-in-law, Aug. 1833; 66, widow, 4 children/3 living, b. Vermont
Johnson, Ellen L, sister-in-law, Sept. 1870, 29, single, b. New Jersey
Johnson, Elva D., boarder, June 1879, 20, single, Maine

After the 1900 census we lose sight of Charles—for the time being.

Except for the next census it is difficult to track Mary Elizabeth (even through the city directories). The 1910[1461] census shows Mary Elizabeth still residing in Everett, but they are now residing at 45 Forest Avenue. Ellen Johnson, age seventy-six, is now listed as the "head" of the family and has her "own income" to support herself. Mary Elizabeth is now forty-eight years old and not employed, while sister Ellen L. Johnson, thirty-nine, works as a librarian at the Everett Library.

Mary Elizabeth Scoville is also noted as "married" for "21" years. Where was Charles?

The records are once again silent until 1915 when Mrs. Mary Elizabeth Scoville is found living in Los Angeles, California, at the Mary Andrews Clark Memorial Home at 336 Loma Drive and is employed as a "watchwoman." According to Wikipedia, this home was built by William A. Clark as a memorial to his mother. The YMCA operated the home from 1913–1987. Mr. Clark's desire was for this building to be a home for "young working women."[1462]

---

1459 Note that the city directories only mentioned Charles by name—Mary Elizabeth is not mentioned at all.

1460 1900 census, *Everett Ward 5, Middlesex, Massachusetts;* Roll: 658; Page: 2A; ED: 0751; FHL: 1240658.

1461 1910 census, *Everett Ward 5, Middlesex, Massachusetts;* Roll: 624_598; Page: 5A; ED: 0812; FHL: 1374611.

1462 For more information on this, see Mary Andrews Clark Memorial Home, https://en.wikipedia.org/wiki/Mary_Andrews_Clark_Memorial_Home.

What caused Mary Elizabeth to go three thousand miles away at the age of fifty-four to a place for "young working women"?

The following year (1916,) Mary Elizabeth's mother died in Everett, Massachusetts, and is buried there. Whether Mary Elizabeth was notified by her sister, or went back for the funeral, is something that cannot be confirmed. What *is* known is the fact that she is still in Los Angeles in 1920 when the census is taken. Mary Elizabeth still considers herself as "married" (even though Charles is nowhere to be found) and is now employed as an "elevator operator," perhaps for the Memorial Home, since it was four stories tall.

For whatever reason, Mary Elizabeth went back east as she is again residing in Everett, Massachusetts, in 1930.[1463] When did she return and why? She is now sixty-eight years old and is working as a hospital dietician. The family with whom she is boarding is "Joseph S. Baker," head of the household, and his daughter and her husband, "Helen and Mortimer Schroeder."[1464]

In 1940, Mary Elizabeth Scoville is back in California, this time living in Pacific Old People's Home at 1055 North Kingsley Drive, Los Angeles. She now gives her marital status as "widowed."

Mary Elizabeth Scoville died July 28, 1949,[1465] aged eighty-eight. She died from a cerebral embolism and heart disease and is buried in Inglewood Cemetery, Los Angles, California.

These are the bare bones facts of what is known of Mary E. Scoville's life. I have not located any newspaper articles or other documents to round out this individual.

~

We will now follow the trail of Charles Merritt Scoville. In this Scoville line alone, there are three distinct Charles <u>M.</u> Scovilles:

Charles Martin Scoville—1835–1864 (son of Franklin Scoville, born 1809)
Charles Merritt Scoville—1867 (son of Albert F. Scoville [son of Franklin, b. 1809])
Charles Mittean Scoville—1874–1947 (son of Franklin Scoville, b. 1850)

We know from the marriage records that Charles Merritt Scoville married Mary Elizabeth Johnson in 1888 in Everett, Massachusetts. We know that Charles was in Everett and Worcester, Massachusetts, from 1888 through 1893. He is referred to as a "stair-builder" and "carpenter" in these records.[1466] In 1895, the city directory states he (or they) removed to Quincy (Massachusetts). I reviewed the 1895, 1896, and 1897 city directories that are available online through *Ancestry*—there are no Scoville names listed.

When I did a wider search for a Charles M. Scoville born in 1867, I kept coming up with the one living in Syracuse, Onondaga, New York. I tracked his line down, and believe he

1463 1930 census, *Everett, Middlesex, Massachusetts;* Page: 12A; ED: 0223; FHL:234053. Ancestry.

1464 Helen Baker Schroeder is the niece of Mary Elizabeth Johnson Scoville. This is based on the obituary notice for Ellen L. Johnson, Mary's sister, who died January 1966 in Everett, Massachusetts. Obit notice located in Wednesday, January 5, 1966, issue of the *Boston Globe.* 16.

1465 My copy of the *State of California, Department of Health, Certificate of Death.*

1466 *U.S. City Directories, 1822–1995.* Ancestry.

belonged to another family. The search for the *right* Charles M. Scoville went on for years. I was no longer spending as much time on genealogical research, and had put this research aside for quite some time.

Since I believe no family line should be left dangling, and as Sherlock Holmes once said in *The Adventures of Beryl Coronet,* "when you have excluded the impossible, whatever remains, however improbable, must be the truth."[1467] I began to focus my research on Charles M. Scoville through a different lens. Fortunately, it was through Ancestry where information began to fall into place. When I originally began researching Charles, the record that opened up research avenues did not exist on the Ancestry website at the time—or at least I may have overlooked it. A copy of a United States passport was now available online for a "Charles M. Scoville." This was an emergency passport "in order that he may proceed to Russia." The date of this passport is May 24, 1910. What caught my eye was this man's date and place of birth: *September 17, 1867, East Canaan, Connecticut.* While I believed that this ***had*** to be the son of Albert Franklin Scoville and brother to Cora Scoville Claflin, I knew I had to pursue further.

Here is the wording of the passport in its entirety:[1468]

> I, Charles M. Scoville, a native and loyal citizen of the United States, hereby apply to the American Legation[1469] at Stockholm for a passport for myself, accompanied by my wife **Eudora**, and minor children as follows: Lula May, born at Haverhill, Mass., on the 26 day of April, **1894**, and Gwendolyn **Cora**, born Summerville, Mass., Jan. 31, **1904**.
>
> I solemnly swear that I was born at **East Canaan**, in the **State of Conn.**, on or about **17 Sept., 1867**, that my father is a native citizen of the United States; that I am domiciled in the United States, my permanent residence being at Boston, in the State of Mass., where I follow the occupation of Superintendent of Building Construction, that I left the United States on the 12 day of May, 1910 and am now temporarily sojourning at Stockholm . . . that I intend to return to the United States within a year . . .

The document goes on to say that he will perform the duties of "citizenship therein" and he desires a passport to visit Russia. Charles M. Scoville took the oath and swore his allegiance to the United States "against all enemies, foreign and domestic."

The passport application also gives a description of Charles M. Scoville. He is listed as 5′ 9 ½″ tall, moustache, ordinary forehead, blue eyes, straight nose, brown hair, ruddy complexion, and an oval face. He gives his age as "43."

There are a number of clues to follow in the passport application; the biggest one is his place and date of birth. Through all my years of genealogical research on the Scoville family, I have never come across another Charles M. Scoville born on September 17, 1867, in East (or North) Canaan,[1470] Connecticut.

1467 Doyle, Sir Arthur Conan; 315.

1468 *U.S., Passport Applications, 1795–1925*; No. 229; Ancestry.

1469 This likely refers to the American Embassy in Stockholm.

1470 Canaan, Connecticut, is a very small town. Whether Charles Merritt Scoville was born in

The *Scovel* book by Holley has one reference to a *Charles Merit Scoville,* however, he was not born in Connecticut and was born six years before the Charles of this record, as well as having a wife named "Olivia." This is ***not*** the same man.

The city directories have been searched in Boston, Quincy, Sommerville, and Haverhill for the possible years that Charles claims in his passport application.

As I have previously written, Charles M. Scoville is not found with his lawful wife, Mary Elizabeth, after 1900. In 1910, Mary Elizabeth is living with her mother and sister. She (Mary) continues to refer to herself as "married."

A man by the name of "Charles M. Scoville" is located in 1910 in Youngstown Township, Mahoning, Ohio, with his family:

120 McKinney Drive, Youngstown

Scoville, Charles M., head, 45, **first marriage**, m. **16 yrs.**, b. **Connecticut, parents born Connecticut**, foreman, Heller Bros. Co., rents.

Scoville, Eudora, wife, 34, first marriage, m. 16 yrs. 2 children born, 2 living, b. Maine

Scoville, Lula M., daughter, 15, single, b. Massachusetts

Scoville, Gwendolyn, daughter, 6, single, b. Massachusetts

You will note the areas in bold that stand out. It appears that Charles is the one who provided the enumerator with this information on the 19th day of April 1910. He is claiming that this is *his first marriage* and that they had been *married for sixteen years*. This would mean that Charles and Eudora were together prior to their daughter Lula's birth (born 26 April 1894).

Also note that Charles states he was born in Connecticut and his parents were born in Connecticut. If this *is* the son of Albert Franklin and Hannah Scoville, this would be a fact.

How do we reconcile the birth of Lula May Scoville, who was born in 1894 in Haverhill, Massachusetts (to Charles M. Scoville and Eudora Steel), to the Charles M. Scoville who was on the 1900 census with Mary Elizabeth Scoville in Everett, Massachusetts? **If** this is a case of bigamy, then the two couples would never have "run" into each other as Everett to Haverhill is approximately thirty-five miles.

After the 1900 census, Charles never lives in Everett or Worcester, Massachusetts, again.

Of course, it is possible that Charles divorced Mary Elizabeth and she continued to list herself as "married" for the sake of propriety;[1471] however, if this was the case, why would he be back with Mary Elizabeth for the 1900 census? I theorize that Charles was living two separate lives since 1894.

Charles is never again on any other census with Mary Elizabeth after 1900. What were the dynamics of this couple? Did Charles come and visit her periodically? Did she know that he had another family? These are questions that will never be answered.

A city directory reference has Charles in Syracuse (NY) in 1908 and employed as a "Superintendent," living at 208 South Crouse Avenue. He and his "second" family were in

---

East or North Canaan, has no bearing on whether this is the son of Albert F. Scoville and husband of Mary Elizabeth Johnson Scoville.

1471 At the time of this writing, many town/city clerks have set aside genealogical requests "until further notice." The only records presently available are those that appear online.

Haverhill, Massachusetts, in 1911 as they had a son born that year; however, the years between 1912–1914 are a mystery. He *was* in Pasadena, California, according to his father's will in 1915. The city directory for Pasadena,[1472] 1915, lists a "Chas. Scoville, contractor, renting at 192 West Colorado." I would conclude that this is the same Charles Scoville who married Mary Elizabeth Scoville in 1888 as he was a "stair-builder," "carpenter," and "contractor" according to various directory listings.

Mary Elizabeth Scoville was in Los Angeles in 1915. There would have been only ten miles between them. Did Charles know that she was there and vice versa?

In the month of January, 1916,[1473] C. M. Scoville, "48," supervisor and manager, born Connecticut, paid $100 to go from New York to British Columbia, Canada. Traveling with him were his wife, Dora, 45, housewife, born in Maine, and their son, Harold, aged 5, born in Massachusetts. The port of entry was White Rock.

In 1920[1474] Charles M. Scoville and Eudora are living in Syracuse, Onondaga, New York. The family was living at 241 Garfield Avenue when the enumerator visited them on January 10th:

Scoville, Charles M. head, rents, 52, married, b. Connecticut/parents: Connecticut, Superintendent-Building.

Scoville, Eudora M., wife, 45, married, b. Maine/parents: Maine.

Scoville, Gwendolyn, daughter, 15, single, b. Massachusetts.

Scoville, Harold, son, 8, single, b. Massachusetts.

Steele, Arthur, nephew, 19, single, b. Maine, mechanic automobile factory.[1475]

You will note that Lula is no longer in the household—her whereabouts are unknown during this time. In addition, a son was born to this couple while they were in Haverhill, Massachusetts, and is now eight years old. A nephew of Eudora's is also living with them.

The couple is still residing on Garfield Avenue in 1921, and in 1922 they were residing at 2003 South Salina Street.[1476] After 1922, there is no trace of Charles or Eudora in the Syracuse city directories.

Where this couple were between 1922–1926 is another mystery.

The death of Eudora Scoville on January 6, 1927, confirms that she/they were living in Syracuse at that time. Eudora Marion (Steele) Scoville dies at the age of fifty-three. There is no obituary; only a brief death notice was published in the *Syracuse Herald*: "Deaths: Thursday, Eudora Scoville, 445 Ellis Street." No mention of husband, children, or any grandchildren. It's as if this family would *vaporize* periodically and then pop up again.

Was Charles with his wife, Eudora, when she died?

---

1472 *U.S. City Directories, 1822–1995;* Ancestry.

1473 *Border Crossing: From U.S. to Canada, 1908–1935.* Ancestry.

1474 1920 census, *Syracuse Ward 19, Onondaga, New York;* Roll: T625_1249; Page: 7B; ED: 222; Image: 317.

1475 This was likely the Franklin Automobile Company. They were marketers of automobiles in Syracuse from 1902–1934. You can read more about this under "Franklin (automobile)" on Wikipedia.

1476 *U.S. City Directories, 1822–1995.* Ancestry.

Charles is mentioned in his aunt Irene Scoville Smith's will. She died on February 9, 1927, and her estate gives a list of all those relatives who would receive a bequest and where they were living at that time. Charles M. Scoville was one of those who was to receive a bequest and he is given as being in Tampa, Florida, during February 1927—a month after Eudora died. His address is a Post Office Box number only. Was he there when Eudora died, or did he leave soon after her death? He is not listed in the 1927 or 1928 city directory for Tampa. So where was he?

The years between the time he was in Tampa in 1927 until his death in 1938 on Staten Island, New York, are a complete blank. I have tried many variations of his name for the 1930 census, and he just does not show up. He had been known to travel, and he may very well have been out of the country, on the road, or somehow the enumerator missed him.

The death certificate for Charles M. Scoville provides the following data:[1477]

Charles M. Scoville
Born: 17 September 1867
Married
Age: 70
Residence: 65 Central Avenue
Died: 14 July 1938 New York City, Richmond (Staten Island)[1478]
Cerebral Hemorrhage, arteriosclerosis
Buried: 16 July 1938—Kenisco Cemetery
Occupation: Binder Construction
Father: Albert
Mother: Mary
Wife: Ellen

Is this the correct Charles M. Scoville who was married to Mary Elizabeth and Eudora? There are three things that point to this being one and the same person: his date of birth, his occupation, and his father's name. Death certificates are not considered primary source evidence as the information comes from whomever the informant was and what they know about the individual.

It would appear (from the death record) that Charles M. Scoville married a woman named "Ellen" and she was the informant. While the name of Charles' father is correct, the mother's name is incorrect (unless she confused "Mary," Charles' first wife's name, as his mother's name). We don't know what Charles may have told Ellen about his past and so I consider this error a non-starter, and I have no doubt that the man who died in 1938 is, in fact, the same one born in 1867 in Connecticut.[1479]

---

1477 *New York, New York, U.S., Index to Death Certificates, 1862–1948*. Certificate No.: 1304; Ancestry.

1478 I've had no success via the city directories in locating Charles in Richmond, Staten Island, New York. The city directory online ends in 1933. In addition, Richmond County, Staten Island, is not to be confused with Richmond, Ontario County, New York. The Find A Grave information threw me off for a while and I was going in the wrong direction.

1479 I also checked for other Charles Scovilles who may have had a wife named "Ellen" but could

I have been equally unsuccessful in finding anything about Ellen Scoville and have decided to leave her as the proverbial question mark—for now.

Going back to Charles' first wife, Mary Elizabeth: the 1940 census now shows her marital status as "widowed." How did she know that Charles had died two years prior? Very curious, but again, no answers, only speculations.

Charles M. Scoville and Mary Elizabeth Johnson were childless.

### *Children of Charles Merritt Scoville and Eudora Marion Steel*

i. Lula Mary Scoville,[8] b. 26 Apr 1894, Haverhill, Middlesex, Massachusetts;[1480] d. 13 Dec 1965, possibly Syracuse, Onondaga, New York;[1481] m. sometime between 1915 and 1917, Andrew Henry Goettel; b. 7 May 1892, Syracuse, Onondaga, New York;[1482] d. unknown; son of Andrew and Henrietta Goettel.

Andrew H. Goettel was a musician, as was his father before him. Lula and Andrew had one daughter, Karoline Goettel (1918–1982); she married Thomas F. Pitfido (1910–1988).

ii. Gwendolyn Cora Scoville,[8] b. 31 Jan 1904, Sommerville, Middlesex, Massachusetts; d. 23 Jun 1931, Gananoque, Ontario, Canada; m. 31 Jan 1922, Salina, Onondaga, New York, Paul Forrester Grassman, b. 26 Nov 1900, Syracuse, Onondaga, New York; d. 17 Oct 1964, Marietta, Onondaga, New York.

According to the 1928 city directory for Syracuse, Paul Forrester Grassman was employed in the advertising department of a firm that was not named in the directory. In 1928, Paul Forrester Grassman, his wife, Gwendolyn, and their one-year-old daughter, Paula, are named on the *Canadian Immigration Service* report. At the time of this record, Paul Grassman was twenty-seven and all of them were born in Syracuse, New York. The admission record asks what "race or people," and Paul and Paula are listed as "German" and Gwendolyn as "Dutch." Their religion was "Presbyterian." Paul Grassman's occupation is difficult to read but it appears to be "multigraph operator" and he states that he is "retired" and had an annual income of $8,000.[1483] Their destination was 272 Jolen (?) Street in Gananoque, Ontario. The port that they entered was Brockville, Ontario, Canada. The town of Gananoque (GAN e NOK Way) is a town of Leeds and Grenville, Ontario, and sits on the St. Lawrence River and has access to 1,864 islands.[1484]

The family was still there in 1931 when Gwendolyn Cora Scoville Grassman was involved in a fatal automobile accident. Existing are two records: her death certificate and *Reports of Deaths of American Citizens Abroad, 1835–1974.*[1485] The details of this report are distressing:

---

not find any. It is possible that Charles M. Scoville remarried after Eudora's death to a woman named Ellen. No records of this have been found to date.

1480 Date of birth is from the passport information for father.

1481 Obituary notice from *Post-Standard,* Syracuse, New York; December 14, 1965, edition.

1482 *U.S., World War I Draft Registration Cards, 1917–1918,* Ancestry.

1483 Eight thousand dollars in 1931 would be equivalent to $146,737 in the current market. He may have received an inheritance and no longer had to work? Later records indicate he was too ill to work.

1484 Wikipedia.org.

1485 Ancestry.

> On June 23, 1931, at 4:30 p.m., Highway #2, Gananoque, Ontario, Gwendolyn Cora Grassman, age 27, native, died from [a] crushed chest, contusion of brain and fractured ribs, caused by motor accident, as certified by Dr. Lockhead, Landsdowne, Ontario.

Her body was taken to Syracuse, New York, for burial, accompanied by her husband.

In the remarks section it states, "Owning to the illness of Mr. Grassman, it has been impossible to get this information before this date." Filed in October 1931. It is unknown what Paul Grassman's illness was, whether it had to do with the combination of the death of his daughter in 1925 and then his wife's tragic death, or if he had some other problem.

A little over a year later, on July 9, 1932, Paul Forrester Grassman married Florence Ann Case in Syracuse, Onondaga, New York. Miss Case was born September 20, 1907, in Verona, Oneida, New York, to J. Arthur Case and Bertha Page. Florence Case was employed as a teacher. Paul Grassman was not employed.

I have not been able to locate this couple on the U.S. censuses for 1930 or 1940; however, in 1933, 1934, and 1935 they are listed as living in Syracuse. Paul F. Grassman is employed as a "printer." The next record that appears for this individual is the *U.S. WWII Draft Cards Young Men, 1940–1947.*[1486] The date of his registration was February 14, 1942. At that time, he and his wife were living at 1902 Euclid Avenue, Syracuse. The question "employer's name" is answered "none (unemployed at request of doctor)." Paul F. Grassman was 5′ 11″ tall with blue eyes, blonde hair, and light complexion.

The only other record that is available is the death record for Paul F. Grassman. At the time of his death, he and his wife were living in Marietta, Onondaga, New York. His death occurred on October 18, 1964, and he is buried in Oakwood Cemetery, Syracuse. Paul F. Grassman and Gwendolyn Cora Scoville had two children: Helen Roberta Grassman (1924–1925) and Paula Grassman Doughty (1927–2008), who married Marshall Kevin Doughty.

iii. Harold Merritt Scoville,[8] b. 15 Mar 1911, Haverhill, Essex, Massachusetts;[1487] d. 3 Dec 1959, Rochester, Monroe, New York;[1488] m. (1) 23 Sept 1936, Allen, Allen, Indiana,[1489] Adrienne Jingozian, b. 23 Sep 1911, Rodosto, (Tekirdag) Turkey;[1490] d. 2 Nov 1997, San Diego, San Diego, California;[1491] m. (2) Bertha Pero.[1492]

Up until 1930, Harold apparently lived with his mother and father. On the census for 1930[1493] he is boarding with the George German family in Syracuse City. He is nineteen years old and is employed as a bank clerk.

On June 22, 1936, Harold M. Scoville married Adrienne Jingozian in Allen, Indiana.

---

1486 Ancestry.

1487 *Massachusetts, Birth Records, 1840–1915; 5;* Ancestry.

1488 *Rochester Democrat and Chronicle,* Sunday, December 6, 1959, edition; 8B. Newspapers.

1489 *Indiana Marriages, 1811–2019*; 239; FamilySearch.

1490 *U.S., Naturalization Records Indexes, 1794–1995;* Images: 1018; Ancestry.

1491 *California, Death Index, 1940–1997.* Ancestry.

1492 The first name of Harold's second wife comes from his obituary notice.

1493 1930 census, *Syracuse, Onondaga, New York;* Page: 26A; ED: 0207; FHL: 2341363. Ancestry.

Adrienne was the daughter of Thaddeus Jingozian and Nuvart Bozian (according to the marriage record). They were likely Armenians who lived in the eastern part of Turkey, and whether they removed to Turkey during the genocide or had been part of the large Armenian population in Turkey prior is unknown.

Adrienne Jingozian attended Wittenberg University in Springfield, Ohio, and belonged to the Beta Beta Beta sorority.[1494] Since Harold was also in Springfield, Ohio, in 1935 (according to the 1940 census) this is where the couple must have met. However, their marriage didn't last very long.

The 1940 census reveals that Harold M. Scoville is boarding with the Spencer Slingerland family in Geneva, Ontario, New York.[1495] His marital status is given as "single," and he is working as a clerk for a shipping company.[1496] Adrienne, on the other hand, is living in Saugatuck, Allegan, Michigan. She gives her surname as "Jingozian" as opposed to "Scoville." Her mother, Nuvart, is also living with her. Adrienne is working as a teacher in a public school during this time.

In 1942 Harold registered for the draft (as was required) and had returned to New York, living at 34 Jefferson Avenue in Geneva, and was working at the Geneva Resuring (?) Company on State Street.

The next record that is available is the divorce record for this couple, which was decreed on July 3, 1946,[1497] in Wayne, Wayne, Michigan. Whether they tried to reconcile throughout the years is difficult to determine. After the divorce, they apparently went their separate ways.

A yearbook for East Commerce High School, Class of 1952,[1498] lists Adrienne Scoville as part of their faculty.

There are no other records that I have been able to locate online for Harold M. Scoville other than his obituary notice. He remarried sometime after his divorce, but I have not been able to find that record either. Harold's obituary appeared in the *Rochester Democrat and Chronicle* in their Sunday edition on December 6, 1959:[1499]

> **Harold Scoville Funeral Today**
> A last rite for Harold Scoville of 188 Charlotte St., an employee of Harper Method Laboratory here, will be held at 2 p.m. today in the Thomas F. Trott Funeral Home, 683 Main St., E.
>
> Mr. Scoville, who moved here about 18 years ago from Syracuse, died Thursday (Dec. 3 1959). He was 48. He leaves his wife, Bertha; a daughter, Holly M. Scoville; a sister, Mrs. Andrew Grettel of Syracuse, and several nieces and nephews. Burial will be at the family's convenience.

---

1494 *U.S., School Yearbooks, 1900–1990.* Ancestry.

1495 According to the 1940 census, in 1935 he was living in Springfield, Ohio. 1940 census, *Geneva, Ontario, New York;* Roll: m_t6027-02706; Page: 4B; ED: 35-27. Ancestry.

1496 I am guessing that this word is "shipping."

1497 *Michigan, Divorce Records, 1897–1952.* Ancestry.

1498 East Commerce High is in Detroit, Michigan. *U.S., School Yearbooks, 1900–1990.* Ancestry.

1499 Newspapers.

I wasn't sure if this was the correct person until I saw Harold's sister's name—Mrs. Andrew Goettel, (spelled incorrectly in the obituary notice). His burial place is unknown.

Through further research on Bertha, it was discovered that she had remarried after Harold M. Scoville's death to Victor R. Brackley on May 28, 1960, in Rochester, New York.[1500] Through this marriage record it gave her birth name as Bertha Louise Pero, daughter of Rufus Pero and Grace L. Gibson. Bertha was born September 11, 1926, in Rochester, Monroe, New York.[1501] The marriage record gives her names as "Bertha Pero" and "Bertha Scoville." To confirm that this is the same Bertha who married Harold M. Scoville I located two obituary notices. One, for Victor Brackley, mentions a "daughter," Holly Goar—the second obituary is for Bertha, which states, " Bertha L. Brackley, Hilton, Peacefully, November 29, 2006, predeceased by first husband, Harold M. Scoville."[1502] This confirms the information in relation to Bertha.

The *California, Death Index, 1940–1997*[1503] lists an Adrienne J. Mandossian, born September 23, 1909, born in "other country," died on November 2, 1997, San Diego, San Diego, California. I believe this to be one and the same person who married Harold M. Scoville. In an article in the *California Courier* about the *Armenian Ladies Club*, it mentions Dr. Adrienne Mandossian and her sister Derouhi Jangozian, "formerly of Detroit." We know that Adrienne Jingozian Scoville was in Detroit, Michigan, in 1940 and teaching at a public school. It is likely that she obtained a doctorate (re: Dr. Adrienne) and had remarried (hence the surname of Mandossian); however, a marriage record, obituary, or any other record for her remains unknown.

Harold Merritt Scoville and Adrienne Jingozian did not have any children.

Harold Merritt Scoville and Bertha Pero had one daughter: Holly M. Scoville, who had married Eric Goar.[1504]

### *40. Florence Mabel Scoville[7] (Albert Franklin,[6] Franklin,[5] Ithamar,[4] Timothy,[3] Stephen,[2] Stephen,[1] Arthur)*

Born 11 April 1886, Worcester, Worcester, Massachusetts;[1505] died 29 October 1964, Worcester, Worcester, Massachusetts; buried Hope Cemetery, Worcester, Massachusetts;[1506] married 20 October 1915, M. E. Church, Worcester, Massachusetts, William Louis Carr;[1507] born

1500 *New York State, Marriage Index, 1881–1967;* Image: 1716. Ancestry.

1501 *New York State, Birth Index, 1881–1942;* Image: 1201; Ancestry.

1502 *Democrat and Chronicle;* Sunday, December 3, 2006; 36. Newspapers

1503 Ancestry.

1504 The obituaries for Bertha Scoville Brackley and Victor R. Brackley mention a daughter, Holly Goar.

1505 *Massachusetts, Birth Records, 1840–1915;* Image: 1508. Ancestry.

1506 Find A Grave.

1507 *Massachusetts, Marriage Records, 1840–1915;* Image: 70. Ancestry.

21 April 1880, Presque Isle, Aroostook, Maine;[1508] died 12 March 1959, Worcester, Worcester, Massachusetts; buried Hope Cemetery; son of Lewis French Carr (1837–1906) and Alice Brannen (1854–1916).

Florence was the daughter of Albert Franklin Scoville and his second wife, Margaret Estella Apperson, and was the only child born to this couple who survived into adulthood. When Florence was seven years old, her mother died in childbirth (as did the baby). A year later, Albert remarried for the third time to Melissa V. Moore, and she would become Florence's mother.

Sometime before 1906[1509] the Carr family moved to 18 Ball Street.[1510] The family was made up of Louis F. Carr, Alice Carr, and William Louis Carr.

William and his mother are listed on the 1910 census[1511] living at the same residence. William is age "twenty-nine" and is employed as a "foreman" in a "blade shop."

Florence continues to live at home with her father and stepmother. Whether William and Florence courted for an extended time is not known. It wasn't until after Florence's father died in May 1915 that she consented to marry William, in October of that same year.[1512]

Florence had received a bequest from her father for $100 (worth approximately $2,715.94 in 2021) and a piano. Her stepmother also received a bequest. William and Florence may have bought the house at 7 Ball Street from Melissa, as by 1920, Melissa was living on her own in another part of town.

When Florence married, she was already twenty-nine years old and was what would have been considered a "spinster" during that time. William was thirty-five at their marriage, but being a bachelor at that age did not hold the same stigma as it did for a female.

Prior to her marriage, Florence worked as a "typewriter" in a department store. After her marriage, she no longer worked outside of the home; whether this was by design, or the decision of her husband is unknown. William Carr was a foreman and likely made an adequate income to support his wife, although in the censuses for 1920 and 1930, the couple had a boarder living with them. Having a boarder would provide for some additional income.

The 1930 census shows that William was employed as a "shipper" for a paper machine company. Based on the available city directories for Worcester, William continued to be employed during the Depression.[1513]

There is very little in the way of newspaper articles regarding this couple other than these two articles that were in the *Evening Gazette:*

---

1508 *Ibid,* and *U.S., World War I Draft Registration Cards, 1917–1918,* Ancestry.

1509 The date is an approximation based on the death date of Louis F. Carr who was a resident of 18 Ball Street when he died on 28 February 1906 (death certificate).

1510 Florence had grown up at 7 Ball Street in Worcester and she remained there until her death.

1511 1910 census; *Worcester, Worcester, Massachusetts;* Ward 7; ED: 1901; Page: 30B. Ancestry.

1512 Albert F. Scoville had been ill prior to his death. Perhaps Florence felt it unseemly to marry during that time and so waited until after her father's death to marry.

1513 I am basing this on the fact that he shows up on the 1930, 1931, and 1939 city directories as being employed as a "shipper clerk" and a "foreman."

Paul Dekhard, 6, of 49 Canterbury Street was slightly injured last night when struck by an automobile operated by William L. Carr of 7 Ball Street. He was treated by Dr. Nugent and taken home.[1514]

On Thursday, April 19, 1928:

Mr. and Mrs. William L. Carr of 7 Ball Street are entertaining Rev. and Mrs. William F. Koons of Holliston during the Methodist Episcopal conference being held at Wesley Church . . .[1515, 1516]

Florence M. Scoville

Florence and William Carr

William Carr retired from Rice Barton Corporation[1517] in 1954 after twenty-eight years of service—he was seventy-four years old.

William Louis Carr died on 12 March 1959 at the age of seventy-eight. He is buried in Hope Cemetery, Worcester, Massachusetts. His wife, Florence, died four years later on 28 October 1964 at the age of seventy-eight. Florence is buried next to her husband in Hope Cemetery. Obituary notices have not been located for either William or Florence. No children were born to this couple.

1514 Friday edition on August 28, 1925, 5; GenealogyBank.com

1515 No page given; GenealogyBank.com

1516 Photos courtesy of Sandra Amador.

1517 Rice Barton is a company that makes papermaking and textile machinery and is still in operation today.

# Eighth Generation

## 41. i. *Charles Mittean Scoville[8] (Franklin,[7] Charles M.,[6] Amasa,[5] Ithamar,[4] Timothy,[3] Stephen,[2] Stephen,[1] Arthur)*

Born 5 January 1874, Ironton, Iron, Missouri; died 28 May 1947, Riverside, Riverside, California;[1518] m. 12 July 1893, St. Joseph, Berrian, Michigan,[1519] Sara "Sadie" Lobdue Jackson; born 10 May 1871, Chicago, Illinois; died 10 January 1962, San Diego, San Diego, California;[1520] daughter of Daniel Jackson and Mary Philbrick.[1521]

This is the last of the "Charles M. Scovilles" that I had mentioned earlier. Charles' middle name—Mittean—likely comes from his mother's side of the family as I have not come across it anywhere in my research on the Scoville family.

At the age of nineteen, Charles married twenty-two-year-old Sara "Sadie" L. Jackson who is purported to be from Chicago, Illinois. They had become engaged in 1892 according to the announcement in the newspaper:

> The engagement of Mr. C.M. Scoville to Miss Lobdue Jackson, both of Chicago, is announced through Chicago papers. Mr. Scoville is the eldest son of Frank Scoville, formerly a resident of Ironton, and well known in this vicinity. Mr. C.M. Scoville holds a position of high responsibility and trust in the employ of his uncle and is much admired by his business associates.
>
> Miss Jackson is the youngest daughter of one of Chicago's pioneers and is quite accomplished. Both are prominent in society and have a vast number of friends.[1522]

The last child to be born in Ironton, Missouri, is Charles' brother Gilbert in 1882. The family must have moved back to Chicago (or surrounding area) sometime after, as the last two children (Mabel and Ethel) were born in Illinois in 1887 and 1890 respectively.

On July 12, 1893, in St. Joseph, Michigan, Charles and Sadie were married. The town of St. Joseph lies on the east side of Lake Michigan and is approximately ninety-four miles from Chicago (and lies on the west side of the lake). It is curious why they traveled there to take their wedding vows instead of the Chicago area, but at the time of their marriage, Charles' parents had already removed to California. Perhaps St. Joseph was where they were to honeymoon and it would have made sense to get married there.

The copy of the marriage record on Ancestry (*Michigan, Marriage Records, 1867–1952)*

---

1518 Birth and death information comes from the *California, Death Index, 1940–1997,* Ancestry.

1519 *Michigan, Marriage Records, 1867–1952;* 258, Record: 1422. Ancestry.

1520 Birth and death information comes from the *California, Death Index, 1940–1997,* Ancestry.

1521 Parents' names are mentioned in the newspaper marriage notice.

1522 *Iron County Register,* Ironton, Missouri; December 29, 1892, issue. No page number given; GenealogyBank.

provides information that confirms that this is the Charles M. who is the son of Franklin Scoville. There is one notation that stands out: the couple is listed as "B" for black. I have not found any other record (primarily the censuses) where they are ever again designated as "black,"[1523] and there is no way to expand on this any further, although this is certainly a curious entry in the marriage book.

A year later, another announcement appeared in the *Iron County Register* regarding the birth of their first child:

> Last Thursday we received by mail, in an envelope post-marked Chicago, a card bearing the following lines: "Catherine Sara Scoville, July 12, 1894, Mr. and Mrs. Charles M. Scoville . . ."[1524]

By the time of the 1900 census,[1525] Charles and Sadie were living in California in Corona City with their two daughters. At this time Charles was a merchant of dry goods and renting their home. By that time, the town of Corona had grown to 1,434 residents with agriculture (lemon and orange groves) as the backbone of the economy (mining came in second).[1526]

Charles and his family were living on Main Street next door to his father in 1910. He was now a bookkeeper for a water company. The 1907 city directory for Corona, Riverside, California, shows that Charles was working as a bookkeeper for the Temescal Water Company in 1906. Charles would remain with this company for a number of years in different capacities.

The Temescal Water Company was organized in Corona in 1888 on one hundred sixty acres of land in Perris Valley. Wells were put in and pumping plants were erected to supply the much-needed water to Corona.[1527]

As early as 1902, Charles M. Scoville was mentioned in many newspaper articles that appeared in the *Riverside Daily Press* and the *Riverside Independent Enterprise.* There are too many articles to be captured here. The articles pertained to luncheons, traveling plans, birthday celebrations, church news, and board meetings. Here is one example that appeared in the Monday edition of the *Riverside Independent Enterprise* newspaper:

> **Reliable Reports From the County**: Charles M. Scoville, prominent and popular Corona business man, says Loyal Kelley[1528] will receive 90 percent or better of the Corona vote. He is a Corona boy, and everyone is with him.[1529]

---

1523 Note that all the other couples on the same page were designated as "W" (white).

1524 Thursday, 26 July 1894, edition; Vol: 28; Page: 6; GenealogyBank.

1525 1900 census, *Corona, Riverside, California;* Sheet 7; ED: 0221; FHL: 1240097; Dwelling: 134; Family: 135.

1526 Information comes from https//www.incorona.com.

1527 Holmes, Elmer Wallace, *History of Riverside County California*, (1912), 160.

1528 Loyal Kelly was running for District Attorney in Corona against his opponent, Walter Davison. The headline read: "**Walter Davison loses against Loyal Kelley by a margin of 45 votes.**" *Riverside Daily Press,* Thursday, August 31, 1922; 2.

1529 *Riverside Daily Press,* August 28, 1922; 4.

By 1913, Charles was working for the Temescal and Corona Water Company as its secretary and continued with that position for some twenty-odd years until he was promoted to the accountant position within the company.

At the age of forty-four his draft registration card was completed on September 12, 1918. He was of stout build and of medium height with blue eyes and dark brown hair. The family was renting a home at 911 Howard Street through the 1930s. By the time of the 1940 census, they had bought a home at 136 South West Boulevard in Corona. Charles was sixty-six years old and still employed at the water company.

Charles Mittean Scoville died on May 20, 1947, and is buried in Sunnyslope Cemetery in Corona. His obituary is very basic for one who was so prominent in the town. From the *Los Angeles Times*:

> Scoville, Charles M. of Corona, husband of Sadie L. Scoville, father of Mrs. John Hardisty and Mrs. Paul D. Burnett of Corona, brother of Harry S. Scoville of Monrovia, grandfather of Charles S. Hardisty of San Diego. Masonic services Saturday 9 a.m. at John L. Brown Funeral Home, Corona followed by services at 10 a.m. at St. John's Episcopal Church, Corona.[1530]

Since the 1950 census is not available as of this writing, it is harder to track Charles' wife, Sadie.

Sadie was born Sara Lobdell (Lobdue?) Jackson. According to the *California, Death Index, 1940–1997,* she was born May 10, 1871, in Illinois—the actual town or city has not been determined via any primary source documentation. Her parents were married in 1861/1862 in Boone County, Illinois.[1531]

Daniel Jackson was born January 13, 1822, in Salem, Washington, New York, and died November 7, 1892, in Cook County, Illinois.[1532] The death record gives his occupation as a "commission merchant" (someone who buys and sells goods for others on a commission basis).[1533]

According to some unsourced family trees on *Ancestry,* the first child of Daniel and Mary Jackson (Benjamin Franklin Jackson) was born January 29, 1861, in Cherokee County, Alabama; all the other children were born in Belvidere, Boone County, Illinois.

Sadie's siblings were Benjamin Franklin, Clara Melvina (1863–1938), and Frank Philbrick (1869–1962). Her mother, Mary Philbrick Jackson, lived from 1835–1912, when she died in Chicago. Husband and wife are buried in Belvidere Cemetery, Belvidere, Illinois.[1534]

---

1530 Thursday, May 29, 1947, edition; 15. Newspapers.

1531 *Illinois County Marriages, 1800–1940.* There is an alternate marriage record for *David* Jackson and Mary F. Philbrick for 11 October 1861, Boone, Illinois; *Illinois Marriage Index, 1860–1920.* Their first child, Benjamin Franklin Jackson, is said to have been born in 1861, but I have not found a birth record to confirm this.

1532 *Cook County Illinois Death Index, 1878–1922.* Ancestry.

1533 www.collinsdictionary.com.

1534 Find A Grave.

Since Sadie L. Scoville died in San Diego, it is possible she lived with or near her daughter Irene M. Burnett, who was also residing in said city. Sadie is buried in Sunnyslope Cemetery in Corona.

The first child of Charles M. and Sadie L. Scoville was Catherine Sadie Scoville (1894–1978), who married John Hardisty (1886–1976). They lived in California. The second was Irene Mitchell Scoville (1899–1980). Her first marriage was to Harry Tate Ashley (1891–1931) in 1919. They divorced in 1922. He worked for the Pacific Electric Railway and, according to the divorce record, he was "intemperate and did not provide for the family."[1535] Irene then married Paul Dover Burnett (1897–1982).

### 42. *II. GEORGE ALBERT SCOVILLE*[8] *(FRANKLIN,*[7] *CHARLES M.,*[6] *AMASA,*[5] *ITHAMAR,*[4] *TIMOTHY,*[3] *STEPHEN,*[2] *STEPHEN,*[1] *ARTHUR)*

Born 21 December 1876, Ironton, Iron, Missouri;[1536] died 14 January 1940, Rochester, Monroe, New York;[1537] married 10 May 1905, Riverside, Riverside, California, Mary Josephine Dyer; born 29 July 1877, perhaps Toulon, Stark, Illinois; died 24 April 1957, Orange, Orange, California;[1538] daughter of Otis Theron Dyer (1844–1898) and Mary Ellen Weed (1844–1919).

I am going to start with the end of George's life as his obituary is filled with many details, many of which I would not have been aware of had I just relied on data from the usual sources. The obituary was published in the *Democrat and Chronicle*, Monday, January 15, 1940.[1539]

Keep in mind that an obituary is not a primary source, and some information may be in error; however, much of the information may have come from his wife and/or business colleagues.

> George A. Scoville, 63, vice president and general manager of the Stromberg-Carlson Telephone Manufacturing Company died yesterday (January 4, 1940) in General Hospital. He was taken ill early in September while on a business trip to Seattle, Washington, but recovered sufficiently three months later to return to his home [on] 108 Sandringham Road, Brighton. Ten days ago, his condition became worse, and he was taken to the hospital.
>
> The record of Mr. Scoville's business activities is filled with a wealth of both engineering and sales experience. He was born in Ironton, Missouri, but spent only a few years in that town, his family moving to Chicago in his early childhood. During his high school years, the family moved to California. He completed his secondary education in Corona High School, Corona, California, then attended Stanford University for two years studying electrical engineering.[1540]

---

1535 *Riverside Daily Press,* Friday, January 23, 1922, edition; 8; GenealogyBank.

1536 *U.S., World War I Draft Registration Cards, 1917–1918.* Ancestry.

1537 Various sources: obituary; *New York, Episcopal Diocese of Rochester Church Records; U.S., Social Security Applications and Claims Index,* Ancestry, and Find A Grave.

1538 Birth and death from *California, Death Index, 1940–1997.* Ancestry.

1539 Page: 11; Newspapers.

1540 While at Stanford, George Scoville belonged to the Varsity Mandolin Club (guitar). He

He spent the next three years in shops of the Western Electric Company in Chicago, after which he returned to Stanford. He graduated in 1903. He spent a year with Southern California Edison Company and then returned to Western Electric Company.

In 1905 several former associates, then with the Kellogg Switchboard and Supply Company, Elyria, Ohio went to the Dean Electric Company in that city, and George Scoville left the Western Electric Company to join them. Two of those men, Ray H. Marson and Sidney A. Beyland, eventually went to Stromberg-Carlson with him.

With the Dean Company he held positions of sales engineer, Pacific Coast manager and sales manager until 1916 when he came to Rochester as a sales manager for Stromberg-Carlson. While at the Dean Company he spent a year in Australia and New Zealand.

In 1920, he was made a director of the company and in 1924 he was named vice-president. He was a directory of the United States Independent Telephone Association and chairman of the telephone manufacturing section, as a chairman of the supervisory agency of the Telephone Manufactures, the group administering the code for the industry and a member of the board of Radio Manufacturing Association.

He was known not only in the telephone industry but was personally acquainted with radio dealers throughout the country, having been connected to the radio business since 1922, when Stromberg-Carlson went into that business.

George Scoville was also a vestryman of the Episcopal Church of the Epiphany and a teacher for many years of its men's class, he was also much interested in philanthropic and civic activities.

For several years he headed the Industrial Employee Division of Rochester Community Chest and was a director of the Rochester Humane Society.

Mr. Scoville was also a member of many clubs, the Genesee Valley Club, the Rochester Club, Oak Hill Country Club, the Rochester Chamber of Commerce and the Stanford Club of New York, and held a membership in the American Institute of Electrical Engineers and the Rochester Engineering Society.

He leaves, besides his wife, three brothers and two sisters, all of California, Charles M. Scoville, Corona; Harry F. Scoville, Monrovia; Gilbert A. Scoville, San Gabriel; Mrs. Earl Thayer, San Diego; and Mrs. Frederick W. Kuster, Corona.

Mrs. Scoville is the former Mary Dyer, a native of California.[1541] The couple were married in 1905. Funeral services will be held in the home at 2:30 p.m. tomorrow. Burial will be in California."[1542]

---

could also play the piccolo and violin. *U.S., School Yearbooks, 1900–1999.* Ancestry.

1541 I believe this to be erroneous information. The Dyer family were living in Toulon, Stark, Illinois, around the time of Mary Dyer's birth.

1542 George A. Scoville is buried in the Dyer Family vault in Olivewood Cemetery, Riverside, California.

GEORGE A. SCOVILLE

George A. Scoville had a wide and varied career with many interests. To obtain this type of information from an obituary is a rarity.

Unfortunately, Mary Dyer Scoville's obituary is not as expansive. From what I can glean from the records her father, Otis Dyer, was born in New York in 1844. His family is then located in New London, Connecticut, in 1850 and then they all headed to Illinois where Mary and her siblings were born. Sometime after the 1880 census in Toulon, Illinois, the family struck out for California. Mary's father died in 1898 at the age of fifty-four from nephritis (kidney disease) and Mary continued to live with her mother (also named Mary) until her marriage to George Scoville.

Mary D. Scoville's obituary does not tell of any interests, clubs, etc., that she was involved with. After George's death, she went to live with her brother-in-law Harry Scoville in Monrovia, California, as well as some other relatives until her passing in 1957. She is buried with the rest of her family in Olivewood Cemetery in the Dyer vault.

This couple did not have children.[1543]

### *43. iii. Harry Franklin Scoville[8] (Franklin,[7] Charles M.,[6] Amasa,[5] Ithamar,[4] Timothy,[3] Stephen,[2] Stephen,[1] Arthur)*

Born 10 May 1880, Ironton, Iron, Missouri;[1544] died 30 August 1963, Pomona, Los Angeles, California; married 12 August 1910, Los Angeles, Los Angeles, California,[1545] Clara Marian Bennett; born 20 May 1885, Missouri; died 30 September 1976, Los Angeles, Los Angeles, California,[1546] daughter of Charles M. Bennett and Mary_______.[1547]

As his brothers before him, Harry F. Scoville had a long and varied career. Once again, I've relied on his obituary notice to outline his business life.

> Like his brother George, Harry attended Stanford University for a law degree[1548] and was admitted to the State Bar of California in 1903 and practiced law for fifteen years

1543 This photo accompanied the obituary notice.

1544 Birth and death information comes from the *California, Death Index, 1940–1997*. Ancestry.

1545 *Monrovia News-Post*, Sunday, October 3 1910; 9. Newspapers.

1546 Birth and death information comes from the *California, Death Index, 1940–1997*. Ancestry.

1547 The 1895 census for Ottawa City Ward 1, Franklin, Kansas, shows a family headed by C. M. Bennett with wife, Mary, and a daughter, Clara, age 9, born in Missouri. Clara's obit states she was born in "Kansas," so the Kansas census for 1895 is most likely Clara Marion Bennett's family. *Kansas, U.S., State Census Collection, 1855–1925*. Family enumerated on 1 March 1895. *Kansas Territory Census;* Roll: v115_49; Line: 11; Dwelling: 342; Family: 344. Ancestry.

1548 While at Stanford Harry Scoville belonged to the Varsity Glee Club as the second tenor. *U.S., School Yearbooks, 1880–2012*. Ancestry.

in Corona and Los Angeles.

However, in 1918 sickness[1549] interrupted his legal career and he went to Monrovia (California), where he purchased a small ranch.

It wasn't long after, Harry Scoville was named Monrovia's first city manager serving in that capacity for approximately three years. He then accepted a position with the Bureau of Efficiency of Los Angeles County and was later the director of the Bureau of Administrative Research. After twenty-three years in top county posts, he retired.

As a businessman he was involved in many organizations such as the Monrovia Kiwanis Club and Masonic Order. He was past president of the Society for Advancement of Management, a member of the Western Government Association, Speakers Club of Los Angeles County and American Society for Public Administration. He was also responsible of Intern System of Public Administration. The Los Angeles Branch of the American Society of Public Administration established the Harry Scoville Award, which goes annually to the young man establishing the best record in public administration in the area.[1550]

As an aside, Harry had also played football in his youth for Corona High School as well as playing the 'E bass' in Terpening's Corona Band, which was organized in March 1909.

Since I have no personal insight into the intimate life of Harry F. Scoville, I can only relay what is available. Where or when Harry met Clara Marion Bennett is a question mark. Through the census records Clara can be found in Kansas from 1895, 1900, and 1905 living with her parents and siblings. Her father was born in Missouri and had been a traveling salesman; her mother was born in Indiana. Her younger siblings were all born in Kansas.

By 1910, Clara was living in Temescal Township, Riverside, California, with the Edward Newton family as a "lodger" and had been teaching in a public school for the last two years. Somewhere along the way she met Harry F. Scoville and they began courting. On August 12, 1910, the couple married.

In 1914 they had a daughter, Elinor Marion, who was their only child. Elinor lived with her parents all her life until her death in 1952.

Since Clara's husband was the major breadwinner of the family she did not work outside of the home. Her "job" was to care for her home and family.

According to her obituary in 1976, she was "quiet and unassuming" and had contributed in many ways to the good of the community. She was a longtime member of the Guild of St. Luke's Episcopal Church and a member of the Monrovia Garden Club. She had been ill for several years prior to her death at the age of ninety-one. It is said her funeral was "well attended" and she had many friends within the community.[1551]

---

1549 There is no mention in the article as to the type of sickness Harry had. It is possible it was the Spanish Flu, but that is only speculation on my part due to the year of death.

1550 The Harry Scoville Award for Academic Excellence is still presented to those who show significant public administration through teaching, research, writing, and related activities.

1551 *Monrovia News-Post*, Thursday, October 7, 1976, 1. Newspapers.

Harry Franklin Scoville died in 1963 at Santa Teresita Hospital following surgery. Funeral services were held at St. Luke's Episcopal Church and he is interred in Live Oak Memorial Park, Monrovia, California.

Their daughter Elinor (Eleanor) Marion Scoville was born January 26, 1914, in Los Angeles[1552] and died February 19, 1952, in Los Angeles.[1553] She was thirty-eight years old. As far as I can tell, she never married and was never employed (according to the census records for 1920, 1930, and 1940). However, the voter registration states that she was a "writer."[1554] She did travel to Hawaii in 1938 on the *S.S. Matsonaa.*[1555] What her cause of death was or where she is buried is unknown as I have not been able to locate an obituary for her.

### *44. iv. Gilbert Lafayette Scoville[8] (Franklin,[7] Charles M.,[6] Amasa,[5] Ithamar,[4] Timothy,[3] Stephen,[2] Stephen,[1] Arthur)*

Born 26 July 1882, Ironton, Iron, Missouri;[1556] died 17 January 1940, San Gabriel, Los Angeles, California;[1557] married 29 June 1910, Petaluma, Sonoma, California, Lulu A. McMahon;[1558] born October 1884, Michigan; died 17 January 1980, San Gabriel, Los Angeles; daughter of Joseph McMahon and Harriett ________.

Like his brothers George and Harry, Gilbert attended Stanford University and his course of study was electrical engineering. Gilbert also was a member of the Kappa Sigma fraternity and graduated from Stanford in 1906.[1559]

The 1910 census shows him in Clatsop, Oregon, living as a lodger on Franklin Street and is employed as a telephone electrical engineer.[1560]

In June of that same year, he married Lulu McMahon, and they settled in Petaluma. Lulu is found on the 1900 census living with her parents in Brockway, Saint Clair, Michigan. Her father emigrated from Ireland in 1856 and was employed as a grocery dealer.[1561]

In the intervening years, the couple had three children born to them: Mary M. (1912–1986), Frank (1915–1991), and Josephine (1916–1999).

Gilbert registered for the draft on September 12, 1918, and was employed as the chief engineer for the C. W. Burkett Pacific Telephone and Telegraph Company in San Francisco.

1552 *California, Birth Index, 1905–1995.* Ancestry.

1553 *California, Death Index, 1940–1997.* Ancestry.

1554 *California, Voter Registrations, 1900–1968.* Ancestry.

1555 *Honolulu, Hawaii, Passenger and Crew Lists, 1900–1959.* Ancestry.

1556 *U.S., World War I Draft Registration Cards, 1917–1918;* Ancestry.

1557 *California, Death, Index, 1940–1997;* Ancestry; Obituary notice.

1558 *California, County Birth, Marriage, and Death Records, 1849–1980.* Ancestry.

1559 *U.S., School Yearbooks, 1880–2012.* Ancestry.

1560 1910 census, *Astoria Ward 2, Clatsop, Oregon;* Roll: T624_1278; Sheet: 9B; ED: 0023; FHL microfilm: 1375291. Ancestry. This Gilbert L. Scoville is said to have been born in "1883" in "Missouri" and father born "Connecticut." This fits the profile of Gilbert L. Scoville and his father.

1561 1900 census, *Brockway, Saint Clair, Michigan;* Roll: 741; Sheet: 11B; ED: 0073; FHL: 1240741; Dwelling: 234; Family: 240. Ancestry.

The family was living at 3037 Capp Street in Oakland, California, during that time.[1562] By the time of the 1930 census, the family had once again relocated, this time to South Pasadena, California, where Gilbert continued to work for the Pacific Telephone and Telegraph Company.

Three days after his brother George died, Gilbert Lafayette Scoville died on January 17, 1940. He was fifty-six years old and had worked for the Pacific Telephone and Telegraph Company for thirty years and was about to retire when he had "taken ill about a year ago."[1563] He is buried in Sunnyslope Cemetery, Corona, California.

Gilbert's wife, Lulu, was living in San Gabriel with their son, Frank, and daughter, Josephine, as shown on the 1940 census. Nothing more is known about Lulu until her death, which, ironically, also occurred on January 17, 1980—forty years after Gilbert died. I have been unsuccessful in locating any further information on her including an obituary or where she is buried.

### *45. v. Mabel M. Scoville[8] (Franklin,[7] Charles M.,[6] Amasa,[5] Ithamar,[4] Timothy,[3] Stephen,[2] Stephen,[1] Arthur)*

Born 3 August 1877, perhaps Belleview, Illinois; died 20 September 1944, San Diego, San Diego, California;[1564] married 20 May 1913, Seattle, King, Washington, Earl Levi Thayer;[1565] born 25 October 1855, Luther, Lake, Michigan;[1566] died 24 January 1939, San Diego, San Diego, California;[1567] son of Thomas Thayer and Cora Ferguson.

Very little is known about Mabel and her husband, Earl. From the online records, Earl Levi Thayer was in the Navy and retired from active service on April 1, 1921, at the age of sixty-six (Earl was twenty-two years older than Mabel). Even after his official retirement, Earl Thayer continued to work as a pay clerk for the Navy.[1568] Since Earl Thayer did not complete a draft registration card, it is presumed he was already in the service of the Navy. The earliest record available from the registries is 1918 where he is listed as the acting pay clerk aboard the *USS Oregon*. "The *Oregon* was commissioned, designated solely as an official battleship for the U.S. Navy. On March 19, 1898, the *Oregon* was called to fight in the Spanish–American War."[1569] It is unknown as of this writing whether Earl participated in the Spanish–American War as I have not found any reference of that to date.

---

1562 This residence still exists, but has been made into separate apartments.

1563 Obituary/Funeral notice; *Petaluma Argus-Courier*, Evening edition, Saturday, January 20, 1940; S. Newspapers.

1564 Birth and death data comes from *California, Death Index, 1940–1997*. Ancestry.

1565 *Washington, Marriage Records, 1854–2013*. Ancestry.

1566 *Michigan, Births and Christenings Index, 1867–1911*. Ancestry.

1567 Find A Grave. Military cemetery.

1568 Records of his Naval service come from *U.S., National Cemetery Interment Control Forms, 1928–1962 and U.S., Naval and Marine Corp Registries, 1814–1992*. Ancestry.

1569 See: https://www.oregonencyclopedia.org>u_s_s_oregon.

The couple had two daughters, Elise S. Thayer (1915–1997), who was married to Lotan Latham Hamilton, and Virginia (1922–2008). She was married to Homer Hayden Brown.[1570]

A very brief obituary was published in the *News Pilot* on Friday, August 11, 1938, under the subtitle **Naval Orders:** "Acting Pay Clerk Earl Levi Thayer, retired, inactive died June 24, 1939 at Shrine Camp, Laguna, California." The full name of the camp was *Al Bahr Mount Laguna Shrine Camp*. The camp was a lodge built by the Shriners in 1925 and members were able to use it to celebrate birthdays, anniversaries, and the like.[1571]

Earl was buried in the Fort Rosecrans National Cemetery, San Diego, California.

Mable Thayer died three years later. Her obituary was posted in the *Monrovia News-Post* on the front-page on Friday, September 22, 1944:

> Mrs. Earl Thayer, sister of Harry F. Scoville of 123 Highland Place, passed away at her home in San Diego very suddenly Wednesday evening of a heart attack. She was the former Mabel Scoville. Mr. Scoville and Mrs. George Scoville are now in San Diego where funeral services will be held tomorrow. Mrs. Thayer will be laid to rest beside her husband who passed away three years ago.

### *46. vi. Ethel May Scoville[8] (Franklin,[7] Charles M.,[6] Amasa,[5] Ithamar,[4] Timothy,[3] Stephen,[2] Stephen,[1] Arthur)*

Born 15 December 1890, perhaps Belleview, Illinois; died 17 March 1941, Riverside, Riverside, California;[1572] married 5 January 1913, Frederick Wilhelm Kuster in California;[1573] born 14 May 1884, Williamsburg, Franklin, Kansas;[1574] died 14 June 1949, Orange, Orange, California;[1575] son of Jacob Kuster and A. B. _______.[1576]

When Frederick (aka "Fritz") Kuster arrived in California is unknown. The earliest I've been able to locate him there is in 1913 in Riverside via the city directories.

Fritz was born in Williamsburg, Franklin, Kansas, to Jacob—a German immigrant—and his wife, A. B. (nothing more is known about Jacob's wife other than that her name could have been Anna or Augusta; Jacob may have been married twice).

Fritz's father appears to have first settled in Wisconsin and then removed to Kansas and, according to the records, Jacob was a druggist/dentist (depending upon which census you read).[1577] One of the difficulties is discerning which Jacob Kuster is the correct one as

---

1570 You can find her details at Find A Grave under "Virginia Thayer Brown."

1571 The lodge and its surrounding cabins were destroyed by the Chariot Fire in 2013; *The San Diego Union-Tribune*, July 9, 2013. Internet version of the article.

1572 Birth and death information comes from *California, Death Index, 1940–1997*. Ancestry.

1573 *California, County Birth, Marriage, and Death Records*. Ancestry.

1574 *U.S., World War II Draft Registration Cards, 1942*. Ancestry.

1575 *California, Death Index, 1940–1997*. Ancestry.

1576 *Kansas State Census Collection, 1855–1925*. Ancestry

1577 The occupational information varies depending upon which census is read. For instance, the 1885 Kansas State census states that he came from Wisconsin. 1885 *Kansas Territory Census;* Roll:

there are a number of men named "Jacob Kuster" in and around the same general area. An advertisement appeared in the *Williamsburg Star* on December 1, 1893.

OLD RELIABLE DRUG STORE.

Medicines, Drugs, School Books,

Stationery, cigars and tobacco. Physicians' prescriptions and family receipts carefully compounded. None but the best and purest drugs used.

DR. J. KUSTER.

When Fritz's father died in 1899 in Williamsburg, he left a substantial estate for his wife and children. Fritz received 498 shares from the Golden Eagle Mining Capital Stock Company, as well as a life insurance policy from Kansas Mutual Life Association.[1578]

I believe after Fritz received his inheritance, he made plans to start his life. I have not been able to locate him in the 1900 or 1910 censuses; however, he does show up in the city directory for 1913 in Corona, California, and is listed as a "rancher," and in subsequent directory listings his occupation is a citrus grower. My belief is this is how Fritz met Ethel Scoville, his future wife. As I recounted prior on the life of Frank Scoville (Ethel's father), he was a well known citrus grower throughout this area. Fritz and Frank Scoville may have had business dealings with one another. In fact, by 1927, Fritz Kuster had teamed up with a G. W. Waterbury and they are both listed together as "citrus growers" in the city directory.[1579]

In 1920[1580] the family was living on El Cerrito Romcho (Rancho?), which is listed as a farm. He did not own the property. The family consisted of Fritz and Ethel and their children Victor S., Frederick W., Jr., and Katherine E. Kuster.

In June of that same year, Fritz applied for a passport[1581] to Mexico for the purpose of buying guano[1582] for importation. His departure was intended for July of 1920 and he intended to remain there for four months doing business in Chihuahua, Durango, Sinaloa, and Sonora. The description of the applicant is that he was "thirty-five years old, 5′ 7″ with a high forehead, blue eyes, long nose, straight mouth, a square, full chin, light brown hair, dark complexion and a square face." A photo does accompany the passport, but it is not very clear. Fritz's partner, Guy W. Waterbury, confirmed his identification.

The passport also contains a notarized letter from his mother, A. B. Kuster, confirming where and when her son was born.

A few articles appeared in the local paper regarding Fritz and his partner, G. W. Waterbury.

**Some Fine Fruit**

Fritz Kuster has brought to the office of the Corona Chamber of Commerce an excellent display of J.H. Hale peaches raised on three-year old tree of the Kuster &

---

KS1885_50; Line: 1. Ancestry.

1578 *Kansas, U.S., Wills and Probate Records, 1803–1987; Vol. A-C, 1863–1906.* Ancestry.

1579 Directory listings are from *U.S., City Directories, 1822–1995.* Ancestry.

1580 1920 census, *Corona, Riverside, California;* Roll:T625_125; Page:11B; ED: 137. Ancestry.

1581 *U.S., Passport Applications, 1795–1925.* Ancestry.

1582 Waste product from bats used for fertilizer.

> Waterbury tract east of Corona. The fruit is large and of good color and a delicious taste . . . [1583]

By 1930 the family had moved to 4020 South Main Street into a home that was now owned by Fritz and Ethel. The value of the home was $10,000. The family grew by one more child—Kenneth—and they now had a maid by the name of Aileen Rollins.

The homestead no longer remains. What was once a citrus farm is a wasteland with wire fences and some type of electrical or cell tower.[1584]

The intervening years between 1930–1940 remain a blank spot as I have not found any other records for that timeframe. The 1940 census shows that the family was now living at 1852 South Main Street in Corona. The family was made up of Fritz, Ethel, Kenneth, Frederick, Jr., and a servant, Lillie Haynes.

On March 17, 1941, Ethel Scoville Kuster died from a heart attack. Her obituary was published the following day in the *Riverside Daily Press*.[1585] Other than naming the various relatives, there isn't any personal information on Ethel.

When Fritz arrived at the local draft board to register for the World War II draft, he gave G. W. Waterbury as the person who would always know where he was.[1586] However, sometime after this he must have remarried as his obituary names his wife Mrs. Lula A. Kuster. While I do not have proof of a marriage record, the *California Voter Registrations, 1900–1968,* provides the addresses of each registered voter:

> 1942—Frederick W. Kuster, 1862 South Main, Corona
> Lula Ann Kuster, housewife, 1862 South Main, Corona

The voter registration records are the same for 1944 and 1946.

While I have not located a marriage record between Frederick W. Kuster and Lula Ann _____, I believe *this* Lula Ann to be the widow of Gilbert L. Scoville, Lula A. McMahon, who married Gilbert L. Scoville (and Frederick Kuster) and died January 17, 1980, in San Gabriel, California.

Fritz W. Kuster died on June 15, 1949, at the age of sixty-four. His obituary was published in the *Monrovia News-Post,* on page one of the Tuesday, June 21, 1949, edition of the newspaper.[1587]

Fritz is buried in Olivewood Cemetery in Riverside, California.

## Monrovians' Relative Dies

Masonic funeral services will be conducted in Corona tomorrow for Frederick W. Kuster of Laguna Beach, brother-in-law of Mr. and Mrs. Harry F. Scoville and Mrs. George Scoville. Mr. Kuster succumbed of a heart attack.

Surviving are his widow, Mrs. Lula Kuster; two sons, Frederick W. Kuster Jr. and Capt. Kenneth Kuster who is arriving by plane tonight from Germany, and a daughter, Mrs. Ray Chambers of Laguna Beach. Mr. and Mrs. Kuster's eldest son, Victor, was killed in an airplane accident two years ago.

A former resident of Corona, Mr. Kuster was a past president of the Rotary Club of that city, past master of the Masonic Lodge and a Knight Templar. He had frequently attended the Monrovia Masonic Beefsteak Feeds and other Masonic events here with his brother-in-law, Harry F. Scoville.

1583 *Riverside Daily Press,* Tuesday, August 21, 1923, edition; 6; GenealogyBank.

1584 Google street view, 2018. Google.com.

1585 Tuesday, March 18, 1941, edition; 15. Newspaper.

1586 *U.S. World War II Draft Registration Cards, 1942.* Ancestry.

1587 Newspapers.com. This newspaper is no longer in publication.

## 47. *AGNES[2] MARY BILLIAN[8] (AGNES,[7] CHARLES MARTIN,[6] FRANKLIN,[5] ITHAMAR,[4] TIMOTHY,[3] STEPHEN,[2] STEPHEN,[1] ARTHUR)*

Born 2 August 1876, New Britain, Hartford, Connecticut;[1588] died 12 October 1960, New Britain, Hartford, Connecticut;[1589] married (1) 15 June 1898, New Britain, Hartford, Connecticut, George Clarence Ferdinand Kumm;[1590] born April 1876, Wallingford, New Haven, Connecticut;[1591] died 9 October 1917, New Britain, Connecticut;[1592] (2) 5 April 1919, New Britain, Hartford, Connecticut, Charles C. Cafferty;[1593] born circa 1870, Connecticut;[1594] (3) 24 January 1925, New Britain, Hartford, Connecticut,[1595] Bert Sanborn.[1596]

Agnes Mary (sometimes noted in the records as "Agnes M. J.") was the first-born child and was born a little over a year after the marriage of her parents (a brother followed the next year).

I presume in her childhood she attended school. Since she was only three years old in 1880 (according to the census) and the census of 1890 is non-existent for Connecticut, it is only speculation that Agnes *did* attend school.

What I know of Agnes' personality is purely anecdotal—impressions and opinions coming from various members of the Billian and Kumm families. Since I did not know Agnes personally (I was seven when she died, and our families were not close), I can only relay these impressions here as best and gently as I can.

Agnes was said to be very loquacious. I can tell you that *my* side of the Billian family were not conversationalists and someone who talked too much was an anathema. An example of this is that certain family members would cross the street when they saw her coming[1597] as they didn't want to be caught up in long, drawn-out conversations. The opinion of one family member would then be the opinion of others in that nuclear family without ever getting to know her.

Agnes' first marriage was to George Clarence Ferdinand Kumm in 1898. His parents had emigrated from "Germany," arriving in New York, New York, on July 23, 1850.[1598] (I believe

---

1588 *U.S., Social Security Applications and Claims Index, 1936–2007.* Ancestry.

1589 *Connecticut Death Index, 1949–2012.* Ancestry.

1590 Newspaper marriage notice, *Meriden Daily Republican,* Wednesday, June 15, 1898. No page given. Newspapers.

1591 1900 census. The Kumm family lived in Wallingford, New Haven, Connecticut, prior to removing to New Britain.

1592 *Connecticut Death Records, 1897–1968,* CSL.

1593 *Connecticut Marriage Records, 1897–1968, CSL.*

1594 Approximate year of birth based on the 1920 census.

1595 *Connecticut Marriage Records, 1897–1968,* CSL.

1596 *Possibly* the Bert Elmer Sanborn who was born 22 February 1882, New Hampshire; died 7 March 1943, Hartford, Connecticut. His wife, Ethel May Dow, died in New Britain on 24 April 1920 (Find A Grave).

1597 This would occur on the main throughfare in downtown New Britain.

1598 They likely came through Castle Garden as Ellis Island didn't officially open as an immigration station until 1892. The Kumms came from an area where the boundaries changed.

the family resided in Wallingford, Connecticut, prior to their moving to New Britain.)

Depending upon what record is reviewed, the first child of Agnes and George Kumm was born on July 4, 1898, or 1899. If born on the former date, Agnes would have been in her eighth month of pregnancy at the time of their marriage. If this was the case, then the couple would marry as soon as they learned of the pregnancy to alleviate any gossip. However, a newspaper article from the *New Britain Herald* confirms Clarence's birth year as 1899:

> **25 Years Ago Today**
> A son made his first Fourth of July appearance at the home of Mr. and Mrs. George C. Kumm of Kensington Avenue yesterday.[1599]

In 1900 Agnes and George C. Kumm were living at 417 Church Street, New Britain. This was a three-family home. Agnes' mother, father, and her youngest brother, Ernest, lived there, as well as Agnes' grandmother, Katie (Schneider Scoville) Gammerdinger.

George C. Kumm is employed at that time as a "plane grinder." He then changed his occupation to a house painter sometime after 1900.

While I know very little about Agnes, I know less about her husband, George. No one I spoke with could provide any first-hand information since George had died long before they were born.

George C. completed the military census form on February 27, 1917. He (and his family) were living at 68 Prospect Street (New Britain). He was a painter and had been previously employed as a machine setter. He was forty years old, 5′ 11″ tall, and 176 pounds. He also states that he has two dependents to support and was in the National Guard in New Britain for four years.

George C. Kumm died eight months later at the age of forty-one. The second son, Harold Clarence Kumm (who had been born approximately eighteen years after his brother, Clarence George Kumm), was a few days shy of his first birthday at the time of his father's death.

While I could not locate an obituary, a funeral notice appeared on page twelve of the *New Britain Herald:*

> The funeral of George C. Kumm will be held at 8:30 o'clock tomorrow afternoon in the Erwin Mortuary Chapel in Fairview Cemetery. All Veterans of Company E. C. N. G. are invited to attend the services. Burial will be in Fairview Cemetery.[1600]

On April 5, 1919, Agnes Billian Kumm married again to Charles C. Cafferty in New Britain. The couple are listed on the 1920 census[1601] as living at 313 Church Street:

---

Some records state they are from Germany; others state Poland or Prussia. *New York, Passenger and Crew Lists* (including Castle Garden and Ellis Island). NARA via Ancestry.

1599 Saturday, July 5, 1924. edition; 7. GenealogyBank.

1600 Thursday, October 11, 1917, edition. The funeral notice is confusing—8:30 o'clock in the afternoon?

1601 1920 census, *New Britain Ward 4, Hartford, Connecticut;* Roll:T625_185; Page:16B; ED:161. Ancestry.

Charles C. Cawferty [sic], 50, b. Connecticut, laborer, ball-bearing company
Agnes Cawferty, 43, wife, b. Connecticut
Harold Cawferty, son, 3, b. Connecticut

It is unknown who gave this information (using the last name "Cafferty" for Harold), but I suspect it was Agnes. You can draw your own conclusions why she did this.

This marriage did not last long. Charles C. Cafferty put a notice in the Monday, November 7, 1921, edition of the *New Britain Herald:*[1602]

Notice—

I hereby give notice that my wife, Agnes Cafferty, having left my bed and board is no longer entitled to credit in my name and I will no longer hold myself responsible for debts of her contracting.

Charles C. Cafferty

There are so many scenarios that could be drawn from the inferences in Charles Cafferty's notice. Whatever the "real" story is, I have no knowledge of what had occurred within their marriage.

Because the name "Charles Cafferty" is quite common, finding the correct man who had been married to Agnes has been difficult. I believe it is beneficial to follow each person's trail to see where it leads, and the only Charles Cafferty I could find who *may* be the man who had been married to Agnes comes from an obituary notice in the *New Britain Herald,*[1603] which appeared in the Monday, November 10, 1924, edition of the newspaper. The obituary mentions that one Charles Cafferty died "aged about 55 years." He lived on Bank Street and was one of "Plainville's best-known residents and lived all his life here . . . survived by five sisters and two brothers."

While I can't confirm that this is the same Charles Cafferty married to Agnes, the date of his death and Agnes' next marriage is curious, for on December 22, 1924, Agnes Billian Kumm Cafferty files for a marriage license with Bert Sanborn "of Middletown." The marriage notice indicates that this is her third marriage.[1604] The actual marriage took place in New Britain on 24 January 1925.[1605]

Again, information on Bert Sanborn has been hard to come by for the fact that his name could have been simply "Bert/Burt," "Albert," or "Herbert/Hubert." Trying all those combinations did not bring any results that could be confirmed as the one who was married to Agnes. There was a man named Bert Elmer Sanborn, born February 22, 1882, in New Hampshire and who died March 7, 1943, in Hartford, Connecticut. He had married Ethel May Dowd in New Hampshire. She died April 24, 1920, in New Britain.[1606] A "Bert Sanborn" married Agnes in 1925 in New Britain, so it is a possibility that this is one and the same man.

1602 Page 13; GenealogyBank.

1603 The obituary has been paraphrased; page 8. GenealogyBank.

1604 *New Britain Herald,* Monday, December 22, 1924; 16; GenealogyBank.

1605 *Connecticut Marriage Records, 1897–1968;* CSL.

1606 Information comes from Find A Grave.

The *U.S., City Directories, 1822–1995* shows a Bert Sanborn in New Britain in 1919, 1922, 1923, and then he removed to Wallingford, Connecticut, according to the 1924 city directory for New Britain.

Agnes' third marriage to Bert Sanborn did not last either as by 1930[1607] she is back to using her first married name of "Kumm" and Bert is not in the household. Agnes lists herself as "widowed" on this census and her son Harold, age 13, is living with her along with a boarder, Charles Goliner,[1608] age 51.

I have not been successful in confirming or denying that Bert Sanborn was married to Agnes either, and whether she was in fact a widow or she was divorced.

Agnes' son Clarence George Kumm became a New Britain police officer and had been out of the household for quite some time; however, her son Harold Clarence Kumm, who was born when Agnes was forty, remained with her until his death in 1937. This is where the other anecdotal information does not put Agnes in a good light. As it was told to me, Agnes was not a good mother, especially to Harold. The person claimed that Harold died from malnutrition, but that is not correct according to his death certificate.

Harold was born with congenital heart disease, Banti's disease (a disease of the spleen), as well as cardiac decompensation (cannot maintain an efficient circulation). It is possible that because he had these diseases, he was not healthy looking, so others thought that he was not being fed. In 1937, the medical field treating these specific diseases was woefully inadequate as the proper treatments were not known at that time.

Agnes lived until October 12, 1960. She had been placed in a convalescent home and died from a "long illness." The following obituary comes from *The Hartford Courant:*[1609]

> **Mrs. A. B. Kumm Dies at Age 84**
> New Britain (Special)
>
> Mrs. Agnes Billion [sic] Kumm, formerly of 561 Main St., died Wednesday afternoon at a local convalescent home after a long illness.
>
> A native and lifelong resident, Mrs. Kumm was the daughter of Fred and Agnes Schofield [sic] Kumm[1610] and the widow of George Kumm.
>
> She leaves two brothers, Fred and Ernest Billion, both of this city: six grandchildren including Police Sgt. Wesley Kumm, and nine great-grandchildren.
>
> Funeral services will be held at 9:30 a.m. Friday at the Ericson-Hansen Funeral Home. The Rev. Edward C. Dahl, pastor of the First Church of Christ Congregational, will officiate and burial will be in Fairview Cemetery. There will be no calling hours.

---

1607 1930 census; *New Britain, Hartford, Connecticut;* Page: 9B; ED: 0160; FHL: 2340001. Ancestry.

1608 I am not certain the name is Goliner—it could be Grenier.

1609 Thursday, October 13, 1960, edition, under "New Britain News;" 30. Newspapers.

1610 This should have read Fred and Agnes Scoville Billian. The number of errors in this obituary is not surprising to me as Agnes' brothers did not have much to do with her, especially my grandfather, Ernest Billian.

***Children of George Clarence Kumm and Agnes Mary J. Scoville***

i. Clarence George Kumm,[9] b. 4 July 1899, New Britain, Hartford, Connecticut;[1611] d. 19 February 1944, New Britain, Hartford, Connecticut;[1612] m. Agnes Amelia/Emelia Hart (Hjert), b. 19 March 1896, Connecticut;[1613] d. 26 March 1983, Windsor, Hartford, Connecticut. They had the following children: Wesley Kumm, Sr. (1920–2003), Roy Kumm (1921–1983), Russell Kumm (1925–2010), George Kumm (1928–2016), Earl Kumm 1931–), and Shirley Kumm (1932–1983).

ii. Harold Clarence Kumm,[9] b. 5 October 1916, New Britain, Hartford, Connecticut; d. 21 November 1937, New Britain, Hartford, Connecticut.[1614] He was "21 yrs., 1 m. and 16 days old." The death certificate notes that he was learning at the Monroe Vocational School. His burial place is unknown, perhaps in an unmarked grave in Fairview Cemetery, New Britain.

Harold Clarence Kumm and his mother, Agnes Billian Kumm

The photo of Agnes and her son Harold shows a mother who loves her son. At least, that is how I see it. Agnes may have caused many of her own problems after the death of her first husband. A woman on her own was not a favorable position to be in. There were plenty of women who did make it on their own; I just don't believe Agnes was capable of doing so.

She had been rejected by her youngest brother because "she talked too much" and she had married three times; because of that, no one on my side of the family ever got to know her.[1615]

## *48. FRED JOE BILLIAN[8, 1616] (AGNES,[7] CHARLES MARTIN,[6] FRANKLIN,[5] ITHAMAR,[4] TIMOTHY,[3] STEPHEN,[2] STEPHEN,[1] ARTHUR)*

1611 Two different birth years. Newspaper article as previously mentioned and the WWI Draft Registration Records.

1612 *Connecticut Death Index, 1949–2012*. Ancestry.

1613 Ancestry.

1614 The birth and death information comes from the death certificate in my possession. Informant: Agnes Kumm, mother.

1615 Photo is from the author's personal collection. Harold appears to be around six or seven years old. Note that he is wearing short pants. This was the norm during the 1920s, and possibly when this photo was taken.

1616 The records alternate between the name usage of Fred Joe or Frederick Billian. I do not have a birth certificate that would verify his birth name.

Born 31 December 1877, New Britain, Hartford, Connecticut;[1617] died 11 September 1963, New Britain, Hartford, Connecticut; married (1) 27 October 1897, Berlin, Hartford, Connecticut, Ada Louise Church,[1618] born August 1879, Connecticut; died_______; daughter of Elijah Church and Sarah Baker;[1619] married (2) circa 1934/35, Agnes Case, New Britain, Hartford, Connecticut;[1620] born 13 May 1889, Connecticut; died 11 March 1980, Berlin, Hartford, Connecticut;[1621] daughter of Charles M. Case and Leonie J. Thorpe.

Other than the available online records, I have no personal knowledge of my great-grand-uncle Fred. This is the only photo of I have of him:[1622]

Fred was born a year after his sister Agnes. Nothing more is known until 1897 when he married a woman by the name of Ada Louise Church. This was not a marriage of "domestic bliss," at least according to Ada.

Fred worked as a box maker per the 1900 census and the couple were living in Berlin, Connecticut.

The following year on August 2, 1901,[1623] a son was born to the couple by the name of Raymond Church Billian.

By 1910[1624] Fred had improved the family's earnings as he was now a foreman in an automobile shop and owned their home outright, which, according to the census, was a farm. At this point and time, the couple had been married for twelve years and the marriage would not last much longer.

According to Ada Billian in her deposition to gain a divorce, Fred deserted the family on November 26, 1912. She had told the judge that her life was "more or less unhappy from the start," and after the marriage she discovered that her husband could neither read nor write and she taught him how to do both.[1625] This information (whether he could read or write) would be contrary to the later census reports (stating he completed grade 8) and his obituary, where his

1617 Birth and death information comes from *U.S., Social Security Death Index, 1935–2014*. Ancestry.

1618 *Connecticut Marriage Records, 1897–1968*. CSL.

1619 Father's name comes from his obituary where Ada Billian is mentioned.

1620 Date of marriage based on Agnes' name on Fred's WWI draft registration in 1918.

1621 Find A Grave and Agnes' obituary.

1622 Photo from author's personal collection. The photo has been cropped and enlarged from the original family photo.

1623 *U.S., World War II Draft Cards, Young Men, 1940–1947.* Ancestry.

1624 1910 census; *Berlin, Hartford, Connecticut;* Roll: T624_130; Sheet: 3A; ED: 0129; FHL: 1374143. Ancestry.

1625 The divorce notice was published in the *Hartford Courant,* Saturday, May 13, 1916; 3. Newspapers.

second wife recounted that her husband attended the local public school. We will never know what the real story was. Divorce were not easy to come by. A spouse usually had to "spill some dirt" on the other spouse (whether true or not) to hope to get what they wanted.

Ada also stated that "since the date of the desertion, the man had not spoken, written or had any communication with her in any way. He had not done anything for her." Fred, however, did contribute "about $100 to the support of his son." While this does not sound like much, one hundred dollars during that time would amount to $2,743.10 in 2021 (based on the average inflation rate). While Fred may not have communicated with his wife, he did support his son.

Ada Billian was granted her divorce and gained custody of their son, Raymond. It wasn't long before Ada remarried. The divorce notice was printed in May 1916 and Ada married Edward Jenks in Berlin on June 17, 1916.[1626]

Edward Laurence Jenks was born February 16, 1876, in Worthington, Massachusetts, to Scott Jenks and Sylvia C. Lincoln.[1627] At the time of his World War I draft registration in 1918, he was a factory guard at Stanley Works in New Britain. The couple lived in Wallingford and Meriden, Connecticut.

The marriage between Edward Jenks and Ada Church Billian Jenks also ended in divorce sometime after 1925 as this is the last time I find them listed together in the city directory for Wallingford, Connecticut.[1628]

On the 1930 and 1940 census, as well as the *Connecticut Death Index, 1949–2012,* Edward's marital status is given as "divorced." Edward died on January 27, 1954, in Meriden, Connecticut. I used all available online sources to locate an obituary, but one could not be located. In addition, information as to where he is buried remains a mystery. It is also a mystery as to what became of Ada L. Church Billian Jenks. It is possible she remarried, moved out of state, and died elsewhere.

Fred Billian remained single throughout the 1920s until the mid 1930s when his second wife, Agnes, appears with him in New Britain in 1936 living on Hart Street. To verify that *this* Agnes was not Fred's mother (also named Agnes), I found Mother Agnes living on Arch Street and listed as "widow of Frederick."[1629]

Agnes Case lived with her parents at 9 Franklin Square (New Britain) until her marriage to Fred. According to the 1930 census, Agnes was a machine operator in a factory. Fred had been living with his mother at 559 Arch Street (New Britain) prior to his second marriage and was employed as a machinist.[1630]

The couple continued to live in New Britain and had owned their own home at 22 Whiting Street. Their house is no longer there, swallowed up by commercialism.

According to Fred's obituary, he retired in 1950 when he was seventy-three years old.

What kind of relationship Fred had with his son, Raymond, is difficult to know since the Billian family was not a close-knit one. Raymond used the surname "Jenks" throughout his

---

1626 *Connecticut Marriage Records, 1897–1968*. CSL.

1627 *U.S., Social Security Application and Claims Index, 1936–2007.* Ancestry.

1628 *U.S., City Directories, 1822–1995*. Ancestry.

1629 Her husband's name should have read "Ferdinand" not "Frederick."

1630 They may have met while working in the same factory.

life, although there are records showing his biological surname as "Billian."

On September 11, 1963, Frederick J. Billian died at the New Britain Memorial Hospital at the age of eighty-five.

> Fred J. Billian, 85, of 272 Rocky Hill Avenue, died Wednesday at New Britain Memorial Hospital. Born here, he attended local schools and was a former Kensington resident. He operated a garage business at one time and was later employed as assistant foreman at Corbin Screw Company, retiring in 1950.
>
> He was a member of First Congregational Church and the American Hardware Corporation Foreman's Club. He leaves his wife, Mrs. Agnes Case Billian; a son, Ray C. Jenks; a brother, Ernest Billian of Middletown and several grandchildren and great-grandchildren.
>
> Funeral services will be held Saturday at 1 p.m. First Congregational Church. Burial will be in Maple Cemetery, Berlin. Calling hours at Carlson Funeral Home will be Friday from 2–4 and 7–9 p.m.[1631]

Agnes L. Billian continued to live on Whiting Street—at least up until 1961, as that is the last online city directory available. Agnes died at the age of eighty-two on March 11, 1980, in New Britain. She is buried with her husband and there is no obituary for her.

Because of their ages at the time of marriage, Fred and Agnes never had any children.

***Children of Frederick J. Billian and Ada L. Church***

*a.i.* Raymond Church Billian,[9] b. 2 Aug 1901, New Britain, Hartford, Connecticut; d. 22 Aug 1983, Madison, New Haven, Connecticut; m. (1) 7 July 1919, Berlin, Hartford, Connecticut, Mildred Gouse;[1632] d. 31 March 1968;[1633] m. (2) 27 Sep 1974, Madison, New Haven, Connecticut, Anna Riva McVeigh;[1634] b. 18 Nov 1916, Connecticut; d. 8 Sep 1998, Hartford, Hartford, Connecticut.[1635]

At the age of thirteen, Raymond was involved in a serious accident. The newspaper headlines read:[1636]

> **Raymond Billian Sustains Serious Injuries in Accident**
>
> Raymond Billian, a thirteen-years-old schoolboy, lies at the home of his parents, Mr. and Mrs. Fred Billian of Kensington, with a compound fracture of his right leg which he received in a peculiar accident on an automobile truck Monday afternoon. Although his condition is very serious, Dr. Clifton Cooley of New Britain, who is

1631 *The Hartford Courant,* September 12, 1963, edition; 30D; Pro-Quest through Connecticut State Library.

1632 *Connecticut Marriage Records, 1897–1968.* CSL.

1633 Death date comes from the grave maker. Find A Grave.

1634 *Connecticut Marriage Records, 1897–1968.* Ancestry.

1635 *Connecticut Death Index, 1949–2012.* Ancestry.

1636 *New Britain Herald,* Friday, January 1, 1915; 10. GenealogyBank.

> attending him, states that his chances of recovery are bright and that there was a marked improvement in his condition today.

Apparently, Raymond and some other boys from the neighborhood spent the afternoon coasting on Hooker's Hill, near his home. The boys spied a "heavy automobile truck" belonging to Eaton Brothers Feed Company (of Plainville) going up the hill. The young boys thought it would be a good opportunity to get carried up the hill by the truck. They "leaped upon the tailboard of the vehicle" and when Raymond attempted to get on board, there was no room for him, so he jumped onto the hub of one of the rear wheels. Raymond's right foot slipped and was "shot in between the spokes." The cries of the children brought the truck to a stop, "probably saving the youngster's life."

Raymond was carried to his home where a doctor was summoned. Raymond had broken his leg in two places and the "lad bore up under the terrible pain with great courage . . ."

> . . . Raymond is a pupil in the sixth grade of the Rockwell school in New Britain and is an unusually bright boy. His many playmates were thrown into gloom by the unfortunate accident.

Other than the data provided here, I know very little about Raymond. In the many conversations I've had with my grandparents and my father over the years about the "old days," his name never came up in those discussions. This should not surprise me seeing that my grandfather and his siblings were not on the best of terms. I also don't know what kind of relationship Raymond had with his own father. He *did* continue to use his birthname of Billian, as in most records he is listed as "Billian Jenks." So perhaps he had some connection to his birth father.

Over the years the city directories have Raymond employed as a cabinet maker, an interior decorator, and, later in life, he was in the upholstery business (Ray C. B. Jenks Upholstery Shop, in New London, Connecticut). He and his first wife, Mildred, had three children: Richard, Beryl, and Ethel. At Raymond's death in 1983, only his daughter Ethel survived him.

When his wife Mildred died in 1968, Raymond remarried in 1974 to Anna Riva McVeigh.

Raymond and Mildred are buried together in Cedar Grove Cemetery, New London, Connecticut. Anna is buried in St. Mary's Cemetery in East Hartford.

### *49.* **ERNEST CLARENCE BILLIAN**[8] *(AGNES,[7] CHARLES MARTIN,[6] FRANKLIN,[5] ITHAMAR,[4] TIMOTHY,[3] STEPHEN,[2] STEPHEN,[1] ARTHUR)*

Born 22 May 1897, New Britain, Hartford, Connecticut;[1637] died 24 October 1980, Middletown, Middlesex, Connecticut; married 16 April 1917, Caroline Linnea Halldin;[1638] born 2 July 1897, New Britain, Hartford, Connecticut; died 23 January 1982, Middletown, Middlesex, Connecticut; daughter of Anders Johan (Andrew John) Halden and Karolina Charlotta

1637 All records of birth, marriage ,and death are from my personal recollections and copies of their death certificates.

1638 The name has variant spellings in the records: Halden and Haldin.

Carlsdotter (Rahm).[1639]

There are three things that I remember about my paternal grandfather: he told corny jokes, he had a tattoo of Jesus on his bicep (which one I do not recall), and he smoked unfiltered Camel cigarettes, which he would tap on any surface to pack the tobacco tighter. I was told that he would also wake in the middle of the night to "light-up."

Ernest Billian

My grandparents lived on Crown Street in the late 1960s and I remember going over there with my parents to visit. I was about thirteen/fourteen years old and, even then, I was interested in family history. I believe it was my father who asked his father (my grandfather) where we were from in Germany. As was typical, my grandfather responded, "My father was from Hamburger and my mother from Frankfurter." Ha-ha, as my grandfather tapped another cigarette on his silver lighter. We never did learn that day where the Billian family was from (and he likely didn't know either).

Outside of the usual historical records, anything written here is based on my observations and what was told to me by my father and other relatives who knew him more intimately than I did. But again, keep in mind these are *their* individual opinions.

My grandfather was born on Kensington Avenue, New Britain, Connecticut, twenty years after his brother, Fred Joe. Ernest's sister and brother were married and living their own lives elsewhere. Ernie was the only child at home and was treated more like a grandchild (at least by Ernest's father, Ferdinand).[1640]

The photo of Ernest in the carriage shows quite an elaborate outfit for one so young (the mortarboard cap is likely a prop from the photographer's studio, as is the carriage) and Ernest was well turned out for his time at the photographer.

My grandfather's early life is unknown to me, and I doubt that he spoke much about it to his children, as there were no recollections from them regarding those years.

Without the photo on the next page, it is doubtful we would know that my grandfather had attended St. Mark's Episcopal Church in New Britain.

Ernest Billian

1639 Karolina's patronym was *Carlsdotter,* however, in this country, the name Rahm or Carlson was used by her and her siblings.

1640 Photos of Ernest Billian in the personal collection of the author.

I don't know if this photo is for his confirmation or whether he was an altar server.

On April 16, 1917, Ernest C. Billian married Caroline L. Halldin. They had known each other for "three weeks" according to the stories that were recounted. However, I don't know what the circumstances were for such a quick marriage. In the parlance of the time, my grandfather would have been considered "tall, dark, and handsome," something that may have attracted my grandmother, Caroline. They barely knew one another, yet they set up housekeeping. Were they escaping from the lives that they had prior to marriage?

My grandmother's life was one of prosperity, then destitution. Her parents were recent immigrants from Sweden. They arrived in the United States in May 1892 and settled in New Britain, Connecticut, as her brothers and sisters had emigrated some years before her. My great-grandfather was a master tailor, having learned the trade in Halden, Norway. When he arrived in New Britain, he established himself as the tailor for all the executives who lived and worked in New Britain. The story goes that he and his wife were in the process of building a house. The housebuilder was a "drinker," and he enticed my great-grandfather into the builder's favorite pastime—drinking liquor. From that point on, the house was never built, and my great-grandfather would disappear for weeks at a time. No money was coming in and the family became destitute. My great-grandfather, Johan Anders Svensson Halden (John Andrew Halldin), committed suicide in 1910—my grandmother was only seven years old.

From that point on the family was in rough shape economically and mentally. My grandmother may have thought that this marriage would be a way out. That is not to say she didn't love my grandfather. The quick marriage fmay have been for her to get out of a depressing situation. My grandfather may also have wanted to get out of his household, as he and his mother did not get on very well.[1641]

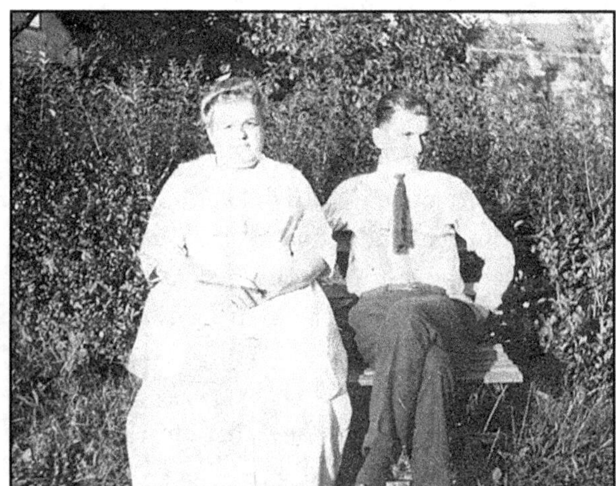

Agnes Scoville Billian and her son Ernest C. Billian

Nine months after my grandparents married, their first son was born, whom they named Howard. At the time of his

1641 Photos in author's collection. This is the only other photo that I have of Agnes Scoville Billian. The photo was probably taken in 1917–1919, or perhaps in the early 1920s. My grandmother may have been between 16–20 in this photo.

Caroline, Ernest, and Howard Billian

Caroline Halldin

birth, they were living at 156 Maple Street in New Britain, and like so many of the older homes in New Britain it was a multi-family dwelling that still stands today.

Sometime after Howard's birth, my grandfather had the idea of buying a farm. The farm that they purchased lay in the Westfield section of Middletown, Connecticut, known as West Road Highland Station.[1642]

Ernest Billian on his farm Westfield, Connecticut

If you recall in the narrative for Agnes Scoville Billian (Ernest's mother), their life as farmers did not last too long as they couldn't make a go of it (which is a theme that followed my grandfather throughout his life). Ernest had been a farmer, a conductor, a carpenter, a sub-contractor, a chauffeur, and raised chickens. His last scheme was owing a pet shop in Meriden, Connecticut, in the 1960s—that too, did not last. I don't believe that my grandfather had the personality or the type of business sense to make a success of any entrepreneurial venture.

My grandparents moved frequently. By the time of my grandfather's death in 1980 he had lived in twenty-six different places between New Britain, Middletown, Westfield, Durham, Kensington, Newington, and Portland, Connecticut.

Times were tough during the Depression, and at times they lived in "cold water flats," which were just as it sounds—there was no running hot water. You had to share a

1642 Photos from the author's collection.

hallway bathroom with your neighbors. Can you imagine having seven children in these circumstances? That is how my grandparents lived, like many other families during that time.

My dad recounted eating onion sandwiches, wearing shoes that didn't fit or had holes in them and where they would use cardboard to insert in the shoe, picking coal to heat the house, and picking scrap metal around the train tracks to sell. Finding work during this time was equally as difficult. Ernest found whatever work he could during this time.

From 1940–1950 my grandparents lived in Middletown (although they moved twice during this time).

As with most families, there were the ups and downs of everyday life. Children died, married, had children of their own, and divorced and remarried.

By 1956 my grandparents were still in Middletown (yes, moving four times). Their final destination was on Bartholomew Road, where my uncle Howard bought a house in 1973 and where he lived with his mom and dad.

I haven't spoken much about my grandmother during this narrative. She was a sweet person and very loving. Being married to my grandfather wasn't easy. Towards the end of her life, my dad and I went to visit her. She was so thrilled that I was interested in her Swedish family (even though it was fraught with tragedies). I don't think she thought anyone would care about her family, but I did, and it made her happy.

I will be honest and say the narrative on my grandfather has been the hardest to write. There are many details that are left unsaid for purposes of privacy and the fact that two of my grandfather's children are still living.

My grandmother when she worked at Goodyear in Middletown.

***The Children of Ernest C. Billian and Caroline L. Halldin***

i. Howard Ernest Billian, born 21 January 1918, New Britain, Hartford, Connecticut; died 20 June 1985, Middletown, Middlesex, Connecticut; never married; drafted 11 July 1942; served Oran, North Africa, Sicily, Italy; served with Battery C, 339$^{th}$ Field Artillery, 88$^{th}$ Division. Howard loved to play chess and was a baseball fan.

ii. **Russell Edward Billian**, born 18 January 1922, New Britain, Hartford, Connecticut; died 21 June 2008, Middletown, Middlesex, Connecticut; married 12 June 1943, Anniston, Alabama, Mildred L. F. Timbrell; born 2 June 1922, Quebec City, Quebec, Canada; died 16 January 2001, Middletown, Middlesex, Connecticut. Russell was drafted in 1943 and served with the 3$^{rd}$ Army, 5$^{th}$ Division, 10$^{th}$ Infantry, First Battalion Headquarters. He was a messenger and received the Silver Star, Bronze Star, and the Good Conduct Medals. Russell participated in the Battle of the Bulge, Metz, Rhineland, and others. He came home in October 1945. Russell loved sports and worked in factories all his life. He had four children, including the author.

iii. Marjorie Billian, born 31 March 1924, New Britain, Hartford, Connecticut; died 3 May 1926 (pneumonia), New Britain, Hartford, Connecticut.
iv. Kenneth E. Billian, born 6 August 1927, New Britain, Hartford, Connecticut; died 27 December 2003, Kenduskeag, Penobscot, Maine; married (1) 2 July 1949, Middletown, Middlesex, Connecticut, Lila-Jeanne Butler; divorced ?; (2) Pearl Athorne; born 24 September 1922; died 8 March 2011, Kenduskeag, Maine. There were four children from Kenneth's first marriage:
v. Eleanor Rose Billian—living.
vi. Leonard F. Billian—living.
vii. Raymond E. Billian, born 29 November 1933, New Britain, Hartford, Connecticut; died 8 December 1971, Hartford, Hartford, Connecticut. Never married and no children.

### *50. Wilbur Henry Raidart*[8] *(George Raidart,*[7] *Julia Scoville,*[6] *Franklin,*[5] *Ithamar,*[4] *Timothy,*[3] *Stephen,*[2] *Stephen,*[1] *Arthur)*

Born 12 August 1891, Riverton, Litchfield, Connecticut;[1643] died sometime after 1942, perhaps Chicago, Cook, Illinois; married 19 April 1929, Zion City, Lake, Illinois, Esther Mae Hedges;[1644] born 24 April 1909, Zion City, Lake, Illinois; died 17 July 1968, Cook County, Illinois.[1645] She married (2) 4 April 1956, Cook County, Illinois, George H. Mettee, who died January 1962.[1646] Esther was the daughter of Paul Hedges and Rosetta Berfield.

Wilbur Henry "Ray" Raidart has been a mystery for a very long time. His children do not know what became of him after he deserted the family. Through much research done by his son, Robert Raidart Berfield, as well as the author of this book, we've never been able to discover where he lived after 1942 and when he died.

Like all mysteries we have to start at the beginning. For the sake of this narrative, I will refer to Wilbur as "Ray," as he apparently used that nickname for himself.

Ray attended school likely in Riverton or Barkhamsted. He was a bright young man and had become an industrial engineer. For the years 1914–1915, Ray was the superintendent for the Winsted Edge Tool Works. This company had been incorporated in 1882 and was in operation until the catastrophic flood of 1955, which destroyed most the village's manufacturing district. The company made various types of chisels, drawknives, and the like.

It is said that Ray was very talented; he could sing and play the organ very well. He may have been involved with church choral groups in the area.

In 1917, Ray registered for the draft. At that time, he was living at 24 Windsor Avenue in Hartford and was the general foreman for the Billings and Spencer Company. This company also made various tools such as wrenches. Ray was still single at this time. He was "tall" with "light blue eyes and light hair."

---

1643 Birth information comes from the *WWI & WWII Draft Registration cards*. Ancestry.

1644 Marriage information, as well as the birth of Esther Hedges, comes from the late son of Wilbur H. Raidart. We corresponded many years ago.

1645 *Cook County Death Records,* File: 621686. Ancestry.

1646 *Cook County Marriage Records;* File: 2392161. Ancestry.

At some point in 1917 he left Connecticut and was in St. Louis, Missouri, until 1922.[1647]

While in St. Louis he met a woman named Mary Armead Stacy, who was born in 1891. Ray and Mary had a son together by the name of Douglas William Raidart, who was born 18 July 1917 in St. Louis. Mary and Ray would have had to have been together by October 1916 for this birth to happen.

This would all be speculation except for the fact that Douglas Raidart names his father as "Wilbur H. Raidart" and "Mary A. Stacy" as his mother on his Social Security Application.[1648]

On the 1920 census[1649] Douglas' mother, Mary, is listed as "Armead" Duncan with husband, Kenneth, in Minneapolis, Minnesota. Douglas is listed as the "son," age two and born in Missouri. By 1930, Douglas is living with his maternal grandparents, Oliver and Mary Stacy, in St. Genevieve, Missouri. Where was his mother, birth father, and stepfather?

Douglas Raidart also had a sister named Armead(a) Raidart who was born in July 1920. She must also be the daughter of Ray Raidart and Mary Armead(a) Raidart.

Where was Wilbur Henry "Ray" Raidart?[1650]

In 1930, Ray Raidart was living in Chicago, Illinois, with his new wife, Esther Hedges Raidart. Ray had married Esther when he was thirty-nine years old. Living with them was Esther's mother, Rosetta. They were living in an apartment/hotel at 912 Dakin Street in the 48th ward.

Ray Raidart and his mother-in-law were both thirty-eight years old and Ray's wife was twenty. No one in this household was employed, yet the rent was seventy-two dollars a month. How were they paying for their expenses?

It was in 1929 that the stock market crashed, and the United States was in the throes of the Great Depression. Chicago was especially hard hit due to the reliance on manufacturing, and the emergency relief funds ran out in 1932. There were "food shortages and rampant homelessness."[1651]

On September 28, 1937, Ray learned that his father had died and had left half of the estate to Ray upon his mother's death. Somehow, Ray found the funds to travel back east to see his

---

1647 This information comes from Ray's son, Robert R. Berfield. While I never located any online records in Missouri for Ray, there is proof that he was there per the birth of a son.

1648 *U.S. Social Security Application and Claims Index, 1936–2007.* Ancestry.

1649 1920, census, *Minneapolis, Hennepin, Minnesota,* Roll: T625_834; Page: 21B; ED: 105. Ancestry.

1650 The late Robert Raidart Berfield sent this photo to me in 2007. He stated that Wilbur Raidart was nineteen when this photo was taken.

1651 https://www.chicagotribune.com/business/081024-great-depression-photogallery-photogallery.html.

mother to request half of the estate. Apparently, there was tension between himself and his mother, and she did not give him any money and told him that he was not welcome there. On October 5, 1937, just one month after his youngest son was born, Ray deserted the family. Family members in Connecticut and Illinois never heard from him after that and never learned where he was.

When Ray's mother died in 1944, she left a bequest of "one dollar to Wilbur for reasons known to him." The rest of the estate went to his sister, Olive.

I have a notation that Wilbur was listed as a "boarder" in Ward 44 in Chicago in 1940; however, when I have tried to go back and search for him, I have not been able to locate him using his name and date of birth, etc. I also tried "wild card" searches as well as reading the 1940 census page by page for Ward 44. A very tedious process.

The last record we have of Ray is the draft registration for World War II. He registered on April 27, 1942, in Chicago. He was living at 949 West Madison Street at the McCoy Hotel and was unemployed. This area was known as "skid row" during this time. Ray noted that the person who would always know where he was would be William Brower, who was employed at the hotel.

During the time that Ray lived on West Madison Street it was a "twelve block stretch of flophouses, gin joints and battered dreams."[1652] Those twelve blocks were filled with derelict men, many sleeping in doorways or anywhere they could find a place to sleep. The Great Depression was likely the catalyst for so many unemployed men who turned to drink to blot out their despair. Was Ray Raidart one of these men?

Esther Mae Raidart subsequently divorced Wilbur for desertion and the divorce was finalized on July 31, 1945. More misfortune was to befall the family as Esther had glaucoma and was slowly going blind and was not able to support and raise her family. Richard Raidart was taken in by a great-uncle in Waukegan, Illinois; Ronald and Renne Raidart were placed in an orphanage for a short time. Renne was eventually adopted by relatives of Esther's uncle and was raised in Chicago and later in Indiana. Robert Raidart was also placed with another great-uncle and aunt. Roger was adopted by friends of the family. Ronald Raidart remained with his mother and grew up in Chicago.

Esther later remarried a man by the name of George Mattee/Mettee in 1955 in Chicago. George Mattee/Mettee died in January 1962. Esther went on to live with her son Ronald in Chicago. Esther is buried in the Elmwood Cemetery, Chicago.

I am hoping that the 1950 census will reveal where Wilbur "Ray" Raidart was living—but I am not counting on it. When and where he died is also a mystery.

***Children of Wilbur H. Raidart and Mary Armead Stacy***

i. Douglas William Raidart, 1917–1994.
ii. Armead Mary Raidart, July 1920—she married Albert Komer, 21 Oct 1941, New York, New York.[1653] This marriage did not last.

---

1652 *Chicago Tribune,* June 13, 2014, galleries.chicagotribune.com/chi-hobos-bums-tramps-unemployed.

1653 *New York, New York, Index to Marriage Licenses, 1908–1910, 1938–1940.* Ancestry.

**_Children of Wilbur H. Raidart and Esther Mae Hedges_**

iii. Richard Henry Raidart, 1930–1992.

iv. Ronald William Raidart, 1932–2000.

v. Robert George Raidart Berfield, 1934–2005. Robert took the name of his adoptive family, who were related to Esther's mother's family.

vi. Renne Yvonne Raidart Lassa, 1936–2003.

vii. Roger Lee Raidart Kurtz, 1937–2003.[1654]

1654 The information on the births and deaths of the children of Wilbur and Esther comes from the wife of Robert George Raidart Berfield.

# The Case of Philo C. Scoville

Philo C. Scoville (*Ithamar,[4] Timothy,[3] Stephen,[2] Stephen,[1] Arthur*),[1655] born circa 1813,[1656] Connecticut;[1657] died 30 December 1889, Brodhead, Green County, Wisconsin;[1658] married 30 September 1856, Janesville, Rock County, Wisconsin;[1659] Mary Kay, born 13 June 1840,[1660] Yorkshire, England, died 28 July 1903, Brodhead, Green, Wisconsin;[1661] she married (2) 27 November 1887, Green, Wisconsin, Charles H. Sidnam.[1662]

Placing Philo as a "son" of Ithamar is based purely on conjecture. I do not have proof that Philo C. Scoville is the son of Ithamar Scoville. It is possible that the Philo mentioned here as the son of Ithamar is actually the son of Philo Scoville, baptized in 1774 (and who was a brother of Ithamar). However, there is no other record found for this brother of Ithamar's. Ithamar could also have named his son after a brother who may have died at a young age. Here are some reasons for putting him here:

1. He is consistently listed as having been born in Connecticut in all the available census records.
2. He is living in New Hartford, Connecticut, in 1850. Philo and Franklin Scoville are the only two Scovilles living in this town at that time—a possible relationship?
3. The 1820 census for Norfolk, Connecticut, show three males under the age of 10 in Ithamar's household. Since the censuses from 1790–1850 do not indicate if any one person is related to the head of the household, we do not know who these three males are. We can eliminate Amasa Scoville, as he would have been 29 years old in 1820. We can also eliminate an unnamed male child born 1803 as he died in 1813. Franklin Scoville would have been the other male "under ten." *If* Philo was one of the three males under the age of ten, then he would fit into this family nicely.

The first record of Philo is on the 1850[1663] census as residing in New Hartford. He is enumerated with the family of Henry Richards, his "wife" Maria Richards, and Thomas Case (1831–1907). Philo's age is given as "thirty-two" years old. This would mean he would have been born in 1818, not 1813; it is well known that the ages on the census reports are often incorrect, but we do have to take this into consideration.

---

1655 This genealogical line is purely hypothetical at this time.

1656 Date based on his age at the time of his death.

1657 Location of birth based on the available census records.

1658 *Wisconsin Death Index, 1820–1907.* Information provided by a professional researcher.

1659 *Index to Registrations of Marriages, 1852–1907,* Fiche# 6331479.

1660 Birth information based on census records.

1661 *Wisconsin Death Records, 1867–1907;* FamilySearch/*Wisconsin, U.S. Death Index 1820–1907,* Ancestry.

1662 *Wisconsin, U.S. Marriage Index, 1820–1907;* Vol: 05; Page: 0253. Ancestry.

1663 1850 census, *New Hartford, Litchfield, Connecticut;* Dw#200; Fam#288.

Philo does not appear on the 1860 census in Connecticut. I did a census search for anyone named Philo Scoville with his approximate birth year and found a Philo Scoville living in Orfordville, Rock County, Wisconsin,[1664] with a wife and daughter. Before going any further, I also reviewed the marriage records and found Philo is listed on the Rock, Wisconsin, marriage record for September 30, 1856.[1665] His wife is Mary Kay.

The marriage was performed by a Justice of the Peace (or minister) Reuben North of "Janesville." The column where the names of the parents would be for the bride and groom is left blank. Philo gives his residence at the time of the marriage as Magnolia (Wisconsin).

Mary Kay was born June 13, 1840, in Yorkshire, England, and at the time of her marriage, she would have been just sixteen years old (Philo was forty-three). Why would such a young girl marry a man so much older? Philo was a farmer/laborer, and was by no means wealthy or even well off. Perhaps there was a lack of marriageable men (or women) and either Philo or Mary decided they needed to find a spouse? Marriages in the nineteenth century were often ones of convenience. That is not to say the emotion of love wasn't a factor; however, a marriage between a girl and a man seems to be one where Mary didn't have any other options open to her and so made the decision to marry Philo.[1666]

1860 census[1667]—Ordfordville, Spring Valley, Rock County, Wisconsin:
Dwelling #168; Family #178

Philo Scoville, 39, farmer, born Connecticut; personal estate: $120
Mary Scoville, 19, born England
Sarah J. Scoville,[1668] 1, born Wisconsin

Wisconsin had state censuses beginning 1855–1905. The unfortunate thing is that they only list the head of household and how many in the household—no names are listed. For 1865, the family has moved to Decatur, Green County, Wisconsin. There are now two males and two females listed.

The family remained in Green County but had moved to the village of Brodhead.

1870 census—Brodhead, Green County, Wisconsin:

Philo Scoville, 54, farmer, born Connecticut
Mary Scoville, 30, born England
Jenny Scoville, 11, daughter, born Wisconsin
James Scoville, 8, son, born Wisconsin

---

1664 1860 census, *Rock County, Wisconsin*, Page: 658.

1665 *Wisconsin, Rock County Registration of Marriages, 1840–1907; Index to Marriages, 1852–1907, 1840–1907*. Fiche #1275527, Book 1, Page 30, Entry #898.

1666 The first thought that would come to mind is that Mary was with child, however, that was not the case, as they did not have any children until 1859.

1667 1860 census, *Spring Valley, Rock, Wisconsin;* Roll: M653_1431; Page: 658; FHL: 805431. Ancestry.

1668 Sarah J. Scoville went by the name "Jenny."

There were no changes to the family for 1875, but the dynamic of the household changes in 1876. Divorce papers are served to Philo Scoville on August 11, 1879.[1669] The document states that in 1876 Philo had "abandoned and deserted the family." Philo was in the township of Spring Grove when the papers were served.

In Mary Scoville's deposition, she stated that "she was a dutiful wife and had supported the family entirely for the last three years. Philo did not want to support the family being only a day laborer, with no other skills, and drank to excess." The document goes on to confirm that there were two children born to the couple.

At the time of the divorce, daughter Jenny, age twenty, confirmed the circumstances surrounding the events that led to the demise of the marriage. Mary obtained custody of Jenny, but there is no mention of having custody of their son, James (called Fred).

James is found living with his father in Brodhead on the 1880 census.[1670]

Philo C. Scoville, 61, divorced, farmer, born Connecticut
James Scoville, 18, son, born Wisconsin

Mary is still living in the same town, dwelling #312; family #328[1671]

Mary Scoville, 40, divorced, born England, dressmaker
Jenny Scoville, 21, daughter, born Wisconsin, dressmaker
Kitty Kay, niece, 8, born Wisconsin
William Kay, father, 65, born England

No other record is available for Philo until December 30, 1889, when Philo succumbed to pneumonia.[1672]

Mary Kay Scoville continued on with her life in Brodhead and on November 27, 1887, she was remarried to Charles H. Sidnam. They were married for sixteen years until Mary's death in 1903. No obituary or burial records have been found, but she did leave a will.[1673]

Mary Kay Scoville Sidnam left "$400 to her husband Charles," as well as many pieces of furniture, i.e., bedding, rockers, chairs, carpets, and the like. To her son, Fred, she bequeathed "$150.00" along with a table, rocker, chairs, curtains, carpet, and homemade rugs.

Her daughter, Jenny, received the rest of the estate, "both real and personal." This included two pieces of property in Brodhead: "Lot 6, block 88" and "all of block 207."

The legal notice was printed in the *Brodhead Independent,* a weekly newspaper.

Charles H. Sidnam died at the age of seventy-two while visiting a sister in New York. The body was brought back to Brodhead and a funeral service was held at the M.E. Church. His interment was in Greenwood Cemetery in Brodhead. The obituary was published on

---

1669 *Green County Courthouse Records;* Vol. 2:109.

1670 1880 *Brodhead, Green, Wisconsin* census, Roll: 1428; Page: 74D; ED: 136. Ancestry.

1671 *Ibid,* 80D.

1672 *Greene County, Wisconsin Death Records,* Vol.1:71; Reel 32, Image 2302. Ancestry.

1673 *Wisconsin U.S. Wills and Probate Records, 1800–1987;* Green, Estate Files: Case: 4817-4874, 1903. Ancestry.

September 12, 1912, in the *Daily Register-Gazette* (Illinois) in the Saturday edition.[1674] It is likely that Mary is also buried in the same cemetery.

***Children of Philo C. Scoville and Mary Kay***

i. Sarah Jenny Scoville, b. 19 January 1859,[1675] perhaps Spring Grove, Green County, Wisconsin; d. sometime after the 1920 census and before the 1930 census, probably in Broadhead; m. 18 March 1881, Wisconsin, George Harris McNitt.[1676] This family is found in Decatur, Green County, Wisconsin, in the 1900 and 1905 censuses. In 1910 the family resided in Avon, Rock County, Wisconsin, and by 1920 they had returned to Broadhead. The 1930 census for Broadhead shows George McNitt as "widowed" and owning his own home. His daughter, Lulu, is living with him and is also listed as "widowed."

***Children of George H. McNitt and Sarah Jenny Scoville***

*a. i.* Harvey McNitt, b. Wisconsin; d. before 1900, Wisconsin.

*b. ii.* Clayton George McNitt, b. 31 May 1890, Spring Grove, Wisconsin; d. 13 December 1977, Broadhead, Green County, Wisconsin;[1677] buried Avon Cemetery, Avon, Rock County, Wisconsin; m. Nettie Ruth Henry (1892–1974). Children: Leila McNitt Haack (1913–1996), Mary Marjorie McNitt Schilling (1917–2005), Beth Irene McNitt Ringen (1919–2010).[1678]

*c. iii.* Lulu Blanche McNitt, b. 11 July 1895,[1679] Spring Valley, Rock Co., Wisconsin; she is listed as "widowed" on the 1930 census, living with her father. She is listed as "Lulu McNitt" on the census. We don't know who gave this information so it could be an error in recording. Death and burial dates are unknown.

ii. James Frederick Scoville, b. either 23 August 1862, Spring Valley Township, Rock County, Wisconsin, or 24 May 1862, Batch Grove, Wisconsin;[1680] d. 21 January 1922, Rocklin, Winnebago, Illinois;[1681] buried in Brodhead, Wisconsin; m. (1) 15 October 1885, Broadhead, Wisconsin, Mary Elizabeth (Lizzie) Noggle,[1682] b. 3 July 1869, Dayton, Richland County, Wisconsin; daughter of Christopher Noggle(s) and Catherine C. Staley; d. 6 January 1941, Evansville, Wisconsin; she divorced James

1674 Page: 12; GenealogyBank.

1675 The birth information for the children of Philo and Mary Scoville comes from a Wisconsin genealogical researcher and, regrettably, the paperwork for this family is missing.

1676 The actual record shows him as "S. H. McNitt."

1677 Find A Grave.

1678 All information on this family comes from Find A Grave.

1679 *Wisconsin Birth Index 1820–1907.* Ancestry.

1680 *Illinois, Deaths and Stillbirths Index, 1916–1947*; Ancestry.

1681 *Ibid* and *Morning Star,* Tuesday, January 24, 1922, edition, Rockford, Illinois, page 3.

1682 *Green County Marriage Records, Vol.6:312.* Marriage and court case records provided by a professional genealogical researcher in 2005.

Frederick Scoville;[1683] m. (2) 4 December 1896, Sophie Elizabeth Miller,[1684] Beloit, Rock County, Wisconsin; m. (3) 18 February 1913, Winnebago, Illinois, Elnora Green, b. circa 1879, daughter of Edwin Green and Jane Kelly.[1685]

James, who sometimes went by the name "Fred," grew up in a dysfunctional household (based on the divorce record account) and lived with his father. Whether he saw his mother and sister after the divorce is difficult to ascertain. All that is known is revealed in the vital records and a divorce record for James' first marriage.

James Frederick and Mary Elizabeth (Lizzie) Noggle married on October 15, 1885, in Brodhead. Lizzie was the daughter of Christopher Noggle(s) and Catherine Staley. Christopher is stated to have been born in Dubuque, Iowa, in 1832 and married Catherine Staley on November 6, 1864, in Green, Wisconsin.[1686] The Noggle family is living in Exeter, Green County, Wisconsin, per the 1870 census. The Noggle household members are Christopher, Catherine, Jones, George Washington, and Eliza (age nine months).

The condition of James and Lizzie's marriage in the beginning is not known, but it did not end well. From all accounts Lizzie's life must have been horrendous in a time when women's shelters did not exist and where sympathy for a battered women may have existed, but nothing was ever done about by the authorities.

The account from the courts is not easy reading. Not only did the wife suffer, but their child did as well. The court records show that "Fred" was a heavy drinker who would "pound her and misuse her." He would not provide wood for warmth or put food on the table. He would often threaten to kill her. He called her "dirty" names and had a "good mind to blow her brains out." Lizzie did try to leave but would always return (there was no place for her to go). Lizzie would often have to rely on the kindness of relatives or neighbors to provide her with food.

An example of extreme cruelty is that, two days after she gave birth to their second child, James "whipped the three-year old boy [Alvie] until he was black and blue because the hired girl didn't feed the animals on time." There are many other such instances that occurred, which I will not go into further here. Suffice it to say that Lizzie and her son Alvie led a very difficult life.

Their son, Alvie James, was sent to Sparta State School, presumably as an "orphan" because his father would not have anything to do with him.[1687] This school was a place for children with no parents or close relatives, or who were suffering from neglect, which was the case here and the mother did not have the power to do anything about this situation.

1683 *Green County Court House, Case H 1162, page 165.*

1684 The couple married at the M.E. Church. Witnesses were John W. Clark and Mrs. Lydia Spafford. Sophie was the daughter of Charles and Sophie Elizabeth Kostuf Miller. Information provided by a genealogical researcher, 2005.

1685 *Illinois County Marriage Records, 1800–1940,* FamilySearch.

1686 Vital record on Christopher Noggle has not been proven. The marriage record comes from *Wisconsin Marriages—pre-1907,* p 16. Ancestry.

1687 Alvie's mother (Lizzie) would have had no say in the matter of her son being sent to the state school. The Sparta State School was also known as the State Public School from about 1889–1938. In 1947 it was renamed Wisconsin Child Center.

While this couple did have a house and a lot, too much was owed on it to provide any support for Lizzie.

The final findings of the court were in favor of Lizzie as she experienced "cruel and inhumane treatment and the [husband] failed to provide for the family." Lizzie was granted an "absolute" divorce and was given custody of their son, Alvie James. The divorce was decreed on October 25, 1895.

The next record for James "Fred" Scoville is another marriage, which occurred on December 4, 1896,[1688] to Sophia "Sophie" Elizabeth Miller. She was born in February 1869[1689] in Beloit, Rock County, Wisconsin, to Charles H. Miller and Sophia Elizabeth Kostof (immigrants from Germany). Although she used her maiden name on this marriage record, she actually had been married two other times. Her first marriage was to John C. Crist onFebruary 1, 1883, in Rock, Wisconsin.[1690] Her second husband was one Joseph C. Frey, who had been born in Pennsylvania according to the marriage record. This couple married on September 19, 1888, in Clinton, Iowa.[1691] Mr. Frey designates himself as "widowed" on the 1905 Iowa

**DECIDE FOR HUTCHINS**

**Industrial Board Renders Important Decision in Rockford Case.**

The Industrial board yesterday handed down a decision in the case of James F. Scoville against A. R. Hutchins under the Workmen's Compensation law in favor of Mr. Hutchins, the board taking the stand that it had no jurisdiction in the case.. The decision is an important one as it establishes a precedent. Hutchins, who conducted a flour and feed business in Beloit, hired Scoville to haul a load of corn for him from Rockton to Beloit, the teamster falling under the wagon and breaking his leg. Suit was started and the defense contended that as the defendant was in business in Wisconsin he could be held under the Illinois law. Attorney Frank E. Maynard represented Mr. Hutchins and Attorney D. D. Madden, Mr. Scoville.

DAY, AUGUST 9, 1916.

**HUTCHINS WON THE DECISION**

**INDUSTRIAL BOARD HOLDS IT HAS NO JURISDICTION IN DAMAGE CLAIM.**

A legal decision which is of far-reaching importance under the Workman's Compensation law was handed down today in a case wherein James F. Scoville, the injured party, was petitioner, and A. R. Hutchins of Harlem boulevard, was respondent.

Hutchins conducted a flour and feed business in Beloit, Wis., and engaged the said James F. Scoville to haul a load of corn for him from Rockton to Beloit. Scoville slipped and the wagon ran over his leg breaking both bones.

Suit was filed under the Workman's Compensation Act by Attorney D. D. Madden, representing Scoville, against A. R. Hutchins who was represented by Attorney Frank E. Maynard.

Attorney Maynard contended that the business of the said Hutchins was in Wisconsin and therefore he could not be held under the laws of Illinois for an injury to an employe, and made a motion to dismiss the case for want of jurisdiction. Attorney Madden contended that as long as the hiring was done in this state, the employer was subjected to the terms of our Compensation law. However, the Industrial board held that they had no jurisdiction of the case and dismissed the suit.

This is the first time such a case has arisen under the Compensation law and the legal questions puzzled the arbitrator, but the decision is of far-reaching effect and is of importance to all attorneys as establishing a precedent along this line.

---

1688 *Green County Marriage Records, Vol.6:312.*

1689 1900 census, *Broadhead, Green County, Wisconsin*; Page: 8; ED: 0120; FH: 1241789. Ancestry. The family was living in a rented house on Thomas Street. James' occupation is a "teamster."

1690 *Wisconsin Marriages 1836–1930,* FamilySearch.

1691 *Iowa Clinton County Marriages, 1838–1934,* FamilySearch. This is the correct marriage as the

(Clinton) State census; ironically, at the same time, Sophie Miller Scoville is living in the household of husband number three, "F. J. Scoville," in 1905, living in Broadhead, Wisconsin.

I haven't been successful in locating any death records for the first two husbands—it is more likely that Sophia divorced one or two of her previous husbands prior to her marriage to James Scoville.

The online records are "silent" after 1905 as to Sophia and James, as I cannot find either of them on the 1910 census in Wisconsin, Iowa, or Illinois. However, I do find another marriage record for James—this time in the *Illinois County Marriages, 1810–1940*: Elnora Green, born circa 1879, daughter of Edwin Green and Jane Kelly, married James F. Scoville in Winnebago, Illinois, on February 18, 1913.[1692]

While seeking additional information on James, I came across two newspaper articles relating to a Workman's Compensation claim made by James Scoville in 1916.

According to these two articles, James F. Scoville suffered a severe injury to his legs from slipping on ice and a wagon rolled over him. This injury incapacitated him to the point where he was not able to work, and his hope was that he would get compensated. However, that was not to be. How he and his wife managed financially after his injury is unknown.

There hasn't been any success in locating him or his wife on the 1920 census in Wisconsin or Illinois—or anywhere for that matter.

On January 24, 1922, in Rocklin, Winnebago, Illinois, James Frederick Scoville died at the age of fifty-nine years.

His obituary:[1693]

**FRED C. SCOVILLE DIES AT ROCKTON**

ROCKTON, Jan. 23.—Fred C. Scoville passed away Saturday afternoon at 5:30 o'clock at his home on the south side of town, after a lingering illness. He leaves the widow, one son, A. J. Scoville of Evansville, Wis., and one daughter Miss Jemine, at home. No arrangements for the funeral have been made, but burial will probably be in Brodhead, Wis.

There are other obituary notices printed that are slightly different in their wording; one states the illness lasted "two-weeks" and others give the name of the daughter alternately as "Jemine," "Jessie," and "Jean." A. J. Scoville is Alvie James. While Fred C. Scoville may have been buried in Brodhead, I haven't found a record of the location of his burial.

His third wife, Elnora Green, has been impossible to find outside of her marriage to James Scoville. The name "Elnora" combined with the name "Green" or "Scoville" is not as uncommon as one may suppose. Curiously, on the 1928 Beloit (Wisconsin) City Directory a "Clara E. Scovelle [sic]" is listed as the "widow of F.C." and residing at 1919 Lenox Avenue. Since James is often listed as "Fred C." it is possible that this reference could be Elnora, going by the name of Clara.

---

parents' names for Sophia are the same as with her first and third marriage.

1692 *Newspaper Article—Morning Star, Rockford, Illinois,* August 10, 1916, edition. GenealogyBank. Images used with the explicit permission of NewsBank, Inc. 16 February 2022.

1693 *Morning Star,* Tuesday, January 24, 1922, edition; 3; Newspapers.com. The image of the death notice is now in the public domain.

Another reference for a woman named Clara Scoville is the 1930 census for Beloit, Wisconsin. This "Clara Scoville" was living with the August Johnson family as the *widowed mother-in-law.* Her age is given as "fifty-one" (born 1879) and she was married for "twenty years." The marriage information would be off by three years,[1694] but that is not enough to disprove that the "Clara Scoville" enumerated on this census is, in fact, Elnora Green Scoville. There is also a daughter living with her by the name of "Jannie Scoville" who was born in 1918 (recall the obituary notice for James Scoville with a daughter by the name of Jermine, Jessie, or Jean). The woman who is married to August Johnson is Hazel, who at the time of this census was aged twenty-nine years, and would have been born circa 1903. This date is prior to the marriage of Elnora and James. I suspect that "Hazel" is a daughter of Elnora from a previous marriage.

Further review of the records found an unsourced record on *FamilySearch*: Clara Elnora Green, born 23 February 1879, Wisconsin; died 14 August 1932, Wisconsin. I must also note that there is a Clara Scoville buried in Eastlawn Cemetery in Beloit, Rock County, Wisconsin.[1695] More research is needed to verify the facts noted here.

Another partially unsourced record on *FamilySearch* for the woman named "Jannie, etal" on the 1930 census: Jennie May Scoville, born 25 June 1914, Rockton, Winnebago, Illinois; died 4 May 1985, Monroe, Green County, Wisconsin.[1696] Father: James Frederick Scoville; Mother: Clara Elnora Green; Spouse: Albert Baerwald.

The obituary for Albert Baerwald[1697] indicates that he was born on 4 March 1915, "in the Town of Eldorado, a son of Albert and Ida Baerwald." Albert Baerwald married Jenny Scoville at Fox Lake, Illinois, on 19 August 1951.

I have not been able locate anything further on this family through the 1940 census, marriage, burial records, etc.

≈

As to what became of Mary Elizabeth (Noggle) Scoville, this can only be told through the census records.

Per the 1905 Wisconsin State Census for Albany, Green County, she is living in the household of Frank B. Chase (45) and his daughter Esther T. Chase (6). Lizzie (36) is a "servant." Where Lizzie was in 1900, I have not been able to ascertain.

1910 census—Albany, Green County, Wisconsin:

Mary E. "Hoggle," 40, housekeeper, divorced,[1698] b. Wisconsin
Frank B. Chase, 50, farmer, b. Wisconsin
Esther Chase, 10, b. Wisconsin

1694 Based on the marriage date of 1913.

1695 Information comes from Find A Grave.

1696 *Wisconsin Death Index, 1959–1997.* Ancestry.

1697 *Fond du Lac Reporter,* Monday, October 30, 1972, edition, 34. Newspapers.

1698 Note that she is listed with her maiden name—albeit misspelled—and lists herself as divorced, which was uncommon to do in that period. Women would usually state that they were single or widowed.

Sometime between the 1910 census and the 1920 census, Frank Chase removed to Idalia, Yuma County, Colorado, and Mary "Lizzie" went with him.

Frank B. Chase, 60, widowed, farmer, b. Wisconsin
Mary E. Hoggle, 52, lodger and home helper, divorced, b. Kansas

In 1930 they are still living in Idalia and were enumerated on 25 April. Mary is back to using her former married name of Scoville.

Mary E. Scoville, housekeeper, 60, divorced, b. Wisconsin
Frank B. Chase, head, widower, 70, b. Wisconsin

On October 17, 1938, Frank B. Chase died.[1699] He was the widower of Laura Bell Taft and left one living child—Esther Taft Chase. He is buried in Maple Hill Cemetery, Evansville, Rock County, Wisconsin.

Mary Elizabeth had been with him for thirty-three years. Whether it was a deep, abiding friendship, or a more intimate relationship, Mary Elizabeth may have finally found some peace after the turmoil she lived in for those ten years with her husband, James "Fred" Scoville.

By the 1940 census[1700] Mary is back in Evansville, Wisconsin, living with her son, Alvie, his wife, and Alvie's mother-in-law.

Alvie Scoville, head, 51, owns own home, value $1500, b. Wisconsin, core maker in a foundry
Verena Scoville, wife, 46, b. Wisconsin
LeRoy Scoville, son, 24, b. Wisconsin, salesman
Mary Scoville, mother, 70, widowed, mentions having lived in Yuma, Colorado
Ellen Huseth, mother-in-law, 69, widowed, b. Wisconsin

Approximately one year later, Mary Elizabeth Noggle(s) Scoville died. The newspaper notice is from the *Wisconsin State Journal,* edition date Monday, January 6, 1941, page 2.

**Mrs. Mary E. Scoville**

EVANSVILLE—Mrs. Mary Elizabeth Scoville, 71, died here Saturday night in the home of Mr. and Mrs. A.J. Scoville, S. Madison St., her son and daughter-in-law, after a week's illness. She has been in poor health for two years. She was born Mary Elizabeth Noggle, July 3, 1869, in Dayton, Green County and was reared in that community. She was married to Fred J Scoville in Brodhead, October 15, 1885, and they lived in that city for several years. After that she lived in Burlington, Colorado for 28 years and returned to live with her son here two years ago. Survivors include the son and a grandson, Leroy, who is a national guard at Fort Knox Ky., returned today for the funeral services. A brother, C.C. Noggle also survives. The body was taken to the Roderick Funeral Home.

---

1699 Find A Grave. Mitchell Addition, Block 2, Lot 49.

1700 1940 census, *Evansville, Rock, Wisconsin,* Roll:m-t0627-04520; Page:66B; ED:53-27. The census was taken on 13 May 1940.

**Children of James Frederick Scoville and Mary Elizabeth Noggle(s)**

i. an unnamed child, probably born before Alvie James. Died in infancy.[1701]

ii. Alvie James Scoville, b. 24 May 1888, Argyle, Lafayette County, Wisconsin;[1702] d. 27 February 1962, Evansville, Rock County, Wisconsin;[1703] married 12 October 1912, Albany, Green County, Wisconsin, Verena Matilda Huset (also written as Huseth); b. on a farm in Mount Horeb, Dan, Wisconsin, 9 April 1894, daughter of Peter Huset and Elsbeth Zweifel; d. 18 May 1980,[1704] Evansville, Rock County, Wisconsin.

As I have previously written, Alvie had a rough childhood. The court deemed that he couldn't take care of himself, and his father wouldn't care for him, and he was treated as an orphan and was sent to the Sparta State School. According to the court records, "Alvie wasn't vicious or bad, he just wanted to go to school." It's impossible to say how long he remained at Sparta School, but by 1914 he had married Verena (a.k.a. Fanny) Huset.

The next record found is the *World War I Draft Registration Cards 1917–1918* via the National Archives and Record Administration. At this point Alvie was twenty-nine years old and living at 304 Cherry Street in Evansville[1705] with his wife and one child. He worked in a foundry as a core-maker and requested an exemption from the service as his wife was "crippled." He was "short," "slender," with blue eyes and brown hair.[1706] Other than the draft registration, I find no military record for him and presume he was exempt from service.

The family was still living in Evansville in 1920 but they had moved to South Madison Street. Their son, LeRoy, was a little over four years old and Alvie was making his living as a core-maker at Factory Motor Works, where several of his neighbors also worked.

By 1930 Alvie owned his own home on Madison Street and was still working in an engine factory. It appears that he and his neighbors have a different employer, but the handwriting of the enumerator is not legible, although it appears to read windmill (?) and engine factory. LeRoy is now fourteen and attending school. Alvie's wife is a homemaker.

The 1940 census has been captured under Alvie's mother's information.

Whether Alvie Scoville has any connection to my Scoville line or not, I have an affection for him and his mother for the hardships and turmoil that they lived through. They seemed to come out of it on the other side with decent, everyday lives, with their ups and downs and losses.

**Children of James Frederick Scoville and Mary Elizabeth Noggle(s) continued . . .**

iii. an unnamed child b. 14 May 1891; d. 20 May 1891.

---

1701 Based on the divorce record where Mary states she had two children that she "lost."

1702 Birth information comes from Find A Grave.

1703 *Wisconsin Death Index, 1959–1997*. Ancestry.

1704 *U.S. Social Security Applications and Claims Index, 1936–2007* and *Wisconsin Death Index 1959–1997*, Ancestry.

1705 As of this writing the house still stands on the corner of Cherry and Water Streets, Evansville, Wisconsin.

1706 A photo of Alvie, his wife, and child can be found on Ancestry.com.

Verena Huseth Scoville, Alvie James Scoville, and LeRoy Scoville. Photo used with permission by Mike Huseth.

***Children of Alvie James Scoville and Verena Huset***

*a.i.* Manlon Alvie Scoville, b. 2 February 1914, Evansville; d. 1914.

*b. ii.* LeRoy Arnold Scoville, b. 30 November 1915, Evansville, Rock County, Wisconsin; d. 24 January 1945 of wounds suffered as a POW. LeRoy never married, but apparently had a girl named Betty Hyne of whom he was fond.[1707] For purposes of this genealogy and the fact that I don't know if this family is connected to my Scoville line, I will only provide an overview of LeRoy's life here. I suggest reading about the life and death of LeRoy Scoville online in its entirety. It is a truly harrowing tale.

LeRoy's nickname was "Scoops" to his friends. He graduated in 1933 from Evansville High School and lived at 464 South Madison Street.

LeRoy joined the Wisconsin National Guard's 32nd Tank Company on 23 September 1940. Two months later, on 28 November 1940, the tank company was called to federal service.

LeRoy was one of the many men who were part of the death march in Bataan and he was held as a POW at Camp O'Donnell. He was constantly being moved around from prison to prison. On September 25, 1944, LeRoy was sent to Bilibid Prison with his friend Jack Merrifield. This was a clearinghouse for those who would be sent to Japan. After he had passed a physical, he and Merrifield boarded a ship, the *Oryoku Maru*. Once it sailed it came under attack by American planes. The ship ran aground, and LeRoy and the other prisoners swam to shore.

More time passed and on January 6, 1945, LeRoy was put on the *Enoura Maru* with 500 POWs. The ship was still docked when it came under attack by American planes on January 9, 1945. LeRoy was badly injured as his right leg and foot were torn to pieces by the bomb. The medics cared for him but since they did not have the medical supplies needed, there wasn't much they could do for him.

LeRoy was placed on a third ship, called "Hell Ship," the *Brazil Maru*, with the other surviving POWs. This is the ship where LeRoy died on the morning of January 24, 1945. Before he died, he asked Robert A. Boehm of A Company to give his parents his last possessions, as he had lost everything else in the sinking of the *Oryku Maru*. As with all soldiers who have died aboard ship, LeRoy's body was released into the sea. LeRoy's name appears on the "Tablets of the Missing" at the American Military Cemetery outside of Manila.

Here is a very brief synopsis of a letter he had written to his parents early in the war:

1707 See *Bataanproject.com* for full details of what 2nd Lt. LeRoy A. Scoville went though.

Dear Mom and Dad and all,

. . . We live in the woods and have learned the numerous was of preparing beds and all types of things for protection. Have faith. Pray for me as I pray for you, and I know that he will take care of us. Should be time to eat soon. I have made an allotment at the bank. If you should need the money, I want you to feel welcome to use it in any way. Please write and tell me about all the folks, those at the store, and our relatives and friends. I presume mail is very difficult to get through. Anyway, Bye now and God bless you all.

Love,
Leroy.

Lastly, before I conclude this particular line, I have reviewed the other Scovilles who were in Wisconsin in the same general area as Philo and his family. One man, named George Scoville, stood out as he was also living in Green County, and I have reviewed the 1850 census. George Scoville was living in the town of Brooklyn, Green County. The census indicates he was "37" years of age and his estimated birth year would be circa "1813." I thought he may be a possible candidate for being related to Philo Scoville for two reasons:

1. He (George) was born in Connecticut.
2. His birth year is close enough to Philo's to be a brother.

Since George Scoville is stated as having been born in Connecticut, I reviewed the 1840 census for a man named "George" who could possibly fit his profile. There was only one George "Scovelle" [sic] who was relevant—a man with the same name who was living in Goshen, Litchfield County, Connecticut. His age was in the category as being between the ages of 20–29; in other words, this person was born between 1811–1820.

The next question is this: are the George on the 1840 census in Connecticut and the George on the 1850 census in Wisconsin the same man? While I do not have any sources to prove this theory that they are one and the same, I can only say that I did not find any other George Scovilles on the 1850 census for Connecticut. I have continued to follow this trail based on the theory that he is the same man who was in Wisconsin in 1850.

According to the census records already mentioned, George Scoville was born between 1811–1813 in Connecticut and Philo was born circa 1813, also in Connecticut. George was living in Goshen (Connecticut) in 1840 and Philo was in New Hartford (Connecticut) in 1850.[1708] The distance between these two towns is approximately seventeen miles, perhaps a little more if we are speaking of the roadways during the timeframe that George and Philo lived in their respective towns.

Provided in the narrative on Philo, we see that he was in New Hartford during the time the

1708 Philo Scoville has not been found on the 1840 census for Connecticut.

census was recorded in 1850, living with the Richards family. He left Connecticut sometime after the census and before his marriage in 1856 in Wisconsin.

Below is a timeline for George and Philo as to where they were living during the census records.

| George Scoville | Philo Scoville |
|---|---|
| 1855—Magnolia, Rock Co. | Possibly Janesville, Rock Co. |
| 1860—Magnolia, Rock Co. | Ordville, Rock Co. |
| 1865—unknown | unknown |
| 1870—Jordan, Green Co. | Broadhead, Green Co. |
| 1875—Jordan, Green Co. | Broadhead, Green Co. |
| 1880—Jefferson, Green Co. | Broadhead, Green Co. |
| 1885—Jefferson, Green Co. | unknown |

While they lived in the same county at different census times, they never lived in the **same town** at the **same time**; however, these towns/villages are not that far apart either, so I would imagine they may have known one another, even if they weren't related.

George Scoville can be followed in Wisconsin until the 1885 census. Online records show that George died in 1889. The grave marker states he was born 29 November 1811, Connecticut, and died 16 April 1889 in Green County, burial in Richland Cemetery, Monroe, Green County, Wisconsin. A short biography states that he lived "77 yrs., 5 mos., 17ds." He had been married twice (Luretta and Althea) and had a total of six children.[1709]

One final note—there is a public tree on Ancestry that states that George Scoville (1811–1899) was the son of Ruben Scoville (1765–1853), who was the son of John Scovill (1738–1807). I personally have not found any proof of this. I checked the various books on the descendants of Arthur Scovel and John Scovill. None of the people noted are found within the pages of these genealogies.

The Philo Scoville[1710] (born circa 1774) and brother of Ithamar, *could* have had a son also named Philo, who had lived for a time in New Hartford near his uncle Franklin Scoville, and then removed to Wisconsin, but nothing more of Philo (son of Timothy Scoville and brother of Ithamar) is known.

In conclusion, after many years of searching for clues and reading census reports and any other record I could find, the parentage of Philo C. Scoville (and George Scoville) remains a mystery. Perhaps someone will take up the mantle of finding out who this Philo C. Scoville belongs to.

1709 Find A Grave.

1710 This Philo Scoville is not to be confused with Philo Scoville, son of Timothy Scoville, who removed from New York to Cleveland, Ohio, in the early 1800s. This particular Philo was a nephew of Ithamar's.

# The Account Book of Ira Scovill

A copy of this book was sent to me many years ago by the late Gary Scovill. This account book gives a glimpse of the daily life of the early Scoville settlers. I have transcribed the entries as the original writer wrote them (spelling errors and all). I have provided clarification of what some of the terms mean in the footnotes.

Norfolk November 17, 1801
Asa Burr[1711]
to two days work at dung.

February 16, 1802
to one day dressing flax[1712]
to ash timber and making troves.

February 1803—to cash
to one day dressing flax
to cash one and eight
to cash for brandy
to cash for brandy
to part of the day dressing flax.

Luther Harrison[1713]
to half day at bridge
to one day plowing
to one days work at [ ]

April 7, 1804
Jesse Whiting[1714]

---

1711 Asa Burr, shoemaker; m. Mary Lockwood, daughter of Seth Lockwood of Goshen. Asa learned the trade from Seth Lockwood, with whom he apprenticed. Asa d. 1852, age 86, and was the son of Oliver Burr. He lived in South Norfolk on the Old Goshen Road.

1712 Dressing flax—separating the fibrous thread from the stalk—this is one of the last steps in a many stepped process. Some of the implements used would be a brake, hatchet, a swinging board, and a knife. The flax would be twisted into bunches and then given to the women to spin, weave, whiten, and make into cloth.

1713 Luther Harrison was a neighbor of Timothy Scoville, their land bordering one another. Luther was the son of Daniel Harrison, who was originally from Branford, CT. Luther Harrison was born about 1770 and died 20 February 1813, age 43, most likely from the spotted fever epidemic. He married Rachel Johnson. She was the daughter of ______ and Olive (Douglas) Johnson.

1714 Jesse Whiting—he is listed on the 1800 census for Norfolk, CT.

May 25
to one days work dressing flax
to one days work heping[1715] [sic] logs

May 26
by payment to Reuben [C][B]rown?[1716]

June 30—to two days pice [sic] chopping.
February 3, 1808—then recond with Jessie Whiting and ballans all book accounts.

to two days chopping wood dove.[1717]
28—to one day making Hare trof.[1718]
to one day chopping sap wood.[1719]
to one pair lether mittings.[1720]
to one days at millis.[1721]
to one day chopping dove. (?)
to one day at apple trees.
to one day work at logs.
to one day a logs heping.
to one day at fence.
to one day heeping logs follar.[1722]
to one half on follar.
to one day by Joshua P.[1723] [page torn]
to one day pealing. [page torn]

1802—Doctor Joseph North[1724]
to Timothy Schovel[1725]

---

1715 I believe this is likely *heaping* logs, putting logs into a pile?

1716 The name here is illegible. There was a Reuben Crown in Cornwall, CT.

1717 The word appears to be "dove," however, it is likely "wood grove."

1718 Hare would certainly mean a rabbit. Perhaps the word "trof" means trap—in other words, an implement to catch wild rabbits.

1719 Saplings? The word is clearly "chopping" so it is doubtful it's tapping for sap (maple syrup)—more likely he is referencing the cutting away of undergrowth and saplings.

1720 Leather mittens.

1721 Not clear if he is referring to a family by the name of Mills, or if he means "one day going to the mill."

1722 Not sure what he is referring to here.

1723 The page is torn, so the last name of "Joshua" it not known.

1724 Dr. Joseph North, d. 22 September 1818 in Cornwall, age 76.

1725 This is probably Timothy Schovel [sic] father of Ira, Ithamar, et al. His son Timothy may have been traipsing through New York State during this time.

to cash paid for settin womans arm.[1726]

May 17—to cash
1817—then recond with Joseph North
June 11—all book account with Joseph North and balance the same (signatures of Dr. North and Ira Schovel).

John Dickeson Dr. To Ira Schovel 1803.[1727]
from the old book.
to sundre days work.[1728]

May 1803 to ox yoke and [ ].
to weaving nine yrds 3 quarter.
to weaving Sixteen yrds & half.
for cronck cut out.[1729]
to weaving seven yrd 3 quarter.
to weaving ten yrds 1 quarter.
to spinning nine run yarn.

June 25—to weaving twenty four 3 qrts.
June 9—to weaving fourteen yrd 3 qt.
Oct 15—to weaving sixteen yrd 1 qt wool.
Oct 26—to weaving [ ] eight yrd 1 qtr.
to fifteen shillings from Roger Foot.[1730]
1804—he says turned on my account.
May—to weaving eight yrds and [ ].

Augt 29, 1804
The reckond [sic] with Ira Schovel and Balens all Book accounts witness my hand [ ] John Dickinson.

---

1726 The woman who broke her arm may have been Timothy's wife, Sarah Rogers Scoville.

1727 John Dickeson—not known who he is. There were a number of people in the town of Cornwall by the name of "Dickinson," but no one named "John."

1728 Sundre (sundry)—refers to a variety of jobs he performed that day.

1729 Not sure what this term is in reference to—something to do with the weaving process? The weaving was typically done by the women.

1730 There are a number of men with the name "Roger Foot(e)" within Litchfield County and New London County, Connecticut. There is a land record for Reuben Dean and Roger Foot (both of Norfolk) regarding the mill. The document was signed by Roger Foot, Roger Foot, Jr., and Samuel Foot.

June 1806—caried Kellogg of Salisbury a calf skin to tan.[1731]
to a quarter of veal wt.
sixteen pound three pence pur pund.[1732]
(page torn at the bottom, much is illegible)
[ ]oseph hovel (probably Joseph Schovel)[1733]
Mentions "butter;" "8 oz. pork."
by three days and half at [ ].
by one quarter of beef.
by two bushel potatoes.
by one qrtr veal wt. ten pound.
by sledding two [ ].[1734]

June [ ] 1803
Then recond with Roger Foot (signed "Roger Foot").

Kelloggs (faded print) Jessie Whiting.
by one days work plowing.
by one day of your boy and oxen.[1735]
by one day work plowing.
by a pig and a tr [ ].
by one day and half [ ].

February 10, 1803—by one day chopping.
by half a day drawing.[1736]
by one day drawing wood.
to two pound tobacco.
by one day plowing.
by two days plowing my plans(?)[1737]
by one day plowing.
by one day plowing field.

1731 "Carried to Kellogg" references Ira Scovill bringing a calfskin to a Mr. Kellogg to do the tanning process. The name Kellogg is prevalent in Litchfield County. Salisbury boarders both Massachusetts and New York.

1732 Note that Ira is still using the currency in pre-Revolutionary terms. In 1792, the Congress Coinage Act established the United States dollar as the country's standard unit of money.

1733 Joseph Scoville was probably the son of Samuel Scoville and Mary Rowland. Samuel was the brother to Timothy (*Stephen,[2] Stephen,[1] Arthur*).

1734 Sledding—a mode of transporting goods.

1735 Not sure if the term "your boy" refers to a son of Kellogg or Jesse Whiting, or is referring to a hired hand.

1736 The term "drawing" refers to moving something.

1737 This word is likely "place"—finally getting around to plowing his own field.

by one day plowing with mare.
by one day with [ ].
by plowing corn.

Philo Clemmons[1738]
To two quarts whiskey.
Ballance (page torn).

A Burr November 31,[1739] 1801
by making me one pair shoes.
by making my king two pair.[1740]
little shoes finding lether.[1741]
by one pair of shoes for wife.

October 26—Number of bushels of wheat raised in 1831 (very faint writing).[1742]
March 9—Mr. Yapbie to thirteen bushels of ashes.[1743]

April 18, 1808—Thaddeus Ford[1744]
to one nine quarter veal wt. thirteen pound one quarter.
Dagant(?) Store.[1745]
by Joel half a day killing [ ][1746]
by one day cradling.[1747]

---

1738 This is likely the Philo Clemmons who is conjectured to have married Ira Scoville's daughter, Clarissa.

1739 The account book clearly states "November 31." Asa Burr was a shoemaker.

1740 Probably should read "by making my *kin* two pair."

1741 Ira looking for leather to make a pair of shoes for a child, and next entry a pair of shoes for his wife, Ruth.

1742 Paper was not wasted, and the account book doesn't flow from one year to the next. If there was an available spot to write something, the keeper of the book would write wherever he could.

1743 I have not found anyone by the name of "Yapbie"—could it be "Maltbie"? While Ira's handwriting is usually legible, there are some words that are seemingly impossible to decipher.

1744 Thaddeus Ford was of Cornwall and is listed on the 1790 Rate (tax) bill. He was married to Sarah______. They had children Levi, Polly, and Tabitha. In early days he had a spinning mill in Cornwall Hollow.

1745 Likely refers to a store in either Cornwall or Norfolk.

1746 Possibly this refers to Joel Harrison of Cornwall. He and his brothers and father were neighbors of the Scovilles in North Cornwall as their land bordered one another.

1747 This term is used throughout the account book. It is a method of harvesting—a cradle was a rake-like scoop with a long handle. It had tines of wood that were pointed sideways to gather the grain. It would then be tied into sheaves.

by one gallon rum.[1748]
by two pound thirteen oz butter.
[ ]by found pound butter.
by one day chopping wood.
by work at stable.
by twenty three pound pork.

Luther Harrison[1749]
by making salool (?).
by four pound quarter chees.
by one bushel of ry loved.[1750]
by [ ] a day chopping wood.
by work at stable.
by twenty three pound pork.

[ ]19, 1801
John Beach[1751]
to one days wok at barn.
July 15—to craddlin five acres of ry.
to cradling one acre and a half.
to thrashing part of acre.
December 19, 1801
to two days chopping logs
to one day chopping logs.

March 1803—to weaving 39 yards.
to weaving twenty-two yrds.
to weaving twenty one yards.
to half a day work road sawyer.[1752]
to one day work at stocks.[1753]

June 2, 1804—to weaving fifteen yrd 3 qr.

---

1748 The early settlers kept liberal amounts of rum, whiskey, and beer on hand for medicinal purposes, as well as for everyday use with meals and special occasions. Cider was liberally consumed on a daily basis by most families.

1749 Luther Harrison (1769–1813), son of Daniel Harrison and Hannah Barker. His wife was Rachel Johnson. He was born in Branford, Connecticut, and removed to Cornwall, where he lived and died.

1750 Possibly rye loaves.

1751 Possibly Deacon John Beach, who lived on a farm on the Old Goshen Road in South Norfolk.

1752 A sawyer is someone who works with wood—either in a sawmill or, in this instance, someone who is clearing trees on the road.

1753 Perhaps a reference to working with farm animals.

At seven pence pr yrd shirtin[1754]
To two hundred and twenty six feet of hemlock bords.

March 1820—Ira Scovil (note the year of this entry. Ira was in New York at this time).
to Fredrick Main[1755]
to two quarts whiskey.
to one quart whiskey.
(torn) quart whiskey.
to two quarts whiskey.
to one quart.
(the rest of the page is torn).

November 1801—Joshua Beach[1756]
to three days work on follar.
to part of day at Stocks.
to one days work shingling.
to one days thrashing.
December 6, 1802—then recond with Joshua Beach all book account and found due to me two shillings to balance book (Signed Joshua Beach).

December 7 (no year recorded, possibly a continuation of 1801).
to half days work.
going to mill and nortons.[1757]
going after midwife.[1758]
go mare to coalbrook.[1759]
to my mare to mill.
to one day at milses at flax.[1760]
to one day at fence.
to one day at your barn corners.
to one day to rises.[1761]

---

1754 Not sure if the word "shirtin" is in reference to a particular type of cloth to make shirts, or "shirrin," referring to "to gather cloth."

1755 Frederick Main—the conjectured husband of Dimmis Scoville, daughter of Ira Scoville.

1756 There was a Joshua Beach who lived in South Norfolk and had a sawmill there. He made cheese casks. It is said that he had 13 children.

1757 Not sure who "Norton" was—a person or a store?

1758 There is no indication who needed the midwife—Joshua Beach's wife?

1759 Colebrook, Connecticut.

1760 See note 1721.

1761 The Webster's Dictionary defines "riser" as the "vertical piece between the steps in a stairway." Since Ira was working on the barn corners, he may have spent time at Joshua Beach's, either repairing or building.

to one day foot logs.
to one day by calop beach.[1762]
to a remnant of sheep skin.
to butchering.
[ ] 22, 1804—then recond with Joshua Beach and balanced all book accounts (signed Joshua Beach).

John Beach
by one barrel brandy.
by fifteen bushel apples.
by one barrel cyder.
by half pound tea.
by nine pound tea.
by half bushel salt.
by two hancercheif.[1763]
by one Canaan do.[1764]

Jonathan Vangorden[1765]
to two quarts whiskey.
to one quart whiskey.
to one pint whiskey.
June 30—to one pint whiskey.
Balance due paid.
(on same page in faded handwriting is written "Myron Scoville"[1766] Rochester, Lorain Co. Ohio).

1801—Dr. Benjamin Welch[1767]
to four pound and half potatoes.
to a womans saddle.

Dr. Joseph North
May 9, 1806—to three days work at wall.
1808—to one cow & calf.
May–June 3—to three days work with oxen.

---

1762 The first name is probably "Caleb." There are two men with this name on the census reports from 1800–1820: one in New Milford and one in Winchester, both towns in Litchfield County.

1763 Handkerchief.

1764 Probably referring to the town of Canaan, but uncertain what this entry refers to.

1765 Jonathan Vangorden—have not been able to locate any information on this individual.

1766 Myron Scoville, youngest son of Ira and Ruth Scoville.

1767 Dr. Benjamin Welch, doctor of Norfolk, Litchfield, Connecticut. He had nine children, five sons—all became doctors, and all settled in Norfolk.

1810 October—to two days work at corn apples.[1768]
September in 1811—to weaving [ ] half.
October—to weaving eleven & half yrd [ ] it first 1892[1769]

1814—to weaving twenty one & half.
May—to weaving twenty yrds forty cloth at a shilling per yrd.
November - Roger Foot
to work at your flax.
to one day at clay morter.
to one day chopping wood.
to one day at your cow hous.
to one Tap Yoke.[1770]

1814 continued . . .
to one days work.
to earthen ware.
to one roster.[1771]
to one bushel potatoes.
to one day chopping.
to one day chopping.
to helping butcher cow.
to five dollars in the way of deal (the rest is illegible).

May 1802—begin six months work for Roger Foot for seventy-five dollars.[1772]
absent two days and a half.
absent one day to mend fence.
to fourteen shillings in part.
pay for plow agreed upon.
absent half a day after shoes.
absent half a day sick.[1773]
absent half a day at brush meadow.
absent three days moing.[1774]
December 27, 1802 then recond with Roger foot all book accounts and found due to me

1768 I have been unsuccessful in finding out if there was such a thing as a "corn apple." This entry may simply mean "to two days work at corn and apples."

1769 This could be a measurement of the woven cloth.

1770 Uncertain what the term "tap yoke" is referring to.

1771 Rooster.

1772 You will note that Ira uses the currency "dollars" but will then revert back to old money terms (pence, shilling, etc.).

1773 First mention of not being able to work due to illness.

1774 Mowing.

nineteen and nine pence, as witness our hands. (signed Roger Foot).

February 1, 1803—to one days chopping wood.
to cash paid to huldah grisoud.[1775]
(page torn) one day making Taptrous.[1776]
(page torn) days work at wall.

Samuel Ovet[1777]
To five hundred bushels of cole at three dollars per hundred.

December 7, 1802—Elias Balcan[1778]
to one day shoat[1779] you say.
by marchant [sic] goods.[1780]
by one bushel and half corn.
by one bushel oats.

August 1804—Joseph Schovel[1781]
to one day cradling.
to one day moing.
to cradling ots.
to one day and half ditching.
to cradling buck wheat.
November 30—to one day work at wall.
to one day work at wall.

July—to two days moing.
to one day moing.
to cradling four half acre ry.
to cradling acre and 1 quarter ots.

---

1775 Possibly the Huldah Griswold of "Norfolk" who was born in 1843 and died in 1935. There were other Huldah Griswolds, but the one mentioned here seems the likely choice.

1776 I have found only one reference of this word in a book entitled *Historical Notices and Records of the Village and Parish of Fincham, in the County of Norfolk* (England—my note), by the Rev. William Blyth, M.A. This book is in both Latin and English. The book states that "taptrous" is a tap trough, which the *Oxford Languages* describes as "a long, narrow open container for animals to eat or drink out of."

1777 Perhaps the Samuel Oviatt who was from Goshen, Connecticut, and died in 1805.

1778 Perhaps the Elias Balcomb who resided in Norfolk, Connecticut.

1779 Shoat = a young, weaned pig.

1780 Purchasing goods from a merchant.

1781 Possibly the Joseph Scoville of Harwinton (*Ezekiel,[2] Stephen,[1] Arthur)* but more likely the Joseph Scoville of Cornwall (*Samuel,[2] Stephen,[1] Arthur)* who had married Lomhomah (Loru) Chapin? 5 July 1782.

January 15, 1806—then recond with Joseph Schovel and found due to him two and six pence to balance book (signed Joseph Scovill).

July—to one day moing.
to two days cradling.
to cradling one acre and half.
to moing half a day.
(the rest of the page is too faded to read).

July 3—Roger Foot.
by cash.
by oxen to get Ithamar[1782] gran.
by three days moing.
by cash for vinegar.

August 7—by cash
by one days of your oxen.
by two days your oxen to plow.
by oxen half a day.
by oxen to drag one day
by oxen to drag.
by oxen to fetch cyder.
by oxen to fetch apples.
by oxen to draw wood.
by hors to rid to town.
by oxen to draw wood.
by oxen and boy to cows.
by oxen part of the day.
by oxen half a day to sled wood.
December 27, 1802 this credit recond by cash.
by cash to bestsa Pettibone.[1783]
Continued . . .

by cash to John Beach.

January 4, 1802—Deacon Mills[1784]
by eight pound chees
(rest of this page is blank).

---

1782 The Ithamar mentioned here is likely Ira's brother, Ithamar: "by oxen to get Ithamar grain."

1783 Betsy Pettibone—probably connected to the Pettibone family in either Norfolk or Cornwall, Connecticut.

1784 Deacon Mills

1801—Levi T[h]om[p]son[1785]
to half a hide wt [ ]
April 15—to ten pound on half sugar.
to two gallons and half molasses.

January 1802—to cash Myron[1786]
June 1801—timothy schovel[1787]
to fetching slabs from Canaan.[1788]
to two days work on barn.
to one days work on barn.
to one days work under barn pinnin.

January 1, 1806—took one heifer to fodder.[1789]
February 20—begin fodder oxen and mares and cow.
March 16—left foddering timothy schovels cattle.
March 21—left of foddering heifer.
stephen schovel[1790]
to four shoats.

March 31, 1820—Jonathan Stroke[1791]
To two quarts whiskey.
Balance due paid in cash.
Find all charges paid by Stroke. I the undersigned certify to this to be a true account is near as I am capable of judging. (signed Myron Scoville).

(there is a page of "doodles" where the name Ira Scoville was written over and over again)
(page torn) and eight bushels wheat [ ].
timothy[1792] ry ground 5 bushels peck thr (the rest is illegible).

---

1785 Levi Thomson—too many men by this name to be able to discern which one is mentioned here.

1786 Myron Scoville—son of Ira, keeper of this account book.

1787 Timothy Scoville—this is probably in reference to Ira's father, Timothy, as opposed to his brother, who is said to have left Cornwall, Connecticut, in 1801.

1788 Canaan, Litchfield, Connecticut.

1789 This is in reference to feeding the livestock.

1790 This is probably Ira's uncle, the brother of his father, Timothy.

1791 This entry is when Ira and his family were residing in Hector, NY. There was a Christopher *Stork* in Cornwall. Anna Scoville (*Samuel,[2] Stephen,[1] Arthur)* married Christopher Stork "of Cornwall." This couple also removed to New York. I have not been able to locate a "Jonathan Stroke" in the records. His last name may actually be "*Stork.*"

1792 If this entry was recorded while in New York, then the Timothy mentioned here would be Ira's brother.

timothy had ten bushels more.
timothy had put up ry.
(there is other writing on this page, but it is illegible).

May 1804—Joseph Schovel
by six pound wheat flr.
by twelve pound & half veal.
by one bushel of ry.
by half a bushel of wheat.

September 7, by cash.
by wheat flower [sic] six pound.
by one bushel of ry.
by one bushel of ry.
by one bushel of buck wheat.
by one bushel of ry.
(this entry continues with mentioning bushels of rye, wheat flour and twelve pounds of veal).

July 3—by bushel of ry.
July 19—by one bushel of ry.
By payment to deming.[1793]
October 12—by two pound of butter.
by two pound 1 quarter butter.
by one dinner pot price.
by one dish kettle price.
(the next page is torn at the top and the date is unknown for the following entry)

to half [ ]
to one day moing.
to one day moing.
to half a day cone from corn.[1794]
to part of a day stacking.
to part of a day for ox work whip.
to half a days work on follar.
to one days work by Berry Beach.[1795]

---

1793 There were many Deming families in Litchfield County. It is not known which Deming he is referring to here.

1794 "Cone from corn"—Unknown meaning.

1795 The name "Berry" could be a nickname as I have not found anyone with that name through the regular sources. There were a number of Beach/Beech names in Norfolk, Connecticut, during the time period of these entries.

to one day plowing follar.
to cash for tramming.[1796]
to one day plowing follar.
to one day dragging follar.
to have a day cutting wood.
to two days work at flax.
to one day by Ithamar flax.

August 1801—then recond with Roger Foot and balance all book accounts [ ] to pay [ ] signed by Roger Foot.

Timothy Schovel
September 1, 1804—to thrashing one bushel wheat.
to thrashing 4 bushel ry.
to thrashing two bushel 2 quarts ry.
by one bushel of ry to eat.
to thrashing three bushel wheat.
to thrashing one bushel and half of ry.

Stephen Schovel[1797]
by one four quarter veal wt.
by one bushel corn.
by two shad.
by one hin(d) quarter veal wt. eighteen pound.
by five bushel potatoes.

March 31, 1820—Daniel Tyler.[1798]
to half pint whiskey.
to two quarts whiskey.
to half pint whiskey.
to one quart whiskey.
to one half pint whisky (page torn)
to half pint whiskey.
in co. with knox.[1799]
to one gil to Isaac.[1800]

---

1796 This word could be "trimming."

1797 This reference is likely the uncle of Ira Scoville.

1798 Ira's daughter Amanda married a Lewis Tyler, and they had a son named Daniel; however, this can't be the same Daniel (son of Amanda and Lewis) as he was born in 1823 in NY. The Daniel Tyler mentioned here could be a relative of Lewis Tyler.

1799 I take this to mean "in company with Knox." Without a first name, it would be difficult to discover who this is.

1800 The Webster's dictionary gives a definition of the word "gill" as a unit of liquid measure.

to one pint whiskey.
(the rest of the page is torn).

____ew Morhons.[1801]
to weaving thirty yrd quarter.
to weaving six half yrds.
to weaving 28 yrds.

November 28, 1804—Benjamin Carier.[1802]
To two days chopping wood.
January 1807—to chopping two thirds of day.
to going to goshen with boots.[1803]

October 1809—Sasa Brown.[1804]
to going to Canaan.
January 1810—at three shillings per week.
November—to going to Norfolk for ____actor.[1805]
____ber—to paing Oliver hotchkin[1806] cash.
April 17, 1812—to one order five dollars on Edward burrels stor.[1807]
July 20, 1813—to six sheep at 8 shillings.

May 1820—Aaron Burges[1808]
to one quart of whiskey.
all settled.

February 3, 1807—Joshua Chace
to one load of wood price.
to one load of wood.

May 1813—Joel Harrison[1809]

---

1801 Possibly Matthew Morhons?

1802 There was a Benjamin Carrier in Cornwall, Connecticut. A possible relation to Elisha Carrier who married Lodemia Scoville?

1803 Goshen, Litchfield, Connecticut.

1804 The name is clearly written "SaSa." This is perhaps a nickname.

1805 Tractor?

1806 Oliver Hotchkin is probably Oliver Hotchkiss—my fourth great-grandfather.

1807 Edward Burrell's store.

1808 The surname could be "Burgess." The 1820 census for Hector, Tompkins, New York, lists an Aaron Burgess with a family of six.

1809 The Harrisons were from Cornwall, Litchfield, Connecticut. The Harrisons' and the Scovilles' land bordered each other during the time that they resided there. Joel Harrison was the

to Ira Schovel for Dimes[1810] work.
nine days muslin.
to washen and shirrin 13 sheep.
to one day repairing fence.
settled up and paid.
March 5, 1842—(rest of the page is blank).

May 1803—Benony Mills[1811]
To a calf [ ].

November 1804—Jason Cole[1812]
to work.
to sledding wood one day.
November 1805—recond and [ ] to me six shillings.
to work on barrick.

February 1806—
to chopping maple tree.
to one day laing wall.
to one day at hay.
to cradling.
Cornwall October I, 1806
then recond with Jason Cole and found due to him sixteen shillings to balance book.
(Signed Jason Cowles).

November
to repairing fence.
to carrying one lod of hay.
to [ ] two chains.
to sledding cyder to Canaan.
to butchering hogs.
to thrashing wheat and having (haying?).
to thrashing ry carrying to Canaan.
to half day cutting sprouts.

May 10—to one quarter of veal wt. 17–8.

---

son of Daniel Harrison and Hannah Barker. Joel married Hannah Beardsley and went to Amenia, New York. E. C. Starr's, *History of Cornwall*, 469.

1810 Uncertain what this term means.

1811 A Benoni Mills (1767–1850) resided in Norfolk, Litchfield, Connecticut.

1812 There was a Jason Cowles/Coles born in 1762 in Colebrook, Litchfield, Connecticut. It is uncertain if this is the same person.

April 1811—to weaving 18 yards 3 quarter.
June 18, Daniel Case.[1813]
Daniel case by 4 pound of Butter.
By David Smoke.[1814]

July 1801—Ithamar Bailey[1815]
to weaving 1 [ ] half.
to weaving 11 and quarter.
Ithamar B.
Oliver Hoskin.

November 5, 1805
to three quarters of a day work chopping.
to one day hoing.
August 21 1806—by agreement (written in the margin of the book "agreed upon with Oliver.")
to cradling two acre three quarter ots at three shilling per acre.

for Abraham hodskin
March 1807—for one day picking corn by Joseph (torn)
to two hundred and thirty hoop poles.[1816]
March 11, 1815 –
to one day sledding wood
to one quarter of veal wt 19.
to two load of wood.
to carrying a lod of wood and fetchin cyder.
to one whip Lask[1817] to your father.
to three bushel flax seed.
to one day sledding wood.

---

1813 The *Case* name is numerous—particularly in Hartford County, Connecticut. Some of them migrated to Litchfield County (CT). There were three "Daniel Cases" in Simsbury (CT) on the 1790 census and a Daniel Case in Hector, NY, in 1820.

1814 The name "Smoke" is a variation of Smoak/Smock. A David Smoke shows up on page 409 with Ira Scoville in 1820 (census) and the next page lists a Jacob Smoke.

1815 I have not been able to find this individual in any of the usual sources.

1816 Hoop poles were "long, straight rods, cut in the woods from ash, hickory, hazel, and white oak saplings or from bushes that had been specifically pruned for the purpose. While they might be cut in spring or fall, farmers often processed them in midwinter, when they were less busy. The bark and shoots, had to be removed. The poles were used on the farm for many tasks, such as rollers to move heavy loads and for temporary floors under haystacks." From: Old Ridgefield (Connecticut). January 30, 2007. www.naturegeezer.com/2007/01/hoop-pole.com.

1817 I have not found a definition of a "whip lask."

to one day sledding wood.

June 5, 1812—to weaving 37 yards and a half at seven pence per yard.
October 15—to weaving 19 and a half at seven pence per yard.
April 4, 1813—then recond with Oliv (torn) and found dew to him to Balance all bo(ook?) acts to this day two pounds and eight shi(illings) (signed Olivir (torn).[1818]

July—to cradling two acre one quarter to pasterin[1819] ram 13 weeks.
November third 1841 (?).
To weaving 26 yards and at eight pound per.

Rachel Harrison[1820]
by douglas half a day chopping.[1821]
by hoing half a day
by hoing one day.
by abner hotchkin 3 quarters of day.
by douglas helping me cart.
by douglas two days hain.
by Isaac feens two days hain.[1822]

April 30—by four hundred of quarter hay.
by three pigs.
by half veal.
by douglas half a day plow.
by one pound 3 quarters butter.
by work.
by five pound cheese half.
by one pound butter.
by three pounds and half butter.
by two pounds hog fat.
by calf skin manda shoes.[1823]

1818 This entry is likely referring to Oliver Hotchkiss.

1819 Pasturing.

1820 Rachel Johnson Harrison was the wife of Luther Harrison, who had been born in Branford, New Haven, Connecticut, son of Daniel Harrison and Hannah Barker. Luther Harrison died 20 February 1813 (probably from the "spotted fever" epidemic). His will confirms that Joel Harrison was his brother, and his father was Daniel. Ira Scoville's land bordered southerly on Luther Harrison's in Cornwall. At the time of this entry, Rachel Harrison was likely a widow.

1821 "Douglas" may be a hired hand.

1822 No information on this person.

1823 This is likely referencing making shoes for his daughter, Amanda, and Ira's wife, Ruth. Asa Burr was the town's shoemaker.

by one pair of shoes for wife.
October 26—Number of bushels of wheat raised in 1831 (very faint writing).
March 9—Mr. Yapbie to thirteens bushels of ashes.

April 18, 1808—Thaddeus Ford[1824]
To one nine quarter veal wt thirteen pound one quarter.
Dagan (?) Store.[1825]
by Joel had a day killing [ ].
by one day cradling.
by one gallon of rum.
by two pound thirteen oz butter.
[ ] by found pound butter.
by one day chopping wood.
by work at stable.
by twenty three pound pork.

Luther Harrison.
by making salool (?)
by four pound quarter chees.
by one bushel ry loved (loafs?)
by [ ] a day chopping.
(next line torn and illegible).
[ ] wagon to camp.
[ ] 19, 1801.

This is the end of the account book of Ira Scoville. He may have continued keeping accounts while he lived in New York and Ohio, but those books did not survive.

Reading these entries may seem tedious; however, they reveal how many of our male ancestors spent their days (it's a shame that there isn't the same type of book kept by the women of these same ancestors), working for other people.

Ira Scoville's son, Myron, also kept an account book, which is also in my possession. Myron writes on the front page that the book was purchased February 184____ in Hector, New York and seems to end in 1859. There are many names noted through his time living in Hector, New York, Penfield, Ohio and Amboy Township, Michigan. Myron's account book uses dollars and cents for each job performed. Here is one example:

1824 Thaddeus Ford was of Cornwall and was listed on the 1790 tax rate bill. He married Sarah_____ and they had the following children: Levi, Polly, and Tabitha. In early days he had a spinning mill in Cornwall Hollow.

1825 A general store that was located in Cornwall or Norfolk, Connecticut.

Penfield—October 14, 1847
I. B. Scovill cr. ("cr." stands for credit)
To 5 pound of pork 61. . . . . . . . . . 30¢
To 7 p 11 oz of pork. . . . . . . . . . . . 48¢
To one pig. . . . . . . . . . . . . . . . . . . . 75¢

Here are two examples of the account books that are in my possession. The first is a well-worn page from Ira Schovel's [sic] book and the second is a drawing from Myron Scovill's account book. Perhaps this is a rendition of a home he was planning to build.

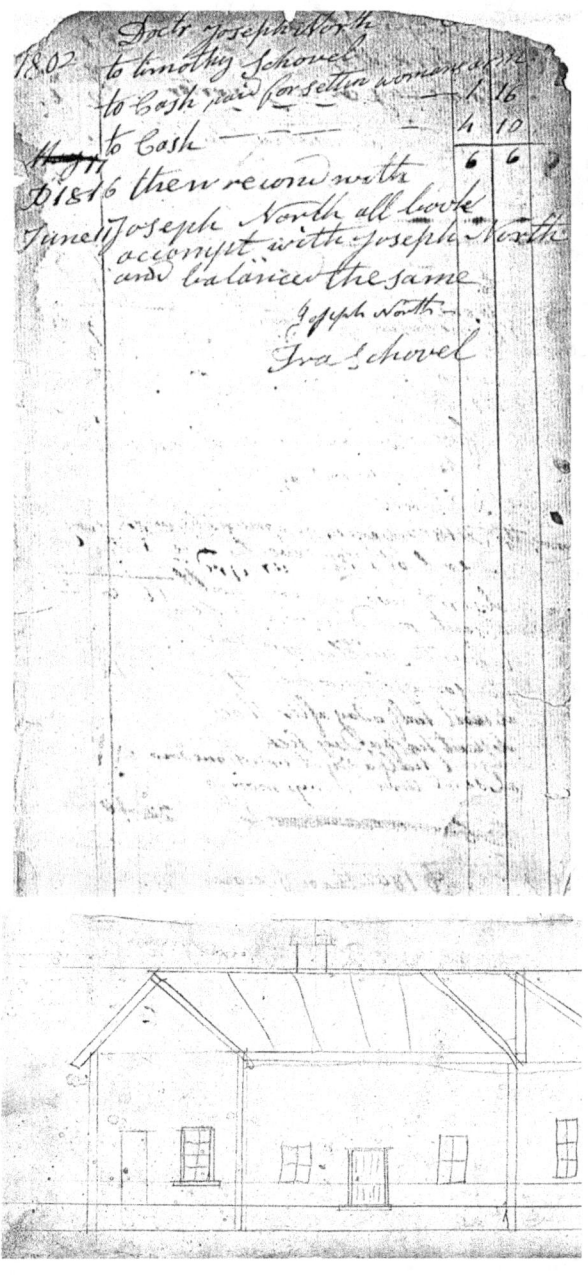

Doctr Joseph North
1802 to timothy Schovel
to Cash paid for setten | 1 | 16
to Cash | 4 | 10
| 6 | 6
1816 then recond with
June 11 Joseph North all book
accompt with Joseph North
and balanced the same
Joseph North
Ira Schovel

# Index

Please note that birthdates are provided when necessary in order to disambiguate similar names. Also, the use of *née* indicates a woman's patronym assigned at birth.


**A**

Abrams, David, 74
Abrams, Jerusha (née Knapp), 74
account books
 of Ira Scoville, 56, 400–419
 of Myron Scoville, 418–419
Ackerson, Martha Clark. *See* Main, Martha Clark
Adam, Abigal, 255
Adam, John, 255
Adam, William, 255
Adams, Carrie (née Benson), 184–187
Adams, Charles E., 186–187
Ahsley, Howard W., 327
Allen, Elijah, 23
Allen, Joseph, 22
Anderson, Ruth Marie (née Kelsey), 291
Andrews, Roxalana/Roxylana. *See* Dean, Roxalana/Roxylana
Apperson, James, 250
Apperson, Jane (née McCausland), 250
Apperson, Margaret Estella. *See* Scoville, M. Estella
Ashely, Irene Mitchell (née Scoville). *See* Burnett, Irene Mitchell
Ashley, Agnes C. (née Moffatt), 323–326
Ashley, Albert, 317
Ashley, Elizabeth, 317
Ashley, Frank, 333
Ashley, Frank V. C., 319–321, 329, 332–335
Ashley, Harry Tate, 361
Ashley, Howard (b. 1862), 247, 316–325, 328, 330
Ashley, Howard Burnett (b. 1894), 309, 318–319, 329, 331–334
Ashley, Howard Wesley (b. 1929), 333–334
Ashley, Iola, 317
Ashley, James, 316–317
Ashley, Laura G. (née Kilpatrick), 331–332
Ashley, Mary (née Moore), 316–317
Ashley, Minnie Irene 1(née Scoville). *See* Linberg, Minnie Irene Ashley
Ashley, Rhoda E. *See* Holmes, Rhoda Ellsworth
Ashley, Ruth (née Dover), 332–334
Athorne, Pearl. *See* Billian, Pearl

**B**

Bachelor, Artemisia (née Heath), 140
Bachelor, Celinda. *See* Kelsey, Celinda
Bachelor, Jeremiah, 140
Bachelor, Lyman, 140
Bachelor, Nelson, 140, 142
Badker, Emma Marie. *See* Gilbert, Emma Marie
Baile, Freda, 275
Baile, Samuel Girven, 275
Bailie, Edward E., 275
Bailie, Everett G., 275
Bailie, Mary Hartford (née Elliot), 273–275
Baird, Andrew, 157, 164
Baird, Anna, 164–165
Baird, Jane (wife of Andrew Baird), 157
Baird, Jane (wife of William Fuller). *See* Fuller, Jane
Baird, Sarah. *See* Scoville, Sarah
Baker, Barbara Winslow, 345
Baker, Sarah. *See* Church, Sarah
Ball, Esther (née Hall), 260
Ball, Jessie Maud. *See* Scoville, Jessie Maud
Ball, Sylvester, 260
Barber, Mindwell. *See* Scoville, Mindwell

Bartelli, Catherine Irene "Kay" (née Miller), 330, 334
Bartelli, Donald "Don," 330
Bear, Lydia Rebecca. *See* Scovill, Lydia Rebecca
Beckwith, Lucy. *See* Scoville, Lucy
Beckwith, Mary (née Scoville) (b. 1720), 15
Bemis, Alice Marie, 114–115
Bemis, Amelia, 113
Bemis, Anna, 114
Bemis, Asaph S., 112
Bemis, Caroline Amelia (née Scovill) (b. 1822), 110, 112–114
Bemis, Edward, 114
Bemis, Elijah St. John, 112–114
Bemis, George A., 115
Bemis, Helen Marion. *See* Wilkes, Helen Marion
Bemis, Katherine "Kate" (née Starkey), 114
Bemis, Margaret K. (née St. John), 112
Bemis, Mary Townsend. *See* Parsons, Mary Townsend
Bemis, Philo S. (son of Philo Scovill Bemis), 114
Bemis, Philo Scovill (b. 1840), 113–114
Bennett, Charles M., 363
Bennett, Clara Marian. *See* Scoville, Clara Marian
Bennett, Mary, 363
Benson, Alice M. *See* Kolling, Alice M.
Benson, Carrie. *See* Adams, Carrie
Benson, Clarissa (née Kelsey), 138, 181–190
Benson, Henry N., 279–282
Benson, Horace, 184, 280
Benson, Howard, 282
Benson, Isaac, 181–182, 187
Benson, Jane (née Bowker), 181
Benson, Juliette. *See* Young, Juliette
Benson, Niles Horace "Henry," 182, 187
Benson, Olive (b. 1896), 282
Benson, Olive I. (née Stowell) (b.1844), 279–282
Benson, Sherman S., 280–282
Benson, Sophie (née Kolling), 282
Benson, Susan Jane. *See* Elliott, Susan Jane
Benson, William, 138, 144, 182–190
Berfeld, Rosetta. *See* Hedges, Rosetta
Berfield, Robert George Raidart, 383, 385–386
Billian, Ada Louise (née Church). *See* Jenks, Ada Louise
Billian, Agnes L. (née Case) (b. 1889), 304, 375
Billian, Agnes Mary (b. 1876). *See* Kumm, Agnes Mary
**Billian, Agnes R.** (née Scoville) (b. 1859), 222–223, 227–229, 231–232, 296–304, 371, 376, 380–381
Billian, Carolina, 303
Billian, Caroline Linnea (née Hallden), 304, 378–383
Billian, Clarence, grandchild of Gammerdinger, 231–232
Billian, Eleanor Rose, 383
**Billian, Ernest Clarence** (b. 1897), 231–232, 302–304, 371, 378–383
Billian, Ferdinand, 229, 232, 298–304, 371
Billian, Frederick Joe "Fred Joe" (b. 1878), 299–301, 303–304, 374–379
Billian, Howard Ernest (b. 1918), 303, 380–382
Billian, Katharina (née Geiger), 232
Billian, Kenneth E., 383
Billian, Leonard F., 383
Billian, Lila-Jeanne (née Butler), 383
Billian, Marjorie, 383
Billian, Mildred L. F. (née Timbrell), 382
Billian, Pearl (née Athorne), 383
Billian, Raymond Church (b. 1901), 231–232, 375–378
Billian, Raymond E. (b.1933), 383
**Billian, Russell Edward**, 382
Billian Catherina (née Geiger), 298
Bissel, Herman, 134
Bissell, Ethel June (née Carrier), 134
Bissell, Grace (née McClintock), 134

Bissell, Sylvester Loy, 134
Bixby, Benjamin, 107–108
Bixby, Jemima. *See* Scoville, Jemima
Bixby, Margaret (née Walker), 107–108
Blake, Jane. *See* Elliot, Jane
Bockway, John, 15
Borden, Elizabeth (née Scoville), d.o. Arthur, 3–5, 7–8
Borden, Sarah. *See* Rogers, Sarah
Borden, William, 4–5, 7–8
Bosker, Jane. *See* Benson, Jane
Bowen, Maud. *See* Roys, Maud
Bozian, Nuvart. *See* Jingozian, Nuvart
Brackley, Bertha (née Pero), 353–355
Brackley, Victor R., 355
Brady, Marjorie (née Miller), 324, 329
Brannen, Alice. *See* Carr, Alice
Breckenridge, Hazel Blance (née Farmer), 89
Bremer, Sophie. *See* Kolling, Sophie
Brockway, Hannah. *See* Champion, Hannah
Brockway, Sarah (née Scoville), 15
Bronson, Jemima. *See* Kelsey, Jemima
Brown, Barbara Winslow. *See* Baker, Barbara Winslow
Brown, Donal Claflin, 345
Brown, Elias, 287
Brown, Elizabeth Amy. *See* Smith, Elizabeth Amy
Brown, Elizabeth (née Winnek), 345
Brown, Emma (née Hudson), 287
Brown, Frank Elias, 287
Brown, Harold Edward, 344–345
Brown, Ida May (née Flint), 211, 287
Brown, Joseph Winslow, 345
Brown, Laura Katherine. *See* Christianson, Laura Katherine
Brown, Marjorie (née Nash), 344–345
Brown, Richard Nash, 345
Brown, Roy William, 287
Brown, Virginia (née Thayer), 367
Bubier, Caroline Elizabeth. *See* Claflin, Caroline Elizabeth
Bubier, Francis Kennard, 338, 340
Bubier, Frank Breed, 338
Bubier, Kenneth, 338
Bubier, Paul Morgan, 338, 340
Bubier, Sylvester, 338
Buck, Amanda (née Hoyt), 199–201
Buck, Amy, 201
Buck, Anson, 198
Buck, Ben, 199
Buck, Charles, 199–200
Buck, David, 198, 201
Buck, Esther (née Springsteen), 198
Buck, Harry, 200–201
Buck, Jane, 198
Buck, Jesse, 200–201, 205
Buck, Lester W., 144, 189, 198–204
Buck, Melissa (née Kelsey). *See* Garlow, Melissa
Buck, Nellie, 199–201
Buck, Rosey, 200
Buck, Willie, 201
Burnett, Irene Mitchell (née Scoville), 361
Burnett, Paul Dover, 361
Burnham, Oliver, 33
Burnham, Sarah (née Rogers), 33
Butler, Lila-Jeanne. *See* Billian, Lila-Jeanne


C


Cafferty, Agnes Mary (née Billian). *See* Kumm, Agnes Mary
Cafferty, Charles C., 304, 370–372
Carier, Mary, 93
Caris, Catherine. *See* Edson, Catherine
Carlsdotter, Charlotta. *See* Hallden, Charlotta
Carlson, Karonlina Charlotta. *See* Halden, Karolina Charlotta
Carr, Alice (née Brannen), 356
Carr, Florence Mabel (née Scoville), 355–357
Carr, Lewis French, 356
Carr, William Louis, 355–357
Carrier, Alice L. *See* Glass, Alice L.
Carrier, Andrew, 25
Carrier, Arthur W., 131
Carrier, Betsy (née Weeks), 92

Carrier, Darrius, 93
Carrier, Edna B., 132
Carrier, Edson Stuart, 133
Carrier, Elisha, 55, 90–93, 126, 128–130
Carrier, Elizabeth "Betsy," 92–93
Carrier, Elmer Edson, 131–132
Carrier, Ethel June. *See* Bissell, Ethel June
Carrier, Frederick Emerson, 133
Carrier, Frederick L., 132–133
Carrier, George W., 92
Carrier, Harold R., 131
Carrier, Harry E., 131
Carrier, Helen M. (née Jones), 92
Carrier, Jennie (née Koon), 132
Carrier, Joseph Lucius, 128–131
Carrier, Lillie, 92
Carrier, Lodema (née Scoville), 55–57, 93, 100–102, 126–134
Carrier, Lola E. (née Cook), 131
Carrier, Lorain, 92
Carrier, Lucile M., 131
Carrier, Lucius, 127–130
Carrier, Mary, 92
Carrier, Mary M (née Edson), 130–131
Carrier, Myra, 92
Carrier, Newton E., 92
Carrier, Nina B., 92
Carrier, Orilla "Amelia/Aurelia" (née Emerson), 128–130
Carrier, Rufus, 92, 127–128
Carrier, S. Gertrude (née Little), 132–133
Carrier, Stuart, 133
Carrier, Triphene/Triphena (née Scoville), 30, 35, 90–93, 126
Carroll, Margaret. *See* Miller, Margaret
Case, Agnes L. *See* Billian, Agnes L.
Case, Arthur J., 353
Case, Bertha (née Page), 353
Case, Charles M., 375
Case, Florence Ann. *See* Grassman, Florence Ann
Case, Hester Kelsey (née Scoville). *See* Rich, Hester Kelsey
Case, Leonie J. (née Thorpe), 375
Case, Lucinda. *See* Cowles, Lucinda
Case, Nathan Gardner, 46
Chamberlain, Miriam. *See* Scoville, Miriam
Chambers, Katherine E. (née Kuster), 367, 369
Chambers, Ray, 369
Champion, Hannah (née Brockway), 9
Champion, Henry, 9, 14
Champion, Sarah. *See* Scoville, Sarah
Champion, Thomas, 10
Chapman, Hester. *See* Kelsey, Hester
Charlton, Elsie G. (née Elliot), 273–274, 277–278
Charlton, Oliver Adair, 274, 277–278
Chase, Maria/Mary Susan M. *See* Little, Maria/Mary Susan M.
Christianson, Laura Katherine (née Brown), 287
Church, Ada Louise. *See* Jenks, Ada Louise
Church, Elijah, 375
Church, Sarah (née Baker), 375
Civil War
- Benson, Henry N., 279–280, 282
- Benson, Isaac, 187–188
- Benson, William, 182–183
- Carrier, Darrius, 93
- Carrier, George W., 92
- Enrollment Act of 1863, 130
- Farmer, Charles Gudson, 89
- Garlow, John W., 207
- Garlow, William, 207
- Kelsey, Philo, 213
- pensions for children of veterans killed in action, 292
- Salisbury Furnace and, 95
- Scovil, Edward J., 89
- Scovill, Ancil Milo, 87
- Scovill, Edward A., 111
- Scovill, Milo, 84
- Scovill, Ransom, 85
- **Scoville, Charles Martin**, 223–227, 242–243
- Scoville, Henry C., 123

Scoville, James a., 159–160
Scoville, William Harrison (b. 1839), 227, 242–243
Young, Abram, 188
Claflin, Anna J. *See* Quick, Anna J.
Claflin, Caroline Elizabeth (née Morgan). *See* Davis, Caroline "Carrie" Elizabeth
Claflin, Charles R. B., Sr., 253
Claflin, Charles Ripley Burnett, Jr., 253, 335–345
Claflin, Cora Irene (née Scoville), 249–250, 253, 335–345
Claflin, Ella Mary (née Tinker), 337–338
Claflin, Emma (née Locke), 253, 340
Claflin, Grace H. *See* Nash, Grace H.
Claflin, Josie, 336
Claflin, Marie Gertrude. *See* Moore, Marie Gertrude
Claflin, Maud, 340
Claflin, Minnie M. Rockwood (née Usher), 337
Claflin, Walter M., 336, 343
Clark, Mary Victoria. *See* Scovill, Mary Victoria
Clark(e), Adeline. *See* Scovill, Adeline
Clemmons, Clarissa (née Scoville), 63–66
Clemmons, Mary E., 65
Clemmons, Philo, 63–65
Clemons, Lyman, 64–65
Clough, Lizzie (née Dunn), 242
colonial life in America
census records, 24–25
childhood mortality, 11
Cold Summer of 1816, 60
courtship and marriage, 25, 34, 54, 66
daily life of settlers, 27
early homes, 26–27
Gunter Chain measurements, 42
hired help in the home, 14, 25
land transfers, 61
male versus female responsibilities, 17, 24, 44–45
military service, 36–39
movements of, 41–43, 67
naming customs of children, 6–7
religious life, 43–44
road systems, 7n9, 26
role of ministry in, 23, 23n51
settlement of Western Lands, 22–23, 26
support of paupers, 49
warnings out of town, 49
women as guardians of their children, 17n32
Conley, Eunice G. "Scovill," 314–315
Connecticut Western Reserve, 61–62, 127
Cook, Lillian, 131
Cook, Lola E. *See* Carrier, Lola e.
Cook, Mary. *See* Scoville, Mary
Cornell, Carrie E. *See* Main, Carrie E.
Corning, Charles Solon, 116
Corning, Kate (née Scovill), 116
Corning, Warren Scovill, 116
Cornish, Sarah. *See* Steele, Sarah
Cotton, Helen Margaret (née Kelsey), 291
Cowell, Edward, 290
Cowell, Isabel. *See* Kelsey, Isabel "Belle"
Cowell, Margaret, 290
Cowles, Elizabeth "Betsy." *See* Kelsy, Elizabeth "Betsy"
Cowles, Elon, 144, 212
Cowles, Lucinda (née Case), 212, 289
Cowles, Ruth. *See* Knapp, Ruth
Cowles Lucinda (née Case), 144
Craig, Ella Mary. *See* Claflin, Ella Mary
Crawford, Cynthia. *See* Scovill, Cynthia
Crocker, Alice (née Swift), 24–25
Crocker, James, 24–25
Crocker, James (son of James), 25
Crocker, Jonathtan, 27
Crocker, Levi, 27
Crocker, Thankful. *See* Scoville, Thankful
Cummings, Bertha L. (née Farmer), 89
Cummings, Ellen Maria, 345
Cushing, Edward Theodore, 167, 174, 270–272
Cushing, Martha, 270
Cushing, Mary Jane (née Scoville), 125, 157,

162, 167, 169, 264, 270–272
Cushing, Natalie S., 270–272
Cushing, Nathan, 270

D

Daniel, Christine H., 342
Davidson, Alveretta (née Garlow), 206–208, 210
Davidson, Burt, 207
Davis, Caroline "Carrie" Elizabeth (née Morgan), 338–340
Davis, Ira B., 339
de Scoville, Ralph, 1–2
Dean, Amasa, 95
Dean, Anne, 94
Dean, Joel, 97
Dean, Lydia, 95
Dean, Roxalana/Roxylana (née Andrews), 25–26, 35, 93, 101–106, 121
Dean, Ruben, 35, 56, 93–105, 121
Dean, Ruth, 94
Dean, Sarah, 95
Dean, Seth, 93–94
Dean Benajah, 95
Dean Joel, 95
Dean Seth, 95
Decker, Rena. *See* Scovill, Rena
Deming, Alice B. (née Raidart), 234–239
Deming, Alice Maude. *See* Raidart, Alice Maude
Deming, Amaret (née Spencer), 238
Deming, Bessie A. (née White), 240
Deming, Daniel, 305
Deming, Earl Lewis, 238, 240
Deming, Faith, 240
Deming, George Gilbert, Jr., 304
Deming, Grace E., 239
Deming, Grove Walter, 237–240
Deming, Grove Walter, Jr., 240
Deming, Harvey, 238
Deming, Irene, 240
Deming, Jenette (née Woodward), 304
Deming, John Allen (b. 1854), 236–240
Deming, John (b. 1615), 305
Deming, Marilla Irene (née Moore), 240
Deming, Marion G. (née Waite). *See* Deming, Marion G.
Deming, Ralph Spencer, 239–240
Deming, Spencer, 240
Dennison, Harriett. *See* Scovill, Harriet
Dennison, Matilda. *See* Main, Matilda
Dickey, Marjorie (née Miller), 331
Dickey, Robert A., 331
Dodge, Sophia. *See* Knapp, Sophia
Doolittle, Sally. *See* Sullivan, Sally
Doughty, Marshall Kevin, 353
Doughty, Paula (née Grassman), 353
Douglas, Benajah, 22
Dover, Emiline Elizabeth (née Penn), 332
Dover, Ruth. *See* Ashley, Ruth
Dover, Solomon Wesley, 332
Duff, Marie Gertrude (née Moore), 337, 337n1396
Duff, Valentine S., 337n1396
Duffey, Edith Arminda (née Scovill), 87
Duffey, Otis, 87
Duncan, Kenneth, 384
Duncan, Mary Armeada (née Stacy), 384
Dunham, Mary Ann. *See* Flint, Mary Ann
Dunn, Lizzie. *See* Clough, Lizzie
Dunn, Mary Catherine. *See* Scoville, Mary Catherine
Dunn, Nellie. *See* Morin, Nellie
Dutton, Rebecca, 16n28
Dyer, Mary Ellen (née Weed), 361
Dyer, Mary Josephine. *See* Scoville, Mary Josephine
Dyer, Otis Theron, 361, 363
Dyer, Zenas, 147–148

E

Eaton, Carl, 290
Eaton, Dora, 290
Eaton, Eula Carrie (née Kelsey), 289–290
Eaton, Francis, 290
Eaton, Gertrude, 290

Eaton, Maurice, 290
Eaton, Priscilla (née Seely), 289
Eaton, William Phillip, 289–290
Eddinger, Nancy M. *See* Scovill, Nancy M.
Edson, Benjamin O., 130
Edson, Catherine (née Caris), 130
Edson, Mary M. *See* Carrier, Mary M.
Elliot, Albert C., 274
Elliot, Clara. *See* Pierce, Clara
Elliot, Elsie G. *See* Charlton, Elsie G.
Elliot, Howard Benson, 273–276
Elliot, Jane (née Blake), 187, 272
Elliot, John, 272
Elliot, Mary Hartford. *See* Bailie, Mary Hartford
Elliot, Mercedes, 276
Elliot, Ruth E., 274
Elliot, Susie E. *See* Gates, Susie
Elliott, Henry Newton, 187, 272–279
Elliott, John, 187
Elliott, Susan Jane (née Benson), 182, 187, 272–279
Ely, Augustus, 44, 46
Ely, Olive S. (née Scoville), 46
Emerson, Joseph, 130
Emerson, Orilla. *See* Carrier, Orilla
Emmons, Mary. *See* Scoville, Mary
Enrollment Act of 1863, 130
Entricon, Mary L. *See* Scovill, Mary L.

**F**

Farmer, Arthur Myron, 89
Farmer, Bertha L. *See* Cummings, Bertha L.
Farmer, Charles Claude, 89
Farmer, Charles Gudson, 89
Farmer, Fred, 89
Farmer, Harry Ernest, 90
Farmer, Hazel Blanche. *See* Breckenridge, Hazel Blance
Farmer, Ivy Leona, 89
Farmer, Lewis McKinley, 90
Farmer, Mabel, 89
Farmer, Mary Almira (née Scovill), 89
Farmer, Pearl M., 89
Farmer, Ruth, 90
Federal Non-Population Schedule, 191–192
Ferguson, Cora. *See* Thayer, Cora
Ferry, Martha. *See* Taylor, Martha
Fischer, Barbara. *See* Schneider, Barbara
Flint, Abner, Jr., 144, 189–197, 211–212
Flint, Althia Almeda (b. 1903). *See* Steward, Althia Almeda
Flint, Althia Almeda (née Hardy) (b. 1865), 210–211, 282–288
Flint, Anna (née West), 189
Flint, Carrie, 283
Flint, Dean, 287
Flint, Dorothy (née Kegler), 288
Flint, Elizabeth Amy. *See* Mead, Elizabeth "Lizzie"
Flint, Eva, 287
Flint, Floyd (b. 1859), 193, 211
Flint, Floyd (b. 1892), 212
Flint, Frank, 286
Flint, Frank (b. 1857), 191–193, 195–197, 210–211, 282–288
Flint, Fred Abner (b. 1898), 211, 283–284, 287
Flint, Harold K., 212
Flint, Hettie Arvilla. *See* Green, Hettie Arvilla
Flint, Ida May. *See* Brown, Ida May
Flint, Ira, 193, 195, 197, 211
Flint, Irvin J., 211
Flint, Keith, 288
Flint, Laura Edna. *See* Gilbert, Laura Edna
Flint, Lena M. *See* Remy, Lena M.
Flint, Leroy, 191, 193, 195, 211
Flint, Marlin, 288
Flint, Martha M. (née Holmes), 211
Flint, Mary Ann (née Dunham), 211
Flint, May, 283–284
Flint, Melissa (née Kelsey). *See* Garlow, Melissa
Flint, Nettie Melissa. *See* Fuller, Nettie Melissa
Flint, Raymond, 287
Flint, Russell, 287
Flint, Susie Camilla. *See* Prindle, Susie Camilla

Foote, Lucy C. *See* Scoville, Lucy C.
Foote, Lucy (née Lord), 55, 122
Foote, Samuel, 55, 122, 168
Ford, Amanda. *See* Scoville, Amanda
Foster, Sadie. *See* Zimmer, Sadie
French, Sarah. *See* Joslyn, Sarah
French and Indian War, 20
Fuller, Adelaide. *See* Scoville, Adelaide
Fuller, Elizabeth, 287
Fuller, Eugene, 287
Fuller, Jane (née Baird), 167
Fuller, Nettie Melissa (née Flint), 211, 283–285, 287
Fuller, Ocea May (née Piper), 287
Fuller, Paul, 287
Fuller, Samuel, 25

**G**

Gammerdinger, Catherine (née Schneider), 152, 220–221, 227–232, 295–296, 298, 371
Gammerdinger, Gotlieb Christian, 152, 227–228, 230, 295
Gammerdinger, Gottfried, 152
Gammerdinger, John, 228
Gammerdinger, Marie Agnes, 152
Garlow, Albert, 206
Garlow, Almeda, 206
Garlow, Almissa, 206, 208
Garlow, Alveretta G. *See* Davidson, Alveretta G.
Garlow, Alvin, 208, 210
Garlow, Clarasa, 206–207
Garlow, Dorcus, 206–207
Garlow, Elizabeth (née Whitaker), 205, 208
Garlow, Emily, 208
Garlow, Gertrude, 208
Garlow, Hannah (née Wheeler), 206–208, 210
Garlow, Henry, 208, 210
Garlow, John (b. ca. 1785), 205–206
Garlow, John W. (b. ca. 1819), 144, 189, 205–209
Garlow, Mary "Polly," 206
Garlow, Medisa, 206
Garlow, Melissa (née Kelsey), 144, 189–197, 203–205, 208–212, 283, 286
Garlow, Olvia, 206
Garlow, Phoebe, 206–207
Garlow, Sally A. (née Glendening), 209
Garlow, Sarah, 206
Garlow, Sarah A. "Sally," 206
Garlow, William, 206–207, 210
Gates, Albert Cassius, 276
Gates, Laborious, 276
Gates, Maria, 276
Gates, Marjorie, 277
Gates, Mary. *See* Scoville, Mary
Gates, Oliver P., 277
Gates, Richard A., 277
Gates, Ruth E., 276
Gates, Susie E. (née Elliot), 273–274, 276–277
Geiger, Katharina, 232
Gibson, Caroline Amelia (née Scovill) (b. 1847), 116
Gibson, George J., 116
Giger, Catherina. *See* Billian, Catherina
Gilber, Russell, 284
Gilbert, Amy (née Kelly), 286–287
Gilbert, Emma Marie (née Badker), 287
Gilbert, James Alfred, 286
Gilbert, Laura Edna (née Flint), 211, 283–286
Gilbert, Peter, 286
Glass, Alice L. (née Carrier), 93
Glass, John M., 93
Glendening, Sally A. *See* Garlow, Sally A.
Goar, Eric, 355
Goar, Holly M. (née Scoville), 354–355
Goettel, Andrew Henry, 352
Goettel, Karoline. *See* Pitfido, Karoline
Goettel, Lula Mary (née Scoville), 348–349, 352, 354–355
Goodwin, Amanda. *See* Smith Amanda
Gordon, John A., 334
Grassman, Florence Ann (née Case), 353
Grassman, Gwendolyn Cora (née Scoville), 348–350, 352–353
Grassman, Helen Roberta, 353

Grassman, Paul Forrester, 352–353
Grassman, Paula, 352
Green, Abram, 211
Green, Edwin, 391, 393
Green, Elnora. *See* Scoville, Elnora
Green, Hettie Arvilla (née Flint), 211
Green, Jane (née Kelly), 391, 393
Guise, Artie. *See* Scovill, Artie
Guise, Lillian. *See* Scovill, Lillian

**H**

Halden, Caroline Linnea. *See* Billian, Caroline Linnea
Halden, Johan Anders Svensson (John Andrew), 304, 378
Halden, Karolina Charlotta (née Carlsdotter), 378–379
Haldin, Caroline Lineea. *See* Billian, Caroline Linnea
Haldin, Charlotta (née Carlsdotter), 304
Hale, John, 20
Hall, David, 249
Hall, Esther. *See* Ball, Esther
Hall, Hannah E. *See* Scoville, Hannah E.
Hall, Lucy, 249
Hall, Mary Ann (née Cotterill), 249
Halldin/Haldin. *See* Halden
Hamilton, Elise S. (née Thayer), 367
Hamilton, Lotan Latham, 367
Hamilton, Mildred (née Corning), 116
Hardisty, Catherine Sadie (née Scoville), 361
Hardisty, John, 361
Hardy, Alitha. *See* Flint, Alitha
Hardy, Althia Almeda. *See* Flint, Althia Almeda
Hardy, Elizabeth Amy (née Moak) (b. 1843), 211, 283
Hardy, John Augustus, 211, 283
Harnden, Abigal. *See* Main, Abigail
Harrison, Luther B., 21, 29
Harrison, Mary Elizabeth (née Scoville), 21
health and illness
  apoplexy, 196
  Banti's disease, 373
  birth defects, 213
  Bright's disease, 245
  cardiac decompensation, 373
  cerebrospinal meningitis, 19n38, 91–92
  chronic interstitial nephritis, 257
  colera infantum, 340
  consumption (tuberculosis), 200–201
  deaf offspring, 21
  dysentery, 213
  paralytic schock, 196
  parletic shock, 196
  scarlet fever, 193
  Spanish Flue epidemic, 274, 328
  spotted fever epidemic, 19n38, 22, 34, 44, 91–92
  sudden infant death syndrome, 262
Heath, Artemisia. *See* Bachelor, Artemisia
Hedges, Esther Mae. *See* Mettee, Ester Mae
Hedges, Paul, 383
Hedges, Rosetta (née Berfeld), 383
Helf, George, 88
Helf, Lucy Jane (née Scovill), 87–88
Helf, Rosa Isabella. *See* Scovill, Rosa Isabella
Hillman, Anna J. (née Claflin). *See* Quick, Anna J.
Hillman, Charles Henry, 340
Hinkle, Inez. *See* Scovill, Inez
Hobson, Charles J., 293, 295
Hobson, Jesse, 291
Hobson, Mariah (née Westbrook), 291–292
Hobson, Rose M. *See* Kelsey, Rose M.
Holmes, Martha M. *See* Flint, Martha M.
Holmes, Rhoda Ellsworth (née Ashley), 247, 310, 318–319, 327–329, 331, 333–334
Holmes, Robert W., 329
Homes, Harold J., 334
homesteading, 280
Hoskins, Salome. *See* Stark, Salome
Hotchkiss, Amarilla. *See* Scoville, Amarilla
Hotchkiss, Oliver, 144, 148–149
Hotchkiss, Rebecca (née Strudevant), 144, 148–149, 233

Howe, Dilly, 20
Howe, Lois (née Stark), 20
Howland, John, 25n58
Hoyt, Amanda. *See* Buck, Amanda
Hoyt, Carrie E. *See* Morgan, Carrie E.
Hubbard, Anna Rachel. *See* Mead, Anna Rachel
Hudson, Emma. *See* Brown, Emma
Hudson, Nathaniel, 4–5, 7
Hudson, Rachel (née Scoville), 3–5
Huggins, Rhoda D. *See* Roys, Rhoda D.
Huset, Elsbeth (née Zweifel), 396
Huset, Peter, 396
Huset, Verena Matilda. *See* Scoville, Verena Matilda
Huseth. *See* Huset

J

Jackson, Benjamin Franklin, 360
Jackson, Clara Melvina, 360
Jackson, Daniel, 358, 360
Jackson, Frank Philbrick, 360
Jackson, Mary (née Philbrick), 358, 360
Jackson, Sarah "Sadie" L. *See* Scoville, Sarah "Sadie" L.
Janes, Meeta. *See* Kegler, Meeta
Jenks, Ada Louise (née Church), 304, 375–376
Jenks, Anna Riva (née McVeigh), 378
Jenks, Beryl, 378
Jenks, Edward Laurence, 376
Jenks, Ethel, 378
Jenks, Mildred, 378
Jenks, Raymond C. *See* Billian, Raymond Church
Jenks, Richard, 378
Jenks, Scott, 376
Jenks, Sylvia C. (née Lincoln), 376
Jennings, Ruhamah. *See* Scoville, Ruhamah
Jingozian, Adrienne. *See* Mandossian, Adrienne J.
Jingozian, Nuvart (née Bozian), 354
Jingozian, Thaddeus, 354
Johnson, Ellen L., 346
Johnson, Ellen Maria (née Cummings), 345–346
Johnson, Elva D., 346
Johnson, John Edgerly, 345
Johnson, Mary Alis. *See* Scovill, Mary Alis
Johnson, Mary Elizabeth. *See* Scoville, Mary Elizabeth
Jones, Helen M. *See* Carrier, Helen M.
Joslyn, Jesse Jane. *See* Scoville, Jesse Jane
Joslyn, Jessie Jayne. *See* Scovill, Jessie Jayne
Joslyn, Richard, 308
Joslyn, Sarah (née French), 308
Judah, Percy. *See* Quick, Anna J.

K

Kasson, Sarah (née Knapp), 74
Kegler, Dorothy. *See* Flint, Dorothy
Kegler, George, 288
Kegler, Meeta (née Janes), 288
Kelly, Jane. *See* Green, Jane
Kelsey, Almira (née Scoville), 55, 134–144, 181, 212
Kelsey, Celinda (née Bacherlor), 140
Kelsey, Charles Edward, 291
Kelsey, Charles Franklin, 214, 288–292
Kelsey, Chloe. *See* Scoville, Chloe
Kelsey, Clarissa. *See* Benson, Clarissa
Kelsey, Daniel, 136
Kelsey, David, 135
Kelsey, Dora (née Seeley), 214, 288, 290
Kelsey, Edward Charles, 290
Kelsey, Elizabeth "Besty" (née Cowles), 139, 144, 212–214, 289, 292
Kelsey, Ella M., 178, 180–181
Kelsey, Eula Carrie. *See* Eaton, Eula Carrie
Kelsey, Flavia, 144
Kelsey, George, 181
Kelsey, Helen Margaret. *See* Cotton, Helen Margaret
Kelsey, Hester (née Chapman), 36, 39
Kelsey, Horace, 55, 134–144, 176, 181, 189, 198, 212
Kelsey, Isabel "Belle" (née Cowell), 288–290

Kelsey, Isabelle Sarah (née Zimmer) (b. 1907), 290–291
Kelsey, Jemima (née Bronson), 136–137
Kelsey, Lyle, 144
Kelsey, Malissa, 139
Kelsey, Margaret Elizabeth. *See* Swartout, Margaret Elizabeth
Kelsey, Marion. *See* Vergason, Marion
Kelsey, Melissa. *See* Garlow, Melissa
Kelsey, Nathan E., 178, 181
Kelsey, Olive (née Parmalee), 136
Kelsey, Patsy/Patty M., 144, 176–177
Kelsey, Philo (b. 1836), 139, 144, 177, 190, 212–214, 289
Kelsey, Philo Lewis "Lew" (b. 1862), 213–214, 289, 291–295
Kelsey, Rose M. (née Hobson), 214, 291–295
Kelsey, Ruth Marie. *See* Anderson, Ruth Marie
Kelsey, Silas, 139, 144, 176–181
Kelsey, William, 36, 39
Kelsey,George, 178
Kelsy, Flavia C., 176–180
Kilbourn, Joseph, 22
Kilpatrick, Amy, 332
Kilpatrick, Harry A., 332
Kilpatrick, Laura G. *See* Ashley, Laura G.
Knapp, Amanda (née Scoville), 62, 72–73, 75–77
Knapp, Charles W., 74
Knapp, David, 62, 73–77
Knapp, Flavia, 74
Knapp, Jerusha. *See* Abrams, Jerusha
Knapp, Ruth. *See* Scoville, Ruth
Knapp, Ruth (née Cowles), 55, 62–63
Knapp, Sarah. *See* Kasson, Sarah
Knapp, Sophia (b. 1826). *See* Mattoon, Sophia
Knapp, Sophia (née Dodge) (b. 1779), 75
Knapp, Timothy, 55, 62
Kolling, Alice M. (née Benson), 282
Kolling, Christian, 282
Kolling, Christian H. (b. 1868), 282
Kolling, Delia H., 282
Kolling, Gretta, 282
Kolling, Henry B., 282
Kolling, Sophie. *See* Benson, Kolling
Kolling, Sophie (née Bremer), 282
Komer, Albert, 385
Komer, Armead(a), 384–385
Koon, Charles, 132
Koon, Ettie (née MacKee), 132
Koon, Jennie. *See* Carrier, Jennie
Kostof, Sophia Elizabeth. *See* Miller, Sophia Elizabeth
Kradel, Alice J., 280
Kradel, Alice J. (née McCl [ ] g), 260
Kradel, Esther Vaughn (née Scoville), 259–260
Kradel, Plummer Charles "Hap," 260
Kradel, Richard L., 260
Kradel, Theodore, 260
Kradel, Thomas H., 260
Kumm, Agnes Mary (née Billian), 299, 304, 370–374
Kumm, Clarence George (b. 1899), 231–232, 371, 373–374
Kumm, George Clarence Ferdinand, 298, 304, 370–374
Kumm, Harold Clarence, 371–374
Kurtz, Roger Lee Raidart, 385–386
Kuster, A. B., 367–368
Kuster, Ethel May (née Scoville), 266, 268–269, 367–368
Kuster, Frederick W., Jr., 368–369
Kuster, Frederick Wilhelm "Fritz" (b. 1884), 269, 367–369
Kuster, Jacob, 367
Kuster, Katherine E., 368
Kuster, Kenneth, 369
Kuster, Lulu/Lula Ann (née McMahon), 269, 365–366, 369
Kuster, Victor S., 368–369

L

Lane, Mary. *See* Scoville, Mary
Lassa, Renne Yvonne (née Raidart), 385–386
Le Senes, Claudia. *See* Philipe, Claudia
Leedy, Ella. *See* Steward, Ella

Light, Rosanna, 78
Linberg, Michael O. "Mike," 316, 322–323, 326–327
Linberg, Minnie Irene (née Scoville), 243–245, 247, 308–309, 316–335
Linborg. *See* Linberg
Lincoln, Sylvia C. *See* Jenks, Sylvia C.
Lindberg. *See* Linberg
Lindberg, Paul Michael, 247
Little, John, 132
Little, Luna, 132
Little, Maria/Mary Susan M. (née Chase), 132
Little, S. Gertrude. *See* Carrier, S. Gertrude
Locke, Emma. *See* Claflin, Emma
Lord, Lucy. *See* Foote, Lucy
Lucas, Mary. *See* Scoville, Mary
Lyon, Florence Octavia. *See* Scovill, Florence Octavia

**M**

McCausland, Jane. *See* Apperson, Jane
McClintock, Grace. *See* Bissell, Grace
McClu [ ] g, Alice J. *See* Kradel, Alice J.
MacKee, Ettie. *See* Koon, Ettie
McMahon, Harriet, 269, 365
McMahon, Joseph, 269, 365
McMahon, Lulu/Lula Ann. *See* Kuster, Lulu/Lula Ann
McNitt, Clayton George, 390
McNitt, George Harris, 390
McNitt, LuLu Blanche, 390
McNitt, Sarah Jenny (née Scoville), 388–390
McVeigh, Anna Riva. *See* Jenks, Anna Riva
Maguire, Maria Agnete, 337
Main, Abigail (née Harnden), 71
Main, Anna B. (née Shaw), 71
Main, Azuba, 72
Main, Carrie E. (née Cornell), 72
Main, Chauncy V., 72
Main, Daniel M., 72
Main, Dimmis (née Scoville), 66, 68–71
Main, Frederick, 66–70
Main, Frederick A. (b. 1823), 72
Main, Jane, 72
Main, Jerome, 71
Main, John D., 72
Main, Jonathan, 67–68
Main, Laura M., 72
Main, Lydia (née Rensier), 72
Main, Martha Clark (née Ackerson), 72
Main, Matilda (née Dennison), 71–72
Main, Norman, 72
Main, Parry J., 71–72
Main, Ruth (née Miller), 72
Maine. *See* Main
Mandossian, Adrienne J. (née Jingozian), 353–355
Marshall, Hannah. *See* Wilson, Hannah
Marshall, Ruby Sema. *See* Scovill, Ruby Sema
Mason, Eunice. *See* Stork, Eunice
Mattee. *See* Mettee
Mattoon, Sophia (née Knapp), 74–75
Mattoon, Spencer John, 74
Mayflower ancestors
  Howland, John, 25n58
  Tilley, Elizabeth, 25n58
  Warren, Richard, 25n58
Mead, Anna Rachel (née Hubbard), 287
Mead, Blanche R. *See* Monnier, Blance R.
Mead, Chester Benton, 287
Mead, Elizabeth "Lizzie" Amy (b. 1886), 211, 283, 285, 287
Mead, Frank Monroe, 285, 287
Mead, Lorran, 287
Mead, Morris, 287
Mead, Velma, 287
Mead, Warren, 287
Meeker, Phineas, 100
Merrill, Olive. *See* Scoville, Olive
Mettee, Ester Mae (née Hedges), 307, 383–386
Mettee, George H., 383
military service
  Ashley, Frank V. C., 332
  Ashley, Howard Burnett (b. 1894), 332
  Benson, Henry N., 279–280, 282
  Benson, Isaac, 187–188

Benson, William, 182–183
Billian, Russell Edward, 382
Carrier, Darrius, 93
Carrier, Frederick L., 133
Carrier, George W., 92
Charlton, Oliver Adair, 277
Dean, Reuben, 95–97
Dean, Seth, 94
Enrollment Act of 1863, 130
Farmer, Charles Gudson, 89
Garlow, John W., 207
Garlow, William, 207
Kelsey, Philo, 213
Scovil, Edward J., 89
Scovill, Ancil Milo, 87
Scovill, Edward A., 111
Scovill, Milo, 84
Scovill, Ransom, 85
**Scoville, Charles Martin**, 223–227, 242–243
Scoville, Henry, 20
Scoville, Henry C., 123
Scoville, James A., 159–160
Scoville, LeRoy, 397–398
Scoville' Timothy, 34, 36–39
Scoville, William Harrison (b. 1839), 227, 242–243
Young, Abram, 188
Millard, Elizabeth (née Smith), 16
Millard, Humphrey, 16
Millard, Matthew, 16–18, 23
Millard, Rebecca (wife of Steven Scoville). *See* Scoville, Rebecca
Millard, Rebecca (wife of Thomas Millard), 16–17
Millard, Thomas, 16–18
Miller. *See* Millard
Miller, Cahterine Irene "Kay." *See* Bartelli, Catherine Irene
Miller, Charles H., 392
Miller, Eugene Lawrence "Heine," 328
Miller, Margaret, 333
Miller, Margaret (née Carroll), 328
Miller, Marjorie. *See* Brady, Marjorie; Dickey, Marjorie
Miller, Rhoda Ellsworth. *See* Holmes, Rhoda Ellsworth
Miller, Roy, 334
Miller, Ruth. *See* Main, Ruth
Miller, Sandra, 329–330
Miller, Sarah Ann (née Main), 70–72
Miller, Sophia Elizabeth (née Kostof), 392
Miller, Sophia "Sophie" Elizabeth. *See* Scoville, Sophia "Sophie" Elizabeth
Miller,Catherine, 329
Miller,Conrad, 328
Moak, Elizabeth Ann. *See* Hardy, Elizabeth Ann
Moffatt, Agnes C. *See* Ashley, Agnes C.
Moffatt, Emily, 324
Monnier, Blanche R. (née Mead), 287
Moore, Joanne Joseph, 337
Moore, Maria Agnete (née Maguire), 337
Moore, Marie Gertrude. *See* Duff, Marie Gertrude
Moore, Marilla Irene. *See* Deming, Marilla Irene
Moore, Mary. *See* Ashley, Mary
Moore, Melissa Viola. *See* Scoviile, Melissa Viola
Morgan, Caroline Elizabeth. *See* Davis, Caroline "Carrie" Elizabeth
Morgan, Carrie E. (née Hoyt), 338
Morgan, John, 338
Morin, Nellie (née Dunn), 242

**N**

Nash, Ernest O., 343–345
Nash, Grace H. (née Claflin), 343–345
Nash, Marjorie, 345
Nash, Myra B. (née Wyre), 343
Nash, Oliver M., 343–344
Nelson, Alveretta (née Garlow). *See* Davidson, Alveretta G.
Noble, Martha Scovill (née Wheeler), 88
Noble, Nathan, 88

Noggle, Catherine C. (née Staley), 390–391
Noggle, Christopher, 390–391
Noggle, Eliza, 391
Noggle, George Washington, 391
Noggle, Jones, 391
Noggle, Mary Elizabeth. *See* Scoville, Mary Elizabeth

**P**

Page, Betha. *See* Case, Bertha
Parmalee, Olive. *See* Kelsey, Olive
Parsons, Abby Catherine, 115
Parsons, Florence L., 115
Parsons, Henry Ethelbert, 115
Parsons, Mary Townsend (née Bemis), 113, 115
Parsons, Samuel Holden, 115
Patent, Philipse, 35
Penn, Emiline Elizabeth. *See* Dover, Emiline Elizabeth
Pero, Bertha. *See* Scoville, Bertha
Peters, William B., 334
Philbrick, Mary. *See* Jackson, Mary
Philipe, Claudia (née Le Senes), 314
Philipe, Eugene, 314
Philipe, Eugenia. *See* Scovill, Eugenia
Philpse Patent, NY, 95
Piatt, Charlotte B., 330
Pierce, Clara (née Elliot), 273, 275
Piper, Ocea May. *See* Fuller, Ocea May
Pitfido, Karoline (née Goettel), 352
Pitfido, Thomas F., 352
Polensky, Frouwina H. *See* Shaffer, Frouwina H.
Potomac Road, 42
Prince, Donald S., 261
Prince, George James, 261
Prince, Jennie Thorpe, 261
Prince, John Lucius, 261
Prince, Julia Irene (née Scoville), 256, 258, 261
Prince, Stanley, 261
Prindle, Dayle, 288
Prindle, Dorinne, 288
Prindle, Doris, 288
Prindle, Dwayne, 288
Prindle, Earl William, 288
Prindle, Susie Camilla (née Flint), 211, 284, 288

**Q**

Quick, Anna J., 344
Quick, Anna J. (née Claflin), 340–342
Quick, Christine H. (née Daniel), 342
Quick, Gloria, 342
Quick, J. W., 342
Quick, Josephine, 342
Quick, Theodore Roosevelt, 340, 342

**R**

Rahm, Karonlina Charlotta. *See* Halden, Karolina Charlotta
Raidart, Alice B. *See* Deming, Alice B.
Raidart, Alice Maude (née Deming), 240, 304–307, 385
Raidart, Armead(a). *See* Komer, Armead(a)
Raidart, Douglas William, 384–385
Raidart, Esther Mae (née Hedges). *See* Mettee, Ester Mae
Raidart, George Henry, 235–238, 240, 304–307
Raidart, Julia Rebecca (née Scoville), 147, 152, 220, 232–240, 306
Raidart, Mary Armeada (née Stacy), 307, 384
Raidart, Olive Mildred. *See* Sears, Olive Mildred
Raidart, Renne Yvonne. *See* Lassa, Renne Yvonne
Raidart, Richard Henry, 385–386
Raidart, Robert George. *See* Berfield, Robert George
Raidart, Roger Lee. *See* Kurtz, Roger Lee
Raidart, Ronald William, 385–386
Raidart, Wilbur Henry "Ray," 306–307, 383–386
Raidart, William Henry, 152, 232–240
Rawson, Grindall, 10n17, 12

Reed, Martha C. *See* Van Deusen, Martha C.
Remy, A. J., 211–212
Remy, Lena M. (née Flint), 211–212
Rensier, Lydia. *See* Main, Lydia
Revolutionary War
Dean, Reuben, 95–97
Dean, Seth, 94
Salisbury Furnace and, 95
Scoville, Timothy, 34, 36–39
Rich, David, 46
Rich, Hester Kelsey (née Scoville), 46
Roberts, Samuel, 22
Roger, Rhoda, 33
Rogers, Arthur, 32
Rogers, Ashael, 31–33
Rogers, John, 31–34
Rogers, Noah, 33
Rogers, Noah, Jr., 33
Rogers, Sarah. *See* Burnham, Sarah; Scoville, Sarah
Rogers, Sarah (née Borden), 31–34
Rogers, Sarah (née Scoville), 21
Routson, Mary. *See* Scovill, Mary
Rowland, Mary. *See* Scoville, Mary
Roys, Edmond Davis, 262–263
Roys, Eugene Edmond, 262
Roys, John M., 262
Roys, Mary Doolittle (née Scoville), 256, 262–263
Roys, Maud (née Bowen), 262
Roys, Rhoda D. (née Huggins), 262

S

St. John, Margaret K. *See* Bemis, Margaret K.
Sanborn, Agnes Mary (née Billian). *See* Kumm, Agnes Mary
Sanborn, Bert, 304, 370–374
Sankey, Ella. *See* Scovill, Ella
Saurman, Lucy. *See* Scovill, Lucy
Schaeffer, Eugenia Philipe. *See* Scoville, Eugenia Philipe
Schaeffer, Eugenie. *See* Scovill, Eugenia
Schneider, Agnes, 229
Schneider, Anthony, 229
Schneider, Barbara (née Fischer), 220–222, 227, 229
Schneider, Catherine. *See* Gammerdinger, Catherine
Schneider, John, 220–222, 229
Schneider, Mary Ann, 229
Scholl, Catherine. *See* Scovill, Catherine
Scholl, Jacob, 111
Scholl, Sarah (née Hyland), 111
Schoval; Scovil; Scovel. *See* Scoville
Schuman, Lucy, 239–240
Scovil, Irene, 147–148
Scovill, Adeline (née Clark), 115
Scovill, Albert S., 78
Scovill, Alfred, 85–86
Scovill, Almanzor, 87
Scovill, Almina M., 89
Scovill, Alyra/Almira Sabrina, 85
Scovill, Amanda, 89
Scovill, Ancil Milo, 86–87
Scovill, Artie (née Guise), 80
Scovill, Burton Baldwin, 88
Scovill, Caroline Amelia. *See* Bemis, Caroline Amelia; Gibson, Caroline Amelia
Scovill, Charles Loren (b. 1866), s.o. John Mitchell, 81
Scovill, Charles Philo, 116
Scovill, Cynthia (née Crawford), 83–84
Scovill, Cyrus Sawyer, 78–79, 85
Scovill, Danvers. B., 85–86
Scovill, Dora. *See* Watkins, Dora
Scovill, Edith Arminda. *See* Duffey, Edith Arminda
Scovill, Edmund Cameron, 88
Scovill, Edward Alexander, 107, 109–112
Scovill, Edward Everett, 87
Scovill, Edward J., 89
Scovill, Edward Tracey, 111
Scovill, Ella (née Sankey), 89
Scovill, Ellsworth Mitchell, 80
Scovill, Eugenia (née Philipe), 247, 308, 312
Scovill, Eulalia Amanda, 88

Scovill, Eunice G. *See* Conley, Eunice G. "Scovill"
Scovill, Everett B., 85–86
Scovill, Everett Bradford, 80
Scovill, Florence Harriet (née Sholes), 111
Scovill, Florence Octavia (née Lyon), 87
Scovill, Frank Ellsworth, 242, 244, 246–247, 307–315, 329
Scovill, Gary, 400
Scovill, Geoge Sawyer, 81
Scovill, George William, 85
Scovill, Harriet (née Dennison), 77–78
Scovill, Herbert C., 85–86
Scovill, Hester. *See* Smith, Hester
Scovill, Inez (née Hinkle), 85–86
Scovill, Ira Bradford, 63–64, 77–82
Scovill, Jemima (née Bixby), 45, 107–114
Scovill, Jessie Jayne (née Joslyn), 307–315
Scovill, John (b. 1738), 399
Scovill, John Mitchell (b. 1841), 78, 80–81
Scovill, Josephine, 116
Scovill, Kate. *See* Corning, Kate
Scovill, Laura. *See* Smith, Laura
Scovill, Letica Electa. *See* Wolfe, Letica Electa
Scovill, Lewis, 89
Scovill, Lillian (née Guise), 80
Scovill, Lucy Jane. *See* Helf, Lucy Jane
Scovill, Lucy (née Saurman), 86
Scovill, Lydia Rebecca (née Bear), 80–81
Scovill, Martha (née Wheeler). *See* Noble, Martha
Scovill, Mary Alis (née Johnson), 87
Scovill, Mary Almira. *See* Farmer, Mary Almira
Scovill, Mary E., 85–86
Scovill, Mary J. (née Vanderhoef), 85
Scovill, Mary Joanna (née Vanderhoof), 79
Scovill, Mary L. (née Entricon), 87
Scovill, Mary (née Routson), 83–84
Scovill, Mary Victoria (née Clark), 79
Scovill, Milo, 83–84
Scovill, Minnie (née Sipes), 85–86
Scovill, Myron Leroy, 87
Scovill, Nancy M. (née Eddigner), 86
Scovill, Newlin Sampson, 87
Scovill, Oliver Comstock "Crockett," 110, 115–116
Scovill, Philo (b. 1791), 107–116
Scovill, Ransom C., 85–86
Scovill, Rena (née Decker), 85–86
Scovill, Rosa Isabella (née Helf), 87
Scovill, Rosanna (née Light), 78
Scovill, Ruby Sema, 81
Scovill, Sara Belle, 85–86
Scovill, Sarah Belle (née Scoville), 80
Scovill, Ulisus Grant, 87
Scovill, Ulysses Sidney, 80
Scovill, Wesley D., 78
Scovill, Wesley Wells, 81
Scovill, William H., 78
Scovill, William Sholl, 111–112
Scovill, Winifred, 88
Scoville, Abner, 21, 32
Scoville, Adelaide (née Fuller), 85–86
Scoville, Adrienne (née Jingozian). *See* Mandossian, Adrienne J.
**Scoville, Agnes R.** *See* **Billian, Agnes R.**
Scoville, Albert A. (b. 1857), 221–222, 227, 229, 231–232, 295–297
Scoville, Albert (b. ca. 1837), 126
b.o. George, 159
Scoville, Albert Franklin (b. 1846), 147–148, 153, 246, 248–250, 335, 356
Scoville, Albert (son of Charles), 149
Scoville, Almira. *See* Kelsey, Almira
Scoville, Alvie James, 391, 396–397
Scoville, Amanda. *See* Knapp, Amanda; Tyler, Amanda
Scoville, Amanda (née Ford), 21
Scoville, Amarilla (née Hotchkiss), 144, 149, 214–215, 217, 233, 241, 254
Scoville, Amasa, 55–57, 93–95, 100–102, 116–126, 154, 156
Scoville, Ancel Cowles, 58, 62, 77
Scoville, Anna. *See* Stork, Anna
Scoville, Artemus, 21

Scoville, Arthur (b. 1635), 1–8
Scoville, Arthur (b. 1663), 3–5, 7
Scoville, Arthur (b. 1710), 15
Scoville, Asube (daughter of Timothy[3]), 30, 35
Scoville, Bertha (née Pero). *See* Brackley, Bertha
Scoville, Catherine (née Schneider). *See* Gammerdinger, Catherine
Scoville, Catherine (née Scholl), 111
Scoville, Catherine Sadie. *See* Hardisty, Catherine Sadie
Scoville, Catherine Sara, 359
Scoville, Charles Foote (b. 1821), 122, 125–126, 154–167, 173, 264
**Scoville, Charles Martin** (b. ca. 1834), 147, 152, 218–232, 241–243, 295, 298, 347
Scoville, Charles Merritt (b. 1867), 253, 345–357
Scoville, Charles Mittean (b. 1874), 269, 347, 358–361
Scoville, Charlie (b. 1868), 249
Scoville, Chloe (née Kelsey), 36, 39, 43, 45–46
Scoville, Clara, 393–394
Scoville, Clara Marian (née Bennett), 269, 363–365
Scoville, Clarissa. *See* Clemmons, Clarissa
Scoville, Clarissa (née Spencer), 122, 154–156, 264
Scoville, Cora Irene. *See* Claflin, Cora Irene
Scoville, Daniel (b. 1718), 15, 32
Scoville, Daniel (b. 1768), 19
Scoville, Dimmis. *See* Main, Dimmis
Scoville, Elinor Marion, 268, 364–365
Scoville, Elizabeth. *See* Borden, Elizabeth
Scoville, Elizabeth (b. 1744), 19–20
Scoville, Ellen "Nellie" Amanda (née Sullivan), 153, 254–263
Scoville, Elnora (née Green), 391, 393
Scoville, Erza, 19
Scoville, Esther Vaughn. *See* Kradel, Esther Vaughn
Scoville, Ethel May. *See* Kuster, Ethel May
Scoville, Eudora Marian (née Steele), 253, 345–346, 348–349, 351
Scoville, Eugenia Philipe (née Schaeffer), 247
Scoville, Ezekiel, 7, 15
Scoville, Florence, 246
Scoville, Frank, 126, 250
Scoville, Frank (b. 1915), 365
**Scoville, Franklin** (b. 1809), 55, 144–153, 214–215, 217, 241, 254
Scoville, Franklin "Frank" (b. 1850), 157, 159, 167, 169, 264–270, 358, 367
Scoville, George Albert (b. 1876), 268–269, 361–363
Scoville, George (b. 1833), 159
Scoville, George (b. ca. 1813), 398–399
Scoville, George E., 125–126, 171
Scoville, Gilbert Lafayette, 266, 269, 358, 365–366
Scoville, Gwendolyn Cora. *See* Grassman, Gwendolyn Cora
Scoville, Hannah (b. ca. 1716), 15
Scoville, Hannah (bap. ca. 1745), 20
Scoville, Hannah E. (née Hall), 153, 248–253
Scoville, Hannah (wife of James), 8
Scoville, Harold Merritt (b. 1911), 350, 353–354
Scoville, Harriet Eliza (b. ca. 1805), 21
Scoville, Harriet (née Winans), 21
Scoville, Harry Franklin (b. 1880), 266, 268–269, 363–365, 369
Scoville, Harry Oliver (b. 1876), 218, 257, 259–260, 263
Scoville, Henry (b. 1740), 19–20
Scoville, Henry C. (b. 1827), 123–125
Scoville, Hester Kelsey. *See* Rich, Hester Kelsey
Scoville, Hezehiah, 15
Scoville, Holly M. *See* Goar, Holly M.
Scoville, Ira, 30, 33, 35, 38, 55–90, 400–419
Scoville, Irene (b. 1748), 19–20
Scoville, Irene (b. 1832). *See* Smith, Irene
Scoville, Irene (d. 1813), 22
Scoville, Irene Mitchell. *See* Burnett, Irene Mitchell

**Scoville, Ithamar**, 34, 46–55, 93, 98–101, 121, 126, 134–135, 149, 176, 387
Scoville, Jacob, 19, 29
Scoville, James A. (b. 1838), 126, 155, 159
Scoville, James (b. 1670), 3–5, 7–8
Scoville, James Frederick (b. 1862), 388–393, 396–397
Scoville, Jemima (née Bixby), 111, 115
Scoville, Jerusha, 15
Scoville, Jesse Jane (née Joslyn), 247
Scoville, Jessie Maud (née Ball), 259–260
Scoville, Joanna, 3–4, 7–8
Scoville, John, 1–8
Scoville, Jonah (son of Samuel), 19
Scoville, Joseph (b. ca. 1765), 19, 29
Scoville, Joseph (b.1862), 223, 232
Scoville, Josephine (b. 1916), 365
Scoville, Julia Irene. *See* Prince, Julia Irene
Scoville, Kate (née Shephard), 264–270
Scoville, Laura, 44
Scoville, Laura Jennie (née Steele), 232, 295–297
Scoville, LeRoy Arnold "Sccops," 396–398
Scoville, Levi U. (b. ca. 1780), 21
Scoville, Lodema. *See* Carrier, Lodema
Scoville, Lucius Edwin, 147, 149, 153, 254–263
Scoville, Lucy, 159
Scoville, Lucy A. *See* Van Deusen, Lucy A.
Scoville, Lucy C. (née Foote), 55, 116, 118, 122, 156, 169
Scoville, Lucy (née Beckwith), 15, 32
Scoville, Lula Mary. *See* Goettel, Lula Mary
Scoville, Lulu/Lula Ann (née McMahon). *See* Kuster, Lulu/Lula Ann
Scoville, Mabel M. *See* Thayer, Mabel M.
Scoville, Manlon Alvie, 397
Scoville, Margaret, 223, 232
Scoville, Margaret Estella (née Apperson), 153, 248, 250, 356
Scoville, Mariah, 268
Scoville, Martha (née Taylor), 20
Scoville, Mary. *See* Beckwith, Mary; Wickwire, Mary
Scoville, Mary (b. ca. 1740), 21
Scoville, Mary (b. ca. 1744), 32
Scoville, Mary Catherine (née Dunn), 153, 224–225, 227, 240–254, 308–310, 324, 329, 333
Scoville, Mary (daughter of Charles F.), 159
Scoville, Mary Doolittle. *See* Roys, Mary Doolittle
Scoville, Mary Elizabeth. *See* Harrison, Mary Elizabeth
Scoville, Mary Elizabeth (née Johnson), 253, 345–347, 349, 352
Scoville, Mary Elizabeth (née Noggle), 390–392, 394–396
Scoville, Mary Jane. *See* Cushing, Mary Jane
Scoville, Mary Josephine (née Dyer), 269, 361–363
Scoville, Mary Kay. *See* Sidnam, Mary Kay
Scoville, Mary Lord. *See* Wilson, Mary Lord
Scoville, Mary M. (b. 1912), 365
Scoville, Mary (née Cook), 1–2
Scoville, Mary (née Emmons), 19
Scoville, Mary (née Gates), 15
Scoville, Mary (née Lane), 21
Scoville, Mary (née Lucas), 7–8
Scoville, Mary (née Rowland), 19
Scoville, Mary "Polly" (b. 1795), 46
Scoville, Melissa Viola (née Moore), 153, 248, 356
Scoville, Mindwell (née Barber), 15
Scoville, Minnie Irene. *See* Linberg, Minnie Irene Ashley
Scoville, Miriam (née Chamberlain), 15, 32
Scoville, Myron, 88, 418–419
Scoville, Nathan, 7, 15
Scoville, Olive Merrill (b. 1823), 21
Scoville, Olive (née Merrill) (b.1779), 21
Scoville, Olive S. *See* Ely, Olive S.
Scoville, Philo (b. ca. 1790), 45
Scoville, Philo (bap. 1774), 35, 387, 399
Scoville, Philo C. (b. 1813), 387–399
Scoville, Phoebe (b. ca. 1740), 21, 32
Scoville, Phoebe (née Willey), 15

Scoville, Rachel. *See* Hudson, Rachel
Scoville, Ransley, 21
Scoville, Rebecca (b. 1773). *See* Thornton, Rebecca
Scoville, Rebecca (née Millard), 15–21, 27
Scoville, Rebeckah, 22
Scoville, Richard, 1–2
Scoville, Roxalana/Roxylana. *See* Dean, Roxalana/Roxylana
Scoville, Ruben, 399
Scoville, Ruhamah (daughter of Timothy[3]), 30, 35
Scoville, Ruhamah (née Jennings), 19
Scoville, Rush, 30
Scoville, Ruth (b. 1760), 30
Scoville, Ruth (née Knapp) (b. 1774), 35, 55, 61–62, 65, 76
Scoville, Ruth (née Squires), 19, 26
Scoville, Sabrina (née Wraight), 21
Scoville, Sally (wife of Levi), 21
Scoville, Samuel (b. 1731), 19, 26, 29
Scoville, Samuel (b. 1758), 19
Scoville, Samuel D. (b. 1827), 123, 154
Scoville, Sara Belle. *See* Scovill, Sarah Belle
Scoville, Sarah. *See* Brockway, Sarah
Scoville, Sarah (b. 1736), 20
Scoville, Sarah (b. 1742), 20
Scoville, Sarah (daughter of Arthur[2]). *See* Rogers, Sarah
Scoville, Sarah Jenny. *See* McNitt, Sarah Jenny
Scoville, Sarah (née Baird), 122, 125, 154, 157–159, 162, 166–167, 264
Scoville, Sarah (née Champion), 5, 8–9, 14–15
Scoville, Sarah (née Rogers), 30–34, 58–59
Scoville, Sarah "Sadie" L. (née Jackson), 269, 358–361
Scoville, Sophia "Sophie" Elizabeth (née Miller) (b. 1869), 391–392
Scoville, Stephen, 19
**Scoville, Stephen** (b. 1706), 9–10, 15–22
Scoville, Stephen (b. 1729), 18, 23
Scoville, Stephen (b. 1752), 20–21, 29
**Scoville, Stephen** (b. ca. 1680), 5–15
Scoville, Stephen (b. ca. 1813), 21
Scoville, Stephen (son of Samuel), 19
Scoville, Sylvester Merrill (b. ca. 1816), 21
Scoville, Thankful (née Crocker), 24–26, 30, 34–35, 93
Scoville, Thomas (b. 1722), 7, 11–12, 14–15
**Scoville, Timothy** (b. 1737), 19–20, 24–25, 27–35, 56–57
Scoville, Timothy (b. 1762), 26, 34, 36–46
Scoville, Triphene/Triphena. *See* Carrier, Triphene/Triphena
Scoville, Trypena (née Terrell), 19
Scoville, Verena Matilda (née Huset), 396–397
Scoville, William, 5–7
Scoville, William Harrison (b. 1839), 134–135, 144, 147–148, 153, 227, 240–254
Scoville family
  origin of name, 1–2
  original settlement in Cornwall, CT, 23
Sears, Elizabeth Raidart, 307
Sears, Olive Mildred (née Raidart), 305, 307, 385
Sears, Ralph Edwin (b. 1899), 307
Sears, Ralph Edwin (b. 1929), 307
Seeley, Charles Barber, 289
Seeley, Dora. *See* Kelsey, Dora
Seely, Priscilla. *See* Eaton, Priscilla
Shaeffer. *See* Schaeffer
Shaeffer, Eunice G. *See* Conley, Eunice G. "Scovill"
Shaffer, Catherine Irene "Kay" (née Miller). *See* Bartelli, Catherine Irene
Shaffer, Charles, 330
Shaffer, Charlotte B. (née Piatt), 330
Shaffer, Frouwina H. (née Polensky), 330
Shaffer, Helen Clare Rink, 330
Shaffer, William S. "Bill," 329–330
Shaw, Anna B. *See* Main, Anna B.
Shepard, Bilbe, 264, 267
Shepard, Kate. *See* Scoville, Kate
Shepard, Lydia Gobel (née Truesdale), 264
Sholes, Florence Harriet. *See* Scovill, Florence Harriet

Sidnam, Charles, 387–390
Sidnam, Mary Kay Scoville, 387–390
Sipes, Minnie. *See* Scovill, Minnie
Smith, Amanda (née Goodwin), 214–215, 217
Smith, Ann, 82–83
Smith, Burr, 82
Smith, Carlo, 214–215
Smith, Chauncey, 82–83
Smith, Eli, 82–83
Smith, Elizabeth. *See* Millard, Elizabeth
Smith, Elizabeth Ann (née Brown), 345
Smith, Elmer Moses, 217
Smith, Emma, 217–218
Smith, Ezekiel Benjamin, 78
Smith, George (b. 1802), 81–82
Smith, George (b. 1840), 82
Smith, Hester (née Scovill), 78
Smith, Horatio Nelson, 215
Smith, Irene (née Scoville) (b. 1832), 149–150, 152, 214–219, 351
Smith, John (b. ca. 1851), 215–216
Smith, John C., 217–219
Smith, Laura (née Scovill), 81–82
Smith, Mary, 82
Smith, Matthew, 16
Smith, Merritt Ellsworth, 149–150, 152, 214–219
Smith Amanda (née Goodwin), 149
Snider; Snyder. *See* Schneider
Snyder/Snider. *See* Schneider
Sourman. *See* Saurman
Spanish-American War
    Carrier, Frderick L., 132
    Charlton, Oliver Adair, 277
    service of Frderick L. Carrier, 132
    *USS Oregon*, 366
Spencer, Amaret. *See* Deming, Amaret
Spencer, Clarissa. *See* Scoville, Clarissa
Spencer, Florence L. *See* Parsons, Florence L.
spotted fever epidemic, 91
Springsteen, Esther. *See* Buck, Esther
Squires, Ruth. *See* Scoville, Ruth
Stacy, Mary, 384
Stacy, Mary Armeada (b. 1891). *See* Raidart, Mary Armeada
Stacy, Oliver, 384
Staley, Catherine C. *See* Noggle, Catherine C.
Stark, Jonathan, 20
Stark, Lois. *See* Howe, Lois
Stark, Salome (née Hoskins), 20
Stark, Sarah, 20
Starkey, Katherine "Kate." *See* Bemis, Katherine "Kate"
Steel, Sarah (née Cornish), 232
Steele, Arthur, 350
Steele, Eudora Marian. *See* Scoville, Eudora Marian
Steele, Laura Jennie. *See* Scoville, Laura Jennie
Steele, Sarah (née Cornish), 295
Steele, Thomas, 232, 295
Steward, Althia Almeda, 288
Steward, Ella (née Leedy), 288
Steward, Orville A. Douglas, 288
Steward, Walter, 288
Stork, Anna (née Scoville), 19
Stork, Christopher Still Moses, 19
Stork, Eunice (née Mason), 19
Stork, Moses, 19
Stowell, Miranda (née Woodruff), 279
Stowell, Olive I. *See* Benson, Olive I.
Stowell, Sherman, 279
Strudevant, Rebecca. *See* Hotchkiss, Rebecca
Sturdevant, James, 150
Sturdevant, William, 150
Sullivan, Ellen "Nellie" Amanda. *See* Scoville, Ellen "Nellie" Amanda
Sullivan, John, 254
Sullivan, Sally (née Doolittle), 254–255
surveyor's chains, 42
Swartout, James J., 290–291
Swartout, Margaret Elizabeth (née Kelsey), 290
Swift, Alice. *See* Crocker, Alice

**T**

Taylor, David, 20

Taylor, Martha. *See* Scoville, Martha
Taylor, Martha (née Ferry), 20
Terrell, Tryphena. *See* Scoville, Trypena
Thayer, Cora (née Ferguson), 366
Thayer, Earl Levi, 269, 366–367
Thayer, Eise S. *See* Hamilton, Elise S.
Thayer, Mabel M. (née Scoville), 266, 268–269, 366–367
Thayer, Thomas, 366
Thayer, Virginia. *See* Brown, Virginia
Thornton, Rebecca (née Scoville), 19–20
Thorpe, Leonie J., 375
Tilley, Elizabeth, 25n58
Timbrell, Mildred L. F. *See* Billian, Mildred L. F.
Tinker, Ella Mary. *See* Claflin, Ella Mary
Truesdale, Lydia Gobel. *See* Shepard, Lydia Gobel
Tyler, Amanda (née Scoville). *See* Knapp, Amanda
Tyler, Charles Dwight, 73
Tyler, Daniel, 62
Tyler, Daniel Henry (b. 1823), 73
Tyler, George Washington, 73
Tyler, Harriet Loisa, 73
Tyler, Ira Lewis, 73
Tyler, Lewis, 73–75
Tyler, Martin Quick, 73
tyler, Merry Melinda, 73
Tyler, Sarah Jane, 73
Tyler, Sylvia Corkin, 73

**U**

Usher, Minnie M. Rockwood. *See* Claflin, Minnie M. Rockwood

**V**

Van Deusen, Egbert, 258
Van Deusen, Frank H., 257–259
Van Deusen, Lucy A. (née Scoville), 256–259
Van Deusen, Martha C. (née Reed), 258
Vanderhoef, Mary J. *See* Scovill, Mary J.
Vanderhoof, Mary Joanna. *See* Scovill, Mary Joanna
Vergason, Marion (née Kelsey), 291

**W**

Waite, Marion G. *See* Deming, Marion G.
Waler, Joseph, 22
Walker, Margaret. *See* Bixby Margaret
Warren, Richard, 25n58
Watkins, Chauncy, 85–86
Watkins, Dora (née Scovill), 85–86
Watkins, Orlyn C., 85–86
Weed, Mary Ellen. *See* Dyer, Mary Ellen
Weeks, Betsy. *See* Carrier, Betsy
Welch, Ellen, 72
West, Anna. *See* Flint, Anna
Westbrook, Mariah. *See* Hobson, Mariah
Wheeler, Hannah. *See* Garlow, Hannah
Wheeler, Martha. *See* Noble, Martha
Whitaker, Elizabeth. *See* Garlow, Elizabeth
White, Bessie A. *See* Deming, Bessie A.
Wickwire, David, 22
Wickwire, Mary (née Scoville), 22
Wilkes, George Henry, 114
Wilkes, Helen Marion (née Bemis), 114
Willey, Phoebe. *See* Scoville, Phoebe
Williams, Helen Clare Rink. *See* Shaffer, Helen Clare Rink
Williams, Nathan, 25
Wilson, Abner Marshall, 122, 167–170
Wilson, Almira, 176
Wilson, Hannah (née Marshall), 168, 170
Wilson, Hiram C., 175–176
Wilson, Mary Lord (née Scoville), 122, 125, 167–176
Wilson, Parliman, 170
Wilson, Roger, 168, 170
Winans, Harriet. *See* Scoville, Harriet
Winnedk, Elizabeth. *See* Brown, Elizabeth
Wolfe, George, 85–86
Wolfe, Letica Electa (née Scovill), 85–86
Woodruff, Miranda. *See* Stowell, Miranda
Woodward, Jenette. *See* Deming, Jenette
World War I

Ashley, Frank V. C., 332
Ashley, Howard Burnett (b. 1894), 332
World War II, Billian, Russell Edward, 382
Wraight, Sabrina. *See* Scoville, Sabrina
Wyre, Myra B. *See* Nash, Myra B.

**Y**

Yelping Hill, 27, 32
Young, Abram, 188
Young, Juliette (née Benson), 182, 184, 188–189
Young, Mary, 188

**Z**

Zimmer, George, 291
Zimmer, Isabelle. *See* Kelsy, Isabelle
Zimmer, Isabelle Sarah. *See* Kelsey, Isabelle Sarah
Zimmer, Sadie (née Foster), 291
Zweifel, Elsbeth. *See* Huset, Elsbeth

www.ingramcontent.com/pod-product-compliance
Lightning Source LLC
Chambersburg PA
CBHW051206290426
44109CB00021B/2362

* 9 7 8 0 5 7 8 3 7 2 0 2 0 *